# MUSIC AND EMOTION

# Series in Affective Science

*Series Editors*
Richard J. Davidson
Paul Ekman
Klaus R. Scherer

*The Nature of Emotion: Fundamental Questions*
edited by Paul Ekman and Richard J. Davidson

*Boo!: Culture, Experience, and the Startle Reflex*
by Ronald Simons

*Emotions in Psychopathology:*
  *Theory and Research*
edited by William F. Flack Jr. and James D. Laird

*What the Face Reveals:*
  *Basic and Applied Studies of*
  *Spontaneous Expression Using the*
  *Facial Action Coding System (FACS)*
edited by Paul Ekman and Erika Rosenberg

*Shame: Interpersonal Behavior,*
  *Psychopathology, and Culture*
edited by Paul Gilbert and Bernice Andrews

*Affective Neuroscience: The Foundations of*
  *Human and Animal Emotions*
by Jaak Panksepp

*Extreme Fear, Shyness, and Social Phobia:*
  *Origins, Biological Mechanisms, and*
  *Clinical Outcomes*
edited by Louis A. Schmidt and Jay Schulkin

*Cognitive Neuroscience of Emotion*
edited by Richard D. Lane and Lynn Nadel

*The Neuropsychology of Emotion*
edited by Joan C. Borod

*Anxiety, Depression, and Emotion*
edited by Richard J. Davidson

*Persons, Situations, and Emotions: An Ecological Approach*
edited by Hermann Brandstätter and Andrzej Eliasz

*Emotion, Social Relationships, and Health*
edited by Carol D. Ryff and Burton H. Singer

*Music and Emotion: Theory and Research*
edited by Patrik Juslin and John Sloboda

# MUSIC AND EMOTION

*Theory and research*

Edited by

**PATRIK N. JUSLIN,**
*Uppsala University, Sweden*

and

**JOHN A. SLOBODA**
*University of Keele, UK*

OXFORD
UNIVERSITY PRESS

# OXFORD
### UNIVERSITY PRESS

Great Clarendon Street, Oxford OX2 6DP

Oxford University Press is a department of the University of Oxford.
It furthers the University's objective of excellence in research, scholarship,
and education by publishing worldwide in

Oxford  New York

Auckland  Bangkok  Buenos Aires  Cape Town  Chennai
Dar es Salaam  Delhi  Hong Kong  Istanbul  Karachi  Kolkata
Kuala Lumpur  Madrid  Melbourne  Mexico City  Mumbai  Nairobi
São Paulo  Shanghai  Taipei  Tokyo  Toronto

Oxford is a registered trade mark of Oxford University Press
in the UK and in certain other countries

Published in the United States
by Oxford University Press Inc., New York

© Oxford University Press, 2001

A catalogue record for this title is available from the British Library

Library of Congress Cataloging in Publication Data

Music and emotion : theory and research / edited by Patrik N. Juslin and John A. Sloboda
(series in affective science)
Includes bibliographical references and index.
1. Music—Psychological aspects.  2. Emotions.  I. Juslin, Patrik N.  II. Sloboda, John A.  III. Series.
ML3830.M695  2001  781.11′038—dc21  2001036068

ISBN 0–19–263188–8 (Pbk)
ISBN 0–19–263189–6 (Hbk)

10 9 8 7 6 5 4

Typeset by J&L Composition Ltd, Filey, North Yorkshire
Printed in Great Britain
on acid-free paper by
Biddles Ltd, King's Lynn, Norfolk

# CONTENTS

## The Performer

## The Listener

## Postlude

# LIST OF CONTRIBUTORS

**Judith Becker** School of Music, University of Michigan, 1100 Baits Drive, Ann Arbor, Michigan 48109 – 2085, USA

**Leslie Bunt** Faculty of Health and Social Care, St. Matthias Campus, University of the West of England, Bristol BS16 2UP, UK

**Annabel J. Cohen** Department of Psychology, University of Prince Edward Island, Charlottetown PE C1A 4P3, CANADA

**Nicholas Cook** Department of Music, University of Southampton, Highfield, Southampton SO17 1BJ, UK

**Stephen Davies** Department of Philosophy, University of Auckland, Private Bag 92019, Auckland, NEW ZEALAND

**Tia DeNora** Department of Sociology, University of Exeter, Amory Building, Rennes Drive, Exeter EX4 4RJ, UK

**Nicola Dibben** Department of Music, University of Sheffield, Sheffield S10 2TN, UK

**Alf Gabrielsson** Department of Psychology, Uppsala University, Box 1225, SE – 751 42 Uppsala, SWEDEN

**Patrik N. Juslin** Department of Psychology, Uppsala University, Box 1225, SE – 751 42 Uppsala, SWEDEN

**Erik Lindström** Department of Psychology, Uppsala University, Box 1225, SE – 751 42 Uppsala, SWEDEN

**Leonard B. Meyer** Department of Music, University of Pennsylvania, 201 SO. 34th Street, Philadelphia, PA 19104, USA

**Susan A. O'Neill** Department of Psychology, University of Keele, Newcastle, Staffordshire ST5 5BG, UK

**Mercédès Pavlicevic** Music Therapy Programme, Department of Music, University of Pretoria, Pretoria 0002, SOUTH AFRICA

**Isabelle Peretz** Department of Psychology, University of Montreal, CP 6128, Succ. Centre-ville, Montreal, Québec H3C 317, CANADA

**Roland S. Persson** School of Education and Communication, Jönköping University, Box 1026, SE – 55 111 Jönköping, SWEDEN

**Klaus R. Scherer** Department of Psychology, University of Geneva, 40 Boulevard du Pont d'Arve, CH – 1205 Geneva, SWITZERLAND

**Emery Schubert**  School of Music and Music Education, University of New South Wales, Sydney, NSW 2052, AUSTRALIA

**Dean Keith Simonton** Department of Psychology, University of California, Davis, CA 95616 – 8686, USA

**John A. Sloboda** Department of Psychology, University of Keele, Newcastle, Staffordshire ST5 5BG, UK

**Andrew Steptoe** Department of Epidemiology and Public Health, University College London, London WC1E 6BT, UK

**Marcel R. Zentner** Department of Psychology, University of Geneva, 40 Boulevard du Pont d'Arve, CH – 1205 Geneva, SWITZERLAND

# ACKNOWLEDGMENTS

The editors would like to thank the authors, all of whom entered into this project with great enthusiasm, professionalism, and efficiency. They did more than write their individual contributions. They willingly engaged with other authors and ourselves to develop and refine a coherent and cross-referring set of papers which, as a result, is considerable greater than the sum of the parts. Crucial to this process was the contribution of a number of referees. Each chapter was reviewed by a least two experts in the field, and their perceptive comments helped authors to refine and update their contributions. Among those who participated in the review process were Emmanuel Bigand, Anne Blood, Warren Brodsky, Claudia Bullerjahn, Alfred Cramer, Ian Cross, Jane Davidson, Walter Dowling, Andrew Gregory, David Hargreaves, Antoine Hennion, Anthony Kemp, Carol Krumhansl, Andreas Lehmann, Jerrold Levinson, Justin London, Clifford Madsen, Peter Martin, Eugene Narmour, Bruno Repp, John Rink, Martin Stokes, William Forde Thompson, Magnus Widesheim, Suzanna Widmer, and Dolf Zillman. In addition, several of the authors provided comments on parts of the book.

We are particularly grateful for the help and support of colleagues at Oxford University Press, for receiving the initial proposal warmly, and encouraging the project at all stages. Martin Baum, our Editor, has taken a close personal interest in all aspects of the project, and his constant attentiveness and readiness to act on behalf of the project has meant a great deal to us.

We acknowledge the support of our respective institutions. Patrik Juslin's work was supported by the Bank of Sweden Tercentenary Foundation. John Sloboda was enabled to devote time and resources to the project by the award of a semester of sabbatical leave under the Keele University Research Investment Scheme.

Finally, we wish to acknowledge two individuals, now retired from full-time academic positions, without whom this project would have been inconceivable. Leonard B. Meyer's brilliant work in the 1950s is the foundation on which almost everything else in this book rests, directly or indirectly. We are delighted that he has supported this project with a contribution which is as fresh and innovative as anything that he has written. Alf Gabrielsson is, in many ways, the father of modern psychological investigations into musical emotions. He was publishing pioneering empirical work relating to emotion and musical expression in the early 1970s, long before any other contributor to this book. He has been profoundly influential for many researchers, not least the editors of the current volume—Juslin through many years of direct collaboration at the Uppsala University, and Sloboda through two decades of collegial support in activities such as the organization of scientific meetings, the nurturing of scholarly scientific bodies, and tireless contributions to the editorial work of books and journals. We salute these two giants, and hope that this book will add to the recognition of their important contributions to the furthering of knowledge.

# FOREWORD

It has often been claimed that music is the language of the emotions. One can interpret this claim in either of two senses. On the one hand, it could be taken to mean that music provides an iconic representation of the affective 'movements of the soul' which is more appropriate to the dynamic flow of emotional experience than symbolic description through verbal labels (which imply steady states). On the other hand, the claim that music is the language of the emotions can also be understood as commentary on the nature of music, specifically the suggestion that music cannot be composed, performed, or listened to without affective involvement. In consequence, the privileged relationship between emotion and music has been the object of much scholarly discussion as well as empirical research. Not surprisingly, then, the topic has been addressed by many different disciplines - philosophy, musicology, literature, psychology, acoustics, anthropology, and neurosciences - as well as by practising musicians, composers and performers alike.

Given its multifaceted nature, the relationship between music and emotion is a topic of central concern for the emerging domain of affective science. The current volume, edited by Patrik Juslin and John Sloboda, will have a major role in establishing the topic as a core research area in this multidisciplinary domain of scientific inquiry. It attempts no lesser feat than bringing together the various concerns with the affective nature of music that have so far been spread over a wide variety of journals and book publications in different disciplines. For all practical purposes, this material has been inaccessible to the non-specialist. In addition, the volume provides a state-of-the-art overview of current thinking and a synthesis of the major research results to date. The editors succeed admirably on both counts.

Following an overview of the various perspectives that have been adopted by the disciplines concerned with the emotional expressiveness and the affective impact of music, the contributions are grouped with respect to their focus on the composer, the performer, and the listener. In an extensive introduction, that helps to structure the issues and define fundamental concepts, as well as in a final commentary, Juslin and Sloboda pull together the various strands and work toward an integration of the different themes. Among the contributors, all established experts in their respective areas, are two of the eminent pioneers in the study of music-emotion relationships - Alf Gabrielsson and Leonard Meyer. This volume is a fitting tribute to their vision.

Given the multitude of perspectives provided in this book and the ensuing enlargement of the horizon for scholars and researchers in the highly specialized disciplines concerned with this topic, one can expect a quantum jump in the sophistication of affective science research on music and emotion. It is equally to be hoped that the fascinating questions and hypotheses detailed in the pages of this volume will recruit a new generation of multidisciplinary-minded researchers to the study of a phenomenon that has intrigued mankind since the dawn of time.

Klaus R. Scherer

PART I

# INTRODUCTION

# CHAPTER 1

# MUSIC AND EMOTION: INTRODUCTION

PATRIK N. JUSLIN AND JOHN A. SLOBODA

Questions about music and emotion have occupied human beings ever since antiquity. It is a topic of considerable interest to laymen and experts alike. Some sort of emotional experience is probably the main reason behind most people's engagement with music. Emotional aspects of music should thus be at the very heart of musical science. It is all the more remarkable then that this topic has been seriously neglected during the last decades. None of the recent books on music psychology, or emotion psychology, have treated emotional aspects of music other than sparingly, despite the fact that some emotion theorists have argued that studies of music might be helpful also in understanding emotions more generally (Gaver & Mandler 1987). The most authoritative handbook of music psychology to appear thus far, *The psychology of music* (Deutsch 1999), does not include a chapter on emotion. Similarly, the most extensive handbook on emotion yet to appear, *Handbook of emotions* (Lewis & Haviland-Jones 2000), also does not contain a chapter on music.

Still, it is probably true that most people experience music—somehow, somewhere— every day of their lives, often with an accompanying affective response of some sort (e.g. nostalgic recognition of a favourite song on the radio while driving a car, frustration directed at the music at the shops, joy when listening to an excellent performance at an evening concert, a sad mood created by the soundtrack of a late night movie). As noted by Dowling and Harwood (1986), 'music arouses strong emotions in people, and they want to know why' (p. 202). However, despite the ubiquity of emotional responses to music, it seems that, for a long time, such reactions have defied psychological explanation.

Without wishing to forestall the different conceptualizations of emotion in this book, it may be useful to provide a preliminary description of how affect is differentiated from other psychological phenomena that occur in relation to music. When an individual engages with music, either as performer, listener, or composer, a very broad range of mental processes and contents may be engaged. The present book focuses on those musical processes and mental contents that have an *evaluative* component. We contrast such phenomena to those processes and contents that are primarily descriptive or *representational*.

Examples of representational processes would include the determination, or awareness, of such properties of a piece of music as metre, rhythm, tonality, harmony, melody, form, and style (whether accomplished explicitly or implicitly). Such representational processes are central to the recognition, identification, and performance of music. They are the focus of the study of music perception and cognition, and, as such, have dominated the scientific literature on musical activity for the last century or more (Deutsch 1999; Sloboda 1985).

Examples of evaluative processes would include the determination, or awareness, of music as eliciting liking or disliking; preference; emotion and mood; and aesthetic, transcendent, and spiritual experiences. We use the term evaluative because it is typical of such processes that they are both *valenced* and *subjective*. Valence refers to the tendency to attach differing degrees of positivity or negativity to whatever is being experienced or processed. Subjectivity refers to the fact that such experiences are affected by labile personal factors such as attitudes, associations, and goals. There is, of course, no absolute dichotomy between representational and evaluative processes. Rather they represent extremes of a continuum. Representation can incorporate evaluative components (particularly in situations of ambiguity, with which music abounds). For instance, hearing the lower rather than the upper line of a two-part invention as 'foreground' may involve preference grounded in subjectivity (this particular listener perhaps prefers focusing on lower parts because he or she is a bass player). Affect can also incorporate representational aspects, especially where some aspect of what is being experienced is deeply embedded culturally or biologically. For example, listeners within a particular culture may have no option but to hear organ music as 'churchy'—with all the emotional connotations that brings—thus appearing to be an 'objective' characteristic of the music. One of the key issues for musical science is to better understand the relationship between the representational and affective processes. Do affective responses always take representations as their starting point, and if so, what other factors moderate between representation and outcome? Unfortunately, musical affect has been the poor relative of contemporary musical science (Sloboda 1995).

## 1.1 The slow progress in the study of music and emotion

Why has the field of music and emotion been so slow to catch up with the other domains of musical science, such as music cognition or musical development? We believe that there are several reasons for this neglect—some that the domain of music and emotion has in common with the field of emotion as a whole, and some that are particular to the music domain. One problem, which has impeded progress in understanding emotions in general, is the difficulty involved in studying emotions in the laboratory (Plutchik 1994, Chapter 1). This is also true of emotional reactions to music, which are difficult to observe under laboratory conditions.

Another reason for the slow progress in the field of music and emotion is the dominant influence of so-called *cognitive science* (Gardner 1985) on psychology in general and music psychology in particular, which has led to a strong emphasis on cognitive aspects of musical behaviour—both in perception (Deutsch 1999; Dowling & Harwood 1986) and performance (Gabrielsson 1999; Palmer 1997). This is illustrated through the titles of some of the main scholarly organizations for music that exist around the world. Most of them contain the word 'cognition'. None contain the word 'emotion' (e.g. Society for Perception and Cognition of Music, European Society for the Cognitive Sciences of Music, International Conference for the Perception and Cognition of

Music). And whereas studies of music cognition have been guided by a common 'paradigm'—the information-processing approach—the study of music and emotion has not yet benefited from any unifying paradigm. Indeed, a number of authors have expressed doubts that current theories of emotion are adequate for dealing with music. Thus it seems to us that the study of musical emotion is pretty much in its 'pre-paradigmatic' phase, to borrow from Kuhn's (1962) terminology. There is still plenty of disagreement in the field about many issues, and at present, it seems that the field is best served by a multiplicity of approaches. A lack of a unifying theoretical framework may explain why no psychologist has attempted to write a book on the topic: it has been too difficult to present a coherent story based on the available literature. However, one important goal for future research could be to try to reach some degree of consensus concerning a common set of concepts, definitions, and methodologies for the study of music and emotion. Indeed, we hope that this very book may contribute to that goal by summarizing a variety of theoretical perspectives and methods in a systematic fashion, highlighting areas of agreement whenever possible.

One reason why many researchers have been reluctant to study musical emotions is that it is a very difficult topic. Most of the early studies in the field were concerned with matching emotion labels to excerpts of music, and for about 50 years, it appeared as if the field would not move beyond such studies. There was no sense of direction in this early work, despite the pioneering studies by Kate Hevner (1935) and others. Perhaps frustrated by a lack of theories and by some difficulties inherent in describing responses to music in words, many researchers simply abandoned the field. Part of the reason for this was also the behaviourist era of the 1940s and 1950s, during which the study of emotions and other 'inner' mental processes were seen as less than scientific. Since then, we believe, there has been a tendency for many researchers to think that the problem of music and emotion is so complex that they would prefer to avoid it altogether—rather than dealing with the problem inadequately, it is better not dealing with it at all. This view has, of course, not improved the state of affairs. As a result, there has been limited progress in the field.

A final reason for the neglect of emotion comes from the fact that much academic study of music takes as paradigmatic a very particular way of listening to music and talking about it that is enshrined in the narrow 'classical concert culture' where, as described by Frith (1996) and others (Cook 1998; Small 1999), audiences are taught to listen 'silently and respectfully' with minimum bodily movement or emotional expression (until the end). 'Appreciation' of music is often taken to mean having an intellectual understanding of the history and form of the musical composition, rather than an articulated emotional response. Even where emotions are valued, they tend to be those rarefied (transcendent or spiritual) forms that are related to 'higher' abstract and aesthetic properties of works, rather than the everyday or full-blooded emotions. As a consequence, there have been few academic discourses available in which to frame and articulate a relevant understanding of the emotions. Such discourses have mainly been relegated to 'the discourse of the hallway' (e.g. Frith 1996), those informal 'off-duty' moments when academics allow themselves to say what they feel about the music they study. It is in the context of increasingly viewing the whole music of the world's cultures as worthy of study (including taking account of the discourses and practices surrounding music making in these diverse cultures) that the possibility of making emotion more central to disciplined talk about music may be increasingly enabled.

## 1.2 Purpose and organization of this book

The present book is, to the best of our knowledge, the first scientific anthology ever devoted specifically to musical emotions. Why should it appear now? Along with a renewal of interest in emotional phenomena in general (e.g. Ekman & Davidson 1994; Lewis & Haviland-Jones 2000) there has been a new surge of interest in music and emotion. Music and emotion is once again at the forefront of music psychology, as reflected in innovative and exciting research all over the world. After a long time of regarding music and emotion as an 'off-limits' topic, scientists are returning to the field to address what may be the most exciting aspect of musical behaviour: its affective consequences. Today, it is almost becoming fashionable again to study emotion. For instance, in August 2000, 94 out of 310 papers (30 per cent) presented at the Sixth International Conference of Music Perception and Cognition (Woods *et al.* 2000) contained the word 'emotion' in the text (as verified by applying a search engine to the CD rom version of the proceedings). By contrast, visual inspection of the proceedings of the First International Conference in the same series (Japanese Society of Music Perception and Cognition 1989) yields only 11 out of 94 papers (12 per cent). The peak of this renaissance is yet to come, we believe.

This book can be characterized by two words. The first word is 'change'. The concept of emotion is intimately related to changes—in particular to significant changes in the social environment (cf. Oatley 1992). Music, too, is about changes. Music takes place in time, in a constant flux. Emotional responses to music are often induced by particular kinds of changes in the music. The field of music and emotion itself has gone through some dramatic changes over the last decade. One of the most significant changes is the increasing diversity of topics, approaches, and methods involved. Another significant change is the increasing concern with theories of music and emotion. Both of these trends are evident in the present volume.

The second word that can be used to characterize this book is 'interface'. Emotions have been conceptualized as the interface between the inner world of goals and plans, and the outer world of objects and events (cf. Scherer 1985). Emotion has also been described as the point where nature meets nurture (Oatley 1992, p. 14)—this is evident in many of the contributions to this volume. Moreover, much of what is interesting about music and emotion takes place at the interface between performance and perception (Juslin 2000). Last but not least, this book represents an interface between researchers from different disciplines. Recent years have seen some important developments in diverse approaches to music and emotion.

Unfortunately, current work is largely scattered across different publications. It is thus difficult to get a sense of the progress in the field, or to grasp what questions researchers are currently debating. The purpose of the present book is to bring together some of the leading researchers of the field for an up-to-date look at the relationship between music and emotion. Fundamental questions addressed by this book include: Why does music induce emotions in its listeners? Are the emotions we experience in relation to music different from the emotions we experience in everyday life? Why are different pieces of music associated with different emotions? Are performers able to communicate specific emotions to listeners? Do emotional responses to music vary as a function of the cultural context? How do emotional responses to music affect the brain and body of listeners?

The purpose of the book is both summative and formative. We aim to summarize what is currently known about music and emotion, but we also aim to stimulate further research in promising directions that have been little researched. The focus is on theory and research on music and emotion rather than practical applications. We believe that, with a few exceptions in the context of music therapy, performance anxiety, and film music, the field of music and emotion has not yet reached a stage where it can provide a consistent body of knowledge for application to a wide range of practical problems (this is incidentally another reason why we prefer to think of the field as being in a 'pre-paradigmatic' phase). However, we believe that the present book covers every major approach to the study of music and emotion.

This volume is organized into four sections following this introduction. The first section provides multidisciplinary perspectives on music and emotion from philosophy, musicology, psychology, biology, anthropology, sociology, and therapy. The next three sections of the book provide research reviews that focus on the composer, the performer, and the listener, respectively. Although, in practice, most musical situations involve some combination of composition, performance, and listening, research has largely tended to focus on one or two of these aspects. (Most research has focused on the listener, and the least on the composer.) Therefore, we have assigned the remaining chapters into sections according to whether their primary focus lies on the composer, the performer, or the listener.

## 1.2.1 Multidisciplinary perspectives

Arguably, emotion is first and foremost a psychological concept (e.g. given the 'mentalistic' nature of the construct and its relation to behaviour). It is not surprising then that the majority of studies on music and emotion to date are psychological. However, the study of music and emotion often transcends the traditional lines of enquiry, and we believe that much can be learned from other perspectives as well. The chapters in Part II of the book are intended to stimulate further research and collaboration in areas that—in some cases at least—have been little studied previously. The chapters are ordered to reflect both historical primacy (philosophy and musicology are arguably the oldest disciplines to consider emotion and music) and also a progression from the more individualist perspectives (as epitomized by psychology and biology) to social and cultural perspectives (as reflected in anthropology and sociology).

One important problem that has plagued theory and research on music and emotion is conceptual confusion. Therefore, an important contribution to the study of music and emotion from philosophy could lie in its ability to resolve conceptual problems. In **Chapter 2, Davies** provides a discussion of philosophical perspectives on music and emotion. After outlining the nature of academic philosophy and discussing philosophical perspectives on emotions, Davies considers three philosophical problems with respect to music and emotion: The first problem concerns the fact that music is often perceived as expressive of emotion—despite the fact that music is not a sentient being. The second problem concerns the listener's emotional response to music in such instances where the listener's response mirrors the music's, despite a lack of beliefs that usually underlie such a response. The third problem concerns why listeners enjoy and revisit pieces of music that, on their own account, incline them to feel sad. In addressing these problems, Davies scrutinizes the major philosophical theories of music's expressiveness—music as symbol, expression theory, arousal theory, music as virtual persona, contour theory—involving the works of Langer, Kivy, Levinson, and Davies himself. Davies further explores the idea that music is a universal language of emotions, and mentions some critical issues that need to be considered in regard to this notion. (This touches upon one of the recurring themes of the book, i.e. the relationship between biological universals and cultural specifics.) Davies' philosophical discussion is framed by a set of constraints that an acceptable theory of music's expressiveness should satisfy, according to Davies. One of these constraints is that the theory must explain how—despite their manifest differences—our non-primary use of emotion words to describe responses to music relates to these words' normal application to the emotions of sentient creatures.

Philosophical concerns about emotion in music have been expressed for almost as long as people have thought about music. Musicological thinking, surveyed by **Cook and Dibben** in **Chapter 3**, also has historical roots stretching back for many centuries (indeed, it could be argued that musicological and philosophical approaches have only been separable in the last three centuries or so). Cook and Dibben's treatment of musicological approaches to music and emotion in Western art music and popular music focuses on theoretical frameworks aimed at understanding how music can embody, express, arouse, or otherwise signify emotional states. Cook and Dibben begin with a historical sketch, tracing some of the developments in thinking about music and emotion that still exert an influence on modern thinking, for instance the ancient notion that music can both represent and induce emotions. An important observation is that our views on musical emotions, throughout history, have been much shaped by contemporary conceptions of emotion in general (e.g. the eighteenth-century affect as a rationalized emotional state, in contrast to the nineteenth-century emotion as personal and spontaneous expression). Cook and Dibben then review a selection of classic music-theoretical approaches to musical emotion (many of which were influenced by linguistic models), including the 'doctrine of affections' and the theories by Cooke, Tagg, Meyer, and others. This leads them to propose that the fundamental problem in musicological approaches to music and emotion is 'to talk about both the emotion and music in a sustained manner'. Cook and Dibben suggest that Hatten's neo-semiotic approach is the most comprehensive attempt to integrate expressive and structural analysis within a coherent critical practice. Cook and Dibben conclude by discussing a 'performative' approach in which music-analytical practices are understood less in terms of how the music *is* and more in terms of how it *might* be heard; the implication is that musicological knowledge actually may shape our perceptions of music. Thus, as Cook and Dibben note, the very act of saying that a certain piece of music is expressive in a certain way well lead us to hear it in that way.

Contemporary psychological approaches to music and emotion have been very much influenced by philosophical and musicological debates. In **Chapter 4, Sloboda and**

**Juslin** describe the essentials of a psychological approach to the study of music and emotion. They suggest that a central aim of psychology is to understand the mechanisms that intervene between music reaching a person's ears and an emotion being perceived, or experienced, by that person as a result of hearing that music. Other important aims involve understanding the roles of emotion in composing and performing music. First, Sloboda and Juslin review the major approaches to conceptualizing emotion in psychology: categorical, dimensional, and prototype approaches. They also show that there are certain underlying and objectively observable characteristics that are present in the set of phenomena we normally describe as 'emotions', and that these same characteristics seem to apply also in the case of music. Then, they consider two primary sources of emotion in music, namely *intrinsic* and *extrinsic* sources. Intrinsic sources are those that are non-arbitrarily embedded in structural characteristics of the music and that contribute to the creation, maintenance, confirmation, or disruption of schematic expectations. Extrinsic sources are of two kinds: (i) iconic sources which come about through some formal resemblance between a musical structure and some event or 'agent' carrying emotional tone; and (ii) associative sources which are premised on arbitrary and contingent relationships between the music being experienced and a range of non-musical factors, which also carry emotional messages of their own. Sloboda and Juslin suggest that failure to see the many ways that music may represent and induce emotions has contributed to the controversies that have characterized the field of music and emotion. No single theory is likely to be able to account for all emotional responses to music. Sloboda and Juslin conclude by suggesting some directions for future research, noting in particular that the psychological approach has tended to ignore the social context of musical behaviour.

**Chapter 5** by **Peretz** outlines a biological approach to music and emotion. This approach is very much rooted in psychology, and uses data from the brain to shed light on the cognitive organization of musical experience. It should be noted that a biological approach to music and emotion may entail evolutionary perspectives, physiological perspectives, or neuropsychological perspectives. It is the last of these that is the focus of Peretz' chapter (an evolutionary perspective is provided by Juslin in Chapter 14, and physiological evidence is reviewed by Scherer and Zentner in Chapter 16). Neuropsychological studies are burgeoning at the moment, with a variety of brain-imaging techniques that can be used to investigate the effects of music on the brain, such as positron emission tomography (PET), functional magnetic resonance imaging (fMRI), and event-related potentials (ERPs). Peretz reviews studies that may shed light on the brain substrates underlying emotional responses to music. Peretz also suggests promising future directions for research, showing what questions, in particular, such studies of music and emotion are most likely to answer. Peretz concludes that emotional appreciation of music is best conceived as the product of a specialized cortical arrangement that is shared by most members of a given musical culture.

Psychology and neuropsychology focus on emotion as experienced and perceived by the individual. The remaining chapters of this section consider musical emotion from a broader social perspective, beginning in **Chapter 6** where **Becker** presents perspectives on music and emotion from music anthropology: the study of modes of music making as a means of cultural expression. Becker challenges some of the unexamined 'ideologies' and presuppositions that have dominated Western theorizing about music and emotion and that—as she demonstrates—do not apply for most of the world. This includes the common view of the listener as inwardly focused and isolated. Becker introduces the concept of 'habitus' of listening to describe the listening habits and expectations that listeners within a particular culture 'accumulate largely unawares'. These habits reveal implicit assumptions in the listening context about what music 'means', what it is for, how it is to be perceived, and what might be 'appropriate' responses. Becker goes on to consider anthropological views on emotion, and reviews evidence of cultural differences in the expression of, motivation for, and interpretation of emotion in relation to musical events. However, she also notes that, through experience and empathy, we can come to understand differing emotional reactions to different kinds of music. Becker then presents examples of different kinds of habitus of listening from her fieldwork and that of others. Becker suggests that autonomic arousal is a human universal related to music making. This leads her to the main theme of her chapter: a plea for a move to transcend the dichotomy between 'scientific universalism' and 'humanistic particularity'. In particular, Becker suggests that biological and cultural approaches to music and emotion may be brought together by understanding music listening as a process in which the relationship between music and emotion extends beyond the minds and bodies of individuals. She argues that this process can be viewed as 'biological', since both performers and listeners undergo a learning process in which they imitate physical and mental gestures that transform both their inner structures and their relationships to everything beyond the boundaries of the body.

The social context of musical behaviour is also central to **Chapter 7** in which **DeNora** presents a sociological perspective on music and emotion. Sociology is concerned with investigating forms of social organization and the relations of these forms to social action, whether 'macro' (large-scale institutions) or 'micro' (interactional processes). DeNora first considers the recent rediscovery of emotion in sociology, which has been linked to sociology's traditional concern with social contexts. (A concern with the social context of music making is another recurring theme in the present book.) Then she describes how the focus of sociological studies of music has changed over the last decade, from preoccupations with music's production—music as an object shaped by social relations—to concerns with how it is consumed and what it 'does' in social life. Within this 'new' sociology of music, she observes, music is conceptualized as a device for the constitution of emotive action in and across a range of social settings. (DeNora traces the origins of this development to the writings of Theodor Adorno and ethnographic studies in the 1970s.) One of the most promising trends in the 'new' sociology, according to DeNora, is the discovery of how music can be used by, and on behalf of, actors as a resource to construct self-identity and to create and maintain a variety of emotions. DeNora illustrates this point by reviewing some recent work by Hennion and herself concerning the uses of music in everyday life. Based on in-depth interviews, these studies reveal that listeners are not merely passively affected by music, but rather are actively constructing their own ability to be moved. Moreover, the studies reveal how people use music to regulate, enhance, and change qualities and levels of emotion. They show considerable awareness about the music they 'need' to hear in different situations and at different times to influence aspects of themselves and their self-concepts. Such uses of music are based on the listeners' perceptions of what they believe the music to 'afford', for instance associations that listeners have made between certain musical materials and extramusical features. DeNora suggests that there may be a useful bridge here between sociology's focus on associations that listeners forge between music and emotions, and musicology's traditional focus on ways in which musical structures lend themselves to particular interpretations.

Ending this section is a contribution which shows how music embedded in a context of social interaction can become an agent of therapy or healing. **Chapter 8** by **Bunt and Pavlicevic** considers the role of music in music therapy, with a particular focus on improvisational music therapy. First, they give a general background to music therapy, discussing different forms of music therapy and showing how the different sources of emotion described by Sloboda and Juslin in Chapter 4 may be observed in clinical practice. A critical aspect to the generating and receiving of emotion in music therapy is the direct experiencing of emotion within the listener or player, as well as the recognition of emotion within the music itself. Therapists' abilities to make emotion judgments from musical improvisations were explored in a study summarized by Bunt and Pavlicevic. The therapists listed a large number of musical parameters that aided the process of judging the emotions (Bunt and Pavlicevic note that these are common features of many musical improvisations made by patients of all ages). Moreover, Bunt and Pavlicevic show how recent work in developmental child psychology by Trevarthen, Trehub, Papoušek, and others, and in particular Stern's so-called 'vitality affects', can provide reference points in understanding the subtle interplay between the personal and the musical in improvisational music therapy. They suggest that the primary locus of any therapeutic change lies in the interpersonal musical relationship built up between therapist and patient. Examples from their own practice show how Pavlicevic's concept of dynamic form can be used to understand how the relationship between the therapist and the patient is defined in real-time improvisations. This chapter complements the scientific perspectives offered by the previous chapters by providing unique insights from clinical practice.

We believe that this multidisciplinary section makes at least two things clear. First, it suggests that multidisciplinary approaches are called for—perhaps even necessary—to make real progress in understanding the relationship between music and emotion in all its richness and complexity. Second, it calls for some humility. Given the broad range of domains that intersect with the study of music and emotion—from brain imaging to sociological studies to analyses of musical structure—we cannot expect any one individual to be able to address the topic from all angles simultaneously. The key word is 'collaboration'. The first section of the book presents a challenge to the reader, with its wide range of disciplines, theories, concepts, and methods. Many of the traditional views on music and emotion are certainly challenged. However, we believe that the reader who is willing to accept this challenge will be rewarded with a fresh look on the topic, and that he or she may be able to look at the other contributions of the book in the light of these multidisciplinary statements.

### 1.2.2 The composer

In Part III, the focus is on the composer and—in particular—the materials or 'building blocks' that the composer can work with. In subsequent sections, the contributions examine emotion as communicated and experienced by the performer, and finally by the end-recipient, the listener.

One of the fundamental emotion dimensions which studies of music listening have identified is *arousal*. The notion of arousal is crucial to **Simonton's Chapter 9**, which links this concept to the act of music composition. In other chapters of the book, the authors have reviewed evidence based on such methods as philosophical enquiry, experiment, observation, brain imaging, interview, and structural analysis. In this chapter, Simonton adopts yet another approach called 'historiometrics', which involves the adaptation of psychometric methods to analyse data about historic individuals. In the case of classical composers, Simonton includes both biographical information about their lives and content-analytical information about their works. Simonton has been using this particular technique to study creativity and aesthetics in classical music. Although this research programme was not directed specifically at investigating musical emotion, some of the empirical results clearly have a bearing on this topic. Simonton begins by defining his concept and measure of 'melodic originality' in musical compositions, and goes on to show that this simple measure—which incidentally seems to encompass more compositional aspects than just melody alone—may be related to a piece's 'arousal potential' as perceived by listeners. Pieces of music scoring high on 'melodic originality' should sound more unpredictable, interesting, or complex (and thus yield more uncertainty, to elaborate on Meyer's views in Chapter 15) than melodies scoring lower. Simonton refers to experimental work that supports this hypothesis, and there is a clear link to Meyer's theory that emotional arousal reflects the violation of musical expectations. Simonton goes on to demonstrate that the relation between arousal potential and aesthetic impact is curvilinear, in accordance with the 'Wundt curve', and that the most popular classical works in the real world are those that evoke an optimum arousal level. However, due to 'habituation', the response to an arousing stimulus will often diminish. Therefore, as Simonton illustrates, composers have a tendency to increase their use of melodic originality as their careers progress. Moreover, Simonton argues (boldly) that the degree of melodic originality also reflects the emotional life of the composer at the time of a work's composition, such that the melodic originality (and hence the 'arousal potential') is larger during periods of life stress. Indeed, Simonton finds a positive relationship between measures of melodic originality and an index of life stress for ten eminent composers of classical repertoire (after controlling for confounding factors). Simonton also discusses the 'Swan song' phenomenon (i.e. the idea that composers exhibit a 'late life' compositional style). Simonton concludes that 'melodic originality', at least to some extent, forms part of the composer's tools for expressing emotions in music. However, he also observes that composers have a great deal more in their 'expressive tool kit' than just the choice of pitches.

Additional aspects of the expressive tool kit that composers can use to express various emotions are dealt with in **Chapter 10**, in which **Gabrielsson and Lindström** present a review of studies—from the end of the nineteenth century to the present day—that have attempted to specify the expressive properties of various elements of musical structure usually indicated in the musical notation of a piece of music (performance aspects are reviewed in Chapter 14 by Juslin). This is, in fact, the domain within which most of the traditional studies of music and emotion tend to fall. Gabrielsson and Lindström first describe different methodological approaches used in studies of expression in music since the late nineteenth century, including different response formats: free description, adjective checklists, adjective ratings, and continuous response (reviewed by Schubert in Chapter 17). Studies also differ with regard to musical stimuli, ranging from brief and simple sound sequences to recordings of entire musical compositions. Then, Gabrielsson and Lindström review findings about the expressive properties of different musical elements, such as interval, mode, rhythm, tempo, melodic direction, harmony, timbre, and form. This review uncovers a number of relationships between musical elements and particular emotions, but also indicates several gaps and ambiguities in the results. In particular, few investigations have considered potential interactions among different elements. Gabrielsson and Lindström conclude by suggesting directions for future research, emphasizing the need to explore more sophisticated manipulations of melody, rhythm, timbre, and harmonic progression. Even so, the findings reviewed by Gabrielsson and Lindström provide a rich source of music-emotion relationships that have been used, or could be used, in a variety of practical contexts such as music therapy or film music.

In **Chapter 11**, **Cohen** considers an applied compositional domain that has a substantial history: the use of music in film. This complements Chapters 8 and 13 which explore applications of knowledge about emotion in the context of music therapy and performance anxiety. The purpose of Cohen's chapter is to address the question of what contribution music makes to the emotional impact of film. Cohen argues that music is one of the strongest sources of emotion in film and intends to open doors to further empirical work that explains why this is so. Cohen begins by establishing a context for discussing emotion in music and film. Then, she presents a historical perspective on film music, from the use of music in silent film to the advent of the sound film in the late 1920s. Cohen also reviews empirical research that has investigated the effects and functions of music in film. These functions of film music include masking extraneous noises, providing continuity between shots, directing attention to important features, inducing mood, communicating meaning and furthering the narrative, enabling the symbolization of past and future events through the technique of leitmotiv, heightening the sense of reality, and adding, as an art form, to the aesthetic effect of the film. Cohen also presents a cognitive framework for understanding musical phenomena of relevance to soundtracks. Finally, she considers the role of the composer as the ultimate source of musical emotion in film, discussing conditions and requirements associated with composing music for film. A hypothesis of Cohen's chapter is that the capacity of music to accomplish its emotional task may be based on the ability of music to simultaneously carry several kinds of emotional information in its harmony, rhythm, melody, timbre, and tonality. Real life often entails multiple emotions, simultaneously and in succession. Miraculously, yet systematically, Cohen argues, this 'emotional polyphony' can be represented by the musical medium.

### 1.2.3 The performer

In Part IV of the book, the focus is on the role of emotion in the performance of music. In **Chapter 12, Persson** makes an excursion into the subjective world of the performer, outlining exploratory research into the 'phenomenology' of emotion in musical performance. This includes such issues as performance motivation and interpretation, and the learning and conceptualization process of constructing musical meaning. Persson acknowledges that there is little previous research in this area, but notes that the present chapter might serve as a basis for future research and provide a preliminary understanding of how performers construe the subjective aspects of musical performance. Persson's overview is based on qualitative and quantitative research by himself and others, as well as on published interviews with famous performers. Persson considers the motivational basis for becoming a performer, asking what made certain individuals choose a musical career. Although a variety of reasons are suggested, a significant finding from Persson's research is that many performers are motivated primarily by a 'hedonic' motive—treasuring music as a means to control and induce positive emotional experiences by means of playing (this theme is also evident in Chapter 6 by Becker). Persson then considers the roles of emotion in interpretation, discussing imagery, conceptualization of musical meaning, and so-called self-induction to altered states of awareness. He concludes by suggesting directions for (much needed) further research concerning the subjective world of performers.

As noted by Persson in Chapter 12, one important reason for performing music is that it induces positive emotions in the performer. In **Chapter 13, Steptoe** considers the flip side of the coin: While performance of music often generates strong positive emotions, it may also induce *negative* emotions in the performer, such as distress and anxiety. Such emotions may impair the quality of performance, and could also have debilitating effects on the performer's career. Steptoe reviews the psychological and medical literature on performance anxiety and also considers other negative emotions related to music performance as a profession, such as social tension, worries about job security, boredom, feeling separated from family, and so forth. Furthermore, Steptoe argues that research on performance anxiety would benefit from regarding performance anxiety as a form of situational stress response, which is similar in certain respects to problems such as social phobia or academic examination stress. By analogy with other work on stress, Steptoe suggests, it may be useful to separate distinct components of performance anxiety. One such component is affect, which forms the central experience of performance anxiety for many musicians. However, there are other important aspects as well, including cognitive responses (e.g. disturbances in information processing), changes in behaviour, and physiological responses. Steptoe reviews some promising treatment methods that have been devised for stress management, and argues that the incorporation of these principles into the training of musicians could be very beneficial.

Numerous studies have investigated emotional expression in pieces of music (these studies are reviewed by Gabrielsson and Lindström in Chapter 10). However, only recently have researchers begun to study how different aspects of the *performance* affect the emotional expression of a piece of music. This topic is reviewed by **Juslin in Chapter**

14. He provides a review of empirical studies of communication of emotion in music performance, and outlines a theoretical framework suitable for organizing the findings. The review of studies focuses on two aspects of the communicative process, namely how well performers succeed in conveying a particular emotional interpretation to a listener, and what acoustic means they use to do this. The relationships between variables in the performance and emotion categories (e.g. sadness) and dimensions (e.g. arousal, activity) are described, with emphasis on 'expressive contours' and so-called 'mixed' emotions. Then, Juslin outlines a theory to account for the origin of the 'code' used by performers. Following the biological approach to music and emotion discussed by Peretz in Chapter 5, Juslin suggests an evolutionary perspective on performers' expressive skills. He argues that the acoustic code of performers reflects both innate 'brain programmes' for vocal expression of emotions, and social learning (for example, learning of links between cues and extramusical aspects through analogies). He further argues that the code used by performers today may be linked—in functional ways—to important cultural activities of the past. Juslin also describes a Brunswikian 'lens model' that can serve to illustrate how music performers communicate emotions to listeners by combining a number of uncertain but partly redundant cues in the performance. The lens model makes it possible to quantitively relate performance to perception in order to better understand the functional relationships between expression and recognition of emotion. Finally, possible mechanisms for the induction of emotion by expressive performance are discussed by Juslin.

### 1.2.4 The listener

In the final part of the book, the focus is on the listener. The contributions are ordered to reflect the progression of Part II (multidisciplinary perspectives). This progression begins with a musicological (and philosophical) contribution, moving to two chapters concerned with the explanation and measurement of individual response, and ends with two contributions which emphasize the effect of social context on listener response.

One of the most influential analyses of musical emotion was given by Meyer (1956) in his book, *Emotion and meaning in music.* In **Chapter 15, Meyer** revisits his theory to provide an updated version of his view on music and emotion. The focus of Meyer's essay is on the role of uncertainty in listeners' emotional responses to music. First, Meyer provides a number of distinctions for the field of music and emotion, observing that the field has lacked conceptual specificity and precision (another theme recurring throughout this book, see, for example, Chapters 4 and 16). Then, he points out that researchers have tended to focus on emotions as states rather than processes. Consequently, Meyer notes, researchers have underestimated the importance of succession in explaining emotional responses to music. In fact, the heart of the emotional experiences of music lies, he argues, in processes that can be understood in terms of creation and minimization of uncertainty (the role of uncertainty is also discussed by Juslin in Chapter 14, but whereas Juslin focuses on the 'textural' resolution of uncertainty via parallel 'cues' to emotion, Meyer focuses on the 'successive' resolution of uncertainty in musical 'episodes'). Meyer distinguishes between 'native' processes (which reflect constraints that are inherent in the human mind and body, e.g. the gestalt laws) from 'syntactic' processes (which depend on learning, having internalized the constraints of a particular style). Both 'native' and 'syntactic' processes generate uncertainty (about what will happen, when it will happen, and how it will happen). Uncertainty, in turn, generates arousal and schematic implications that are disrupted, delayed, or confirmed. Ultimately, Meyer observes, this process reflects the human need to envisage in order to choose. But whereas we try hard to avoid uncertainty in everyday life, in the arts—including music—we frequently cultivate and relish a considerable amount of uncertainty. But uncertainty itself is not an emotion, according to Meyer. Uncertainty is rather one of the sustaining conditions for emotions. The uncertainty is a function of the amount of information the mind is required to process. Therefore, as the number and strength of implied musical alternatives increase, so does the uncertainty.

**Scherer and Zentner** in **Chapter 16** present a theoretical framework for studying emotional effects of music in which they include very stringent criteria for distinguishing different kinds of affective response: mood, emotion, preference, attitude, personal trait, and interpersonal stance. Scherer and Zentner propose that we should theoretically define the effects of music on the listener in the form of 'rules', which specify the relative contribution of different features (such as musical structure, performance, listener personality and mood, and context). The bulk of their chapter deals with production rules, outlining those mechanisms that can be theoretically expected to produce, or induce, changed emotional states in the listener (e.g. appraisal, memory, empathy, or proprioceptive feedback). Scherer and Zentner suggest that it is important to clarify exactly which type of state can be produced by music and what criteria should be used to determine the presence of the respective states empirically. Then, they review the literature pertinent to this issue, and examine the effects of music on cognition, physiological arousal, motor expressive behaviour, action tendencies, and subjective experience. Scherer and Zentner argue that, ideally, the claim that music can induce emotions should be instantiated by studies showing that listening to a piece of music reliably leads to a *synchronization* of cognitive, physiological, expressive, motivational, and experiential processes. Few studies of this kind are currently available, although Scherer and Zentner review a large number of studies of separate components, which provide preliminary evidence of emotional responses. One theme in the chapter is that researchers should be open to new ways of conceptualizing affective responses to music. Scherer and Zentner also suggest that an important goal for future research might be to develop a vocabulary of emotion specifically for the domain of music. They conclude by making suggestions for theoretically based and methodologically sound future research on emotion production.

One of the themes of Meyer (Chapter 15) is that researchers have tended to underestimate the importance of succession in explaining emotional responses to music. Following this lead from Meyer, **Schubert** (in **Chapter 17**) presents an overview of recent attempts to address this problem by means of 'continuous response methodology'. The comprehensive research agenda proposed by Scherer and Zentner (Chapter 16) also requires the development of such methodologies. First, Schubert considers different response formats used in continuous response research—checklists, open-ended formats, and rating scales—noting some of the problems associated with particular formats. He argues that rating scales based on emotion dimensions like *valence, activity*, and *arousal* are most useful in continuous measurement of emotional response. Schubert goes on to discuss the different uses of continuous response methods in the literature: validation of various response formats, comparative investigations (e.g. comparing the responses of musically trained and untrained listeners), stimulus-response investigations (i.e. exploring which musical parameters predict changes in response), and system-dynamics investigations (i.e. studying the dynamic nature of emotional responses over time). Schubert also provides a critical discussion of problems concerning the design, validity, and reliability of continuous response instruments (e.g. the coding of musical features, response coding, synchronization of music and response, sampling rate, lag structure, and statistical analysis). Schubert argues that researchers using continuous response methods must become more aware of the analytical problems created by continuous response data, and suggests some solutions for dealing with these problems. He concludes that the main advantages of continuous response methodology—the abilities to study moment-to-moment changes in the relationship between musical structures and emotional responses and the 'lag' structure of listeners' response to music—are yet to be fully exploited by researchers.

Scherer and Zentner argue in Chapter 16 that future work on the emotional effects of music must pay greater attention to motivational constructs that are specific to music (e.g. 'why do people listen to music?'), because these are the motivational urges that need to be taken into account when we attempt to assess goal conduciveness or obstruction in cognitive appraisals of musically induced emotions. A fresh perspective on this motivational terrain, the uses and functions of music in everyday life, is provided in **Chapter 18** by **Sloboda and O'Neill**. They build on the foundation laid out by DeNora in Chapter 7, pointing out that music is a cultural resource in the social construction of emotions. Music, they observe, is heard in a particular place and time, with or without other persons being present, and with other activities taking place at the same time. Thus, an account of emotional responses to music must recognize the interaction among these different factors. The purpose of Sloboda and O'Neill's chapter is to discuss research on habitual and routine modes of engagement with music, including as much of the social context as possible. By definition, everyday uses of music are difficult to study in the laboratory. Further, they tend to be unmemorable and, hence, unsuitable for retrospective report of the kind used by Gabrielsson (in Chapter 19). The solution adopted by Sloboda and O'Neill is called the 'experience sampling method'. This involves the use of electronic pagers that subjects carry with them during the waking hours, along with a booklet that they fill in on each paging. A study by Sloboda and co-workers using this method indicated that there was a 44 per cent likelihood of music being experienced in any 2-hour period—confirming the common claim that music pervades everyday life. More importantly, the study showed how music was used in a wide range of everyday activities. One of the working assumptions made by Sloboda and O'Neill is that music can have different 'emotional functions' in different situations, and they present evidence that listeners use music to manage their moods in a number of different ways. Indeed, this deliberate use of music to achieve specific psychological outcomes can be described in terms of 'self-therapy'—a practice partly corresponding to the professional uses of music to that same end in music therapy (see Bunt and

Pavlicevic, Chapter 8). One notable finding from Sloboda and O'Neill's pager study is that the majority of episodes that involved music resulted in the listeners feeling more positive and alert. That is, music made them feel better. However, Sloboda and O'Neill also review evidence of negative emotions in memories of childhood experiences, often related to an evaluative context and hence reminiscent of the negative emotions experienced by some adult performers (Chapter 13). Sloboda and O'Neill conclude that musical activities are enmeshed in a social and cultural world which involves a number of 'hidden' practices and assumptions about musical activity. Only by uncovering the 'hidden' meanings of these practices, Sloboda and O'Neill argue, can we hope to gain a better understanding of emotional responses to music in everyday life.

In **Chapter 19**, **Gabrielsson** reviews findings about emotional reactions to music based on free phenomenological description of strong experiences of music. Gabrielsson begins by discussing the notion of *peak experience*, made famous by the humanistic psychologist Abraham Maslow. Gabrielsssson then describes his research project on strong experiences of music (SEM), the purpose of which was to get some sense of what phenomena are contained in such experiences, and to study how SEM are related to the properties of the music, the individual, and the situation. Gabrielsson is also concerned with the long-term consequences of such experiences. To address these questions, Gabrielsson adopts an approach involving written self-reports by listeners of their strongest experiences of music. Content analysis of several self-reports yielded an overall classification of SEM into physical and behavioural aspects, perceptual aspects, cognitive aspects, emotional aspects, motivational aspects, existential/transcendental aspects, and developmental aspects. In the present chapter, Gabrielsson explores in depth the emotional aspects, providing a large number of examples of emotional reactions to music from the listeners' reports. The examples include so-called 'basic' emotions as well as 'aesthetic' and 'transcendental' emotions. These descriptions provide fascinating glimpses into the peak experiences that many people treasure. Gabrielsson notes that positive emotions dominate in the reports, often in the form of euphoria that borders on ecstasy, but that there are also examples of strong negative emotions. Finally, Gabrielsson considers some implications of these findings for theories of emotional responses to music, and also mentions certain problems associated with retrospective, verbal description of music experience, such as memory distortions and individual differences in verbal fluency.

## 1.3 Concluding remarks

The peer-reviewed contributions of the present book will reveal how much progress there has been in this field since Meyer's (1956) classic book, *Emotion and meaning in music*. Besides providing research overviews, many of the chapters also set forth significant paths for future theory and research. *Music and emotion* may thus serve many functions. First, it may provide a research source for what is currently known about music and emotion. Second, it may serve as a starting point for investigating the field. Third, and as already noted, it can be a source of interdisciplinary dialogue. The chapters in this volume represent the history of the study of music and emotion, its present state, and its future. This scope is reflected in the age range of the contributors. At the time of writing, the youngest of the contributors is 30 years old and the oldest is 82 years old. Throughout the work on this book we have often been struck by the enthusiasm with which the authors have shared their ideas about music and emotion; we hope that this enthusiasm will come through in their contributions.

Last but not least, we would like to describe one of our personal reasons for bringing together this anthology. We are dedicating this book to Alf Gabrielsson to coincide with his retirement in June 2001. Alf has made an enormous contribution to the field of music research—both as a researcher and as a teacher—as many of his colleagues would be willing to attest. Of more direct relevance for the present volume, Alf was one of the (relatively few) people who repeatedly stressed the importance of studying emotional aspects of music, long before it became fashionable to do so. We sense an increase of interest in affective processes in music at the moment and hope that the twenty-first century will be the time when the domain of music and emotion finally catches up with the other domains of musical science. This would surely help us to gain a better understanding of the manifold ways that music enriches all of our lives.

## References

Cook, N. (1998). *Music: A very short introduction.* Oxford, UK: Oxford University Press.

Deutsch, D. (ed.) (1999). *The psychology of music,* (2nd edn). San Diego, CA: Academic Press.

Dowling, W. J. & Harwood, D. L. (1986). *Music cognition.* New York: Academic Press.

Ekman, P. & Davidson, R. J. (ed.) (1994). *The nature of emotion: Fundamental questions.* New York: Oxford University Press.

Frith, S. (1996). *Performing rites: On the value of popular music.* Oxford, UK: Oxford University Press.

Gabrielsson, A. (1999). The performance of music. In *The psychology of music,* (2nd edn) (ed. D. Deutsch), pp. 501–602. San Diego, CA: Academic Press.

Gardner, H. (1985). *The mind's new science. A history of the cognitive revolution.* New York: Basic Books.

Gaver, W. W. & Mandler, G. (1987). Play it again, Sam: On liking music. *Cognition and Emotion,* 1, 259–82.

Hevner, K. (1935). Expression in music: A discussion of experimental studies and theories. *Psychological Review,* 42, 186–204.

Japanese Society of Music Perception and Cognition (1989). *Proceedings of the First International Conference on Music Perception and Cognition.* Kyoto City, Japan: University of Arts, Department of Music.

Juslin, P. N. (2000). Cue utilization in communication of emotion in music performance: Relating performance to perception. *Journal of Experimental Psychology: Human Perception and Performance,* 26, 1797–813.

Kuhn, T. S. (1962). *The structure of scientific revolutions.* Chicago: University of Chicago Press.

Lewis, M. & Haviland-Jones, J. M. (ed.) (2000). *Handbook of emotions,* (2nd edn). New York: The Guilford Press.

Meyer, L. B. (1956). *Emotion and meaning in music.* Chicago: University of Chicago Press.

Oatley, K. (1992). *Best laid schemes. The psychology of emotions.* Cambridge, MA: Harvard University Press.

Palmer, C. (1997). Music performance. *Annual Review of Psychology*, **48**, 115–38.

Plutchik, R. (1994). *The psychology and biology of emotion.* New York: Harper-Collins.

Scherer, K. R. (1985). Vocal affect signaling: A comparative approach. In *Advances in the study of behavior*, (Vol 15) (ed.J. Rosenblatt, C. Beer , M-C. Busnel, & P. J. B. Slater), pp. 189–244. New York: Academic Press.

Sloboda, J. A. (1985). *The musical mind. The cognitive psychology of music.* Oxford, UK: Oxford University Press.

Sloboda, J. A. (1995). Psychology of music today: The need for applicable psychology. In *Psychology of music today*, (ed. M. Manturzewska, K. Miklaszzewski, & A. Biatkowski), pp. 19–24. Warsaw, Poland: Frederyk Chopin Academy of Music.

Small, C. (1999). Musicking: the meanings of performance and listening. A lecture. *Music Education Research*, **1**, 9–21.

Woods, C., Luck, G., Brochard, R., Seddon, F., & Sloboda, J. A. (ed.) (2000). *Proceedings of the Sixth International Conference on Music Perception and Cognition, August 2000* (CD rom). Keele, UK: University of Keele, Department of Psychology.

# Part II

# MULTIDISCIPLINARY PERSPECTIVES

# CHAPTER 2

# PHILOSOPHICAL PERSPECTIVES ON MUSIC'S EXPRESSIVENESS

STEPHEN DAVIES

## 2.1 Philosophy and its method

Sometimes philosophy seems to psychologists to be psychologizing in a fashion that is uninformed and unrestrained by empirical data. (That's alright, sometimes psychology looks to philosophers like unskilled philosophizing!) As this is the only chapter by a philosopher, I begin with an introduction outlining the nature of academic philosophy.

For most questions, one (or more) of the following strategies supplies the answer: fact finding, scientific theorizing, calculating, voting, and legislating. The natural and social sciences rely on the first three of these methods. Some questions are not satisfactorily resolved by their use, however. The issues these questions present are neither empirical nor merely matters of opinion—they are 'philosophical'. 'Philosophy' comes to connote the recalcitrant residue of questions which remain after all the (other) branches of knowledge and taste have taken the questions they are equipped to answer. The fact that philosophical questions are immune from empirical data suggests, perhaps, that they arise from deep conceptual confusions or subtleties, and that it is the purpose of philosophy to untangle these knotted skeins.

Some of the questions of philosophy are distinctive to it, such as many of those addressed by metaphysics, ethics, and logic. But, also, philosophical queries are generated by consideration of foundational issues in all areas and disciplines, and so there is philosophy of art, of science, of mathematics, of feminism, of medicine, of mind, and so on.

Some classic examples of philosophical questions are these: What is truth? Is causality a natural relation or, instead, merely how constant conjunction sometimes is interpreted by human observers? What is identity? Is more than one consideration (such as merit and need) relevant to justice and, if so, are these different aspects mutually commensurable? How is the good to be characterized? What is time? A few moment's reflection should make clear that the answers cannot be settled by an investigation looking at the sorts of facts tested by science. The usual scientific methods of enquiry typically presuppose certain answers to such questions, and the use of such approaches thereby prejudges the outcome of the study. To take another case, how could science analyse the nature of scientific facts without begging the outcome? And another: if empirical facts underdetermine the explanatory theories we apply to them, we cannot choose between theories, as we will want to do in distinguishing pseudo-science and psycho-babble from legitimate disciplines, solely by citing the facts, because what counts as a fact and how it is significant is disputed between the contested theories. Also, if we are indeed enmeshed in some subtle confusion about a topic, we may be confused in how to describe and respond to (further) empirical evidence.

To say that philosophical method is non-empirical is not to imply that philosophy is indifferent to the facts of science. Philosophical analyses must be consistent with the facts, or with interpretations of what these are. But philosophical analyses must go beyond the facts in resolving the problems, paradoxes, and inconsistencies they can seem to generate. What is needed often is not more facts, but a clarification of the issues raised by those that are available. The most familiar notions can produce conceptual puzzles, and then it is not more facts but a deepening of our current understanding, or new interpretations of the resident data, that is needed. Sometimes philosophical investigations are suggestive of new empirical questions, and here science takes over again. At other times, a grasp of unexpected conceptual connections or distinctions enables us to overcome the mental cramps that formerly afflicted us.

To bring out their non-empirical nature, philosophical puzzles often describe two things that are alike in their appearance or empirical features but which strike us as conceptually very different, and then asks what makes that difference. For instance, Descartes wondered how he knew he was not presently dreaming, given that he could dream that he was dreaming. Others have explored how we are to describe the distinction between one's arm's being moved and the action of one's moving one's arm, or how Marcel Duchamp's ready-mades could be artworks where their lookalike, unappropriated counterparts were not.

It could be that nothing hangs on how we answer the philosophical questions before us. In that case, we will come to see that it is for us to decide which way to go, since there is no truth of the matter to be discovered. And it can be that, on examination, philosophical questions turn out to be nonsensical. But it cannot be assumed from the beginning, however, that all philosophical questions are empty, trivial, or silly. In many cases, how we propose to resolve a philosophical question can have far-reaching implications for other cases, for overall consistency within our folk practices, for the power and fecundity of our explanatory models, and for coherence and consistency in our theories.

Not all philosophical questions are weighty. 'Is the karaoke singer a co-performer with the people on the accompanying DVD?' is a philosophical question that provokes us to consider the individuating conditions of performances and recordings, but it is not in the same league as 'what is the meaning of life?' And not all weighty questions are as exciting as this last. Also, the significance of the topic under discussion is often not apparent in the examples in terms of which it is discussed. These frequently are mundane or commonplace, either because it is appropriate to begin with uncontroversial paradigms or to avoid illustrations that attract attention to themselves, rather than to what is at issue. Philosophers who discuss the expression of emotion in music regularly offer the slow movement of Beethoven's *Eroica* as illustrating musical sadness. This does not mean they deny that other pieces are expressive, or that other emotions can be expressed in music. Instead, it indicates that even such a humdrum case already presents in a graphic form the puzzle that troubles the philosopher.

Sometimes, Anglo-American analytical philosophy, which is the approach of this chapter, is contrasted with continental philosophy. The differences are largely matters of degree or style. In terms of the philosophy of music, Continental approaches sometimes describe an entire metaphysical system and consider music in order to locate it within that system; or they view music in terms of larger sociopolitical or psychological models of human behaviour, such as Marxist or psychoanalytic ones; or, again, they approach it from the perspective of general theories that are semiotic, structuralist, or deconstructionist. And when they do focus on music as such, they are likely to emphasize the subjective response and the phenomenology of musical experience. By contrast, analytic philosophy is less theory-driven and politically motivated. It is centred on perceived 'problems' or 'questions', rather than on a canon of works by great philosophers. The approach is (often) piecemeal, tackling issues one by one as their relevance emerges. The focus falls on interpersonal judgments and public criteria, rather than the idiosyncratic or personal.

In what follows, I concentrate on philosophical discussions of music's expressive character. An obvious question asks how music could be expressive of emotion, which is how we seem to experience many pieces, when it is non-sentient. Depending on how we answer this first query, we are led to others. For instance, if we argue that expressive predicates apply only metaphorically to music, we might then be puzzled at the strength of the response music is capable of eliciting from the listener.

The topic on which I focus, that of music's expressiveness, has been a dominant one in music aesthetics, but many subjects not covered here have also attracted detailed examination by philosophers. These include the ontology of musical works (Goehr 1992; Gracyk 1996; Levinson 1990), performances and their relation to works (Godlovitch 1998; Thom 1993), the notion of 'authentic' performance (Davies 1987; Kivy 1995; Levinson 1990), musical representation (Davies 1994; Kivy 1988), ways in which music can be said to be meaningful and the kind of understanding it invites (Davies 1994; Kivy 1990; Levinson 1990, 1997a), music's value (Budd 1995; Davies 1994; Goldman 1995a; Higgins 1991; Kivy 1990, 1997), and music's social significance and ethical dimension (Goehr 1998; Higgins 1991). For recent collections covering many of these topics, see Alperson (1994, 1998), Robinson (1997), and Hjort and Laver (1997).

## 2.2 Ways in which music's expression of emotions is philosophically problematic

In this chapter I consider three puzzles, the first of which has dominated philosophical discussions about music and emotion over the past two decades. It observes that purely instrumental music is not the kind of thing that can express emotions.[1] Music is not

---

[1]   The focus falls on instrumental music simply because the problem of music's expressive powers is at its most acute where music is divorced from words, narrative, and drama.

sentient and neither is its relation to occurrent emotions such that it could express them. The second problem concerns the listener's response, where this mirrors the music's expressive character. When listeners are saddened by the music's sadness, apparently they lack the beliefs that normally underpin such a reaction; for example, they do not think the music suffers, or that the music's expressiveness is unfortunate and regrettable. The third perplexity concerns negative responses elicited by music, such as the sad one just mentioned. Why do listeners enjoy and revisit works that, on their own account, incline them to feel sad? (For a summary of philosophical approaches to these three topics and more besides, see Levinson 1997*b*, 1998.) Before addressing these puzzles, it is useful to examine philosophical theories regarding the nature of the emotions.

## 2.3 Theories of the emotions

It was once thought, by Descartes for instance, that emotions involve the subject's awareness of the perturbations of his or her animal spirits. It was the dynamic structure of this inner motion, along with the feeling of pleasure or displeasure with which it was apprehended, that distinguished the various emotions. Call this the 'hydraulic theory' of the emotions. In this view, emotions are experiences passively undergone by the subject; they are only contingently connected to their causes and to their behavioural manifestations; they are essentially non-cognitive.

In the latter half of the twentieth century, an alternative account, usually called the 'cognitive theory', has been developed (see Lyons 1980; Gordon 1987; Solomon 1976).[2] This allows that emotions possess a phenomenological profile, but regards this as only one element among several, all of which are necessary and none of which is sufficient alone for an emotion's occurrence. Emotions may be characterized by physiological changes, but, more importantly, they are object-focused. Emotions are directed toward their objects. This means they are usually outward facing, as when I fear the lion that is before me, though the emotion's object also may be one's own sensations or emotions, as when I am alarmed by how tense I feel or where I am ashamed that I am angry. Moreover, emotions involve the categorization of their objects; for instance, if the emotion is one of fear its object must be viewed as harmful, and if the emotion is one of envy its object must be viewed as something both desirable and not already controlled or possessed. In addition, they include attitudes toward their objects; for example, though I judge you to be injured, my emotional response will depend on whether this is a source of concern, satisfaction, or indifference to me. Also, particular emotions find expression in typical behaviours; if I pity you I will try to comfort you and to change your situation for the better, and if I fear you I will fight, flee, or seek protection.

Philosophers disagree in the versions of the cognitive theory they espouse. Some insist that emotions require a belief in their objects' existence, while others think that cognitive

---

[2]  The term 'cognitive' has a somewhat different meaning in philosophical theories of emotion than it has in psychological theories. In the latter, the term implies a focus on underlying information-processing mechanisms, whereas in philosophical theories, it refers to beliefs, imaginings, thoughts, intentions, desires, and like states of consciousness.

attitudes, such as make belief, also can play the role of securing the emotion's object. Some hold that emotions can be individuated in terms of their sensational patterns, without reference to the emotion's propositional component, whereas others regard its cognitive ingredient as crucial to its identification. (For a useful summary of the literature, see Deigh 1994.)

Many of these disputes can be resolved by acknowledging that emotions do not constitute a homogenous class. For instance, some, such as disgust, might be primitive, automatic responses that are not susceptible in their operation to changes in the subject's cognitive state, whereas others, such as patriotism, are marked more by their self-conscious, intellectual content than their sensational character. Even if there is a continuum of cases between these extremes, it is useful to distinguish between emotions (such as jealousy, hope, and remorse) in which the cognitive elements are prominent, malleable, and sophisticated from those (such as lust, fear, and disgust) in which the cognitive elements may not be present to awareness and the reaction is inclined to be automatic and inflexible.[3]

Some further distinctions that may be useful are those between emotions and moods, and between emotions and mere sensations (or mere feelings). These distinctions are drawn roughly within folk psychological discourse along the following lines. Moods are not object-directed and involve rather general feelings. There can be moods of dread, depression, and happiness, but not of embarrassment or remorse, because these latter lack a distinctive experiential character and are distinguished more in terms of what is cognized about their objects. Meanwhile, emotions may involve bodily sensations but are not reducible to them. A person who sits too close to the fire might experience exactly the same sensations as another who is acutely embarrassed, but it is only the latter who feels an emotion.

## 2.4 Constraints on the theory

Before outlining philosophers' theories of musical expressiveness, it is helpful to consider the desiderata that an acceptable theory must satisfy.

We could not account for the interest and value of expression in music, or for the emotional responses music calls from the listener, unless terms like 'sad' and 'happy' retain their usual meanings in connection with music's expressiveness. So a principal

--------

[3]  Griffiths (1997) argues that the emotions do not form a 'natural kind' and that the cognitive theory applies to only some. He is impressed by experimental data supposedly showing that the neural structures dealing with the emotions are modular and cognitively opaque, thereby generating evolutionarily adaptive quick, dirty, and conservative reactions to affective stimuli. (For work on this wavelength, see LeDoux 1998.) But it seems to me that the cognitive theory is not so easily dismissed. Propositional attitudes—beliefs, desires, intentions—can be in play without being held before the mind. Yesterday I believed that the earth is round, though I did not bring the relevant thought to consciousness at any time. Nevertheless, though I suspect the experimental data referred to by Griffiths might be interpreted in ways consistent with cognitivism, as I have just indicated, later I argue that some of the most common emotional responses to music's expressiveness do not fit the cognitive model.

task will be to indicate how, despite their manifest differences, music's expressing an emotion parallels the default case in which a person expresses an emotion they feel. In other words, an account explaining and justifying our attribution to music of predicates such as 'sad' and 'happy' must make clear how this non-primary use relates to these words' normal application to the occurrent emotions of sentient creatures.

As I see it, this constraint quickly rules out three approaches to the topic. It will not do to attempt to reduce music's expressiveness to a catalogue of technicalities and compositional devices. Even if it is true that all, and only, music in minor keys sounds sad, it cannot be that 'sounds sad' *means* 'is in a minor key'. Even if one can make sad music by composing it in the minor key, there must be more to the analysis of music's expressiveness than acknowledgment of this, for it is by no means clear how the music's modality relates to the very different kinds of things that make it true in the standard case that a person is expressing sadness. Musical features ground music's expressiveness, and it is interesting to discover what features those are, but identifying them is, at best, only an initial step toward an informative theory of musical expressiveness.

Another of the disallowed strategies claims that music's expressiveness is metaphorical and declines to unpack the metaphor.[4] The claim here is not merely that, as a figure of speech, music can be described metaphorically. It is, rather, that the music itself is metaphorically expressive. While this last assertion obviously locates expressiveness squarely with the music, its meaning is quite mysterious. The idea that musical expression is metaphorical must itself be a metaphor, since metaphor primarily is a linguistic device depending on semantic relations for which there is no musical equivalent. This approach indicates what is puzzling about music's expression of emotions—that it is hard to see how emotion terms could retain their literal sense when predicated of music, though clearly their application to music trades somehow on their literal meaning—but it offers no solution to that puzzle.

Also unacceptable is the theory insisting that music's expressiveness is *sui generis*; that is, of its own kind and not relevantly comparable to the default case in which occurrent emotions are expressed. That approach is not offering a theory, but, rather, is rejecting the philosophical enterprise that seeks one. I do not deny that, when it comes to expressiveness, music does its own thing. This is only to be expected: its medium is that of organized sound, not that of a biological organism evolved and educated to engage emotionally with its environment. What I repudiate is the suggestion that an analysis of music's expressiveness can avoid addressing if and how the musical medium realizes a kind of expressiveness that is equivalent to the biological one.

## 2.5 The qualified listener

One assumption common to the theories discussed below should be made explicit: listeners must be suitably qualified if they are to be capable of detecting and appreciating music's expressiveness. (Unprepared listeners may miss, or misidentify, the music's

---

[4] In its strongest version, the theory denies the possibility of analysing the crucial metaphor. For theories to which this claim is central, see Goodman (1968) and Scruton (1997).

expressive character.) Qualified listeners are at home with the type of music in question, with its genre, style, and idiom. They know when the melody begins and ends, and when the piece is over. They can recognize mistakes and can distinguish predictable from unusual continuations. They may not be able to articulate this knowledge, most of which is acquired through unreflective exposure to pieces of the relevant kind. Indeed, the majority of qualified listeners have no formal music education and are not familiar with the musicologist's technical vocabulary (Davies 1994; Kivy 1990; Levinson 1996).

## 2.6 First problem: the expression of emotion in music

When we say that something expresses an emotion, usually we mean that it publicly betrays or indicates a state that it feels. People's tears express their sadness only if they are experiencing sadness. Therefore, only sentient creatures can express emotions. Musical works are not sentient, so emotions cannot be expressed in them. Yet many of them do express emotions such as sadness and happiness. How could that be?

### 2.6.1 Music as a symbol

A first theory suggests that music operates as a symbol or sign, the import of which is purely associative and conventional. Though it bears no natural relation to an emotion, it comes to denote or refer to an emotion, and then to characterize it, by virtue of its place within a system. In this view, music picks out and conveys something about emotions after the manner of linguistic utterances; that is, through combining elements according to rules with the function of generating and communicating a semantic or propositional content (Coker 1972). Musical signs, like linguistic ones, are both unlike and opaque to their referents.

Quasi-vocabularies sometimes have been described for music in its relation to the emotions, and music is highly organized according to quasi-syntactic rules governing the well-formedness of musical strings (Lerdahl & Jackendoff 1983; Meyer 1956), yet there is not a semantics in music. Without that, the parallel with linguistic and other symbol systems collapses. It is not the case that music points or refers to emotions which it then goes on to describe. There are no plausible equivalents in music to predication, to propositional closure, or to any of the other functions and operators that are essential to the meaningful use of linguistic and other truth-functional systems.

An alternative theory would have it that music refers to the emotions not within the framework of a symbol system, but as a result of *ad hoc*, arbitrary designations and associations. For instance, certain musical gestures or phrases happen to be linked saliently with texts expressive of a given emotion and retain that connection over many years, so that purely instrumental music comes to be heard as expressive when it includes the relevant gesture or phrase (Cooke 1959). Or music of certain kinds is linked with rites or events that otherwise are emotionally charged, and these ties persist, becoming commonplaces of musical expressiveness. In this theory, expressiveness involves techniques like those followed by Wagner in his use of leitmotiv, except that the relevant conventions are available to many composers and occur in many works, so widespread and entrenched are the associations that underpin them.

There is no denying that some aspects of music's expressiveness—for instance, the links between instruments and moods, as between the oboe and bucolic frames of mind, the organ and religiosity, or the trumpet and regality or bellicosity—seem to be arbitrary and conventional in ways that may depend on historical associations. Such cases notwithstanding, this last account is no more plausible or attractive than the first. It reduces music's expressiveness to something like brute naming; it indicates how music might refer to an emotion but not how it could characterize it.

These theories regard expressive music as referring beyond itself. As with language or signs relying on arbitrary associations, features intrinsic to the music are of interest only in so far as they happen to be relevant to its role as a symbolic vehicle. Though the music mediates contact with the emotion that is symbolized, listeners should not be distracted by its intrinsic qualities from pursuing its referential target. Because it is radically different from the emotions it symbolizes, it is opaque with respect to them, yet the music is of interest only in its symbolic import.

This account is seriously at odds with the phenomenology of listeners' experiences of music's expressiveness. Registering music's expressiveness is more like encountering a person who feels the emotion and shows it than like reading a description of the emotion or than like examining the word 'sad'. While the dinner bell might, through association, lead us to salivate, we do not think of it as tasty. By contrast, we experience the sadness of music as present within it. Emotion is transparently immediate in our experience of music and our awareness of its expressiveness is not separable from, or independent of, our following the music's unfolding in all its detail. Moreover, the listener's connection is not with some general, abstract conception of the emotions, but with a specific and concrete presentation.

Any theory of musical expressiveness must acknowledge and respect the phenomenological vivacity and particularity with which music presents its expressive aspect. Here, then, is a further constraint on acceptable theories of music's expressiveness, and it is one that is failed by the theories discussed so far. Music is not merely a vehicle for referring beyond itself in a fashion that largely ignores the intrinsic and unique character of its individual works.

The semiotic theory can respond to this objection if the link between music and emotion is transparent because it is natural, not arbitrarily conventional. Here is a first suggestion: there is a synaesthetic quality to certain timbres. The trumpet's upper notes are bright and the clarinet's low register is dark; the tone of the celesta is ethereal, while high string harmonics are brittle. Even if these connections are widely made, however, they lack the temporally extended complexity that could account for music's expressiveness. They might contribute to the work's emotional ambience, but they could not generate it.

A stronger form of natural connection is that of similarity, and this is emphasized in theories regarding music as an iconic or exemplificatory symbol. If music vividly resembles the emotions it expresses—indeed, if it depicts them in virtue of these resemblances—then it would be natural to respond to the symbol much as we respond to that for which it stands. Iconic symbols (such as representational paintings) are more transparent to their referents than are signs that rely on arbitrary associations or symbol systems (such as that of a natural language) to establish the connection. We regularly talk of pictures as if we are in the presence of what they depict, though this is not to say we are deceived by them. We do not react to linguistic descriptions in the same way. Both Langer (1942) and Goodman (1968) have suggested that music is symbolic precisely because it is experienced as resembling or exemplifying what it denotes.

What is it about the emotions that music resembles? Not their thought components if, as was just argued, purely instrumental music is not equipped to convey the contents of proposition. It has been suggested that expressive instrumental music recalls the tones and intonations with which emotions are given vocal expression (Kivy 1989), but this also is dubious. It is true that blues guitar and jazz saxophone sometimes imitate singing styles, and that singing styles sometimes recall the sobs, wails, whoops, and yells that go with ordinary occasions of expressiveness. For the general run of cases, though, music does not sound very like the noises made by people gripped by emotion. A more plausible source of resemblance lies in the music's dynamic structure than in its sound as such. We experience movement and pattern in music; we hear in music a terrain shaped by ongoing interactions between its parts, which vary in their highness, complexity, teleological impetus, energy, texture, inertia, tension, and so on. If music resembles an emotion, it does so by sharing the dynamic character displayed either in the emotion's phenomenological profile, as Addis (1999) maintains, or in the public behaviours through which the emotion is standardly exhibited.

The first of these suggestions assumes that the phenomenological profile of some emotions is distinctive enough to provide for their individuation. I am doubtful both that cognitively rich emotions, like hope or jealousy, survive being divorced from their cognitive elements and that there is anything to distinguish the internal dynamics of bursting with joy from blowing one's top. Moreover, to suggest that music symbolizes the 'general form of emotions' (Langer 1942), not particular kinds or their instances, enfeebles the account. To those who have abandoned the hydraulic in favour of the cognitive theory of the emotions, it is more promising to compare music with the outward expressions of emotions than with their experiential shape. A number of emotions have standard behavioural expressions that are partly constitutive of their nature, rather than dispensable concomitants, and these have distinctive dynamic physiognomies. A downcast bearing and slow movements go with sadness, whereas joy is upbeat and lively. Sometimes we can tell what a person is feeling from the carriage of their body, without knowing the cause of their feeling, their cognitive state, or the object of their emotion.

A fatal problem remains in explaining music's expressiveness in terms of this or any other resemblance between music's features and properties displayed by emotions: in the normal case, the pertinent behaviours are expressive only if they stand in the relevant relation to an instance of the appropriate emotion. Someone might always display the behaviour without feeling the way their behaviour leads us to suppose. In that case, no occurrent emotion is expressed. And if a given physiological state is not accompanied by relevant thoughts, attitudes, desires, or behavioural dispositions, the experience of that state would not normally be regarded as an emotion. No matter how powerful the resemblance, the analogy fails to go through, since it cannot be supposed that music experiences or undergoes the emotions expressed in it.

Theories regarding music as a sign or symbol referring to the emotions accept the conclusion of the argument with which I commenced: occurrent emotions cannot be expressed in musical works. They look for some other, more abstract, way music can connect with the affective life. But semiotic theories inevitably leave a gap between music and emotion. In consequence, they do not do justice to the direct and unmediated fashion in which emotional expression imposes itself on our experience of the music.

### 2.6.2 Experiencing subjects: composers, listeners, and imagined personas

Most theorists accept that only sentient creatures can express occurrent emotions, but deny that this counts against music's expressiveness. They hold that, when emotion is expressed in a piece of music, that piece stands to a sentient being's occurrent emotion as expressing it. Accordingly, they seek a sentient being whose emotion is given expression by the music. The prime candidates are the composer (or performer) or a persona represented in the music. Alternatively, they maintain it is the occurrent feelings of the listener, ones caused by his or her attention to the music, that license the judgment that the music is expressive.

The *expression theory* analyses the music's expressiveness as depending on the composer expressing his or her occurrent emotion through the act of composition. The chief difficulty for this theory is conveyed by O. K. Bouwsma's aphorism: 'The sadness is to the music rather like the redness to the apple, than it is like the burp to the cider' (1950, p. 94). In other words, we experience music's expressiveness not as a residue of feelings discharged in the compositional process but as resident in its nature.

The expression theory seems to be empirically false as not all expressive music is written by composers who feel emotions and try to express them. A more philosophical point is this: in the default case, sadness is expressed by weeping and the like, not by musical composition. The connection between the composer's emotions and the work he or she writes is by no means as natural or transparent as that between his or her emotions and the behaviours, like weeping or whooping, that vent them. So, even if composers sometimes express their emotions in the works they write, this fact, rather than accounting for the music's expressiveness, needs to be explained. Indeed, in the most plausible account, the composer appropriates the music's expressiveness in order to make the connection with his or her own emotions. In other words, the composer is like the person who expresses his or her feelings, not by showing them directly, but by making a mask that wears an appropriate expression. Just as the mask is expressive whether or not it is used in this sophisticated act of self-expression, so too is the music. If composers occasionally match the expressiveness of the music to their own feelings, that is possible only because the music can present expressive aspects apart from its being appropriated in this fashion.[5] (For further criticism of the expression theory, see Davies 1987, 1994; Goldman 1995*b*; Kivy 1989; Tormey 1971.)

The *arousal theory* explains the music's expressiveness as its propensity to evoke the corresponding emotion in the listener. What makes it true that grass is green is that it

---

[5] Similar arguments can be ranged against the version of the expression theory that identifies the performers as the ones who express their emotions through their rendering of the music. Performers need not feel the emotions they present, and when they do, there is matching rather than direct expression.

arouses certain experiences in (human) observers under standard conditions; grass's greenness is its causal power to bring about appropriate experiences. Similarly, what makes it true that music is sad or happy is its causal power to bring about these or related responses in the listener (Matravers 1998).

I doubt that the correspondence between listeners attributing sadness to music and their experiencing feelings or emotions of sadness in response to it is sufficient to make the arousal theory plausible. In the case of colour, the experience inevitably goes with the judgment and the two are pulled apart only when the observer or the conditions of observation are abnormal. The 'standard conditions' for music to produce its effects are those in which a qualified listener pays attention to the music. Those conditions are often satisfied. When they are, the arousal of a response in listeners who correctly judge the music to be expressive is not nearly as regular as the arousal theory requires. And it is unconvincing to claim that the relevant feelings, or dispositions to them, can be so weak as to escape the listener's notice. In fact, we have a clear sense of the music's expressive character as quite distinct from our (very variable) responses to it. This is not to deny that the music sometimes can cause an emotional reaction. What is denied is that this reaction is what makes it true that the music is expressive. Normally, we regard the connection as reversed: it is because the expressiveness is apparent in the work that we are moved by the music.

Many theorists (but cf. Beever 1998) would subscribe to the following proposition: if we were never moved by music, we would not find it expressive. This involves no commitment to the arousalist's programme for analysing music's expressiveness, though. Usually the conditional is regarded as reversible: if we never found music expressive, we would not be moved by it. In other words, it identifies the close and mutual dependence of our experience of music and the judgments we make concerning its features; it does not imply that one takes explanatory precedence over the other.

Expression and arousal theories go hunting for an experiencing subject to whom the music might stand, either as the expression of his or her (the composer's) occurrent emotion or as the cause of his or her (the listener's) emotion-like response. Instead of actual persons and emotions, perhaps we should consider imagined ones. In the case of works generating fictional worlds, such as novels and films, we engage imaginatively with characters inhabiting that world. Maybe music's expressiveness connects to fictional or make-believe experiences of emotion. There are two possibilities. In the first, listeners imaginatively ascribe emotions to themselves on the basis of their make-believe engagement with the world of the work. In the second, listeners make believe that the work generates a fictional world to which they are external observers; they imagine of the music that it presents a narrative concerning the emotional life of a persona.

Both views are presented by Walton (1988), but it is his version of the first that I will consider. He suggests that a passage is expressive of sadness if the listeners imagine of their hearing of it that it is a cognizance of their own feelings of sadness. Listeners take their awareness of their auditory sensations to be an awareness of their own feelings, and it is these feelings that the music can be said to express.

Even if one charitably allows that awareness of music's expressiveness could be as self-centred and introspective as this, the theory remains implausible. Reflecting on one's auditory sensations is not plainly similar to experiencing emotions, so it is difficult to see how what one imagines can be connected back to and controlled by the music, so that, ultimately, it is the music's expressiveness that is revealed.

The thesis that, in hearing expressiveness in music, we sometimes imagine a persona who is subject to a narrative that unfolds in the music, is widely supported (Budd 1985; Karl & Robinson 1995; Ridley 1995; Vermazen 1986; Walton 1988, 1990). The idea could be offered as a heuristic—as a way of helping people recognize the music's expressiveness—or as a claim applying only to particular works. The strongest position insists that this manner of hearing is always required for appreciation of the music's expressiveness. Levinson (1996) comes nearest to the strong position by defining musical expressiveness such that a passage is expressive of an emotion if, and only if, it is heard (by appropriately experienced listeners) as the expression of that emotion by an imagined human subject, the music's persona.

A first objection denies that all qualified listeners imagine a persona as a condition of their awareness of the music's expressiveness. They might be able to say what it would be suitable to imagine, even if they do not imagine it themselves, but they do this in terms of an awareness of the music's expressive character that is not mediated by the imagination. Besides, I contend that what the listener imagines is too little constrained by the course and detail of the music to provide a theory regarding music's expressiveness as an objective property, which is what Levinson intends. In the case of novels and films, a great deal of information about the fictional world is conveyed to the audience, even if its members must entertain the reality of this world. Those data control what is to be imagined, and why and how, in following the story. Because it does not convey a definite propositional or depicted content, and hints at such things (if at all) only in the vaguest and most general fashion, purely instrumental music cannot direct and channel the content of the listener's imagining (Davies 1997). For instance, what is to determine how many personas he or she should make believe, or the background of relations that might hold between different personas? Inevitably, what is imagined reveals more about the listener than about the music's expressiveness.

### 2.6.3 The contour theory

A final view, the *contour theory*,[6] abandons the attempt to analyse music's expressiveness as depending on its connection to occurrent emotions. It observes that certain behaviours, comportments, and physiognomies are experienced as expressive without giving expression to, or being caused by, occurrent emotions. Some faces, gaits, or movements are happy-looking. They present an emotion characteristic in their appearance. St Bernards are sad-looking dogs, but this is to say nothing about how they feel. The use of emotion terms to name the expressive characteristics of appearances is secondary, but it bears an obvious connection to those terms' primary use: the behaviours that display an emotion characteristic unconnected with an occurrent emotion are the same (or very similar) to the

---

[6] Kivy's version of the theory (1989) often is called 'cognitivism' as a way of acknowledging his commitment to a cognitive theory of the emotions, especially as these concern the listener's response. His theory of music's expressiveness does not invoke the cognitive theory of the emotions, however, because it denies that the music expresses occurrent emotions.

ones that, where the emotion is occurrent, give direct and distinctive expression to it. Only those emotions that can be recognized solely on the basis of the outward expressions that betray them have corresponding emotion characteristics in appearance.

Turning now to music, the contour theory proposes that pieces present emotion characteristics, rather than giving expression to occurrent emotions, and they do so by virtue of resemblances between their own dynamic structures and behaviours or movements that, in humans, present emotion characteristics. The claim is not that music somehow refers beyond itself to occurrent emotions; music is not an iconic symbol of emotions as a result of resembling their outward manifestations. Rather, the claim is that the expressiveness is a property of the music itself. This property resides in the way the music sounds to the attuned listener, just as happy-lookingness can be a property displayed in a creature's face or movements. Because music is a temporal art, its expressive character is revealed only gradually, and can be heard only through sustained attention to its unfolding. It takes as long to hear the music's expressive properties as it takes to hear the passages in which those properties are articulated.[7]

Consider Fig. 2.1. The car and the puppet are happy looking, and the dog and the weeping willow are sad looking. These attributions apply to the appearances the depicted items present, not to occurrent emotions. Only the dog is sentient, and there is no reason to think it feels as it looks. (Besides, dogs do not display feelings of sadness, when they have them, in their *faces*.) These looks present emotion characteristics because they resemble bearings or expressions which, were they shown by people under appropriate circumstances, would express those people's occurrent emotions. I maintain that, when we attribute emotions to music, we are describing the emotional character it presents, just as we do when we call the willow sad or the car happy. In the case of music, this 'appearance' depends on its dynamic topography, as this unfolds through time. In general, music resembles gaits, carriages, or comportments that are typically expressive of human occurrent emotions, rather than facial expressions.

In discussing the theory that regards music as an iconic symbol or depiction of emotions, I have already considered objections to the view that music resembles expressions of the emotions. I concluded that the resemblance claim is at its most plausible when it compares music's dynamic pattern to that apparent in non-verbal, behavioural expressions of emotion. Yet even if this is accepted, a further objection notes that resemblance alone could not ground music's expressiveness. Resemblances, which are symmetrical and, anyway, can be found between music and many things besides expressive appearances, are insufficient to explain why we experience music as powerfully expressive of emotion.

One might reply, as Kivy does, that we are evolutionarily programmed to 'animate' what we perceive. Or one might simply say 'yet this is how we hear it', without committing oneself to an account of the mechanisms and triggers that underlie the response. Not just music, but many things, are experienced as redolent of emotions, despite lacking

---

[7] In outline, this is the theory presented in Kivy (1989), as well as in Davies (1994), though the terms in which it is formulated are closer to my account than Kivy's. As observed earlier, Kivy is more inclined than I to find an expressive resemblance between music and the human voice (see also Juslin, this volume). For further discussion of our differences, see Davies (1994) and Kivy (1999) and for critical commentaries, see Goldman (1995b), Levinson (1996, 1997b), and Madell (1996).

(a)

(b)

(c)

(d)

**Figure 2.1** Appearances with various emotion characteristics: (a) car, (b) puppet, (c) dog, and (d) weeping willow.

the feature one would assume to be crucial; namely, sentience. There can be no denying that crude representations of the human face can be emotionally compelling in their expressive power, though such responses are not strictly entailed by the resemblances that can be found. Consider the masks of comedy and tragedy, or a simple drawing such as Edvard Munch's 'scream' face.

If these last observations are not fully satisfying, that does not reflect worse on the contour theory than on other analyses. For instance, the arousalist is reduced ultimately to saying 'simply, this is how music affects us'; and philosophers who regard music as an iconic symbol, or as calling on us to make believe a narrative about a persona, are no better equipped than the contour theorist to go beyond the perceived resemblances that are central to their accounts of music's expressiveness.

A different line of objection doubts that the contour theory can explain the significance we attach to expressiveness in music, or the energy with which music engages our emotions. What can we learn from, and why should we be moved by, mere appearances of emotion that are not expressions of occurrent, deeply felt emotions? One answer draws attention to the fact that music is intentionally and ingeniously designed to be as it is. Though expressiveness is a property of the piece's sounds, we encounter it not as an accident of nature but as deliberately created and used, which adds considerably to its potential importance. Another response could question if it is true that music is valued as a source of knowledge about the emotions, rather than for the experience it provides, where this experience takes in much more than only its expressiveness.

### 2.6.4 Universalism

The contour theory, more than any other, lends itself to the idea that music is a universal 'language of the emotions'; that is, to the suggestion that expressiveness can be recognized cross-culturally. If, as some psychologists have claimed (Ekman 1980), certain emotions have characteristic appearances that are universally understood, and if music is experienced as expressive as a result of its recalling these same appearances in its dynamic character, then cross-cultural appreciation of music's expressiveness should be possible. And perhaps it is sometimes. When the musical systems of different cultures are parallel (for instance, in their principles of scalar organization and modalities), there may be sufficient transparency to allow members of one culture to correctly recognize expressiveness in the music of the other culture. Many Westerners can access sub-Saharan African music, and not only because it provided the seeds from which a number of popular Western musical types emerged.

Often, though, the music of one culture is expressively opaque to outsiders. There are several reasons why this can be so. The emotions appropriate to given circumstances can differ, so that one group sees death as an occasion for sadness where another views it as a cause for joyous celebrations. Until one appreciates the belief systems that determine the significance of the social settings in which emotions are situated, and then recognizes the connection of music with all this, it will not be a simple matter to read off expressiveness from foreign music. Even if music's expressiveness implicates 'natural' resemblances to behaviours that are transcultural in their import, these then are structured according to historically malleable musical conventions of genre and style, so that they are no longer apparent to those who lack familiarity with the culture's music. To take a crude example, whether a given pitch is 'high', 'middle', or 'low' depends on the range that is deemed available for use, and that can vary arbitrarily from musical type to type. The contour theory, no less than other analyses, supposes that qualified listeners can become such only by immersing themselves in the kinds of music that are their focus, and that listeners have no guaranteed access to the properties of foreign music, including its expressive ones, until they become appropriately experienced.

## 2.7 Second problem: mirroring responses to music's expressiveness

People often respond emotionally to musical works. While there is nothing odd about a listener being moved by the work's beauty, it is strange that he or she should respond with sadness to the sadness it expresses. The listener's sad response appears to lack beliefs of the kind that typically go with sadness. When I am sad because the dog has died, or because it is raining on your parade, or because you are depressed, I believe the death of the dog, or the rain, or your depression, are unfortunate occurrences, but when the sadness of the music makes me feel sad I do not believe there is anything unfortunate about the music. Moreover, the response to another's emotion often does not mirror it. Another's anger is as likely to produce in me fear, or disappointment, or irritation, as it is likely to precipitate my anger. Yet the listener is not as liable to feel pity, or compassion, or evil delight at the music's sadness as he or she is liable to feel sadness. How is the listener's response appropriate to the music?

The problem is not a general one. Many of our emotional reactions to music conform neatly to the cognitivist model. We can marvel at the music's complexity, and be shocked by its discordant novelty. These responses, in taking the music as their object, involve beliefs or thoughts of the kinds that normally accompany marvelling and shock. The problem case is the one in which listeners mirror in their reactions what the music expresses; where they are saddened by sad music, or cheered by happy music.

Kivy (1989) denies the problem's existence: people are mistaken when they claim to be saddened by sad music.[8] They are moved by the music, certainly, but not to sadness. This explains why concert audiences neither display nor act as if they are sad about the music; simply, that is not how they feel. People are not often wrong about the identity of their emotions (cf. Griffiths 1997), however, and Kivy's position will fail so long as some people sometimes react to the music's expressiveness by mirroring it in their own feelings. For these reasons, and by appeal to their own experience, most philosophers reject Kivy's stance (for discussion, see Davies 1994; Goldman 1995b). Any alternative theory that can deal with the problem without denying the phenomenon will be preferable.

If the listener believed music expresses a sadness felt by its composer (or performer), there would be no special puzzle about his or her reaction, for such beliefs are appropriate to a sad response. In this case, however, the object of the response would not be the music, but the composer or performer. When we react to a person's emotional state, our response is directed to them, not to their expressive behaviour as such, even if it was this behaviour that alerted us to their condition. This account does not after all address the problem case, that in which the listeners' responses are solely to the music's expressive character. To have this reaction, they need not believe that the music expresses emotions experienced by its composer; it can be sufficient that they acknowledge the music's expressive appearance, without supposing this to be connected to anyone's occurrent emotions.

According to the theory in which a persona is the human subject of the imaginary act of expression we hear as going on in the music, the problem response can be approached as follows: if that response is directed to the persona, then it will be targeted at the music, for it is in the world of the music that the persona is imagined to exist. And if we hear the persona as undergoing the emotional vicissitudes outlined in the music, then we entertain thoughts about the situation of the persona that are appropriate for mirroring reactions. Admittedly, these thoughts are make believed, not believed, but if this presents no special difficulty in accounting for our reactions to fictional characters (as argued in Carroll 1998), then the response also is unproblematic in the musical case. So long as the cognitive theory of the emotions allows that the cognitive connection between the emotion and its object can be secured by the imagination in some cases, as

---

[8] Addis (1999) agrees that listeners are not aroused to sadness by sad music. He differs from Kivy, though, in holding both that they are aroused to a uniquely musical experience—a kind of stirring—and that this response does not take the music as its intentional object, though it is caused by the music.

well as by belief in others, the listener's response can be seen to be consistent with the cognitive theory of the emotions.

The claim that attitudes other than belief can play the cognitively central role in emotions is not accepted by all who support the cognitive theory of the emotions. And it might be thought that it is one thing to imagine of the emotion's object that it has emotion-pertinent features that one does not believe it to have, yet quite another to make believe that the emotion's object exists when one does not believe it to do so. In addition, there is the concern mentioned earlier: that it is not clear that what is entertained is sufficiently controlled by what happens in the music to count as belonging to the world of the work.

The arousalist maintains that what makes it true that the music is sad is that it arouses sadness in the listener; the listener's response is not to some expressive property possessed independently by the music. While the arousalist might deny that the listener's responses *mirror* an expressiveness that is independent of their reaction, still he or she must hold that the response correlates with the music's expressiveness by licensing the judgment that the music is expressive of what is felt by the listener. Given this, and also the fact that the causal relation between the music and the listener's response need not be informed by cognitions beyond those involved in tracking the unfolding of the music, a problem remains for the arousalist in characterizing the listener's reaction as emotional.

In a recent defence of arousalism, Matravers (1998) acknowledges that the crucial response is a feeling, not an emotion as such, because it lacks the cognitive contents that characterize the emotions. For instance, the response feels like sadness or pity, and this makes it true that the music expresses sadness, but the response is not an object-directed, cognitively founded emotion. This explains why listeners are not strongly inclined to act on their feelings; the prime motivators for action are beliefs and desires directed to an emotional object, but these are absent in the musical case. Because only a few feelings have distinctive phenomenologies, music can arouse only rather general feelings, and thereby is capable of expressing only a limited range of emotions.

I endorse this approach, which can be disassociated from arousalism: if the listener does mirror the music's expressiveness, that response is caused by and tracks the music, but does not take the music, or any other thing, as its emotional object. This is not to agree, however, with the arousalist's claim that it is the listener's reaction that licenses the judgment that the music is sad.

My account can appeal to one resource that is not available to the arousalist. Earlier I suggested that inanimate appearances often strike us as expressive. To this it can be added that sometimes we find expressive characteristics in appearances highly evocative of responses of the mirroring kind (Davies 1994), not only in the musical case but in others (see Hatfield *et al.* 1994). Whether through empathy or sociality, we often 'catch' the mood prevailing around us. Both high spiritedness and despondency can be 'contagious'. The same applies sometimes, I claim, when we are confronted with powerfully expressive appearances that are not connected to occurrent emotions. There is no reason why appearances of sadness should make me feel gloomy if I do not think they show how anyone feels (and often they do not do so); which is to say, mere appearances of sadness are not a suitable object for sadness, since they are not thought to be unfortunate and the rest. Nevertheless, if I am roused to an emotion under those circumstances, it will be a mirroring one, because, in the absence of relevant cognitions, it is only through a kind of contagion or osmosis that my feelings are engaged.[9]

## 2.8 Third problem: negative responses

Yet if we accept that music expressive of negative emotions sometimes produces an echo in feelings experienced by the listener, another problem emerges. People avoid sad experiences where they can, because these are unpleasant. Those who are under no duty to listen to sad music often choose to do so. They report that such music gives rise to a negative emotional response, yet they offer this in praise of the music. Rather than fleeing, they are attracted to the music, and they willingly return to it, despite predicting that it will again make them feel sad. Given that music lovers are not masochists, how is this to be explained?

For Kivy (1990) there is again no problem. Listeners to sad music do not experience negative feelings, or if they do, these are of the ordinary kind—as when one is disappointed in the poverty of the work's ideas, or by its execrable execution—and provide reason for avoiding the emotion's object, the work, or the performers, in the future. Those who think that music can lead the listener to a negative, mirroring response cannot avoid the issue, though. Three argumentative strategies are available.

The first notes that there can be much to enjoy about musical works that arouse negative emotions; for instance, the work's beauty, the composer's treatment of the medium, and so forth. In addition, because it lacks 'life implications', one can savour and examine one's response, thereby coming to understand the emotion better while being reassured of one's own sensitivity (Levinson 1982). In this view, the negative elements are outweighed by positive ones. We listen to music that arouses negative emotions because it also does much more, and the overall balance is on the credit side.

The position is not entirely convincing in its present formulation. If we can get the same or similar benefits from works that do not make us feel unhappy, we should prefer them. We should shun skilful, interesting works that make us feel sad in favour of equally skilful and interesting works that make us feel happy. To reply to this objection, the original view can be developed (as in Levinson 1982) by arguing that at least some of the benefits cannot be obtained from works other than those that are liable to induce negative feelings. The Aristotelian position, according to which we are better off for purging negative feelings in the context of art, pursues this line, as does the theory that our experiences of artworks educate us about the emotions in a setting that insulates us from the practical demands and dangers of

---

[9] The view presented here requires rejection or revision of the cognitive theory of the emotions sketched earlier, since it countenances emotions that lack the appropriate beliefs or make beliefs, the desires, and behavioural dispositions that would follow from these, and the relevant emotional object. As indicated, Matravers (1998) and Addis (1999) also deny that the mirroring response takes the music as its emotional object. Of course, this is not to deny that the music is the focus of attention and perceptual object of the response, which is a point apparently missed by Madell (1996).

the real world. In this connection, it is also often held that the feelings experienced in regard to artworks are muted and undemanding compared to equivalents provoked by real-world situations.

These ways of addressing the objection are more convincing in the discussion of our reactions to narrative and representational artworks, not instrumental music, I find. If the response to music lacks the cognitive content of emotions, it is difficult to see how it could be a source of education or insight, or how it is easier to tolerate than similarly unpleasant feelings caused by real-world phenomena. If music does not generate a contentful fictional world, the reaction to its expressive properties is not less a response to 'real-world' features than is, say, that in which an especially vivid shade of lime green induces sensations of dyspepsia in its observer.

The second approach to the issue derives from Hume (1912), who argued of the experience of tragedy that its negative aspects are transformed to positive ones through the delight taken in the narrative's construction, the natural attractiveness of representation, and so on. It is far from clear, though, what is the character of this conversion, or how feelings such as sad ones could remain sad while becoming intrinsically pleasant. Perhaps what Hume was driving at is better articulated by the third strategy, which offers the strongest possibility for justifying the interest of someone whose sensitivities incline him or her to negative feelings on hearing music in which negative emotions are presented.

Even if we accept that the negative aspects of experience are unpleasant, and that this gives a reason for avoiding them, it is plain that, for many, this reason is not always overriding. For music, that which is negative often is integral to the whole. Provided our desire to understand and appreciate the work is strong enough, we may be prepared to face those negative elements. The experience that results is not just good on balance; it is not as if the work would be better if we could ignore its negative aspects, for then we would not be engaging with it as such. In other words, experience of, and reaction to, music's negative expressiveness, where that expressiveness is important to the work, is something to be accepted if our goal is to understand and, through understanding, to appreciate the music. There is nothing irrational in pursuing that goal, though the experience to which it gives rise can be unpleasant in parts.

There is a different way of getting at the same point. It simply is not true that people always duck the avoidable negative aspects of life. These are recognized as essential components of many things we like and value. They come along with the territory, not solely as something to be endured but also as contributing to its being the territory it is. This is true of the most important components of our lives: intimate personal relationships, child rearing, self-realization, career. To achieve a fulfilling life, the individual must honestly and seriously face these in all their dimensions, both positive and negative. Yet it also is true of the way we live generally, even apart from the big issues of survival and flourishing. Thousands of amateurs train for endurance races, such as marathons and triathlons. Other hobbies and activities, in which the challenge of the negative is no less central, are pursued with the same passionate commitment by other people, though they are under no compulsion to do so. Against this background, surely it is safe to deny there is a special problem about the fact that people willingly engage with something so rewarding as music, though they know that doing so will expose them to expressions of negative emotions, which are liable to cause feelings that are unpleasant to experience.[10]

## References

Addis, L. (1999). *Of mind and music.* Ithaca, NY: Cornell University Press.

Alperson, P. (ed.) (1994). *What is music? An introduction to the philosophy of music.* University Park, PA: Pennsylvania State University Press.

Alperson, P. (ed.) (1998). *Musical worlds: New directions in the philosophy of music.* University Park, PA: Pennsylvania State University Press.

Beever, A. (1998). The arousal theory again? *British Journal of Aesthetics,* **38**, 82–90.

Bouwsma, O. K. (1950). The expression theory of art. In *Philosophical analysis,* (ed. M. Black), pp. 71–96. Englewood Cliffs, NJ: Prentice-Hall.

Budd, M. (1985). *Music and the emotions: The philosophical theories.* London: Routledge.

Budd, M. (1995). *The values of art: Pictures, poetry, and music.* London: Penguin Press.

Carroll, N. (1998). *A philosophy of mass art.* New York: Oxford University Press.

Coker, W. (1972). *Music and meaning: A theoretical introduction to musical aesthetics.* New York: Free Press.

Cooke, D. (1959). *The language of music.* London: Oxford University Press.

Davies, S. (1987). Authenticity in musical performance. *British Journal of Aesthetics,* **27**, 39–50.

Davies, S. (1994). *Musical meaning and expression.* Ithaca, NY: Cornell University Press.

Davies, S. (1997). Contra the hypothetical persona in music. In *Emotion and the arts,* (ed. M. Hjort & S. Laver), pp. 95–109. Oxford, UK: Oxford University Press.

Deigh, J. (1994). Cognitivism in the theory of the emotions. *Ethics,* **104**, 824–54.

Ekman, P. (1980). Biological and cultural contributions to body and facial movements in the expression of the emotions. In *Explaining emotions,* (ed. A. O. Rorty), pp. 73–101. Los Angeles: University of California Press.

Godlovitch, S. (1998). *Musical performance: A philosophical study.* London: Routledge.

Goehr, L. (1992). *The imaginary museum of musical works: An essay in the philosophy of music.* Oxford, UK: Clarendon Press.

Goehr, L. (1998). *The quest for voice: On music, politics, and the limits of philosophy.* Oxford, UK: Clarendon Press.

Goldman, A. H. (1995*a*). *Aesthetic value.* Boulder, CO: Westview Press.

Goldman, A. H. (1995*b*). Emotion in music (a postscript). *Journal of Aesthetics and Art Criticism,* **53**, 59–69.

Goodman, N. (1968). *Languages of art.* Indianapolis, IN: The Bobbs-Merrill Company.

Gordon, R. (1987). *The structure of the emotions.* Cambridge, UK: Cambridge University Press.

Gracyk, T. A. (1996). *Rhythm and noise: An aesthetics of rock music.* Durham, NC: Duke University Press.

Griffiths, P. (1997). *What emotions really are.* Chicago: University of Chicago Press.

---

[10] I thank the editors, Jerrold Levinson, and an anonymous referee for comments on this chapter, and Vivian Ward for help with the artwork.

Hatfield, E., Cacioppo, J. T., & Rapson, R. L. (1994). *Emotional contagion.* New York: Cambridge University Press.

Higgins, K. (1991). *The music of our lives.* Philadelphia, PA: Temple University Press.

Hjort, M. & Laver, S. (ed.) (1997). *Emotion and the arts.* Oxford, UK: Oxford University Press.

Hume, D. (1912). Of tragedy. In *Essays moral, political and literary,* (Vol. 1) (ed. T. H. Green & T. H. Grose), pp. 258–65. London: Longmans, Green, & Co (originally published 1777).

Karl, G. & Robinson, J. (1995) Shostakovitch's tenth symphony and the musical expression of cognitively complex emotions. *Journal of Aesthetic and Art Criticism,* **53**, 401–15.

Kivy, P. (1988). *Osmin's rage: Philosophical reflections on opera, drama and text.* Princeton, NJ: Princeton University Press.

Kivy, P. (1989). *Sound sentiment.* Philadelphia, PA: Temple University Press.

Kivy, P. (1990). *Music alone: Philosophical reflection on the purely musical experience.* Ithaca, NY: Cornell University Press.

Kivy, P. (1995). *Authenticities: Philosophical reflections on musical performance.* Ithaca, NY: Cornell University Press.

Kivy, P. (1997). *Philosophies of art: An essay in differences.* New York: Cambridge University Press.

Kivy, P. (1999). Feeling the musical emotions. *British Journal of Aesthetics,* **39**, 1–13.

Langer, S. K. (1942). *Philosophy in a new key.* Cambridge, MA: Harvard University Press.

LeDoux, J. E. (1998). *The emotional brain.* London: Weidenfeld & Nicolson.

Lerdahl, F. & Jackendoff, R. (1983). *A generative theory of tonal grammar.* Cambridge, MA: MIT Press.

Levinson, J. (1982). Music and negative emotion. *Pacific Philosophical Quarterly,* **63**, 327–46.

Levinson, J. (1990). *Music, art, and metaphysics.* Ithaca, NY: Cornell University Press.

Levinson, J. (1996). *The pleasures of aesthetics.* Ithaca, NY: Cornell University Press.

Levinson, J. (1997*a*). *Music in the moment.* Ithaca, NY: Cornell University Press.

Levinson, J. (1997*b*). Emotion in response to art: A survey of the terrain. In *Emotion and the arts,* (ed. M. Hjort & S. Laver), pp. 20–34. Oxford, UK: Oxford University Press.

Levinson, J. (1998). Emotion in response to art. In *Routledge Encyclopedia of Philosophy,* (Vol. 3) (ed. E. Craig (chief ed.) & M. Budd (subject ed.)), pp. 273–81. London: Routledge.

Lyons, W. (1980). *Emotion.* New York: Cambridge University Press.

Madell, G. (1996). What music teaches about emotion. *Philosophy,* **71**, 63–82.

Matravers, D. (1998). *Art and emotion.* Oxford, UK: Clarendon Press.

Meyer, L. B. (1956). *Emotion and meaning in music.* Chicago: University of Chicago Press.

Ridley, A. (1995). *Music, value and the passions.* Ithaca, NY: Cornell University Press.

Robinson, J. (ed.) (1997). *Music and meaning.* Ithaca, NY: Cornell University Press.

Scruton, R. (1997). *The aesthetics of music.* Oxford, UK: Clarendon Press.

Solomon, R. C. (1976). *The passions.* Garden City, NY: Anchor Press/Doubleday.

Thom, P. (1993). *For an audience: A philosophy of the performing arts.* Philadelphia, PA: Temple University Press.

Tormey, A. (1971). *The concept of expression.* Princeton, NJ: Princeton University Press.

Vermazen, B. (1986). Expression as expression. *Pacific Philosophical Quarterly,* **67**, 196–224.

Walton, K. L. (1988). What is abstract about the art of music? *Journal of Aesthetics and Art Criticism, 46,* 351–64.

Walton, K. L. (1990). *Mimesis as make-believe: On the foundations of the representational arts.* Cambridge, MA: Harvard University Press.

# CHAPTER 3

# MUSICOLOGICAL APPROACHES TO EMOTION

NICHOLAS COOK AND NICOLA DIBBEN

## 3.1 Defining musicology

Writing about music may well go back as far as writing itself, but to speak of 'musicology' before about 1800 is to court anachronism. In the centuries before then, there were in the West two broadly distinct traditions of writing about music: on the one hand more or less practical manuals addressed in general to (and generally by) composers and performers, and on the other hand more or less speculative writings that, to modern eyes, can at times resemble cosmology with a musical vocabulary. The emergence of 'musicology' (a term not used in English until the twentieth century, but borrowed from the earlier French term *musicologie*) can, then, be traced to two circumstances: first, the new relationship between compositional theory and practice that resulted from a general growth in historical awareness and the establishment of a canon of 'masterworks'; and second, the increasing systematization of what in the course of the nineteenth century became known (especially in Germany) as the human sciences.

In its original form, and to some extent still in common British parlance, 'musicology' means simply the study of and knowledge about all aspects of music, taking in, for example, the systematic approaches to musical organization collectively known as 'music theory'; American usage of the term is distinctly narrower: in Joseph Kerman's words, 'the study of the history of Western music in the high-art tradition' (Kerman 1985, p. 11). In the 1990s, however, the self-imposed limitations of this version of musicology were seriously challenged by the so-called 'new' musicology (a development foreshadowed by Kerman's critique of the traditional discipline's formalist and positivist tendencies). There is, then, no single, universally accepted definition of the discipline's scope.

This poses problems in determining the scope of this chapter. A genuinely inclusive treatment of musicological approaches to emotion would not restrict itself to the work of 'musicologists' in any narrow sense, but might encompass the views of performers, composers, aestheticians, and others who wrote on music before 1800; similarly, it might take in not only present-day musicological writing but also the ethnomusicological, philosophical, psychological, or sociological perspectives that inform it. (It might also recognize the existence of other traditions of systematic thinking about music, other musicologies, outside the Western orbit.) But that would take a book and not a chapter! More modestly, then, we discuss here a selection of musicological or music-theoretical approaches to the expression of emotion in Western 'art' and popular music, most of them written since 1950, emphasizing in particular those that set out general frameworks within which to understand how specific pieces of music embody, express, arouse, or otherwise signify emotional states. (We recognize, and readers should be aware, that other authors might well have made a different selection.) Bearing in mind the likelihood that many of our readers will be unfamiliar with the discipline, however, we precede this with a whistlestop tour of thinking about music and emotion since around 1600: this will serve as much to contextualize musicology as to identify issues and points of reference that will be drawn on later in the chapter.

## 3.2 A historical sketch

While comparatively little is known of the nature and practice of ancient Greek music, classical writings about music have formed a constant point of reference for subsequent theorists and have accordingly exerted a lasting influence. One could almost frame a history of thinking about music and emotion in terms of the two principal functions which the Greeks ascribed to music: on the one hand *mimesis* (the imitation or transformation of an external reality) and, on the other, *catharsis* (the purification of the soul through emotional experience). The first term values music for its representational function, in this sense embracing it within the theory of knowledge, whereas the second locates music's value in the effect it makes upon the experiencing subject. At issue are two fundamentally different conceptions of what sort of thing music is. As might be expected, however, such philosophical concerns did not greatly impinge upon the practice of working musicians, who were less likely to discuss issues of music's emotional powers than simply to take them for granted; a comprehensive history of pre-musicological approaches to emotion would have to be extracted from a multitude of oblique references hidden in the nooks and crannies of a wide range of texts.

The rise of opera around 1600, with which we begin this overview, was associated with a long period of ascendancy in the idea of music as *mimesis*. (It is perhaps not irrelevant that the Florentine *camerata* responsible for this development saw themselves, however misguidedly, as reconstructing the practices of ancient Greek drama.) The function of music in baroque opera is to reflect or heighten the expression of the emotions signified by the words and presented by means of staged action; we can talk of the music 'expressing' emotion just to the extent that the emotion is located not within the music as such, but within an external reality (whether actual or imagined) which the music references. Music, in short, represents reality, just as language does. It is not surprising, then, that baroque musicians borrowed wholesale from contemporary thinking about language, seeking to understand even instrumental music as a form of discourse and, in particular, applying to it the principles of classical rhetoric: an eighteenth-century example is Mattheson (1981), who traced the operation in music of such rhetorical devices as repetition, variation, or counterstatement, seeing them as serving to project or heighten emotional content in the same way that, in language, the devices of rhetoric colour or inflect propositional content. And in each case the aim was persuasion: just as legal or political orators would seek to persuade their listeners of the case being presented, so musicians sought to convince audiences of their emotional veracity. Like actors, musical performers had themselves to feel the emotions they wanted to convey to their listeners: as C. P. E. Bach put it in his *Essay on the true art of playing keyboard instruments*, 'A musician cannot move others unless he too is moved' (Bach 1974, p. 152).

During the seventeenth and eighteenth centuries, vocal music—that is, music allied to words—was understood as the paradigm case for music in general. It was through heightening verbal signification that music itself acquired meaning; purely instrumental music by contrast had no meaning, or at best signified at second hand, functioning as a more or less pale reflection of texted music. Unsurprisingly, then, music fared badly in the formulation of the eighteenth-century discipline of aesthetics; music can arouse emotions, Kant admitted, but it amounts to no more than 'a play with aesthetic ideas . . . by which in the end nothing is thought'. (He added that the pleasure it creates 'is merely bodily, even though it is aroused by ideas of the mind, and . . . consists merely in the feeling of health that is produced by an intestinal agitation corresponding to such play'.[1]) It is in this light that the much vaunted rise around 1800 of autonomous instrumental music has to be understood: the point is not that people did not play purely instrumental music up to that time, but that it was not the paradigm case for music that it became by the middle of the nineteenth century. Lydia Goehr has characterized this conceptual transformation as a conjunction of a '*formalist* move which brought meaning from the music's outside to its inside' and a '*transcendent* move from the worldly and the particular to the spiritual and the universal' (Goehr 1992, p. 153).

The formalist move to which Goehr refers is most famously represented in the writings of the Viennese critic Eduard Hanslick, the first edition of whose short book *On the musically beautiful* appeared in 1854. In describing the 'content' of music as 'tonally moving forms' (Hanslick 1986, p. 29), Hanslick was claiming that questions about musical meaning, which had long been formulated in terms of representation, should be reformulated as questions about the intrinsic properties of the music itself. The clearest indication of what is at stake here is to be found in those later writers, such as the turn-of-the-century Viennese theorist Heinrich Schenker, who sought to build systems of musical analysis on Hanslickian foundations: commenting on C. P. E. Bach's prescriptions of how the improviser is to excite or soothe the passions, Schenker claims that 'One must not seek in Bach's word 'passions' [*Leidenschaften*] what certain aestheticians of the doctrine of affections bring to it . . . [Bach] means by it simply the consequences of a change in diminution: pure musical effects which have nothing in common with the amateurishly misunderstood and so grossly exaggerated ideas of the aestheticians' (Schenker 1994, p. 5).[2] (This development of the scope of musical analysis, in effect elaborating on the structural potential of 'tonally moving forms', might be seen as a definitive rebuttal of Kant's dismissive reduction of music to the level of intestinal

---

[1]  This passage (from Kant's *Critique of judgement*) is quoted and discussed by Kivy, who scornfully encapsulates Kant's image of music as 'the sonic counterpart of Tums for the tummy' (Kivy 1993, pp. 258–9).

[2]  The passage in Bach's *Essay on the true art of playing keyboard instruments* to which Schenker refers is on pp. 438–9 of Mitchell's translation (Bach 1974).

agitation.) It is in this sense that, as Goehr puts it, meaning was brought from the music's outside to its inside.

Released from its representational function, music is no longer seen as describing specific emotions within specific situations (the Count's mounting jealousy in Act 1 of Mozart's *Marriage of Figaro*, say), but rather as abstracting the essence of phenomena; this is the move from the particular to the transcendental of which Goehr speaks. Just as in the work of early romantic artists like Caspar David Friedrich, personal emotions are subsumed within a generalized aesthetic yearning for the universal and the spiritual; for the influential writer E. T. A. Hoffmann, writing in the early years of the nineteenth century, music's power lay precisely in its ability to transcend the conditions of ordinary existence, a view echoed in Hanslick's statement that the composer creates 'something which has no counterpart in nature and hence none in the other arts, indeed none in this world' (Hanslick 1986, p. 74). Seen in this light, music, once the poor relation of the visual and literary arts, could be considered uniquely privileged within the aesthetic hierarchy: the very lack of specificity that formerly consigned it to a subordinate role was now construed as an infinite suggestiveness. It is precisely because of its lack of direct reference to the specifics of everyday existence that the art historian Walter Pater (1910, p. 135) wrote that 'All art constantly aspires to the condition of music'.

But it is at this point that the story takes a series of unexpected turns, which between them can be seen as accounting for the fragmented and in many ways contradictory nature of present-day thinking about music, and particularly about musical meaning. For no sooner had music made itself independent of the word than the word began to re-establish itself, only this time outside rather than inside the musical text. It was during the nineteenth century that the consumption of music began to be routinely surrounded by a variety of informative and interpretative texts: programme notes, music appreciation texts, and, today, CD liners, broadcasts, and magazines. This development was largely associated with the reception of Beethoven's instrumental music, and in particular the increasingly idiosyncratic, not to say erratic, works of his late period. Some contemporary listeners put their hermetic style down to the composer's now profound deafness. Others felt that, behind the music's apparent contradictions (such as the consistent mixing of genres in the Ninth Symphony) there must lie some intention, some deeper message. And so there emerged a plethora of commentaries on the music, each attempting to work from the musical text to the meaning assumed to lie behind it. The most influential of these commentaries understood the music in autobiographical terms. In 1828, for example, Franz Joseph Fröhlich published a review of the Ninth Symphony, interpreting it as the expression of Beethoven's struggle with deafness and his ultimate transmutation of suffering into joy (Wallace 1986). Fröhlich even brought this interpretation to bear upon the bar-by-bar details of the music: bars 1–30 of the first movement, he explained, represent in succession tender longing, heroic strength, pathos, and a vision of joy—all of them complementary aspects of Beethoven's own, complex personality.

Commentaries of this kind, which maintained their popularity among the concert-going public during the remainder of the nineteenth century, set up a number of striking paradoxes. The first we have already referred to by implication: in Scott Burnham's words, 'music no longer in need of words now seems more than ever in need of words' (Burnham 1999, p. 194). Secondly, and related to this, music now vindicated as the most abstract of the arts is explained in the most concrete terms; it is worth observing how the music programme tradition which runs from Berlioz and Liszt to Richard Strauss (and from there, arguably, into film music) in effect brought such explanations back within the music itself, so setting itself up in opposition to the prevailing aesthetic of autonomous instrumental music. Thirdly, meaning now understood as located within the musical text (the very term applied to such commentaries, 'hermeneutics', is borrowed from traditions of biblical exegesis) is explained through the construction of an authorial persona whose experiences the music represents. Most telling of all, however, is the manner in which music is now construed as an expression of what might be termed bourgeois subjectivity.

As presented in baroque and classical opera, emotion belongs to the public sphere; to put it another way, it is conceived dramatically. The paradigm of nineteenth-century literature, by comparison, is the novel, where emotion subsists in private, subjective experience, to which the various characteristic devices of the novel give the reader access. In the same way, the emotion which nineteenth-century commentators read into Beethoven's music belongs to the private sphere, unmistakably so when Wagner describes the Ninth Symphony as Beethoven's attempt to reach out from the solitude of his deafness: 'When you meet the poor man, who cries to you so longingly, will you pass him on the other side if you find you do not understand his speech at once?' (Wagner 1899, p. 203). Music is still understood as expression, just as under the principle of *mimesis*, but this now takes the form of self-expression, the attempt of the artist to make contact with others and, so to speak, with himself or—more rarely—herself. However dated its origins, this is a concept that has never really lost currency in the years since the 1820s, though it is nowadays perhaps most evident in popular music: music videos, for instance, promise the fan a means of intimate access to the star, while the values of authentic self-expression are central to the carefully constructed persona of an artist like Bruce Springsteen (Cavicchi 1999).[3] It is in the contrast which Adorno once drew between the emotional qualities of Schoenberg's music and the earlier model of dramatic representation, however, that the idea of music as self-expression reaches its apogee: 'Passions are no longer simulated', he wrote, instead, 'genuine emotions of the unconscious—of shock, of trauma—are registered without disguise through the medium of music' (Adorno 1973, pp. 38–9). For the composer, then, and perhaps for the listener too, music provides something akin to the purification of the soul through emotional experience that the Greeks associated with it, and so assumes the function of *catharsis*.

Nowadays, formalism and hermeneutics are seen as opposite ends of the critical spectrum. But as we have explained, it was not always so: formalism, the idea that music is autonomous and should be understood in its own terms, was originally associated with the sense of music's other-worldliness and consequent spiritual value. Nor did Hanslick seek to deny music's emotional powers, although later formalists often read him this way. (Hence his statement in the foreword to the eighth edition of *On the musically*

---

[3] For a study of the bourgeois subject that takes in both romantic *Lieder* and rock, see Bloomfield (1993); for an example of popular music which problematizes this expressive norm, see Dibben (2001).

*beautiful*—published in 1891, 37 years after the book's first appearance—that 'I share completely the view that the ultimate worth of the beautiful is always based on the immediate manifestness of feeling' (Hanslick 1986, p. xxii).) He did, however, seek to qualify its ability to represent specific emotions, putting forward an early version of what is nowadays called the cognitive theory of the emotions (Kivy 1993, pp. 270, 284; see also Davies, this volume). You cannot feel love, Hanslick claims, without thinking of the loved one; the emotion is inextricably tied up with its object. But depending on the circumstances 'its dynamic can appear as readily gentle as stormy, as readily joyful as sorrowful, and yet still be love'. His point is that 'music can only express the various accompanying adjectives and never the substantive, e.g. love itself' (Hanslick 1986, p. 9). But how does it do this? In order to answer this question, Hanslick asks another (p. 11):

What, then, from the feelings, can music present, if not their content? Only that same dynamic . . . It can reproduce the motion of a physical process according to the prevailing momentum: fast, slow, strong, weak, rising, falling. Motion is just one attribute, however, one moment of feeling, not the feeling itself.

His conclusion, then, is that it is these purely musical motions, and not the feelings with which they may be associated, that must form the focus of any meaningful theory or criticism of music.

It would be possible to argue that what Hanslick means is that only when you can fully explain music in *motional* terms is there any point in trying to do so in *emotional* ones. Because you can never fully explain anything in the arts, however, that is a recipe for infinite deferral. At all events, and whatever Hanslick himself may have intended, he laid the foundations for a formalism that grew in strength during the later part of the nineteenth century and survived through the greater part of the twentieth, according to which issues of musical meaning and expression were regarded as off limits for purposes of serious academic discussion. This change in the nature of formalism coincided with the development of increasingly abstract and powerful methods for musical analysis (through the work of not only Schenker but also Schoenberg and Hindemith in the first half of the twentieth century, for example, and Babbitt, Forte, and Lerdahl in the second half), the aim of which was to provide complete and self-sufficient explanations of music in exclusively structural terms. That did not necessarily entail a denial that music might have emotional powers. Lerdahl and Jackendoff (1983, p. 8) specifically state that

To approach any of the subtleties of musical affect, we assume, requires a better understanding of musical structure. In restricting ourselves to structural considerations, we do not mean to deny the importance of affect in one's experience of music. Rather we hope to provide a stepping stone toward a more interesting account of affect than can at first be envisioned. [4]

But the practical effect is, of course, the indefinite postponement of consideration of music's expressive qualities to which we have already referred. In what follows, we shall consider the viability of the separation that this implies between structural analysis and expressive interpretation. For now it is worth just noting its apparent similarity to the traditional piano teacher's advice formulated by Ralph Kirkpatrick as 'Learn the notes

---

[4] Cf. Edward T. Cone's claim that 'If verbalization of true content—the specific expression uniquely embodied in a work—is possible at all, it must depend on close structural analysis' (Cone 1982, p. 233).

and then put in the expression'; tellingly, Kirkpatrick continues, 'My admonition is to learn the notes and understand their relationships, and then to draw the expression out' (Kirkpatrick 1984, p. 128).

By the 1980s there was a growing view that this narrowness of analytical purview, coupled to a parallel reluctance to enter upon aesthetic interpretation on the part of music historians, had resulted in an apparently unbridgeable schism between the concerns of professional musicologists on the one hand, and those of practically everyone else who had an interest in music on the other: as Kerman put it, 'Along with the preoccupation with structure goes the neglect of other vital matters—not only the whole historical complex . . . but also everything else that makes music affective, emotional, expressive' (Kerman 1985, p. 73). In this context one can see the 'new' musicology that followed as less new than revisionary, aiming to reinstate something of the more generous purview of musical interpretation as practised in the middle of the nineteenth century. Indeed one of the vehicles of the 'new' musicology was the revival of a self-styled hermeneutic criticism tacitly modelled on the nineteenth-century version.[5] Leo Treitler has made the acid observation that such criticism is 'not different in form or verisimilitude from the sort of nineteenth-century hermeneutic that interpreted Beethoven's Ninth Symphony in images drawn from Goethe's *Faust*' (Treitler 1999, p. 370).[6]

There is a crucial difference, however, for the 'new' musicological revival of hermeneutics was supplemented by a strain of social critique deriving primarily from the work of Adorno. It was most conspicuous in the work of Susan McClary, who gained a great deal of notoriety through her critical interpretations of the war-horses of the symphonic repertory: most famously, she likened parts of the Ninth Symphony to a rapist's murderous fantasy (McClary 1991, pp. 128–9), contrasting what she saw as the violent and misogynous emotions expressed by Beethoven's music with the altogether more accommodating and socialized expression found in the music of the contemporary but (arguably) homosexual Schubert. One might see this as a frivolous or mischievous application of traditional hermeneutical procedures, involving the construction of a clearly unhistorical compositional persona (and McClary has been criticized on precisely these grounds). But that is to miss her substantial point, which is that music serves to express not only personal emotions but also social ideologies, in this case a characteristic attitude to women or, more generally, to sociocultural differences. While many aspects of McClary's work have been subject to critique, the broadened musicological purview represented by her work has been widely accepted. And as a result, the long marginalized topic of musical meaning has become central to the discipline.

## 3.3 Some classic approaches

As we have seen, one strand which has dominated thinking about musical expression is a reliance on linguistic models. The notion of a shared musical 'language' is particularly

---

[5] See, for instance, Kramer (1990), along with McClary (1991), one of the key texts of the 'new' musicology; for a brief overview, focusing on issues of gender representation, see Cook (1998a, Chapter 7).

[6] The reference is to the programme note that Wagner drew up for his 1846 performance of the symphony in Dresden.

prominent in baroque music treatises which, influenced by newly rediscovered Greek and Roman doctrines of oratory and rhetoric, provided instruction on how the composer was to 'move' the 'affections' or emotions of the listener.

A primary aesthetic goal in baroque music was to achieve stylistic unity based on the representation of a single emotion—a phenomenon exemplified by the da capo aria, so called because its final section repeated the first one da capo, 'from the top'. Affections were conceived as typified and static attitudes of mind, expressed in music through specific figures and compositional techniques identified and discussed in contemporary theoretical sources (one of the earliest was Burmeister's *Musica Autoschediastike* of 1601). The approach derived from the rhetorical concept of *decoratio*, that is, rules and techniques for embellishing the ideas of an oration and infusing it with passion. Applied to music, devices such as melodic repetition, fugal imitation, and the use of dissonance were invoked in order to explain and justify irregular contrapuntal writing, in much the same way that nineteenth-century commentators proposed hermeneutical explanations for the idiosyncrasies of Beethoven's style. Gesturing was also part of rhetorical delivery (itself an object of study for politicians, ministers, and actors), and was theorized in the form of treatises on gestures in everyday life, and on rhetorical delivery and opera acting (Fig. 3.1) (Solomon 1989). The

**Figure 3.1** Gestures with the hand and face: (a) astuteness, (b) beauty, (c) carefulness, (d) deception, and (e) the negative (from Andrea di Joria, *La mimica degli antichi investigata nel gestire napoletano*, Napoli, 1832, reproduced in Solomon 1989).

precise bodily gestures and movements associated with the representation of specific attitudes of mind outlined in these texts seem perversely static and unreal from the standpoint of nineteenth- and twentieth-century constructions of subjectivity; in the same way, the da capo aria has long been criticized for the artificial nature of its return to the opening, as if emotions could be repeated to order. All this reflects a fundamental shift of conception: whereas the eighteenth-century affection is a rationalized attitude of mind, the nineteenth-century understood emotion as a personal and spontaneous expression or experience. (The listeners of Fig. 3.2, eyes turned away from the performers or head buried in hands, embody the migration of emotion from the outer to the inner world.)

In the later part of the eighteenth century, there was a shift from the earlier emphasis on *decoratio* to a lexicon of affective types or 'topics', as they have been termed by Ratner (1980); this was linked to an increasingly dynamic view of musical expression, whereby a single piece might encompass different emotions, or the transition between one emotion and another. (For contemporary listeners this was one of the most striking and innovatory features of Mozart's operatic arias and ensembles.) Basing his work on contemporary treatises as well as the study of musical texts, Ratner showed how classical compositions evoked, often in kaleidoscopic succession, a more or less fixed repertory of melodic, rhythmic, textural, and other types, each of which had its own specific connotation. Such types might refer, for example, to particular dances (minuet, gigue),

**Figure 3.2** Beethoven playing for his friends (lithograph by Albert Graefle, c. 1877).

styles (the 'brilliant' style, the 'Turkish' style), compositional procedures (the 'learned' style), or extramusical associations (the hunt).

This notion of an affective lexicon has been further developed by means of semiotic theory, in relation to both 'art' music (Agawu 1991; Allanbrook 1983) and popular music (Tagg 1982); it has also been interpreted in terms of cognitive theory (Gjerdingen 1988). All such approaches understand expressive meaning as the product of historical usage: music signifies through reference to established syntactical types (the V–I progression and motivic liquidation that encode closure in a Mozart string quartet, say), to other music and its circumstances of performance (the parade ground, for instance, in the case of an orchestral march), or to some kind of extramusical reality. It is crucial to such approaches that these meanings were deliberately employed by composers and understood as such by contemporary audiences. For example, Agawu (1991, p. 31) cites a letter from Mozart to his father in which he discusses his compositional strategy in the opera *Die Entführing aus dem Serail*, and the likely impact of particular features on the audience. Mozart refers specifically to his use of the 'Turkish' style to create a comic effect during the scene in which Osmin expresses his rage, as well as to the use of syntactical features such as a change of key and metre at the end of a particular aria in order to surprise his audience.[7]

Because of the assumption that musical meaning results from historical sedimentation, the application of any given lexical approach of this kind is necessarily restricted to a specific repertory. By contrast, the aim of Deryck Cooke's *The language of music*, first published in 1959, is to provide not only a lexicon of but also an explanatory basis for the emotional meanings of Western 'art' music in general (and perhaps even, as we shall see, for music as a universal phenomenon). In Cooke's words, his book 'attempts to show that the conception of music as a language capable of expressing certain very definite things is not a romantic aberration, but has been the common unconscious assumption of composers for the past five-and-a-half centuries at least' (Cooke 1959, p. xi). He locates his basic expressive lexicon in the tonal and intervallic 'tensions' embodied in specific scale steps and the patterns of motion between them, seeing other musical dimensions such as timbre and texture as 'characterising agents', that is, as merely modifying the tensions established through pitch, time, and dynamics (Cooke 1959, pp. 37–8). He substantiates his theory by citing large numbers of extracts taken from vocal works, the texts of which embody similar expressive meanings. The assumption is that the emotional associations of particular musical formations apply equally when these formations occur in autonomous instrumental music. After going through this process with each of the different scale steps, he draws up a summary of what he terms 'the basic

---

[7] Such lexicons had a kind of after-life in early cinema history, in the form of the cue sheets, manuals, and handbooks that provided guidance to the performers, usually pianists, who accompanied silent films. These volumes contained both transcriptions from the classical repertoire and originally composed music, categorized according to the narrative situations and emotions engendered by it (see also Cohen, this volume). One of the earliest anthologies (*Motion picture piano music: Descriptive titles to fit the action, character or scene of moving pictures*, cited in Marks 1992, p. 68) contains 51 short pieces with titles such as 'Aged Colored Man, Aged Persons, Ancient Dance, Andante, Antique Dance, Apparitions', listed alphabetically.

expressive functions of all twelve notes of our scale', beginning as follows (Cooke 1959, pp. 89–90):

*Tonic:* Emotionally neutral; context of finality. *Minor Second:* Semitonal tension down to the tonic, in a minor context: spiritless anguish, context of finality. *Major Second:* As a passing note, emotionally neutral. As a whole-tone tension down to the tonic, in a major context, pleasurable longing, context of finality. *Minor Third:* Concord, but a 'depression' of natural third: stoic acceptance, tragedy. *Major Third:* Concord, natural third: joy'

Philip Tagg's (1982) application of semiotic theory to popular music is reminiscent of Cooke's approach in both concept and method. He identifies a range of signs in popular music, equating particular emotions, moods, and meanings with particular harmonies, melodies, timbres, and so forth, and referring to them as 'musemes' or minimal units of musical meaning; the term is based on 'phoneme', and is thus a further illustration of the indebtedness of theories of musical emotion to linguistic models.[8] Tagg verifies his interpretations in two ways. The first of these is what he calls 'inter-subjective comparison', by which he simply means establishing the consistency of attributions of meaning to the same music played to different respondents. The second and better known is what he terms 'inter-objective comparison' (IOC): this means the substitution for a given museme of others drawn from comparable expressive contexts, especially ones involving words, in order to confirm their semantic equivalence. (Again the reference to texted music provides a link with Cooke's method.) Tagg demonstrates his theory through the detailed analysis of specific pieces of music, the most extended examples being his analyses of the *Kojak* TV theme tune and the Abba hit *Fernando*. The readings that result are more complex than Cooke's in that they do not simply bring to light emotional contents but attempt to define an attitude towards the ostensible meaning of the lyrics: in the case of *Fernando*, for instance, Tagg concludes that the music gives the lie to the revolutionary sympathies expressed by the words.

There are a number of criticisms which can be levelled equally at Cooke and Tagg.[9] One is that both their methods are heavily dependent upon extramusical aspects, particularly accompanying lyrics or other programmatic elements. Although such elements are obviously important where present, how do we know what happens in music from which they are absent and the connotations of which are therefore less clear (Middleton 1990, p. 234)? How confident can we be that what applies in the one case applies in the other? (Does music derive its emotional meanings from purely historical associations with certain texts, or were those texts associated with the music because of some

---

[8]   Tagg's concept of sign, however, is broader than Cooke's: as well as 'style indicators', which refer to compositional 'norms', and 'genre synecdoche', referring to a 'foreign' style and hence to the genre and culture to which it belongs, Tagg identifies 'anaphones', which share a structural homology with the sonic, kinetic, or tactile events that they signify, and 'episodic markers', which designate structural functions (Tagg 1992).

[9]   See, for example, Middleton (1990), Davies (1994, with many references), and Shepherd and Wicke (1997). Scruton (1997, pp. 203–8) offers a trenchant critique of the parallel between music and language implicit in Cooke's approach.

emotional quality inherent in the music?) Related to this is an objection which applies to all lexical approaches to musical meaning: the emotional or other signification of musemes may vary according to the musical contexts within which they are articulated (in other words, it may not be possible to draw so confident a distinction between the 'semantic' and the 'syntactical' aspects of music).[10] Lexical approaches, in short, may endow the music with a false semblance of semantic fixity.

Other criticisms apply to one method but not the other. For example, one problem with Tagg's IOC technique is that it is so laborious, if it is to be done properly, as to verge on the impractical. As Allan Moore (1993, p. 158) puts it, 'it is so time-consuming that I have never seen it properly undertaken in equivalent studies' (other than by Tagg, that is to say). Again, Tagg has been criticized for drawing comparisons between contemporary popular styles and the European 'art' repertory, so implicitly assuming that they form part of a common cultural tradition (Middleton 1990, p. 234). This may be a reasonable assumption in the case of some film and television music: several commentators have traced the appropriation of semantic elements from late nineteenth- and early twentieth-century 'art' music by the Hollywood film industry (Eisler [and Adorno] 1947; Flinn 1992). Analyses of popular music also sometimes reveal the influence of 'art' traditions. An example is Walser's linkage of heavy metal music with the ideologies and even some of the performance practices of nineteenth-century Romanticism (Walser 1993). However, it would be clearly wrong to claim that traditions such as blues, rock, rap, or dance music derive primarily from 'art' music. So it becomes necessary to define just what the relevant frame of reference is for any particular repertory or piece, and that of course raises questions of who is doing the defining and to what ends. Nor is that the only problem. If you set out to identify the different stylistic traditions within which different musemes operate, how are you going to decide where to stop? (Are there specific musemes applicable to popular music? Or to pop but not rock? Or just to dance music? house? garage? jungle? Bristol jungle?)

Such problems may not be insoluble in principle, but they are certainly hard to solve in practice. In such a context, there is something very tempting about Cooke's attempt to derive the emotional expression of music directly from natural principles. As we have seen, he explains expression in terms of intervallic tensions, and he explains intervallic tensions in terms of basic acoustic principles, specifically the overtone series. 'That the major third should be found to express pleasure should surprise no one', he writes, since it appears 'early on in the harmonic series: it is nature's own basic harmony, and by using it we feel ourselves to be at one with nature' (Cooke 1959, p. 51). He admits that tradition builds on tradition, that is, that there is a historical element in musical meaning, but he insists that traditions arise in the first place because of the natural principles built into the music (Cooke 1959, pp. 40–1); for him, then, there was emotional mean-

---

[10] Cf. Jenefer Robinson's criticism (also voiced, for example, by Anthony Newcomb) that 'most philosophical theorists of musical expression have either ignored or underemphasized . . . the fact that the musical expression of complex emotions is not a function of a few isolated measures here and there, as in Kivy's examples in *The corded shell*; rather it is very often a function of the large-scale formal structures of the piece as a whole. We cannot understand the expression of complex emotions in music apart from the continuous development of the music itself' (Robinson 1998, p. 19).

ing in music before texts were associated with it. And, of course, principles like the overtone series do not vary from one culture to another. It is in this sense that, although limiting his examples to Western 'art' traditions, Cooke implicitly sets out a universal model of emotion in music: the laws of nature apply in China and in Africa as they do in Europe and America, and therefore the same principles should govern musical expression. Such thinking has become deeply unfashionable, because of its potentially essentializing and ethnocentric nature, and few present-day scholars would probably be prepared to sign up to this aspect of Cooke's theory. (Approaches to emotion and meaning in the ethnomusicological literature, while falling outside the scope of this chapter, are almost invariably rooted in the 'thick' description of specific cultures and contexts.[11]) Perhaps the most telling symptom of Cooke's ethnocentricity, however, lies in the way in which he unquestioningly identifies meaning with the expression of personal emotion—in which he understands it, in short, in terms of bourgeois subjectivity. A strong argument could be made that Cooke's approach, valid as it may be for Schubert or Schumann, is misleading in relation not just to Chinese or African music, but to Monteverdi's and Handel's too.

Despite the difficulties to which we have referred, Cooke's work was important in placing emotion firmly within the musicological agenda, and in attempting to do so on a principled basis. Much the same might be said of Leonard B. Meyer (1956), whose first book, *Emotion and meaning in music*, appeared 3 years before Cooke's (indeed, Kivy has described it, perhaps rather sweepingly, as 'the book that taught many of us for the first time that you can talk about music without talking nonsense' (Kivy 1987, p. 153)). Whereas Cooke attempted to ground the emotional expression of music in natural-scientific principles, thereby as it were short-circuiting cultural mediation, Meyer drew upon a range of sources in psychology. His overall interpretation of musical structure, which he has continued to develop in the ensuing 40 years (cf. Meyer, this volume), is based on gestalt principles: listeners are drawn to perceive musical patterns as wholes, as tending towards closure, and compositional techniques can be understood as ways of both stimulating and challenging such perceptions. In essence, Meyer sees music as setting up expectations in the listener (or, to put it another way, implications in the music) which are in general fulfilled or realized, but often only after postponement or apparent diversion. It is here that Meyer's approach to emotion comes in. The basic principle, which Meyer also drew from contemporary psychology, is that 'Emotion or affect is aroused when a tendency to respond is arrested or inhibited' (Meyer 1956, p. 14). To take a very simple example, a dominant seventh chord implies resolution; the longer resolution is postponed the more affect will be created, and if when it comes the resolution is to *vi* (an interrupted cadence), further postponing the return to *I*, there will be a further heightening of affect. Because the implications created by any given piece of music, and the manner in which they are or are not realized, fall clearly within the domain of structural analysis, the result is that emotion is incorporated within the latter. In effect, the analysis of musical emotion plugs into that of musical structure.

[11] For representative examples—one chapter-length, one book-length—see Tolbert (1994) and Feld (1982). See also Becker (this volume).

For all its neatness, however, this approach creates a number of difficulties. One concerns the relationship between emotions as normally understood—hope, joy, grief, and so on—and the kind of undifferentiated affect or feeling tone (in effect a unidimensional variable) that Meyer's theory predicates. Some commentators have doubted whether Meyer's theory can properly be considered as pertaining to the emotions at all (e.g. Budd 1985). Davies (1994, p. 288), by contrast, observes that 'for Meyer the possibility of the listener's differentiating the feeling tone is a real one', and he elaborates and justifies Meyer's position by arguing that the feeling tone can itself take on a kind of mimetic function:

There are, within any culture, groups of emotions having a common pattern of behavioral expression. For instance, the dynamics of the behavioral expressions of sadness, grief, disappointment, and regret are similar and can be distinguished from the behavioral expressions of joy, happiness, and enthusiasm. Music can be heard as imitating the dynamics of behavior. As listeners we hear these dynamics and imagine that the music is through them expressive of, say, sadness. In so doing we (imaginatively) make the music the emotional object in terms of which our feeling tone can be differentiated.

In saying this, Davies is invoking the Hanslickian idea that feelings are characterized by specific dynamic qualities. As we saw above, Hanslick argues that music cannot specify love, but through its motional qualities it can specify such adjectival properties as the joyful or sorrowful quality of love. In effect, Davies is suggesting that Meyer's undifferentiated affect conveys such adjectival properties, which we are led to attribute to the music itself (that is why it is common, if arguably misleading, to talk of the music being happy or sad, as if it were a sentient being). Since Hanslick's day the idea that music expresses emotion through somehow mirroring the dynamics of our inner life has become a commonplace in writing on the topic; the classic formulation is Langer's claim that 'there are certain aspects of the so-called "inner life"—physical or mental— which have formal properties similar to those of music—patterns of motion and rest, of tension and release, of agreement and disagreement, preparation, fulfilment, excitation, sudden change, etc.' (Langer 1942, p. 228).[12] When we said that music 'somehow' mirrors the dynamic of inner life, however, we meant to signal a crucial vagueness in such thinking: without entering into details, the problem lies in specifying what sort of entity the 'dynamics of our inner life' might actually be, or how it might be measured. In the absence of adequate answers to these questions, the appeal to such impalpable dynamics has little explanatory force.

A second line of criticism is that Meyer's approach is too narrow and exclusive. Davies, for instance, complains that it 'overemphasizes the status of the unpredictable at the expense of the structural significance of similarity' (Davies 1994, p. 289), while Keil (1994) similarly complains that it ignores the significance of repetition and performance skills. Underlying these complaints is a suspicion that, through incorporating them within a psychologically based theory, Meyer is lending a spurious

---

[12] Davies (1994, pp. 123–4) offers a critique, along with an extensive though by no means complete listing of similar claims by other writers (p. 230, n. 33). The basic approach, of course, links with earlier ideas of music 'moving' listeners' affections.

generality to principles grounded in the modernist aesthetic, with its valorization of innovation and the unique. This charge would be not altogether fair, because the link he makes between psychological principles and musical meaning is not a simple or direct one. For one thing, Meyer recognizes the extent to which listeners' expectations reflect not only the properties of the musical stimulus but also the culturally specific stylistic codes that are acquired through enculturation. For another, he took pains to explain on the very first page of *Emotion and meaning in music* (1956) that the kind of musical meaning we have so far discussed is not the only one: he distinguishes 'embodied' meaning, which is the result of the realization or frustration of expectation, from 'designative' meaning, which involves reference to objects, concepts, or events outside music (a distinction corresponding to Jakobson's 'introversive' and 'extroversive semiosis'; see Jakobson 1971, pp. 704–5), emphasizing that the latter reflects not just culture-specific associations but the listener's personal experiences and disposition, too. Nevertheless, embodied meanings play a far larger role in Meyer's work than designative ones, and it is not hard to see why, for his theory *explains* musical meaning (rather than simply acknowledging its existence) only to the extent that it can be reformulated in terms of relationships between musical elements. Or to put it another way, explaining meaning means translating it into music-structural terms; it is a one-way process. There is something symbolic in the fact that Meyer's first book is the only one he wrote specifically about musical emotion and meaning, the others all focusing on issues of structure and style.

## 3.4 Structural and expressive vocabularies

The basic problem we have diagnosed in Meyer is that of talking about both the emotion and the music in a sustained manner: you may start off talking about the emotion, but you seem to end up talking about the music in more or less the usual way. Of the admittedly limited amount of musicological or music-theoretical work in this area since 1956, much is open to the same criticism. So it is of interest to consider a more recent critique of such work by a professional philosopher (Kivy 1993). Kivy takes as his starting point a critical reading of Schumann's Second Symphony by a writer loosely associated with the early stages of the 'new' musicology (Newcomb 1984). Newcomb's essay is a good example of the revival of a hermeneutical approach to which we previously referred, and indeed sets out to reconstruct a nineteenth-century perception of Schumann's symphony (which was more highly rated in its own time than is generally the case today). Newcomb attempts to achieve this through consideration of the expressive trajectory of the piece, which he characterizes as 'suffering leading to healing or redemption', and relates these emotional characteristics to the difficult circumstances of Schumann's life as he sketched the work. He also points out that many other compositions from around the same period exhibit a similar trajectory (an example to which we have already referred being the 'transmutation of suffering into joy' in Beethoven's Ninth Symphony), and suggests that we might think of this as a 'plot archetype', in other words a generic category in terms of which individual instances may be understood.

Kivy (1993) applauds Newcomb's aims (indeed he sees in them the seeds of a 'new music criticism'), but identifies what he sees as serious methodological failings. In particular, Kivy objects that Newcomb is trying to add an additional, interpretative layer to structural analysis, whereas the whole project of interpreting autonomous instrumental music is built on a fallacy. 'Pure' music cannot represent anything, Kivy claims, and therefore the symphony cannot contain the meaning Newcomb ascribes to it; in other words, as soon as Newcomb started talking about Schumann's biography, he stopped talking about the music. (As a musicologist rather than a philosopher, Newcomb might very well reply that nineteenth-century listeners clearly *did* interpret the music in just this way, and that the question of whether they were philosophically justified in doing so is irrelevant to an exercise in historical reconstruction.) But in that case, you might ask, how *are* we to build emotional expression into music criticism? Kivy (1993, p. 316) replies:

The new way is not to amplify criticism by adding interpretation to analysis but, rather, by amplifying analysis itself. For once one ceases to see expressive properties of music as semantic or representational properties, it becomes clear that they are simply *musical* properties: they are phenomenological properties of music, and as such a proper subject of musical analysis.

In other words, he is saying, when we analyse music we should analyse its expressive properties alongside its structural ones. And he offers some examples of what he has in mind. In Mozart's 'Dissonance' Quartet, he says, the relationship between the dark, anguished character of the introduction (which gives the quartet its soubriquet) and the light, sunny character of the allegro that follows creates an effect of strong, expressive resolution; take away the expression and you weaken the resolution. Or again, there is an expressive difference between a Haydn symphony movement that goes from tonic minor to relative major to tonic minor (that is, from dark to light to dark), and one that ends in the tonic major (so that its overall trajectory is from dark to light). Because these are directly experienced aspects of the music, Kivy concludes, 'an analysis . . . that leaves out the expressive contrast, is incomplete in a musically non-trivial way' (1993, p. 319). But does this solve the problem of how to talk about both the music and the emotion in a sustained manner? The answer turns on whether Kivy has identified expressive properties as distinct from structural ones, or whether he is simply talking about structural properties but giving them expressive names. In the Mozart case, is the effect of resolution created by the passage from dark to light actually different from that created by the passage from the dissonance of the opening to the diatonicism of the main movement? Or are these just different ways of talking about the same thing? (If so, then in what sense are you leaving out the expression in speaking only of dissonance and diatonicism?) Again, in the Haydn case, just what does it mean to speak of the passage from dark to light over and above what it means to speak of the passage from minor to major? If the conclusion is that the one terminology can be simply substituted for the other, then there must be a suspicion at least that Kivy's 'new music criticism' is just the old music criticism with an updated (some music theorists might say outdated) vocabulary.

Of course, it might just be that Kivy applies his expressive terminology in too literal a manner. That, at any rate, is suggested by the comparison with another study, this time a collaboration between a philosopher and musicologist, which interprets Shostakovitch's Tenth Symphony as 'a progression from dark to light or struggle to victory' (Karl &

Robinson 1997, p. 166). In using these terms, the authors are not referring to anything as simple as a major or minor mode, or dissonance versus consonance. They are referring to the composite properties of a complex musical structure, and, indeed, their main purpose is to show how the large-scale musical unfolding of the third movement is central to the construction of its expressive message, which they see as one of hope (and more than that, false hope). While their argument begins with structural analysis and ends with expressive analysis—the same sequential approach that Kivy criticized in Newcomb—it would not be fair to describe Karl and Robinson as simply building expression onto structure, like icing on a cake. The very characterization of complex, large-scale passages as 'light' or 'dark' stimulates the attempt to explain these expressive qualities in terms of the music's structural properties; again, the authors set out what they call the 'cognitive content' of hope (which involves looking forward to, and striving towards, a happier but uncertain future) and then match the structural properties of the music against these criteria, in effect using them as an analytical framework. In this way their interpretative strategy involves what they describe as 'a complex interplay among a variety of different sorts of observations' (1997, p. 170), both formal and expressive. There is, however, a certain ambiguity at this point. On the one hand, the authors write that 'we consider this dichotomy [between the formal and the expressive] ill-conceived, because often the formal and expressive threads of a work's structure are so finely interwoven as to be inextricable' (1997, p. 176). On the other, they claim that 'the formal and expressive elements of musical structure are so thoroughly interdependent that the formal function of particular passages can often be accurately described only in *expressive* terms' (1997, p. 177). The second statement seems to start by saying the same as the first but to end up saying the opposite: if you can describe a particular passage in expressive but not structural terms, or for that matter vice versa, then this seems to reinstate the dichotomy between them (an implication which becomes still clearer when the authors continue 'there is no 'strictly formal' or purely musical explanation for why our focal passage unfolds as it does in the central section of the third movement').[13] The relationship between structure and expression remains unclear.

This issue has been explicitly addressed by another musicologist, Fred Maus. In an article entitled 'Music as drama' (Maus 1988), he launches a systematic attack on the sequential, structure-to-expression approach, and then proceeds to offer an analysis of the opening of Beethoven's String Quartet, Op. 95, combining analytical and expressive

---

[13] Karl and Robinson make a related point in a footnote on p. 173, where they explain that 'a listener schooled in the epic symphonic tradition might expect that the tension of the third movement should be swept away at the beginning of the finale ... Upon finding this expectation frustrated, he or she may then feel tense, impatient, or bewildered ... The listener's feelings of impatience or frustration, while poorly mirroring the expressive structure of the work, may nonetheless provide the initial clues that something is amiss ... providing an impetus to interpretation'. In this way the frustration of expectation which Meyer saw as the source of affect functions as an interpretative cue: implicit in this is a distinction between the listener's emotional response and the expressive properties of the music *per se*. (This distinction bulks large in philosophical writing on the subject, particularly Kivy's, but falls outside the scope of this chapter.)

vocabulary and commenting self-consciously on his analytical strategies as he does so.[14] The conclusion that Maus draws from this analysis—as much an analysis of analysis as of Beethoven—is that music has neither structural nor emotional content. Rather it consists of a series of *events*, which we make sense of by regarding them as the *actions* of imaginary agents, so attributing intentions or motivations to them. His Beethoven analysis, Maus claims, '*explains* events by regarding them as *actions* and suggesting *motivation, reasons* why those actions are performed, and the reasons consist of combinations of psychological states' (1988, p. 67). It is this imagined dramatic content that both structural and expressive vocabularies seek to represent, each in their own way: as Maus (1988, p. 69) explains,

the technical language and the dramatic language offer descriptions of *the same events*. That event at the opening of the quartet, according to the analysis, is an outburst and it is also a unison passage with an obscure relation between metrical hierarchy and pitch hierarchy. The technical vocabulary of the analysis describes the actions that make up the piece.

While referring to the same musical content, then, the two vocabularies construct it in different ways, filter it differently, and the analyst can exploit the asymmetries between them in order to gain purchase on the music. It is for this reason, presumably, that Maus observes that 'Both sorts of description—"technical" or music-theoretical, "dramatic" or anthropomorphically evocative—belong, interacting, to the analysis' (1988, p. 63), and Robert Hatten uses the same word when he writes of 'the interaction of expressively significant . . . thematic, motivic, or topical events with structurally significant voice-leading events' (Hatten 1994, p. 320, n. 8). Hatten's book is, to date, the most comprehensive attempt to incorporate expressive and structural analysis within a coherent critical practice, and it brings together many of the approaches we have described so far. As his reference to topics suggests, Hatten builds on the documentary evidence that historical listeners (his book focuses on Beethoven) not only identified topical references in the music they heard but also saw them as one of the main ways in which it conveyed emotional or other meaning; to this extent Hatten's work, like Agawu's, links with the tradition of understanding emotion as a public, rationalized state, which as we have seen goes back to the baroque affections. Unlike Agawu's work, however, Hatten's also embraces nineteenth-century conceptions of emotion as a private, subjective experience, and indeed the book is easily read as a contribution to the hermeneutic tradition (like Newcomb, Hatten claims to be reconstructing historical practices of listening, and his concept of 'expressive genre' corresponds closely to Newcomb's 'plot archetype'). More centrally, it brings together extroversive and introversive approaches within a unified theoretical framework drawn from present-day semiotic theory. The question on which we wish to focus, however, is the extent to which Hatten succeeds in theorizing the interaction between structure and expression to which he refers.

The immediate impression of Hatten's working procedure is that, once again, he starts with structural analysis, and then adds in the interpretation. The first ten pages of his analysis of the first movement of the Quartet, Op. 130, for instance, consist of structural

---

[14] For detailed discussion of the relationship between structural and expressive vocabularies in critical writings which draw analogies between music and narrative, see Maus (1997).

analysis, while the final page offers an expressive interpretation in terms of a quasi-Hegelian synthesis of opposed emotions (Hatten 1994, pp. 134–45). And while he does sometimes begin with a provisional and intuitive identification of the music's expressive content, following this with structural analysis and then a refinement of the expressive interpretation based on that analysis, it is significant that Hatten never goes on to the next stage (that is, returns to and refines the structural analysis on the basis of the expressive one). To this extent the relationship between structure and expression is still an unequal one: as usual in musical analysis, the cards are stacked in favour of structure. In other contexts, however, such as his account of the *Cavatina* from the same quartet, Hatten's treatment is more even-handed. He makes use of vocabulary that applies equally well to structure or expression (undercutting, irruption, or reversal, for example). He mingles structural and expressive vocabulary (1994, p. 213):

A strong wedge motion in m. 5 expands registrally to the apex on the downbeat of m. 6, which is negated as a climax by the more intensely expressive crux created by the unexpected reversal (registral collapse) on the second beat. The 'willed' (basically stepwise) ascent takes on a hopeful character supported by the stepwise bass'.

At other times, he offers parallel structural and expressive interpretations; on p. 214 he writes of bar 12 that 'As the vi region of E♭ major, C minor would appear to be an appropriate choice in light of the harmonic emphasis it has already received in m. 6. The region could also be motivated by the expressive value of the relative minor as an emotionally troubled opposition to the serenity of the major'.

But most revealing is the way in which he stresses what, in 'purely musical' terms, might be seen as points of abnormality or incoherence, and siezes upon them as interpretative opportunities. For instance, he says of the repeated $iv^7$ chords on the second beats of bars 15 and 16, following anomalously on cadential six-four chords, that they support (1994, p. 215)

a construal as 'parenthetical' or outside the normal course of time, thus akin to 'insight' in that it comes without logical necessity or sequential train of thought . . . Interactively interpreting these inflections of meaning, one might understand the resulting trope as 'tragically weighted insight or reflection, expanding an instant that seems frozen within the flow of time'.

Expanding the same principle to the scale of the movement's formal unfolding, he provides a figure showing 'unconvincing formal analyses' (1994, p. 209, Fig. 8.1): the very incoherence of the movement when understood in purely formal terms becomes a source of its overall expressive meaning, which Hatten sees as a kind of metaphorical blend of tragic insight and faith, each illuminating the other. In this way, expression is not seen as simply a gloss on structure; it works in counterpoint with it.

Writers such as Karl and Robinson, Maus, and Hatten demonstrate that it is possible to use structural and expressive vocabularies together in a way that does not simply map the one onto the other, in the manner of Kivy's 'new music criticism'. It might be going too far to say that any of them succeeds in talking in a sustained manner about both the music and the emotion (even Hatten sometimes gives the impression of lurching from one to the other). But they manage to do so in flashes, and the result is illuminating.

## 3.5 Conclusion: discourse and emotion in music

In the work of some writers, the distance between technical and 'anthropomorphically evocative' interpretation, to borrow Maus's phrase, becomes much greater. A good illustration is provided by a pair of curiously similar essays: by Charles Fisk on the first movement of Schubert's Sonata in B♭ major, D. 960 (Fisk 1997), and by Marion Guck on—among other things—the second movement of Mozart's G minor Symphony, K. 550 (Guck 1994). Each begins with a single, portentous moment in the piece:[15] the left hand trill in the seventh bar of Schubert's sonata, and the C♭ in bar 53 of the symphony movement. And each constructs out of this moment a similar story: that of an alien element, an 'outsider' who after a succession of vicissitudes becomes accepted within the larger context represented by the piece—is accepted, in other words, as an 'insider'. The link that each author makes between music on the one hand, and on the other the narrative of rejection and acceptance, alterity and assimilation, builds on the expressive properties of the music and at the same time brings new expressive properties, new connotations of positive or negative emotion, to bear upon it. Neither author, of course, is claiming that the original music was in any sense 'about' immigration. Like Newcomb in the case of Schumann's Second Symphony, and Karl and Robinson in the case of Shostakovitch's Tenth, Fisk invokes the circumstances of Schubert's life to add credibility to, or at least to deepen, his interpretation: maybe, he says, the (again arguably) homosexual Schubert felt himself to be an outsider in his own society and so 'took solace, at least unconsciously' from his own parable of integration (Fisk 1997, p. 200). Whereas Karl and Robinson give the impression of speaking from a position of interpretative authority, however ('Shostakovich, ever mistrustful of happy endings, undercuts its optimistic qualities' (Karl & Robinson 1997, p. 178)), Fisk claims to be doing no more than telling a story, offering 'a naively poetic description of what happens in the music' (Fisk 1997, p. 195), and the personal and provisional nature of his interpretation is highlighted in the title: 'What Schubert's last sonata might hold' (further glossed, on the final page of the article, as 'what Schubert's last sonata holds for me'). Guck similarly introduces her account as 'a story about C♭' (Guck 1994, p. 67).

Then what, you might ask, is the point of all this? Fisk tells his story in order to substantiate an argument that every listener projects his or her own emotional experiences into the music, which in turn moulds those experiences so that they become in some sense purely musical emotions (Fisk 1997, p. 182). The limitation of his approach, however, is that he begins with technical analysis, goes on to unfold his narrative (showing how it can be fitted to the framework of the analysis)—and then stops. Guck, by contrast, structures her article through a process of oscillation between technical and expressive interpretation. She begins with her perception of the C♭'s portentousness, an observation which (as she puts it) 'incorporates a conceptual structure that is covert' (Guck 1994, p. 71). The purpose of constructing the parallel narrative, she continues, is that 'the conceptual structure of the immigrant's tale is revealed in the process of its telling'; in other words, the story renders the structure explicit, and so initiates the

---

[15] Both authors use this word 'portent'/'portentous': Fisk (1997, p. 184) and Guck (1994, p. 63).

process of answering the analytical question '*why* is the C♭ portentous?'. But to complete the answer it is necessary to return to the text, to the plane of technical analysis, understanding and experiencing the music in light of the narrative: as Guck puts it, her story 'suggests a strategy for hearing not only the highlighted events but also the lines of development in which they participate, which is to say that it provides a means of codifying and enriching the hearing of the whole piece' (1994, p. 71). The point of the analysis, in short, is not just to describe how you experience the music, but to *change* how you experience it, both in technical terms and emotionally.

It is not only Fisk's and Guck's analyses which do this. We mentioned above that Hatten presents his work as, in essence, an exercise in the reconstruction of historical listening practices. However, this is not the only nor necessarily the most productive way of reading it, and indeed Hatten does not embark upon the systematic kind of historical reconstruction of period perception, based on contemporary documentation, that has been attempted for instance by Johnson (1995). The alternative is to read Hatten's work as a sustained argument about how we might most fruitfully hear Beethoven's music today. Understood this way, Hatten's book becomes an attack on the etiolated listening practices brought about by what he refers to as the 'errors of formalism' (Hatten 1994, p. 228); by contrast, he is offering a richer, more complex, more human way to hear the music, and one which (as a bonus) perhaps recreates something of the manner in which Beethoven's first listeners heard it. Another way to express this is that it is not simply a matter of hearing emotions out of the music—that is, hearing the meanings that were always there within it—but, so to speak, of hearing them *into* it. Understood this way, analytical and critical practices are less concerned with how the music *is* than how it might be heard to be; they aim less at proof than at persuasion (as Guck puts it, 'Truth is replaced by the plausibility of the narrative'; 1994, p. 72). This is the basis of what we term a 'performative' approach to music and expressive meaning.[16]

There is a sense in which writing about music has always been performative, and one of the most common ways of misinterpreting the documents of music history is by reading them as descriptions of actual practice rather than interventions in it. This is obvious in the case of the treatises of the baroque and classical periods, which prescribed how their readers were to compose, perform, or understand music (and in some cases the music they were to compose, perform, or understand, too).[17] Equally, musicological knowledge can shape perceptions: Spitzer (1987) has shown how divergent accounts by different critics of the same piece of music (*Sinfonia Concertante* in E♭,

---

16 The concept of the performative derives from speech act theory (Austin 1962) and is particularly influential in performance and gender studies (see, respectively, Schechner 1988 and Butler 1990). Central to it is the idea that meaning is constructed through performative acts: whereas the meaning of 'the sky is blue' is referential (it refers to an external reality), when you say 'I promise' you are not referring to something but actually *doing* it by virtue of what you say. The term therefore has no direct link with performance in the musical sense (which is not to say that performative approaches do not have much to offer the study of musical performance).

17 For an example of the role of performance pedagogy in the construction of musical experience, see Blasius (1996). Blasius argues that, along with other discursive domains, early nineteenth-century piano method is a realization of the eighteenth-century project to systematize affect and rhetoric.

attributed to Mozart) are not simply due to differences in taste, but reflect debate over the work's authenticity. (Not only do critics tend to write more positively when they think the music is by Mozart, Spitzer found, but they tend to focus on the same passages and use the same metaphors in describing them.) And one might equally claim that, to misquote Judith Butler, all the approaches to musical emotion outlined in the previous sections have helped to bring about the very responses and practices which they purport to describe.[18] Or to use the language of social constructionism, discourse about music (by which we mean principally, but certainly not exclusively, verbal discourse) actively constructs rather than simply reconstructs its expressivity. The very act of saying that a certain piece of music is expressive in a certain sort of way leads you to hear it that way, and so one can think of dominant interpretations of particular compositions (Tovey's interpretation of the first movement recapitulation of the Ninth Symphony as the embodiment of cosmic catastrophe, for instance, or for that matter McClary's interpretation of the same passage in terms of a rapist's fantasy) as exercises in the creation and not merely the reporting of expressive meaning.

There was a strong awareness of the performative value of criticism among certain writers associated with the 'new' musicology (in particular, Kramer and Abbate[19]). More generally, and reflecting parallel trends in cultural studies, the ethnomusicologist Philip Bohlman (1993) argued in his significantly named article 'Musicology as a political act' that the discipline as a whole is as much involved in the generation as the analysis of the values and meanings that are ascribed to music. Attempts to develop explicit theoretical models for the attribution of meaning to music, however, are a more recent development and arise out of a promising intersection of music theory, psychology, and cognitive science. Zbikowski (1999), for instance, has drawn on conceptual blending theory (itself representing the intersection of linguistics and literary theory) in order to analyse three separate settings of the same poem, Müller's *Trockne Blumen*. Without entering into details, the basic idea is that there are aspects of shared structure (what Zbikowski calls a 'common topography') between the words and the music, which enables us to map the one onto the other as we listen to the song.[20] The result is a blending of the attributes of each, which gives rise to emergent meaning—meaning, that is, which is not present in either words or music separately but arises out of their interac-

---

[18] '[Gender] identity is performatively constituted by the very 'expressions' that are said to be its results' (Butler 1990, p. 25).

[19] See, in particular, Kramer (1990) and Abbate (1991). More recently, Monson (1996) has applied the same principle to the analysis of jazz performance, arguing that 'emotion is constituted or constructed through social practices . . .. Music, it seems to me, is a particularly powerful constructor of emotion . . . a powerful activity that can produce a 'community of sentiment' binding performers and audiences into something larger than the individual' (p. 178).

[20] The analysis involves the creation of a graphic diagram or 'conceptual integration framework' (CIN) which shows four interrelated 'spaces'. These are the 'text space' and 'music space', which show the corresponding features on which the mapping is based; the 'generic space', which indicates the dimension within which it takes place; and the 'blended space', where attributes of the text and music spaces are combined to create new meaning. For further explanation of CINs, which derive from the work of Mark Turner and Gilles Fauconnier, see Zbikowski (1999, pp. 310–14).

tion. In this way the emotional associations of the words are transferred to the music: as Zbikowski says, 'We can easily imagine outward physical expressions of the miller's torment—facial contortions, hand wringing, pacing—mirroring his internal conflict' (1999, p. 309). The point is that these become as much properties of the music as of the words,[21] so that once again there is a sense in which we are talking about emotional content even as we analyse musical structure. Up to now such approaches have been principally applied to the analysis of multimedia texts (Cook 1998b builds a general theory of multimedia on a similar basis), but there is no reason why this should be the case: you can equally well use them to compare Tovey's and McClary's interpretations of the first movement recapitulation of the Ninth Symphony, demonstrating the manner in which each interpretation creates new meaning (Cook, 2001). Used this way, the conceptual blending approach reveals how meaning is constructed through the interaction between musical texts and the invisible web of discourse, ranging from books and CD liners to television and concert-interval chatter, that surrounds them.

Coming from a different direction but converging with the conceptual blending approach is another, drawn this time from psychology—specifically, from James Gibson's (1979) 'ecological' approach to perception (which musicologists and music theorists are only now beginning to explore). Traditional approaches to music perception see it as built up in succession from basic elements such as tones, scale patterns, chords, and so on, with expressive or social meaning representing, to repeat our earlier phrase, the icing on the cake. (This corresponds to the sequential approach we have criticized: first analysing the structure, and then interpreting the meaning.) By contrast, the ecological approach seeks to understand perception in terms of its function, that is to say the means by which any organism grasps and interacts with its environment, and from this perspective the semantic properties of any stimulus, including its emotional properties, are just as basic—just as much properties of the music—as any acoustic ones. Emotional properties, in short, are not deduced through interpretation of the music, but directly specified by it. But this does not represent a reversion to earlier ideas that meaning is 'locked into the sounds', to borrow Moore's phrase (1993, p. 157), just waiting to be unlocked by listeners, because meaning emerges from a mutual relationship between perceiver and perceived in which any number of personal, historical, or critical influences come into play. It is this mutual relationship that becomes the object of analysis. As most conspicuously represented by Clarke's (1999) study of subject position in music by Frank Zappa and P. J. Harvey, the aim is very much the same as we have described in the work of Zbikowski: to find a way of talking about music which articulates the emotional properties that keep us listening to it, while at the same time conforming to the requirements for intersubjective intelligibility in the absence of which writing about music becomes a critical free-for-all where anything goes.

New as they may be, at least to musicology, such approaches address an old problem: how to speak about music and emotional meaning at the same time, without changing the subject. In addition, they emphasize the intrinsic reflexivity of critical activity—

---

[21] This links with Fisk's claim, mentioned in the previous section, that listeners' emotions are so moulded by music as to become purely musical emotions.

what we say about music's meaning contributes to bringing that meaning into being. If the further development of musicological approaches to emotion depends on continued cross-fertilization with other disciplines, then (to misquote Butler again) this book may itself contribute to the very thinking we have attempted to describe.

## References

Abbate, C. (1991). *Unsung voices: Opera and musical narrative in the nineteenth century.* Princeton, NJ: Princeton University Press.

Adorno, T. W. (1973). *Philosophy of new music.* London: Sheed & Ward.

Agawu, V. K. (1991). *Playing with signs.* Princeton, NJ: Princeton University Press.

Allanbrook, W. J. (1983). *Rhythmic gesture in Mozart.* Chicago: University of Chicago Press.

Austin, J. L. (1962). *How to do things with words.* Cambridge, MA: Harvard University Press.

Bach, C. P. E. (1974). *Essay on the true art of playing keyboard instruments* (trans. W. J. Mitchell). London: Eulenberg Books (originally published 1959–1962).

Blasius, L. D. (1996). The mechanics of sensation and the construction of the Romantic musical experience. In *Music theory in the age of Romanticism*, (ed. I. Bent), pp. 3–24. Cambridge, UK: Cambridge University Press.

Bloomfield, T. (1993). Resisting songs: Negative dialectics in pop. *Popular Music,* 12, 13–31.

Bolhman, P. (1993). Musicology as a political act. *Journal of Musicology,* 11, 411–36.

Budd, M. (1985). *Music and the emotions: The philosophical theories.* London: Routledge.

Burnham, S. (1999). How music matters: Poetic content revisited. In *Rethinking music* (ed. N. Cook & M. Everist), pp. 193–216. Oxford, UK: Oxford University Press.

Butler, J. P. (1990). *Gender trouble: Feminism and the subversion of identity.* New York: Routledge.

Cavicchi, D. (1999). *Tramps like us: Music and meaning among Springsteen fans.* New York: Oxford University Press.

Clarke, E. F. (1999). Subject-position and the specification of invariants in music by Frank Zappa and P. J. Harvey. *Music Analysis,* 18, 347–74.

Cone, E. T. (1982). Schubert's promissary note. *19th–Century Music,* 5, 233–41.

Cook, N. (1998a). *Music: A very short introduction.* Oxford, UK: Oxford University Press.

Cook, N. (1998b). *Analysing musical multimedia.* Oxford, UK: Clarendon Press.

Cook, N. (2001). Theorizing musical meaning. *Music Theory Spectrum,* 23, 170–95.

Cooke, D. (1959). *The language of music.* London: Oxford University Press.

Davies, S. (1994). *Musical meaning and expression.* Ithaca, NY: Cornell University Press.

Dibben, N. (2001). Pulp, pornography and voyeurism. *Journal of the Royal Musical Association,* 126, 83–106.

Eisler, H. [and Adorno, T. W.] (1947). *Composing for the films.* London: Dennis Dobson.

Feld, S. (1982). *Sound and sentiment: Birds, weeping, poetics, and song in Kaluli expression.* Philadelphia, PA: University of Pennsylvania Press.

Fisk, C. (1997). What Schubert's last sonata might hold. In *Music and meaning*, (ed. J. Robinson), pp. 179–200. Ithaca, NY: Cornell University Press.

Flinn, C. (1992). *Strains of utopia: Gender, nostalgia, and Hollywood film music.* Princeton, NJ: Princeton University Press.

Gibson, J. J. (1979). *The ecological approach to visual perception.* Boston: Houghton-Mifflin.

Gjerdingen, R. O. (1988). *A classic turn of phrase.* Philadelphia, PA: University of Pennsylvania Press.

Goehr, L. (1992). *The imaginary museum of musical works: An essay in the philosophy of music.* Oxford, UK: Clarendon Press.

Guck, M. A. (1994). Rehabilitating the incorrigible. In *Theory, analysis and meaning in music,* (ed. A. Pople), pp. 57–73. Cambridge, UK: Cambridge University Press.

Hanslick, E. (1986). *On the musically beautiful: A contribution towards the revision of the aesthetics of music* (trans. G. Payzant). Indianapolis, IN: Hackett (originally published 1854).

Hatten, R. (1994). *Musical meaning in Beethoven: Markedness, correlation, and interpretation.* Bloomington, IN: Indiana University Press.

Jakobson, R. (1971). *Language in relation to other communication systems. Selected writings,* (Vol. 2). The Hague: Mouton.

Johnson, J. H. (1995). *Listening in Paris: A cultural history.* Berkeley, CA: University of California Press.

Karl, G. & Robinson, J. (1997). Shostakovich's Tenth Symphony and the musical expression of cognitively complex emotions. In *Music and meaning* (ed. J. Robinson), pp. 154–78. Ithaca, NY: Cornell University Press.

Keil, C. (1994). Motion and feeling through music. In *Music grooves* (ed. C. Keil & S. Feld), pp. 53–76. Chicago: University of Chicago Press.

Kerman, J. (1985). *Musicology.* London: Fontana Press. (= *Contemplating music: Challenges to musicology.* Cambridge, MA: Harvard University Press).

Kirkpatrick, R. (1984). *Interpreting Bach's 'Well-Tempered Clavier': A performer's discourse of method.* New Haven, CT: Yale University Press.

Kivy, P. (1987). How music moves. In *What is music? An introduction to the philosophy of music* (ed. P. Alperson), pp. 149–62. University Park, PA: Pennsylvania State University Press.

Kivy, P. (1993). *The fine art of repetition: Essays in the philosophy of music.* Cambridge, UK: Cambridge University Press.

Kramer, L. (1990). *Music as cultural practice, 1800–1900.* Berkeley, CA: University of California Press.

Langer, S. K. (1942). *Philosophy in a new key.* Cambridge, MA: Harvard University Press.

Lerdahl, F. & Jackendoff, R. (1983). *A generative theory of tonal music.* Cambridge, MA: MIT Press.

McClary, S. (1991). *Feminine endings: Music, gender and sexuality.* Minnesota, MN: University of Minnesota Press.

Marks, M. M. (1992). *Music for the silent film: Contexts and case studies 1895–1924.* Oxford, UK: Oxford University Press.

Mattheson, J. (1981). *Der vollkommene Capellmeister* (trans. E. C. Harris). Ann Arbor, MI: UMI Research Press (original work published 1739).

Maus, F. E. (1988). Music as drama. *Music Theory Spectrum,* **10,** 56–73.

Maus, F. E. (1997). Narrative, drama and emotion in instrumental music. *Journal of Aesthetics and Art Criticism,* **55,** 293–302.

Meyer, L. B. (1956). *Emotion and meaning in music.* Chicago: University of Chicago Press.

Middleton, R. (1990). *Studying popular music.* Milton Keynes, UK: Open University Press.

Monson, I. (1996). *Saying something: Jazz improvisation and interaction.* Chicago: University of Chicago Press.

Moore, A. F. (1993). *Rock: The primary text.* Buckingham, UK: Open University Press.

Newcomb, A. (1984). Once more 'between absolute and program music': Schumann's Second Symphony. *19th-Century Music,* 7, 233–50.

Pater, W. (1910). *The Renaissance: Studies in art and poetry.* London: Macmillan (Original work published in 1873).

Ratner, L. G. (1980). *Classic music: Expression, form and style.* New York: Schirmer.

Robinson, J. (1998). The expression and arousal of emotion in music. In *Musical worlds: New directions in the philosophy of music* (ed. P. Alperson), pp. 13–22. University Park, PA: Pennsylvania State University Press.

Schechner, R. (1988). *Performance theory* (rev. edn). New York: Routledge.

Schenker, H. (1994). The art of improvisation (trans. R. Kramer). In *The masterwork in music: A yearbook. Volume 1 (1925),* (ed. W. Drabkin), pp. 2–19. Cambridge, UK: Cambridge University Press (originally published 1925).

Scruton, R. (1997). *The aesthetics of music.* Oxford, UK: Clarendon Press.

Shepherd, J. & Wicke, P. (1997). *Music and cultural theory.* Cambridge, UK: Polity Press.

Solomon, N. (1989). Signs of the times: A look at late 18th-century gesturing. *Early Music,* 17, 551–61.

Spitzer, J. (1987). Musical attribution and critical judgement: The rise and fall of the Sinfonia Concertante for Winds, K. 279b. *Journal of Musicology,* 5, 319–56.

Tagg, P. (1982). Analysing popular music: Theory, method and practice. *Popular Music,* 2, 37–67.

Tagg, P. (1992). Towards a sign typology of music. In *Secondo Convegno Europeo di Analisi Musicale,* (ed. R. Dalmonte & M. Baroni), pp. 369–78. Trento, Italy: Università degli studi di Trento.

Tolbert, E. (1994). The voice of lament: Female vocality and performative efficacy in the Finnish-Karelian *itkuvirsi.* In *Embodied voices: Representing female vocality in Western culture,* (ed. L. C. Dunn & N. A. Jones), pp. 179–94. Cambridge, UK: Cambridge University Press.

Treitler, L. (1999). The historiography of music: Issues of past and present. In *Rethinking music,* (ed. N. Cook & M. Everist), pp. 356–77. Oxford, UK: Oxford University Press.

Wagner, R. (1899) *Prose works,* (Vol. 8) (trans. W. A. Ellis). London: Reeves.

Wallace, R. (1986). *Beethoven's critics: Aesthetic dilemmas and resolutions during the composer's lifetime.* Cambridge, UK: Cambridge University Press.

Walser, R. (1993). *Running with the Devil: Power, gender and madness in heavy metal music.* Hanover, NH: Weslyan University Press.

Zbikowski, L. M. (1999). The blossoms of 'Trockne Blumen': Music and text in the early nineteenth century. *Music Analysis,* 18, 307–45.

CHAPTER 4

# PSYCHOLOGICAL PERSPECTIVES ON MUSIC AND EMOTION

JOHN A. SLOBODA AND PATRIK N. JUSLIN

## 4.1 The psychological approach

In the context of a multidisciplinary work, it may be appropriate for us to briefly set out what we consider to be the essentials of a psychological approach, so as to show its distinct orientation, alongside the other disciplines represented here. Yet, we are also mindful of the apocryphal tale of a young colleague of William James who was asked by the master to take an introductory course in psychology while James was away, and thought he would begin by defining psychology, and was still struggling to do that when James returned 12 weeks later!

So as not to delay our treatment of emotion for too long, let alone its intersection with music, we shall confine our remarks on psychology to a set of rather dogmatic statements. We believe that in broad outline they describe what most psychologists do, although there is much dispute over the details, with differing schools and periods placing differing emphasis on the various subcomponents (Leahey 1987). More importantly for the present chapter, perhaps, these statements reflect our own perceptions of what it is to do psychology, of both music and emotion, and form some sort of underlying framework for the material we present here.

1. Psychology is concerned with the explanation of human behaviour. Behaviour includes overt action as well as 'inner' behaviour, such as thought, emotion, and other reportable mental states. It can include behaviour of which the agent is not fully or even partly aware, such as the dilation of the pupils of the eye.

A psychological approach to music and emotion therefore seeks an explanation for how and why we experience emotional reactions to music, and how and why we experience music as expressive of emotion.

2. The explanations sought by psychologists are essentially causal and organismic. They are causal in the sense that they seek both to discover antecedents to the behaviours requiring explanation and uncover or postulate mechanisms whereby the antecedents interact to bring about the observed behaviours. They are organismic in that the primary interest of psychology is in mechanisms which are internal to the organism. External causes, such as historical or social factors, are only relevant to a

psychological framework where, even if only in sketched in principle, there is a route by which these may impact on the internal mechanisms.

In the study of music and emotion, a central aim of psychology is to understand the mechanisms that intervene between music reaching a person's ears and an emotion being experienced or detected by that person as a result of hearing that music. Other important aims involve understanding the roles of emotion in composing and performing music.

3. There are different levels at which organismic explanations can operate. These include the physiological and the phenomenological. A physiological explanation attempts to describe the causal pathway in terms of mechanisms within the nervous system, the endocrine system, and other biological constellations. A phenomenological explanation, on the other hand, attempts to describe the causal pathway in terms of the intentions, meanings, and interpretations that the individual concerned places on his or her own behaviours. There is, however, an explanatory level intermediate between these extremes, which is the core concern of psychology. A term commonly used for this level of explanation is 'cognitive'. Another term is 'computational'. The concern of a cognitive explanation is more in the functional logic of the mechanism (what it does—the 'software') than the precise neural location and instantiation (how it does it—the 'hardware'). However, this is not simply a redescription of the phenomenological level, because some of the most significant advances made by the psychological approach relate to aspects of behaviour which are pre-conscious and therefore could not—even in principle—be incorporated at the phenomenological level.

We shall try to be explicit about the level of explanation that is being used at various points in the psychological arguments that we describe and critique.

4. Psychology is a materialist science. Psychology is materialist because it holds some version of reductionism (or mind-brain identity). Every event describable at a phenomenological level (e.g. an intention) is, at the same time, assumed to be describable as a set of physical events (e.g. a particular constellation of biological events). Psychology is a science because it only allows explanations to survive in the long term when they have withstood repeated, critical interactions with observed data. The organization and interpretation of such interactions are collectively known as 'the scientific method' (Neale & Liebert 1986).

Emotional responses to music are material phenomena whose components are correlated with observable phenomena in law-governed ways. We aim in this chapter to demonstrate the relationships between scientific observations and the development of theory.

5. Whilst psychology operates within a materialist framework, it is—at least tactically—not reductionist in its programme. Many psychologists believe that seeking links between biological events and behavioural or phenomenological events does not always lead to scientific progress. For instance, showing a lawful correspondence between a set of behavioural and biological events (which is rarely easy to do) does not in itself yield an explanation of how the biology and the behaviour

are causally linked. Psychological explanations have sufficient explanatory and pre-dictive power that few psychologists currently operate on the ambition to render psychological explanations obsolete in favour of biological ones. Indeed, psycho-logical explanations allow certain kinds of understanding that biological explana-tions cannot easily support (see next point).

In this chapter, we shall centre our account at the psychological level, leaving detailed treatment of other levels to other authors.

6. Psychological explanations are particularly successful at incorporating teleological or functional perspectives. Understanding a behaviour requires more than knowing how it was caused. It also requires knowing something about the ends that the behaviour serves. What, in other words, does the behaviour and the psychological mechanisms that support it allow the organism to achieve? Functional explanations may also be offered at different levels. At the most distal, functions can be considered in terms of the survival of the individual, or even of the species. However, more proximally, functions may be considered in terms of individual goals and plans, which may be very short term and malleable.

An adequate psychological theory of emotional responses to music should, therefore, explain how such emotions reflect the ways that emotions serve to fulfil psychological goals and outcomes. It is not enough to simply demonstrate law-like relationships between musical antecedents and emotional consequents.

Before considering the enduring issues of music and emotion from a psychological perspective, we briefly review emotion concepts and major approaches to emotion. This serves to anchor our subsequent discussion of music and emotion.

## 4.2 What is an emotion?

Emotion is one of the most pervasive aspects of human existence, related to practically every aspect of human behaviour—action, perception, memory, learning, and decision making. It is thus all the more remarkable that the study of emotion has been neglected throughout much of psychology's brief history. Although the scientific study of emo-tions dates back to the nineteenth century (Darwin 1872; James 1884; Wundt 1897), studies of emotion have often been eclipsed by studies concerned with the 'higher' forms of mental processes, such as reasoning, problem solving, and decision making. As noted by Lazarus (1991, p. 4), 'Failure to give emotion a central role puts theoretical and research psychology out of step with human preoccupations since the beginning of recorded time.' Almost every great philosopher has been concerned with the nature of emotions. Writers, artists, and musicians have always attempted to appeal to the emo-tions, to influence and move the audience through emotional communication.

What is an emotion? This question, which incidentally was the title of one of William James's (1884) most famous papers, has not yet received a definitive answer. There are many reasons for this state of affairs. One reason is that emotions are difficult to define and measure. As pointed out by Fehr and Russell (1984, p. 464), 'everyone knows what an emotion is, until asked to give a definition'. Another reason may be the 'disruptive' role ascribed to emotions as motivators of human behaviour. Although our view of the emotions has changed considerably throughout history, one of the prevailing views has been that rationality can be hijacked by the pirates of emotion (Cacioppo & Gardner 1999). Only recently have researchers seriously reconsidered the role played by emotions in human rationality (Damasio 1994; De Souza 1987; Johnson-Laird & Oatley 1992; Simon 1967). This has reached the point where scientists today readily speak of 'emotional intelligence' (e.g. Mayer & Salovey 1993), a notion that would have been inconceivable during the heyday of behaviourism!

Emotion is both an everyday concept and a scientific construct. As such it involves both an implicit and an explicit body of knowledge (e.g. Plutchik 1980). The implicit knowledge is embodied in the so-called 'folk theories' of emotion. We all know something about emotions. We think that they are powerful forces that affect our behaviour and thoughts in powerful ways, that some emotions feel good and some bad, and that some people are more 'emotional' than others. The explicit knowledge is based on studies of problems such as how emotions develop, whether emotions are associated with physiological changes, and how well we judge emotions from facial or vocal expressions. Emotion as a scientific construct is inferred from three kinds of evidence: (a) self-reports; (b) expressive behaviour; and (c) physiological measurement.

The most common—and deceptively simple—way to measure emotional responses in human adults is by means of *self-report*: adjective checklists, rating scales, questionnaires, or free descriptions. This approach is associated with numerous problems, such as the imperfect relationship between emotions and words that denote emotions, and the problem of choosing which words to include in checklists or scales. At the same time, self-reports are probably the most direct form of evidence, and it is conceivable that certain aspects of emotional life (e.g. 'peak' experiences, see Gabrielsson, this volume) cannot be reached in any other way.

Because the use of self-reports is not always possible—or reliable, some would say—another approach has been to measure different forms of *expressive behaviour*, or products of expressive behaviour (such as drawings; see, for instance, Smith & Williams 1999). This may include facial expressions, vocalizations, and body language (e.g. gestures). The most famous example is perhaps Ekman's (1973) cross-cultural studies of facial expression of emotion. One problem with this form of evidence is that emotions are not always accompanied by expressive behaviours. Furthermore, expressive behaviours often occur in the absence of emotions, because people use such behaviours intentionally to communicate information to other individuals.

The third kind of evidence that is used to infer emotions involves various *physiological measures* of emotion. This kind partly reflects the early work of William James, who claimed that emotion was basically a perception of internal bodily changes. Since then, researchers of emotion have used a number of physiological indices to measure emotion, including heart rate, respiration, skin conductance, muscle tension, electrocadiagram (EKG), blood pressure, and electroencephalograph (EEG) (for a review, see Cacioppo *et al.* 1993). There are many problems with physiological measures, the most serious of which is probably that autonomic changes often occur even in the absence of emotions (primarily because each physiological system has many different functions within the body). Therefore, it is difficult to establish clear-cut relationships between emotional states and physiological responses.

Based on these three kinds of evidence, theorists have proposed a number of different definitions of emotion during the past 100 years. For example, Kleinginna and Kleinginna (1981) identified 92 definitions found in textbooks, articles, dictionaries, and other sources. Based upon a review of these definitions they proposed the following consensual definition (Kleinginna & Kleinginna 1981, p. 355):

Emotion is a complex set of interactions among subjective and objective factors, mediated by neural/hormonal systems, which can (a) give rise to affective experiences such as feelings of arousal, pleasure/displeasure; (b) generate cognitive processes such as perceptually relevant effects, appraisals, labeling processes; (c) activate widespread physiological adjustments to the arousing conditions; and (d) lead to behavior that is often, but not always, expressive, goal-directed, and adaptive.

Many researchers like to think of emotion as a sequence of events: emotions are triggered by our cognitive appraisals of significant events; these appraisals evoke strong reactions of most of our bodily systems; the bodily reactions generate subjective experiences of feeling; and the subjective experiences yield action tendencies and expressive behaviour. However, researchers often disagree about the precise sequence of events, and about where such an episode begins or ends (Scherer 1993).

As even a superficial reading of the literature on emotion would show, scientists have used a number of different terms to denote the phenomena of interest in this chapter—affect, emotion, mood, feeling, arousal, etc. We think that much of the confusion and controversy in the field of music and emotion has been caused by the lack of clear definitions of these terms. Whereas most researchers of music appear to have used the terms affect, emotion, and mood interchangeably—lay people certainly do that—there is a growing consensus among emotion researchers that the three terms should be differentiated from one another. Affect is seen as a more general term than emotion or mood (Oatley & Jenkins 1996, p. 124). Affect refers to the positive or negative valence of the emotional experience. Many researchers consider affective valence as the most basic feature of emotional life, and believe that affect is phylogenetically and ontogenetically more primitive than emotion or mood (cf. Batson *et al.* 1992). Emotions are often said to differ from moods in three ways. First, emotions are said to be brief, whereas moods last much longer. Second, many researchers think that emotions usually have an identifiable stimulus event, whereas moods do not. Third, some researchers have proposed that emotions are accompanied by distinct facial expressions, whereas moods are not (Ekman & Davidson 1994, pp. 51–96).

Davidson (1994), however, suggests that it is more useful to differentiate emotion and mood in terms of their functions. He proposes that 'emotions bias action, whereas moods bias cognition' (p. 54). Emotions arise most often when adaptive action is needed. Moods, on the other hand, tend to shift the 'mode' of information processing in ways that influence memory, decision making, and evaluative judgments (see Bless & Forgas 2000). In this way moods can alter the probability that particular emotions will be triggered. Thus, emotions can be viewed as *phasic* perturbations that are superimposed on the *tonic*, affective background provided by the mood (Davidson 1994).

*Arousal* is often considered to be an important aspect of emotional reactions, and this term has figured prominently in many theories of emotion (e.g. Mandler 1984), and also in many accounts of music and emotion (Berlyne 1971; Gaver & Mandler 1987; Meyer 1956; see also Simonton, this volume). Sometimes, the term is used more generally to refer to the level of emotional intensity of the response, other times it is used to refer specifically to the sympathic activation of the nervous system. The relationship between the two meanings of the term is not clear. For example, there is evidence that people can feel intense emotion, without showing autonomic arousal (Harrer & Harrer 1977).

A major element in both folk theories and scientific theories of emotion is that emotions are subjective feelings that people experience—the word 'emotion' comes from a Latin word which means 'move' or 'to stir up' (Plutchik 1994). But how many emotions are there, and how do different emotions relate to each other?

## 4.3 Major approaches to emotion

The ways that emotions are experienced and expressed help both scientists and lay people to conceptualize emotions and differentiate among them. In this section, we describe the most prominent approaches to conceptualizing emotion: the categorical approach, the dimensional approach, and the prototype approach. We also consider an additional class of affects—the vitality affects—which we believe could be useful in explaining listeners' responses to music.

### 4.3.1 The categorical approach

According the categorical approach, people experience emotions as categories that are distinct from each other. Essential to this approach is the concept of *basic emotions*; that is, the idea that there is a limited number of innate and universal emotion categories from which all other emotional states can be derived (see Ekman 1992; Izard 1977; Oatley 1992; Plutchik 1994; Power & Dalgleish 1997; Tomkins 1962). Each 'basic' emotion can be defined functionally in terms of a key appraisal of goal-relevant events that have occurred frequently during evolution (Table 4.1). Thus, basic emotions are regarded as adaptive in dealing with life emergencies without resorting to time-consuming processing: 'When no fully rational solution is available for a problem of action, a basic

Table 4.1 Key appraisals for basic emotions adapted from Oatley[1] (1992) and Lazarus[2] (1991)

| Emotion | Juncture of plan[1] | Core relational theme[2] |
| --- | --- | --- |
| Happiness | Subgoals being achieved | Making reasonable progress towards a goal |
| Anger | Active plan frustrated | A demeaning offense against me and mine |
| Sadness | Failure of major plan or loss of active goal | Having experienced an irrevocable loss |
| Fear | Self preservation goal threatened or goal conflict | Facing an immediate, concrete, or overwhelming physical danger |
| Disgust | Gustatory goal violated | Taking in or being close to an indigestible object or idea (metaphorically speaking) |

emotion functions to prompt us in a direction that is better than a random choice' (Johnson-Laird & Oatley 1992, p. 201). Basic emotions solve problems with speed rather than precision. They may be viewed as 'fast and frugal algorithms' that cope with conditions of limited time, knowledge, or cognitive capacities (Gigerenzer & Goldstein 1996).

Some general criteria for distinguishing basic emotions from 'secondary' or 'complex' emotions have been suggested. The most important of these are that basic emotions: (a) have distinct functions that contribute to individual survival; (b) are found in all cultures; (c) are experienced as unique feeling states; (d) appear early in development; (e) are associated with distinct patterns of physiological changes; (f) can be inferred in other primates; and (g) have distinct emotional expressions. A considerable body of evidence supports the case for a concept of basic emotions as defined by these criteria (see Ekman 1992; Izard 1977; Oatley 1992; Panksepp 1992; Power & Dalgleish 1997). 'Secondary' emotions are usually believed to be founded on basic emotions, but involve 'blends' of basic emotions (Plutchik 1994), or particular cognitive evaluations that occur together with a basic emotion (Oatley 1992).

The notion of basic emotions has been criticized on a number of grounds, most notably because different researchers have come up with different sets of basic emotions (Ortony & Turner 1990). However, as noted by Oatley (1992) 'this issue is not about voting, it is about theory' (p. 104). It all depends on how we *define* emotions. Therefore, if one takes a closer look at the researchers who consider emotions in terms of their functional significance, one finds that there is reasonable agreement among researchers with regard to at least five basic emotions: happiness, sadness, anger, fear, and disgust (Kemper 1987; Plutchik 1994; Power & Dalgleish 1997). For an example of how the basic emotions approach has been applied in the case of music, see Juslin (this volume).

### 4.3.2 The dimensional approach

The categorical approach focuses mainly on the characteristics that distinguish emotions from one another. In contrast, the dimensional approach focuses on identifying emotions based on their placement on a small number of dimensions, such as *valence*, *activity*, and *potency*. The search for the dimensional structure of emotions dates back to Spencer (1890; cited in Izard 1977), but more influential formulations of this same notion were provided by Wundt (1897), Woodworth (1938), and Schlosberg (1941). A dimensional structure can be derived from any type of response data, although the most common sources are similarity judgments of emotion words or facial expressions that are analysed using factor analysis or multidimensional scaling.

Russell's (1980) *circumplex model* has generated the most research (Fig. 4.1). This model consists of a two-dimensional, circular structure involving the dimensions of *activation* and *valence*. Within this structure, emotions that are across the circle from one another, such as sadness and happiness, correlate inversely. The circumplex model captures two important aspects of emotions: that they vary in their degree of similarity and that certain emotions (e.g. happy, sad) are often thought of as bipolar. About the same circular structure has been found in a large number of different domains— including music (Thayer 1986)—suggesting that the circumplex model really captures something fundamental about emotional responses.

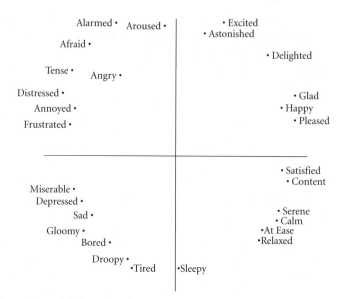

**Figure 4.1**  A circumplex model of emotion (from Russell 1980). (Copyright ©1980 by the American Psychological Association. Reprinted with permission.)

Among the strengths of the circumplex model is that it suggests a simple yet powerful way of organizing different emotions in terms of their affect appraisals (pleasant or unpleasant) and physiological reactions (high or low arousal). On the other hand, dimensional approaches have been criticized on the grounds that they blur important psychological distinctions and therefore obscure important aspects of the emotion process (cf. Lazarus 1991). In Russell's circumplex model, for example, emotions that are placed in the same position in the circular matrix may, in fact, be very different. Thus, anger and fear are two emotions that are highly correlated within the model, because they are both high in activity and unpleasantness. Yet, they are very different in terms of their implications for the organism (see Table 4.1).

Notably, many researchers regard categorical and dimensional approaches to emotion as complementary to each other (Nyklicek *et al.* 1997) and both receive some support from neurophysiological data (Damasio 1994). Dimensional models may be especially useful for capturing the continuous changes in emotional expression that occur during a piece of music. For examples of response methods based on the dimensional approach to emotion, see Schubert (this volume).

### 4.3.3 The prototype approach

The prototype approach to emotions is based on the work by Rosch (1978). Essential to this approach is the idea that language, and knowledge structures associated with language, shape how people conceptualize and categorize information. A basic principle is that membership in a particular category is determined by resemblance to prototypical exemplars. The prototype itself is an abstract image that consists of a set of weighted features that represent the exemplar of a family of instances. Thus, for example, robins are presumably more prototypical of birds than ostriches. Similarly, some emotions (e.g. elation) are probably better exemplars of joy than others (e.g. relief), depending on related features such as elicitors, cognitive appraisals, and physiological reactions.

The prototype approach provides an interesting compromise between categorical and dimensional approaches to emotion—it addresses both the contents of individual categories and the hierarchical relationships among categories. An example of a proto-type structure is shown in Fig. 4.2. The vertical dimension of the structure shows the hierarchical relationships among categories. The most general level is the *superordinate* level, which is defined by the positive or negative valence of the emotions within a par-ticular category. The middle level represents the basic-level categories, or *prototypes*, of emotions, which anchor our mental representations of all emotions within a given cate-gory. The *subordinate* level consists of all other emotions related to a particular proto-type. Finally, the horizontal dimension shows the relations among members of the same prototype category (Shaver *et al.* 1987).

Critics of the prototype approach have argued that people's accounts of emotions are insufficient for capturing the underlying structure of emotions. For instance, the proto-type structure presented in Fig. 4.2 includes surprise among the prototypes, despite the fact that many researchers would not consider surprise an emotion (cf. Oatley 1992; Plutchik 1994). Critics also complain that there is disagreement about which emotions qualify as basic-level prototypes, and that emotions may cross boundaries in the proto-type structures. However, supporters of the prototype approach accept that boundaries between emotion categories are sometimes 'fuzzy', and argue that emotions cannot be defined in terms of a set of necessary and sufficient conditions.

### 4.3.4 The vitality affects

Apart from the more traditional approaches to emotion, there is another class of qual-ities that, although their status as emotions may be called into question, seems to be particularly relevant in the case of music. Stern (1985) introduced the concept of *vitality affects* to describe a set of elusive qualities related to intensity, shape, contour, and movement. These characteristics are best described in dynamic terms such as crescendo, fleeting, explosive, diminuendo, etc. These qualities are not emotions, but rather abstract 'forms' of feeling that occur both together with, and in the absence of, proper emotions. The vitality affects are 'amodal' in the sense that they are common to all modes of expression. Stern (1985) suggests that the vitality affects are of a particu-lar importance in the early communicative acts of mother and infant. Mother and infant respond to one another by constantly adapting and adjusting the intensity, tim-ing, and contour of their expressive acts. This process of constant matching of gestur-al events is referred to as *attunement*. Lack of capacity to enter into such interpersonal synchrony is often regarded as symptomatic of mental illness (Bunt & Pavlicevic, this volume).

Although the notion of vitality affects is admittedly vague, it seems to capture something important about music's expressiveness. Often when researchers speak about affect in music, they seem to be thinking about something akin to the vitality affects rather than true emotions. Vitality affects, with their dynamic changes and patterns of events, are somewhat reminiscent of philosopher Susanne Langer's (1951)

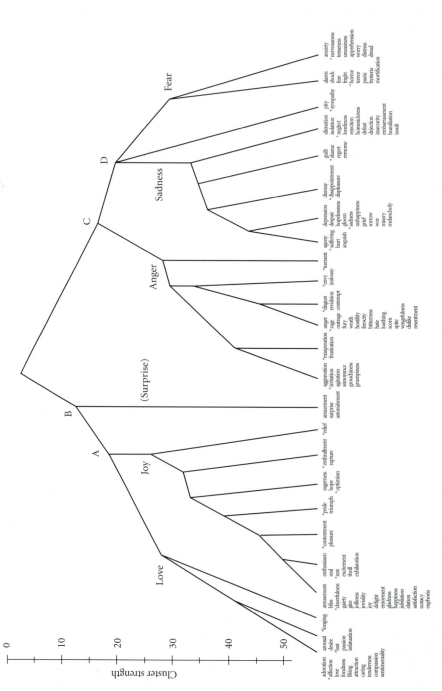

**Figure 4.2** A prototype analysis of emotion words (from Shaver et al. 1987). (Copyright © 1987 by the American Psychological Association. Reprinted with permission.)

notion of music as expressive of the forms of feeling. Music, suggests Langer, represents the *dynamic form* of emotional life, not specific emotions. When Langer observes that 'some musical forms seem to bear a sad and happy interpretation equally well' (Langer 1951, p. 202), this might be because vitality affects are not emotions themselves, and because some vitality affects are common to many different emotions.

Of all art forms, no one may be better equipped to capture vitality affects than music, in particular classical music. For an example of how the notion of vitality affects can be applied to a phenomenological description of music experience, see Imberty (1997). Imberty argues that musical style is ultimately 'an architecture of vitality affects', and goes on to discuss the role of vitality affects in the protonarrative character of musical time. The notion of vitality affects is also important in accounts of emotional processes in music therapy, in which dynamic form in improvisation is used to communicate a statement of the self (Bunt & Pavlicevic, this volume).

Having briefly reviewed the major approaches to emotion, we are ready to look more closely at the relationship between music and emotion.

## 4.4 The study of emotion in relation to music

Although emotions have been studied scientifically for a century, treatises on emotion rarely consider emotional reactions to music (for a few notable exceptions, see Fridja 1989; Lazarus 1991; Oatley 1992; Zajonc 1994). This may reflect the assumption that emotions experienced while listening to music are in some sense different from other emotions. To be sure, there are important differences between musical emotions and other emotions, both in antecedents and consequences, although this in itself does not imply that the emotions themselves are different. Another reason for the neglect of music in the emotion literature could be that such emotions are somehow considered less important—perhaps because scientists have failed to realize that music fulfils vital functions in many people's daily lives (Sloboda & O'Neill, this volume).

Aesthetic emotions—emotional reactions to films, drama, music, or paintings—have never been in the 'mainstream' of psychology (Lazarus 1991). Although psychologists have acknowledged that art may evoke strong emotional reactions despite its illusory nature, few scientists seem to have considered this problem worthy of study. Even in contemporary music psychology, the study of emotion has occupied a peripheral existence (cf. Gabrielsson 1993). However, we sense an increased interest in music and emotion at the moment, and today it is almost fashionable among music scientists to move into the emotion field. We believe that this interest may reflect an increasing awareness that music psychology has made limited progress regarding the problem that should be closest to its heart—how people experience music.

Musical emotions are, at a first glance, of two kinds: first, there are those emotions that concern the aesthetical value of music. Psychologists have, on the whole, embarrassingly little to say about the aesthetics of music, whereas philosophers have been discussing this topic for centuries (Budd 1985). It has been suggested that an aesthetic response is an intense personal experience that provides insight into the nature of life, and that involves emotional, cognitive, and social components (Konečni 1979). In the field of 'new' empirical aesthetics, however, researchers have focused on more mundane

relations between liking, or preference, and such informational properties of the stimulus as its complexity, expectedness, or familiarity (e.g. Berlyne 1971; North &
Hargreaves 1997; for a review of musical preferences, see Russell 1997).

Second, there are those emotions that are induced or expressed by the music, more or
less apart from the aesthetical value of the music. These are the emotions with which we
will mainly concern ourselves in this chapter. However, the two classes of emotion are
not wholly independent of each other, and we believe that an understanding of psychological aspects of music and emotion requires that researchers make the connection
between the two explicit.

The study of emotion in relation to music is problematic in many ways. First, emotional reactions are commonly understood in terms of their adaptive functions related
to biological survival. Since emotional reactions to music are not as directly related to
biological survival, they seem to be difficult to explain within existing theories of emotion (Dowling & Harwood 1986). Second, scientists who wish to study emotional reactions to music are faced with the problem that there is great variability between
individuals, and across time within individuals (Sloboda 1996). Third, experiments that
attempt to measure listeners' affective responses to music may impact so much on the
listening process that the task destroys the very thing it is supposed to measure—the
problem of *reactivity* (Neale & Liebert 1986).

On the other hand, some authors have suggested that music is an excellent medium
for studying emotion. For example, Gaver and Mandler (1987) have argued that using
musical stimuli to study emotion is ecologically valid, because people are used to making judgments about music and their affective responses to music. They also note that
music has a structure that is rich, and yet fairly well known, and that understanding the
structure of an event may help in understanding an emotional reaction to it. Yet
another advantage of using music as a stimulus is that it avoids many of the ethical concerns associated with other kinds of stimuli.

A review of the literature on music and emotion reveals the atheoretical nature of
much of this work. Music psychologists have been strikingly reluctant to turn to emotion psychology for theoretical guidance (Juslin 1997a). One reason for this could be
that the field of emotion has presented such a confusing picture that many researchers
have found it difficult to distil something useful from this research. Another reason may
be that researchers have considered current theories of emotion inadequate for explaining emotional responses to music—a view also evident in the work of some philosophers (e.g. Kivy 1990). In our view, however, the problem does not lie in current
theories of emotion, but in the fact that most researchers have not made serious
attempts to apply the theories to their problems. It is significant that one of the most
influential analyses of music and emotion to date, namely that of Meyer (1956), was
partly based on a theory of emotion (Dewey 1894).

One of the primary questions in the field of emotion is whether there are some
underlying and objectively observable characteristics that are invariably present in the
class of phenomena we normally describe as emotions. In the following section, we
describe typical characteristics of emotion and show how these apply in the case of
music.

## 4.5 Typical characteristics of emotions

### 4.5.1 Emotions are functional despite their apparent non-instrumentality

Fridja (1986) has provided one of the most influential psychological analyses of the behavioural characteristics that lead one to impute emotion to a person. His analysis is particularly valuable because it is not circular—it does not smuggle in the very concepts it is supposed to explain. He says the following (Fridja 1986, p. 2):

At some moments when observing behaviour, that behaviour seems to come to a stop. Effective interaction with the environment halts and is replaced by a behaviour that is centered, as it were, around the person himself, as in a fit of weeping or laughter, anger or fear. Or interaction with the environment may go on but seems peculiarly ineffective. When someone smashes the dinner plates, the broken plates would hardly seem to be the end result the person had in mind. Other behaviour that invites emotion words seems to contain a surplus that is not needed for the end result: superfluous emphasis in speed and scope of movement, or hesitation and undue toning down, or a smile that, in someone who is stroking a child, does not add to the tenderness of the touch.

To capture this aspect of emotion Frijda uses the notion of 'non-instrumentality', in that the emotional phenomena do not seem to be linked in any direct way towards the achievement of immediate goals and plans. A major purpose of emotion science is therefore to explain what functionality emotions do have. Are they useful to us, and if so how? Most researchers seem to believe they are (Keltner & Gross 1999). There is some consensus that the primary function of emotions is to guide behaviour; emotions evolved because they enabled successful interaction with the environment. But how does the idea of functionality apply in the case of music?

First, the view of emotions as functional adaptations has important implications for how we should understand and explain emotional responses to music (Juslin 1997a). Specifically, the functional architecture of emotions should *constrain* our responses to music, such that our responses to music can be explained by the ways that emotions have been shaped by biological evolution. Thus, for example, some of our emotional responses to music might be understood in terms of selective pressures favouring our ability to employ acoustic cues in our environment—particularly the social environment—to make useful inferences about the probable behaviours of other individuals (e.g. Juslin, 2001). Such mechanisms have presumably been favoured by biological evolution because they contribute to individual survival.

A second, and by no means less important, sense in which the functionality of emotions should be considered is the functions that music serve in everyday life, an aspect which is still obscure and poorly understood (Sloboda & O'Neill, this volume). Until we have a clear notion of what a person's involvement in music is for, then we are not going to know whether or not the emotions it evokes are or are not instrumental or functional, and in what way. It has been suggested that music may serve a mood-optimizing function in people's lives (Zillman 1988). However, the mere fact that emotional responses to music are so puzzling—even to the very people who often experience and value such emotions—suggests that musical emotions share in the apparent non-instrumentality of other emotions.

### 4.5.2 Emotions have behavioural, physiological, and experiential components

Although it may seem self-evident that we experience emotions to music, it is really an open question whether the conditions for ascribing emotion in music are the same as in other areas of emotional life. We noted in Section 4.2 that emotion is usually inferred from three kinds of evidence—self-reports, expressive behaviour, and physiological behaviour. It seems pertinent to ask, then, to what extent these kinds of evidence can be obtained also in connection to music.

The most basic observations arguably come from studies that use self-reports. These studies have yielded evidence that people experience emotions while listening to music, and that they perceive music as expressive of emotions. An interesting example is Pike's (1972) phenomenological analysis of music experience. Pike asked a number of musically untrained participants to listen to different pieces of music. After hearing each piece, which lasted no more than 5 minutes, the participants were asked to write down their responses. Through content analysis, the listeners' responses were reduced to a small set of common experiential factors (listed in the order of their frequency of occurrence): (a) feeling of pleasure (96 per cent); (b) perception of stable moods (86 per cent); (c) feeling of oneness with the music (83 per cent); (d) perception of spontaneous and transient emotional states (72 per cent); and (e) feeling of movement (65 per cent). This finding suggests that emotional responses to music—like emotional responses to other stimuli—include stable moods, transient emotions, and feelings of pleasure. Many other studies provide evidence from self-reports that listeners experience emotions in relation to music (e.g. Behne 1997; Gabrielsson 1991; Krumhansl 1997; Sloboda 1991, 1992; Waterman 1996).

We also have some evidence of expressive behaviour in responses to music. For example, Gabrielsson (1991), Waterman (1996), and Sloboda (1991) have shown that people really do cry when listening to some music. Furthermore, studies using facial electromyography (EMG) have suggested that people react with subliminal facial expressions towards expressive music (Witvliet & Vrana 1996). Kenealy (1988) found that a music mood-induction procedure yielded significant effects on behavioural measures, such as decision time, distance approximation, and writing speed (behaviours believed to be affected by moods). Moreover, there are many social contexts in which music provides a rich stimulus for expressive behaviours (e.g. rock concerts).

There is also evidence of physiological reactions to music (Bartlett 1996). Krumhansl (1997) has reported that the constellation of physiological responses occurring while people listen to music generally judged to be sad, fearful, or happy, under laboratory conditions (i.e. still and silent) are similar, although not always identical, to those constellations identified by other researchers as present when people experience these emotions to non-musical events—particularly in situations involving behavioural suppression (cf. Cacioppo et al. 1993; Gross & Levinson 1993). Nyklicek et al. (1997) have reported evidence of cardiorespiratory differentiation of music-induced emotions (happy, serene, sad, agitated). Finally, a few studies have explored a special kind of intense emotional responses to music called 'thrills' or 'chills', indicating that such responses to music are quite common, and are more prevalent for sad than for happy pieces of music (see Goldstein 1980; Panksepp 1995). For a review of physiological studies, see Scherer and Zentner (this volume).

Regardless of the particular method used, all these studies have provided evidence that emotional responses to music involve what Scherer (1993, p. 3) has termed the classic 'reaction triad' of subjective feeling, expressive behaviour, and physiological reaction.

### 4.5.3 Emotions have proximal elicitors

Frijda (1986, p. 4) again gives an influential expression to this feature: 'Emotions are elicited. The eliciting events appear to fulfill a special role: they are not just stimuli. They appear to act through their significance, their meaning, their rewarding or aversive nature.'

This characteristic of emotions seems to be necessary in order to distinguish them from other classes of affective phenomena. For instance, sadness which is pervasive and prolonged tends to be seen as a mood or a disposition rather than an emotion, according to its duration and the relative difficulty of isolating a specific proximal stimulus. However, the distinctions are necessarily imprecise. Clearly, weeping on first news of the death of a loved one is part of an emotional reaction to that event. A year later, a predominant and pervasive sense of sadness would not easily be characterized as an emotional reaction to the death, but rather a mood (although even at that distance a specific instance of weeping might well be viewed as an emotion if a proximal reminder of the loved one could be identified as a proximal elicitor).

A particularly interesting set of issues arise with respect to the assertion that eliciting stimuli should have significance or meaning to the person experiencing the emotion. Is it necessary that this person should be able to know, consciously, what meanings mediate the emotion? Is it, in other words, plausible to attribute emotion in the case that a stimulus occurs, the experience of sadness follows, the person believes that the stimulus has caused or triggered his or her response, and yet the person experiencing this response has no knowledge of why this stimulus should cause the reaction it does? This is an important issue for the application of emotion to the musical domain, because a great deal of what looks like emotional response to music is not accompanied by any strong sense of where the significance lies. A person can be reduced to tears by a particular passage of music, yet be completely unable to specify, even in outline, any objective feature of the music which would account for its grief-inducing qualities.

Fortunately, music is not unique in this respect. Research has shown that people often perceive and process emotional information in a pre-conscious or automatic manner. LeDoux (1996), for example, has recently described a neurophysiological system consisting of parallel-processing perceptual mechanisms, or modules, that react to simple stimulus features. LeDoux has found a direct neural link from auditory nuclei in the thalamus to the 'fear effector system' in the amygdala, which provides immediate information about simple features of emotionally relevant auditory stimuli. This 'quick and dirty' route of transmission bypasses the thalamocortical pathway, which gives full meaning to the stimuli. The perceptual system outlined by LeDoux (1996) provides some support for Zajonc's (1980) controversial slogan that 'affect precedes inference', and shows how emotions can be elicited outside conscious awareness.

Of particular interest is the fact that people implicitly perceive emotional expressions, which subsequently influence their behaviour (Niedenthal & Showers 1991). This means that implicit perception of the emotional expression of a piece of music may affect us emotionally although we are not consciously aware of this process. Much has been made by some music psychologists of the resemblance of certain musical sounds to signals that human infants may be biologically 'pre-programmed' to respond emotionally to (see Juslin, this volume).

Another class of implicit stimuli are those which obtain their emotional charge through resemblance to characteristics of events which the person can no longer remember (whether through Freudian repression, or normal processes of forgetting). One of the present authors has an overwhelming fear of being submerged in water, but no memory for any event which could account, even non-rationally, for that fear. The fear survives successful contemporary non-damaging experiences of submersion. In a similar fashion, musical stimuli might arouse strong emotions through conditioned responses, the origin of which we cannot remember.

### 4.5.4 Emotions are intrinsically social

Although emotions can occur when a person is alone, their full manifestation very often seems to require other people. For instance, it is well known that young children (e.g. pre-verbal) will look to a nearby adult for a cue concerning how to respond to some events, such as a fall or graze. If the adult looks upset and concerned, the infant will cry. If the adult appears calm and confident, the infant is less likely to cry. This process is referred to as *social referencing* (Sorce *et al.* 1985), and illustrates that others' emotional expressions are important sources of information which may influence our behaviour.

In another well-known series of studies, Schacter and Singer (1962) placed participants whose arousal levels had been artificially elevated into different social situations, where actor confederates of the experimenter appeared to express particular strong emotions. In general, the participants experienced the emotion displayed by the confederate. All these studies indicate that we are extremely ready to 'catch' ourselves the emotions we observe in others. Emotions are 'contagious' (Hatfield *et al.* 1994).

This tendency may be internalized in the self-regulation of emotions. For instance, a person may ask him or herself 'what would X feel in this situation' and use the stored answer to such a question to influence how he or she responds. In other situations, we identify another person's emotions not so much to align our emotional state with them, but to determine how we should respond to them. If I detect another person as uncontrollably angry, I may well become afraid of what that person might do to me, and withdraw. I might become afraid of what that person might do to someone else, become apprehensive for that person's welfare, and so attempt to help her avoid hurt.

For such reasons, identification of the emotion present in other people is a key priority for us in most situations, and therefore we have very well-developed mechanisms for scanning the environment for any cues that would allow us to both attribute emotion to others and determine whether we should feel that same emotion ourselves. These cues do not necessarily come from direct observation of another person's behaviour. We may deduce something about a person's emotional state from the way that they have affected the environment, for instance, arranged the contents of a room or written a note. People in some cultures have read emotions of unseen beings (such as gods) into such natural phenomena as storms. An angry human may throw small objects around, and so when big objects (such as trees) get thrown around, it is natural to ascribe anger to a superhuman being. It is not only facial expression, gesture, and vocalizations that suggest emotions to us, but material phenomena which may be the outcome of, or in some sense resemble, those expressions, gestures, and vocalizations.

Music, it could be argued, has many of the requisite qualities that incline us to ascribe emotions to it. There is a great deal of evidence on this point. In general, the experimental technique has been to present a participant with a musical extract and then ask him or her to select, from a smaller or larger list of emotion-related words, those words which most closely match the extract (e.g. Gabrielsson & Juslin, in press). All of these studies confirm that there are some extract-emotion combinations which generate high agreement among listeners, even when they may not have engaged explicitly in such tasks previously. Levinson (1996) has given particularly strong form to this argument through his claim that pieces of music are often construed by listeners as a 'virtual persona'.

Sloboda (2000, p. 227) has suggested that music probably creates an environment in which the distinction between attributing detected emotion to oneself as opposed to an outside source or agent is particularly fluid: 'If I detect some piece of music as containing elements appropriate to anger, then there is a sense in which I am pretty free to ascribe that anger where I will. I may ascribe it to the composer, or to the performer, to myself, to God. None of these ascriptions need to bring me up against any of the immediate constraints or contradictions provided by a real-life event in which my own interests and relationships figure.'

### 4.5.5 Emotions invoke action tendencies

Emotions change the probabilities associated with subsequent behaviours (Fridja *et al.* 1989). For instance, fear renders it more probable that one will avoid (or seek to avoid) the eliciting stimulus. Frijda (1986) uses the term 'action tendency' rather than 'intention' or 'plan' because the emotion does not contain within it a specific outcome, but rather directs the person experiencing it towards one category of behaviours rather than another.

So, for instance, a fearful person may simply close her eyes, so as not to see the fear-inducing stimulus, feeling that it cannot be avoided; she may run away from it (but with no specific end-location in mind); she may move towards a known place of safety; or she may develop plans to destroy or render harmless the fearful stimulus. These actions are distinct from the set of actions which might be primed by an emotion of tenderness towards the same eliciting stimulus (e.g. a mouse). In both cases, however, the precise action that occurs is not specified from within the emotion itself. This will depend on subsequent appraisals, and the intentions, skills, and knowledge of the subject.

From this analysis comes the most generally accepted theory of what emotions are for, that is why we have developed them. Frijda's (1986, pp. 77–8) formulation is, once again, seminal:

Action tendencies ... originate in discrepancies: in mismatch or in perception of potential match. Action tendencies terminate in unresolvable mismatch or in match. Mismatch, potential match, and match must be assumed to give rise to signals indicating that action is called for, is likely to succeed, or can terminate. We may identify these signals with feelings of pain, pleasure, and desire. These are the signals that initiate, maintain, and terminate action tendency. They constitute the direct source of 'being set' for change or continuation of the given situation. At the same time, they confer an 'aim' upon action tendency: they provide such tendency with an end point, the functional equivalent of a goal. Action tendency continues until the mismatch signals that initiate and maintain it die down; action tendency remains aligned when potential match signals resound, and terminates where match signals indicate success.

In effect, emotions are biologically embedded mechanisms that ensure that, in general, our psychological energies are directed to the meeting of primary needs, both physical and psychological. They are 'non-negotiable' and force our attention onto the eliciting stimulus until the action tendency is realized. But emotions by themselves do not guarantee effective solutions to life's challenges, particularly in the complex and rapidly changing material and social environments that human beings have constructed for themselves. Such solutions are developed by learning and the establishment of a repertoire of problem-solving strategies.

Understanding the links between one's emotions and effective behaviour has recently been described as an important aspect of 'emotional intelligence' (Mayer & Salovey 1993). The development of effective responses to emotionally challenging situations can be helped through various kinds of 'off-line' activities, such as role playing (observed as spontaneous 'pretend play' in children), and story telling. Stories present the observer with a series of situations which elicit emotions in the protagonist, and by empathy or identification, in the reader or listener. By exploring the interactions between situations, emotions, and actions in a simulated environment, we can develop and test different strategies that might be deployed in real situations, but without the potentially harmful consequences of 'getting it wrong'.

It is in the context of such considerations that emotional responses to many art forms are rendered partly explicable. Novels, plays, operas, and films can provide opportunities to feel emotions with and for the protagonists, and explore consequences of different ways of acting on these same emotions. This is true even in the Western art culture, where the passive and immobile 'respectful silence' of the audience has such paradigmatic status. There is a strange paradox in the typical public performance, where much emotion is experienced (as evidenced by self-report of audience members) but almost none is displayed.

On the other hand, many other social contexts in which music and drama has occurred through the ages has provided opportunities for, and even encouraged, action. Pop concerts, for instance, provide a typical context and stimulus for exuberant and joyful bodily and vocal expressions among audience members. Indeed, the urge to participate seems to be a natural and early occurring phenomenon. Young children seem to spontaneously break into motion when they hear certain types of music (Moog 1976). Even when suppressing an overt response to music, listeners may still be engaging in subliminal physical action (e.g. Fraisse *et al.* 1953; Harrer & Harrer 1977). There is also evidence that soothing music yields more helpful behaviour in subjects than music that is aversive in nature (Fried & Berkowitz 1979). So action tendencies are by no means absent in emotional responses to music.

Perhaps more puzzling is the question of the underlying motivation for the action tendencies. If Frijda's analysis is correct, then music-engendered emotions, just like any other emotions, should involve the awareness of match, potential match, or mismatch between the current situation and some envisaged situation. Emotion should be initiated, maintained, or terminated by key events or actions which bring about transitions from match to mismatch or vice versa. A central problem for music psychology is to characterize and explain the various ways in which musical events can be interpreted by the human cognitive system as marking these transitions, while not directly 'telling a story'. Not only does music achieve this, but it often achieves it spectacularly well. The emotions felt by many people to music are equal in intensity to the emotions they experience to life events. And in some circumstances, people have reported that these emotions have propelled them towards significant personal change (Bunt & Pavlicevic, this volume; Gabrielsson & Lindström 1993; Sloboda 1992).

### 4.5.6 Emotions change during the course of human development

All researchers who study emotion seem to agree that emotions do change with development (e.g. Ekman & Davidson 1994). However, researchers differ among themselves with regard to their views on what changes occur, and why these changes occur. Although the number of proposed changes in emotions as a function of development is too large to permit a thorough overview, they include maturational changes of the nervous system, changes in the stimulus conditions eliciting emotions, changes in emotion regulation and coping skills, changes in the relationship between cognition and emotion, changes in expressive behaviour as a consequence of mothers' communication styles, and changes associated with cultural influences, including language. Theories of emotional development typically describe how emotions develop from pleasure and displeasure to successively more differentiated emotional states (Harris 1989).

To what extent does emotional development apply to the case of music? Unfortunately, individual differences in emotional responses to music within age cohorts have by and large not been systematically examined. However, there is a stream of developmental research that has concerned the development of perception of emotional expression in music (e.g. Cunningham & Sterling 1988; Dolgin & Adelson 1990; Kastner & Crowder 1990; Kratus 1993; Terwogt & van Grinsven 1988). These studies used pictures of facial expressions and asked children to select the face that matches the music's emotional tone most closely. The results indicate that even children 3 or 4 years of age can recognize certain emotions—joy, sadness, anger, and fear—in music with an accuracy better than chance. This ability seems to increase with age, however, particularly up to the age of six.

Developmental studies show that increasingly sophisticated music-emotion associations are acquired through childhood, and suggest that recognition of emotional expression in music depends on the general development of emotions (Gembris 1995). Very little is known about the development beyond childhood. However, the simple fact that listeners' preferences for music change over the life span (Russell 1997) could partly reflect the fact that certain types of music resonate better with certain phases of life in terms of the associated emotions. Rock music, for instance, with its focus on emotions like sexuality, anger, and rebellion may have a special appeal to adolescents, for which these same emotions are especially salient.

### 4.5.7 Emotions involve cognitive appraisals of organism-environment relationships

For an organism to be able to seek pleasure and avoid displeasure, it has to be able to evaluate its immediate environment. Thus, most theorists believe that emotions involve some kind of cognitive appraisal. However, theorists differ in their views on how much cognitive processing is minimally required for an emotion to occur (see, for example, Lazarus 1982; Zajonc 1980). Early theorists of emotion paid limited attention to the precise analyses of the elicitors of emotion, and the 'cognitions' associated with these elicitors. However, a number of recent 'appraisal theories' (Scherer 1999) hold that the precise nature of the emotional reaction is a result of appraisal processes undertaken on the elicitor of the emotion, and the way that elicitor is construed.

Ortony *et al.* (1988) have suggested a tripartite division of elicitors into events, agents, and objects. Developing one of their examples, one could consider a person's emotional reactions to a recently acquired new car which has broken down. As object, the car may elicit valenced reactions as a result of its aesthetic qualities (shape, colour, design). These would elicit liking or disliking. As event, the breakdown would elicit pleasure or displeasure as a result of its perceived consequences for self or others. Thus, for instance, I might be pleased with the breakdown if it prevented me from making an unwelcome journey. As agent, the car would be attributed with personality or intention, and so I might feel angry with the car for not working (irrational but common!).

On such a view, the basic emotional categories would be those given in Table 4.2. Note that the emotions contained there are relatively non-specific. Ortony *et al.* place other emotions in subcategories of the basic categories in respect of further more specific qualifying conditions of the appraisal. Thus, for instance, anger turns out to be one of the more complex emotions, being, at the very least, 'disapproval of the action of an agent in causing an event which has negative consequences for oneself'.

**Table 4.2** Basic emotional appraisal categories (adapted from Ortony *et al.* 1988)

| Valence | Proximal elicitor construed as | | |
| --- | --- | --- | --- |
| | Event | Agent | Object |
| Positive | Pleasure | Approval | Liking |
| Negative | Displeasure | Disapproval | Disliking |

Waterman (unpublished, reported in Sloboda 1991) derived a list of emotion words designed to exhaustively sample the emotion space proposed by Ortony *et al.*, and asked his participants to identify which of them they had ever felt to music, and if they had not felt it, how plausible it would be for a piece of music potentially to elicit it. These data suggested that music is capable of eliciting both positive and negative emotions relevant to all three types of construals—music can be appraised as event, action of agent, and object.

However, the more complex and specific the qualifying conditions, the less likely the emotion was to be experienced (or judged as possible for experiencing) to music. So, for instance, music elicits happiness quite easily, but almost never elicits gloating, although both emotions involve positively valenced reactions to something appraised as 'event'. Gloating denotes pleasure in the very specific context of the belief that someone else has been less fortunate than oneself. It is this precise cognitive context that defines the emotion. Music seems ill-suited for carrying such specific messages.

Rather clear examples of the three major categories of construal are provided by the study of Waterman (1996). He asked participants to listen to prerecorded pieces of music in a comfortable and quiet laboratory situation. They were asked to press a button each time they 'felt something'. After the music ended, the recording was played back, and stopped at each point where they had pressed, with a request to explain what had been going through their minds when they pressed. Event-related appraisals often concerned structural awareness (e.g. 'I knew the end was coming'). Action-of-agent appraisals often related to the performer or composer (e.g. 'her technique fascinated me'). Object-related appraisals included evaluations of the piece as a whole (e.g. 'I liked it') or of specific aspects of it (e.g. 'I didn't like the singer's voice'). What is particularly interesting about Waterman's study is that, although different listeners tended to press the 'felt something' button at the same point in the music, their stated reasons for pressing were very different from one another. This suggests that in music there may be a partial decoupling between the mechanisms that determine intensity of affect and those that determine emotional content, the former being predominantly determined by structural characteristics of the music (*intrinsic emotion*), the latter being determined more strongly by contextual factors, including the memories, associations, and priorities of the person hearing the music (*extrinsic emotion*).

Having established that responses to music involves true instances of emotion, we move on to consider the sources of emotion in more detail.

## 4.6 Sources of emotion in music

### 4.6.1 Intrinsic emotion

There is now an accumulating body of knowledge that shows that there is a lawful relation between the intensity of emotional qualities experienced in music and the specific structural characteristics of the music at a particular point in time. The intensity of emotional response to a piece of music often rises and falls as the music unfolds. Musical discourse, both formal and informal, talks of climaxes and points of repose, tension, and relaxation. In other words, there are peaks, where intense emotions (or other affective sensations) are prone to be experienced, and troughs, where the intensity is weak.

Sloboda (1991, 1992) has identified a set of structural characteristics that are associated with the elicitation of bodily and behavioural manifestations of emotion, such as weeping or piloerection ('thrills' or 'shivers') (Goldstein 1980; Panksepp 1995). These characteristics include syncopations, enharmonic changes, melodic appoggiaturas, and other music-theoretical constructs, which have in common their intimate relationship to the creation, maintenance, confirmation, or disruption of musical expectations. The positing of a central role for such constructs in generating emotional responses to music has characterized the accounts of a number of influential musicological theorists (e.g. Meyer 1956; Narmour 1991; see also Meyer, this volume). It is only in the last decade, however, that their intuitions have been substantiated by scientific data.

The term 'intrinsic' seems appropriate because it is only with reference to other musical events and structures that particular events become more or less expected. These expectations may reflect learning, or may operate at the level of primitive perceptual processes, such as the 'gestalt laws' of perception, where, for instance, movement in a particular direction creates expectation for further movement in that direction (law of good continuation) (Meyer 1956). Narmour (1990) provides a particularly detailed theoretical working out of these ideas in the context of melodic perception and expectancy. Other expectations may arise as a function of exposure to a large body of music sharing a set of structural regularities. Some expectations relate to the entire body of, for instance, tonal music; others may relate to specific styles or genres (e.g. AABA song form, sonata form).

Sloboda (2000) has discussed some of the issues that need to be resolved before strong predictions can be made about the intensity of emotional responses on the basis of structural analysis. Thus, for example, almost every note in a piece of music confirms or violates *some* expectancy. Therefore, in order to predict actual emotional responses, further parameters must be added to the basic model. These may include density of eliciting events, positioning within the compositional architecture, and what Sloboda has called 'asynchrony of levels'—an event which simultaneously confirms an expectation on one level while violating it on another. None of these factors has yet been the subject of scientific investigation. However, some preliminary models of musical expectancy have recently been tested (Eerola & North 2000).

If musical expectation is really the key to emotional intensity, how is it that we can feel emotions to music we are highly familiar with? First, many of the violations of expectations may occur on a subconscious level, involving modules for music processing that are denied conscious access (cf. Fodor 1983). Second, even when the musical 'narrative' is familiar to us, we may still be able to enjoy it. Much like when re-watching a great movie, we can appreciate the twists and turns of a good story in music, even though we already know how the story is going to end. Third, iconic and associative sources of emotion, such as emotional contagion and memories, may remain much the same throughout repeated listening to the same piece of music (many of our emotional responses to music may simply reflect the fact that we find the music beautiful, and this beauty may be perceived each time we listen to the piece). Fourth, a basic principle says that familiarity with an object itself mght increase our liking of that object up to a certain point (Gaver & Mandler 1987). Finally, it is possible that some effects of music processing are executed by a processor, whose responses are 'hard-wired' in regard to certain perceptual primitives. If this processor is 'sealed' from other more labile parts of the system, then it may be possible that however well one knows the piece, expectation, suspense, and surprise can still occur within the processor, because the processor is always hearing the piece 'for the first time' (Jackendoff 1992).

A theory of emotional responses to music in terms of 'musical expectations' has clear explanatory value in relation to Frijda's (1986) notion of emotions as a function of monitoring match and mismatch. Most compositional systems, such as the tonal system, provide a set of dimensions that establish psychological distance from a 'home' or 'stability point'. Proximity or approach to this resting point involves reduction of tension; distance or departure involves increase of tension. Distance can be measured on a number of dimensions, including rhythm and metre (strong beats are stable, weak beats and syncopations are unstable), and tonality (the tonic is stable, non-diatonic notes are unstable). There is now much experimental evidence that the human listener is sensitive to such features, and represents music in relation to them (e.g. Bharucha 1994; Krumhansl 1990). These features provide reference points against which the emotional system can plausibly compute match or mismatch in terms of envisaged end-points.

One problem with this approach is that it cannot without some difficulty explain why people experience different emotions in relation to pieces of music. The interplay of tension, release, surprise, and confirmation does not amount yet to a full-blown emotion. It is better characterized as 'proto-emotion', because it has a strong tendency to grow into emotions through the addition of further mental content (e.g. appraisal, valence). For instance, if the surprise is appraised as pleasurable, then an emotion of joy or elation may emerge (a similar point has been made by Ortony *et al.* 1988). What is needed to turn the structure-induced proto-emotions into full-blown emotions is semantic content. They need to be about something. Theory and evidence suggest two sources of content—iconic and associational. Because they both refer outside the music, we call these sources extrinsic.

### 4.6.2 Extrinsic emotion

*Iconic sources of emotion*

Iconic relationships come about through some formal resemblance between a musical structure and some event or agent carrying emotional 'tone' (e.g. Dowling & Harwood 1986). So, for instance, loud and fast music shares features with events of high energy and so suggests a high energy emotion such as excitement.

Iconic relationships are closely associated with the abundant literature on expression in music. Throughout history, there has been a number of different views on what music is able—or unable—to express. Music has, for example, been regarded as expressive of: (a) emotion; (b) motion; (c) beauty; (d) Christian faith; (e) tension and release; (f) things and events; (g) human character; and (h) political and social conditions. Empirical research has touched on only a few of these aspects. At some level, the common denominator for all these aspects may be human feeling, of one kind or another. Thus, it is perhaps not so surprising that psychological research has focused mainly on iconic relationships between musical features and particular emotions (for an extensive review, see Gabrielsson & Juslin, in press).

Empirical studies have shown that iconic relationships may specify particular emotions, and that they thus supply emotional content to the non-specific sensations of surprise, tension, and arousal engendered by the listener's engagement at the purely structural level of the music. Examples of studies of such iconic correspondences between musical variables and emotions are seen in Bruner (1990), Hevner (1935), Juslin (1997*b*), Rigg (1964), Scherer and Oshinsky (1977), and Wedin (1972). One recent strand in this work has been the suggestion that certain musical devices directly suggest gestural and other expressions of emotions by the human body (e.g. Clynes 1977; Scherer 1995). Another development has been studies of how performers communicate emotions to listeners through their performance of a piece of music (Gabrielsson & Juslin 1996; Juslin 1997*a*, 2000).

Unfortunately, most of these studies have measured only a few musical parameters and their main effects, whereas intercorrelations and possible interaction effects have been largely unexplored. Generally, the amount of study carried out on a particular musical parameter is inversely related to the difficulty of quantifying it. Therefore, most studies have not taken into consideration the dynamic changes in emotional expression that take place during a piece of music. Only recently have music researchers devised new techniques to capture the moment-to-moment changes in emotional expression (for a review, see Schubert, this volume). For a review of associations between composed structure and emotional expression, see Gabrielsson and Lindström (this volume). For a review of associations between performance features and emotional expression, see Juslin (this volume).

Study of emotional expression in music is probably the most common of all approaches to music and emotion in psychology—perhaps because of the relative ease with which such studies are carried out. A number of generalizations have emerged from this research. First, listeners seem to find it natural to attach emotion labels to pieces of music. Second, listeners are often consistent in their judgments and agree about the emotional expression of the music. Third, the veridicality of the judgments is rarely studied due to a lack of sufficient criteria of composers' intentions. Fourth, iconic representation of emotions in music seems to operate on a broad level of emotion categories, perhaps corresponding to the 'basic' emotion categories (cf. Dowling & Harwood 1986; Juslin 1997c; Krumhansl 1997). Fifth, listeners' judgments of emotion are influenced by such musical parameters as tempo, dynamics, rhythm, timbre, articulation, pitch, mode, tone attacks, and harmony.

The term 'iconic' seems particularly appropriate for this set of relationships, because the resemblances between a musical event and its non-musical referent is, in some sense, obvious to anyone who is familiar with the non-musical referent. Therefore, as a number of studies have shown (e.g. Juslin 1997a), recognition of iconic emotional meaning does not seem to require specific musical training. Non-musicians access iconic meanings just as easily as do musicians.

A second feature of iconic relationships is that, like the intrinsic relationships described in the previous section, they are non-arbitrarily embedded in specific structural characteristics of the music. If you change the structures then, perforce, the iconic meanings change. This means that iconic sources mediate moment-to-moment changes in emotional experience as a piece of music unfolds. Iconic relationships contribute to the ebb and flow of music-entrained emotion.

*Associative sources of emotion*

Associative sources of emotion are those that are premised on arbitrary and contingent relationships between the music being experienced and a range of non-musical factors which also carry emotional messages of their own. A memorable formulation of a key exemplar of associative sources is that of Davies (1978) who identifies associative theories as 'Darling, they're playing our tune' theories.

There are certain types of stimuli (e.g. music, smells, and tastes) which seem to become associated in human memory with particular contexts or events in earlier life, and provide a trigger to the recall of these events. This seems particularly so when the earlier events were, in themselves, occasions of strong emotion (Dutta & Kanungo 1975). Many investigators (e.g. Gabrielsson 1991; Sloboda 1991) have found examples of specific pieces of music that trigger strong emotion in this way. Such emotions tend to lead attention away from the present music onto the remembered past event.

Waterman (1996) has demonstrated that even when music does not directly trigger past experiences, many of the emotional processes are self-referring in some way (e.g. 'I should have recognized that', 'this is not my type of music'). Because these feelings are linked to the life histories of individuals they are often completely idiosyncratic. However, common cultural experiences can sometimes lead to shared emotions which still are fundamentally extrinsic, for example, the extreme negative emotions felt by many Jews after the Second World War on hearing the music of Richard Wagner; the strong emotional identification of generational cohorts with the popular music prevalent in their teenage years (e.g. Holbrook & Schindler 1989); and the cultural associations formed by film-music pairings, such as Johann Strauss' 'Blue Danube' waltz, with the spaceship docking sequence in Stanley Kubrick's film *2001: A Space Oddesey*.

Unlike the intrinsic and iconic sources of emotion, associative sources are often bound non-specifically to entire pieces or passages, and do not require any particular feature of the music for their binding (i.e. other than some means of identifying the music in question as the relevant music rather than a different piece or genre). Although associative sources of emotion are obvious and pervasive, there is little scientific research into them. This may be because the intrinsic idiosyncrasy of these associations renders control and generalizability problematic.

### 4.6.3 Interactions between different sources of emotion

In the foregoing, we noted that emotional responses to music reflect both intrinsic emotion that is locally focused, and extrinsic emotion that is more globally context-dependent. Furthermore, music both induces emotions in listeners and is perceived by listeners as expressive of emotion. This means that emotional responses to music may come about in a large number of different ways, and failure to recognize this fact may account for some of the past disagreements in the field. In each listening situation, (a) all, (b) only some, or (c) none of the different sources of emotion may be present. Much of the richness of emotional responses to music comes from this multitude of sources of emotion. Moreover, different sources of emotion may interact in interesting ways. For example, the mood of a particular piece of music (iconic signification) may evoke mood-congruent memories (associative signification) through so-called 'spread of activation' in neural networks associated with emotional reactions (Bower 1981). Similarly, the manner in which a particular section of a piece of music builds up tension through musical expectations (intrinsic affect) may remind us of the patterns of tension and release in a certain extramusical context (extrinsic affect). Furthermore, different sources of emotion may support or contradict one another, thus creating either clarity or ambiguity in the emotional impact of the music. The emotional ambiguity of certain pieces of music is, of course, reminiscent of the mixed emotions we often experience in many other domains of life (Oatley & Duncan 1994).

Music (instrumental music, at least) often suggest emotions in a vague fashion. Sloboda (2000, p. 226) notes that music:

can suggest or resemble certain types of human gestures and actions. Given shared experience and understandings, it is easy to see how a group of people might be able to extrapolate specific emotions from such cues. It is equally easy to see how there is room for ambiguity and imprecision. Very often we feel that there is an emotion present, we know it is of one general type rather than that of another, but we cannot quite tie it down. In such a state of ambiguity and cue-impoverishment we may well expect the profound and semi-mystical experiences that music seems to engender. Our own subconscious desires, memories, and preoccupations rise to the flesh of the emotional contours that the music suggests. The so-called 'power' of music may very well be in its emotional cue-impoverishment. It is a kind of emotional Rorschach blot.

## 4.7 Implications and future directions

This chapter has suggested a multitude of ways in which emotional processes may occur in relation to music. Yet, this chapter has provided only a small glimpse of all the work that has been carried out within the psychological approach to music and emotion. One implication of the foregoing overview is that emotional responses to music have very much in common with emotional responses to other stimuli. However, in the case of a non-musical stimulus, emotion is usually generated via appraisal of the capacity of the stimulus to affect the interests, values, and goals of the perceiver. Because music has no direct capacity to further or block such goals, a challenge for theorists of music and emotion has been to provide an alternative but plausible account of the casual path between musical features and experienced emotion, for instance in terms of musical expectations or various extramusical associations.

Given the emphasis on emotional responses to music in this chapter, we should perhaps note that music does not always arouse emotional responses in listeners. Often, we may listen to a piece of music without feeling anything in particular. In fact, some people claim that they rarely, if ever, experience emotional reactions to music. Unfortunately, there is little research so far on the *epidemiological* aspects of musical emotions; in other words, how often people experience emotions to music under various circumstances. This represents a crucial area for future research. We should attempt to delineate the conditions (including the music, person, and situation) under which a listener is most likely to react emotionally to music. This might involve the kind of diary approach that have been used in earlier research on epidemiological aspects of emotions (Oatley & Duncan 1994).

Psychological studies of music and emotion have largely ignored the interaction among three factors: the listener, the music, and the context (cf. Gabrielsson, this volume). Previous research has focused mainly on factors in the music. We know quite a lot about the ways that factors in the music can induce and represent emotions. However, the fact that different styles of music may yield very different emotional responses in listeners has received little attention. Therefore, it should be acknowledged that theoretical explanations of emotional responses relevant to one particular style of music (e.g. classical music) may not apply equally well to a different style (e.g. blues).

A fair amount of research has focused on factors in the individual that might influence emotional responses to music. Listeners' affective responses to music are likely to depend to some extent on their age, gender, personality, training, current mood, and so forth (Abeles & Chung 1996). Interactions between music and listener may involve the listener's familiarity with the music (North & Hargreaves 1997) and his or her musical preferences (Holbrook & Schindler 1989; Russell 1997).

The factor that has been mostly ignored in previous research is the context—including everything from the concrete situation in which the musical activity takes place, to the wider social and cultural context. Konečni (1982) has strongly criticized previous empirical studies for having treated aesthetical responses as if they occur in a social, emotional, and cognitive 'vacuum'. Emotional responses to music are likely to depend on what the music is used for. To understand emotional responses to music, we should consider the social functions of the music in its particular context. Hargreaves and North (1999) have suggested that the social functions of music manifest themselves in three main ways: (a) the formulation and expression of self-identity (our responses to some musical styles may partly reflect what they stand for in the larger social context); (b) the establishment and maintenance of personal relationships (e.g. prestige effects and conformity); and (c) mood management (music tastes reflect situationally determined goals of 'mood optimization'). Studies of music and emotion have recently begun to address these issues (e.g. DeNora 2000, this volume; North & Hargreaves 1997; Sloboda & O'Neill, this volume).

One example of the strong social influence is the kind of emotion that arises from what one has been told, and therefore may come to believe, about the music in question. A seminal study by Weick *et al.* (1973) manipulated the reputation of the composer of a jazz orchestra piece by telling some players it was by an established jazz composer and others that it was by a dance band arranger (not exactly a high prestige genre for jazz players). This manipulation clearly affected emotional and motivational involvement with the piece. Players who thought the piece was by an established composer both liked the piece more and devoted more effort to learning it. As suggested by this study, almost every piece of music is given a cultural value by members of the community within which it is experienced, produced, and discussed. Therefore, there is little music that we come to 'blind'. Our hearing of a Beethoven Symphony cannot now be dissociated from the ubiquitous discourse (available on programme notes, CD cases, radio stations, etc.) that assigns him a pre-eminent position of 'greatness' in the canon of masterworks. Because greatness has been ascribed to Beethoven, our emotional response to hearing a famous Beethoven work is conditioned by cultural attitudes appropriate to 'greatness' (e.g. reverence). We may rebel against these tendencies, but we cannot ignore them.

Such considerations lead us into the heart of contemporary debates in musicology (see Cook 1998). Traditional musicology has become increasingly under fire for being unreflexive about the cultural and social sources of its own attitude toward the music it was studying, an attitude which could lead to the assumption that Beethoven's greatness was 'for all times and all places' and had nothing to do with the particularities of nineteeth- and twentieth-century European societies into which his music has been received and championed. The increasing self-critical reflexivity of the musicological community augurs well for developments in psychology. Many psychologists have been 'victims' of the same cultural unawareness that dominated mid twentieth-century musicology, and this may be one reason why this area has not been well researched. Psychologists have not really grasped the nature of the problem. To put the problem in its most acute form, one of the most prevalent cultural discourses about music concerns its emotional power. This discourse surrounds all of us from our earliest years. We, therefore, approach any new music already expecting (even willing) it to have an emotional content. One answer to the question 'why is music so emotionally powerful' is that we have decided to construe it thus. At one very important level of analysis, music is not inherently emotional. It is the way we hear it that makes it so (see Becker, this volume).

Because the concept of emotion itself relies on research from such diverse domains as philosophy, psychology, sociology, biology, anthropology, and physiology, we believe that interdisciplinary collaborations provide the royal road to progress in this field. Juslin (1997c, pp. 15–16) notes that music researchers have approached questions of music and emotion with empirical rigor but that:

this has unfortunately not been matched by an equal sophistication concerning conceptual problems. There are often vague references to the 'musical emotions', without further clarification of the meaning of this concept. Philosophers may, of course, contribute to these conceptual problems through thoughtful analyses, but too often they are not familiar with the latest developments in emotion psychology, which means that their ground premises may be wrong. In the end, it may turn out that we can make progress in this area only through the combined efforts of different disciplines.

We believe that psychologists must learn to draw from the knowledge currently available in related disciplines—philosophy, sociology, anthropology, biology, and musicology.

Given the problems of the study of music and emotion, we think it is also desirable for music researchers to follow closely the developments in the emotion domain more generally. Recent debates in emotion psychology have involved: (a) the role and limits of self-reports in the study of emotion; (b) cross-cultural agreement in emotion judgments; (c) the nature and existence of basic emotions; (d) individual differences in emotion disposition; (e) the tracking of phasic aspects of emotion; (f) linguistic analyses of emotion; and (g) relationships between emotion and cognition (Cacioppo & Gardner 1999), all of which have a direct bearing on the study of emotion in music. The implication is that music researchers cannot escape from the theoretical and methodological problems confronted by other researchers who study emotion. Studies of music and emotion that measure emotions in multiple channels simultaneously (self-report, physiology, expressive behaviour), and over time, is clearly an important goal for future research. Such an endeavour may have to involve a switch from the traditional agrarian-based inferential statistics to non-linear, dynamic models that are better suited to the time-dependent nature of emotional responses to music.[1]

---

[1]   We thank Carol Krumhansl and Klaus Scherer for useful comments on a preliminary version of this chapter.

# References

Abeles, H. F. & Chung, J. W. (1996). Responses to music. In *Handbook of music psychology* (2nd edn) (ed. D. A. Hodges), pp. 285–342. San Antonio, TX: IMR Press.

Bartlett, D. L. (1996). Physiological reactions to music and acoustic stimuli. In *Handbook of music psychology* (2nd edn) (ed. D. A. Hodges), pp. 343–85. San Antonio, TX: IMR Press.

Batson, C. D., Shaw, L. L., & Oleson, K. C. (1992). Differentiating affect, mood, and emotion: Toward functionally based conceptual distinctions. In *Review of personality and social psychology: Emotion*, (ed. M. S. Clark), pp. 294–326. Newbury Park, CA: Sage.

Behne, K. E. (1997). The development of 'musikerleben' in adolescence: How and why young people listen to music. In *Perception and cognition of music*, (ed. I. Deliége & J. A. Sloboda), pp. 143–59. Hove, UK: Psychology Press.

Berlyne, D. E. (1971). *Aesthetics and psychobiology.* New York: Appleton Century Crofts.

Bharucha, J. J. (1994). Tonality and expectation. In *Musical perceptions*, (ed. R. Aiello, & J. A. Sloboda), pp. 213–39. New York: Oxford University Press.

Bless, H. & Forgas, J. P. (ed.) (2000). *The message within. The role of subjective experience in social cognition and behavior.* Hove, UK: Psychology Press.

Bower, G. H. (1981). Mood and memory. *American Psychologist*, **36**, 129–48.

Bruner, G. C. (1990). Music, mood, and marketing. *Journal of Marketing*, **54**, 94–104.

Budd, M. (1985). *Music and the emotions. The philosophical theories.* London: Routledge.

Cacioppo, J. T. & Gardner, W. L. (1999). Emotion. *Annual Review of Psychology*, **50**, 191–214.

Cacioppo, J. T., Klein, D., Berntson, G. G., & Hatfield, E. (1993). The psychophysiology of emotion. In *Handbook of emotions*, (ed. M. Lewis & J. M. Haviland), pp. 119–42. New York: Guildford Press.

Clynes, M. (1977). *Sentics: The touch of emotions.* New York: Doubleday.

Cook, N. (1998). *A very short introduction to music.* Oxford, UK: Oxford University Press.

Cunningham, J. G. & Sterling, R. S. (1988). Developmental changes in the understanding of affective meaning in music. *Motivation and Emotion*, **12**, 399–413.

Damasio, A. (1994). *Descartes' error. Emotion, reason, and the human brain.* New York: Grosset/Putnam.

Darwin, C. (1872). *The expression of the emotions in man and animals.* London: John Murray.

Davidson, R. J. (1994). On emotion, mood, and related affective constructs. In *The nature of emotion: Fundamental questions*, (ed. P. Ekman & R. J. Davidson), pp. 51–5. New York: Oxford University Press.

Davies, J. B. (1978). *The psychology of music.* London: Hutchinson.

DeNora, T. (2000). *Music in everyday life.* Cambridge, UK: Cambridge University Press.

De Sousa, R. (1987). *The rationality of emotions.* Cambridge, MA: MIT Press.

Dewey, J. (1894). The theory of emotions. I. Emotional attitutes. *Psychological Review*, **1**, 553–69.

Dolgin, K. & Adelson, E. (1990). Age changes in the ability to interpret affect in sung and instrumentally-presented melodies. *Psychology of Music*, **18**, 87–98.

Dowling, W. J. & Harwood, D. L. (1986). *Music cognition.* New York: Academic Press.

Dutta, S. & Kanungo, R. N. (1975). *Affect and memory: A reformulation.* New York: Pergamon Press.

Eerola, T. & North, A. C. (2000). Expectancy-based models of melodic complexity. In *Proceedings of the Sixth International Conference on Music Perception and Cognition, August 2000*, (CD rom) (ed. C. Woods, G. Luck, R. Brochard, F. Seddon, & J. A. Sloboda). Keele, UK: Keele University.

Ekman, P. (ed.) (1973). *Darwin and facial expression.* New York: Academic Press.

Ekman, P. (1992). An argument for basic emotions. *Cognition and Emotion*, **6**, 169–200.

Ekman, P. & Davidson, R. J. (ed.). (1994). *The nature of emotion: Fundamental questions.* New York: Oxford University Press.

Fehr, B. & Russell, J. A. (1984). Concept of emotion viewed from a prototype perspective. *Journal of Experimental Psychology: General*, **113**, 464–86.

Fodor, J. A. (1983). *The modularity of the mind.* Cambridge, MA: MIT Press.

Fraisse, P., Oleron, G., & Paillard, J. (1953). Les effets dynamogeniques de la musique. *L'Anée Psychologique*, **53**, 1–34.

Fridja, N. H. (1986). *The emotions.* New York: Cambridge University Press.

Fridja, N. H. (1989). Aesthetic emotions and reality. *American Psychologist*, **44**, 1546–7.

Fridja, N. H., Kuipers, P., & ter Schure, E. (1989). Relations among emotion, appraisal, and emotional action readiness. *Journal of Personality and Social Psychology*, **57**, 212–28.

Fried, R. & Berkowitz, L. (1979). Music that charms ... and can influence helpfulness. *Journal of Applied Social Psychology*, **9**, 199–208.

Gabrielsson, A. (1991). Experiencing music. *Canadian Journal of Research in Music Education*, **33**, 21–6.

Gabrielsson, A. (1993). Music and emotion. *ESCOM Newsletter*, **4**, 4–9.

Gabrielsson, A. & Juslin, P. N. (1996) Emotional expression in music performance: Between the performer's intention and the listener's experience. *Psychology of Music*, **24**, 68–91.

Gabrielsson, A. & Juslin, P. N. (in press). Emotional expression in music. In *Handbook of affective sciences*, (ed. R. J. Davidson, H. H. Goldsmith, & K. R. Scherer). New York: Oxford University Press.

Gabrielsson, A. & Lindström, S. (1993). On strong experiences of music. *Jarbuch der Deutschen Gesellschaft für Musikpsychologie*, **10**, 114–25.

Gaver, W. W. & Mandler, G. (1987). Play it again, Sam: On liking music. *Cognition and Emotion*, **1**, 259–82.

Gembris, H. (1995). The development of perception of emotional expression in music: A review. Paper presented at the ESCOM Conference, Jahrestagung Deutsche Gesellschaft für Musikpsychologie, Bremen, 15–17 September 1995.

Gigerenzer, G. & Goldstein, D. G. (1996). Reasoning the fast and frugal way: Models of bounded rationality. *Psychological Review*, **103**, 650–69.

Goldstein, A. (1980). Thrills in response to music and other stimuli. *Physiological Psychology*, **8**, 126–9.

Gross, J. J. & Levinson, R. W. (1993). Emotion suppression: physiological, self-report, and expressive behaviour. *Journal of Personality and Social Psychology*, **64**, 970–86.

Hargreaves, D. J. & North, A. (1999). The functions of music in everyday life: Redefining the social in music psychology. *Psychology of Music*, **27**, 71–83.

Harrer, G. & Harrer, H. (1977). Music, emotion, and autonomic function. In *Music and the brain. Studies in the neurology of music*, (ed. M. Critchley & R. A. Henson), pp. 202–16. London: William Heinemann Medical Books.

Harris, P. L. (1989). *Children and emotion.* Oxford, UK: Basil Blackwell.

Hatfield, E., Cacioppo, J. T., & Rapson, R. L. (1994). *Emotional contagion.* New York: Cambridge University Press.

Hevner, K. (1935). Expression in music: A discussion of experimental studies and theories. *Psychological Review,* 42, 186–204.

Holbrook, M. B. & Schindler, R. M. (1989). Some exploratory findings on the development of musical tastes. *Journal of Consumer Research,* 16, 119–24.

Imberty, M. (1997). Can one seriously speak of narrativity in music? In *Proceedings of the Third Triennial ESCOM Conference, 1997,* (ed. A. Gabrielsson), pp. 13–22. Uppsala, Sweden: Department of Psychology, Uppsala University.

Izard, C. E. (1977). *The emotions.* New York: Plenum Press.

Jackendoff, R. (1992). Musical processing and musical affect. In *Cognitive bases of musical communication,* (ed. M. R. Jones & S. Holleran), pp. 51–68. Washington, DC: American Psychological Association.

James, W. (1884). What is an emotion? *Mind,* 9, 188–205.

Johnson-Laird, P. N. & Oatley, K. (1992). Basic emotions, rationality, and folk theory. *Cognition and Emotion,* 6, 201–23.

Juslin, P. N. (1997*a*). Emotional communication in music performance: A functionalist perspective and some data. *Music Perception,* 14, 383–418.

Juslin, P. N. (1997*b*). Perceived emotional expression in synthesized performances of a short melody: Capturing the listener's judgment policy. *Musicae Scientiae,* 1, 225–56.

Juslin, P. N. (1997*c*). Can results from studies of perceived expression in musical performances be generalized across response formats? *Psychomusicology,* 16, 77–101.

Juslin, P. N. (2000). Communication of emotion in music performance: Relating performance to perception. *Journal of Experimental Psychology: Human Perception and Performance,* 26, 1797–1813.

Juslin, P. N. (2001). A Brunswikian approach to emotional communication in music performance. In *The essential Brunswik: Beginnings, explications, applications,* (ed. K. R. Hammond & T. R. Stewart), pp. 426–430. New York: Oxford University Press.

Kastner, M. P. & Crowder, R. G. (1990). Perception of the major/minor distinction: IV. Emotional connotations in young children. *Music Perception,* 8, 189–202.

Keltner, D. & Gross, J. J. (1999). Functional accounts of emotions. *Cognition and Emotion,* 13, 465–6.

Kemper, T. D. (1987). How many emotions are there? Wedding the social and the autonomic components. *American Journal of Sociology,* 93, 263–89.

Kenealy, P. (1988). Validation of a music mood induction procedure: Some preliminary findings. *Cognition and Emotion,* 2, 41–8.

Kivy, P. (1990). *Music alone: Philosophical reflections on the purely musical experience.* Ithaca, NY: Cornell University Press.

Kleinginna, P. R. & Kleinginna, A. M. (1981). A categorized list of emotion definitions, with a suggestion for a consensual definition. *Motivation and Emotion,* 5, 345–71.

Konečni, V. J. (1979). Determinants of aesthetic preference and effects of exposure to aesthetic stimuli: Social, emotional, and cognitive factors. In *Progress in experimental personality research,* (Vol. 9) (ed. B. A. Maher), pp. 149–97. Orlando, FL: Academic Press.

Konečni, V. J. (1982). Social interaction and musical preference. In *The psychology of music,* (ed. D. Deutsch), pp. 497–516. San Diego, CA: Academic Press.

Kratus, J. (1993). A developmental study of children's interpretation of emotion in music. *Psychology of Music*, 21, 3–19.

Krumhansl, C. L. (1990). *Cognitive foundations of musical pitch*. Oxford, UK: Oxford University Press.

Krumhansl, C. L. (1997). An exploratory study of musical emotions and psychophysiology. *Canadian Journal of Experimental Psychology*, 51, 336–52.

Langer, S. (1951). *Philosophy in a new key*. (2nd edn). New York: New American Library (original work published 1942).

Lazarus, R. S. (1982). Thoughts on the relations between emotion and cognition. *American Psychologist*, 37, 1019–24.

Lazarus, R. S. (1991). *Emotion and adaptation*. New York: Oxford University Press.

Leahey, T. H. (1987). *A history of psychology. Main currents in psychological thought*, (2nd edn). Englewood Cliffs, NJ: Prentice Hall.

LeDoux, J. (1996). *The emotional brain*. New York: Simon & Schuster.

Levinson, J. (1996). *The pleasures of aesthetics*. Ithaca, NY: Cornell University Press.

Mandler, G. (1984). *Mind and body. Psychology of emotions and stress*. New York: Norton.

Mayer, J. D. & Salovey, P. (1993). The intelligence of emotional intelligence. *Intelligence*, 17, 433–42.

Meyer, L. B. (1956). *Emotion and meaning in music*. Chicago: Chicago University Press.

Moog, H. (1976). *The musical experience of the pre-school child*. London: Schott.

Narmour, E. (1990). *The analysis and cognition of basic melodic structures*. Chicago: University of Chicago Press.

Narmour, E. (1991). The top-down and bottom-up systems of musical implication: Building on Meyer's theory of emotional syntax. *Music Perception*, 9, 1–26.

Neale, J. M. & Liebert, R. M. (1986). *Science and behavior*. Englewood Cliffs, NJ: Prentice Hall.

Niedenthal, P. M. & Showers, C. (1991). The perception and processing of affective information and its influences on social judgment. In *Emotion and social judgments*, (ed. J. P. Forgas), pp. 125–43. Oxford, UK: Pergamon Press.

North, A. C. & Hargreaves, D. J. (1997). Experimental aesthetics and everyday music listening. In *The social psychology of music*, (ed. D. J. Hargreaves & A. C. North), pp. 84–103. Oxford, UK: Oxford University Press.

Nyklicek, I., Thayer, J. F., & van Doornen, L. J. P. (1997). Cardiorespiratory differentiation of musically-induced emotions. *Journal of Psychophysiology*, 11, 304–21.

Oatley, K. (1992). *Best laid schemes. The psychology of emotions*. Cambridge, MA: Harvard University Press.

Oatley, K. & Duncan, E. (1994). The experience of emotions in everyday life. *Cognition and Emotion*, 8, 369–81.

Oatley, K. & Jenkins, J. M. (1996). *Understanding emotions*. Oxford, UK: Blackwell.

Ortony, A, Clore, G. L., & Collins, A. (1988). *The cognitive structure of the emotions*. New York: Cambridge University Press.

Ortony, A. & Turner, T. J. (1990). What's basic about basic emotions? *Psychological Review*, 97, 315–31.

Panksepp, J. (1992). A critical role for affective neuroscience in resolving what is basic about basic emotions. *Psychological Review*, 99, 554–60.

Panksepp, J. (1995). The emotional sources of 'chills' induced by music. *Music Perception*, 13, 171–208.

Pike, A. (1972). A phenomenological analysis of emotional experience in music. *Journal of Research in Music Education*, 20, 262–7.

Plutchik, R. (1980). A general psychoevolutionary theory of emotions. In *Emotion: Theory, research, and experience. Vol 1. Theories of emotion*, (ed. R. Plutchik & H. Kellerman), pp. 3–33. New York: Academic Press.

Plutchik, R. (1994). *The psychology and biology of emotion.* New York: Harper Collins.

Power, M. & Dalgleish, T. (1997). *Cognition and emotion. From order to disorder.* Hove, UK: Psychology Press.

Rigg, M. G. (1964). The mood effects of music: A comparison of data from earlier investigations. *Journal of Psychology*, 58, 427–38.

Rosch, R. (1978). Principles of categorization. In *Cognition and categorization*, (ed. E. Rosch & B. B. Loyd), pp. 27–48. Hillsdale, NJ: Erlbaum.

Russell, J. A. (1980). A circumplex model of affect. *Journal of Personality and Social Psychology*, 39, 1161–78.

Russell, P. A. (1997). Musical tastes and society. In *The social psychology of music*, (ed. D. J. Hargreaves & A. C. North), pp. 141–58. Oxford, UK: Oxford University Press.

Schacter, S. & Singer, J. E. (1962). Cognitive, social, and physiological determinants of emotional states. *Psychological Review*, 69, 379–99.

Scherer, K. R. (1993). Neuroscience projections to current debates in emotion psychology. *Cognition and Emotion*, 7, 1–41.

Scherer, K. R. (1995). Expression of emotion in voice and music. *Journal of Voice*, 9, 235–48.

Scherer, K. R. (1999). Appraisal theories. In *Handbook of cognition and emotion*, (ed. T. Dalgleish & M. Power), pp. 637–63. Chichester, UK: Wiley.

Scherer, K. R. & Oshinsky, J. S. (1977). Cue utilization in emotion attribution from auditory stimuli. *Motivation and Emotion*, 1, 331–46.

Schlosberg, H. (1941). A scale for the judgment of facial expressions. *Journal of Experimental Psychology*, 29, 497–510.

Shaver, P. R., Schwartz, J., Kirson, D., & O'Connor, C. (1987). Emotion knowledge: Further exploration of a prototype approach. *Journal of Personality and Social Psychology*, 52, 1061–86.

Simon, H. (1967). Motivational and emotional controls of cognition. *Psychological Review*, 74, 29–39.

Sloboda, J. A. (1991). Music structure and emotional response: Some empirical findings. *Psychology of Music*, 19, 110–20.

Sloboda, J. A. (1992). Empirical studies of emotional response to music. In *Cognitive bases of musical communication*, (ed. M. Riess-Jones & S. Holleran), pp. 33–46. Washington, DC: American Psychological Association.

Sloboda, J. A. (1996). Emotional responses to music: A review. In *Proceedings of the Nordic Acoustical Meeting*, (ed. K. Riederer & T. Lahti), pp. 385–92. Helsinki: The Acoustical Society of Finland.

Sloboda, J. A. (2000). Musical performance and emotion: Issues and developments. In *Music, Mind, and Science*, (ed. S. W. Yi), pp. 220–38. Seoul, Korea: Western Music Research Institute.

Smith, L. D. & Williams, R. N. (1999). Children's artistic responses to musical intervals. *American Journal of Psychology*, 112, 383–410.

Sorce, J., Emde, R., Campos, J, & Klinnert, M. (1985). Maternal emotional signalling: Its effect on the visual cliff behavior of one-year olds. *Developmental Psychology*, **21**, 195–200.

Stern, D. (1985). *The interpersonal world of the infant. A view from psychoanalysis and developmental psychology*. New York: Basic Books.

Terwogt, M. M. & van Grinsven, F. (1988). Musical expression of mood states. *Psychology of Music*, **19**, 99–109.

Thayer, J. F. (1986). Multiple indicators of affective responses to music. *Dissertation Abstracts International*, **47**, 12.

Tomkins, S. (1962). *Affect, imagery, and consciousness: The positive affects*. New York: Springer.

Waterman, M. (1996). Emotional responses to music: Implicit and explicit effects in listeners and perfomers. *Psychology of Music*, **24**, 53–67.

Wedin, L. (1972). A multi-dimensional study of perceptual-emotional qualities in music. *Scandinavian Journal of Psychology*, **13**, 1–17.

Weick, K. E., Gilfillian, D. P., & Keith, T. A. (1973). The effect of composer credibility on orchestra performance. *Sociometry*, **36**, 435–62.

Witvliet, C. V. & Vrana, S. R. (1996). The emotional impact of instrumental music on affect ratings, facial EMG, autonomic response, and the startle reflex: Effects of valence and arousal. *Psychophysiology Supplement*, **91**.

Woodworth, R. S. (1938). *Experimental psychology*. New York: Holt.

Wundt, W. (1897). *Outlines of psychology* (trans. C. H. Judd). Lepzig: Englemann.

Zajonc, R. B. (1980). Feeling and thinking: Preferences need no inferences. *American Psychologist*, **35**, 151–75.

Zajonc, R. B. (1994). Emotional expression and temperature modulation. In *Emotions: Essays on emotion theory*, (ed. S. H. M. Van Goozen, N. E. Van de Poll, & J. A. Sergeant), pp. 3–27. Hillsdale, NJ: Erlbaum.

Zillman, D. (1988). Mood management: using entertainment to full advantage. In *Communication, social cognition, and affect*, (ed. L. Donohew, H. E. Sypher, & E. T. Higgens), pp. 147–71. Hillsdale, NJ: Earlbaum.

# CHAPTER 5

# LISTEN TO THE BRAIN: A BIOLOGICAL PERSPECTIVE ON MUSICAL EMOTIONS

## ISABELLE PERETZ

The functioning of the brain is fascinating. It fascinates for the obvious reason that the brain is the commander of all our actions, thoughts, and motivations. By studying its functioning, the hope is to obtain crucial information about the biological determinants of human cognition and emotion. Neuropsychology is the discipline concerned with these questions. As its name indicates, neuropsychology aims to relate neural mechanisms to mental functions. It is an old discipline, dating back to the discovery that speech was related to the functioning of a small region of the left brain by Broca in 1861. Following this discovery, the neural correlates of musical abilities were similarly scrutinized (for a recent review, see Marin & Perry 1999). Although the neuropsychological approach to music is a century old, progress has been slow. However, the recent advances made in brain-imaging techniques, as well as the current trend of viewing most human activities from a biological perspective, has intensified research activities in the field.

As a result of this biological trend, neuropsychology has been recently renamed 'cognitive neuroscience'. This change in terminology reflects the intention to include neuropsychology within the vast domain of neuroscience. Since neuroscience covers a large spectrum of disciplines, going from the physiological study of single neurons in the turtle retina (Sernagor & Grzywacz 1996) to the brain organization subserving the sense of humour in humans (Shammi & Stuss 1999), 'cognitive' has qualified the 'neuroscience' term. The qualifier is unfortunate because 'cognitive' usually excludes emotion. Cognition is often seen as antagonistic to emotion. For example, Kivy (1990) in his influential essay on the meaning of music coined the term 'cognitivist' to refer to the position that holds that music simply expresses emotions without inducing them. The opposite position, called 'emotivist', holds that music elicits emotional responses in listeners.

The antagonism between 'cognitivists' and 'emotivists' is not limited to music psychology. It has a long history starting with Descartes' early separation of emotion and reason. Still, today, the majority of experimental psychologists and neuropsychologists are 'cognitivists' by default. They have simply ignored emotions. This neglect partly reflects the information-processing approach that started in the early 1960s (e.g. Neisser 1967) and that used the computer as a metaphor for mental functions. Following this approach, the brain is a machine, devoid of emotions.

Recently, neuropsychologists have become more concerned with emotions. Although neuropsychologists do distinguish between emotional and cognitive processes, they no longer reject the emotional part as being too obscure or subjective to be scientifically studied. On the contrary, emotions are now studied for their own sake. In their two popular books published in 1994 and 1996, respectively, Damasio and LeDoux have greatly contributed to the *rapprochement* between cognition and emotion in neuropsychology. Reason is no longer seen as the human-specific activity that controls emotional irrationality. As Damasio (1994) has shown, emotional processes are an integral part of decision making and are no longer confined to subcortical brain structures that are shared with other animals. Emotions recruit portions of the frontal lobes, which are the largest and latest brain structures to develop in the human brain. Thus, neuropsychologists are currently studying emotions in the same way as any other mental function worthy of enquiry.

The objective of this chapter is to present current knowledge about musical emotions from a biological perspective. I will introduce this topic by first covering neuropsychological data accumulated on facial expressions of emotions. This area of investigation has made remarkable progress recently. An outline of the major findings will allow me to illustrate a number of principles that characterize the field of neuropsychology in general. After this excursion into the facial processing domain, I will cover what is currently known about the neural correlates of musical emotions. Then, I will address the possibility that musical emotions follow similar paths to vocal emotions (the emotional expressions produced by non-verbal inflections of the human voice) by reviewing the relevant literature. Although the neuropsychological study of musical emotions lags behind, drawing parallels across domains should benefit the musical endeavour and, hopefully, promote cross-fertilization.

## 5.1 An illustration of the rise of affective neuroscience: facial expressions

Emotions have generally been considered too personal, elusive, and variable to be studied scientifically. *A fortiori*, emotions could hardly be conceived as subserved by a neuro-anatomical arrangement that can be shared by all members of the same species. The work of Paul Ekman on human facial expressions has contributed to convince the scientific community that the above view is inadequate. In what follows, I will summarize his work and the subsequent research done on the neural substrates of human facial expressions, because it has spurred my own interest in studying the neural basis of musical emotions. Above all, it will allow me to introduce basic concepts about the neuroanatomical substrates of emotions and the major technologies by way of an example rather than as a disembodied general model associated with a series of techniques without objects.

### 5.1.1 Facial expressions: universality and innateness
Like music, facial expressions are non-verbal communicative displays, which can be very subtle but none the less quickly and easily appreciated by humans. Infants show a precocious ability to respond to different facial expressions of emotions (Field *et al.*

1982). Darwin (1872) was the first to hypothesize the innateness and universality of facial expressions of emotions, but his proposal received little attention. It was only in the late 1960s, with the work of Ekman (Ekman 1994; Ekman *et al.* 1969) and Izard (1971), that Darwin's position regained credibility. At the time Ekman and Izard began their studies, it was thought that facial expressions of emotions are socially learned and therefore variable from culture to culture. Ekman and his collaborators dismissed the idea that facial expressions are pure social constructs, in showing that a variety of emotions are expressed cross-culturally by the same facial movements (even though there might be culture-specific variations as captured by Ekman's concept of 'display rules').

For example, Ekman and collaborators (1987) reported a study in which facial expressions were examined in Japanese and Americans while they watched stress-inducing films (e.g. body mutilations) and neutral films (nature scenes). When the subjects in each culture watched the films alone, unaware of a hidden camera, the same negative facial responses were emitted regardless of culture. However, when a scientist was present while they watched the films, the Japanese more than the Americans masked their expressions with smiles. This study illustrates how universal expressions of disgust on faces can manifest themselves, beyond cultural differences, in their display. In other studies, the same group of researchers has convincingly demonstrated that facial expressions of 'basic' emotions (for a further explanation of this concept, see Sloboda & Juslin, this volume), such as happiness, sadness, anger, and fear, are easy to recognize by members of widely different and isolated cultures. The general rules and processes subserving facial expressions appear universal.

The universality of emotion expressions is necessary but not sufficient for considering them to be innate or biologically determined, as initially posited by Darwin (1872). Universality can arise as common learning experiences because all infants are exposed to the same situations, such as pain, being left alone, or reassured, across cultures. However, as summarized by Oster and Ekman (1978), even premature newborns are capable of producing all the discrete facial muscle movements involved in the expressions of basic emotions such as disgust, endogenous smiling, and sadness. Children born deaf and blind show similar facial expressions to those of hearing and seeing children (e.g. Eibl-Eibesfeldt 1973). Before 1 year of age, infants demonstrate meaningful relations between events and expressions of joy, sadness, fear, disgust, and anger. It is unlikely that young infants could have learned all these complex muscular patterns of facial expressions so quickly. The notion that facial expressions are learned lacks plausibility. Rather, facial expressions appear constrained by innate mechanisms. Thus, the innateness and universality of facial expressions appears sufficiently robust to consider Darwin's hypothesis established.

### 5.1.2 Facial expressions: brain specialization

The fact that facial expressions of emotion exhibit universality and innateness is important from a neuropsychological perspective. More specifically, brain organization is expected to differ for functions that respond to cultural pressure and for functions that meet biological requirements. Functions resulting from social conventions might be implemented in neural networks that vary across individuals. Depending on the quality and quantity of familiarization with a skill, various brain regions might be mobilized to different degrees in individuals. Driving a car, an obvious cultural and recent acquisition in the human behavioural repertoire, would be expected to be subserved by variable, not specialized, neural networks. In order to drive a car, a person would be expected to borrow functional principles and neural resources from other skills, such as navigating, and to adjust them to their processing needs. In contrast, biologically important functions are likely to be subserved by a fixed and specialized neural architecture. This is probably the case for both expression and recognition of emotions in faces, since they exhibit universality and precociousness. Hence, the neural basis of facial expressions is expected to exhibit the same functional and neuroanatomical specialization across human brains. Accordingly, specification of the functional neuroanatomy underlying facial expressions should be relatively easy.

The first neural property that facial expressions should possess is brain specialization. That is, recognition of emotional expressions should be isolable in the brain. This property is indeed verified. Selective losses in the ability to recognize emotions from faces have been reported after focal brain damage (e.g. Calder *et al.* 1996; Etcoff 1984; Parry *et al.* 1991; Sprengelmeyer *et al.* 1996; Young *et al.* 1993). Such patients can recognize all known faces and infer the age of unknown faces, but are unable to see variations in emotional expressions. Conversely, other patients remain capable of discriminating and identifying various facial expressions, while being entirely unable to recover the identities of familiar faces of relatives and even of themselves (e.g. Tranel *et al.* 1988).

The study of the effects of brain lesions on a particular mental function is the oldest method used in neuropsychology. The observed disorders reveal both how the function under study is organized functionally and what part of the brain is *necessarily* involved in its processing. The idea is that the disorder is not arbitrary, but rather reveals the organization of the brain prior to the accident. Assumptions and methods have become extremely sophisticated over the past 20 years, so the patient-based approach remains one of the major sources of information in cognitive neuroscience (see Rapp 2001, for a new textbook devoted to just this: what deficits reveal about the human mind). One of the landmarks of this approach is its power to reveal functional and neural specificity, often referred to as 'modularity'. It is this phenomenon of functional specificity that is illustrated here in the recognition of facial expressions of emotion relative to the recognition of the identity of the face.

The neural segregation of facial emotion and facial identity that emerges from lesion studies has been confirmed by functional brain imaging. For example, Sergent and collaborators (1994) have shown that different brain regions are involved in the analysis of identity and expression by measuring variations of regional cerebral blood flow in normal brains with the positron emission tomography (PET) technique.

The PET technique and the functional magnetic resonance imaging (fMRI) technique are two recent tools that are most often used today for studying the functioning of *normal* brains. PET is more invasive than fMRI because it involves the injection of radioactive substance. However, PET scanning is less noisy, and hence more appropriate for studying music perception. Fortunately, new means have been developed to facilitate auditory testing in the MRI machine. One such means consists in clustering volume acquisition (and hence noise) by acquiring all images of the brain in rapid succession for about 1 second, every 10 seconds, and so providing a period of quiet during which the stimuli may be presented uninterrupted and uncontaminated by cortical responses to the noise (e.g. Edmister *et al.* 1999). Both PET and fMRI are valuable neuropsychological tools because they allow the measurement of variations of cerebral blood flow in three dimensions in the brain of a participant who is performing a task. Local variations in blood flow, or oxygen consumption, respond to different needs at any given time during the performance. However, measurements of cerebral blood flow changes are slow relative to the speed of information processing—requiring 2–3 minutes or 4–5 seconds with PET and fMRI scanning methods, respectively. All measures are taken after transformation of the magnetic resonance images of each individual into a standardized stereotaxic space. This manipulation eliminates any differences attributable to global differences in overall brain size or shape.

Using the PET technique with visual presentations of faces, Sergent and her co-workers were able to show that the processing of facial identity is associated with the ventromesial region of the right hemisphere (i.e. the fusiform gyrus and the lingual gyrus) and the parahippocampal gyrus, whereas facial emotion (covering happiness, sadness, fear, disgust) mostly engages the lateral part of the right occipital cortex and the cingulate gyrus (located in the limbic system). The regions are indicated in Fig. 5.1. Similarly, in the monkey, cells selective for facial identity and expression are found in different brain areas; cells which respond to face identity tend to be located in the inferior temporal gyrus, whereas cells whose responses are modulated preferentially by expression are located within the monkey's superior temporal sulcus (e.g. Hasselmo *et al.* 1989).

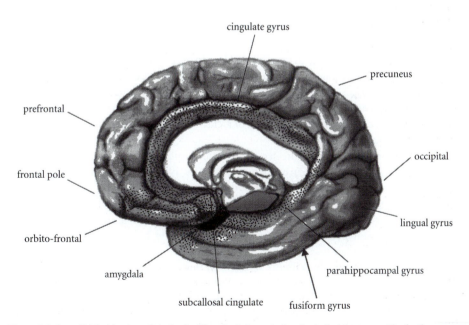

**Figure 5.1** A medial inside view of the brain. The stippled area is the classic limbic system. The fusiform gyrus is hidden inside the temporal lobe. The amygdala, represented in black, is found deep inside the medial part of the temporal lobe.

### 5.1.3 Facial emotions: the role of the amygdala

We have seen that the processing of facial emotions is isolable in the brain. This does not mean facial emotions are subserved by a unique neural pathway. Rather, neural systems appear specialized for the recognition of specific emotions. The clearest evidence comes from studies of patients with damage to the amygdala, a brain structure long thought to play an important role in emotion. The amygdala is located in the limbic system (see Fig. 5.1). This system, named 'le grand lobe limbique' by Broca (1878), corresponds to subcortical structures that appeared early in evolution and remained relatively stable across species. The limbic system was designated as the substrate of emotions by Broca over a century ago, and later also by Papez (1937). Since then, the concept has gradually developed to include many more regions, both cortical and subcortical (Damasio 1994; LeDoux 1996). Emotions are no longer confined to the functioning of the limbic system, although the latter retains its fundamental role in emotion.

In the limbic system, the amygdala has been identified as the brain structure most implicated in fear. Bilateral amygdala damage impairs the recognition of unpleasant emotions, especially fear, in facial expressions (Adolphs *et al.* 1994, 1995; Broks *et al.* 1998; Calder *et al.*, 1996; Young *et al.* 1995); but not always (see Hamann *et al.* 1996). Such patients can see happiness and sadness in faces, but have severe problems with fearful expressions.

Additional support for the selective involvement of the amygdala in perceiving fear in facial expressions has been gathered in recent functional imaging studies of normal brains. Increased neural activity has been observed within the amygdala when subjects are viewing facial expressions of fear as opposed to happiness (Breiter *et al.* 1996; Morris *et al.* 1996; Whalen *et al.* 1998), disgust (Phillips *et al.* 1997), and anger (Blair *et al.* 1999).

The involvement of the amygdala is not limited to facial expressions of fear. The amygdala also plays a key role in conditioned fear in both humans and rats (Bechara *et al.* 1995; LeDoux 1996), as well as in fear-related behaviours such as uncontrollable rage reactions (Davis 1992). Moreover, direct stimulation of the human amygdala with in-depth electrodes evokes similar reactions (Halgren *et al.* 1978), further suggesting that the amygdala is critical to the processing of a class of emotions, namely those related to threat and danger.

The amygdala is strongly connected to the autonomic nervous system, which induces changes in physiological measures such as heart rate, blood flow, and respiration. This connectivity, coupled with the selectivity, of the emotional response, suggests that the amygdala is appropriately located in the brain to enable reactions to threat and danger, without the necessity of higher-level processing. The idea is that an expression of fear on the face of a conspecific may trigger an automatic and quick response to potential danger via the amygdala.

The role of the amygdala is highly selective. It does not participate in the evaluation of all negative emotions expressed by faces. For instance, the amygdala is not as actively engaged in perceiving disgust. Disgust rather involves the basal ganglia and the anterior insula. Increased activation of the insula has been observed in a functional brain-imagery study (Phillips *et al.* 1997), while impairments in disgust have been reported in patients with Huntington's disease, which is a neurological disorder that initially affects the basal ganglia (Gray *et al.* 1997; Sprengelmeyer *et al.* 1996). Disgust is another distinct facial expression that has clear survival value, as does fear. Recognition of disgust allows avoiding contamination by offensive stimuli, and, in particular, the avoidance of ingestion of potentially harmful food. The neural response to facial expressions of disgust appears closely related to another, but related, sensory organ, namely taste. In humans, the anterior insula is particularly activated by aversive tasting (e.g. Zald *et al.* 1998). Altogether, the localization of the neural structures involved in disgust confirms common sense—that disgust is closely related to the perception of unpleasant tastes and smells.

The major implication of the relative engagement of the amygdala in perceiving fear relative to disgust in facial expressions is that it raises the possibility that different basic emotions have different underlying neural substrates. Basic emotions serve important and distinct functions, and the brain appears to be organized so as to respond to these distinct functions with distinct neural systems.

### 5.1.4 Facial expressions: the contribution of the cortical systems

The cortical systems are the neural structures that are evolutionarily more recent, and are particularly developed in the human brain. These cortical systems involve the occipital, temporal, parietal, and frontal cortex (Fig. 5.2). Another characteristic of these cortical structures is that they exhibit functional specialization within and across the two cerebral hemispheres. For example, it is well established that regions of the left hemisphere of the brain are much more essential for speech comprehension and expression than the right side of the brain.

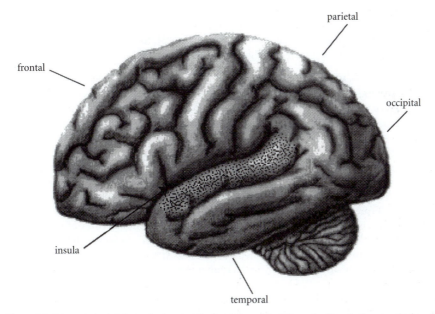

**Figure 5.2** A lateral view of the brain showing the four lobes of the left cerebral hemisphere in which several structures of interest are indicated. The stippled area corresponds to the superior temporal gyrus (see text for explanation).

With respect to emotions, there is currently a debate involving two alternative views. One view is that the right hemisphere is specialized for processing *all* emotions, by containing all 'modules' for non-verbal affect computation (e.g. Bowers *et al.* 1993). This position is known as the 'right hemisphere hypothesis'. The opposing view is the 'valence hypothesis' according to which the right hemisphere is more involved in negative emotions and the left hemisphere more engaged in positive emotions (e.g. Davidson 1992). Both hypotheses have been discussed with regard to the expression and recognition of emotion, as well as the experience of emotion.

The first observations related to the emotional competence of each cerebral hemisphere go back to Jackson (1878), who noticed that emotional language is often preserved in aphasic patients. He attributed the source of the preserved affective utterances to the contribution of the right hemisphere. This dissociation between propositional and affective language has often been reported since. However, it is difficult to reconcile with another classic pattern in clinical neurology that identifies each hemisphere with a distinct affective style. A lesion in the right hemisphere often produces indifference (anosognosia) and a tendency to joke. In contrast, an injury in the left hemisphere often leads to depressive–catastrophic states. The former is obviously less comprehensible than the latter as a reaction to the brain accident. The two emotional modes of responding have been associated with differences in 'affective styles' of the cerebral hemispheres. The left and right frontal cortex would be mediating approach and avoidance, respectively (for a recent review, see Davidson & Irwin 1999).

The valence hypothesis accounts more convincingly for expression and experience of emotions than for perception of emotions. For the latter, the bulk of the evidence seems to favour the right hemisphere hypothesis. In the study of normal adults' perceptual asymmetries, a left visual field (i.e. right hemisphere) superiority is typically found for both positive and negative expressions (see Best *et al.* 1994, for a recent review and additional data on adults' perception of infants' emotional expressions).

Perceptual asymmetries can be easily measured in normal right-handed subjects, in all modalities. In the visual modality, which is used for face presentation, facial expressions are typically and quickly presented to the left or to the right of a central fixation point. A left visual field advantage is inferred if the subjects process more accurately or more quickly the facial expressions presented on the left side of the screen than the expressions presented on the right side. Since the left visual field is directly projected to the right cerebral hemisphere, the advantage is taken to reflect a right hemispheric superiority for the task under study. The same logic applies to the auditory modality with which we will be concerned in the next section. This technique, often referred to as *dichotic listening*, consists of presenting different auditory stimuli in each ear, simultaneously. A right ear advantage is interpreted as a left hemispheric superiority, because it is well established that the information that enters in one ear reaches mostly the primary auditory cortex of the opposite hemisphere. It should be noted that although laterality measures are convenient and non-invasive tools for testing hemispheric specialization, they are less used nowadays because they have low sensitivity and low reliability, particularly in the auditory modality.

Lesion studies are compatible with both the right hemisphere hypothesis and the valence hypothesis. In a recent study involving a large sample of brain-damaged patients, Adolphs and his collaborators (1996) found that lesions of the right hemisphere led to impairments in recognizing negative emotions, such as fear and sadness, but spared recognition of happy expressions. However, there are fewer positive than negative emotions regarded as basic emotions. Positive emotions, such as happiness, may simply be easier to distinguish from negative expressions than are negative emotions from each other. For example, a single prototypical feature (smile) distinguishes happiness from all other emotions.

Although the nature of each hemispheric contribution to the perception of facial expression remains to be determined, the presence of hemispheric advantages highlights the contribution of non-limbic cortical structures. It is plausible that the cortical contribution is related to both the demands of the perceptual analysis of the input (e.g. detailed facial features) and the contribution of memory, such as factual knowledge about emotions.

### 5.1.5 Facial expressions: a lesson and challenge

We have seen that recognition of facial expressions is the result of an adapted behavioural system that is implemented in a distributed neural network involving the limbic system, the amygdala in particular, but that it is not limited to this system. Recent research suggests additional and differential implication of the left and right prefrontal cortex, the anterior cingulate (see Fig. 5.1), and the insular cortex (see Fig. 5.2). Each of these regions appears to play a distinct function in emotional appraisal, with different distributed networks underlying different emotions such as fear and disgust.

Just as cognitive neuroscience has demonstrated the necessity to fractionate global functions, such as face processing or music recognition (Rapp 2001), into more elementary constituents whose neural substrates can be identified, so too modern research in the neuroscience of emotions suggests fractionation of affective processes. This conclusion highlights what is often not obvious to psychologists. It shows why the study of neural correlates in general, and brain localization in particular, is of importance. Examination of brain correlates can shed light on more general assumptions, by requiring that complex brain functions be decomposed into simpler processes so that simple components can be localized anatomically and studied in relative isolation. This fractionation into elementary localized mechanisms can then serve to test current models of emotional functioning or contribute to the building of new models.

## 5.2 Neural correlates of musical emotions

We have seen how facial emotions have become a tractable problem in the neurosciences. The central question is now to examine whether the neuropsychological study of musical emotions will hold similar promises.

### 5.2.1 Which musical emotions and what for?

Like facial expressions, certain musical emotions can be categorized as happiness, sadness, anger, and fear. The happy and sad emotional tones tend to be among the easiest ones to communicate in music (e.g. Gabrielsson & Juslin 1996; Krumhansl 1997). Like facial expressions, these emotions might be expressed by similar structural features across musical styles and cultures. But the claim cannot be made forcefully, since the search of universals in the expression of musical emotions has just begun (Balkwill & Thompson 1999; but see also Juslin, this volume). In contrast, there is increasing evidence that musical emotions are quickly and easily perceived by members of the same culture. For example, ordinary adult listeners need less than a quarter of a second of music (e.g. one chord or a few notes) to reliably distinguish the tone of the whole musical excerpt as happy or sad (Peretz *et al.* 1998a). Moreover, and more generally, we were struck by the systematicity and reliability of the judgment data collected with ordinary listeners. Emotional judgments exhibit a high degree of consistency, suggesting that perception of emotions in music is natural and effortless for the large majority of listeners.

*Developmental perspectives*

Perception of emotion in music is also a skill that appears early in life. Recent empirical research suggests that music plays an important role in emotion regulation and emotional communication between care-givers and infants (e.g. Trehub & Trainor 1999). From birth, care-givers around the world sing to their infants, with the intuition (or instinct?) that music has the power to regulate the infant's state (e.g. comforting) or the quality of interaction (e.g. attention getting). The care-givers nicely mirror infants' perceptual abilities by singing more slowly, at higher pitch, with exaggerated rhythm, and in a more loving or emotionally engaging manner than when singing alone (e.g. Trainor *et al.* 1997). Responsiveness to such infant-directed singing appears inborn. Two-day-old hearing infants, born from congenitally deaf parents (who sign and do not sing or speak), prefer infant-directed singing to adult-directed singing (Masataka 1999).

Care-givers also speak to infants in a special, singing manner, so-called 'baby talk' or 'motherese' (see Bunt & Pavlicevic, this volume). Nevertheless, infants seem to discriminate between infant-directed speech and infant-directed music. Trehub (2001) reports a study in which 6-month-old infants viewed videotaped performances of their own mothers (recorded while singing or speaking to their infants). The infants showed more sustained attention to their mothers' singing episodes than to their speaking episodes. Infants were 'hypnotized' by these sung performances, remaining 'glued' to the monitor for extended periods. Mothers' speaking was not as engaging as their singing. The fact that infants are particularly responsive to the emotional messages of music directed toward them suggests an adaptive value of maternal singing. Mother–infant emotional communication is crucial to survival.

It is also remarkable how skilled the young children are in emotional perception. From the age of 3 years, they show the ability to recognize happiness in elaborate, art music of their culture, and by the age of 6 years they show adult-like abilities to identify sadness, fear, and anger in music (Cunningham & Sterling 1988; Terwogt & van Grinsven 1988, 1991; but for later emergence, see Dolgin & Adelson 1990). Furthermore, the child competence can be related to abstraction of specific musical features. At 5 years of age, children are able to discriminate between happy and sad excerpts by relying on tempo differences (fast vs. slow). At 6, children show evidence of using both tempo and mode (major vs. minor) like adults do. Although the results suggest that sensitivity to tempo precedes sensitivity to mode, it is remarkable that by the age of 6 years, children show full knowledge of the rules that govern the happy–sad character of surrounding music. This ability seems to remain generally unchanged over a lifetime (Dalla Bella *et al.* 2001; Gerardi & Gerken 1995; Gregory *et al.* 1996; Kastner & Crowder 1990; Kratus 1993). Therefore, with consistency and precociousness, musical emotions resemble facial emotions.

*Evolutionary perspectives*

Musical emotions also seem to respond to important needs of the organism, even though considerable controversy surrounds the questions of the origin, biological significance, and function of music (e.g. Pinker 1997). In other words, music may have adaptive significance. Two main evolutionary explanations have been offered. The initial account was provided by Darwin himself (1871), who proposed that music serves to attract sexual partners. This view has been recently revived by Miller (2000), who reminds us that music making is still a young male trait. However, the dominant view of the adaptive value of music lies at the group level rather than at the individual level, with music helping to promote group cohesion. The initial step for this bonding effect of music could be the mother–infant interactive pattern created through maternal singing. The individual- and group-level roles attributed to music do not need to be mutually exclusive. As pointed out by Kogan (1994), individuals taking the lead in gatherings by virtue of their musical and dance prowess can achieve leadership status in the group, a factor that contributes to reproductive success (for other formulations of these evolutionary issues, see Wallin *et al.* 2000).

In support of the contention that music has an adaptive value, particularly for the group, is the fact that music possesses two design features that reflect an intrinsic role in communion (as opposed to communication, which is the key function of speech). Pitch intervals allow harmonious voice blending when sounding together, and temporal regularity facilitates motor synchronicity. These two musical features are highly effective in promoting simultaneous singing and dancing (Brown 2000). The design is specific to music; it is certainly not shared with speech, which requires individuality for its intelligibility. These special features fit with the important criterion, discussed by Buss and collaborators (1998), that for a system to qualify as 'adaptive' it must offer effective solutions to a problem. The system must have a 'special design'. The bonding problem in the case of music is to override 'selfish genes' for the benefit of the group.

For neuropsychologists, this evolutionary perspective on music is essential. As mentioned earlier, the fact that musical emotions are viewed as adaptive responses that can be aroused similarly in every human being is best conceived as the product of neural structures that are specialized for their computation. Furthermore, if biologically important, these emotions can even be seen as *reflexes* in their operation. That is, musical emotions would occur with rapid onset, through automatic appraisal, and with involuntary changes in physiological and behavioural responses. This conception would correspond to the fact that 'we often experience emotions as happening to us, not as chosen by us. We do not simply decide when to have or not have a particular emotion' (Ekman 1994, p. 17).

### 5.2.2 Musical emotions: brain specialization

Support for the existence of specialized neural networks for music processing is presently compelling (for reviews, see Peretz 2001*a*, 2001*b*). However, the evidence relies on the detailed study of music perception and memory, that is on the processing of music as a special auditory structure, not as an emotional medium. Emotional appreciation of music is a new research avenue in neuropsychology. Hence, the data are scarce, albeit consistent and promising.

First of all, musical emotions appear isolable in the human brain. By isolable, I mean that musical emotions can be selectively either lost or spared, usually as a consequence of a brain accident occurring at an adult age. There are a number of case reports that describe musicians who retained their musical skills, but who complained that they lost interest in music because it sounded 'flat' or without emotion (Mazzoni *et al.* 1993; Mazzuchi *et al.* 1982). Unfortunately, the reports are anecdotal. No attention was paid to the emotional complaints of the two patients because of 'the highly subjective nature of the symptom concerned' (Mazzuchi *et al.* 1982, p. 646) or because 'disturbances of this type are, unfortunately, difficult to view objectively because of their highly subjective nature' (Mazzoni *et al.* 1993, p. 322).

However, recent progress made in affective neuroscience in general, and in the study of facial expressions in particular, has encouraged us to go beyond anecdotal reports and study emotional responses in the laboratory. In doing so, we have been able to discover mirror cases, that is, patients who manifest selective sparing of musical emotions. The case of one patient, IR, who suffers from longstanding bilateral brain damage to the auditory cortex (see panel A in Fig. 5.3) is given here. The case is remarkable in that 15 years after the brain damage, IR still experiences severe difficulties with music while her language abilities and her general intellectual and memory abilities are normal (Peretz *et al.* 1997; Peretz & Gagnon 1999). Despite her severe musical deficits, she reports that she still enjoys music, listening regularly to prerecorded music in the car. This possible preservation of emotions for music appeared to us as paradoxical, given the severity of IR's perceptual disorders with music. Therefore, we decided to study her emotional judgments in detail. Three independent studies have been completed with her that will be summarized here.

The goal of the first study (Peretz & Gagnon 1999) was to verify experimentally IR's insights. To do so, IR was presented with popular melodies, half of which are familiar in Québec where the study was conducted. IR performed two judgments: in the emotional judgments, she classified the melodies as 'happy' or 'sad'. In the non-emotional 'control' task, she performed a 'familiar–unfamiliar' classification task. The results confirm her report. She is able to classify melodies as 'happy' and 'sad' as normal controls do, while she fails to reach normal performance in classifying these same melodies for familiarity. For example, when presented with the melody of 'Happy Birthday' without its lyrics, IR would say 'I don't know that tune but it sounds happy'. Similarly, CN, another patient with severe recognition problems for melodies that were once highly familiar to her (Peretz 1996), had an interesting reaction. When listening to the famous adagio of Albinoni taken from her own record collection, CN first said that she had never heard that piece before. Suddenly, she said: 'it makes me feel sad . . . the feeling makes me think of Albinoni's adagio' (R. Kolinsky, personal communication). CN, who was totally

(A)

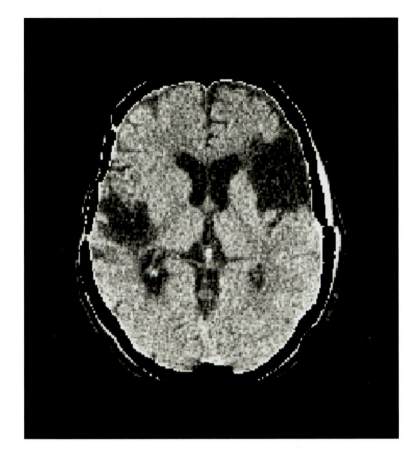

(B)

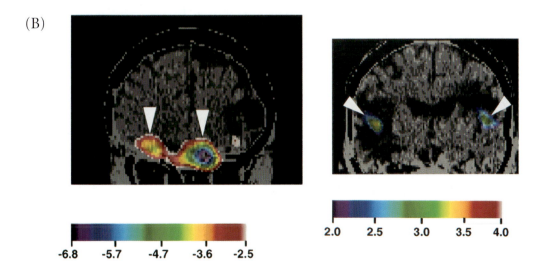

-6.8   -5.7   -4.7   -3.6   -2.5

2.0   2.5   3.0   3.5   4.0

CT scan of I.R.'s brain, transformed into the standardized stereotaxic space. For a more detailed caption see Fig. 5.3 on p.117.

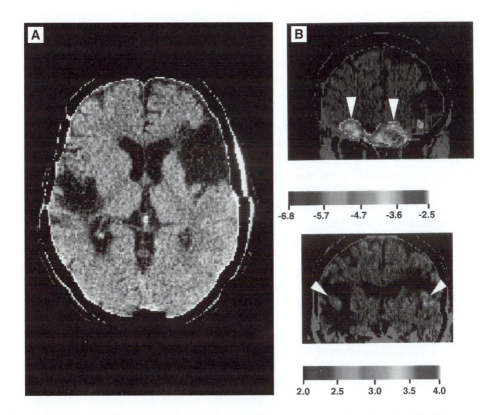

**Figure 5.3** CT scan of IR's brain, transformed into standardized stereotaxic space. The right side of the scan corresponds to the right side of the brain. (A) Horizontal slice showing the differing locations of temporal and frontal lobe damage (i.e. darker areas correspond to damaged tissue) in the left and right hemispheres, and (B) coronal slices showing PET data from a group of normal non-musicians (Blood *et al.* 1999*a*) superimposed on the CT scan of IR's brain. The top panel shows areas whose cerebral blood flow (CBF) changes are related to pleasantness judgments; the arrowheads show the subcallosal area and the left orbitofrontal areas. None of the paralimbic or neocortical regions recruited by the dissonance manipulation in normals overlapped with the lesions in IR's brain. The panel below illustrates areas of significant CBF increase in the subtraction of a highly consonant stimulus condition with a matched noise baseline condition. This illustrates the areas of activity within the superior temporal gyri bilaterally (indicated by arrowheads). Note that these regions overlapped significantly with the lesions in IR's brain. The *t*-statistic ranges are coded by the colour scale below the corresponding panel. (Adapted from Peretz *et al.* 2001.) (See also colour section).

unable to recognize melodies that were highly familiar to her before the brain accident, was able to do so via her emotional responses. This is probably not an isolated finding. However, we did not pursue our work in that direction. Rather, we wished to establish more firmly the dissociation observed in IR between emotion and perception.

In a follow-up study of IR (Peretz *et al.* 1998*a*), we were interested in explaining how she could derive the emotional tone from melodies, while her ability to recognize and discriminate melodies is so limited. One intriguing possibility, derived from the animal work of LeDoux (1996) and from the theoretical position of Zajonc (1984), is that emotions need no cortical mediation. That is, basic emotional responses might function like subcortical reflexes. These emotional responses would be immediate but superficial. They would not require the additional time taken by elaborate processing of the signal in cortical structures. Since IR's lesions are vast, but limited to cortical structures, perhaps her intact limbic system is responsible for her spared ability to distinguish happy from sad music.

To assess the nature of this spared emotional pathway in IR, and to further assess its independence from the rest of her processing system for music, we tested her in a series of experiments employing the same set of excerpts taken from the classical repertoire (e.g. Albinoni's adagio). These were selected to unambiguously convey a 'happy' or 'sad' tone, and were presented under various transformations and with different task demands. At first sight, IR's results seemed to conform to the separate pathways view. As with normals, IR was able to use both the mode and the tempo characteristics to derive the 'happy' or 'sad' tone of the music. Moreover, as with normals, IR's judgments were immediate. In contrast with the relatively sophisticated emotional processing of the musical excerpts, IR showed impaired performance in her non-emotional assessment. Specifically, she performed well below normal controls in the discrimination of these musical excerpts in a 'same–different' classification task that was very easy for controls. Likewise, she failed to detect most errors purposely inserted on either the pitch or time dimension of the musical excerpts, although these mistakes were obvious to control subjects. Thus, IR's pattern of results suggests that perceptual analysis of the musical input is intact for emotional purposes and defective for non-emotional ones.

The relative independence of the emotional pathway from non-emotional processing of music is consistent with previous data of ours that were obtained with neurologically intact students. We showed in a series of experiments that exposure effects differed for recognition and liking judgments (Peretz et al. 1998b). Similarly, we showed that IR can process melodies for emotion recognition, but not for identity recognition (Peretz & Gagnon 1999) or discrimination (Peretz et al. 1998a). However, IR's spared emotional processing cannot be easily accommodated with the isolated functioning of a subcortical pathway. IR is able to use a change of mode, from major to minor and vice versa, in elaborate musical structures. This ability can hardly be conceived as the result of the operation of a primitive subcortical system. Furthermore, as we will see later, there is presently little support for the involvement of a subcortical 'short cut' in emotional processing of music. Rather, musical emotions seem to require cortical mediation. Therefore, all we can conclude from these studies with IR and CN is that severe deficits in perceptual processing and memorization of music can leave emotional judgments of music unimpaired. Such a spectacular isolation of emotional judgments of music suggests the presence of a specialized cortical arrangement for it.

### 5.2.3 Musical emotions: hemispheric specialization

As mentioned above, there are indications that emotional judgments require cortical mediation. The participation of cortical structures seems to depend on the cerebral hemisphere concerned, as observed for facial expressions. Likewise, the available data are divided between the two current hypotheses regarding the nature of this specialization.

Support for the valence hypothesis has been obtained in two recent studies measuring brain electrical activity—the electroencephalogram (EEG)—from scalp electrodes in normal listeners (Schmidt & Trainor 2001; Tsang *et al.* 2001).

EEG methods are non-invasive measurements of the ongoing electrical activity that can be captured by electrodes located on the scalp of the listener. Various measurements are made possible with the recent increases in computer power. The EEG method used in the studies by Schmidt and Tsang that are cited here consists of recording the EEG variations over extended periods of time, in the order of 60 seconds, while the subject is listening to a piece of music. The EEG signal is then decomposed into particular frequency bands, such as the alpha bands taken to reflect variations in activation. Another EEG method that is increasingly exploited in neuropsychology is the evoked response potential (ERP) (for a review of its use with regard to music, see Besson 1997). This method consists of averaging EEG signals time-locked to a particular category of events. The advantage of the ERP is that it is an on-line measure of processing that has a high temporal resolution window, of the order of a few milliseconds. By increasing the number of electrodes over the scalp, and by exploiting sophisticated algorithms to locate the neural source responsible for the observed response, it is now possible to obtain information about brain localization.

Asymmetrical frontal EEG activity has been found to distinguish the valence of musical excerpts taken from the classical repertoire. Subjects exhibit greater relative left frontal activity to music expressing joy and happiness and greater relative right frontal EEG activity to music expressing fear and sadness (Schmidt & Trainor 2001). Subsequently, the same group of researchers (Tsang *et al.* 2001), using the same EEG technique, were able to replicate and relate the EEG findings to musical structure, using our set of musical excerpts used with IR (Peretz *et al.* 1998a). They observed that changes in both tempo and mode in the happier direction resulted in greater relative left frontal activation, whereas changes in both tempo and mode in the sadder direction resulted in greater relative right frontal activation.

In a similar vein, Gagnon and Peretz (2000) have observed ear asymmetries in normal listeners that are compatible with the notion that the left hemisphere contributes more to the perception of positive emotions and the right hemisphere more to negative emotions in listeners. Non-musicians were required to classify tonal and atonal melodies as pleasant and unpleasant in one condition. In a non-affective 'control' condition, the same subjects were required to judge if the melodies sounded correct or not. Listeners exhibited a left-ear superiority effect, taken to reflect the predominance of the right hemisphere, when judging atonal melodies as unpleasant while they displayed a tendency towards the right ear when judging tonal melodies as pleasant. This pattern of ear asymmetries was specific to emotional judgments since a different pattern was obtained when the same melodies had to be classified for 'correctness'.

However, the valence account of cerebral asymmetries is not systematically observed. Two studies are more supportive of the right hemisphere hypothesis. The first one measured ear asymmetries in normal subjects who were judging minor and major melodies as eliciting positive or negative emotions (Bryden *et al.* 1982). In that study, an overall left ear (i.e. right hemisphere) advantage was observed across positive and negative emotional judgments. The second study measured changes in regional cerebral blood flow with the PET technique as a function of pleasantness judgments for chord sequences varying in degree of dissonance (Blood *et al.* 1999*a*). In that study, the activated neural structures by pleasantness judgments were found primarily in the right hemisphere. Moreover, reciprocal activation was found between particular neural structures and the valence of the musical stimulus. However, these reciprocal activations did not occur between hemispheres but rather between the parahippocampal and frontal regions.

### 5.2.4 Musical emotions: contribution of distributed neural structures

Up to now, we have reviewed data suggesting that emotional appreciation of music is subserved by a distinct neural pathway that probably requires cortical mediation. Cortical mediation appears to involve primarily the right hemispheric structures, with a possible contribution of the left frontal regions, depending on the valence of the perceived emotion. More specific localization suggestions have been made by Blood and collaborators (1999*a*), using dissonance as the emotion-eliciting stimulus and PET scanning as the brain-recording measure.

In that PET study, regional cerebral blood flow changes were obtained in several distinct paralimbic and neocortical regions of the brain. Most activated areas depend on the valence of emotion. Activity in the right parahippocampal gyrus and precuneus regions is associated with increasing dissonance, whereas activity in the bilateral orbitofrontal, medial subcallosal cingulate, and right frontal polar cortex correlates with decreasing dissonance (or increasing consonance). In contrast, activity in the superior temporal cortices is observed bilaterally, independently of dissonance level. All implicated regions are indicated in Fig. 5.1.

One powerful means to determine which neural region is essential in a given function is to compare brain-imaging data with brain-lesion data. To this aim, we tested IR, our case with bilateral lesions to the auditory temporal cortex, with consonant and dissonant music (Peretz *et al.* 2001). In fact, IR is unable to distinguish consonant from dissonant versions of the same musical excerpts in pleasantness judgments, although she is able to judge the 'happy–sad' character of the music. This is a striking disorder. Preference of consonant over dissonant music is widely shared by ordinary listeners, beginning with 4-month-old infants (see, for example, Trainor & Heinmiller 1998; Zentner & Kagan 1996). IR has lost this ability. Localization of the responsible damage cannot be easily determined in her brain. As can be seen in Fig. 5.3, IR's lesions are extensive and asymmetrically localized in her cerebral hemispheres. Therefore, it is not clear which of these damaged areas can be taken as responsible for the observed deficit in responding to dissonance. By combining information about IR's lesion localization with normal cerebral regions that are implicated in judging dissonance, we might be able to isolate the critical neural regions.

Therefore, we co-registered images of IR's brain with the activated brain regions found in normal brains. We found that the complex network involving paralimbic and neocortical regions associated with the affective evaluation of dissonance did not overlap with IR's lesions (see top panel B in Fig. 5.3). In contrast, significant overlap was found between IR's lesions and the pattern of activity elicited by all musical stimuli, irrespective of dissonance level (see bottom panel B in Fig. 5.3). The damaged areas in IR's brain coincided with the regions located in the superior temporal gyri that were involved in the perceptual analysis, including those related to dissonance, of the chord sequences in normal brains. Therefore, we can infer that the critical networks for dissonance appraisal are located bilaterally in the superior temporal gyri. Furthermore, we can ascribe IR's indifference to dissonance to a perceptual defect.

That IR's problem with dissonance lies at the perceptual level is consistent with a number of independent observations. First, in general, IR's emotional processes appear fairly normal. Second, the neural network specifically associated with emotional evaluation of dissonance, which involves the subcortical–frontal areas, seems largely spared in IR's brain. Third, IR was unable to discriminate the different versions of the same musical sequence that only differed in degrees of dissonance. Therefore, a plausible account of IR's lack of responsiveness to dissonance is simply that she does not perceive it. Had she perceived it correctly, she would have judged its emotional valence accordingly. If this interpretation is correct, affective responses to dissonance are mediated via an obligatory cortical perceptual relay.

In summary, the present findings suggest a particular functional architecture underlying emotional interpretation of music. Taken together, the results suggest that the musical input first reaches the superior temporal gyri, where perceptual organization is taking place. The perceptual output is then relayed to emotional systems in the paralimbic structures or more frontal areas, depending on its valence. This two-stage model suggests that emotion and perception are not taking place along two parallel and independent pathways as some models (LeDoux 2000; Zajonc 1984) posit. However, caution is required because this model only derives from the study of a single emotional dimension, relating dissonance to unpleasant judgments.

## 5.3 Fractionation of musical emotions

As seen with facial expressions, neuropsychological methods are most productive for dissecting emotions and their neural substrates into elementary components. Unfortunately, research has just begun with musical emotions. Hence, the power of the methods cannot be fully appreciated in the musical domain. In what follows, I will raise a few questions that, I believe, are important to address using neuropsychological methods. Since these questions do not have an answer yet, their outlining should be regarded as guidelines for future research.

### 5.3.1 Single or multiple emotional systems for music?

In theory, lesion studies and functional brain imagery should provide evidence regarding the possibility that there is not a single but multiple emotional systems that can be aroused by music, depending on its content. Although parsimonious, the notion of a single emotional system is difficult to hold given the diversity of emotions and their differential functionality for the organism. This was illustrated earlier with the neuropsychological separation of fear from disgust with regard to facial expressions. The problem with musical emotions is that their functionality is not settled, and *a fortiori* the principles along which musical emotions may fractionate remain open. But neuropsychology may, in principle, provide relevant cues.

For example, there are indications that musical emotions can be studied in relative isolation from each other. The 'happy–sad' character of music can be studied independently from a valence ('pleasant–unpleasant') dimension. As shown in the study of IR, discrimination of happiness and sadness in music can be preserved in the presence of a lost sensitivity to dissonance. Although this dissociation has a perceptual rather than an emotional origin, it highlights one clear advantage of studying musical emotions over other domains, such as facial and vocal expressions. In music, it is easier to manipulate structural characteristics systematically so that the same music can express different emotions gradually. For example, tempo increase and decrease are easy to apply without altering other aspects of the musical structure (e.g. Gagnon & Peretz 2001, within certain limits). We can also manipulate two emotional dimensions orthogonally, as previously done with the same set of stimuli, by modifying mode (from major to minor and vice versa) and dissonance, independently (Peretz *et al.* 2001). There is such a close relationship between structural characteristics and certain emotional expressions in music that the domain lends itself to experimentation. This is hardly a new finding (see Gabrielsson & Lindström, this volume; Juslin, this volume). Yet, it is often overlooked in the literature.

Finally, musical emotions present interesting peculiarities. Sadness in music is a good example. It is pleasurable in music while perceived as unpleasant in most other channels. By studying the neural correlates of certain musical emotions, like sadness, the generalization and neuropsychological validity of various taxonomies of emotions can be advantageously tested. It may turn out that some musical emotions are unlike any other type of emotion. If that is the case, the evidence will in all likelihood come from neuropsychology, since the discipline is perfectly suited to reveal functional specificity.

### 5.3.2 Are emotional systems domain-specific?

As indirectly suggested, musical emotions might differ from other emotions in numerous aspects. However, there is as yet no theoretical or empirical reason for assuming such specificity. Inversely, musical emotions are frequently compared to vocal expressions (Juslin, this volume), with the idea that the two expressive channels may derive ontogenetically and phylogenetically from a unique and common mode of communication. In this context, it may seem curious that up to now I have only considered the advances made in the domain of facial expressions. The reason is simply that progress has been much slower in the domain of vocal expressions of emotions.

Perhaps vocal expressions of emotions have not yet received sufficient theoretical attention (but see Johnstone & Scherer 2000, for a recent summary of promising findings). Despite the obvious biological significance of vocal emotions, there is no consensus over an evolutionary-based theory of it. This lack of theoretical development, compared to, say, the domain of facial expressions, might in turn explain why the topic of vocal expressions has had a limited impact in the recent shaping of the neuropsychology of emotions. This is certainly not due to lack of interest. The literature is abundant, as summarized below.

*Vocal emotions: neural correlates*

Just as musical expressions of emotions can be conveyed by variations in pitch and articulation, emotions can be expressed by modulations of the tone of the voice.

Emotion expressions through vocal sounds can take two different forms in humans. It can be conveyed by the tone of voice in speaking or by non-verbal expressions such as in laughing, crying, and screaming. There has been a greater interest in the first category of vocal expressions, and it is usually referred to as *affective prosody*. However, there is as yet no empirical or theoretical basis for distinguishing these two classes of vocal expressions of emotions, and thus they will not be treated separately in what follows.

The most remarkable neuropsychological property of the system underlying both kinds of vocal expressions of emotions is its specificity. The neural system appears highly specialized, both functionally and neuroanatomically. Firstly, despite the obvious link between facial and vocal expression of emotions, emotional evaluation of the tone of voices is dissociable from the emotional evaluation of faces. Some patients can infer the emotional tone of vocal expressions but not of facial expressions, whereas others show the opposite pattern (e.g. Hornak *et al.* 1996). This dissociation is not due to differences related to the modality of input, because the patient's ability to process other aspects of faces and voices is spared. The separability of vocal from facial emotions is impressive, given that they typically signal emotions in a consistent manner at any given time. Yet, the two modes of expressions seem to be captured by independent neural systems.[1]

Secondly, within the speech signal, the recognition of vocal cues that are emotionally meaningful is clearly dissociable from the recognition of vocal cues that are semantically informative. As mentioned previously, Jackson (1878) was the first to notice the separability of affective prosody from propositional speech. The distinction has been made several times in perception as well. For example, in dichotic listening studies with normal adults, Ley and Bryden (1982) have found a left ear (right hemisphere) advantage for the perception of the emotional tone of voice, and a right ear (left hemisphere) superiority for the recognition of the actual content of the words from the same set of sentences. Similarly, patients who can no longer understand speech, but who are still able to infer the emotion conveyed by vocal cues, have been reported (e.g. Barrett *et al.* 1999). These findings show that emotional processing of speech signals can take different routes, one determined by semantic content and one determined by vocal form.

Finally, the tone of the voice is not analysed just for affective purposes. Prosodic cues can provide important person-specific information (e.g. identity, age, and sex) and linguistic, non-semantic information (i.e. differentiating a question from a statement). Once again, the use of these non-affective cues can dissociate from their emotional use. Brain lesions can interfere with the identification of vocal emotions of happiness, sadness, and fear and spare the identification of prosodic differences marking questions, exclamations, and assertions in spoken sentences (e.g. Heilman *et al.* 1984). Similarly, functional imaging of neurologically intact brains points to the involvement of distinct neural regions in the recognition of emotions and of the speaker's identity in spoken sentences (Imaizumi *et al.* 1997). Together, these findings highlight the fine tuning and specialization of the neural system underlying the emotional interpretation of vocal sounds.

--------------------------------------------------------------------------------

[1] This conclusion requires more systematic work, realized in more comparable testing situations. Computer facilities allow the testing of participants with dynamic events where facial expressions and vocal emissions can be studied jointly. To my knowledge, such testing situations have not yet been exploited with brain-damaged patients or with functional brain imaging.

This highly specific system mostly recruits cortical structures of the right hemisphere. Right hemispheric lateralization has been frequently reported after the seminal work of Heilman and collaborators (1975) in brain-damaged patients (for a review, see Etcoff 1989). It has been observed in normal listeners tested either with laterality paradigms (e.g. Ley & Bryden 1982), as described above, or with functional brain-imaging techniques (e.g. George *et al.* 1996; but see Morris *et al.* 1999, for negative findings relative to hemispheric asymmetry). Within the right hemisphere, and at times in the left hemisphere as well, various cortical and subcortical structures have been identified as contributing to the emotional evaluation of vocal sounds. These structures are the temporal cortex, the insula, the basal ganglia, the caudate nucleus, and the ventral prefrontal cortex (for example, for recent brain-imaging data, see Morris *et al.* 1999, and for recent lesion data, see Hornak *et al.* 1996). Thus, the neural basis of vocal emotions appears rather distributed and complex. Specification of the role of each contributing structure remains a task for the future.

Nevertheless, it is worth noting that attempts to find evidence for the involvement of the amygdala have been negative (Adolphs & Tranel 1999; Anderson & Phelps 1998; but see also Scott *et al.* 1997). Patients with selective bilateral damage to the amygdala, who show evidence of impaired recognition of fear in faces, show preserved recognition of fearful voices. This lack of convergence in recruiting the amygdala across non-verbal communication channels in response to danger is consistent with the general conclusion that the vocal emotional system is subserved by distinct neural structures.

### Are vocal emotions separable from musical emotions?

Because the neural organization underlying the recognition of vocal expression of emotions appears highly specialized, I find it difficult to conceive how it might also serve musical emotions. However, this is a highly speculative and controversial issue. Juslin (this volume) argues that if the neural circuitry used in the recognition of emotion in vocal expression is used also in music, it can be only for those aspects of music's expressiveness that are common to speech and musical performance, that is, cues like speed, intensity, and timbre. However, music's expressiveness does not derive solely from such cues, but also from intrinsic sources of emotion (cf. Sloboda & Juslin, this volume) having to do with the internal structure (e.g. harmonic progression), and so it would not be surprising to find that perception of musical emotions involves neural substrates over and above those involved in the perception of vocal expressions. Panksepp (1995) sees similarities in the emotional 'chills' evoked by sad music and those engendered by 'distress calls' of young children and animals. Yet, Blood and collaborators (1999*b*) suggested the implication of the septum, a region typically associated with pleasure, in emotional 'chills' for self-selected music. In any case, neuropsychological methods are ideally suited for comparing vocal and musical emotions. As a result of advances in neuroscientific procedures and improved digital-processing techniques, findings obtained in the coming years should prove especially informative for our understanding of emotional processing through the vocal and musical channel.

### 5.3.4 Is emotion recognition dissociable from emotion experience?

A crucial question that I have left for the end is to what extent all the evidence reviewed in prior sections is related to emotional experience. What was said above mainly derived from tasks requiring emotion recognition, rather than emotion experience. Thus, results may just reflect emotional knowledge, not felt emotions. In theory, all emotions, including fear, may be perceived, recognized, known, described, and mimicked, without being felt. I can see fear in the face displayed on the screen, I can recognize that the Albinoni's adagio expresses sadness in an exquisite manner. Yet, it may leave me cold, particularly in impoverished experimental settings that are of typical use in current research. In this perspective, the study of emotions remains 'cognitivist', contributing little to the building of affective neuroscience as a new discipline.

The debate around the separability of emotion recognition from emotion experience has a long history in the musical domain (cf. Cook & Dibben, this volume). Although the problem seems easy to conceptualize, it is difficult to solve empirically. One solution is to exploit more 'objective' or 'direct' measures of emotions. By objective measures, it is generally meant those measures that cannot be under the voluntary control of the subject. The measures typically pertain to the domain of psychophysiology. In fact, it is well established that emotions are accompanied by physiological changes that occur automatically without voluntary control. It takes talent or intensive training to control physiological expressions of emotions. Musical emotion is no exception. Music may be particularly powerful in eliciting such changes, particularly 'chills' or 'shivers' (e.g. Goldstein 1980). More commonly, music can elicit changes in heart beat, electrodermal responses, respiration, skin temperature, etc. (e.g. Krumhansl 1997). A review of physiological changes is provided by Scherer and Zentner (this volume; see also Bartlett 1999).

Physiological measures do not solve all problems, however. They have their own limitations. First, their 'objectivity' should not be equated with 'specificity'. Just because physiological changes occur without voluntary control this does not mean that they reveal emotions unequivocally. Physiological measures are notorious for their lack of selectivity in addition to their limited sensitivity (e.g. it is common to reject half the subjects because they are 'non-responders'). Physiological changes do not easily discriminate among emotions. For instance, different types of music (happy, sad, fearful) may all produce physiological changes, but the changes may be in the same direction compared with baseline (Krumhansl 1997; but see Nyklicek *et al.* 1997, for a recent example where physiological measures did discriminate among emotions). Nevertheless, physiological changes represent an interesting complement to other brain-related measurements of emotion. Convergence of measurements is highly desirable, probably more in the emotional domain than in any other field.

Does this mean that if we combine behavioural judgments with physiological measurements and both converge, we can safely conclude that the emotion under study was not only recognized but also experienced? Probably. However, the setting is costly in terms of sample size and of technological sophistication. Fortunately, there are other solutions worthy of investigation. One promising alternative is to study emotions *indirectly* or implicitly.

Musical emotions have been typically studied in a direct and explicit way, by asking listeners to judge, label, or categorize music in emotional terms, or by inviting performers to interpret a musical piece with a particular emotion. The impact of musical emotions is rarely assessed indirectly by the way it affects other tasks or behaviours, without awareness. There are different means to probe emotional judgments indirectly. One procedure that has been successfully used with facial expressions was to require a gender decision (e.g. 'Is this a face of a woman or of a man?', which can be difficult to answer when hair and accessories are removed from the picture). The key variable was that some of the faces displayed an emotion, such as fear or disgust, with various degrees of intensity. The indirect influence of the facial expression can then be measured in a graded fashion on both the timing of the gender decision and the resulting changes in cerebral blood flow as measured by functional brain imagery (for a review of their work done with this procedure, see Dolan & Morris 2000).

The advantage of indirect measurement is that emotional responding is studied as a spontaneous, automatic response of the organism. This is what emotions are: spontaneous responses that are difficult to disguise and that may occur without awareness. However, the question is to what extent these spontaneous responses arise from the operation of the same mechanisms as those implicated in emotional judgments or rather reflect the functioning of different systems. Curiously, this question of consciousness, which has been addressed in various domains such as memory and face recognition, has as yet attracted little attention in affective neuroscience.

My intuition, and experience as illustrated below, is that musical emotions typically occur without consciousness or willingness. For example, a few years ago, I felt obliged to accompany a friend to a Broadway show, featuring 'Mrs Butterfly'. I do not like those shows; I find them boring and caricatural. Yet, at the end of the show, I found myself in tears. The show was not of any better quality than any other one, I found. However, my disliking was probably a cultural response, whereas my emotional reaction was a biological reflex.

To summarize, it is possible, at least in theory, that emotions can be recognized without being experienced. To bypass this problem, one can take different routes. These include brain-related and physiological measurements but also consideration of *indirect* measures. There is an obvious need to go beyond conventional means of studying emotions.

## 5.4 Other issues related to musical emotions

There are a number of issues related to the neural correlates of musical emotions that have not been addressed in this chapter because of insufficient relevant data. One of these issues is the possible exploitation of *neurochemical correlates* of musical emotions. Neurochemicals are neurotransmitters and hormones that alter the response properties of sets of neurons. Music is apparently effective in eliciting such responses, as suggested by the action of the antagonists of endorphins (Goldstein 1980) and cortisol measures (Trehub 2001). The study of these neurochemicals would provide yet another neuropsychological avenue to better understanding of the nature and brain organization of musical emotions (for reviews, see Buck 1999; Panksepp 1998).

A completely different neurological condition that can help in understanding the nature of musical emotions is the study of individuals suffering from *autism* and *Williams' syndrome*. Both disorders are usually associated with intellectual deficiency and a relatively high level of musical proficiency (Don *et al.* 1999; Levitin & Bellugi 1998; Miller 1989). However, the two disorders diverge in several ways. The most apparent distinctive feature concerns sociability. Autistic individuals are socially handicapped, avoiding contacts and interactions with others. In contrast, individuals with Williams' syndrome are very friendly and avid of social exchanges. Since both forms of neurological disorders spare musical skills to a large extent, it would be interesting to compare the consequences of the two disorders for the ability to recognize and express musical emotions.

My prediction is that only individuals with Williams' syndrome, not autistic individuals who are matched for cognitive and musical skills, will be able to interpret music emotionally. Specifically, music is above all seen as a function serving social ends. Because autistic individuals are handicapped at this level,[2] it seems reasonable to expect them to have failed to develop an emotionally responsive system for music. Music would have a different meaning for autistic individuals. Although music performance by 'musical savants' has been qualified at times as 'mechanical' (Mottron *et al.* 1999; Sloboda *et al.* 1985), it has never been experimentally assessed. The only empirical study that has been undertaken in relation to musical emotions in autism has reported negative results (Heaton *et al.* 1999). That is, autistic children were found to be able to distinguish musical excerpts as 'happy' or 'sad'. However, performance was generally poor in that study and measured in a single test. Further investigation is worth undertaking, preferably by coupling different types of measurements, as advocated earlier.

## 5.5 Conclusion

The neuropsychology of musical emotions is in its infancy. One of the most vexing issues in this respect is the lack of consensus of what music is for (see, for example, Sloboda & O'Neill, this volume). Knowing better the functionality of music would certainly help neuroscientists to identify the musical emotions that are most probably hard-wired in the brain. Nevertheless, this lack of knowledge has not prevented researchers from making progress in understanding what are the neural bases underlying both our intuitions of what emotions are and what music appreciation might be.

The current evidence is pointing to the existence of a specific neural arrangement for certain musical emotions, such as happiness and sadness. It is also apparent that there is not a single, unitary emotional system underlying all emotional responses to music. For instance, most of the neural pathway underlying pleasantness judgments as related to consonance has been delineated, and involves a complex and distributed system in the brain. Yet, this pleasant-consonant pathway is distinguishable from the happy–sad

---

[2] One collorary assumption is that music deprivation should lead to social deficiencies. This prediction might be difficult to test since music deprivation almost never occurs. Even deaf individuals manage to dance based on what they can perceive as musical.

neural system. Finally, both forms of emotional judgments require cortical mediation and confirm recent conceptualization of emotions as being subserved by evolved brain structures.

Important advances are to be expected in the near future. This progress will be mostly due to the flourishing of new brain-imaging techniques, but will also reflect the new interest in the domain of emotions in neuroscience. The motivation for understanding the biological foundations of music is also currently high in the scientific community (see, for instance, the two target articles bearing on the biology of music in *Science*, 5 January 2001). There is increasing awareness of the social value of music, particularly with respect to its effectiveness in communicating emotions. Nowadays, music plays an even more powerful and unique role in human life than ever, with wide-ranging effects on many aspects of functioning besides its obvious social function. Music has become such a key element in the human behavioural repertoire that it might be considered as a defining human attribute. In fact, music is so highly valued that very few people are willing to acknowledge a lack of emotional responsiveness to music.[3]

# References

Adolphs, R., Damasio, H., Tranel, D., & Damasio, A. (1996). Cortical systems for the recognition of emotion in facial expressions. *Journal of Neuroscience*, 16, 7678–87.

Adolphs, R. & Tranel, D. (1999). Intact recognition of emotional prosody following amygdala damage. *Neuropsychologia*, 37, 1285–92.

Adolphs, R., Tranel, D., Damasio, H., & Damasio, A. (1994). Impaired recognition of emotion in facial expressions following bilateral damage to the human amygdala. *Nature*, 372, 669–72.

Adolphs, R., Tranel, D., Damasio, H., & Damasio, A. (1995). Fear and the human amygdala. *Journal of Neuroscience*, 15, 5879–92.

Anderson, A. & Phelps, E. (1998). Intact recognition of vocal expressions of fear following bilateral lesions of the human amygdala. *Neuroreport*, 9, 3607–13.

Balkwill, L.-L. & Thompson, W. F. (1999). A cross-cultural investigation of the perception of emotion in music: Psychophysical and cultural cues. *Music Perception*, 17, 43–64.

Barrett, A., Crucian, G., Raymer, A., & Heilman, K. (1999). Spared comprehension of emotional prosody in a patient with global aphasia. *Neuropsychiatry, Neuropsychology and Behavioral Neurology*, 12, 117–20.

Bartlett, D. (1999). Physiological responses to music and sound stimuli. In *Handbook of music psychology*, (ed. D. Hodges), pp. 343–85. San Antonio, TX: IMR Press.

Bechara, A., Tranel, D., Damasio, H., Adolphs, R., Rockland, C., & Damasio, A. (1995). Double dissociation of conditioning and declarative knowledge relative to the amygdala and hippocampus in humans. *Science*, 269, 1115–18.

Besson, M. (1997). Electrophysiological studies of music processing. In *Perception and cognition of music*, (ed. I. Deliège & J. A. Sloboda), pp. 217–50. Hove, UK: Psychology Press.

---

[3]  I wish to acknowledge the assistance of Nathalie Gosselin and Daniel Saumier in creating the figures. My research summarized in this chapter has been supported by research grants from the Natural Sciences and Engineering Research Council of Canada and from the Canadian Institutes of Health Research.

Best, C., Womer, J., & Queen, H. (1994). Hempispheric asymmetries in adults' perception of infant emotional expressions. *Journal of Experimental Psychology: Human Perception and Performance*, 20, 751–65.

Blair, R., Morris, J., Frith, C., Perrett, D., & Dolan, R. (1999). Dissociable neural responses to facial expressions of sadness and anger. *Brain*, 122, 883–93.

Blood, A., Zatorre, R., Bermudez, P., & Evans, A. (1999*a*). Emotional responses to pleasant and unpleasant music correlate with activity in paralimbic brain regions. *Nature Neuroscience*, 2, 382–7.

Blood, A., Zatorre, R., & Evans, A. (1999*b*). Intensely pleasant emotional responses to music correlate with CBF modulation in paralimbic and other subcortical brain regions. *Society of Neuroscience Abstracts*, 25, 2146.

Bowers, D., Bauer, R., & Heilman, K. (1993). The nonverbal affect lexicon: Theoretical perspectives from neuropsychological studies of affect perception. *Neuropsychology*, 7, 433–44.

Breiter, H., Etcoff, N., Whalen, P., Kennedy, W., Rauch, S., Buckner, R. *ET AL.* (1996). Response and habituation of the human amygdala during visual processing of facial expression. *Neuron*, 17, 875–87.

Broca, P. (1861). Remarques sur le siège de la faculté du langage articulé, suivies d'une observation d'aphémie (Perte de la parole) [Remarks on the seat of the faculty of articulate language, followed by an observation of aphemia]. *Bulletin de la Société Anatomique*, 6, 330–57.

Broca, P. (1878) Anatomie comparée des circonvolutions cérébrales. *Revue d'Anthopologie*, 1, 385–498.

Broks, P., Young, A., Maratos, E., Coffey, P., Calder, A., Isaac, C. *ET AL.* (1998). Face processing impairments after encephalitis: Amygdala damage and recognition of fear. *Neuropsychologia*, 36, 59–70.

Brown, S. (2000). The 'musilanguage' model of music evolution. In *The origins of music*, (ed. N. Wallin, B. Merker, & S. Brown), pp. 271–300. Cambridge, MA: MIT Press.

Bryden, P., Ley, R., & Sugerman, J. (1982). A left-ear advantage for identifying the emotional quality of tonal sequences. *Neuropsychologia*, 20, 83–7.

Buck, R. (1999). The biological affects: A typology. *Psychological Review*, 106, 301–36.

Buss, D., Haselton, M., Shackelford, T., Bleske, A., & Wakelfield, J. (1998). Adaptations, exaptations, and sprandels. *American Psychologist*, 53, 533–48.

Calder, A., Young, A., Rowland, D., Perrett, D., Hodges, J., & Etcoff, N. (1996). Facial emotion recognition after bilateral amygdala damage: Differentially severe impairment of fear. *Cognitive Neuropsychology*, 13, 699–745.

Cunningham, J. G. & Sterling, R. S. (1988). Developmental change in the understanding of affective meaning in music. *Motivation and Emotion*, 12, 399–413.

Dalla Bella, S., Peretz, I., Rousseau, L., & Gosselin, N. (2001). A developmental study of the affective value of tempo and mode in music. *Cognition*, 80, B1–B10.

Damasio, A. (1994). *Descartes' error: Emotion, reason, and the human brain*. New York: Avon Books.

Darwin, C. (1871). *The descent of man, and selection in relation to sex*. London: John Murray.

Darwin, C. (1872). *The expression of the emotions in man and animals*. London: John Murray (reprinted Chicago: University of Chicago Press, 1965).

Davidson, R. J. (1992). Emotion and affective style: Hemispheric substrates. *Psychological Science*, 3, 39–43.

Davidson, R. J. & Irwin, W. (1999). The functional neuroanatomy of emotion and affective style. *Trends in Cognitive Sciences*, **3**, 11–21.

Davis, M. (1992). The role of the amygdala in fear and anxiety. *Annual Review of Neuroscience*, **15**, 353–75.

Dolan, R. & Morris, J. (2000) The functional anatomy of innate and acquired fear: Perspectives from neuroimaging. In *Cognitive neuroscience of emotion*, (ed. R. Lane & L. Nadel), pp. 225–41. New York: Oxford University Press.

Dolgin, K. G. & Adelson, E. H. (1990). Age changes in the ability to interpret affect in sung and instrumentally-presented melodies. *Psychology of Music*, **18**, 87–98.

Don, A., Schellenberg, E.G., & Rourke, B. (1999). Music and language skills of children with Williams syndrome. *Child Neuropsychology*, **5**, 154–70.

Edmister. W., Talavage, T., Ledden, P., & Wesikoff, R. (1999). Improved auditory cortex imaging using clustered volume acquisitions. *Human Brain Mapping*, **7**, 89–97.

Eibl-Eibesfeldt, I. (1973). The expressive behaviors of the deaf-and-blind-born. In *Social communication and movement*, (ed. M. von Cranach & I. Vine), pp. 163–94. New York: Academic Press.

Ekman, P. (1994) All emotions are basic. In *The nature of emotions. Fundamental questions*, (ed. P. Ekman & R. J. Davidson), pp. 15–19. New York: Oxford University Press.

Ekman, P., Friesen, W., O'Sullivan, M., Chan, A., Diacoyanni-Tarlatzis, I., Heider, K. ET AL. (1987). Universals and cultural differences in the judgments of facial expressions of emotion. *Journal of Personality and Social Psychology*, **53**, 712–17.

Ekman, P., Sorenson, E., & Friesen, W. (1969). Pan-cultural elements in facial displays of emotions. *Science*, **164**, 86–8.

Etcoff, N. (1984). Selective attention to facial identity and facial emotion. *Neuropsychologia*, **22**, 281–95.

Etcoff, N. (1989). Asymmetries in recognition of emotion. In *Handbook of neuropsychology*, (Vol. 3) (ed. F. Boller & J. Grafman), pp. 363–82. New York: Elsevier.

Field, T., Woodson, R., Greenberg, R., & Cohen, D. (1982). Discrimination and imitation of facial expressions by neonates. *Science*, **218**, 179–81.

Gabrielsson, A. & Juslin, P. N. (1996). Emotional expression in music performance: Between the performer's intention and the listener's experience. *Psychology of Music*, **24**, 68–91.

Gagnon, L. & Peretz, I. (2000). Laterality effects in processing tonal and atonal melodies with affective and non-affective task instructions. *Brain and Cognition*, **43**, 206–10.

Gagnon, L. & Peretz, I. (2001). Mode and tempo relative contributions to 'happy–sad' judgments in equitone melodies. *Cognition and Emotion*, (forthcoming).

George, M., Parekh, P., Rosinsky, N., Ketter, T., Kimbrell, T., Heilman, K. ET AL. (1996). Understanding emotional prosody activates right hemisphere regions. *Archives of Neurology*, **53**, 665–70.

Gerardi, G. M. & Gerken, L. (1995). The development of affective response to modality and melodic contour. *Music Perception*, **12**, 279–90.

Goldstein, A. (1980). Thrills in response to music and other stimuli. *Physiological Psychology*, **8**, 126–9.

Gray, J., Young, A., Barker, W., Curtis, A., & Gibson, D. (1997). Impaired recognition of disgust in Huntington's disease gene carriers. *Brain*, **120**, 2029–38.

Gregory, A., Worral, L., & Sarge, A. (1996). The development of emotional responses to music in young children. *Motivation and Emotion*, **20**, 341–9.

Halgren, E., Walter, R., Cherlow, D., & Crandall, P. (1978). Mental phenomena evoked by electrical stimulation of the human hippocampal formation and amygdala. *Brain*, 101, 83–117.

Hamann, S., Stefanicci, L., Squire, L., Adolphs, R., Tranel, D., Damasio, H. *ET AL.* (1996). Recognizing facial emotion. *Nature*, 379, 497.

Hasselmo, M., Rolls, E., & Baylis, G. (1989). The role of expression and identity in the face-selective responses of neurons in the temporal visual cortex of the monkey. *Behavioural Brain Research*, 32, 203–18.

Heaton, P., Hermelin, B., & Pring, L. (1999). Can children with autistic spectrum disorders perceive affect in music? An experimental investigation. *Psychological Medicine*, 29, 1405–10.

Heilman, K., Bowers, D., Speedie, L., & Coslett, H. (1984). Comprehension of affective and non-affective prosody. *Neurology*, 34, 917–21.

Heilman, K., Scholes, R., & Watson, R. (1975). Auditory affective agnosia. *Journal of Neurology, Neurosurger and Psychiatry*, 38, 69–72.

Hornak, J., Rolls, E., & Wade, D. (1996). Face and voice expression identification in patients with emotional and behavioral changes following ventral frontal lobe damage. *Neuropsychologia*, 34, 247–61.

Imaizumi, S., Mori, K., Kiritani, S., Kawashima, R., Sugiura, M., Fukuda, H. *ET AL.* (1997). Vocal identification of speaker and emotion activates different brain regions. *Neuroreport*, 8, 2809–12.

Izard, C. (1971). *The face of emotions*. New York: Appleton-Century-Crofts.

Jackson, J. (1878). On the affections of speech from disease of the brain. *Brain*, 1, 304–30.

Johnstone, T. & Scherer, K. R. (2000). Vocal communication of emotion. In *Handbook of emotions*, (2nd edn) (ed. M. Lewis & J. M. Haviland-Jones), pp. 220–35. New York: Guilford Press.

Kastner, M. P. & Crowder, R. G. (1990) Perception of the major/minor distinction: IV. Emotional connotations in young children. *Music Perception*, 8, 189–202.

Kivy, P. (1990). *Music alone. Philosophical reflections on the purely musical experience*. Ithaca, NY: Cornell University Press.

Kogan, N. (1994). On aesthetics and its origins: Some psychobiological and evolutionary considerations. *Social Research*, 61, 139–65.

Kratus, J. (1993). A developmental study of children's interpretation of emotion in music. *Psychology of Music*, 21, 3–19.

Krumhansl, C. L. (1997). An exploratory study of musical emotions and psychophysiology. *Canadian Journal of Experimental Psychology*, 51, 336–53.

LeDoux, J. (1996). *The emotional brain*. New York: Simon & Schuster.

LeDoux, J. (2000). Cognitive–emotional interactions: Listen to the brain. In *Cognitive neuroscience of emotion*, (ed. R. Lane & L. Nadel), pp. 129–55. New York: Oxford University Press.

Levitin, D. & Bellugi, U. (1998). Musical abilities in individuals with Williams' syndrome. *Music Perception*, 15, 357–90.

Ley, R. & Bryden, P. (1982). A dissociation of right and left hemispheric effects for recognizing emotional tone and verbal content. *Brain and Cognition*, 1, 3–9.

Marin, O. & Perry, D. (1999). Neurological aspects of music perception and performance. In *The psychology of music*, (2nd edn) (ed. D. Deutsch), pp. 653–724. San Diego, CA: Academic Press.

Masataka, N. (1999). Preference for infant-directed singing in 2-day-old hearing infants of deaf parents. *Developmental Psychology*, 35, 1001–5.

Mazzoni, M., Moretti, P., Pardossi, L., Vista, M., Muratorio, A., & Pugliolo, M. (1993). A case of music imperception. *Journal of Neurology, Neurosurgery and Psychiatry*, 56, 322–4.

Mazzuchi, A., Marchini, C., Budai, R., & Parma, M. (1982). A case of receptive amusia with prominent timbre perception defect. *Journal of Neurology, Neurosurgery and Psychiatry*, 45, 644–7.

Miller, G. (2000). Evolution of human music through sexual selection. In *The origins of music*, (ed. N. Wallin, B. Merker, & S. Brown), pp. 329–60. Cambridge, MA: MIT Press.

Miller, L. (1989). *Musical savants. Exceptional skill in the mentally retarded*. Hillsdale, NJ: Erlbaum.

Morris, J., Frith, C., Perrett, D., Rowland, D., Young, A., Calder, A., & Dolan, R. (1996). A differential neural response in the human amygdala to fearful and happy facial expressions. *Nature*, 383, 812–15.

Morris, J., Scott, S., & Dolan, R. (1999). Saying with feeling: Neural responses to emotional vocalizations. *Neuropsychologia*, 37, 1155–63.

Mottron, L., Peretz, I., Belleville, S., & Rouleau, N. (1999). Absolute pitch in autism: A case-study. *Neurocase*, 5, 485–501.

Neisser, U. (1967). *Cognitive psychology*. New York: Appleton-Century-Crofts.

Nyklicek, I., Thayer, J. F., & van Doornen, L. J. P. (1997). Cardiorespiratory differentiation of musically-induced emotions. *Journal of Psychophysiology*, 11, 304–21.

Oster, H. & Ekman, P. (1978). Facial behavior in child development. In *Minnesota Symposia on Child Psychology*, (Vol. 11) (ed. W. Collins), pp. 231–76. Hilldsdale, NJ: Erlbaum.

Panksepp, J. (1995). The emotional sources of 'chills' induced by music. *Music Perception*, 13, 171–208.

Panksepp, J. (1998). *Affective neuroscience*. New York: Oxford University Press.

Papez, J. (1937). A proposed mechanism for emotion. *Archives of Neurology and Psychiatry*, 38, 725–43.

Parry, F., Young, A., Saul, J. S., & Moss, A. (1991). Dissociable face processing impairments after brain injury. *Journal of Clinical and Experimental Neuropsychology*, 13, 545–58.

Peretz, I. (1996). Can we lose memories for music? The case of music agnosia in a nonmusician. *Journal of Cognitive Neurosciences*, 8, 481–96.

Peretz, I. (2001a). Music perception and recognition. In *The handbook of cognitive neuropsychology*, (ed. B. Rapp), pp. 519–40. Hove, UK: Psychology Press.

Peretz, I. (2001b). Brain specialization for music: New evidence from congenital amusia. *Annals of the New York Academy of Sciences*, 930, 153–156.

Peretz, I., Belleville, S., & Fontaine, F. S. (1997). Dissociations entre musique et langage après atteinte cérébrale: Un nouveau cas d'amusie sans aphasie. *Revue Canadienne de Psychologie Expérimentale*, 51, 354–67. [Dissociation between music and language after brain damage: a new case of the amusia without aphasia. *Canadian Journal of Experimental Psychology*.]

Peretz, I, Blood, A., Penhune, V., & Zatorre, R. (2001). Cortical deafness to dissonance. *Brain*, 124, 928–940.

Peretz, I. & Gagnon, L. (1999). Dissociation between recognition and emotional judgment for melodies. *Neurocase*, 5, 21–30.

Peretz, I., Gagnon, L., & Bouchard, B. (1998a). Music and emotion: Perceptual determinants, immediacy, and isolation after brain damage. *Cognition*, 68, 111–41.

Peretz, I., Gaudreau, D., & Bonnel, A.-M. (1998b). Exposure effects on music preference and recognition. *Memory and Cognition*, 26, 884–902.

Phillips, M., Young, A., Senior, C., Brammer, M., Andrew, C., Calder, A. *et al.* (1997). A specific neural substrate for perceiving facial expressions of disgust. *Nature*, 389, 495–8.

Pinker, S. (1997). *How the mind works*. New York: Norton.

Rapp, B. (ed.) (2001). *The handbook of cognitive neuropsychology. What deficits reveal about the human mind*. Philadelphia, PA: Psychology Press.

Schmidt, L. & Trainor, L. (2001). *Frontal brain electrical activity (EEG) distinguishes valence and intensity of musical emotions*. Manuscript submitted for publication.

Scott, S., Young, A., Calder, A., Hellawell, D., Aggleton, J., & Johnson, M. (1997). Impaired auditory recognition of fear and anger following bilateral amygdala lesions. *Nature*, 385, 254–7.

Sernagor, E. & Grzywacz, M. (1996). Influence of spontaneous activity and visual experience on developing retinal receptive fields. *Current Biology*, 6, 1503–8.

Sergent, J., Ohta, S., MacDonald, B., & Zuck, E. (1994). Segregated processing of facial identity and emotion in the human brain: A PET study. *Visual Cognition*, 1, 349–69.

Shammi, P. & Stuss, D. (1999). Humour appreciation: A role of the right frontal lobe. *Brain*, 122, 657–66.

Sloboda, J. A., Hermelin, B., & O'Connor, N. (1985). An exceptional musical memory. *Music Perception*, 3, 155–70.

Sprengelmeyer, R., Young, A., Calder, A., Karnat, A., Lange, H., Hömberg, V. *et al.* (1996). Loss of disgust: Perception of faces and emotion in Huntington's disease. *Brain*, 119, 1647–65.

Terwogt, M. M. & van Grinsven, F. (1988). Recognition of emotions in music by children and adults. *Perceptual and Motor Skills*, 67, 697–8.

Terwogt, M. M. & van Grinsven, F. (1991) Musical expression of moodstates. *Psychology of Music*, 19, 99–109.

Trainor, L., Clark, E., Huntley, A., & Adams, B. (1997). The acoustic basis of preferences for infant-directed singing. *Infant Behavior and Development*, 20, 383–96.

Trainor L. & Heinmiller, B. (1998). The development of evaluative responses to music: Infants prefer to listen to consonance over dissonance. *Infant Behavior and Development*, 21, 77–88.

Tranel, D., Damasio, A., & Damasio, H. (1988). Intact recognition of facial expression, gender and age in patients with impaired recognition of face identity. *Neurology*, 38, 690–6.

Trehub, S. (2001). Music predispositions in infancy. *Annals of the New York Academy of Sciences*, 930, 1–16.

Trehub, S. & Trainor, L. (1998). Singing to infants: Lullabies and play songs. In *Advances in infancy research*, (ed. C. Rovee-Collier), pp. 43–77. Greenwich, CT: Ablex.

Tsang, C., Trainor, L., Santesso, D., Tasker, S., & Schmidt, L. (2001). Frontal EEG responses as a function of affective musical features. *Annals of the New York Academy of Sciences*, 930, 439–442.

Wallin, N., Merker, B., & Brown, S. (ed.) (2000). *The origins of music*. Cambridge, MA: MIT Press.

Whalen, P., Rauch, S., Etcoff, N., McInerney, S., Lee, M., & Jenike, M. (1998). Masked presentations of emotional facial expressions modulate amygdala activity without explicit knowledge. *Journal of Neuroscience*, 18, 411–18.

Young, A., Aggleton, J., Hellawell, D., Johnson, M., Broks, P., & Hanley, J. (1995). Face processing impairments after amygdalotomy. *Brain*, 118, 15–24.

Young, A., Newcombe, F., de Haan, E., Small, M., & Hay, D. (1993). Face perception after brain injury. Selective impairments affecting identity and expression. *Brain*, 116, 941–59.

Zald, D., Lee, J., Fluegel, K., & Pardo, J. (1998). Aversive gustator stimulation activates limbic circuits in humans. *Brain*, 121, 1143–54.

Zajonc, R. (1984) On the primacy of affect. In *Approaches to emotion*, (ed. K. R. Scherer & P. Ekman), pp. 259–70. Hillsdale, NJ: Erlbaum.

Zentner, M. R. & Kagan, J. (1996). Perception of music by infants. *Nature*, 383, 29.

# CHAPTER 6

# ANTHROPOLOGICAL PERSPECTIVES ON MUSIC AND EMOTION

JUDITH BECKER

The study of anthropology is the study of the modes of being human, while the study of ethnomusicology is the study of the modes of music making as a means of cultural expression and as sources of meaning. Both are concerned with human behaviour and the cultural ideologies that inform behaviour; both tend to rely upon ethnographic research and techniques of participant observation, with the results later written and published as a monograph. Within each discipline there are 'universalists' who tend to look for commonalities of behaviour and beliefs, and 'particularists' who are more interested in how we differ one from another, one group from another group.

Whatever the difference of perspective, nearly all anthropologists and ethnomusicologists subscribe to the dictum that one must attempt to understand behaviours and belief systems from within, that is, the necessity for making the effort to understand other musics and other styles of emotional expression from the perspective of their owners. This is related to, but not the same thing as, what is called 'cultural relativism,' which is taken to mean a refusal to make value judgments about beliefs and practices of peoples outside one's own group. A commitment to trying to comprehend the motivations and underlying paradigms of another's actions certainly delays or impedes a 'rush to judgment'. In the case of music and emotion, the ethnographic approach involves both looking closely at the cultural construction of emotion and at the cross-cultural differences in the uses, purposes, and meanings of musical expression.

In this chapter, I will present a theoretical frame for the cross-cultural exploration of music and emotion, provide specific examples, and conclude with a section on the possibility of conjoining humanistic and scientific approaches.

## 6.1 Culturally inflected listening

Studies on music and emotion conducted by Western scholars and scientists nearly always presume a particular image of musical listeners: silent, still listeners, paying close attention to a piece of music about which they communicate the type of emotion evoked by the piece to an attendant researcher. Communication of the emotion may be immediate in a laboratory setting, or retrospective, recalling the emotion after the musical event.

What is wrong with this image?

Nothing, if the intent is to describe the emotional responses to decontextualized performances by middle-class American or European listeners to music while seated quietly, in the second half of the twentieth century or the early twenty-first century. The laboratory situation may reflect the habit of many current Western listeners, possibly even more so now than in the past as so much musical listening takes place attached to headphones, rather than at live performances. Silent, still, focused listening is also the habit in some other musical traditions, notably the north Indian Hindustani 'classical' tradition, where one sits quietly, introspectively listening to the gradually developing filigree of the musical structure of a *raga*, played, perhaps, on a sitar. Thoughts and feelings are turned inward. The setting is intimate, conducive to introspection, and a distancing from one's fellow listeners.

But if the intent is to delineate something more general about the relationships between musical event and musical affect, the image of an inwardly focused, isolated listener is inadequate. This portrayal of listener and listening presents a set of unexamined ideologies and presuppositions that would not apply for most of the world. The unasked questions include: What constitutes 'listening' to music? What are the appropriate kinds of emotions to feel? What kind of subjectivity is assumed? Who is it that is 'having' the emotions? How is the event framed?

Anthropology and ethnomusicology have contributed to the study of music and emotion an expanded notion of the possibilities that constitute the relationship between the musical event and the listener, and the degree to which emotional response to musical events is culturally inflected. Musical performances and listeners find themselves in a relationship in which they define each other through continuous, interactive, ever-evolving musical structures and listener responses. Meaning resides in the mutual relationship established at any given moment in time between particular listeners and musical events. A group of listeners develops a 'community of interpretation' (Fish 1980), not necessarily uniform, but overlapping in some salient features. This community of listening means that when presented with a musical event, this community will approach the music with a pre-given set of expectations, a 'forestructure of understandings' (Gergen 1991, p. 104). Every hearer occupies a position in a cultural field not of his or her own making: every hearing is situated.

We accumulate our listening habits and expectations largely unawares; only when confronted with an alternate kind of listening are we likely to reflect upon our own conventionalized mode. Listeners can shift modes in different contexts, such as the ways in which one listens to music at a chamber music recital, or at a rock concert, or a jazz club, or a cinema, or at a salsa club (Becker 1983). Cross-culturally, modes of listening may add features not shared by us, or may not involve features that we take for granted. What is appropriate to say about musical affect, what one does *not* say, what one feels, and what one does *not* feel may reveal underlying assumptions surrounding musical listening. What is *not* assumed in one mode (such as bodily movement in Western classical listening) may become central in another mode (such as dancing while listening to a salsa band). To sit quietly focused on musical structure at a salsa concert is as inappropriate as swing dancing to a Schubert quintet.

We need a term to express the temporal and spacial situatedness of the hearer which is the aural equivalent of the visual term for modes of seeing; that is, *the gaze*. Frequently a feminist challenge to the dominance of *the male gaze* in literature (Kern 1996), film (Zizek 1991, p. 88), painting (Hebdige 1995), photography (Slater 1995), television (Morley 1995), psychoanalysis (Zizek 1996, p. 90), medicine (O'Neill 1995), and advertising (Barnard 1995), the term *gaze* is now used in a wide variety of contexts to exemplify the situatedness of looking, the historical and psychological specificity of any one visual approach, and the complex imbrication of modes of seeing with rhetorical and institutional structures and beliefs (Brennan & Jay 1996; Gamman & Marshment 1988; Jenks 1995).

Modes of *looking* imply habits of seeing that change not only across space (Mitchell 1986), but also at different historical periods within a single culture (Baxandall 1974; Goldhill 1996). Similarly, modes of *listening* vary according to the kind of music being played, the expectations of the musical situation, and the kind of subjectivity that a particular culture has fostered in relation to musical events (Johnson 1995). Even more than modes of looking, modes of listening implicate not only structures of knowledge and beliefs, but intimate notions of personhood and identity. Listening addresses interiors; listening provides access to what is hidden from sight.

Styles of audition, of aural perception, of aural awareness, of *listening* in response to musical events directly impinge upon studies of music and emotion. A given community will foster a particular comportment to listening; a comportment not only of attitude, affect, and expectation, but also bodily gesture. Emotional responses to music do not occur spontaneously, nor 'naturally', but rather, take place within complex systems of thought and behaviour concerning what music means, what it is for, how it is to be perceived, and what might be appropriate kinds of expressive responses. We need a word like Bourdieu's (1977) *habitus*, coined as an alternative to terms such as 'culture' which seemed too static, and sometimes seemed to imply a rigidity, an all-inclusiveness that obscured individual, idiosyncratic, or innovative modes of thought and behaviour. Still left with the need to refer to the ways in which beliefs and behaviours seem relatively stereotypical within a given society, Bourdieu (1977, p. 72) proposed the term habitus to do the theoretical work formerly carried by the word 'culture':

The structures constitutive of a particular type of environment (e.g. the material conditions of existence characteristic of a class condition) produce *habitus*, systems of durable, transposable *dispositions* . . . that is, as principles of the generation and structuring of practices and representations which can be objectively 'regulated' and 'regular' without in any way being the product of obedience to rules, objectively adapted to their goals without presupposing a conscious aiming at ends or an express mastery of the operations necessary to attain them and, being all this, collectively orchestrated without being the product of the orchestrating action of a conductor.

Bourdieu (1977, p. 214, f. 1) goes on to define what he means by *dispositions*:

The word *disposition* seems particularly suited to express what is covered by the concept of habitus defined as a system of dispositions. It expresses first the *result of an organizing action*, with a meaning close to that of words such as structure; it also designates a *way of being, a habitual state* (especially of the body and, in particular, a *predisposition, tendency, propensity,* or *inclination*.

Habitus is an embodied pattern of action and reaction, in which we are not fully conscious of why we do what we do; not totally determined, but a *tendency* to behave in a certain way. Our habitus of listening is tacit, unexamined, seemingly completely 'natural'. We listen in a *particular* way without thinking about it, and without realizing that it even is a particular way of listening. Most of our styles of listening have been learned through unconscious imitation of those who surround us and with whom we continually interact. A habitus of listening suggests, not a necessity or a rule, but an inclination, a disposition to listen with a particular kind of focus, to expect to experience particular kinds of emotion, to move with certain stylized gestures, and to interpret the meaning of the sounds and one's emotional responses to the musical event in somewhat (never totally) predictable ways. Scholars working within the disciplines of anthropology or ethnomusicology typically assume that the stance of the listener is not a given, not *natural*, but necessarily influenced by place, time, the shared context of culture, and the intricate and unreproduceable details of one's personal biography.

The term I have adapted from Bourdieu, habitus of listening, underlines the interrelatedness of the perception of musical emotion and learned interactions with our surroundings. Our perceptions operate within a set of habits gradually established throughout our lives and developed through our continual interaction with the world beyond our bodies, the evolving situation of *being in the world*.

## 6.2 Emotion as a cultural construct

But recognition of the fact that thought is always culturally patterned and infused with feelings, which themselves reflect a culturally ordered past, suggests that just as thought does not exist in isolation from affective life, so affect is culturally ordered and does not exist apart from thought. (Rosaldo 1984, p. 137)

This view, while in the ascendancy among cultural anthropologists and ethnomusicologists, has not gone unchallenged within the discipline of anthropology:

I can make no sense of a line of thought which claims that 'passions' are culturally defined. From my prejudiced position as a social anthropologist this passage reveals with startling clarity the ultimately radical weakness of the basic assumption of cultural anthropology, namely, that not only are cultural systems infinitely variable, but that human individuals are products of their culture rather than of their genetic predisposition. (Leach 1981, p. 16)

These two quotations, starkly put and differentiated by nationality, gender, and perspective—the American, female, cultural anthropologist and the British, male, social anthropologist—state baldly the issue at hand: the cultural relativism of emotion and thought, or the universality of emotion and thought. (Leach was not a racist, but rather a believer in the commonality of mankind. See also Brown 1991; Goodenough 1970, p. 122; Levi-Strauss 1962, p. 161; Spiro 1984; Turner 1983). These contesting views have elicited penetrating dialogues on both sides of the divide and continue to evoke considerable emotion in their defenders. There are good reasons for these passions: much is at stake.

Informing our beliefs about the universality or, conversely, the culturally conditioned aspects of music and emotion, the path of Western intellectual history leads in both directions; one direction taken by the sciences that stresses general laws and instances, the other taken by the humanities and cultural anthropology that stresses cases and interpretations (Geertz 1983*a*).

One way to understand the divide between the scientific and the cultural approach is to look at its development from the eighteenth-century Enlightenment onwards. One of the great contributions of the Enlightenment was the propagation of the idea (already taught by religion, but little observed by society) that humankind shared a basic natural state, independent of geography, chronology, or personality ('We hold these truths to be self evident: that all men are created equal'; Jefferson 1994). In its day, this doctrine was dazzlingly liberal and liberating. It led, in spite of all the detours to the contrary, to the end (almost) of institutionalized slavery in the Western world. A sentence from a history book of the eighteenth-century vividly presents a theatrical metaphor for the belief in the commonality of human life and human nature.

The stage-setting [in different periods of history] is, indeed, altered, the actors change their garb and their appearance; but their inward motions arise from the same desires and passions of men, and produce their effects in the vicissitudes of kingdoms and peoples. (J. J. Mascou, *Geschichte der Teutschen*, quoted in Lovejoy 1948, p. 173)

While elegantly simple, and a vast improvement over earlier views concerning 'The Great Chain of Being' (Lovejoy 1964), this view, in practice, led to the assumption that all peoples everywhere thought and felt like educated, male, Europeans and Americans. Post-colonial studies (Appadurai 1996; Spivak 1988) and gender studies (McClary 1991; Solie 1993) have brought home the bias in such views. We have come to appreciate the nuanced differences of emotion with different stage settings, garbs, and appearances. The 'desires and passions of men' have come to be seen as *not* producing identical 'inward motions'. Partly through the cumulative effects of works by cultural anthropologists writing in the 1970s (Geertz 1973, p. 36; Myers 1979), the 1980s (Levy 1984; Lutz 1986, 1988; Rosaldo 1984; Shweder & Bourne 1984), and the 1990s (Irvine 1990; Lutz & Abu-Lughod 1990), scholars who have championed the concept of the cultural construction of emotion, social scientists and psychologists are increasingly sensitive to the cultural component in the categorizing of, the interpretation of, and the expression of emotion (Davidson 1992; Ekman 1980, p. 90; Ortony *et al.* 1988, p. 26; Russell 1991*a*, 1991*b*).

If we accept Leach's version of the uniformity of human passions, we condone the silences imposed upon subalterns of all times and places whose feelings were assumed to be isomorphic with those of the persons who controlled the writing of history, and we ignore the developing body of data supporting the cultural inflection of the emotions. If we accept the idea of the social construction of knowledge, of morality, and emotion, we seem to be abandoning the idea of a *human* nature, a bond of mind, emotion, and meaning that enfolds us all, and binds us to one another. We may also be in danger of losing sight of the individual as he or she slips into the constructed conventionality of cultural appearance, behaviour, beliefs, and desires and disappears altogether. Persons may become exemplars, instances of this or that cultural model.

I would like to propose that both approaches have incontrovertible empirical support, and that rather than choose sides, we need to accept the paradox that, in fact, we cannot do without either perspective (Needham 1981; Nettl 1983, p. 36; Shweder 1985; Solomon 1984). Cultural difference in the expression of, the motivation for, and the interpretation of emotion in relation to musical events has been persuasively demonstrated over and over again; for example in music from South Africa (Blacking 1973, p. 68), Liberia (Stone 1982, p. 79), Brazil (Seeger 1987, p. 129), New Guinea (Feld 1982, p. 32), Peru (Turino 1993, p. 82), South India (Viswanathan & Cormack 1998, p. 225), Java (Benamou 1998), and Arabic music (Racy 1998, p. 99). Likewise, the fact that most of us can, with experience and empathy, come to understand differing expressive reactions to different kinds of music as reasonable and coherent demonstrates some level of commonality and universality in relation to both music and emotion. It may be that we come into the world with the full range of human emotional expression available to us (Geertz 1974, p. 249). Through continual patterns of interaction with (primarily) close family members in the early years, we develop particular patterns of emotional feelings and expressions in relation to the events of our lives. For the most part, habituated responses and actions delimit the range and type of any one person's emotional responses. Yet, it would appear that we can imaginatively enter into a much wider palette of human emotional possibilities. We need to make a Hegelian move and transcend the dichotomy between scientific universalism and humanistic particularity and embrace both as necessary to the study of music and emotion.

## 6.3 Person as a cultural construct

The 'subjectivity' we are discussing here is the capacity of the speaker to posit himself as 'subject'. It is defined not by the feeling which everyone experiences of being himself (this feeling, to the degree that it can be taken note of, is only a reflection) but as the psychic unity that transcends the totality of the actual experiences it assembles and that makes the permanence of the consciousness. (Benveniste 1971, p. 224)

Benveniste has argued that the sense of person is a product of 'languaging', as have many others, most notably, Buddhist philosophers. (The gerund 'languaging' is a form favoured by scholars who wish to differentiate language activity from the structure of language, see Becker 1995, p. 9; Maturana & Varela 1987, p. 234; Smith & Ferstman 1996, p. 52). While the sense of personhood seems inextricably tied to the development of language, one's sense of bodily boundaries—our sense of what (somatically) belongs to us and where our bodies end—seems to escape the linguistic formation of person and takes shape in areas of the brain not directly involved with languaging (Damasio 1999, p. 108; Melzack 1992). The literature on subjectivity is vast and cannot be dealt with here. None the less, an important aspect of any particular habitus of listening is the way in which the listener thinks of him or herself as a person, how he or she establishes identity in relation to other persons and the phenomenal world.

A classic definition of Western identity is that formulated by Clifford Geertz (1983b, p. 59):

The Western conception of the person as a bounded, unique, more or less integrated motivational cognitive universe, a dynamic center of awareness, emotion, judgment, and action organized into a distinctive whole and set contrastively both against other such wholes and against its social and natural background, is, however incorrigible it may seem to us, a rather peculiar idea within the context of the world's cultures.

Among others, the philosopher Charles Taylor (1989) has written about the development of this style of personhood in the West, from Plato to the present day (see also Gergen 1991, p. 18):

Our modern notion of the self is related to, one might say constituted by, a certain sense (or perhaps a family of senses) of inwardness . . . The unconscious is for us within, and we think of the depths of the unsaid, the unsayable, the powerful inchoate feelings and affinities and fears which dispute with us the control of our lives, as inner . . . But as strong as this partitioning of the world appears to us, as solid as this localization may seem, and anchored in the very nature of the human agent, it is in large part a feature of our world, the world of modern, Western people. The localization is not a universal one, which human beings recognize as a matter of course, as they do for instance that their heads are above their torsos. Rather it is a function of a historically limited mode of self-interpretation, one which has become dominant in the modern West and which may indeed spread thence to other parts of the globe, but which had a beginning in time and space and may have an end. (Taylor 1989, p. 111)

It is almost a truism of contemporary cultural anthropology that the nature of subjectivity, of the sense of self, varies cross-culturally. This is a profoundly anti-intuitive notion, and one that has strong objectors in philosophy from St Augustine (von Campenhausen 1964, pp. 226–7) to Bertrand Russell (Seckel 1986, p. 96). As with the issue of 'emotion', to say that subjectivity is culturally constructed seems to deny the basic humanity of mankind. Yet, differences seem to remain in how persons think of themselves in relation to other persons, and these differences are often markedly cultural (Shweder & Bourne 1984, p. 191).

## 6.4 Person and emotion in the habitus of listening

The particular subjectivity of the listeners described in psychological studies, the prototypical Western, middle-class listener to music is likely to be some variant of the following: an individual with a strong sense of separateness, of uniqueness from all other persons, an individual whose emotions and feelings are felt to be known in their entirety and complexity only to him or herself, whose physical and psychic privacy is treasured, and whose emotional responses to a given piece of music are not felt to be in relation to anything outside of his or her own particular self-history and personality: The emotion, for us, belongs to the individual, not to the situation or to relationships. Emotion is the authentic expression of one's being, and is, in some sense, natural and spontaneous. The emotion is interior, may or may not be shared with anyone else, and may be a guide to one's inner essence. Leo Treitler (1993, p. 48) has written about one way in which this style of subjectivity can relate to listening to music:

It is that interaction of the selves of the listener with those in the music—no, better put: the awareness of the self (selves) in the music through its (their) interaction with the listener's self—that interests me here; musical communication as a function of the interaction of identities.

The differing identities of the listening subject, and those projected by the music become the focus of interest for Treitler. One common variant of this Western kind of subjectivity while listening to music is to identify with the different identity projected by the music. Listening to music offers the opportunity to temporarily be another kind of person than one's ordinary, everyday self. This interpretation segues into theories concerning one's fantasy life and seems to be a fruitful approach to the kind of emotion associated with music that one finds, for example, among adolescents (Frith 1987, p. 143; Shepherd & Giles-David 1991), and may help to explain their profound identification with the popular music of their times. Musical listening may offer the opportunity of experiencing relief from one's own presentation of everyday self (Goffman 1959) by trying on another self-presentation (see also DeNora, this volume).

### 6.4.1 Being a griot

How different is the subjectivity, the habitus of listening of the Western listeners to the Wolof griots of Senegal as described by Judith Irvine (1990). Among the Wolof, the musical expression of emotion is dialogical and situational, not personal and interior. Griots, low-caste individuals, are believed to be highly expressive, highly excitable, 'volatile and theatrical'. The nobles are believed to be the opposite: composed, 'cool', detached, and somewhat bland in affect. It is the duty of the griots to stimulate the nobles to action, nobles who might otherwise be given over to lethargy. The highly expressive, emotional performances of the griots are intended, in part, to provide the energy to the nobles that they might carry out their governing duties. Irvine relates that a frequent image in Wolof oral poetry and epic narratives involves the playing of an ensemble of drums and iron clappers to awaken the king 'lest his royal duties go unfulfilled' (Irvine 1990, p. 134). The emotion of the musicians and dancers is contrasted to the lack of emotion of their primary audience, the nobles. Both the emotion of the griots and its absence in the nobles are public, dialogical, and situational; not private and hidden. One of the primary manifestations of subjectivity among Europeans and Americans, emotions are not personal attributes for the Wolof griots and nobles in the same way. For us, emotional responses to music are not considered to be assigned by virtue of one's class and profession, but to be an inalienable characteristic of a bounded, inviolate individual. This is not at all to say that Wolof nobles do not feel strong personal emotions, or that a griot is necessarily always highly extroverted and volatile. It is only to say that these are the *dispositions,* the *inclinations* that are likely to be fulfilled more often than not. The key participants in these musical events exhibit a habitus of listening and a type of subjectivity that largely conforms to Wolof cultural expectations.

### 6.4.2 The habitus of listening to the sitar, tambura, and tabla

Earlier, mention was made of the similarity of the habitus of listening of the listener of Hindustani 'classical' music and the Western middle-class listener in terms of physical stillness, focused attention, and inner withdrawal. Furthermore, both traditions would claim that music can *represent* emotion. In his autobiography, Ravi Shankar (1968, pp. 23, 27) describes his own subjectivity as a musician, a style of personhood that seems concordant with what I or most readers of this essay might feel as performing musicians:

A *raga* is an aesthetic projection of the artist's inner spirit; it is a representation of his most profound sentiments and sensibilities, set forth through tones and melodies . . . I may play *Raga Malkauns*, whose principal mood [*rasa*] is *veera* [heroic], but I could begin by expressing *shanta* [serenity] and *karuna* [compassion] in the *alap* and develop into *veera* and *adbhuta* [astonishment] or even *raudra* [anger] in playing the *jor* or *jhala*.

The inner spirit of the artist, functioning within culturally constructed categories of emotion, is made manifest in the outward expressions of his musical presentation. Bringing yet another dimension of similarity to the two listening situations is the fact that emotion (*rasa*) experienced in listening to Hindustani classical music is distanced and impersonal. One can feel the emotion without the troublesome immediacy and consequences of an emotion that compels action (Abhinavagupta in Gnoli 1968, pp. 82–5; Masson & Patwardhan 1969, p. 46). June McDaniel (1995, p. 48), writing of *rasa* in the Indian province of Bengal, uses the metaphor of the glass window separating the experiencer from the emotion while still allowing a clear view:

*Bhava* is a personal emotion; *rasa* is an impersonal or depersonalized emotion, in which the participant is distanced as an observer. Why is a depersonalized emotion considered superior to a personal one? Because the aesthete can experience a wide range of emotions yet be protected from their painful aspects. Emotion is appreciated through a glass window, which keeps out unpleasantness. Though the glass is clear, thus allowing a union of sorts with the observed object, the window is always present, thus maintaining the dualism.

The following description is a Western mirror-image of the way to experience *rasa*:

When people listen, say, to 'Questi i campi di Tracia' from Monteverdi's *Orfeo* . . . they do not directly perceive the anguish and guilt of the twice-widowed singer. Listeners only hear a *representation* [italics mine] of the way his voice moves under the influence of his emotions. Nevertheless, this can give listeners important insights into a type of emotional response. Monteverdi skillfully displays the contortions through which Orpheus's voice goes. When listeners know how a voice moves under the influence of an affect, they are given (if they are familiar with the conventions of the music, and otherwise qualified) an immediate demonstration of something about the affect. A good performance of this aria immediately demonstrates to a sensitive audience something about what it is like to feel guilt, remorse, and despair. (Young 1999, p. 48)

In both the Hindustani and the Western classical listener, an emotion evoked by listening to music can be contemplated with a certain deliberation and calmness. But at some point the congruencies between the habitus of listening of each breaks down. The Western observer may well, as Treitler suggests, be involved with comparing identities, or with constructing a more glamorous self in relation to the music heard, or with contemplating 'what it is like to feel guilt, remorse, and despair'. The Indian, however, may be performing a very different act, a somewhat strenuous religious exercise, a kind of refining of emotional essence, a distillation of his or her emotion that will lead to a transformation of consciousness to a higher level of spirituality. Listening to music for the Hindustani classical music devotee should not be, according to canon, a passive act, but requires the active will and mind of the listener to carry consciousness to a higher plane, closer to the divine (Coomaraswamy 1957, p. 39). Western references to *inspiration* or *genius*, which at one time perhaps indicated a holy possession, have become largely metaphoric rather than literal expressions of sacred connections between musical performance and musical listening. In Indian classical traditions, the pursuit of emotion, of *rasa*, in relation to listening to music, may be a path to greater awareness, leading one to cosmic insight. Dance can share as well in this configuration of emotion as a stepping stone to a higher gnosis. One of India's most revered Bharata Natyam dancers has written the following:

> It is here that Bharata Natyam, the ancient and holy art of Indian dance, cuts deeply into the conscious and subconscious levels and revealingly brings to the forefront the fact that it is ultimately and intimately oriented to the nucleus, *atman* [the universal self]. It is a revelation not only to the performing artist, but in an equal measure to the audience as well . . . By the inexplicable power born of the union of melody, lyric, rhythm and gesture, the emotions are released from their limited secular locus and are expanded to universal proportions where there is only pure spirit with nothing of the sensual. (Balasaraswati 1985, pp. 2–3)

According to the Bengali version of the theory of *rasa*, intense emotions, not milder 'aesthetic emotions', are the appropriate vehicle to lead one to mystical knowledge of life's meaning and purpose. Emotions are compared to water that can best be understood by immersion in an ocean rather than by the delicate feel of a raindrop (McDaniel 1995, p. 51). What we might call emotional excesses become pregnant possibilities for greater spiritual attainment for an Indian music listener. While the quiet stance and introverted demeanor of the listener in the prototypical Western case and the Hindustani classical listener is similar, the understanding and interpretation of what is supposed to happen in each case differs. In one case, the listener may be exploring the emotional nuances of his or her inner self or identifying with the emotional interiors presented by the music: In the other, the listener is trying to bring about a kind of 'sea' change, a different self altogether, one that comes closer to divinity.

## 6.5 Arousal: a human universal

Particularities relating to the cultural construction of personhood and of emotion may obscure certain physiological constants that are the correlates of listening to music. Arousal, defined in its most narrow sense as stimulation of the autonomic nervous system (ANS), is one of the most important aspects of musical performance and plays into nearly all studies of music and emotion (see Meyer, this volume; Scherer & Zentner, this volume; Sloboda & Juslin, this volume). The heart beats faster, the pulse rises, breathing becomes shallower, the skin temperature rises, and the pattern of brain waves becomes less regular. All these changes have been observed without any necessary reference to the affective, interpretive component of arousal. They may occur in relation to sexual activity, to exercise, or as a result of drugs or alcohol, as well as to musical listening.

In his famous and controversial theory of the emotions, William James claimed that the physiological component of arousal is primary and precedes the interpretation of the subsequent emotion (James 1950, pp. 442–85). The 'feeling' of anger is the feeling that results from an angry facial expression, bodily stance, shallow breathing, etc. Anger, the emotion, *is*, according to James, what one *feels* when enacting this display. Following

James, but with much more knowledge of the neurophysiology of emotion, Damasio (1999, p. 79) claims that the term 'emotion' should be applied to ANS arousal, and that 'feeling' which follows 'emotion' should be applied to the complex cognitive, culturally inflected interpretation of 'emotion'. Both the Polish Grotowski school of acting (Grotowski 1968) and the Indian Kathakali theatre tradition (Schechner 1988, p. 270) seem to support the theories of James and Damasio. Training a Kathakali actor, or a Western actor of the Grotowski tradition, begins with *mimesis*, recreating the bodily gestures of an emotion, not with delving into one's memories to recreate a 'feeling', as in Stanislavsky's school of 'method' acting (Stanislavsky 1958, p. 1977).

In any case, it is useful analytically to separate physiological arousal ('emotion' for James and Damasio) from the more cognitive concept of 'feeling'. Unlike feelings that directly relate to judgments and beliefs learned within a cultural context and rely upon linguistic categories which are often incommensurable across languages, arousal is more clearly a universal response to musical listening. Combined with a concentrated religious focus, musical arousal can contribute to extreme states of emotion.

Happiness is the emotion most frequently associated with musical listening and may constitute one of the 'universals' of cross-cultural studies of music and emotion. From the 'polka happiness' of the Polish-American parties of Chicago (Keil 1987, p. 276), to the !Kung of the Kalahari desert: 'Being at a dance makes our hearts happy' (Katz 1982, p. 348), to the Basongye of the Congo who 'make music in order to be happy' (Merriam 1964, p. 82), to the extroverted joy of a Pentecostal musical service, music has the ability to make people feel good (cf. Gabrielsson, this volume; Sloboda & O'Neill, this volume). The happiness of listening to music, however one construes 'happiness', is in part the simple result of musical arousal. We tend to feel better when we are musically aroused and excited. The emotion may be attributed to some other aspect of the event, such as the text or our own dancing; none the less, the musical stimulation should not be minimized. Music can be a catalyst for a changing state of consciousness (cf. Persson, this volume).

The following section includes three examples of extreme emotion contextually situated within a religious ceremony in which music is an essential element; all three are sites of the author's fieldwork.

### 6.5.1 Music and ecstasy: the Sufis

The strongest version of happiness in relation to musical listening and an example of extreme arousal is ecstasy. (See Rouget 1985 for descriptions of music and trancing in many time periods and geographical locations.) Usually associated with religious rituals, ecstasy, as extreme joy, almost by definition involves a sense of the sacred (although musical ecstasy can justly be claimed by some attendees at secular musical events such as rock concerts). The degree to which Muslim Sufi orders have formalized and institutionalized musical ecstasy has seldom been exceeded. The works of the eleventh-century Persian Sufi mystic al Ghazzali about music and ecstasy are still basic pedagogical texts for contemporary Sufis in Iran, Afghanistan, Pakistan, and north India.

The heart of man has been so constituted by the Almighty that, like a flint, it contains a hidden fire which is evoked by music and harmony, and renders man beside himself with ecstasy. These harmonies are echoes of that higher world of beauty which we call the world of spirits, they remind man of his relationship to that world, and produce in him an emotion so deep and strange that he himself is powerless to explain it. (Ghazzali 1991, p. 57)

Sufi musicians, called *qawwal* in Pakistan and north India, play for religious cere-monies in which the devotees may reach toward a pinnacle of ecstasy that will bring them into close communion with Allah. The *qawwals* move from song to song, eliciting reactions from the devotees such as moaning, sighing, swaying, even rising up and turn-ing in place as a certain text line speaks directly to the spiritual condition of a particular devotee (Qureshi 1986, p. 119). For a devout Sufi, his ecstasy is a preview, a foretasting of his ultimate union: and though he may weep, he weeps from excess of joy.

Sufi doctrine interprets the music as supportive, as secondary to the all important text, the religious poetry (Qureshi 1986, p. 83). Yet the question remains: to what degree is the arousal stimulated by the sensual overload of intensifying rhythms and soaring phrases sung over and over again at the top of the *qawwal's* range? (For examples, listen to any of the many CDs of Nusrat Fateh Ali Khan.)

A Sufi habitus of listening at a musical religious ceremony involves a sequence of feeling and action that could be called a 'script' (Russell 1991*a*, 1991*b*). Initially, while sitting quietly and reverently, the listener may hope that he or she will be touched by a particular line of text that seems directly applicable to his or her personal situation. If the lead *qawwal* catches the subtle indications of arousal in a listener, he will begin repeating the verse over and over again. The Sufi script then calls for swaying, weeping, rising up, moving to the centre of the room, and slowly turning in place (Fig. 6.1). The emotion of the script, when fully acted out, is the ultimate joy of a direct and personal knowledge of Allah. Musical emotion in the listener changes both its form and its intensity as the script progresses.

### 6.5.2 Music and rage: Balinese bebuten trancing

In Bali, an exorcist ceremony is performed when misfortune befalls a village in which the negative powers of the divine witch Rangda must be neutralized for the well-being of the community. The elaborate mask of the witch Rangda will be brought from its storage place in the temple, blessed and infused with spirit in a potent ceremony con-ducted by a priest. An exceptionally tall and spiritually strong man will be chosen to undergo the trance of *becoming* the witch. A number of men will volunteer to undergo another kind of trance called *bebuten*, from the root *buta*, which means a creature of base instincts, low on the ladder of sentient beings, often translated as *demon*. These men will confront the witch and ultimately neutralize her power with the help of a mag-ical beast called Barong. *Bebuten* trance is not ecstasy. It is a feeling of rage directed toward the witch Rangda, and may leave the trancer feeling embarrassed later by his behaviour during the trance and with an exhaustion that may last for several days (Eiseman 1989, p. 153). Yet, the trancing is a social obligation which he fulfills voluntar-ily, surrendering his own comfort for the betterment of his community. He experiences a kind of homicidal rage (or, rather, 'theo-cidal' rage). One experienced trancer (I Wayan Dibia) passionately described his feelings while listening to the music of the gamelan (Fig. 6.2) upon encountering the witch:

**Figure 6.1** Dancing Sufis From the Divan (Book of poems) of Hafiz (Walters Art Gallery, Baltimore).

When I come up to that tower, when the curtain opens like that, as soon as I step up to approach Rangda, I see a strong fire coming from her eyes! I just—Oh! [slaps his hands together]—I do this! I just jump! I feel myself floating—because of the excitement! . . . Whenever they pick up the music [sings 'jangga jangga jangga'], whenever you sing that song [sings a bit of the gamelan piece that accompanies the trance] people just go crazy! I want to attack Rangda!!!' (I Wayan Dibia, interview, 1996)

**Figure 6.2** Gamelan musicians accompanying a Rangda/Barong ritual (photo by Judith Becker).

Neither the trance, nor the ceremony, nor the pacification of the witch can happen without the gamelan music (Fig 6.3). The habitus of listening of I Wayan Dibia upon encountering Rangda would have to include a description of not only the gamelan music and the presence of the witch, but a complex of beliefs about the negative forces of the universe, their effects upon human communities, the embodiment of these forces in the divine witch Rangda, and the methods by which she may be contained and controlled. His own emotion, culturally constituted but felt interiorly, is a necessary component of the maintenance of community well-being. His murderous passion has little to do with an interiorized self, with the identity of I Wayan Dibia. His rage, in part musically induced, is in the service of his community. Like the Wolof griots, musical emotion for the trancer in a Balinese Rangda exorcism is public, situational, predictable, and culturally sanctioned.

Figure 6.3  Musical transcription of the 'encounter' theme from a Rangda/Barong ritual.

### 6.5.3 Pentecostal arousal: 'music brought me to Jesus' (Cox 1995, p. 139)

Pentecostal religions were formally constituted at the beginning of the twentieth century, and are now rivalled only by Islam in their spread to all parts of the globe (Cox 1995, p. 15). Pentecostalism constitutes a faith that is dependent upon music to structure its religious services and to validate its system of beliefs by provoking intense emotional reactions within its most devote practitioners, leading them to 'testify'. To dance in The Spirit, to be possessed by the Holy Ghost, is demonstration that one is accepted into the congregation of those who will experience the final act of history, the reappearance of Jesus Christ and the establishment of the Kingdom of God on earth (Abell 1982). Music is the driving force for this emotional apotheosis. From softly played passages underlining a sermon or a prayer, to swinging, driving choruses sustaining a wave of religious emotionalism, music is rarely absent from the hours-long services. Pentecostal musical offerings shape a musical/emotional/religious arc that carries the congregation along with it. A service will begin with quiet, slow, soothing music: 'Music gets people in the attitude of worship. It helps them to forget outside influences and to focus on the Lord' (Interview with Jerry Trent, Church of God, Willow Run, Michigan, 1996).

Pentecostal churches may use a wide variety of musical instruments, often including piano, electric organ, synthesizer, guitars, and drumset to back up their driving, repetitive gospel hymns. As the music becomes louder, more rhythmic, and more repetitive, its driving quality supports, propels, and sustains the hand-waving, hand-clapping, foot-stomping choruses of 'Amen!' as the emotional temperature of the congregation gradually rises. High on the trajectory of the musical arc, worshippers may come forward to the altar to pray, and some may dance or trance. As in the Sufi services, the musical support will continue at a high intensity until all worshippers have worked through their transport and regained their normal composure. Religious ecstasy is always accompanied by great joy as it is a confirmation of the salvation of the worshipper. He or she has become a part of the historical narrative of millenarial Christianity and will join fellow believers and Jesus at the last day. The music never flags as some members are moved to tears, to dance, to quiver and jerk in the uncoordinated gestures of some religious trances. As religious passions subside, so does the music, until every last ecstatic has become quiet—exhausted and joyful. 'And it was terrific', exclaimed one worshipper at a service marked by intense, sustained, high-energy music, dancing, and trancing, 'and we really *got down* here. I mean we really *had church*' (Cox 1995, p. 268).

The musical listener at a Pentecostal service is expectant, alert, and waiting for the song leader, the musicians, the singing congregation, and the pastor to transport him or her to the point of experiencing the Holy Spirit in his or her own body. The attitude is one of surrender and openness. No critical irony, no mental busyness, or aesthetic evaluation can be allowed to interfere with a process of holy possession called 'Slain in the Spirit'.

Similar to the Sufi listener and the Balinese *bebuten* trancer, for a Pentecostal listener, the habitus of listening involves a scripted sequence of actions, emotions, and interpretations. Within each of these three scripts, musical, behavioural, and emotional events will occur within a certain predictable frame. Simultaneously, each individual event will be unique and non-repeatable. The listeners to a Wolof griot, an Indian sitar player, a group of *qawwali* singers, a Balinese *bebuten* trancer, or a Pentecostal worshipper have all developed habits of mind and body in response to specific musical events. These habits are acquired throughout their life experiences of interaction with others in similar situations. The emotions are private *and* public, interior *and* exterior, individual *and* communal.

## 6.6 Music, emotion, and 'being': conjoining anthropology, ethnomusicology, psychology, and neurophysiology

It seems clear to this author that a common ground needs to be explored between the more humanistic, cultural anthropological approach and the more scientific, cognitive psychological approach. I see the bringing together of the scientific and cultural approaches to the study of music and emotion as one of the great challenges of our fields. While the styles of argument and the criteria for evidence may remain distinct, the conclusions need to be comparable and not incommensurable. Both disciplinary areas may have to give up some of their established scholarly practices.

### 6.6.1 Single brain/body approaches

For those approaching the study of the emotional effect of musical listening on the brain, the unit of analysis is usually the brain or body of a single listener. From the early studies of music and the brain, such as Neher's early work in the 1960s (Neher 1961, 1962) analysing the brain rhythms of subjects listening to drum beats in a laboratory, to the more recent works of Clynes (1986), Wallin (1991), Peretz (this volume), and many others, musical scholars have adopted the scientific model and studied single brains or bodies in isolation. Studies in music cognition have largely followed the empirical models of cognitive studies in general in their efforts to model the algorithms of single brains processing music (Lerdahl & Jackendoff 1983; Raffman 1993). Neurophysiologists and psychologists of consciousness likewise follow the dictates of their scientific training, isolating and narrowing the problem as much as possible in order to have some control over the variables. In fact, some of the most exciting advances in the understanding of the mind are coming from scientists and philosophers who have focused on single minds/brains (Churchland 1986; Dennett 1991; Edelman 1992). The development of technologies such as magnetic resonance imaging (MRI) and positron emission tomography (PET) scanning have reinforced the practice of the study of single minds in the attempt to unravel the mysteries of conscious experience (see Peretz, this volume). The choice of a single human brain as the unit of analysis has larger implications as well. The emphasis upon the primacy of the self-contained individual has been a treasured credo of Western intellectual pursuits in all fields for many centuries. Contemporary examples include the cognitive sciences, Piaget's genetic epistemology, and Freudian psychoanalysis.

Without intending to denigrate any of these fields, and while fully acknowledging their enormous contributions, I am suggesting that the scripts of music and emotion, the habitus of listening, can be helpfully understood as a process which is supraindividual (Nunez 1997), in which the relationship between music and emotion needs to be understood as extending beyond the minds and bodies of single musicians and listeners, that is as a contextually situated social practice. Emotions relating to music are culturally embedded and socially constructed and can usefully be viewed as being about an individual within a community, rather than being exclusively about internal states. First-person descriptions of music and emotion are rife with tropes of interiority, yet the understanding of how music affects interiors takes place within consensual, shared views of what makes up 'reality'. Musical events set up an aural domain of coordination that envelops all those present.

### 6.6.2 Rhythmic entrainment

A familiar example of a changed interior, personal consciousness in a musical domain of coordination is the phenomenon of *rhythmic entrainment* (Chapple 1970, p. 38; Condon 1986; Hall 1977, p. 61; McNeill 1995, p. 6; Neher 1961, 1962; Rider & Eagle 1986; Vaughn 1990; Walter & Walter 1949). Bodies and brains synchronize gestures, muscle actions, breathing, and brain waves while enveloped in musicking. (The gerund 'musicking' is preferred for the same reasons as 'languaging'. The activity, the process, the experiencing of music is foregrounded; see Small 1998.) Many persons, bound together by common aims, may experience revitalization and general good feeling. The situation is communal and individual, the music descends upon all alike, while each person's joy is his or her own.

> . . . it is no wonder that our words fumble when seeking to describe what happens within us when we dance or march. The initial seat of excitement is far removed from our verbal capabilities. It centers instead in those parts of the nervous system that function subconsciously, maintaining rhythmic heartbeat, digestive peristalsis, and breathing, as well as all the other chemical and physiological balances required for the maintenance of ordinary bodily functions. (McNeill 1995, p. 6)

### 6.6.3 Habitus of listening: culture and biology

An enactive approach to meaning and cognition based in biology has recently been proposed by Maturana and Varela (1987), Varela *et al.* (1991), Nunez (1997), and Foley (1997)—a group including biologists, linguists, and psychologists. While Bourdieu (and others) developed the analytical tool of habitus from an anthropological and sociological perspective, these scholars are reaching toward phenomenology to develop a comparable biological model which transcends the division between the cultural and the biological; between phenomenology and scientific materialism. The two approaches (Bourdieu and this group) are strikingly similar. While wishing to examine the relationships between music and emotion as supraindividual, one may still view the scripts associated with the habitus of listening as a biological process.

A biological process is a process that has an autopoietic organization (i.e. it is self-producing), a process that has boundaries between itself and the enveloping environment, the components of which (people) are dynamically related in a network of ongoing interactions that change the structure of the individuals as well as the structure of their interactions. Further criteria for biological processes are that they are autonomous, that is, that they can specify their own laws, and that they only allow changes to occur dependent upon maintaining the viability of their own structures (Maturana & Varela 1987, pp. 47–52). Groups of people who are focused on a common event and who share a common history of that event act, react, and to some extent think in concert, without sacrificing their bounded personal identities.

Viewing music and emotions as scripts that involve supra-individual biological processes, one can describe the changes that occur in these time sequences as having evolved over time through a historical process called 'structural coupling' (Maturana & Varela 1987, pp. 75–80). 'Structural coupling' describes the internal, structural changes that occur within an organism as a result of interaction with other organisms and with a world; changes of one's being or one's ontology. These changes become new domains of knowledge, knowledge gained through interactive behaviours, through doing. Music listeners as well as musicians undergo a learning process in which they imitate physical and mental gestures that ultimately transform both their inner structures as well as their relations to everything beyond the boundaries of their skins. Music and emotion are part of a larger processual event that includes many other people doing many other things while the whole event unfolds as a unity that has been organized and reorganized over time by small structural changes within the participants.

We are accustomed to thinking of biological processes as extending from a single cell, to multicellular organisms such as a tree, to animals, and to a single human being. When groups of people are acting in some kind of accord, we tend to say that the phenomenon is social, or psychological, or political, but not biological. If we think of music making and music listening within a process that may also include quiet introspection or, conversely, include preaching, glossolalia, and dancing, or the murmuring of mantras, as all part of a biological process that has had a long history of structural coupling, or continual self-recreation, we can begin to think of the music, the emotion, and every other aspect of the process as contributing to bringing forth the activities of each other, as bringing forth a world or a reality in which certain emotions and actions are expected and appropriate, and in which the reality brought forth by all is enacted by all (Dreyfus 1991). A musical event is not just in the minds of the participants, it is in their bodies; like a vocal accent in speaking, emotion in relation to musical listening is personally manifested, but exists supra-individually. Each person, both musicians and listeners, seem to be acting as self-contained, bounded individuals, and indeed they experience whatever they experience as deeply personal and emotional, but the event as a whole plays itself out in a supra-individual domain.

This embodied understanding, including dispositions in the habitus, is tacit knowledge and hence one can only be subsidiarily aware of it; this accounts for why so much of the habitus is preconscious and unable to be reflected on or modified. This conservatism leads to the practices generated by the dispositions of the habitus being transmitted from generation to generation, in other words they are potentially *cultural practices*. Culture in this view is that transgenerational domain of practices through which human organisms in a social system communicate with each other. These practices may be verbal or non-verbal, but they must be communicative in the sense that they occur as part of ongoing histories of social structural coupling and contribute to the viability of continued coupling ... Culture, then, consists of the things people do to communicate in ongoing transgenerational histories of social interaction. (Foley 1997, p. 14)

Emotion is an enactment, not a representation in the mind. It is a way of *being-in-the-world*, not a way of thinking about the world.

The experience of anything out there is validated in a special way by the human structure, which makes possible 'the thing' that arises in the description. This circularity, this connection between action and experience, this inseparability between a particular way of being and how the world appears to us, tells us that *every act of knowing brings forth a world* ... All this can be summed up in the aphorism *All doing is knowing, and all knowing is doing*. (Maturana & Varela 1987, p. 26)

Language, music, and dance become one system of ontogenic coordination of actions. Together, they bring about changes in being and changes in the music event involved. While it is the individual who experiences the emotion, it is the group and its domain of coordinations that triggers the emotion. The changes in the neurophysiology of the listener are not attributable simply to the brain/body of a self-contained individual. They occur through the group processes of recurrent interactions between co-defined individuals in a rhythmic domain of music.

Thinking of the relationship of music and emotion as a biological process with a co-defined, historically enacted ontology, as a group creation in which self-contained individuals have undergone structural changes through their interaction with other self-contained individuals helps to provide an embodied analysis of the relationship of music and emotion and the mysteries of musical affect. The domain of musicking and emotion is intrinsically social, visibly embodied, profoundly cognitive, and biologically consistent with the created domains of many other kinds of living creatures.

This type of analysis is aided by technologies such as film and video. One needs to be able to see everything at once, and to have the opportunity to replay the event. Qureshi's skilful score-like transcriptions of the multiple events at a Sufi religious ceremony demonstrate one method of researching music and emotion that does not focus on individual emotions, but on individual emotions within the context of many other individual emotions (Qureshi 1986, pp. 143–16). One can study her scores and literally *see* how the musicians interact with the congregants, and one can imagine how the emotions of one listener may have stimulated the emotions of another, leading to the ultimate reaction, an enactment of trancing (Fig 6.4).

### 6.6.4 What is gained by claiming that these processes are biological?

We may claim that special modes of conscious experience such as emotional responses to music listening, a habitus of listening, emerges as a phenotypic feature of humankind, as a biological development in the evolution of the species, emerging from both genetic and environmental influences. Music and emotion, viewed as evolving together in the interaction of each individual with performances throughout his or her life, dissolves intractable dichotomies concerning nature versus culture, and scientific universalism versus cultural particularism.

Furthermore, for those of us who want to use the word 'culture' but are inhibited by all the recent attacks upon the term relating to essentialism, historical stasis, and reified, abstracted psychology, culture can be restored as a more precise, more useful term. Culture (redefined) can be understood as a supra-individual biological phenomenon—a transgenerational history of social interactions that become embodied in the individual and transmitted through future actions.

No habitus of listening is entirely stable nor entirely fluid. As interactions change, so do the interiors of those who are interacting. We may have developed a habitus of listening that inclines us to introspectively contemplate the colourful fluidity of changing emotional states in response to Bach's *Musical Offering*, but if it would not disturb the viability of our own structures, we could learn to dance ecstatically in The Spirit with the Pentecostals.

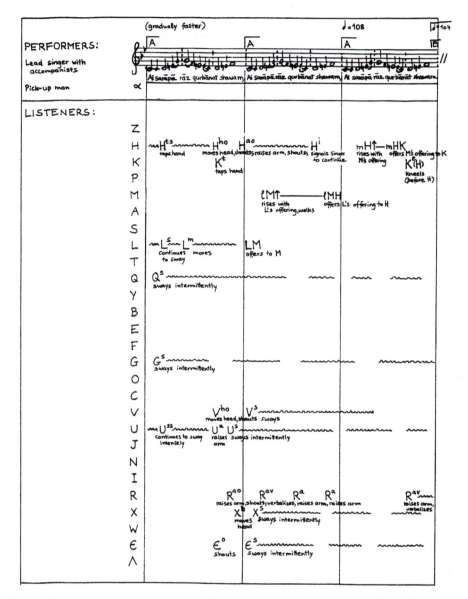

**Figure 6.4** Transcription (excerpt) of music/participant interactions in a north Indian Sufi ritual (from Qureshi 1986, p. 171).

# References

Abell, T. D. (1982). *Better felt than said: The Holiness-Pentecostal experience in southern Appalachia.* Waco, TX: Markham Press.

Appadurai, A. (1996). *Modernity at large: Cultural dimensions of globalization.* Minneapolis, MN: University of Minnesota Press.

Balasaraswati, T. (1985). The art of bharata natyam: a personal statement. In *Dance as cultural heritage, 2, Dance Research Annual XV,* (ed. B. T. Jones), pp. 1–7. New York: Congress on Research in Dance.

Barnard, M. (1995). Advertising: The rhetorical imperative. In *Visual culture,* (ed. C. Jenks), pp. 26–41. London: Routledge.

Baxandall, M. (1974). *Painting and experience in fifteenth century Italy: A primer in the social history of pictorial style.* New York: Oxford University Press.

Becker, A. L. (1995). *Beyond translation: Essays toward a modern philology.* Ann Arbor, MI: University of Michigan Press.

Becker, J. (1983). 'Aesthetics' in late 20th century scholarship. *World of Music,* 25, 65–80.

Benamou, M. (1998). *Rasa in Javanese musical aesthetics* (PhD dissertation: Musicology). Ann Arbor, MI: UMI Company.

Benveniste, E. (1971). Subjectivity in language. In *Problems in general linguistics* (trans. M. E. Meek), pp. 223–30. Coral Gables, FL: University of Miami Press.

Blacking, J. (1973). *How musical is man?* Seattle, WA: University of Washington Press.

Bourdieu, P. (1977). *Outline of a theory of practice* (trans. R. Nice). Cambridge, UK: Cambridge University Press.

Brennan, T. & Jay, M. (ed.) (1996). *Vision in context: Historical and contemporary perspectives on sight.* London: Routledge.

Brown, D. E. (1991). *Human universals.* Philadelphia, PA: Temple University Press.

Chapple, E. D. (1970). *Culture and biological man: Explorations in behavioral anthropology.* New York: Rinehart & Winston.

Churchland, P. S. (1986). *Neurophilosophy: Toward a unified science of the mind-brain.* Cambridge, MA: MIT Press.

Clynes, M. (1986). When time is music. In *Rhythm in psychological, linguistic and musical processes,* (ed. J. Evans & M. Clynes), pp. 169–224. Springfield, IL: C. C. Thomas.

Condon, W. S. (1986). Communication: Rhythm and structure. In *Rhythm in psychological, linguistic and musical processes,* (ed. J. Evans & M. Clynes), pp. 55–77. Springfield, IL: C. C. Thomas.

Coomaraswamy, A. K. (1957). *The dance of Shiva.* New York: Noonday Press.

Cox, H. (1995). *Fire from heaven: The rise of Pentecostal spirituality and the reshaping of religion in the twenty-first century.* Reading, MA: Addison Wesley.

Damasio, A. R. (1999). *The feeling of what happens: Body and emotion in the making of consciousness.* New York: Harcourt Brace & Co.

Davidson, R. J. (1992). Prolegomenon to the structure of emotion: Gleanings from neuropsychology. *Cognition and Emotion,* 6, 245–68.

Dennett, D. (1991). *Consciousness explained.* Boston, MA: Little, Brown & Co.

Dreyfus, H. L. (1991). *Being-in-the-world: A commentary on Heidegger's being and time, Division I.* Cambridge, MA: MIT Press.

Edelman, G. (1992). *Bright air, brilliant fire: On the matter of the mind.* New York: Basic Books.

Eiseman, F. B. (1989). *Bali: Sekala and niskala. Vol. 1: Essays on religion, ritual, and art.* Singapore: Periplus Editions.

Ekman, P. (1980). Biological and cultural contributions to body and facial movement in the expression of emotions. In *Explaining emotions*, (ed. A. Rorty), pp. 73–101. Berkeley, CA: University of California Press.

Feld, S. (1982). *Sound and sentiment: Birds, weeping, poetics, and song in Kaluli expression.* Philadelphia, PA: University of Pennsylvania Press.

Fish, S. (1980). *Is there a text in this class? The authority of interpreting communities.* Cambridge, MA: Harvard University Press.

Foley, W. A. (1997). *Anthropological linguistics: An introduction.* Oxford, UK: Blackwell.

Frith, S. (1987). Towards an aesthetic of popular music. In *Music and Society: The politics of composition, performance and reception*, (ed. R. Leppert & S. McClary), pp. 133–49. Cambridge, UK: Cambridge University Press.

Gamman, L. & Marshment, M. (ed.) (1988). *The female gaze: Women as viewers of popular culture.* London: Women's Press.

Geertz, C. (1973). The impact of the concept of culture on the concept of man. In *The interpretation of cultures*, pp. 33–54. New York: Basic Books.

Geertz, C. (1983*a*). Blurred genres: The refiguration of social thought. In *Local knowledge: Further essays in interpretive anthropology*, pp. 19–35. New York: Basic Books.

Geertz, C. (1983*b*). 'Native's point of view': Anthropological understanding. In *Local knowledge: Further essays in interpretive anthropology*, pp. 55–70. New York: Basic Books.

Geertz, H. (1974). The vocabulary of emotion: A study of Javanese socialization processes. In *Culture and personality: Contemporary readings*, (ed. R. LeVine), pp. 249–64. Chicago: Aldine.

Gergen, K. J. (1991). *The saturated self: Dilemmas of identity in contemporary life.* New York: Basic Books.

Ghazzali, A. H. M. (1991). *The alchemy of happiness* (trans. C. Field & Rev. E. Daniel). London: M. E. Sharpe.

Gnoli, R. (1968). *The aesthetic experience according to Abhinava Gupta.* Varanasi: Chowkhamba Publications.

Goffman, E. (1959). *The presentation of self in everyday life.* Garden City, NY: Doubleday/Anchor Books.

Goldhill, S. (1996). Refracting classical vision: Changing cultures of viewing. In *Vision in context: Historical and contemporary perspectives on sight*, (ed. T. Brennan & M. Jay), pp. 17–28. London: Routledge.

Goodenough, W. H. (1970). *Description and comparison in cultural anthropology.* Chicago: Aldine.

Grotowski, J. (1968). *Towards a poor theatre.* New York: Simon & Schuster.

Hall, E. (1977). *Beyond culture.* Garden City, NY: Anchor Books.

Hebdige, D. (1995). Fabulous confusion! Pop before pop? In *Visual culture*, (ed. C. Jenks), pp. 96–122. London: Routledge.

Irvine, J. T. (1990). Registering affect: heteroglossia in the linguistic expression of emotion. In *Language and the politics of emotion* (ed. C. Lutz & L. Abu-Lughod), pp. 126–61. Cambridge, UK: Cambridge University Press.

James, W. (1950). *The principles of psychology*, (Vol. 2). New York: Dover Publications (Originally published in 1890).

**Jefferson, T.** (1994). *Declaration of independence and the constitution of the United States of America: the texts.* Washington, DC: National Defense Press (Originally published in 1776).

**Jenks, C.** (ed.) (1995). *Visual culture.* London: Routledge.

**Johnson, J. H.** (1995). *Listening in Paris.* Berkeley, CA: University of California Press.

**Katz, R.** (1982). Accepting 'boiling energy': The experience of !Kia healing among the !Kung. *Ethos: Journal of the Society for Psychological Anthropology,* 19, 348.

**Keil, C.** (1987). Participatory discrepancies and the power of music. *Cultural Anthropology,* 2, 275–83.

**Kern, S.** (1996). *Eyes of love: The gaze in English and French painting and novels: 1840–1900.* London: Reaktion Books.

**Leach, E.** (1981). A poetics of power. *New Republic,* 184, 14.

**Lerdahl, F. & Jackendoff, R.** (1983). *A generative theory of tonal music.* Cambridge, MA: MIT Press

**Levi-Strauss, C.** (1962). *The savage mind.* London: Wiedenfeld & Nicholson.

**Levy, R. I.** (1984). Emotion, knowing, and culture. In *Culture theory: Essays on mind, self, and emotion,* (ed. R. Shweder & R. LeVine), pp. 214–37. Cambridge, UK: Cambridge University Press.

**Lovejoy, A. O.** (1948). *Essays in the history of ideas.* Baltimore, MD: John Hopkins Press.

**Lovejoy, A. O.** (1964). *The great chain of being: a study of the history of an idea.* Cambridge, MA: Harvard University Press (Originally published in 1936).

**Lutz, C. A.** (1986). Emotion, thought, and estrangement: Emotion as a cultural category. *Cultural Anthropology,* 1, 287–309.

**Lutz, C. A.** (1988) *Unnatural emotions: Everyday sentiments on a Micronesian atoll and their challenge to Western theory.* Chicago: University of Chicago Press.

**Lutz, C. A. & Abu-Lughod, L.** (1990). Introduction: emotion, discourse, and the politics of everyday life. In *Language and the politics of emotion,* (ed. C. A. Lutz & L. Abu-Lughod), pp. 1–23. Cambridge, UK: Cambridge University Press.

**McClary, S.** (1991). *Feminine endings: Music, gender, and sexuality.* Minneapolis, MN: University of Minnesota Press.

**McDaniel, J.** (1995). Emotion in Bengali religious thought: Substance and metaphor. In *Emotions in Asian thought: A dialogue in comparative philosophy* (ed. J. Marks & R. T. Ames), pp. 39–63. Albany, NY: State University of New York Press.

**McNeill, W. H.** (1995). *Keeping together in time: Dance and drill in human history.* Cambridge, MA: Harvard University Press.

**Masson, J. L. & Patwardhan, M. V.** (1969). *Santarasa.* Poona: Bhandarkar Oriental Research Institute.

**Maturana, H. & Varela, F. J.** (1987). *The tree of knowledge: The biological roots of human understanding.* Boston: New Science Library.

**Melzack, R.** (1992). Phantom limbs. *Scientific American,* 266, 120–6.

**Merriam, A. P.** (1964). *The anthropology of music.* Evanston, IL: Northwestern University Press.

**Mitchell, W. J. T.** (1986). *Iconology: Image, text, ideology.* Chicago: University of Chicago Press.

**Morley, D.** (1995). Television: Not so much a visual medium, more a visible object. In *Visual culture,* (ed. C. Jenks), pp. 170–89. London: Routledge.

**Myers, F. R.** (1979). Emotions and the self: A theory of personhood and political order among Pintupi aborigines. *Ethos: Journal of the Society for Psychological Anthropology,* 7, 343–70.

**Needham, R.** (1981). Inner states as universals. In *Circumstantial deliveries,* pp. 53–71. Berkeley, CA: University of California Press.

Neher, A. (1961). Auditory driving observed with scalp electrodes in normal subjects. *Electroencephalography and Clinical Neurophysiology*, **13**, 449–51.

Neher, A. (1962). A physiological explanation of unusual behavior in ceremonies involving drums. *Human Biology*, **34**, 151–60.

Nettl, B. (1983). *The study of ethnomusicology: Twenty-nine issues and concepts*. Urbana, IL: University of Illinois Press.

Nunez, R. E. (1997). Eating soup with chopsticks: Dogmas, difficulties and alternatives in the study of conscious experience. *Journal of Consciousness Studies*, **4**, 143–66.

O'Neill, J. (1995). Foucault's optics: The (in)vision of mortality and modernity. In *Visual culture*, (ed. C. Jenks), pp. 190–201. London: Routledge.

Ortony, A., Clore, G. L., & Collins, A. (1988). *The cognitive structure of emotions*. Cambridge, UK: Cambridge University Press.

Qureshi, R. B. (1986). *Sufi music of India and Pakistan: Sound, context and meaning in qawwali*. Cambridge, UK: Cambridge University Press.

Racy, A. J. (1998). Improvisation, ecstasy, and performance dynamics in Arabic music. In *In the course of performance: Studies in the world of musical improvisation*, (ed. B. Nettl), pp. 95–112. Chicago: University of Chicago Press.

Raffman, D. (1993). *Language, music, and mind*. Cambridge, MA: MIT Press.

Rider, M. S. & Eagle, C. T. (1986). Rhythmic entrainment as a mechanism for learning in music therapy. In *Rhythm in psychological, linguistic and musical processes*, (ed. J. Evans & M. Clynes), pp. 225–48. Springfield, IL: C. C. Thomas.

Rosaldo, M. Z. (1984). Toward an anthropology of self and feeling. In *Culture theory: Essays on mind, self, and emotion*, (ed. R. Shweder & R. LeVine), pp. 137–57. Cambridge, UK: Cambridge University Press.

Rouget, G. (1985). *Music and trance: A theory of the relations between music and possession* (trans. B. Beibuyck). Chicago: University of Chicago Press.

Russell, J. A. (1991*a*). Culture and the categorization of emotions. *Psychological Bulletin*, **110**, 326–450.

Russell, J. A. (1991*b*). In defense of a prototype approach to emotion concepts. *Journal of Personality and Social Psychology*, **60**, 37–47.

Schechner, R. (1988). *Performance theory* (rev. edn). London: Routledge.

Seckel, A. (ed.) (1986). *Bertrand Russell on God and religion*. Buffalo, NY: Prometheus Books.

Seeger, A. (1987). *Why Suya sing: A musical anthropology of an Amazonian people*. Cambridge, UK: Cambridge University Press.

Shankar, R. (1968). *My music, my life*. New Delhi: Vikas Publications.

Shepherd, J. & Giles-David, J. (1991). Music, text and subjectivity. In *Music as social text*, pp. 174–85. Cambridge, MA: Polity Press.

Shweder, R. A. (1985). Menstrual pollution, soul loss, and the comparative study of emotions. In *Culture and depression: studies in the anthropology and cross-cultural psychiatry of affect and disorder*, (ed. A. Kleinman & B.Good), pp. 182–215. Berkeley, CA: University of California Press.

Shweder, R. A. & Bourne, E. J. (1984). Does the concept of the person vary cross-culturally? In *Culture theory: Essays on mind, self, and emotion* (ed. R. Shweder & R. LeVine), pp. 158–99. Cambridge, UK: Cambridge University Press.

Slater, D. (1995). Photography and modern vision: The spectacle of 'natural magic'. In *Visual culture*, (ed. C. Jenks), pp. 218–37. London: Routledge.

Small, C. (1998). *Musicking: The meanings of performing and listening.* Hanover: Wesleyan University Press.

Smith, J. C. & Ferstman, C. (1996). Knowledge and the languaging body. In *The castration of Oedipus: Feminism, psychoanalysis, and the will to power,* (ed. J. Smith), pp. 52–79. New York: New York University Press.

Solie, R. A. (1993). *Musicology and difference: Gender and sexuality in music scholarship.* Berkeley, CA: University of California Press.

Solomon, R. C. (1984). The Jamesian theory of emotion in anthropology. In *Culture theory: Essays on mind, self, and emotion,* (ed. R. Shweder & R. LeVine), pp. 238–54. Cambridge, UK: Cambridge University Press.

Spiro, M. E. (1984). Some reflections on cultural determinism and relativism with special reference to emotion and reason. In *Culture theory: Essays on mind, self, and emotion,* (ed. R. Shweder & R. LeVine), pp. 323–46. Cambridge, UK: Cambridge University Press.

Spivak, G. C. (1988). *In other worlds: Essays in cultural politics.* New York: Routledge.

Stanislavsky, K. (1958). *Stanslavski's legacy: A collection of comments on a variety of aspects of an actor's art and life,* (ed. and trans. E. R. Hapgood). New York: Theatre Arts Books.

Stone, R. (1982). *Let the inside be sweet: The interpretation of music events among the Kpelle of Liberia.* Bloomington, IN: Indiana University Press.

Taylor, C. (1989). *Sources of the self: The making of the modern identity.* Cambridge, MA: Harvard University Press.

Treitler, L. (1993). Reflections on the communication of affect and idea through music. In *Psychoanalytic explorations in music, Second Series,* (ed. S. Feder, R. Karmel, & G. Pollock), pp. 43–62. Madison, CT: International Universities Press.

Turino, T. (1993). *Moving away from silence: Music of the Peruvian altiplano and the experience of urban migration.* Chicago: University of Chicago Press.

Turner, V. (1983). Body, brain, and culture. *Zygon,* **18,** 221–45.

Varela, F. J., Thompson, E., & Rosch, E. (1991). *The embodied mind: Cognitive science and human experience.* Cambridge, MA: MIT Press.

Vaughn, K. (1990). Exploring emotion in sub-structural aspects of Karelian lament: Application of time series analysis to digitalized melody. *Yearbook for Traditional Music,* **22,** 106–22.

Viswanathan, T. & Cormack, J. (1998). Melodic improvisation in Karnatak music: The manifestation of raga. In *In the course of performance: Studies in the world of musical improvisation,* (ed. B. Nettl & M. Russell), pp. 219–33. Chicago: University of Chicago Press.

Von Campenhausen, H. (1964). *The fathers of the Latin church* (trans. M. Hoffman). London: Adam & Charles Black.

Wallin, N. L. (1991). *Biomusicology: Neurophysiological, neuropsychological, and evolutionary perspectives on the origins and purposes of music.* Stuyvesent, NY: Pendragon Press.

Walter, V. J. & Walter, W. G. (1949). The central effects of rhythmic sensory stimulation. *Electroencephalography and Clinical Neurophysiology,* **1,** 57–86.

Young, J. O. (1999). The cognitive value of music. *Journal of Aesthetics and Art Criticism,* **57,** 1–54.

Zizek, S. (1991). *Looking awry: An introduction to Jacques Lacan through popular culture.* Cambridge, MA: MIT Press.

Zizek, S. (1996). 'I hear you with my eyes'; or, the invisible master. In *Gaze and voice as love objects,* (ed. R. Saleci & S. Zizek), pp. 90–126. Durham, NC: Duke University Press.

CHAPTER 7

# AESTHETIC AGENCY AND MUSICAL PRACTICE: NEW DIRECTIONS IN THE SOCIOLOGY OF MUSIC AND EMOTION

TIA DENORA

## 7.1 The sociological approach

If psychology is concerned with human behaviour (Sloboda & Juslin, this volume), sociology is concerned with forms of social organization and the relation of these forms to social *action*, by which is usually meant, to paraphrase Max Weber (1978, Vol. 1, p. 4), conduct (real or hypothetical) that is meaningfully orientated in its course and outcome. The scope of material that falls within sociology's compass is wide, and perhaps it is because of its substantive breadth that sociology is a diverse—some would argue, fragmented—field.

Sociologists have traditionally employed a range of empirical strategies and theoretical perspectives, and have tended to engage in a high degree of intradisciplinary opposition such that is probably impossible to speak of 'a' sociological paradigm. For example, some sociologists seek to identify and quantify causes of collective and/or individual behaviour and to predict behavioural trends, while others seeks to understand meanings and meaning systems using ethnographic and qualitative methods of observation. The fissures within sociology are legion—*macro* (concern with large-scale institutions and trends) versus *micro* (focus on interactional process), *quantitative* versus *qualitative*, *structuralist* (focus on social forces and trends) versus *interpretive* (focus on meaning-making activity), to name a few. With that caveat, it is none the less possible to caricature the field by saying that sociology takes as its substantive focus a concern with action, intersubjectivity, the production of culture and knowledge, institutions, organizations and their conventions, and the implications of all these things for the social lives and life chances of individuals.

Whereas some psychologists might suggest that these topics are 'external' to the human organism, some sociologists, particularly those concerned with the sociology of the body, would counter that the nature/culture divide is ripe for dissolution (Birke 1992; Featherstone *et al.* 1991; Haraway 1985), to be replaced with a focus on how organismic features, cultural and material-cultural systems are reflexively linked.

Similarly, Foucauldian-inspired sociologists who have taken inspiration from post-structuralism and post-modern theory often suggest that our images of psychological 'interiority' owe much to post-Enlightenment discourses and discourse practices through which psychological subjects are constituted (Giddens 1991; Law 1994; Smith 1992). Put plainly, interior experience (here understood as the perception and self-perception of that experience) is shaped with reference to conventional, culturally, and historically specific categories that help to articulate and contain that experience. To be sure, these intra- and interdisciplinary conundrums can be explored most interestingly through the topic of emotion; adding music to the equation is even more useful because it allows for core sociological issues that centre around *agency* (here defined as a capacity for, and ability to, formulate action and experience) to be explored and advanced in a focused manner, in particular issues that concern agency's aesthetic and emotional dimension.

To that end, this chapter begins by considering the status of the emotions within sociology's paradigms. It moves from there to a discussion of music's position within sociology and focuses in particular on the changing conception of music's link to social life that has emerged within sociology of music over the past decade. From there, I survey classic works in the sociology of music as these illuminate music as a 'device' for the constitution of subjectivity and emotion in a range of settings. Throughout these discussions, my aim is to demonstrate how new approaches within the sociology of music help to highlight a congenital feature of sociology writ large, namely, the concern with social action, its sources, and its structures.

## 7.2 The rediscovery of emotion within sociology

There has been a longstanding interest within sociological theory in the emotions. One strand has developed out of Tönnies' (1957) concepts of *Gemeinschaft* and *Gessellschaft*. Tönnies used these terms to distinguish between social bonds built upon communal, emotional, traditional, and personal grounds versus those produced via rational and administrative procedures. The distinction, and with it a concern with the 'feeling' bases of social organization, has persisted and has established itself across a range of sociological perspectives. Max Weber's concern with the affective action (Weber 1978, Vol 1, pp. 24–8), Max Scheler's (1992) concern with the emotional flashes of insight that lead to knowledge (Remmling 1967, p. 33), Vilfredo Pareto's discussion of sentiments and non-logical aciton (Pareto 1963, p. 161), the 'human relations management' of Elton Mayo (Mayo 1933), Charles Horton Cooley's 'looking glass self' and its focus on emotion as the outcome of imaginative co-operation with external images (Cooley 1983), and Randall Collins' treatment of emotion in relation to rational choice theory (Collins 1993) have all highlighted emotion's role in relation to action and social structure.

And yet, despite this interest (and despite the formation of a thriving section on sociology of the emotions within the American Sociological Association), the affective dimension of human social being was, throughout the 1980s, mostly relegated to sociology's periphery. Particularly in the United States, where the discipline was dominated by rational actor models, and an attendant preoccupation with rule following, choice, and free will (Barnes 2000), the sociology of emotions was typically viewed as an off-shoot of 'micro' sociology and so disconnected from structuralist and 'macro' concerns. Within sociology's dominant disciplinary frameworks, phenomena such as revolution and war, diplomacy, occupations, social and class rivalry, political and economic activity, organizational and institutional behaviour, the rise and fall of social movements, and the exercise of social control were all portrayed as if they took place in passionless corridors, executed by agents who possessed reason but who did not *feel*.

Over the past 5 years or so, more sensitive sociological portraits of action have begun to emerge. With them, the status of the emotions as a topic has been elevated. From a number of subdisciplinary directions has come a new concern with the 'feeling' component of social action. This emphasis can be seen in current approaches to the sociological study of social and political movements and the emerging focus on the affective character of identification with a movement (Melucci 1996*a*, 1996*b*) and 'structures of feeling' as these are entered into, adopted, and adapted in the course of identity politics and movement activity (Hetherington 1998). This emotion renaissance is also evident in new work on political affiliation, for example on the processes by which citizens transfer feelings of 'belonging' from nations to global entities (Berezin 1999). It has been further fuelled by a rapidly growing sociology of the body (Featherstone *et al.* 1991; Turner 1984) and embodied experience (Bourdieu 1998; Williams 1996, 1998).

Thus, sociology is now much more closely affiliated with concerns and topics traditionally lodged within the purview of social psychology. But this trend toward motivation and emotion has simultaneously been linked to sociology's abiding concern with social contexts—situations, occasions, institutions, and organizations—and with the hitherto 'macro' sociological terrain of collective and institutional action. The result is that sociology has begun to eradicate a bifurcation that has been both its hallmark and impediment for more than a century, namely, the distinction between 'micro' and 'macro' levels of analysis. In place of this division, prominent figures within sociology have moved toward a position that brings the feeling component of action—and hence some of the non-rational bases of social order—to the fore. As Alberto Melucci (1996*b*, p. 1) has expressed it:

Each and every day we make ritual gestures, we move to the rhythm of external and personal cadences, we cultivate our memories, we plan for the future. And everyone else does likewise. Daily experiences are only fragments in the life of an individual, far removed from the collective events more visible to us, and distant from the great changes sweeping through our culture. Yet almost everything that is important for social life unfolds within this minute web of times, spaces, gestures, and relations. It is through this web that our sense of what we are doing is created, and in it lie dormant those energies that unleash sensational events.

The playing out of social change, politics, social movements, and relations of production are experienced and renewed from within this 'web', as Melucci calls it; it is from within the matrix of 'times, spaces, gestures and relations' that these 'larger' things are realized. Put differently, it is on the platform of the mundane and the sensual that the specificity of social experience is rendered and patterns are renewed.

A common thread running throughout nearly all of the recent focus on emotions within sociology has consisted of a focus on the interplay between emotions in lived experience and cultural forms. Inspired by the emphasis within post-structuralist and post-modernist theory on discourse and by the concurrent emphasis on texts and artefacts as they imply readers, users, and 'subject positions' (particular and convention-ally understood emotional stances, styles, or niches), sociologists across a wide range of specialist areas have devoted themselves to the question of how material-cultural and aesthetic media may be understood to provide models or candidate structures for the production and achievement of emotion and feeling within specific social settings. This focus has been clear within areas such as gender and sexuality and its concern with the cultural construction of desire and sexual practice (Jackson 1996, 1999), the study of spoken discourse in real time encounters (Frazer & Cameron 1989), organizational behaviour (Witkin 1995), and the sociology of material culture (Akrich 1991; Latour 1991; Law 1994; Moore 1997; Woolgar 1997).

It is from within this framework that the sociology of music can be seen to interact with the broader sociological focus on emotion. Having undergone significant transfor-mation in the past decade, socio-music studies have moved from preoccupations with music's production to concerns with how it is consumed and what it 'does' in social life. In this regard, developments within the sociology of music merge with developments in the sociology of the arts more widely (Bowler 1994). Recent developments within the field have examined connections between musical consumption and musical experience as a means of producing and sustaining social ordering in real time, over the life course, and with reference to organizational and collective spheres of action. These develop-ments have helped to return the sociology of music to the systematic concerns laid out early on in the area by figures such as Max Weber (1958), T. W. Adorno (1967, 1973, 1976, 1999), and Alfred Schutz (1964)—who is of particular interest because of his focus on music's relation to, and ability to, configure 'inner time' (pp. 172, 174). They have helped to renew the sociology of music's emphasis on fundamental questions concerning music's role as an active ingredient of social formation, its traditional and common sense role as the medium *par excellence* of emotion construction. In short, there is now a place at the top of sociology's table for the study of music.

Such a project involves considerable sweep: it encompasses matters that are usually desegregated—a focus on systems of music production and distribution, on organiza-tional ecology and management, and on subjective experience as it is configured in rela-tion to musical media.

## 7.3 Music and social structures: the movement toward conceptual symmetry

From the 1970s to fairly recently, the sociology of music and the sociology of culture more broadly have been concerned with how music is *produced*, with its occupational–politics–distribution systems, and with semiotic readings of musical forms. The empha-sis was upon music as an object shaped by social relations. What remained tacit was any symmetrical attempt to conceive of music as a potentially dynamic medium, or to con-sider what music may 'do' in, to, and for the social relations in which it is embedded. Thus, only one half of the equation was present, albeit a crucial half, focusing on how musical works take shape in ways that are enabled and constrained by their cultures and worlds of production. As a result, apart from some notable exceptions discussed below, the matter of musical experience, and music's links to emotion, passion, and energy, and to the phenomenological and existential features of social life, were all uncharted waters within sociology's paradigm. Even when sociologists considered music consumption, the focus was directed less to the matter of musical experience than to the ways in which tastes, musical values, and listening practices served as symbolic boundaries for status groups and status differences (Bourdieu 1984; Bryson 1997; DeNora 1995; DiMaggio 1982; Lamont 1992; Peterson & Simkus 1992).

As Peter Martin has observed (1995, p. 1), music is ubiquitous in modern societies, yet the significance of music's ubiquity often goes unnoticed within social sciences. In recent years, music's role as an active ingredient of social formation and subjectivity has been restored. Within this 'new' music sociology of emotions, it is possible to conceptualize music as a device for the constitution of emotive action in and across a range of social settings. This concern with *emotion construction* (through musical practice) offers an avenue into sociology's new concerns with the non-cognitive dimensions of agency (e.g. its emotional dimension) and also illuminates the relationship between culture and agency. In the remainder of this chapter, I seek to develop this perspective. I begin, in the next section, with reference to two, originally distinct, strands within the discipline that can be understood to provide the bedrock for more recent work: Adorno's theory of music as a medium of social organization and the more overtly empirical and ethnographic studies of music and lifestyle practice as propounded by Paul Willis in the 1970s.

## 7.4 Music, emotions, and subjectivity: sociology's classic models

For Theodor Adorno, music was inextricably connected to habits of mind, to social structural organization, and to modes of subjectivity. The music of Arnold Schoenberg, for example, he viewed as able to foster critical consciousness because its material organization went against the grain of musical convention and cliché. Conversely, in the age of 'total administration', music was also a medium that 'trains the unconscious for conditioned reflexes' (Adorno 1976, p. 53). Jazz, Tin Pan Alley, and nearly every other popular music genre was linked, in Adorno's view, to forms of regression and infantile dependency (Adorno 1990).

Adorno's work explores the idea that music interiorizes and is able to instigate forms of social organization in and through the ways that it works on and configures its subject-recipient. Put bluntly, Adorno conceived of music as active, indeed formative, in relation to consciousness. In this regard, his work makes some of the strongest claims on behalf of music's power in any discipline. But because Adorno provided no machinery for conceptualizing music's power empirically, his work is also frustrating; it never operationalizes the claim that music 'trains' the unconscious, nor points the way toward how these matters might be observed at the grounded level of musical practice. Adorno's work remained in the safe haven of theory and semiotic 'readings' of (primarily art music) works; it ventured but little into the realm of empirical analysis and the sphere of music consumption (indeed, Adorno's comments on music reception are mainly devoted to delineating a hierarchy of listener types). In its refusal to go out and look at the world, Adorno's work suffers at times from parochialism (e.g. his views on jazz, his unilateral condemnation of popular culture, and his tendency to prescribe musical taste).

During the 1970s, more empirically orientated work on 'music and society' provided an alternative to Adorno's hypothetical approach. The originally British tradition of cultural studies, ethnographically conceived, was directed at exploring connections between music and lived experience—identity creation, feeling, and the social constitution of embodied action and its parameters. Moreover, these explicitly ethnographic works may be read, with hindsight, to have presaged current developments.

Within the classic studies of young people and their intimate involvement with music, in books such as Paul Willis' *Profane culture* (1978), and Simon Frith's early monographs, *Sound effects* (1981) and *The sociology of rock* (1978), music's social presence was illuminated. Rereading these works with their characteristic focus on the experience of music, it is possible to see music providing a resource in and through which agency, identity, and peer culture are produced. Indeed, these studies can be seen to be compatible with Adorno's concern with music's link, and ability to instigate, social being. But this time, the music–social structure nexus was specified in a manner amenable to observation and in terms of how music was actually consumed and used. Music's structuring properties were understood as actualized in and through the practices of musical use, through the ways music was used and referred to by actors in their ongoing attempts to produce their social situations and themselves.

For example, in his report on the culture of the 'bikeboys', Willis noted that the boys' preferred songs were fast-paced and characterized by a strong beat, a pulsating rhythm. Willis showed how the boys established connections between music and social life. Structural similarities—homologies—between music and social behaviour were forged through the bikeboys' cultural practices and classifications.

Willis's focus was directed at the question of how particular actors make connections or, as Stuart Hall (1980, 1986) later put it, 'articulations' between music and social phenomena and how this process of linking music with forms of social life is part of actors' ongoing constitution of their life worlds and themselves. Although he never described his project as such, Willis's work on the bikeboys and on music's role as part of 'profane culture' more widely served to establish no less than an interactionist version of Adorno's original vision, that is an approach to the question of music's link to subjectivity, to cognitive style, and to actors' ontological orientations. Key, however, was that Willis's approach captured music's social impact as it was achieved by the ways in which actors themselves made 'articulations' or links between forms of music and forms of social life. It drew upon the basic interactionist tenet within sociology that agents attach connotations to things and orientate to social circumstances on the basis of perceived meanings. And it highlighted, through ethnographic description, the way in which social forms of organization are made through reference to aesthetic materials. This focus on the social process of world making (and the role of cultural media in this process) signalled an important shift in focus from aesthetic objects and their 'content' (static) to the cultural practices in and through which aesthetic materials were appropriated and used (dynamic) to produce social life. It simultaneously served to justify the need for 'symmetrical' conceptualizations of the relationship between music and social structure.

The bikeboys' music, as Willis noted, did not leave its recipients 'just sit[ting] there moping all night' (1978, p. 69). On the contrary, it invited, perhaps incited, movement.

As one of the boys put it, 'if you hear a fast record you've got to get up and do something, I think. If you can't dance any more, or if the dance is over, you've just got to go for a burn-up [motorcycle ride]' (1978, p. 73). Willis's work was thus pioneering in its demonstration of how music does much more than 'depict' or embody values. It portrayed music as active and dynamic, as constitutive not merely of 'values' but constitutive of trajectories and styles of conduct in real time. As one of the boys observed, 'you can hear the beat in your head, don't you . . . you go with the beat, don't you?' (1978, p. 72). This insight was germane to more recent developments in the field, for it points to the ways in which music, as it is heard or imagined, may serve to organize or 'configure' its users. Willis showed, for example, how music was implicated in the temporal structure of the bikeboys' evening, how it took them from—or provided the fulcrum for—one state (sitting around) to another (dancing as the music plays) to another (riding as the music plays in memory). Viewed in this way, music can be conceived of as a kind of aesthetic technology, or an instrument of social ordering.

It is precisely this interactionist conception that has been rediscovered by younger sociologists and sociologically minded scholars of music and subjectivity (it also lives on in the recent work of its pioneers; see Frith 1996; Willis 2000). For example, Sarah Cohen was one of the first to call for a renewal of an ethnography of musical practice in her insistence that 'focus upon people and their musical practices and processes rather than upon structures, texts or products illuminates the ways in which music is used and the important role that it plays in everyday life and in society generally' (Cohen 1993, p. 127). Similarly, Georgina Born argued, in her ethnography of IRCAM, that it is necessary to focus on 'the actual uses of technologies [she could just as well have said 'musics'], which are often depicted in idealised, unproblematic, and normative ways' (Born 1995, p. 15). In common with all instruments and technological devices, then, music needs to be understood in terms of its (non-verbal) capacities for enabling and constraining its user(s). Within current sociology, this focus has been directed at how individuals come to appropriate musical forms, and how musical forms feature within social settings as organizing materials of action. How, then, can this idea be developed and how can music's structuring powers be illuminated at the level of social experience? In the remaining sections of this chapter, I present two more examples of recent work concerned with music's role as a resource for the constitution of emotional experience. This discussion should be read in conjunction with the chapter by Sloboda and O'Neill (this volume) on emotions in everyday listening to music.

## 7.5 Music and emotion work: producing feeling in daily life

One of the most promising trends in current music sociology has been the focus on how music may be used—with varying degrees of conscious awareness by and on behalf of actors as a resource—to construct self-identity and to create and maintain a variety of feeling states. This work clearly connects with pioneering efforts within social psychology (De Las Heras 1997; Neilly 1995; Sloboda 1992, 1999) and ethnomusicology (Crafts *et al.* 1993; see also Becker, this volume). But it also speaks to an explicitly sociological concern with organizational aesthetics and with the social distribution of emotion and conventional notions concerning feeling structures within particular social settings (for example, matters such as who is entitled to feel what type of emotion, where, when, and how).

The distinctively sociological quality of this concern is its focus on how individuals are produced or produce themselves as social agents with attendant styles of feeling and emotional stature. Thus, from within sociology, emotions are regarded as 'socially constituted' so that the study of music reception and consumption connects with recent discussions within sociology of 'aesthetic reflexivity' (Lash & Urry 1994, Chapter 4) and 'aesthetic agency' (DeNora 1997, 2000; Witkin & DeNora 1997). These terms highlight the consumption of aesthetic media as a means for self-interpretation and self-constitution, for the doing, being, and feeling that is the matrix of social experience. They simultaneously call for an overtly ethnographic turn in the study of aesthetic reception and thus interact with developments in the sociology of media and the plastic arts (Press 1994; Radway 1988; Tota 1997, 1999).

### 7.5.1 Music as a technology of emotion construction

Two recent studies illustrate this point. The first focuses upon music consumption in France (Gomart & Hennion 1999; Hennion & Maisonneuve 1998), the second on England and the USA (DeNora 1999, 2000). Both draw on roughly 50 in-depth interviews and both have concentrated on music's role in relation to the achieved character of feeling, to the ways in which actors' adoption of emotional stances, subject positions, and states are simultaneously the objects of actors' cultural practices in specific settings. In this regard, these works have begun to pave the way for a new sociology of music and emotions, one that conjoins an ethnomethodological focus (on the procedures and practical activities in and through which social orderings are accomplished in real time and in particular social contexts; Garfinkel 1967; Heritage 1984; Law 1994) with a focus on emotions in terms of how they are crafted and experienced within social situations.

In a piece that compares the love of music with the love of taking drugs, and which draws upon in-depth interviews with music lovers and with drug addicts, Gomart and Hennion (1999) examine actors as they engage in 'techniques of preparation' that produce forms of attachment so as to clarify the mechanisms that produce 'disposition'. In so doing, they shift the focus of their particular theoretical persuasion, 'actor network theory', from action to the study of interaction between people and things, and with this shift they make a concomitant move away from the overly general category of 'action' to the more specific concept of 'event'. They highlight 'what occurs' when, as part of the musical—or narcotic—experience, the self is 'abandoned' or given over to sensation and/or emotion. They are interested in no less than an ethnographic sociology of the production of passion.

With regard to the music lovers, they delineate the various practices involved in preparing for aesthetic experience. For example, Gomart and Hennion describe how their interviewees describe becoming 'ready in one's head' for the ear to hear and the body to respond (1999, p. 232), or how they employ particular listening strategies and rhythms so as to be ready to respond in preferred or expected ways. This process is akin to 'tuning in' or attempting to produce, through fine tuning practices, a signal's power and clarity. Listeners, they suggest, like drug users, 'meticulously *establish conditions* [emphasis in original]: active work must be done in order to be moved' (1999, p. 227).

Listeners are by no means simply 'affected' by music but are, rather, active in constructing their 'passivity' to music—their ability to be 'moved'. The music 'user' is thus deeply implicated as a producer of his or her own emotional response—that is, one who:

strives tentatively to fulfil those conditions which will let him be seized and taken over by a potentially exogenous force. 'Passivity' then is not a moment of inaction—not a lack of will of the user who suddenly fails to be a full subject. Rather passivity adds to action, potentializes action. (Gomart & Hennion 1999, p. 243)

Gomart and Hennion were attuned to the question of how 'events' of musical passion and emotional response—the being 'taken over' by music—is reflexively accomplished by music lovers. Similarly, DeNora's study deals with music's role in the day-to-day lives of American and British women as they used music to regulate, enhance, and change qualities and levels of emotion. Nearly all of these women were explicit about music's role as an ordering device at the 'personal' level, as a means for creating, enhancing, sustaining, and changing subjective, cognitive, bodily, and self-conceptual states. Levels of musical training notwithstanding, the respondents exhibited considerable awareness about the music they 'needed' to hear in different situations and at different times, drawing upon elaborate repertoires of musical programming practice, and were sharply aware of how to mobilize music to arrive at, enhance, and alter aspects of themselves and their self-concepts. Part of their criteria for the 'right' music was how well it 'fitted' or was suitable for the purpose or situation they wished to achieve, or for achieving a particular emotional state (see the discussion of 'fit' in Sloboda and O'Neill, this volume). For example, as one respondent, Lucy, put it describing how she came to take time out to listen to some of the Schubert *Impromptus* (quoted in DeNora 2000, p. 16).

I was feeling very 'stressed' this morning 'cause we're in the throes of moving house and its, you know, we're not, we haven't sold our house yet, and its moving, you know, and, um, so I actively decided to put on Schubert's *Impromptus* because they were my father's favourite—you might want to come along to that again, because Schubert's *Impromptus* have a long history with my life—and I thought, my husband had just gone off to work and I thought well, about half an hour before I come up here [to her place of paid work], I'll just listen to them. So, the speakers are [she gestures] there and there on either side of what used to be the fireplace and I sit in a rocking chair facing them, so I get the sound in between the speakers, and I just sat there and listened [sighs, gentle laughter].

Q. [gentle laughter]

A. But I needed it. It was only ten minutes or so, you know, I didn't listen to them all. I just listened to the bits I wanted to listen to.'

Here, the music's powers to instigate emotion are constituted by Lucy herself; the music's power derives from the ways she interacts with it (Fig 7.1). The *Impromptus*, for Lucy, bear meaning on many levels. Their character as physical sound structures and their relation to a body of musical-stylistic convention is interpolated with, for Lucy, equally important biographical connotations and with a history of use such that the pieces calm her not only because they embody musical calm, but because they restore to Lucy a sense of her own identity. First, for Lucy, the works are associated with comfort; they are bound up with a complex of childhood memories and associations. Her late father, to whom she was close, used to play the piano after dinner and these works, wafting up the stairs, were ones Lucy used to hear as she was falling asleep. Second, the material culture of listening is also an accomplice, in this example, of music's power to shift Lucy's mood on the morning she describes. Lucy's listening is conducted in a quiet room. She sits in a rocking chair placed between the speakers and so is almost nestled in the, as she perceives it, calm and nurturing music. (The vocabulary of nurturing is Lucy's. As she puts it, music 'soothes me', 'I retreat into music when I can't bear the rest of the world, you know', 'you can go into [music] and have it around you or be in it', quoted in DeNora 2000, p. 42.)

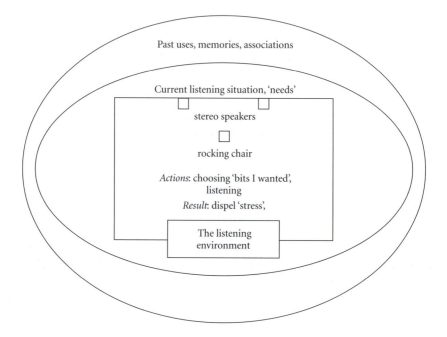

**Figure 7.1** Ten to 15 minutes spent with music: 'Lucy' and Schubert's *Impromptus.*

This example typifies the kind of practical knowledge respondents exhibited repeatedly in their accounts of (often tacit) music practices. Through these practices, respondents produced themselves as coherent social and socially disciplined beings. As in the French data reported by Gomart and Hennion (1999), the British and American respondents routinely engaged in various practices of 'tuning in', of producing a musical event that would be capable of 'moving' them, and this production of passivity in the face of music, and its subsequent emotional 'effect' was achieved through an assemblage of musical practices. These included the choice of specific recordings, volume levels, material-cultural and temporal environments of listening (for example choosing to listen in bed, in a rocking chair, in the bath in the evening, in the morning, or while preparing to go out), and the pairing and compiling of musical works, memories, and previous and current contexts of hearing, such that the respondents could often be conceived as—and spoke of themselves as—disk jockeys to themselves (Fig 7.2).

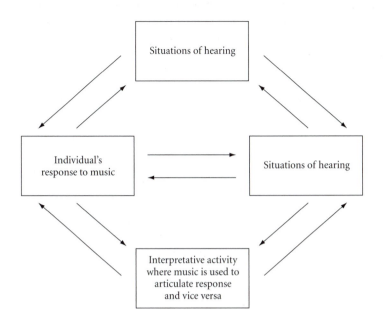

**Figure 7.2** The reflexive constitution of emotional states or events through reference to music in social situations.

Thus, in both the French and the British/American studies, music can be seen as a medium or device for achieving 'emotional work'. First coined by Arlie Hochschild (1983) to describe practices within the workplace where workers were required to produce not only material goods or services, but also to produce themselves as types of emotional agents acting under the organizational cultural auspices (and bearing a strong resemblance to Cooley's conception of emotion constitution in his discussion of 'looking glass self', see above), the concept of emotional work has since been adopted more widely within sociology, where emotion is conceived as a 'bodily co-operation with an image, a thought, a memory—a co-operation of which the individual is aware' (Hochschild 1979, p. 551, quoted in Williams 1996, p. 129). Respondents described how they used music both routinely and in exceptional circumstances to regulate moods and energy levels, to enhance and maintain desired states of feeling and bodily energy (e.g. relaxation, excitement), and to diminish or modify undesirable emotional states (e.g. stress, fatigue).

For example, in their own words, the British and American women interviewed by DeNora described how music's specific properties such as rhythms, gestures, harmonies, and styles provided them with referents or representations of 'where' they wish to 'be' or 'go', emotionally, physically, and so on:

Like with my R&B, um, most of the time I listen to it when I'm, you know, trying to relax. I'm gonna sleep, sometimes I'll throw on a few tracks to wake me up, nice 'n slow and then I'll throw on, something else. And then, sometimes, you know, if I'm not really not in that relaxed mood,

I'm like, you know, 'I don't wanna listen to that' and I'll throw something fast on, or, something fast is playing and I'm like 'that's too chaotic for me right now, I have to put something slow on'. (Latoya, New York City, quoted in DeNora 2000, p. 49)

Respondents made, in other words, articulations between musical works, styles, and materials on the one hand, and desired modes of agency on the other, and then used music to presage, inspire, elaborate, or remind them of those modes of agency and their associated emotional forms. When respondents chose music as part of this care of self, they often engaged in self-conscious articulation work, thinking ahead about the music that might 'work' for them. And their articulations were made on the basis of what they perceived the music to afford. This perception is in turn shaped by a range of matters. Among these are previous associations respondents have made between particular musical materials and other things (biographical, situational), their understandings of the emotional implications of conventional musical devices, genres, and styles, and their perceived parallels (articulations/homologies) between musical materials/processes and social or physical materials/processes.

With regard to this last issue, the popular music scholar Richard Middleton (1990) has provided a useful bridge between sociology's focus on the articulations actors forge between music and feeling and musicology's focus on the ways in which temporal, rhythmic, and harmonic structures may lend themselves to particular interpretations, and how they may afford or instigate particular responses (see also Cook & Dibben, this volume). Middleton discusses what he refers to as 'exosemantic correspondences' between music and spatial or emotional structures/forms (e.g. slow and quiet: 'relaxed'; minor mode: 'depressed'), and develops semiotic concepts of 'primary' and 'secondary' signification (1990, pp. 220–32). The former refers to music's internal references and relationships, its arrangement of structural elements, and to the ways in which its relationships become terms in which to map, frame, and configure (in this case) emotions: '. . .as this note is to that note, as tonic is to dominant, as ascent is to descent, as accent is to weak beat (and so on), so X is to Y' (1990, p. 223). The latter refers to music's connotative level, its ability to invoke or symbolize images, emotions, and ideas.

While, as Middleton (1990) rightly emphasizes, music's material specificity comes to be implicated in emotion construction, music's capacity to engender emotion is by no means preordained. A characteristic of the perspectives on music and emotions discussed so far is their circumvention of, on the one hand, essentialist conceptions of subjectivity (as if feeling arises from internal processes) and, on the other, the notion that music is a 'cause' of emotional states. By contrast, these 'subject-object' dichotomies are bypassed by considering music as part of—a resource for—the reflexive constitution or working up of emotional states or events (see Fig 7.2). Here, music is not conceived as a 'stimulus' nor does it, *pace* Langer (1942), merely 'resonate' with some pre-existing subjective or mental state to which it exists in parallel. Indeed, this view, of which Langer is an exponent, has been subject to criticism from within sociology by Shepherd and Wicke (1997, pp. 12–14) who, though they endorse the idea that homologies exist or are forged between emotions and musical structures, suggest that the insights from musicology on the ways in which music's structures symbolize emotional structures do not 'stretch to an explanation of the mechanisms through which musical processes and processes of subjectivity are involved with one another' (1997, p. 13). In contrast with musicological conceptions that confine analytical focus to, for the most part, the musical 'object', most of the sociologists discussed so far tend to conceive of music as providing a *resource* for emotional states and their achievement. Neither a cause nor a parallel of emotional states, music is conceived within sociology as providing a candidate simulacrum, or contrast structure, against which feeling may be formulated in real time. To speak of music in this way is to speak of it as a material against which 'how one feels' may be identified, elaborated, and made into an object of knowledge. One may, for example, say in reference to a musical example, '*this* is how I feel', and thereby grow tense and relax as the music does, when the music does, or in ways that are modelled, often without conscious awareness, on the music. It is here, then, that music's vital, and indeed, moral dimension—as declaimed by classical philosophers such as Plato ('in music that the guardians will build their guardhouse'; Plato 1966, p. 72) and Aristotle ('what we have said makes it clear that music possesses the power of producing an effect on the character of the soul'; Aristotle 1980, p. 24) can be seen: musical structures and representations are drawn, by actors themselves, into the vortex of feeling production; they literally 'get into' action and subjectivity.

In short, recent studies of music in relation to the achievement of emotional states and events points to music's use in real social settings as a device that actors employ for entraining and structuring feeling trajectories. Music is a resource to which agents turn so as to regulate themselves as aesthetic agents, as feeling, thinking, and acting beings in their day-to-day lives. Achieving this regulation requires a high degree of practical reflexivity. The respondents in both the French and the English/American case studies show how actors often perceive their 'need' for this regulation and know the techniques of auto-emotion work. These techniques may be found inadvertently (e.g. something is tried once and 'works' and so is later repeated and thus becomes part of an individual repertoire), or they may be suggested through culture and the media (and so be, at least initially, imitative), or they may be handed down by associates (and so exist as part of group or family culture), or initially encountered in a social setting—all of these technique locations were mentioned by respondents.

The natural history of the processes through which feeling states are identified and 'expressed' (i.e. enacted to self or other over time) is, moreover, a topic to be developed as it concerns the question of how aesthetic agency is configured in real time, as passion is choreographed and entrained. Holding on to this focus, but widening it from the individual experience of culture (and the social regulation of emotion in and through reference to cultural materials) to music's role in relation to the organization of collective action and its emotional component is but the next step within this programme. In the remainder of this chapter, I survey classic and recent work devoted to music's regulatory role in relation to emotional conduct between two actors engaged in intimate conduct, and between more than two actors, using the case of social movement activity.

## 7.6 Music and emotions in close interaction

Studies of gender and musical taste have long directed their focus to music's connections to love and to courtship. Shepherd and Giles-Davis (1991), for example, have reported on the consumption and use of music by a small number of middle-class

English-speaking teenage girls in Montreal, showing how music provides a kind of template for the formation of sexuality and emotional state. More recently, focus has shifted to the question of how music is actually used during intimate occasions and how it may draw bodies into temporal trajectories (rhythms, pulses, corporeal grammars, movement styles, and feeling grammars). Here, music is viewed as a non-verbal accomplice for particular intimate action forms (DeNora 1997), such that 'who puts what on the record player' as a prelude or backdrop for intimacy is overtly conceived as a question of love's real-time construction and its politics.

Many of the interviewees in DeNora's study (in particular the two younger age groups) described, through a rich series of examples from their daily lives, how they sought to structure both the grammar and style of intimate interaction through musical means and also to reproduce feeling styles and forms by using music that had served as the soundtrack on prior intimate occasions. The typical category for this activity was the concept of 'background' or 'mood' music and the interviewees were unanimous on one point: the music should not be fast paced, loud, or jolting. On the contrary, respondents spoke of how they valued the temporal structures and embodied practices commensurate with a slow pace, with leisured intimate activity. Their responses overlapped with what has already been observed in relation to gender and musical taste (Bryson 1997; Frith & McRobbie 1990; Peterson & Simkus 1992). 'Setting is very important' as one respondent put it, because getting the music 'right' is simultaneously a way of trying to make the action 'right', not merely in the embodied and technical sense, but as a way of prospectively calling out forms of emotional and embodied agency that are comfortable and preferable, that 'feels' right in emotional and embodied terms. (Such agency, of course, includes specific material practices, e.g. a 'light' touch or an 'unhurried' approach, and the music can be perceived as providing 'primary significations' of these things and hence employed as a model or blueprint for action):

I think, last night, it was really funny, it was like 'mood setting' in a way. Cause, like, he had Enya on, and like, as people call that, 'chick music' [i.e. 'women's' music that young men may choose to play when entertaining women because they think it is what women prefer] . . . and he was trying to produce a relaxed atmosphere and um, I think in a way it does promote physical, or just intimacy in general because it's just like, certain music's more calming and, I remember like I think Stigma or Hyper came on and we were like, 'no no no, we don't want that!' and we like tried to get this piece, like I had him play the *First Night* sound track which I love, and there's like, a love song I, there, that's so beautiful, but everything else is like, 'bu bu de bah' [she sings here a triplet followed by a whole note the interval of a fifth higher than the triplet figure] and I'm like, 'no, no, this is not good' but I do, I think it was just very, it's very calming, very intimacy . . .

Q. So it's part of what creates an intimate atmosphere?

Melinda: Yeah, definitely. I think it's, setting is very important, and like music is a very big part of that. (quoted in DeNora 2000, p. 112)

## 7.7 Music and collective action: the case of social movements

Outside the sphere of intimacy, music can also be seen to serve as a model for emotional agency. One of the key areas where this perspective has been developed is within the area of social movements, where new work has sought to draw together the sociology of emotions and the sociology of collective action. Taking inspiration from anthropologist Victor Turner's (1981) concern with 'action paradigms' (cultural materials such as narratives and imagery that may be used in ways that 'emplot' courses of action), Ron Eyerman and Andrew Jamieson (1998, p. 23) have attempted to specify how music may be understood to play an organizing role in the structure of collective action:

> To the categories of action discussed by sociologists we wish to add the concept of exemplary action. As represented or articulated in the cognitive praxis of social movements, exemplary action can be thought of as a specification of the symbolic action discussed by Melucci and others. The exemplary action of cognitive praxis is symbolic in several senses; but it is also 'more' than merely symbolic. As real cultural representations—art, literature, songs—it is artefactual and material, as well. What we are attempting to capture with the term is the exemplary use of music and art in social movements, the various ways in which songs and singers can serve a function akin to the exemplary works that Thomas Kuhn characterised as being central to scientific revolutions: the paradigm-constituting entities that serve to realign scientific thinking and that represent ideal examples of fundamentally innovative scientific work (Kuhn, 1970). The difference between culture and science, however, is that the exemplary action of music and art is lived as well as thought: it is cognitive, but it also draws on more emotive aspects of human consciousness.

As with the examples of individual feeling work discussed by DeNora (1999, 2000) and Hennion (Gomart & Hennion 1999; Hennion & Masisonneuve 1998), Eyerman and Jamieson (1998) describe how music may serve, within the context of social movement activity, as a prescriptive device of agency. Within music's structures, its perceived connotations, and its sensual parameters (dynamics, sound envelopes, harmonies, textures, colours, etc.), actors may 'find' or compose themselves as agents with particular capacities for social action.

For example, Eyerman and Jamieson (1998) describe how Todd Gitlin, a president of the Students for a Democratic Society (SDS) in the 1960s, described the SDS's identification with the music of Bob Dylan ('we followed his career as if he were singing our song; we got in the habit of asking where he was taking us next'; p. 116). In this sense, music may be conceptualized as akin to what Robert Witkin (1974) calls a 'holding form'—a set of motifs that proceed, and serve as a reference point for, lines of feeling and lines of conduct over time. Viewed as such, music plays a role that is similar to that of memory artefacts, as discussed by Urry (1996) and Radley (1990): musical motifs are orientated to for the ways they encapsulate and provide a container for what might otherwise pass as a momentary impulse to act, or a momentary identification of some kind. Holding forms thus provide a touchstone to which actors may return as they engage in collective expressive activity. They are the templates within which agency takes shape and to which actors may refer to renew themselves as types of agents and emotional agents.

Seen in this light, the study of how music is appropriated for emotion work illuminates a fundamental topic within sociology: it provides a way of exploring how social reality, with its forms and relations of feeling, are produced in real time and within specific social milieu. Critical then is the issue that held Adorno and which concerns music's role in modern societies, the matter of how the aesthetic environments that come to afford agency's production are themselves produced. And so the study of consumption returns full circle to the study of production and dissemination as complementary enterprises. Especially with regard to the public spaces where agency is produced, music's role here has grown massively over the past two decades. If music is a device of social ordering, if—in and through its manner of appropriation—it is a resource against which holding forms, templates, and parameters of action and experience are forged, if it can be seen to have 'effects' upon bodies, hearts, and minds, *then* the matter of music in the social space is, as I have discussed above, an aesthetic-political matter. This is why matters of musical taste have, throughout history and across culture, often been contentious.

## 7.8 Conclusion

It seems fair to characterize current sociology of music as involved in two projects with regard to the emotions. The first is to produce portraits of music 'in action', that is, ethnographic documentaries of actors' musical practices and of the role these practices play in the production of emotion in real time and specific social settings. The second is to use these ethnographic reports to generate grounded hypotheses of how music functions in social life, what it does, and how it is reflexively implicated in the creation and recreation of social realms, events, and states.

With regard to this second aim, current work on music as a dynamic medium in social life has highlighted music's role as providing a structure or container for feeling, one whose specific properties contribute to the shape and quality of feeling as it is articulated and sustained in real time within and between individuals as part of the fabrication of ongoing social existence. In short, music is a resource for the practical constitution of entities we know as 'selves' and also for emotions and states that we refer to as 'intersubjective'. It is also a resource for the prospective structuring of action and a material that actors may employ as a referent or template as they elaborate and fill in, to themselves and to others, the modes of agency and subjective stances and identities that are structure-in-action. New work in the sociology of music and the emotions has been devoted to revealing music as it 'gets into' and is incorporated into action and to illuminating this process as it is achieved in and through actors' musical practices. This sociology of the 'musical composition' of subjectivity should be distinguished from more general post-structuralist or postmodernist theories of subjectivity and its 'cultural construction' that deal with emotions and subjectivity in monolithic ways and often leave little space for actors' creative and adaptive practices of emotion work. By contrast, the new sociology of music is devoted to a task that far exceeds assertions about music and the subject positions it may place on offer. It is concerned with specifying these matters at the level of action and action's 'heart' where actors are involved in the production of their social 'experience' and also in the mobilization of cultural and aesthetic materials for being, doing, and feeling. Anything less than this cannot address or begin to account for the mechanisms through which cultural materials 'get into' social psychological life and provide building materials of action.

# References

Adorno, T. W. (1967). *Prisms* (trans. S. Weber & S. Weber). London: Neville Spearman.

Adorno, T. W. (1973). *Philosophy of modern music* (trans. W. Blomster). New York: Seabury.

Adorno, T. W. (1976). *Introduction to the sociology of music* (trans. E. B. Ashby). New York: Seabury.

Adorno T. W. (1990). On popular music. In *On record: Rock, pop and the written word*, (ed. S. Frith & A. Goodwin), pp. 301–14). London: Routledge (originally published 1949).

Adorno, T. W. (1999). *Sound figures.* Stanford, CA: Stanford University Press.

Akrich, M. & Latour, B. (1991). A summary of a convenient vocabulary for the semiotics of human and nonhuman assemblies. In *Shaping technology/building society: Studies in sociotechnical change,* (ed. W. E. Bijker & J. Law), pp. 259–64. Cambridge, MA: MIT Press.

Aristotle (1980). *The politics.* Oxford, UK: Oxford University Press.

Barnes, B. (2000). *Understanding agency: the institution of responsible action.* London: Sage Publications.

Berezin, M. (1999). Emotions unbound: Feeling political incorporation in the new Europe. Paper presented at special session on Emotions and Macrosociology, American Sociological Association, August 1999.

Birke, L. (1992). In pursuit of difference: Scientific studies of men and women. In *Inventing women: Science, technology and gender,* (ed. G. Kirkup & L. Smith Keller), pp. 81–102. Cambridge, UK: Polity Press.

Born, G. (1995). *Rationalizing culture: IRCAM, Boulez, and the institutionalization of the musical avant-garde.* Berkeley, CA: University of California Press.

Bourdieu, P. (1984). *Distinction: A social critique of the judgement of taste* (trans. R. Nice). Cambridge, UK: Polity Press.

Bourdieu, P. (1998). *La domination masculine.* Paris: Seuil.

Bowler, A. (1994). Methodological dilemmas in the sociology of art. In *The sociology of culture,* (ed. D. Crane), pp. 247–66. Oxford, UK: Blackwell.

Bryson, B. (1997). 'Anything but heavy metal': Symbolic exclusion and musical dislikes. *American Sociological Review,* 61, 884–99.

Cohen, S. (1993). Ethnography and popular music studies. *Popular Music,* 12, 123–38.

Collins, R. (1993). Emotional energy as the common denominator of rational choice. *Rationality and Society,* 5, 203–30.

Cooley, C. H. (1983). *Human nature and the social order.* New Brunswick, NJ: Transaction (originally published 1902).

Crafts, S., Cavicchi, D., & Keil, C. (1993). *My music.* Hanover, NH: Wesleyan University Press.

De Las Hera, V. (1997). *What does music collecting add to our knowledge of the functions and uses of music?* Unpublished MSc Dissertation, Department of Psychology, Keele University.

DeNora, T. (1986). How is extra-musical meaning possible? Music as a place and space for 'work'. *Sociological Theory,* 4, 84–94.

DeNora, T. (1995). *Beethoven and the construction of genius: musical politics in Vienna 1792–1803.* Berkeley, CA: University of California Press.

DeNora, T. (1997). Music and erotic agency—sonic resources and social-sexual action. *Body and Society,* 3, 43–65.

DeNora, T. (1999). Music as a technology of the self. *Poetics: Journal of Empirical Research on Literature, the Media and the Arts,* **26,** 1–26.

DeNora, T. (2000). *Music in everyday life.* Cambridge, UK: Cambridge University Press.

DiMaggio, P. (1982). Cultural entrepreneurship in nineteenth-century Boston: The creation of an organizational base for high culture in America. Parts 1 and 2. *Media, Culture and Society,* **4,** 35–50, 303–22.

Eyerman, R. & Jamieson, A. (1998). *Music and social movements: Mobilizing tradition in the 20th century.* Cambridge, UK: Cambridge University Press.

Featherstone, M., Hepworth, M., & Turner, B. S. (ed.) (1991). *The body: Social process and cultural theory.* London: Sage Publications.

Frazer, E. & Cameron, D. (1989). On knowing what to say. In *Social anthropology and the politics of language,* (ed. R. Grillo), pp. 25–40. London: Routledge.

Frith, S. (1978). *The sociology of rock.* London: Constable.

Frith, S. (1981). *Sound effects: Youth, leisure, and the politics of rock 'n' roll.* New York: Pantheon.

Frith, S. (1996). *Performing rites: Evaluating popular music.* Oxford, UK: Oxford University Press.

Frith, S. & McRobbie, A. (1990). Rock and sexuality. In *On record: Pop, rock and the written word,* (ed. S. Frith & A. Goodwin), pp. 371–89. London: Routledge.

Garfinkel, H. (1967). *Studies in ethnomethodology.* Cambridge, UK: Polity Press.

Giddens, A. (1991). *Modernity and self identity.* Cambridge, UK: Polity Press.

Gomart, E. & Hennion, A. (1999). A sociology of attachment: music amateurs, drug users. In *Actor network theory and after,* (ed. J. Law & J. Hazzart), pp. 220–47. Oxford, UK: Blackwell.

Hall, S. (1980). Recent developments in theories of language and ideology: A critical note. In *Culture, media, language: Working papers in cultural studies 1972–79,* (ed. S. Hall, D. Hobson, A. Lowe, & P. Willis), pp. 157–62. London: Hutchinson.

Hall, S. (1986). On postmodernism and articulation: An interview with Stuart Hall. *Journal of Communication Inquiry,* **10,** 45–60.

Haraway, D. (1985). A manifesto for cyborgs: Science, technology and socialist feminism in the 1980s. *Socialist Review,* **80,** 5–107.

Hennion, A. & Maisonneuve, S. with Gomart, E. (1998). *Figures de l'amateur: Formes, objects et pratiques de l'amour de la musique aujourd'hui.* Paris: Ministere de la culture.

Hennion, A. & Meadel, C. (1989). Artisans of desire. *Sociological Theory,* **7,** 191–209.

Heritage, J. (1984). *Garfinkel and ethnomethodology.* Cambridge, UK: Polity Press.

Hetherington, K. (1998). *Expressions of identity: Space, performance, politics.* London: Sage Publications.

Hochschild, A. (1979). Emotion work, feeling rules and social structure. *American Journal of Sociology,* **85,** 551–75.

Hochschild, A. (1983). *The managed heart.* Berkeley, CA: University of California Press.

Jackson, S. (1996). Heterosexuality as a problem for feminist theory. In *Theorizing heterosexuality,* (ed. D. Richardson), pp. 20–38. Milton Keynes, UK: Open University Press.

Jackson, S. (1999). *Questioning heterosexuality.* London: Sage Publications.

Lamont, M. (1992). *Money, morals, and manners.* Chicago: University of Chicago Press.

Langer, S. (1942). *Philosophy in a new key.* Cambridge, MA: Harvard University Press.

Lanza, J. (1995). *Elevator music: A surreal history of muzak, easy-listening and other moodsong.* London: Quartet Books.

Lash, S. & Urry, J. (1994). *Economies of signs and space.* London: Sage Publications.

Latour, B. (1991). Where are the missing masses? A sociology of a few mundane artefacts. In *Shaping technology/building society: Studies in sociotechnical change,* (ed. W. E. Bijker & J. Law), pp. 225–58. Cambridge, MA: MIT Press.

Law, J. (1994). *Organizing modernity.* Cambridge, UK: Polity Press.

McElrea, H. & Standing, L. (1992). Fast music causes fast drinking. *Perceptual and Motor Skills,* 75, 362.

Martin, P. (1995). *Sounds and society: Themes in the sociology of music.* Manchester, UK: Manchester University Press.

Mayo, E. (1933). *The human problems of an industrialized civilization.* Cambridge, MA: Harvard University Graduate School of Business.

Melucci, A. (1996a). *Challenging codes: Collective action in the information age.* Cambridge, UK: Cambridge University Press.

Melucci, A. (1996b). *The playing self: Person and meaning in the planetary society.* Cambridge, UK: Cambridge University Press.

Middleton, R. (1990). *Studying popular music.* Milton Keynes, UK: Open University Press.

Milliman, R. E. (1986). The influence of background music on the behavior of restaurant patrons. *Journal of Consumer Research,* 13, 286–9.

Moore, L. J. (1997). It's like you use pots and pans to cook with. *Science, Knowledge and Human Values,* 22, 434–71.

Moores, S. (1990). *Interpreting audiences.* London: Sage Publications.

Neilly, L. (1995). *The uses of music in people's everyday lives.* Unpublished undergraduate dissertation, Department of Psychology, Keele University, UK.

Pareto, W. (1963). *Treatise on general sociology.* New York: Dover.

Peterson, R. & Simkus, A. (1992). How musical tastes mark occupational status groups. In *Cultivating differences: Symbolic boundaries and the making of inequality,* (ed. M. Lamont & M. Fournier), pp. 152–86. Chicago: University of Chicago Press.

Plato (1966). *The Republic,* (ed. and trans. I. A. Richards). Cambridge, UK: Cambridge University Press.

Press, A. (1994). The sociology of cultural reception: notes toward an emerging paradigm. In *The sociology of culture,* (ed. D. Crane), pp. 221–46. Oxford, UK: Blackwell.

Radley, A. (1990). Artefacts, memory and a sense of the past. In *Collective remembering,* (ed. D. Middleton & D. Edwards), pp. 00–00. London: Sage Publications.

Radway, J. (1988). Reception study: ethnography and the problems of dispersed audiences and nomadic subjects. *Cultural Studies,* 2, 359–76.

Remmling, G. (1967). *The road to suspicion.* New York: Appleton-Century-Crofts.

Roballey, T. C., McGreevy, C., Rongo, R. R., Schwantes, M. L., Steger, P. J., Winninger, M. A., & Gardner, E. B. (1985). The effect of music on eating behavior. *Bulletin of the Psychonomic Society,* 23, 221–222.

Scheler, M. (1992). *On feeling, knowing, and valuing: selected writings,* (ed. and introduction H. J. Bershady). Chicago: University of Chicago Press.

Schutz, A. (1964). Making music together. *Collected papers. Vol 2.* The Hague: Martinus Nijhoff.

Shepherd, J. & Giles-Davies, J. (1991). Music, text and subjectivity. In *Music as Social Text,* pp. 174–87. Cambridge, UK: Polity Press.

Shepherd, J. & Wicke, P. (1997). *Music and cultural theory.* Cambridge, UK: Polity Press.

Sloboda, J. A. (1992). Empirical studies of emotional response to music. In *Cognitive bases of musical communication*, (ed. M. Riess-Jones & S. Holleran), pp. 33–46. Washington, DC: American Psychological Association.

Sloboda, J. A. (1999). Everyday uses of music listening: a preliminary study. In *Music, mind and science*, (ed. S. W. Yi), pp. 354–69. Seoul, Korea: Western Music Research Institute.

Smith, D. (1992). *Texts, facts and femininity: Exploring the relations of ruling.* London: Routledge.

Tönnies, F. (1957). *Community and society.* New York: Harper (originally published 1887).

Tota, A. L. (1997). *Etnografia dell'arte: Per una sociologia dei contesti artistici.* Rome: Logica University Press.

Tota, A. L. (1999). *Sociologie dell'arte: Dal museo tradizionale all'arte multimediale.* Rome: Carocci.

Turner, B. S. (1984). *The body and society.* Oxford, UK: Blackwell.

Turner, V. (1981). Social dramas and stories about them. In *On narrative*, (ed. W. J. T. Mitchell), pp. 137–64. Chicago: University of Chicago Press.

Urry, J. (1996). How societies remember the past. In *Theorizing museums: Representing identity and diversity in a changing world*, (ed. S. Macdonald & G. Fyfe), pp. 45–68. Sociological Review Monograph. Oxford, UK: Blackwell.

Weber, M. (1958). *The rational and social foundations of music.* Carbondale, IL: Southern Illinois University Press (originally published 1921).

Weber, M. (1965). *The sociology of religion* (trans. E. Fischoff). London: Methuen.

Weber, M. (1978). *Economy and society*, (ed. G. Roth & C. Wittich and trans. E. Fischoff *et al.*). Berkeley, CA: University of California Press.

Williams, S. J. (1996). The 'emotional' body. *Body and Society, 2*, 125–39.

Williams, S. J. (1998). Modernity and the emotions: Reflections on the (ir)rational. *Sociology, 32*, 747–69.

Willis, P. (1978). *Profane culture.* London: Routledge.

Willis, P. (2000). *The Ethnographic Imagination.* Cambridge, UK: Polity Press.

Witkin, R. W. (1974). *The intelligence of feeling.* London: Heineman.

Witkin, R. W. (1995). *Art and social structure.* Cambridge, UK: Polity Press.

Witkin, R. W. (1998). *Adorno on music.* London: Routledge.

Witkin, R. W. & DeNora, T. (1997). Aesthetic materials and aesthetic action. *Culture: The Newsletter of the American Sociological Association,* October, 1–5.

Woolgar, S. (1997). Configuring the user: Inventing new technologies. In *The machine at work*, (ed. K. Grint & S. Woolgar), pp. 65–94. Cambridge, UK: Polity Press.

Yelanjian, M. (1991). Rhythms of consumption. *Cultural Studies,* January, 91–7.

# CHAPTER 8

# MUSIC AND EMOTION: PERSPECTIVES FROM MUSIC THERAPY

LESLIE BUNT AND MERCÉDÈS PAVLICEVIC

This chapter focuses on the relationship between music and emotion from within what is generally called 'improvisational music therapy' and aims to explore how a music therapist begins to generate and receive patients' emotional responses to the music in music therapy. We do not attempt to duplicate existing literature by reviewing the clinical and research literature of music therapy, nor do we provide an overview of the profession and the various applications of music as therapy. Instead, the chapter is divided into three main sections. We begin with some general background to music therapy and how connections with emotions are observed in clinical practice. Then follows a summary of a study that investigated how music therapists are able to judge the intended presentation of a series of basic emotions by listening to short improvisations played live by colleagues. This hopefully sheds light on the complex range of emotions within the more natural interplay of the patient's and therapist's improvised music. In the final section, we explore this world of co-created music with patients in music therapy by examining recent work on early infant development and elaborating on the connections between the musical and personal in improvisational music therapy using the theoretical concept of dynamic form.

## 8.1 Some background to music therapy

Music as a therapy provides patients of all ages with an effective means of exploring and communicating a wide range of emotions. As a contemporary discipline, music therapy has developed consistently over the last 50 years, with rapid strides over the last couple of decades in Europe, North and South America, and more recently in the Far East, Australia, New Zealand, and South Africa. Historically, the music therapy profession emerged from work with children and adults where difficulties in communication resulted from profound disabilities or mental health problems (e.g. Alvin 1975; Nordoff & Robbins 1971, 1977; Priestley 1975). A steady profusion of texts during the 1990s indicates how the range of work has developed in various settings: preschool centres and nurseries for children; special schools and units for children with varied learning difficulties; hospitals and special units for adults with learning difficulties, physical disabilities, mental health and neurological problems; hospital units and centres for older people and for people with visual or hearing impairments; hospices and specialist centres for people living with terminal illness; and the prison and probation service (Aldridge 1996, 1999, 2000; Ansdell 1995; Bruscia 1991; Bunt 1994; Heal & Wigram 1993; Lee, 1995, 1996; Pavlicevic 1999*a*; Wigram & de Backer 1999*a*, 1999*b*; Wigram *et al.* 1995).

Examples of research into the clinical efficacy of music therapy with different populations are reported in these texts, as well as, for example, in the *British Journal of Music Therapy* and the US-based *Journal of Music Therapy*. These journals regularly present the results of both outcome and process-based studies, including, for example, studies on music therapy with preadolescents (Montello 1998), autistic children (Edgerton 1994), adult psychiatric patients (Heaney 1992; Pavlicevic & Trevarthen 1989, 1994), as well as the use of music therapy in paediatric oncology settings (Standley & Hanser 1995). Current research uses a proliferation of research techniques drawn from both quantitative and qualitative perspectives (for a review, see Wheeler 1995). Some researchers consider a qualitative approach as being more in keeping with the nature of music therapy practice (for a review, see Langenberg *et al.* 1996). Others propose that music therapy researchers need to continue using both, with different contexts and questions necessitating different perspectives (e.g. Smeijsters 1997). It is interesting that this debate has evolved out of a context of a more established clinical base, with practice preceding research.

### 8.1.1 Active and receptive approaches

Psychological responses to music are the bedrock of much that takes place in music therapy. People of all ages with wide-ranging health care needs come to music therapy and make fundamental connections between their emotions and the music that they experience either as active participants or as listeners. In music therapy, we can observe how music can be used to both express and arouse a wide gambit of emotions.

In an essentially active approach, patients are encouraged to articulate their emotions externally by forming musical gestures and structures. This process can be observed most clearly in improvised music making where the roles of composer and performer merge. Here there are also very close connections in the chain of communication between the originator of the music and the recipient. In a receptive approach, various emotions can be aroused while listening to pre-composed music played live by the therapist or on a recording—and this could include recording of previous improvisations.

Further levels of complexity are inherent in music therapy because emotions emerge alongside the facilitating presence of a music therapist who engages with the patient(s) in active musical involvement, by playing music to the patient(s), with the patient(s), or by listening to music together. Any of these scenarios finds a context within individual or group work. The overlapping links between music and emotions, therapeutic relationship, and the various needs of patients are featured in many definitions of music therapy, for example: 'Music therapy is the use of sounds and music within an evolving relationship between child or adult and therapist to support and encourage physical, mental, social and emotional well-being' (Bunt 1994, p. 8).

The complex interactions between the various musical and personal dynamics within music therapy can be illustrated with a quotation from Francis, a musician and patient who lived with AIDS. His voice is a crucial part of Lee's (1996) extensive case study. Discussing the importance of his music therapy Francis said:

I feel this is almost like a testament. It is the only expression I have of a spiritual journey. The only time that I feel that I am living and communicating. The only time that I feel I'm living the time I have left is when I am improvising. The rest of the time I'm wondering what the hell I'm doing. Time is a limited factor. When I'm doing these sessions with you I am actually living a moment; I'm actually living with somebody and producing something and revealing myself. When I'm improvising, when we are improvising together, I feel that I am saying something and living—and it's terribly important to me. (Lee 1996, pp. 77–8)

Francis talks here of the importance of living in the present moment of making music (cf. Sloboda and O'Neill, this volume). The music therapy sessions are a means for Francis to gain more understanding about his emotions, and to contribute towards a greater sense of self. It is important that his music is heard not in isolation but in the context of sessions that involve a relationship with the therapist. The quote from Francis relates in several ways to Christopher Small's use of the term 'musicking' (1999, p. 13):

The act of musicking brings into existence among those present a set of relationships, and it is in those relationships that the meaning of the act of musicking lies. It lies not only in the relationships between the humanly organized sounds that are conventionally thought of as being the stuff of music, but also in the relationships that are established for the duration of the performance between the participants within the performance space.

Small observes how these relationships can model relationships in the world outside the performance space: 'relationships between person and person, between individual and society, between humanity and the natural world and even perhaps the supernatural world' (Small 1993, p. 13). Parallels can be drawn here with therapist and patients in improvisational music therapy: the musical relationship that develops between the players is personally intimate and relationally significant—for both therapist and client. Moreover, it has direct links with patients' lives outside the therapeutic space, offering patients opportunities to explore, extend, and gain meaning into their emotional lives, both within and outside the therapeutic relationship, and to make connections between their individual and social lives.

### 8.1.2 Musical material in therapy

The range of musical material used to generate a therapeutic relationship is, naturally, context-dependent. One day a music therapist may be facilitating a group improvisation that evolves naturally from a song of emotional significance sung by an elderly patient. The next day may see the same music therapist with a profoundly disabled child working with very elemental sounds or short phrases of music. Here, in addition to the limited musical gestures, any responses and communication of emotions may be via eye blinks, changes in breathing, or subtle shifts in body posture. The therapist's musical and personal response to, and matching of, a patient's musical and personal presentation is in keeping with a well-established principle used in music therapy, namely the 'iso-principle' (Altshuler 1954).

In improvisational music therapy, the improvised music emerging from a session with a group of young children with language problems and limited attention will be qualitatively different from a session with a group of adults with mental health problems (and will also have different emotional significance). In terms of explaining the efficacy of music therapy, the group of language-delayed children may be so motivated to play the instruments and vocalize that their shifts in levels of excitement, quality of relationship, and emotional experiences and expressions may generalize outside of the sessions into further use of vocal sounds, gestures, and a corresponding rise in self-esteem. Likewise, the group of adults with mental health problems may be able to explore the shifting patterns of relating to one another and to the therapist in music and, with the therapist's help, draw analogies to more personal systems of interaction—both within and outside the music therapy setting.

Each of these scenarios presents a complex and multilayered generating, expressing, and conveying of emotional feelings and is dependent upon the music therapist's capacity to generate, judge, and read emotional responses to the music by patients within therapy. Understandably, the development of attentive listening, awareness, and empathy are some of the core qualities needed to work as a music therapist. But before exploring in more detail the various aspects of emotion in music therapy, we first make a brief detour to explore some of the recent research into music and emotion highlighted in this volume. Such thinking is potentially enriching to music therapy discourse and practice.

## 8.2 Sources of emotion in music therapy

Sloboda and Juslin (this volume) review different sources of emotion in music. There are examples of these meeting points between music and emotion in music therapy.

### 8.2.1 Associative connections

We are familiar with this connection, the 'Darling, they're playing our tune' notion (Davies 1978), in passive or receptive music therapy. Here, the music is a very powerful trigger that can set off a whole range of associations with specific events and places, memories of certain people, particularly if the experiences or people have been significant in a patient's life. The associations are generally highly individual, making it difficult to predict how different people will associate with different musical repertoires (Pavlicevic 1997). This necessitates much work on the music therapist's part to discover the musical preferences and history of the individual patient. This kind of emotional association is often the focus of work with elderly patients, when music can be used as a kind of reminiscence therapy (Odell-Miller 1995). It is also apparent in hospices and palliative care work where sensitive discovery of a patient's personal musical history is often a starting point of the treatment programme (Aldridge 1999; Lee 1995, 1996).

### 8.2.2 Iconic connections

Listening to a particular sound or series of sounds, whether improvised or pre-composed, can link musical characteristics to some external musical event or human feeling. For example, a group of children with learning problems can relate a general build-up of loud and fast sounds with a growing storm at sea or some other such high energy event. Improvising to an external theme provides members of a group in a cancer unit, for example, with opportunities to channel and shift levels of energy, to begin to release deep-set levels of tension and to work together towards a common aim (Bunt & Marston-Wyld 1995; Burns *et al.*, 2001). Such a group may wish to improvise to a given theme or pair of emotions, for example to represent shifts from darkness to light, sorrow to joy, etc. Patients may decide to give a specific feeling-based label to an improvisation after hearing a recording of the piece. Not all patients are comfortable making such connections. Some patients are drawn to the very ambiguous nature of music, preferring to perceive the musical experience as an event in itself. They may acknowledge the emotional power of a musical improvisation or listening experience, but wish to contain the experience within the music and not wish to explore any external associations.

### 8.2.3 Intrinsic connections

There are many examples in music therapy practice—in both active and receptive approaches—when connections can be observed between the emotional experiences of the patients and both surface and deep structural aspects of the music. For example, we can observe how intrinsic features of the musical structures evoke different emotions in the specific listening approach, guided imagery in music (GIM):

This does not happen in any simplistic one to one symbolic or causal correspondence between one musical gesture and the creation of an image but in an on-going organic and interactive way. In any series of GIM sessions we can observe similarities between different musical structures and processes and certain structures and processes in the imagery. At the same time of hearing the music the client is also creating an instantaneous link between image and music. It is as if the client is experiencing the music at different levels from the surface to the deep structural, reaching into the music to find the level that matches and resonates with the image. (Bunt 2000, p. 46)

GIM, created by Helen Bonny, involves listening to specifically programmed sequences of recorded music in a deeply relaxed state. The 'traveller' is invited to share the experience and any images or feelings with the therapist/guide (e.g. Bonny & Savary 1973; Bruscia 1995; Clark 1999; Erdonmez Grocke 1999). The images evoked by the music may be visual in nature but also body-based; they may open up a particular pattern of thought or various levels of emotional response. In many ways GIM demonstrates the interaction between the three kinds of connections discussed in this section. A particular melodic detail or surface musical detail may trigger a number of personal associations, memories, and images. Iconic associations may be made between aspects of the music and non-musical events. GIM therapists also witness patients making intrinsic connections between layers of musical expectations and deep structures and the forms and patterns of their internal emotions. The selection of the music used in GIM is indicative of the attention paid to the potential for these kinds of interactive connections.

One of the authors recalls a powerful emotional experience working through Bonny's programme entitled 'peak experience.' The sequence of music is: the 'Adagio' from Beethoven's Fifth Piano Concerto; the 'Et in Terra Pax' from Vivaldi's *Gloria*; the 'Adagio' from Bach's Toccata, Adagio and Fugue in C; the 'In Paradisum' from Fauré's *Requiem*, and the Prelude to Act I of Wagner's *Lohengrin*. A review of the written transcript of the session indicates how certain moments in the music triggered personal associations, memories, and evoked external images. In addition to these links there were many intrinsic connections. The overall order of the pieces created a mood of expectancy and deepening feelings of awe and wonder. Body-based reactions—changes in breathing, shudders, tension in the stomach, or feelings of lightness, etc.—were closely entrained with the formal aspects of the music—phrasing, changes in pitch, sudden harmonic shifts, shifts in loudness levels, density of the textures, etc. The climactic moments of the Prelude to *Lohengrin* corresponded with the most illuminating and profoundly moving moments of the session, the powerful memory of which has proved long lasting and in many ways transformative.

As a link to the next two sections of the chapter it is worth recalling Bruscia's (1989) useful distinction between 'active' music therapy, generally understood as based on the playing of music—whether pre-composed or improvised—and 'receptive' music therapy, generally understood as listening to music. We have already discussed some receptive approaches and shall now comment further on the use of active music therapy.

## 8.3 Active music therapy: the example of improvisational music therapy

Improvisational music therapy is a generic term for those approaches in which the act of improvisation is understood as the locus of the therapeutic encounter between therapist and patient, in either individual or group work. Patients in music therapy improvise; the music therapist improvises. The participants in any improvisation make personal variations within the musical forms, the process of deciding what to play and how to shape musical events changing moment by moment. The music therapist values and attends to all the musical communications made by the individual or group member—there is no 'right' or 'wrong' way of playing. In the psychologically and physically safe context of a therapeutic setting, the different forms of improvisation can also help an individual to try out different aspects of relating both within the self (intramusical and intrapersonal) and between people (intermusical and interpersonal) (e.g. Bruscia 1987, 1989). We can view improvisation as a means of negotiating both old and new meanings.

For example, in a group therapy setting with adult patients, instruments such as drums, cymbals, marimbas, xylophones, guitars, and bongos focus the initial musical curiosity of a group of chronically ill patients referred to a music therapy group by the hospital's psychiatrist. The adults begin to explore the instruments and try out the different sounds. The therapist creates an initial sense of security by suggesting an opening improvisation based on a repeating steady pulse. Gradually, members of the group improvise patterns around the pulse. The group members grow in confidence as they explore freer kinds of improvisation. They pass musical messages to one another and play in small groups. The improvisations release a wide range of feelings and verbal exchange takes place in between the improvisations. After a lengthy discussion, the group decides to improvise on a theme, one that moves from despair to hope. Further discussion ensues exploring the emotions brought to the surface during the long group improvisation. A final improvisation adds a sense of closure for the group.

Music therapists respond instantaneously to the sounds that emerge in improvisations. How will the therapist be able to understand the sound gestures? How will the child or adult be able to use the instruments as a direct and authentic expression of different emotions? How can any communications be read, interpreted, and met or engaged in the therapist's authentic music? Can there be any sense of shared meaning? These are some of the challenges that daily confront a practising music therapist. The therapist will also bring to the music therapy room a range of previous experiences, both personal and musical, that will inform how such musical gestures are read. In addition, these gestures will most likely be framed within a particular philosophical, psychological, or therapeutic perspective which could include anthropological, behavioural, cognitive, developmental, humanistic, medical, musicological, psychodynamic, or transpersonal approaches (see overviews by Aigen 1998; Aldridge 1996; Ansdell 1995; Bruscia 1987; Bunt 1994, 1997; Pavlicevic 1997; Ruud 1980). A therapist working within a psychodynamic framework, for example, will be making use of the dynamics of transference and countertransference in understanding the various relationships between the patient and the music, the patient and the therapist, and, in group work, the patient and other patients (see Bruscia 1998; Priestley 1994).

We shall now focus in more detail on aspects of the generating and receiving of emotion through music in the realms of clinical improvisation and in Pavlicevic's development of her theory of dynamic form in music therapy.

## 8.4 Generating and judging emotion in short improvisations: a small study

A critical aspect to the generating and receiving of emotion in music therapy is the direct experiencing of emotion within the listener/player, as well as the recognition of emotion within the music itself.

### 8.4.1 Background to the study: improvisation and emotions

Research by Gabrielsson and Juslin (1996) which investigated the connections between the performer's expressive intention and the listener's experience was the inspiration behind a simple classroom exercise to explore the kind of instantaneous observations music therapists make to judge the intended emotional content of short improvisations. We explored how a limited number of emotions—happiness, sadness, tenderness, anger, and fear—were judged. These emotions have been regarded as 'basic' by many researchers (see Sloboda and Juslin, this volume).

Deciding to use short examples of improvised music played live by individual music therapists to the listening groups was an essential feature of this study. Would the music therapists playing the short improvisations be able to communicate the intended emotion? Would the therapists listening to the improvisations be able to judge the correct emotional intention? What musical parameters would the listeners use to decode the emotional expression of each improvisation? Behrens and Green (1993) have pointed out some advantages of using improvisations as compared to pre-composed music in judging the affective content of musical examples. There is no question of familiarity;

the emotional intention of each composer/improviser is known in advance; the length can be controlled, and each presentation can represent a complete musical idea. The use of live, as opposed to prerecorded, examples in our study added additional variables, namely the influence of visual and other non-verbal cues (for example, facial expressions, body movements, posture) in communication of the intended emotion.

### 8.4.2 Procedure

Two groups of music therapists took part in this study. The first was a group of thirteen music therapy students in their final stages of training, the second a group of eleven music therapy researchers and teachers. The student group was divided into two groups of six and seven and the researchers worked together as one group. The same procedure was used for both the student and researcher groups (referred to as S and R, respectively, in Table 8.1). Descriptions of the five emotions were written on cards and placed face down on a table. Individual therapists from both groups were invited to make a random selection of a card and to improvise freely within the prevailing emotion indicated for a period up to 2 minutes. The improviser could choose from within a wide range of tuned and untuned percussion instruments (e.g. xylophone, drum, cymbal, bells) as well as the therapist's own instrument (e.g. flute, piano). The therapist was asked to spend a few moments trying to access the particular emotion before selecting an appropriate instrument or group of instruments. Some therapists chose also to sing. The improvising therapist then played or sang to the listening group with the intention of expressing the emotion from the card, the title only being shown to the study's convenor.

After each improvisation, the listening music therapists were asked to rate each improvisation for the expression of each emotional state using the scale: 0 = improvisation does not express the state to 4 = improvisation does express the state (the same range as used in the Behrens and Green study). A score was required for each of the five emotions for each musical improvisation since overlaps were expected in decoding certain emotions. For later descriptive analysis, the listeners were also asked to list both musical and other reasons for their judgment of the main emotional state being communicated. There was a total of 26 improvisations (Table 8.1).

### 8.4.3 Results

The columns in Table 8.1 are used to designate the intended emotional expression of each improvisation and the rows the corresponding adjectives used by the listeners to rate each improvisation. The mean ratings of the respondents are used for each improvisation and total means are tabulated. F-tests were used to test for intended expression. The results were highly significant and provide strong evidence that the responses vary between descriptions.

Looking at the mean responses, clearly happy and angry descriptions correspond to happy and angry intended expressions. We can note that there were some overlaps in the ratings of certain emotions, for example sadness/tenderness and angry/fearful. The music therapists also listed the musical parameters and other observations that aided the process of decoding the intended emotions (Table 8.2).

**Table 8.1** Mean ratings for each improvisation and group totals

| Description | Intended expression | | | | |
|---|---|---|---|---|---|
| | Happy | Sad | Tender | Angry | Fearful |
| Happy | S(a) **3.6** | S(g) 0 | S(j) 0 | S(p) 0.7 | S(r) 1.6 |
| | S(b) **4.0** | S(h) 0 | S(k) 0 | S(q) 0.5 | S(s) 0 |
| | S(c) **3.8** | S(i) 0 | S (l) 1.6 | R(e) 0 | S(t) 0.3 |
| | S(d) **3.6** | R(b) 0 | S(m)1.0 | | R(f) 0 |
| | S(e) **4.0** | R(c) 0.1 | S(n) 0.2 | | |
| | S(f) **4.0** | R(d) 0 | S(o) 0.2 | | |
| | R(a) **3.3** | | | | |
| | $t = 3.76$ | $t = 0.02$ | $t = 0.5$ | $t = 0.4$ | $t = 0.47$ |
| Sad | 0 | **3.0** | 1.6 | 0.2 | 0 |
| | 0 | **1.0** | 2.2 | 0 | 0.2 |
| | 0 | **3.3** | 0.8 | 0.2 | 0.5 |
| | 0 | **2.0** | 1.7 | | 1.0 |
| | 0 | **3.7** | 2.7 | | |
| | 0 | **3.1** | 2.2 | | |
| | 0 | | | | |
| | $t = 0$ | $t = 2.68$ | $t = 1.87$ | $t = 0.13$ | $t = 0.42$ |
| Tender | 0 | 2.8 | **2.8** | 0 | 0 |
| | 0.2 | 3.2 | **4.0** | 0 | 0.6 |
| | 0.6 | 2.0 | **3.6** | 0 | 0 |
| | 0 | 1.1 | **3.7** | | 0.5 |
| | 0.2 | 1.5 | **3.0** | | |
| | 0.2 | 1.8 | **3.6** | | |
| | 0 | | | | |
| | $t = 0.17$ | $t = 2.07$ | **t = 3.45** | $t = 0$ | $t = 0.27$ |
| Angry | 0.2 | 0.2 | 0.2 | **3.5** | 3.0 |
| | 0.2 | 0 | 0 | **4.0** | 0 |
| | 0 | 0 | 0 | **3.8** | 3.0 |
| | 1.0 | 0.1 | 0 | | 1.0 |
| | 0 | 0 | 0 | | |
| | 0 | 0.6 | 0 | | |
| | 0.4 | | | | |
| | $t = 0.26$ | $t = 0.15$ | $t = 0.03$ | $t = 3.77$ | $t = 1.75$ |
| Fearful | 0.2 | 1.8 | 1.0 | 1.2 | 1.0 |
| | 0 | 1.2 | 0.6 | 0.8 | **4.0** |
| | 0 | 2.0 | 0 | 1.0 | 3.7 |
| | 0 | 2.1 | 0 | | 3.5 |
| | 0 | 0.4 | 2.2 | | |
| | 0 | 1.8 | 0.4 | | |
| | 0 | | | | |
| | $t = 0.03$ | $t = 1.55$ | $t = 0.7$ | $t = 1.0$ | $t = 3.05$ |

R, research improviser; S, student improviser; t, total mean for each series of improvisations. The bold type indicates the correct judgment of intended emotion.

**Table 8.2** Various parameters used by music therapists in decoding basic emotions

*Happy*
Tempo and rhythm: fast, flowing tempi; lively, skipping, dotted rhythms; firm pulse
Pitch and melody: high pitches, rising melodies
Tonality and harmony: major tonality, clear structured harmony
Timbre, texture and style: bright textures and timbre, much staccato
Loudness level: no major shifts, mainly middle ground
Phrasing and structure: clear, predictable, many short 'flourishes'
Non-verbal communication: smiling, free body movements, foot tapping, bouncing, clapping, upright posture with no apparent tension, a 'twinkle in the eye'
Other: feeling of abandonment, much communication of high levels of energy, meeting cultural expectation of feeling happy

*Sad*
Tempo and rhythm: slow pulse (absence at times), gentle rhythms
Pitch and melody: wandering, hesitant and unfocused melodies
Tonality and harmony: minor tonality, small intervals, some dissonances, no sustained tension
Timbre, texture and style: sustained, legato, use of single sounds, flat timbre with blurring of sounds, slow vibrato
Loudness level: predominantly soft, small range from *pp* to *mf*
Phrasing and structure: falling phrases
Non-verbal communication: little movement, flat expression, slow breathing, concentration in the eyes, head hanging low
Other: feeling of being unresolved, general look of sadness and introspection

*Tender*
Tempo and rhythm: gentle, slow pulse, lilting rhythms
Pitch and melody: gradual rise and fall to the melody, frequent glissandi, lyrical
Tonality and harmony: major and minor alternation; use of modes, supportive accompaniment with broken chords and gentle arpeggios
Timbre, texture and style: a light touch and texture, sustained
Loudness level: soft
Phrasing and structure: legato, use of pauses
Non-verbal communication: stillness, enclosed posture, head hanging low
Other: communication of relaxed and reflective state

*Angry*
Tempo and rhythm: quick tempi, jerky rhythms, sudden changes in rhythmic patterns with accents
Pitch and melody: low sounds, unpredictable or absence of melody, clusters
Tonality and harmony: minor tonality, atonality, feeling incomplete
Timbre, texture and style: fragmented sounds; strident, harsh and percussive timbres
Loudness level: very loud, distorted sounds, strong and forceful
Phrasing and structure: some repetitions, absence of order, shape and form
Non-verbal communication: aggressive body movements
Other: much construed from strong level of energy and shape of opening musical gesture

*Fearful*
Tempo and rhythm: rapid and jerky tempi and rhythms
Pitch and melody: low sounds, minor tonality or lacking a sense of tonality
Tonality and harmony: random and tense dissonant harmonies, strong chords and clusters
Timbre, texture and style: fragmented, heavy textures
Loudness level: sudden bursts of loud playing building to climaxes
Phrasing and structure: pauses creating feeling of unrest, general lack of organization, no clear pattern or shape
Non-verbal communication: jumpy movements, weighty feeling to the body
Other: cultural stereotypes, e.g. tremolandi; sense of confusion, chaos, hesitation and disconnection; fear read in players' faces

### 8.4.4 Discussion

Clearly, the music therapists who played or sang these short improvisations were able to communicate the intended emotions to the listeners. The listening music therapists were able for the most part to judge accurately the intended emotional expression. The detailed musical parameters were used almost instantaneously as evidence before selection of the main intended emotion was made: evidence preceding the inference. The improvisers were able to communicate some of the very basic emotions: happiness, sadness, tenderness, anger, and fearfulness. These are very common features of many musical presentations made by patients of all ages. An interaction was observed between tender and sad, alerting music therapists to the need to be particularly cautious in jumping to quick judgments with these and other more than basic emotions. We may describe an improvisation as tender and can pick up the general feeling, but it is hard to be more specific. The students found close links between both sad and tender and between angry and sad. These mixed responses are a feature of the interaction effects of even the most basic of emotions (for further elaboration, see Juslin, this volume). There were also discrepancies picked up when a player appeared to find it difficult to articulate a particular emotion. To some extent, this study was also a judgment on how well each improviser was able to communicate the intended expression.

The musical parameters and other behaviours used to describe how each intended emotion was judged indicate the subtle interaction between musical and other cues. Clearly, visual cues are highly relevant in adding meaning to an emotional gesture. It would be interesting to repeat the exercise with the listeners closing their eyes. Music therapists also often enter into the musical world of their patients by playing music with them. This provides a far closer and resonant means of relating directly with the expression of a specific emotion. The emotion may then be embodied in the joint action of interactive music making. The therapeutic situation also differs from the classroom setting of this study in the fact that a more spontaneous and natural expression of emotions can be observed.

In the next section of this chapter, the concept of dynamic form in music therapy is presented, exploring the personal/emotional and musical/emotional interface in clinical improvisation.

## 8.5 Dynamic form

### 8.5.1 Understanding improvisation in music therapy

Explaining the emotional nature of improvisation in improvisation music therapy models (Bruscia 1989) presents complex issues for music therapists and music psychologists because of the musical, psychological, and relational dimensions of the improvisatory act. Music therapists generally understand the spontaneous act of 'improvisation' as being 'more than'—or 'other than'—music improvisation as an 'artistic' event; and as having personal and interpersonal significance. Such improvisation is labelled 'clinical' and is defined by the Association of Professional Music Therapists (UK) as: 'Musical improvisation with a specific therapeutic meaning and purpose in an environment facilitating response and interaction' (quoted in Odell-Miller 1988, p. 54).

At the same time, however, the act of improvisation in music therapy may well draw stylistically from the 'musical' repertoire (for example, the therapist, being a skilled musician, may well use idioms from jazz, blues, modes, boogie-woogie, romantic or baroque music, or free improvisation). This duality of the 'personal' and 'musical' in clinical improvisation has given rise to much debate between therapists, especially with regard to whether or not verbal interpretations of psychological material are necessary, and how words can explain the musical act itself (e.g. Aigen 1999; Ansdell 1995; Pavlicevic 1997; Streeter 1999).

As well as drawing directly from allied theoretical frameworks, as stated earlier, music therapists also describe and explain clinical improvisation using a variety of discourses, including those from behavioural theory (Madsen *et al.* 1968); musicological theory (Ansdell 1997; Lee 1989, 1990); psychoanalytic theory (Brown 1999; Priestley 1994; Robarts 1996; Streeter 1999; Tyler 1998); the medical literature (Aldridge 1996); psychology (Aigen 1999; Bunt 1994; Nordoff & Robbins 1971; Pavlicevic 1997); anthropology (Ruud 1998*a*, 1998*b*); and semiotics (Styge 1999).

### 8.5.2 A brief scenario

Andrew, a teacher suffering from depression as a result of a family bereavement, arrives for a first therapy session and is presented with a room full of various percussion instruments. He has no formal musical training, and last played music at school. He has been referred to music therapy by his general practitioner, to help alleviate Andrew's depression. At the therapist's invitation, Andrew chooses to play an African Conga drum, and begins to beat it somewhat tentatively, erratically, using both hands in a rather clumsy manner. The music therapist listens closely to what Andrew is playing, and hears the tentativeness in his rhythmic patterns, the dull timbre, the slow and erratic pulse, the uneven dynamic level: somewhere between mezzo-piano and mezzo-forte, with the occasional sforzando thud.

Soon she begins to play with him, on the vibraphone, meeting his playing on the Conga. Even though Andrew's beating is erratic, she can detect some fundamental pulse, which she reflects in her own spontaneous playing. She also matches his dynamic level and reflects aspects of his rhythmic patterns, attempting to establish a therapeutic relationship through musical sounds. Soon after beginning to play with Andrew, the dorian mode comes into the therapist's mind, influenced, perhaps, by an aspect of their joint rhythmic forms which remind her of a folk tune. She begins to improvise in this style, while at the same time continuing to meet Andrew's tempo, rhythm, dynamic level, and so on.

To an uninformed listener, their joint playing might well sound like a 'musical event'. Music therapists, however, are able to distinguish between music therapy improvisation (in which the emphasis is on the interpersonal, emotional communication between the players) and 'non-clinical' music improvisation (in which the emphasis is on the musical content and processes). Indeed, an exploratory study reports that 'blind' music therapist listeners asked to identify music therapy and non-music therapy improvisation are able to identify each of these correctly. Moreover, they report being able to 'hear therapeutic thinking' when listening to music therapy improvisations. In contrast, they describe non-clinical improvisation as being musically driven (Brown & Pavlicevic 1997). But how is

music. Dynamic form is elicited within, and as part of, the clinical–musical relationship, using the communicative and expressive mechanisms of basic emotions, that is, those of intensity, contour, tempo, rhythm, timbre, and dynamics. Dynamic form is generated by both therapist and patient, who relate intimately and directly with one another through jointly created sounds (Pavlicevic 1990, 1997, in press). These musical sounds correspond to the mechanisms of 'non-verbal communication', enabling the therapist to 'receive' and directly (and viscerally) experience patients' musical utterances as a presentation of themselves—and also as a presentation of their clinical pathology (Pavlicevic & Trevarthen 1989; Pavlicevic *et al.* 1995). Adult psychiatric patients suffering from conditions that interfere with their capacity to express and communicate emotion—and form relationships with others—portray this collapsed relational capacity in clinical improvisation. Both self and interactional synchrony can be regarded as measures of health with illness and disease occurring when a person becomes out of synchrony—both physically and mentally—with the self and the surrounding environment (Capra 1983; Pavlicevic 1991).

Although clinical improvisation may be heard as musical, the therapist's skill is not solely a 'musical' one, as has been assumed (Schögler 1998*)*. Rather, music therapists' skills lie in their capacity to interface the personal and music in music therapy improvisation; to 'read' music therapy improvisation as an interpersonal event (in the way that mothers and babies read one another's acts not as musical or temporal, but as emotionally expressive and communicative); and to support, develop, and extend the jointly created improvisation according to personal and therapeutic, rather than musical–aesthetic, needs and dictates. It is this direct knowing by one person of the other that enables the therapist to gain a direct experience of the patient, uncluttered by words—and replicating, to some extent, the psychotherapeutic dyad, in which the relationship between therapist and patient is itself the fertile ground for the patient's self-growth and knowing.

If we now return to the opening moments of Andrew's clinical improvisation with the therapist, we can think of each of them as presenting themselves through spontaneously created sounds, using the very ingredients of non-verbal communication—which are essentially musical in character. In the first moments of playing, Andrew portrays aspects of his 'vitality affects' through the musical relationship, using the very modality that directly captures, and portrays to another person, the essence of who he is. However, the jointly created clinical improvisation (once the therapist joins in with him on the vibraphone) elicits much more than this. By joining in with him, the therapist provides the basis for an interpersonal therapeutic relationship, enabling Andrew to express himself, to release deep-seated feelings to which he may, as yet, have no awareness, and to communicate through a powerful, non-verbal, medium: that of music. This musical experience bypasses (and complements) his 'talking' about his feelings—and enables him to gain new insights about himself—which may, or may not, need to be interpreted through words. This direct therapeutic musical event will hopefully enable him to resolve, and be released from, his feelings of loss, and to help him shift from his depressed state (Champion 1992; Pavlicevic 1999*b*). Although, like most music therapy patients, Andrew has no idea about how clinical improvisation 'works', his innate, biological, and neurological preverbal musicality—present from birth—is engaged by the therapist's clinical musicianship: enabling and inviting his sounds to become personal and interpersonal.

Critical, here, is that not just any musical improvisation will do. The therapist needs to elicit dynamic form between herself and Andrew. Were they simply to play music together, however spontaneously, their focus would be on the sounds, tunes, and rhythms of their music, rather than on playing themselves. Through his depression, Andrew's 'vitality affects' have become narrowed and somewhat stuck: this is revealed in his playing which is erratic, tentative, and somewhat clumsy. His depression means that his experience of the world is slow, cloying, dark, and unshifting. These qualities are experienced directly by the therapist when she plays with him, and she then works with the dynamic form, using clinical techniques to stabilize his beating, extend his tempo, introduce rubatos, accelerandos, diminuendos and crescendos, and so on. This is not in order to make him into a better musician, but rather, to grow his expressive, emotional vocabulary, to 'loosen him up' emotionally, and to help him to access the feelings under-lying his depression. At this point, music therapy may (or may not) move into verbal interpretation, with the therapist helping Andrew towards gaining insight into his life, depression, and bereavement. However, many music therapy clients are unable to speak because of their conditions, and even with verbal clients like Andrew, their work might be essentially in the musical event—the gaps between meaning and emotion in clinical improvisation and in words are far from being convincingly explicated in the music therapy literature (Ansdell 1996).

However, a case for the emotional richness of clinical improvisation is made in the final part of this chapter: a transcribed musical excerpt of dynamic form shows, through a brief microanalysis, the interactive mechanisms of communication and rela-tionship between the therapist and client. Neither of their playing can be taken in isola-tion from the other's—hence the insistence of dynamic form being a feature of their joint playing, rather than of simply the patient's in clinical improvisation.

### 8.5.6 A musical example

Figure 8.1 shows 19 s of an improvisation by a music therapist (T) with a depressed patient (P) who is an adult amateur musician. The therapist and patient are seated opposite one another with a marimba between them, taking turns to play—hence the one melodic line. The instrument faces the patient, so that the therapist is playing 'upside down'. Although the excerpt shows the two players reflecting aspects of one another's rhythmic motifs (the excerpt has a compound rhythm), melodic line, dynamic levels, and timbre, the duration of the therapist's eleventh statement (T11) is 300 cs, while the patient's eleventh statement of 602 cs is discrepant in duration. This discrep-ancy exists despite both T11 and P11 comprising ten notes each, and despite the patient's other musical features (i.e. melodic contour, dynamic level, timbre), which clearly show an awareness by the patient of the therapist's preceding statement. The dis-crepancy is caused by the patient delaying the fourth note of her statement (i) as well as the conclusion of her statement at (ii). The delays within P11 'unbalances' the improvi-sation, resulting in an asynchronous interaction—this is somewhat perplexing if we consider that the patient is an amateur musician, but not unusual for someone suffering from depression.

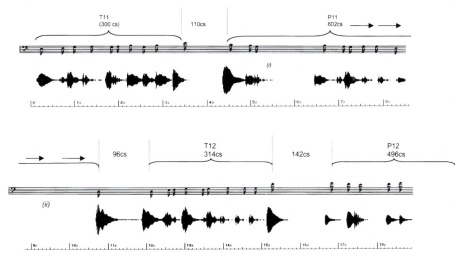

**Figure 8.1** Turn-taking on the marimba by a therapist (T) and depressed patient (P).

Other interesting aspects in this brief excerpt are that when the therapist plays again at T12, her statement acknowledges that the patient has reflected some of the material in T11, which encourages the therapist to offer a similar statement to T11 in her twelfth statement (T12). Also of interest is that the patient is contracting her phrase to 496 cs in P12, suggesting some interpersonal responsiveness and flexibility—despite her depression. The therapist's statement at T12 is almost a repeat of her eleventh statement—and this can be understood as her offering the patient a stable and unambiguous musical structure, with predictable rhythm and pulse: a temporal beacon for the patient. Were the therapist to simply reflect the patient's uneven playing, and offer some rhythmic variation in T12, this might have the effect of destabilizing the patient. Instead, the therapist offers the patient a potential relational and communicative environment to expand into, leading, possibly, to a more fluid interpersonal (and personal) expressiveness. Here is dynamic form as an observable, explicit phenomenon with all the mechanisms of interpersonal timing, contour, motion, shape, and phrasing. It is the 'music between' (Ansdell 1995) the therapist and patient that generates and reveals emotion in music therapy—through the therapist's skill at eliciting, and working with, clinical improvisation.

## 8.6 Conclusion

An emotional response to music is a fundamental aspect of music therapy. It appears as a central link for people of all ages with wide-ranging clinical needs. Music therapists demonstrate the capacity to judge effectively the intended basic emotions of short improvisations played live. The musical parameters used in their judgments are similar to those used when listening to recorded pre-composed music. Recent work in developmental child psychology, in particular Stern's (1985) 'vitality affects', provides reference points in understanding the subtle interplay between the personal and the musical in improvisational music therapy. Here is perhaps where we have the primary locus of any therapeutic change, in the interpersonal musical relationship built up between therapist and patient. Tuning in to our patients with a focused attention and sense of listening to every emotional nuance being expressed are prerequisites of the work of a vigilant music therapist.[1]

## References

**Aigen, K.** (1998). *Paths of development in Nordoff–Robbins music therapy*. Gilsum, NH: Barcelona.

**Aigen, K.** (1999). The true nature of music-centered music therapy theory. *British Journal of Music Therapy*, 13, 77–82.

**Aldridge, D.** (1996). *Music therapy research and practice in medicine*. London: Jessica Kingsley.

**Aldridge, D.** (1999). *Music therapy in palliative care*. London: Jessica Kingsley.

**Aldridge, D.** (2000). *Music therapy in dementia care*. London: Jessica Kingsley.

**Altshuler, I. M.** (1954). The past, present and future of music therapy. In *Music therapy*, (ed. E. Podolsky), pp. 24–35. New York: Philosophical Library.

**Alvin, J.** (1975). *Music therapy*. London: John Clare.

**Ansdell, G.** (1995). *Music for life: Aspects of creative music therapy with adult clients*. London: Jessica Kingsley.

**Ansdell, G.** (1996). Talking about music therapy: a dilemma and a qualitative experiment. *British Journal of Music Therapy*, 10, 4–16.

**Ansdell, G.** (1997). Musical elaborations: what has the new musicology to say to music therapy? *British Journal of Music Therapy*, 11, 36–44.

**Beebe, B., Jaffe, J., Feldstein, S., Mays, K., & Alson, D.** (1985). Interpersonal timing: the application of an adult dialogue model to mother–infant vocal and kinesic interactions. In *Social perception in infants*, (ed. T. M. Field & N. A. Fox), pp. 217–47. Norwood, NJ: Ablex.

**Behrens, G. A. & Green, S. B.** (1993). The ability to identify emotional content of solo improvisations performed vocally and on three different instruments. *Psychology of Music*, 21, 20–33.

**Bernieri, F. J. & Rosenthal, R.** (1991). Interpersonal coordination: behavior matching and interactional synchrony. In *Fundamentals of nonverbal behavior*, (ed. R. S. Feldman & B. Rim), pp. 401–32. Cambridge, UK: Cambridge University Press.

**Bonny, H. L. & Savary, L. M.** (1973). *Music and your mind*. New York: Station Hill.

**Brown, J. J. & Avstreih, Z. A. K.** (1989). On synchrony. *Arts in Psychotherapy*, 16, 157–62.

**Brown, S.** (1999). Some thoughts on music, therapy, and music therapy. *British Journal of Music Therapy*, 13, 63–71.

**Brown, S. & Pavlicevic, M.** (1997). Clinical improvisation in creative music therapy: musical aesthetic and the interpersonal dimension. *Arts in Psychotherapy*, 23, 397–405.

---

[1] We are grateful to Mollie Gilchrist, Faculty of Health and Social Care, University of the West of England, for help with the statistical analysis.

Bruscia, K. E. (1987). *Improvisational models of music therapy.* Springfield, IL: Charles C. Thomas.

Bruscia, K. E. (1989). *Defining music therapy.* Spring City, PA: Barcelona.

Bruscia, K. E. (1991). *Case studies in music therapy.* Phoenixville, PA: Barcelona.

Bruscia, K. E. (1995). Modes of consciousness in guided imagery and music (GIM): A therapist's experience. In *Listening, playing, creating: essays on the power of sound,* (ed. C. B. Kenny), pp. 165–99. Albany, NY: State University of New York.

Bruscia, K. E. (1998). *Dynamics of music psychotherapy.* Gilsum, NH: Barcelona.

Bunt, L. (1994). *Music therapy: An art beyond words.* London: Routledge.

Bunt, L. (1997). Clinical and therapeutic uses of music. In *The social psychology of music,* (ed. D. J. Hargreaves & A. C. North), pp. 249–67. Oxford, UK: Oxford University Press.

Bunt, L. (2000). Transformational processes in guided imagery and music. *Journal of the Association for Music and Imagery,* 7, 44–69.

Bunt, L. & Marston-Wyld, J. (1995). Where words fail music takes over: A collaborative study by a music therapist and a counsellor in the context of cancer care. *Music Therapy Perspectives,* 13, 46–50.

Burns, S. J., Harbuz, M. S., Huckelbridge, F., & Bunt, L. (2001). A pilot study into the therapeutic effects of music therapy at a cancer help centre. *Alternative Therapies in Health and Medicine,* 7, 48–56.

Capra, F. (1983). *The turning point.* London: Fontana.

Champion, L. (1992). Depression. In *Adult psychological problems,* (ed. L. A. Champion & M. J. Power), pp. 26–49. London: Falmer Press.

Clark, M. (1999). The Bonny method of guided imagery and music and spiritual development. *Journal of the Association for Music and Imagery,* 6, 55–62.

Condon, W. S. & Ogston, W. D. (1966). Sound film analysis of normal and pathological behavior patterns. *Journal of Nervous and Mental Diseases,* 143, 338–47.

Davies, J. B. (1978). *The psychology of music.* London: Hutchinson.

Edgerton, C. L. (1994) The effect of improvisational music therapy on the communicative behaviors of autistic children. *Journal of Music Therapy,* 31, 311–62.

Erdonmez Grocke, D. (1999). The music which underpins pivotal moments in guided imagery and music. In *Clinical applications of music therapy in psychiatry,* (ed. T. Wigram & J. De Backer, J.), pp. 197–210. London: Jessica Kingsley.

Feldstein, S. & Welkowitz, J. (1979) A chronography of conversation: In defense of an objective approach. In *Nonverbal behavior and communication,* (ed. A. W. Siegman & S. Feldstein), pp. 329–278). Hillsdale, NJ: Erlbaum.

Gabrielsson, A. & Juslin, P. N. (1996). Emotional expression in music performance. Between the performer's intention and the listener's experience. *Psychology of Music,* 24, 68–91.

Heal, M. & Wigram, T. (ed.) (1993). *Music therapy in health and education.* London: Jessica Kingsley.

Heaney, C. J. (1992). Evaluation of music therapy and other treatment modalities by adult psychiatric inpatients. *Journal of Music Therapy,* 29, 70–86.

Langenberg, M., Aigen, K., & Frommer, J. (ed.) (1996). *Qualitative music therapy research: Beginning dialogues.* Gilsum, NH: Barcelona.

Langer, S. (1942). *Philosophy in a new key.* Cambridge, MA: Harvard University Press.

Langer, S. (1953). *Feeling and form.* London: Routledge.

Lee, C. A. (1989). Structural analysis of therapeutic improvisatory music. *Journal of British Music Therapy*, 3, 11–19.

Lee, C. A. (1990). Structural analysis of post-tonal therapeutic improvisatory music. *Journal of British Music Therapy*, 4, 6–20.

Lee, C. A. (ed.) (1995). *Lonely waters*. Oxford, UK: Sobell.

Lee, C. A. (1996). *Music at the edge: The music therapy experiences of a musician with AIDS*. London: Routledge.

Madsen, C. K., Cotter, V. M., & Madsen, C. H. (1968). A behavioural approach to music therapy. *Journal of Music Therapy*, 5, 69–71.

Malloch, S. N. (1999). Mothers and infants and communicative musicality. *Musicae Scientiae*, **Special Issue 1999–2000**, 29–54.

Montello, L. (1998). Effects of active versus passive group music therapy on preadolescents with emotional, learning, and behavioral disorders. *Journal of Music Therapy*, 35, 49–67.

Nordoff, P. & Robbins, C. (1971). *Therapy in music for handicapped children*. London: Gollancz.

Nordoff, P. & Robbins, C. (1977). *Creative music therapy*. New York: John Day.

Odell-Miller, H. (1988). A music therapy approach in mental health. *Psychology of Music*, 16, 52–61.

Odell-Miller, H. (1995). Approaches to music therapy in psychiatry with specific emphasis upon a research project with the elderly mentally ill. In *The art and science of music therapy: A handbook*, (ed. T. Wigram, B. Saperston, & R. West), pp. 83–111. Langhorne: Harwood Academic Press.

Papoušek, M. (1989). Determinants of responsiveness to infant vocal expression of emotional state. *Infant Behavior and Development*, 12, 505–22.

Papoušek, M. (1996). Intuitive parenting: A hidden source of musical stimulation in infancy. In *Musical beginnings*, (ed. I. Deliège & J. A. Sloboda), pp. 88–112. Oxford, UK: Oxford University Press.

Papoušek, H. & Papoušek, M. (1991). Innate and cultural guidance of infants' integrative competencies: China, the United States and Germany. In *Cultural approaches to parenting*, (ed. M. H. Bornstein), pp. 23–44. Hillsdale, NJ: Erlbaum.

Pavlicevic, M. (1990). Dynamic interplay in clinical improvisation. *British Journal of Music Therapy*, 4, 5–9.

Pavlicevic, M. (1991). *Music in communication: Improvisation in music therapy*. Unpublished doctoral dissertation, University of Edinburgh, Scotland.

Pavlicevic, M. (1995). Music and emotion: aspects of music therapy research. In *Art and music: Therapy and research*, (ed. A. Gilroy & C. Lee), pp. 51–65. London: Routledge.

Pavlicevic, M. (1997). *Music therapy in context: Music, meaning, and relationship*. London: Jessica Kingsley.

Pavlicevic, M. (1999*a*). *Music therapy—intimate notes*. London: Jessica Kingsley.

Pavlicevic, M. (1999*b*). With listeners in mind: creating meaning in music therapy dialogues. *Arts in Psychotherapy*, 26, 85–94.

Pavlicevic, M. (2000). Improvisation in music therapy I: Human communication in sound. *Journal of Music Therapy*, xxxvii, 270–85.

Pavlicevic, M. & Trevarthen, C. (1989). A musical assessment of psychiatric states in adults. *Psychopathology*, 22, 325–34.

Pavlicevic, M., Trevarthen, C., & Duncan, J. (1995). Music therapy in the rehabilitation of persons suffering from chronic schizophrenia. *Journal of Music Therapy*, 31, 86–104.

Priestley, M. (1975). *Music therapy in action*. London: Constable.

Priestley, M. (1994). *Essays on analytical music therapy.* Phoenixville, PA: Barcelona.

Robarts, J. (1996). Music therapy for children with autism. In *Children with autism,* (ed. C. Trevarthen, K Aitken, D. Papoudi, & J. Robarts), pp. 134–60. London: Jessica Kingsley.

Robb, L. (1999). Emotional musicality in mother–infant vocal affect, and an acoustic study of postnatal depression. *Musicae Scientiae,* **Special Issue 1999–2000,** 123–51.

Ruud, E. (1980). *Music therapy and its relationship to current treatment theories.* St Louis: Magnamusic-Baton.

Ruud, E. (1998a). *Music therapy: Improvisation, communication, and culture.* Gilsum, NH: Barcelona.

Ruud, E. (1998b). Science as metacritique. *Journal of Music Therapy,* 35, 218–24.

Schögler, B. (1998). Music as a tool in communications research. *Nordic Journal of Music Therapy,* 7, 40–9.

Small, C. (1999). Musicking: the meanings of performance and listening. A lecture. *Music Education Research,* 1, 9–21.

Smeijsters, H. (1997). *Multiple perspectives: A guide to qualitative research in music therapy.* Phoenixville, PA: Barcelona.

Standley, J. M. & Hanser, S. B. (1995). Music therapy research and applications in pediatric oncology treatment. *Journal of Pediatric Oncology Nursing,* 12, 3–8.

Stern, D. (1985). *The interpersonal world of the infant.* London: Academic Press.

Streeter, E. (1999). Finding a balance between psychological thinking and musical awareness in music therapy theory—a psychoanalytic perspective. *British Journal of Music Therapy,* 13, 5–20.

Styge, B. (1999). Perspectives on meaning in music therapy. *British Journal of Music Therapy,* 12, 20–8.

Trehub, S. E. & Trainor, L. J. (1993). Listening strategies in infancy: The roots of music and language development. In *Thinking in sound: The cognitive psychology of human audition,* (ed. S. McAdams & E. Bigand), pp. 278–327. Oxford, UK: Oxford University Press.

Trevarthen, C. (1993). The self born in intersubjectivity: An infant communicating. In *Ecological and interpersonal knowledge of the self,* (ed. U. Neisser), pp. 121–73. New York: Cambridge University Press.

Trevarthen, C. (1999). Musicality and the intrinsic motive pulse: evidence from human psychobiology and infant communication. *Musicae Scientiae,* **Special Issue 1999–2000,** 155–211.

Trevarthen, C. & Aitken, K. J. (1994). Brain development, infant communication, and empathy disorders: Intrinsic factors in child mental health. *Development and Psychopathology,* 6, 599–635.

Tyler, H. (1998). Behind the mask: An exploration of the true and false self as revealed in music therapy. *British Journal of Music Therapy,* 12, 20–8.

Unyk, A. M., Trehub, S. E., Trainor, L. J., & Schellenberg, E. G. (1992). Lullabies and simplicity: A cross-cultural perspective. *Psychology of Music,* 20, 15–28.

Wheeler, B. (ed.). (1995). *Music therapy research: Quantitative and qualitative perspectives.* Phoenixville, PA: Barcelona.

Wigram, T. & De Backer, J. (ed.) (1999a). *Clinical applications of music therapy in develpmental disability, paediatrics and neurology.* London: Jessica Kingsley.

Wigram, T. & De Backer, J. (ed.) (1999b). *Clinical applications of music therapy in psychiatry.* London: Jessica Kingsley.

Wigram, T., Saperston, B., & West, R. (ed.) (1995). *The art and science of music therapy: A handbook.* Langhorne: Harwood Academic Press.

# PART III

# THE COMPOSER

# CHAPTER 9

# EMOTION AND COMPOSITION IN CLASSICAL MUSIC: HISTORIOMETRIC PERSPECTIVES

DEAN KEITH SIMONTON

The compositions that constitute the classical music tradition of the Western world probably have many different functions. Yet among those functions is probably some kind of emotional expression or communication. That is, when aficionados of classical music attend a concert or turn on their stereo, they usually expect to be 'moved'. Furthermore, listeners often believe that these emotional reactions are what the composer intended—that the work is a vehicle for emotional communication. As Beethoven once put it, 'Coming from the heart, may it go to the heart' (quoted in Scherman & Biancolli 1972, p. 951).

What makes these expectations somewhat surprising is the fact that classical music constitutes a fairly abstract form of aesthetic expression. Indeed, the concert halls are often dominated by purely instrumental forms—such as the symphony, concerto, quartet, and sonata—in which not a single word or programme gives any clue what the piece is actually about. Moreover, looking at a music score does not help render a classical composition any less abstract. On the contrary, musical notation is far more precise, rarified, and refined than can be found in any other form of artistic expression. Superficially at least, a score has more in common with a mathematical proof than with a painting, poem, or sculpture. This mathematical abstraction even holds for vocal forms, such as opera, oratorio, cantata, and song, where the words to be sung occupy a relatively small space on the page relative to all those meticulously placed symbols indicating pitch, duration, rhythm, dynamics, and other essential features of a composition. No wonder Claude Debussy could claim that 'music is the arithmetic of sounds as optics is the geometry of light' (quoted in *Who said what when*, Anon 1991, p. 252).

These observations thus lead to the following question: how do the abstractions of classical music evoke emotional reactions? There are many useful routes to addressing this issue. One option is to engage in a detailed musicological analysis, such as Leonard Meyer (1956) did in his important book on *Emotion and meaning in music*. Alternatively, one can conduct a laboratory experiment in which the emotional responses of listeners are assessed directly. An excellent example is Krumhansl's (1997) psychophysiological

study of the reactions of college students to musical excerpts from the classical repertoire. These musicological and experimental enquires have contributed a great deal to
our understanding of the emotional impact of classical music. Yet they by no means
exhaust the available methodological approaches.

Here, in fact, I adopt a distinctive analytical strategy that is far less common than
either musicological analysis or laboratory experiments. This approach entails the historiometric study of the composers and compositions that define the classical repertoire. By historiometrics, I mean the adaptation of psychometric methods to examine
data about historical individuals (Simonton 1990, 1999b; cf. Woods 1909, 1911). In the
case of classical composers, these data can include both: (a) biographical information
about their lives; and (b) content-analytical information about their works. In a series
of articles published since 1977, I have been using this specific technique to study creativity and aesthetics in classical music (e.g. Simonton 1977b, 1991, 1995). This
research was part of a broader series of studies devoted to understanding the psychology of creative genius. Although this research programme was not directed specifically
at investigating emotional expression in music, some of the empirical results might
possibly shed a little light on how this phenomenon operates, at least within the classical
music tradition.

I begin by describing an objective and quantitative measure of a composition's
melodic originality. I then show that scores on this computerized measure have certain
aesthetic consequences; consequences apparently consistent with the assumption that
the measure gauges something of a composition's 'arousal potential'. These content-
analytical scores are next shown to relate to the composer's biography in a manner
seemingly compatible with the same assumption. I then conclude with a general evaluation about what this research programme may possibly suggest about music and
emotion.

## 9.1 Melodic originality

The original impetus for this research came from an unexpected direction: the issue of
musical style. Those with lots of performing or listening experience with classical music
eventually learn to identify the distinctive styles of particular composers. Not only does
Beethoven's music sound different in comparison to that of Monteverdi, Handel,
Tchaikovsky, or Bartók, but it is even recognizably different from fellow composers of
the classical period, such as Haydn and Mozart. But what makes one composer noticeably different from another, even when they both are composing in the same period
style?

To answer this question, Paisley (1964) developed an idea taken from those art critics
who try to identify the creators of certain unsigned Renaissance paintings. What the
critics learn to look for are certain 'minor encoding habits', such as the way a particular
painter depicts ears, hands, or stones. Because these objects are rather secondary in
importance relative to the composition as a whole, they will often be executed in a
mechanical, almost mindless manner. Minor encoding habits have also proven useful in
identifying the unknown authors of various literary texts (Holsti 1969). These habits
include favourite function words, such as preferred prepositions and conjunctions.

Paisley wished to determine whether classical composers betrayed their identity through analogous encoding habits.

Paisley's (1964) specific solution was to perform a content analysis of the melodies or themes that make up almost any musical composition. Taking the first four notes of each theme, he then determined which combinations of notes were the most common for particular composers. Paisley found that different composers had distinctive ways of constructing their thematic material, and that these encoding habits could be used to predict the identity of the composer of anonymous test samples. Using this technique, Beethoven's work could be easily distinguished from that of other classical composers, including the works of Haydn and Mozart.

If composers can reveal their identity from just the first four notes of their melodies, what else can be learned from the content analysis of their melodic ideas? I decided to develop Paisley's approach to an objective and quantified assessment of an important property of music, namely its melodic originality.

### 9.1.1 Computerized measurement: two-note transition probabilities

The first task was to obtain a large and representative sample of classical composers. The sampling began with all those whose music could be found in a two-volume dictionary of musical themes (Barlow & Morgenstern 1948, 1950). This dictionary included all the classical music that was recorded up to the middle of the twentieth century. After deleting anonymous compositions and other problematic works, the sample consisted of 15 618 themes by 479 composers (Simonton 1980b). This could hardly be called a 'sample' at all, given its size. In fact, according to one study based on performance data, only 100 composers account for 94 per cent of the music that has any place whatsoever in the standard repertoire of classical music (Moles 1968; see also Simonton 1991). So the sample was exhaustive when it came to major composers. In addition, the sample was fairly exhaustive when it came to the principal compositions by the tradition's major figures. For instance, among the 15 618 themes were those coming from *all* of Beethoven's symphonies, concertos, string quartets, and piano sonatas (for a complete listing, see Barlow & Morgenstern 1948, 1950).

Following Paisley (1964), the thematic dictionaries that generated the sample also provided the foundation for the content analysis. For each theme, the dictionaries give the beginning notes, all transposed to a C tonic. In other words, all melodies in the major mode had been transposed into C major, and all those in the minor mode had been transposed into C minor. Although Paisley accomplished a lot with only the first four notes, I decided to use the first *six* notes of each of the 15 618 melodies. These data were all entered into a huge machine-readable data file. The next step was to have a computer calculate the two-note transition probabilities. That is, the first six notes contain five two-note transitions (first to second, second to third, etc.). The partial results of this computerized content analysis are shown in Table 9.1 (for a more complete table, see Simonton 1984, Table 1).

Clearly, some two-note transitions are far more common than others. On the one hand, the dominant–dominant (GG), tonic–tonic (CC), and dominant–tonic (GC) together account for about 17 per cent of all two-note combinations. On the other hand, combinations involving sharps and flats are much more rare—all occurring less

**Table 9.1** Two-note transition probabilities from the first six notes of 15 618 classical themes

---

$P \geq 0.06$: GG (0.067)

$P \geq 0.05$: CC (0.053)

$P \geq 0.04$: GC (0.049) and CD (0.044)

$P \geq 0.03$: CB (0.032), CG (0.032), GF (0.031), EE (0.030), ED (0.030), and DC (0.030)

$P \geq 0.02$: GE (0.029), GA (0.029), EF (0.028), EG (0.026), DE (0.024), BC (0.023), CE (0.022), FG (0.021), FE (0.021), GA (0.021), and AG (0.020)

$P \geq 0.01$: E♭D (0.018), EC (0.016), DE♭ (0.014), AB (0.012), BA (0.011), A♭G (0.011), and DD (0.011)

---

Probabilities given in parentheses are averaged across the first five two-note transitions (extracted from the more complete listing in Simonton 1984).

than 2 per cent of the time. Moreover, those that do appear, namely E♭ and A♭, are not chromatic, but rather are representative of the minor mode. Truly chromatic notes (those that depart from either the major or the minor mode) are even more improbable, only F# occurring with any frequency whatsoever.

It should be pointed out that the probabilities presented in Table 9.1 were averaged across all five two-note transitions. Slightly different results obtain when the two-note probabilities are calculated separately for each of the five transitions. For instance, two-note combinations involving the tonic and dominant decline in frequency from the first to the sixth note. Thus, over 11 per cent of the time the first transition contains the dominant–dominant (GG) pairing, but this figure decreases to less than 5 per cent by the fifth transition. In contrast, those transitions that involve other notes of the scale increase in frequency. Apparently, when composers first begin constructing a melody, they usually start by defining the theme's key with the most definitive notes of the scale before incorporating the other notes of the diatonic scale, such as the mediant, sub-dominant, and leading tone.

These latter, transition-specific probabilities were then used to construct a quantitative measure of melodic originality (Simonton 1980*b*). For each of the 15 618 themes, the probability of each of its five transitions was calculated, and then an average taken. The result is a number that represents the mean percentage of times a particular theme's five two-note transitions appear in the entire repertoire. To illustrate, the second movement of Haydn's Symphony No. 94 (the 'Surprise') opens with an extremely simple theme that begins CCEEGG. All of the component two-note transitions are extremely commonplace: the average transition probability is 0.040. A similar degree of predictability is found in the main theme of the concluding movement of Beethoven's 'Waldstein' Sonata, which begins GGEDGC, yielding a mean transition probability of 0.041. By comparison, the opening theme of the introduction to Mozart's 'Dissonant' Quartet commences with AGF#GAB♭, with a mean probability of 0.005. The theme that initiates Liszt's Faust Symphony is even more unlikely: A♭GBE♭F#B♭, yielding an average two-note probability of less than 0.001 (for more examples, see Simonton 1984, Table 3). In any case, given these numbers, a measure of each theme's melodic originality can be defined as one minus the mean probability (i.e. $1 - \sum P_i/5$). The higher this number, the higher is the assigned score for melodic originality.

This computerized measure may seem very crude. To begin with, the measure concentrates solely on the melody, thereby completely ignoring instrumentation, counterpoint, harmony, formal structure, and text (if any). The implicit assumption being made is that 'melody is the main thing', to quote Haydn (Landowska 1964, p. 336). But even with respect to melody alone, the computer-generated score ignores the theme's key, its rhythmic structure, and many other significant features. Instead, the measure concentrates on the relationships between consecutive pitches. Nevertheless, it turns out that this objective and quantitative score is not only perfectly reliable—the reliability coefficient is necessarily unity—but in addition it enjoys enough validity for research purposes.

### 9.1.2 Measure validation

The melodic originality measure was validated several ways. One very direct validation involved the direct comparison of the measure based on two-note transition probabilities with an alternative measure based on three-note transition probabilities (see Table 2 in Simonton 1984). These two measures correlate so highly that they yield practically the same results (Simonton 1980*a*). Perhaps this should not be too surprising, given that the most likely three-note transitions tend to be made up of the most common two-note transitions (e.g. GGG and CCC). In addition, originality scores based on the probabilities specific to each consecutive two-note transition produce almost the same outcomes as those based upon probabilities that are averaged across all transitions for all 15 618 themes (Simonton 1984). Hence, this gauge of melodic originality is not contingent on the particular operational definition adopted.

Another route to validation was to see if melodic originality correlates with other characteristics of the composition in a manner consistent with expectation. These correlations can be grouped into two categories: general correlates with other characteristics of the composition and those correlates that may more specifically link the measure with emotional expressiveness (Simonton 1994).

*General correlations with compositional characteristics*

The melodic originality of the themes in a composition is associated with other aspects of that composition. These linkages suggest that the computer content analysis has captured something that has musical significance. In particular, consider the following four empirical findings:

1. Originality is higher for those themes that are also more metrically complex (Simonton 1987). By metric complexity I mean melodies in less common metres, such as 3/2 or 9/8 rather than 2/4 or 4/4 time. Thus, as the two-note transitions become more unpredictable, the beats that contain the corresponding pitches become less simple. This hints that the originality measure might indirectly encompass more compositional effects than just melody alone.

2. Originality is higher for themes from instrumental works than those from vocal works (Simonton 1980*b*). Part of this relation may reflect the superior flexibility of most musical instrumental instruments relative to the human voice (e.g. the virtuoso violin versus a coloratura soprano). But another part may be ascribed to the fact that in vocal compositions, the text has part of the responsibility for communicating content (including any emotional expression).

3. Originality is higher for themes from chamber compositions than those from orchestral compositions, the latter in turn having more original themes than those from theatrical works, such as ballet (Simonton 1980b). In chamber compositions, such as sonatas and quartets, largely the thematic material carries the burden of maintaining listener interest. As the instrumental resources increase, as in symphonies, tone poems, and overtures, the opportunities rendered by orchestration can assume more importance in maintaining such appeal and attention. In theatrical compositions, extramusical stimulation becomes prominent as well, such as costumes, sets, and choreography. This renders melodic originality even less necessary.

4. Originality is higher in the outer movements of multimovement compositions than in the inner movements (Simonton 1987). For instance, symphonies and quartets will most often contain four movements: the first usually in sonata–allegro form, the second a slow movement in song or theme-variation form, a third a minuet (or scherzo) and trio, and a fourth that is in sonata–allegro, rondo, or variation form. The first movement contains the themes with the highest melodic originality, followed by the last movement. The middle movement, or movements, features the themes with the lowest melodic originality. Evidently, once the composer has got the listener's attention, originality can relax momentarily, until the intensity picks up again in the work's conclusion.

*Specific correlations with emotional expression and impact*

Although the melodic originality measure was not designed to tap the emotional content of a composition, two empirical findings suggest that some connection might exist:

1. Originality is higher for themes in minor keys than for those in major keys (Simonton 1987). As is apparent from Table 9.1, transitions containing the notes that define the minor mode have lower probabilities than those from the major mode, which gives minor-key themes their higher originality scores. This fits the subjective experiences of many music listeners, who tend to find themes in the minor mode more exotic, strange, or unusual in some way (Meyer 1956). That impression reflects the greater unpredictability of melodies that necessarily flow by less predictable transition probabilities. Perhaps as a consequence, composers frequently choose the minor mode for emotionally expressive compositions. Representative examples include Chopin's F Minor Fantasia, Mozart's G Minor String Quintet, Rachmaninoff's C Minor Piano Concerto No. 2, or Tchaikovsky's B Minor *Pathétique* Symphony. 'The minor mode is not only associated with intense feeling in general but with the delineation of sadness, suffering, and anguish in particular', observed Meyer (1956, p. 297). Later in this chapter, Meyer's assertion will receive some historiometric support.

2. Scores on the melodic originality measure can be directly compared with the subjective experiences of human listeners. Melodies that score higher in melodic originality should sound more unpredictable, interesting, or complex than melodies that score much lower. Anyone familiar with the themes mentioned ear-

lier should agree that this is the case. The Haydn theme sounds very much like a simple nursery tune (*Twinkle, Twinkle, Little Star*, in its English version), whereas the Mozart theme was so incomprehensible to Mozart's contemporaries (including Haydn) that the quartet which it opens with has been known as the 'dissonant' ever since. More important, one experimental investigation found that the originality scores correspond with subjective assessments of a theme's 'arousal potential' (Martindale & Uemura 1983). The originality scores were calculated using the two-note transition probabilities for themes by 252 composers, with one theme per composer. Naïve listeners then made an independent assessment of the arousal potential of each theme after listening to recordings made by a professional violinist. Those themes that scored higher on the objective measure of melodic originality tended to be those that also scored higher on the subjective measure of arousal potential. In other words, melodic originality predicts whether a theme will be perceived as exciting, stimulating, or arousing. Admittedly, the correlation was only 0.21 ($P < 0.001$), but this coefficient was probably attenuated by two factors. The first factor is that the transition probabilities were based on only 252 themes rather than 15 618. The second attenuating factor is that the variance in melodic originality would probably be truncated, given that only 252 themes by 252 composers were examined instead of 15 618 themes by 479 composers. If this correlation is then taken as the lower bound for the true correlation, it seems reasonable to conclude that, within the entire classical repertoire, those themes that contain more original two-note transition probabilities will be more likely to evoke emotional reactions in listeners.[1]

## 9.2 Aesthetic consequences

If the hypothesized linkage between melodic originality and arousal potential has some justification, then the content-analytical measure should bear a theoretically meaningful association with: (a) a composition's aesthetic impact on listeners; and (b) changes in aesthetic style within a composer's career and within the history of classical music. The reasons for these expectations will become clear below.

### 9.2.1 Compositional impact

Research in experimental aesthetics has suggested that the aesthetic success of any work of art is in part a function of its capacity to evoke emotional arousal (e.g. Berlyne 1971, 1974). The arousal potential of a given work is associated with such things as the complexity, novelty, surprisingness, and ambiguity of the aesthetic stimulus. The more complex, novel, surprising, or ambiguous the stimulus, the higher the magnitude of arousal elicited. However, the functional relation between arousal potential and aesthetic

---

[1] Tuomas Eerola (personal communication, 26 March 1999) informed me that he had found a correlation of 0.93 between the melodic originality measure and an alternative measure of melodic complexity derived from research on music perception. This constitutes another independent validation of the computer-generated scores.

impact is not linear, but rather curvilinear. That is, the relation is described by what has been called the 'Wundt curve' (Berlyne 1971). The most successful works are those that evoke an optimal level of arousal. In contrast, compositions with low arousal potential will prove to be predictable, commonplace, or obvious—and hence boring. And compositions that provoke excessive arousal will induce a state of stress, anxiety, or even fear (e.g. the notorious debut of Stravinsky's *Rite of Spring*). A number of investigations in experimental aesthetics have in fact found curvilinear inverted-U relations between measures of arousal potential and aesthetic preferences (e.g. Kammann 1966; Steck & Machotka 1975; Vitz 1964).

However, most of these experimental studies have used artificial 'art-like' stimuli, which were then rated by college students in somewhat unnatural laboratory conditions (Berlyne 1974). This may help explain why the results are not always consistent with theoretical expectation (e.g. Martindale & Moore 1989). Therefore, it behoves us to ask whether the same Wundt curve can be found under more natural circumstances. In particular, is the aesthetic success of real compositions in the classical repertoire partially determined by the melodic originality of the themes those compositions contain? If this content-analytical measure can really be taken as an approximate gauge of a theme's arousal potential, then scores should predict a composition's aesthetic impact. This is in fact the case for both objective and subjective indicators:

*Objective ratings* were based on the actual success of the composition in the classical repertoire (Simonton 1980*a*, 1980*b*, 1983). That is, these ratings gauged the frequency that a musical product is likely to be heard in the concert hall, opera house, and recording studio (for a psychometric assessment of such indicators, see Simonton 1998*a*). The relationship between this objective measure and melodic originality is neither linear positive nor linear negative but rather curvilinear. In particular, the relationship is best described as an inverted backward-J curve, as shown in Fig. 9.1 (Simonton 1980*b*). The most popular works are those that have moderate levels of melodic originality, whereas the most unpopular works are those with the highest levels of melodic originality—the pieces with low melodic originality having more middling popularity. This curvilinear function demonstrates that the Wundt curve provides an adequate description of what happens in the real world of music listening. At least, this function holds for the 15 618 themes that define the classical repertoire. The same function has also been shown to hold for the 593 themes that Beethoven contributed to the classical repertoire (Simonton 1987).[2]

---

[2] Here, as in the rest of this chapter, I am more precisely speaking of *repertoire* melodic originality, that is, the unpredictability of the sequence of pitches when compared with the entire standard repertoire of classical music. Another kind of originality has been defined, namely *Zeitgeist* melodic originality (Simonton 1980*b*). In this case, originality is gauged according to whether a particular theme's construction fits the stylistic norms at the time the work was composed. This distinction is crucial, because the two kinds of melodic originality do not correlate the same way with other variables. For example, the popularity of a composition is a U-shaped function of its *Zeitgeist* melodic originality (Simonton 1980*b*). The most successful works are those that depart (in either direction) from the level of repertoire melodic originality most typical of the day.

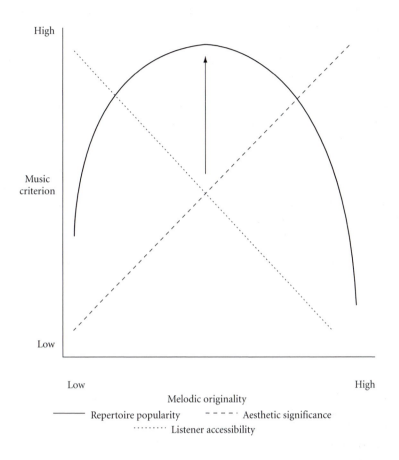

**Figure 9.1** The graph summarizes the empirical results regarding how a theme's melodic originality (as computed from two-note transition probabilities) is associated with three musical criteria: objective repertoire popularity (a composite measure of the performance and recording frequency of the composition which contains the theme) and subjective assessments of its aesthetic significance and listener accessibility (according to Halsey 1976). The arrow indicates the explanatory hypothesis that the peak of the curvilinear function might reside where the product of aesthetic significance and listener accessibility may be maximized.

*Subjective ratings* were taken from Halsey (1976), who rated thousands of classical compositions on two dimensions, namely aesthetic significance and listener accessibility. Melodic originality was correlated with both of these measures, albeit in opposite directions, as also indicated in Fig. 9.1 (Simonton 1986). Aesthetically significant compositions are those that were deemed sufficiently profound that they could withstand repeated listening. They cannot be fully appreciated in a single, superficial hearing. Such pieces score high on the melodic originality of their thematic material. Accessible compositions, in contrast, can be understood at once, and thereby lend themselves to music appreciation courses taught at schools and colleges. Not surprisingly, works that score high on listener accessibility tend to score low on melodic originality. Highly unpredictable themes would only interfere with making an immediately favourable impression.

Note that the functions for the objective ratings were curvilinear, whereas those for the subjective ratings were linear and in opposed directions. Do these results contradict each other? I do not think so. Although aesthetic significance and listener accessibility correlate differently with melodic originality, they both correlate in the same positive direction with repertoire popularity. Accordingly, one could argue that the peak of the Wundt curve represents the point that maximizes the joint contribution of aesthetic significance and listener accessibility to repertoire popularity. At low levels of melodic originality, the music is very predictable and thus accessible, but the music is also considered of trivial aesthetic importance. At high levels of melodic originality, the aesthetic significance is not so much in doubt as the ability of listeners to appreciate the composition. At middle levels of originality, the works are still reasonably accessible while at the same time they are above the norm in significance. The vertical arrow in Fig. 9.1 represents the hypothesis that the highest popularity is to be found where the product of aesthetic significance and listener accessibility is maximal.

Interestingly, because low melodic originality is preferred over high melodic originality in terms of repertoire popularity, aesthetic significance appears to have less weight than listener accessibility. On the whole, at least with respect to emotional arousal, listeners would rather be quietly entertained than anxiously provoked.

### 9.2.2 Stylistic transformations

If the relation between aesthetic impact and melodic originality is mediated by the emotional arousal that highly original compositions evoke, then this relation could be moderated by another basic psychological process: *habituation*. With repetition, the response to an arousing stimulus will often diminish (Berlyne 1971). As a consequence, over time, increasingly higher levels of melodic originality may be required in order to elicit the same optimal level of arousal in music listeners (Martindale 1990; for literary illustration, see Kamman 1966). According to trend analyses of all 15 618 themes by 479 composers, this upward movement manifests itself in two ways (Simonton 1997).

First, composers tend to steadily increase their use of melodic originality as their careers progress (Simonton 1980*b*). Originality is lowest at the beginning of the career, but at once begins to increase. The only exception to this upward growth occurs at around the 56th year of life, where originality tends to reach a peak. After this a modest decline sets in. Beethoven enthusiasts may find the peak at 56 the most intriguing. Beethoven died at that age, which means that he should have been publishing his most original work then, if his career followed the same pattern as 478 other classical composers. A hearing of his Late Quartets suggests that this was indeed the case.

Second, there exists an overall tendency for melodic originality to increase from the Renaissance to the twentieth century (Simonton 1980*b*). This upward trend suggests that each generation of composers feels compelled to produce work that overcomes habituation to a given level of originality, just as predicted by Martindale's (1990) theory of stylistic change. However, just as an exception to the general positive trend was found for composer's careers, so are curious departures found across the history of the classical music tradition. Specifically, superimposed over the positive linear trend are cyclical fluctuations. Melodies in the Renaissance were highly predictable, but by the time of Monteverdi and Gesualdo, originality had reached a maximum point, with a degree of chromaticism that was to be unmatched for nearly three centuries. After that, themes became more predictable again, albeit not as predictable as during the Renaissance. The trough occurred during the time of the 'classical period'—Haydn, Mozart, and Beethoven—when thematic material would be constructed from basic chords (e.g. the opening of Beethoven's *Eroica* Symphony). With the advent of the 'romantic period', melodic originality increased, most notably with the chromaticism of Chopin, Brahms, and Wagner (e.g. the famous prelude to *Tristan und Isolde*). This trend reached a new height about the time of the First World War. It was this peak that witnessed the emergence of the atonal and serial music of Arnold Schoenberg, such as his *Pierrot Lunaire*. Then melodic originality saw another decline, although again not going as low as the two previous lows. The music of Aaron Copland and Sergei Prokofiev is indicative of this retrogression.

The superimposed oscillation would seem to contradict the basic proposition that arousal potential has tended to increase over time. Yet, if this cyclical pattern is examined more closely, it becomes evident that the momentary declines in melodic originality tend to come during those periods in which composers acquire new ways to increase the arousal potential of their works besides increasing the novelty, complexity, surprisingness, and ambiguity of the thematic material. Rather than augment the magnitude of chromaticism, for example, the composer may have access to novel forms, rhythms, and orchestration. In partial support for this conjecture, not only is melodic originality lower in those forms giving the composer greater resources (as noted earlier), but also the relation between melodic originality and repertoire popularity is moderated by the size of the work (Simonton 1980*b*). The larger the form in which the composer writes, the weaker is the relation between originality and the composition's impact.

In any event, once alternative techniques for evoking emotional reactions become fully incorporated in the repertoire, the composers must again resort to melodic originality as a primary means to overcome the pressures produced by jaded tastes. Furthermore, it is essential to recognize that as the history of classical music unfolds, the troughs in originality get less deep and the crests become more elevated. Hence, the musical history of melodic originality never really repeats itself.

## 9.3 Biographical antecedents

For a chapter that purports to deal with music and emotion, the results so far may seem a bit cold. Granted, the objective and quantified indicator of melodic originality may indeed correspond with a theme's capacity to stimulate arousal—and that stimulation may shape a composition's aesthetic impact. But emotion in music is often seen as entailing much more than the simple activation of the human sympathetic nervous system. Emotion is also seen as a form of expression, as a means of communicating emotions between a creative artist and an audience. Yet so far we have treated melodic originality as some compositional quality that a composer must manipulate in order to keep listeners from falling asleep—or from running out of the concert hall in disgust or terror.

Fortunately, research using computerized measures has provided ample reason for believing that melodic originality may reflect the emotional state of the composer at the time of a work's composition. For example, the composer's use of melodic originality is noticeably altered when a composition is created during traumatic political events, such as international war (Simonton 1986, 1987; see also Brook 1969; Cerulo 1984). In particular, compositions penned during times of warfare exhibit much greater variation in melodic originality, extremely unpredictable and extremely predictable themes being found in the same work. It is almost as if such highly stressful events polarize emotional reactions, inspiring vast mood swings between resignation and despair, hope and fear. Shostakovitch's notable (and notorious) *Leningrad Symphony* provides a graphic auditory illustration of the magnitude of this polarization of trite and profound.

More significant, however, is the impact of highly personal events in the life of the composer. Below I treat two potential instances of this personal connection: biographical stress and late-life effects.

### 9.3.1 Biographical stress

Of special interest to any emotional expression hypothesis is the relation between the amount of stress occurring in a composer's personal life and the amount of melodic originality appearing in work created during the same period. If 'music sounds the way emotions feel' (Pratt 1954, p. 296, italics removed), and if stressful events provoke strong emotions, some correspondence between the two should be found. Moreover, the measure of melodic originality would seem to capture some of the attributes of music that contribute to its emotional expressiveness. An excellent example is chromaticism, or the use of notes beside those that define the theme's key. Chromatic notes are often used to express emotions, the unpredictability of the melodic line reflecting the turmoil of our internal emotional state (Meyer 1956). Indeed, this usage is not even confined to the classical music tradition, as the expressive use of chromatic 'blue notes' in blues and jazz illustrates (La Rue 1970).

To test the hypothesized linkage between life stress and melodic originality, I took advantage of an earlier data set that had been compiled for a different purpose (Simonton 1977a). The careers of classical composers were scrutinized to determine the factors that affect a composer's output across the lifespan. The particular composers were the ten most eminent according to a large survey of musicologists (Farnsworth 1969), namely, Bach, Handel, Haydn, Mozart, Beethoven, Schubert, Chopin, Wagner, Brahms, and Debussy. Among the potential predictors of compositional productivity was the occurrence of stressful or traumatic events in the composer's life. To obtain a measure of these events, a chronology of such events was first compiled from the extensive biographies available for these illustrious contributors to the classical repertoire. The next step was to convert these raw facts into a quantitative measure of the degree of stress experiences by each composer during consecutive periods of his life. This conversion was achieved by adapting the social readjustment rating scale, which has proven its utility in research on psychosomatic illnesses (Holmes & Holmes 1970; Holmes & Rahe 1967; see also Simonton 1998b). Table 9.2 shows some of the biographical events and the weights they were each assigned in the resulting tabulations.

**Table 9.2**  Biographical stress coding scheme designed for ten classical composers

*Legal difficulties*: Litigation or lawsuit (30); Detention in jail or exile to avoid arrest (63)

*Economic problems*: Major loan (20); Trouble with creditors (30); Aversive change in financial state or business readjustment (38)

*Educational changes*: Change in schools (20); Begin or terminate formal schooling (26)

*Vocational changes or problems*: Job change (20); Trouble with employer or superior (23); Change in responsibilities at work (29); Begin or end work but not fired or retired (36); Retirement (45); Fired from work (47)

*Mobility*: City or town of permanent residence changed (30 per move); Nation of permanent residence changed (40 per move)

*Interpersonal problems*: Duels, fights, and other physical confrontations (10); Argument with friend (10); Disappointed or unrequited love (15); Onset or termination of a reciprocated love affair (30); Death of a close friend (37)

*Family problems*: Gain of a new family member, including adoption (39); Change in health or behaviour of family member (44); Death of close family member, except children under 3 (63)

*Marital difficulties*: Marital reconciliation (45); Marriage (50); Marital separation (65); Divorce (73); Death of spouse, unless separated (100)

The points assigned to each life-change stress are given in parentheses.

Given these previously calculated assessments, it was a relatively simple matter to estimate the relation between a theme's melodic originality and the amount of stress the composer had experienced during the period of composition (tabulated in cumulative 5-year periods). The association was found to be positive, even after introducing controls for other confounding factors, such as the composer's age at the time a work was conceived (Simonton 1980*a*). This finding was replicated and extended in a second study that concentrated just on the career of Beethoven (Simonton 1987). Besides replicating the positive association between stress and originality, this investigation tabulated a measure of the lifespan fluctuations in Beethoven's physical health (cf. Porter & Suedfeld 1981; Simonton 1998*b*). This latter measure was also found to correspond to the melodic originality found in Beethoven's compositions. When the composer was experiencing robust health, originality tended to be relatively low, whereas when the composer's health failed, originality was likely to be high. Given that physical illness can be considered a major source of life stress, this finding reinforces what was found for biographical stress. The thematic material found in a composer's works may indeed communicate to the listener the composer's underlying emotional life at the time of their composition.

### 9.3.2 Late-life effects

Biographical stress and physical illness serve to heighten levels of melodic originality. Yet sometimes certain life events can operate in a contrary manner. This contrast is found in a study conducted of what was called the 'swan-song phenomenon' (Simonton 1989). There has been much speculation about whether artistic creators exhibit a 'late-life' or 'old-age' style (e.g. Arnheim 1986; Münsterberg 1983), and even some empirical evidence suggests that these speculations have captured a grain of truth (Lindauer

1993). Analogous speculations have been advanced regarding supposed last-work effects in classical music (Einstein 1956). So, do late-life compositions exhibit any consistent stylistic shifts? This question was addressed by examining melodic originality in 1919 works by 172 classical composers, and a striking developmental pattern was identified (Simonton 1989). In the years immediately preceding death, a composer's compositions exhibit rapidly declining levels of melodic originality. In other words, the thematic material becomes much more predictable. Significantly, this effect survived statistical control for the composer's age. Hence, the decline is a consequence of the proximity of death rather than old age. Composers who died young, such as Mozart and Schubert, could thus display the same swan-song effects as those who died at relatively advanced ages, like Vaughan Williams and Stravinsky.

But what is the psychological basis for this swan-song phenomenon? One possibility is to dismiss this effect as an example of the mental deterioration that too often occurs towards the end of any person's life (e.g. Suedfeld & Piedrahita 1984). Consistent with this interpretation, not only do the melodies tend to be less original in last works, but in addition the works themselves are of shorter duration on average (Simonton 1989). Even so, this negative interpretation does not seem very compatible with other empirical results: the closer to the composer's death a work appears, the more frequently it is performed in the classical repertoire and the higher the rating it receives in aesthetic significance. Hence, swan songs may be shorter and have more simple melodies, but they are also more successful in terms of popular and critical appraisal!

Given the sum total of these findings, it seems more likely that the lower melodic originality in late works is deliberate rather than negligent. If high originality is associated with highly emotional states, then low originality may reveal low levels of emotionality. For a composer who may feel that the end is quickly and inevitably approaching—as perhaps indicated by terminal illnesses or the frailties of old age—that low arousal state may hint that he has resigned himself to his fate. That resignation, that acceptance then takes the form of powerful and expressive swan songs that communicate the most with the least. This communication of internal peace can itself be considered a form of emotional expression. To get a direct sense of that feeling, we need only listen to the final chorale of Bach's *The Art of the Fugue*, Mozart's *Ave Verum Corpus*, Brahms' Four Serious Songs, or Richard Strauss' Four Last Songs.

## 9.4 Conclusion

The research just reviewed has many limitations, two of which are especially critical here. First, none of these studies were specifically dedicated to scrutinizing the relation between music and emotion. Instead, their primary purpose was to comprehend more generally the creativity of composers and the aesthetic impact of their compositions. In only one investigation was emotional impact directly assessed, and then only in the rather stripped-down form of 'arousal potential' (Martindale & Uemura 1983). The differentiated emotional states seen in other investigations, such as happiness and sadness, have no direct representation in this historiometric literature (cf. Krumhansl 1997). Furthermore, emotional reactions were mostly introduced as intervening variables to predict or explain the empirical relations between observed variables. Thus, the positive association between biographical stress and melodic originality was predicted under the assumptions that: (a) stress produces emotional states; and (b) such emotional states influence the composer's melodic creativity (e.g. the use of chromaticism). Likewise, the expected curvilinear relation between melodic originality and repertoire popularity was directly based on Berlyne's (1971) optimal-arousal model of the relation between collative variation and aesthetic preference—and the Wundt curve that it theoretically predicts.

Fortunately, none of the empirical findings contradicted the two-fold supposition that melodic originality both influenced listeners' emotional response and reflected the composer's emotional states. In addition, a strong agreement exists between many of these findings and what Meyer (1956) argued on the basis of a detailed, sophisticated analysis of a select number of representative scores (e.g. the relation between emotion and the violation of melodic expectations). None the less, to make a stronger case for this supposition, these historiometric results should be tied more closely with findings from laboratory experiments. For instance, I have previously suggested using the two-note transition probabilities to construct artificial musical stimuli (Simonton 1984). Experiments can then gauge whether these stimuli influence both physiological responses and subjective appraisals of participants (e.g. as in Krumhansl 1997; see also Scherer & Zentner, this volume). This extension would introduce the experimental controls so obviously lacking in historiometric enquiries.

The second limitation concerns the fact that the correlations between melodic originality and other significant factors are far from perfect. At no time can we say that even a quarter of the variance is accounted for by any one relationship, and more often the effects hover around one or two per cent. Yet we should not expect it to be otherwise. Musical creativity, like other forms of creative behaviour, is a complex, multidetermined phenomenon (Simonton 1999a). It probably would take hundreds of variables to fully describe what happens when a composer puts notes on a piece of paper—or when a listener emotionally responds to their performance. In addition, it must be reiterated that the computerized assessment of melodic originality remains only a crude approximation. Composers have a great deal more in their expressive toolkit than the choice of pitches. It certainly makes a difference in emotional impact whether the tempo is adagio or presto, the rhythm regular or syncopated, the dynamics pianissimo or fortissimo, the melody line played on a violin or tuba (cf. Gabrielsson & Lindström, this volume). Indeed, when the current scheme is compared with various alternative content-analytical measures, its simplicity becomes quite obvious (see, for example, Cerulo 1988, 1989). A certain price has been paid to quantify efficiently and objectively so many themes and their corresponding compositions.

All that admitted, the fact remains that the discovered relationships, whatever their limitations, hold for all of the works that dominate the classical repertoire. Certainly, 15 618 themes by 479 composers constitute a far more representative sample than seen in any other investigation, whether musicological or experimental. Therefore, it may be worthwhile to lend serious consideration to the findings that connect the computer-generated melodic originality with a provocative array of variables. Scores on this content-analytical attribute have been empirically linked with various characteristics of classical works, including their key, rhythm, medium, form, and compositional structure. Even more pertinent here, melodic originality seems to bear some connection with a theme's emotional expressiveness. This latter consequence, however modest, has implications for understanding: (a) how compositions vary in their repertoire popularity, listener accessibility, and aesthetic significance; and (b) how melodic originality changes during the development of a composer's career and during the evolution of musical history. At the same time, the melodic originality of particular themes appears to have some foundation in the life experiences prevailing at the time the works were created by the composer. Stressful and even traumatic events tend to intensify the level of melodic originality in concomitant compositions.

All of these empirical relationships imply that melodic originality, at least to some degree, forms part of the composer's tools for expressing emotion. It seems most likely that more sophisticated methods of assessing the expressive qualities of music will reinforce rather than contradict this conclusion.

## References

**Anon** (1991). *Who said what when: A chronological dictionary of quotations.* New York: Hippocrene Books.

**Arnheim, R.** (1986). *New essays on the psychology of art.* Berkeley, CA: University of California Press.

**Barlow, H. & Morgenstern, S.** (1948). *A dictionary of musical themes.* New York: Crown.

**Barlow, H. & Morgenstern, S.** (1950). *A dictionary of vocal themes.* New York: Crown.

**Berlyne, D. E.** (1971). *Aesthetics and psychobiology.* New York: Appleton-Century-Crofts.

**Berlyne, D. E.** (ed.) (1974). *Studies in the new experimental aesthetics.* Washington, DC: Hemisphere.

**Brook, B. S.** (1969). Style and content analysis in music: The simplified 'Plaine and Easie Code'. In *The analysis of communication content*, (ed. G. Gerbner, O. R. Holsti, K. Krippendorff, W. J. Paisley, & P. J. Stone), pp. 287–96. New York: Wiley.

**Cerulo, K. A.** (1984). Social disruption and its effects on music: An empirical analysis. *Social Forces,* **62**, 885–904.

**Cerulo, K. A.** (1988). Analyzing cultural products: A new method of measurement. *Social Science Research,* **17**, 317–52.

**Cerulo, K. A.** (1989). Variations in musical syntax: Patterns of measurement. *Communication Research,* **16**, 204–35.

**Einstein, A.** (1956). *Essays on music.* New York: Norton.

**Farnsworth, P. R.** (1969). *The social psychology of music,* (2nd edn). Ames, IW: Iowa State University Press.

**Halsey, R. S.** (1976). *Classical music recordings for home and library.* Chicago: American Library Association.

**Holmes, T. S. & Holmes, T. H.** (1970). Short-term intrusions into the life style routine. *Journal of Psychosomatic Research,* **14**, 121–32.

**Holmes, T. S. & Rahe, R. H.** (1967). The social readjustment rating scale. *Journal of Psychosomatic Research,* **11**, 213–18.

**Holsti, O. R.** (1969). *Content analysis for the social sciences and humanities.* Reading, MA: Addison-Wesley.

**Kammann, R.** (1966). Verbal complexity and preferences in poetry. *Journal of Verbal Learning and Verbal Behavior,* **5**, 536–40.

Krumhansl, C. L. (1997). An exploratory study of musical emotions and psychophysiology. *Canadian Journal of Experimental Psychology,* 51, 336–52.

La Rue, J. (1970). *Guidelines for style analysis.* New York: Norton.

Landowska, W. (1964). *Landowska on music,* (ed. and trans. D. Restout). New York: Stein & Day.

Lindauer, M. S. (1993). The old-age style and its artists. *Empirical Studies and the Arts,* 11, 135–46.

Martindale, C. (1990). *The clockwork muse: The predictability of artistic styles.* New York: Basic Books.

Martindale, C. & Moore, K. (1989). Relationship of musical preference to collative, ecological, and psychophysical variables. *Music Perception,* 6, 431–46.

Martindale, C. & Uemura, A. (1983). Stylistic evolution in European music. *Leonardo,* 16, 225–8.

Meyer, L. B. (1956). *Emotion and meaning in music.* Chicago: University of Chicago Press.

Moles, A. (1968). *Information theory and esthetic perception* (trans. J. E. Cohen). Urbana, IL: University of Illinois Press (originally published 1958).

Münsterberg, H. (1983). *The crown of life: Artistic creativity in old age.* San Diego, CA: Harcourt-Brace-Jovanovich.

Paisley, W. J. (1964). Identifying the unknown communicator in painting, literature and music: The significance of minor encoding habits. *Journal of Communication,* 14, 219–37.

Porter, C. A. & Suedfeld, P. (1981). Integrative complexity in the correspondence of literary figures: Effects of personal and societal stress. *Journal of Personality and Social Psychology,* 40, 321–30.

Pratt, C. C. (1954). The design of music. *Journal of Aesthetics and Art Criticism,* 12, 289–300.

Schermann, T. K. & Biancolli, L. (ed.) (1972). *The Beethoven companion.* Garden City, NY: Doubleday.

Simonton, D. K. (1977*a*). Creative productivity, age, and stress: A biographical time-series analysis of 10 classical composers. *Journal of Personality and Social Psychology,* 35, 791–804.

Simonton, D. K. (1977*b*). Eminence, creativity, and geographic marginality: A recursive structural equation model. *Journal of Personality and Social Psychology,* 35, 805–16.

Simonton, D. K. (1980*a*). Thematic fame and melodic originality in classical music: A multivariate computer-content analysis. *Journal of Personality,* 48, 206–19.

Simonton, D. K. (1980*b*). Thematic fame, melodic originality, and musical zeitgeist: A biographical and transhistorical content analysis. *Journal of Personality and Social Psychology,* 38, 972–83.

Simonton, D. K. (1983). Esthetics, biography, and history in musical creativity. In *Documentary report of the Ann Arbor Symposium,* Session 3, pp. 41–8. Reston, VA: Music Educators National Conference.

Simonton, D. K. (1984). Melodic structure and note transition probabilities: A content analysis of 15,618 classical themes. *Psychology of Music,* 12, 3–16.

Simonton, D. K. (1986). Aesthetic success in classical music: A computer analysis of 1935 compositions. *Empirical Studies of the Arts,* 4, 1–17.

Simonton, D. K. (1987). Musical aesthetics and creativity in Beethoven: A computer analysis of 105 compositions. *Empirical Studies of the Arts,* 5, 87–104.

Simonton, D. K. (1989). The swan-song phenomenon: Last-works effects for 172 classical composers. *Psychology and Aging,* 4, 42–7.

Simonton, D. K. (1990). *Psychology, science, and history: An introduction to historiometry.* New Haven, CT: Yale University Press.

Simonton, D. K. (1991). Emergence and realization of genius: The lives and works of 120 classical composers. *Journal of Personality and Social Psychology*, **61**, 829–40.

Simonton, D. K. (1994). Computer content analysis of melodic structure: Classical composers and their compositions. *Psychology of Music*, **22**, 31–43.

Simonton, D. K. (1995). Drawing inferences from symphonic programs: Musical attributes versus listener attributions. *Music Perception*, **12**, 307–22.

Simonton, D. K. (1997). Products, persons, and periods: Historiometric analyses of compositional creativity. In *The social psychology of music*, (ed. D. J. Hargreaves & A. C. North), pp. 107–22. Oxford, UK: Oxford University Press.

Simonton, D. K. (1998*a*). Fickle fashion versus immortal fame: Transhistorical assessments of creative products in the opera house. *Journal of Personality and Social Psychology*, **75**, 198–210.

Simonton, D. K. (1998*b*). Mad King George: The impact of personal and political stress on mental and physical health. *Journal of Personality*, **66**, 443–66.

Simonton, D. K. (1999*a*). *Origins of genius: Darwinian perspectives on creativity.* New York: Oxford University Press.

Simonton, D. K. (1999*b*). Significant samples: The psychological study of eminent individuals. *Psychological Methods*, **4**, 425–51.

Steck, L. & Machotka, P. (1975). Preference for musical complexity: Effects of context. *Journal of Experimental Psychology: Human Perception and Performance*, **104**, 170–4.

Suedfeld, P. & Piedrahita, L. E. (1984). Intimations of mortality: Integrative simplification as a predictor of death. *Journal of Personality and Social Psychology*, **47**, 848–52.

Vitz, P. C. (1964). Preferences for rates of information presented by sequences of tones. *Journal of Experimental Psychology*, **68**, 176–83.

Woods, F. A. (1909). A new name for a new science. *Science*, **30**, 703–4.

Woods, F. A. (1911). Historiometry as an exact science. *Science*, **33**, 568–74.

# CHAPTER 10

# THE INFLUENCE OF MUSICAL STRUCTURE ON EMOTIONAL EXPRESSION

## ALF GABRIELSSON AND ERIK LINDSTRÖM

The expressive qualities of music have been a matter of discussion by philosophers and music theorists ever since antiquity and, more recently, by music psychologists. Many kinds of expression have been proposed, but expression of emotion is undoubtedly the most frequent. Likewise, most empirical research has focused on emotional expression in attempts to find out, on the one hand, which emotions can be reliably expressed in music (reviewed in Gabrielsson & Juslin, in press) and, on the other hand, which factors in music contribute to the perceived emotional expression. The latter refer to factors in the composed musical structure represented in the musical notation, such as tempo, loudness, pitch, mode, melody, rhythm, harmony, and various formal properties.

While it is a popular conception, and sometimes perhaps true, that composers express their present feelings in their compositions (cf. Cook & Dibben, this volume; Simonton, this volume), a more plausible view is that composers try to use various structural factors in order to achieve certain intended expressions, different in different works, with little or no direct connection to their present feelings. 'A composer . . . knows the forms of emotions and can handle them, "compose" them' (Langer 1957, p. 222). Tchaikovsky, usually considered a very 'emotional' composer, wrote that 'Those who imagine that a creative artist can—through the medium of his art—express his feelings at the moment when he is *moved*, make the greatest mistake. Emotions—sad or joyful—can only be expressed *retrospectively* . . . a work composed in the happiest surroundings may be touched with dark and gloomy colors' (cited in Fisk 1997, p. 157). For further discussion of these questions, see, for instance, Davies (1994, Chapters 4–6; see also Davies, this volume).

The purpose of this chapter is to review empirical research concerning the influence of different factors in musical structure on perceived emotional expression. However, because listeners usually judge perceived expression of composed music as realized in performance, there is a confounding of the properties of the composed structure and properties of the actual performance. As a rule, performance involves various modifications of the notated structure, for instance, variations of tempo, loudness, articulation, intonation, deviations in note timing, etc. (for a review, see Gabrielsson 1999). Perceived expression is thus dependent both on factors in the composed structure and factors in the performance. Only recently have the influence of the latter been subject to systematic investigations (see Juslin, this volume). Listeners' perception of emotional expression—for instance, to perceive a piece of music as 'happy'—should be distinguished from listeners' own emotional reactions—for instance, to feel happy. Listeners' emotional reactions are treated elsewhere in this volume (Gabrielsson; Scherer & Zentner; Sloboda & O'Neill).

In Section 10.1, we review different methodological approaches to study the influence of musical structure on perceived emotional expression. The results are summarized in Section 10.2, and implications for future research are discussed in the final section.

## 10.1 Different methodological approaches

Empirical studies of musical expression had a cautious start in late nineteenth century, and it was not until the 1930s that they became more common. Subjects listened to pieces of music or other tonal stimuli and reported the perceived expression by either: (a) free phenomenological descriptions; (b) choice among descriptive terms, adjectives, or nouns, provided by the investigator; or (c) ratings of how well such descriptive terms applied to the music in question. Free descriptions were subjected to content analysis. Listeners' choice among descriptive terms was analysed regarding the frequency with which each term was chosen and regarding intersubject agreement. Ratings were usually analysed by multivariate techniques, such as factor analysis, cluster analysis, and multi-dimensional scaling in order to find a limited number of fundamental descriptive dimensions. Recently, various techniques for continuous and/or non-verbal recording of perceived expression have been developed.

Stimuli were usually recordings of selected pieces of music. However, before common use of modern sound recording the pieces were performed live by one or more musicians (e.g. Downey 1897; Gilman 1891; Hevner 1935a; Rigg 1937). The relationship between the composed structure and perceived expression was studied *post hoc* by analysing the musical scores (e.g. Gundlach 1935; Nielsen 1983) or having musical experts judge the selected pieces with regard to structural properties (e.g. Kleinen 1968; Watson 1942; Wedin 1972c).

Studying emotional expression using real music (see Section 10.1.1) means good ecological validity; on the other hand, conclusions regarding the effects of separate structural factors can only be tentative since they are confounded. In contrast to this, there are studies in which the researcher systematically varies one or more structural factors (e.g. loudness, pitch level) in short sound sequences without musical context (see Section 10.1.2). Ecological validity is then limited, but the systematic variation allows more definite conclusions regarding the effects of separate factors. A compromise between these two approaches is to use systematic manipulation of various factors within a musical context (see Section 10.1.3), for instance, to systematically vary tempo, mode, or melodic direction in real pieces of music and thus try to combine the advantages of the before-mentioned strategies. However, some types of manipulation may result in musically unnatural stimuli, thus jeopardizing ecological validity.

### 10.1.1 Studying emotional expression using real music

*Free descriptions and choice among descriptive terms*

The earliest reported empirical investigations on musical expression may be those by Gilman (1891, 1892) and Downey (1897). Their subjects listened to live performances on the piano, or piano and violin, of classical music and gave free phenomenological reports on perceived expression. A variety of emotions was reported and some tentative relationships were noted, for instance, descending thirds in an aria by Handel to indicate sadness.

Gundlach (1935) presented 40 musical phrases from different classical compositions to listeners, who were instructed to determine 'what mood or attitude the composer has succeeded in expressing' (p. 628) by choosing one or more out of 17 descriptive terms. From his analysis Gundlach concluded that speed was by far the most important factor for perceived expression, followed by rhythm, interval distribution, orchestral range, loudness, mean pitch, and melodic range.

Rigg (1937) used 20 short phrases played on the piano that were supposed to express either joy, lamentation, longing, or love. Listeners answered the question 'What emotion is suggested to you by each passage?' either by giving free descriptions or by choosing among the above emotion terms plus anger, fear, and disgust. Rigg discussed the advantages and disadvantages of these procedures. With free descriptions, responses may be scattered, but coherence in listeners' responses would be of more significance than if they merely checked terms in a list. With choice among descriptive terms, responses may be nicely bunched and easier to treat but will partly be a product of the given terms. For instance, love was not often mentioned in free descriptions but more frequently chosen when given as an alternative among the emotion terms. Expression of joy was convincingly indicated by the listeners, and some musical characteristics of the joy excerpts were rapid tempo, major mode, simple harmony, staccato notes, and forte dynamics.

Watson (1942) had 20 musical experts mark which out of 15 selected adjectives were appropriate for each of 30 musical examples. They also judged the examples, using a five-step scale, regarding pitch (low–high), loudness (soft–loud), tempo (slow–fast), sound (pretty–ugly), dynamics (no quick changes in loudness–very many changes), and rhythm (regular–irregular), thus enabling a study of the relationships between these factors and perceived expression. For instance, high pitch and fast tempo tended to express happiness and excitement; low pitch and slow tempo, sadness; high loudness, excitement; and small dynamic range, expression of dignity, sadness, and peacefulness.

*Ratings and multivariate analysis techniques*

In studies by Kleinen (1968), Wedin (1969, 1972*a*), Gabrielsson (1973, Experiments 4–5), and Nielzén and Cesarec (1981, 1982) subjects judged selected pieces of music using a large number of rating scales. The correlations between the scales were subjected to factor analysis in order to obtain a limited number of fundamental factors. These were given similar interpretations in all studies: tension/energy, gaiety–gloom, and solemnity–triviality (Wedin 1969, 1972*a*); intensity–softness, pleasantness–unpleasantness, and solemnity–triviality (Wedin 1972*b*, 1972*c*; in these studies using multidimensional scaling techniques); tension–relaxation, gaiety–gloom, and attraction–repulsion (Nielzén & Cesarec 1981); gay/vital–dull and excited–calm (Gabrielsson 1973); '*Heiterkeit-Ernst*' (cheerful–serious) and '*Robustheit-Zartheit*' (strong/powerful-soft/tender) (Kleinen 1968).

Musical experts rated the respective pieces of music with regard to structural properties. For example, Wedin (1972*c*) used five-point scales for rating intensity (*pp–ff*), pitch (bass–treble), rhythm (outstanding–vague), tempo (fast–slow), rhythmic articulation (firm–fluent, staccato–legato), harmony (dissonant/complex–consonant/simple), tonality (atonal–tonal), modality (major–minor), melody (melodious–unmelodious), type of music (serious–popular), and style (date of composition).

To avoid listeners' dependence on descriptive terms chosen by the investigator, Imberty (1979) had 80 non-musical subjects freely choose any adjectives which came to their mind while listening to excerpts from Debussy's *Préludes* for the piano. Out of a total of 1063 adjectives, 172 were retained for analysis by correspondence analysis, resulting in a joint representation of the musical excerpts and the adjectives on a number of dimensions. The first two dimensions were *Les schèmes de tension et de détente* (tension vs. relaxation) and *Les schèmes de résonances émotionelles* (positive vs. negative emotions). Imberty went on to construct indices for formal complexity and *dynamisme géneral* in the used musical stimuli by combining, in various ways, variables as note duration, *intervalle métrique* (duration between two accented notes), density of notes per time unit, loudness, accents, syncopations, and certain characteristics of melodic, harmonic, and rhythmic motives. Using these indices, he claimed that: (a) low complexity combined with average dynamism means formal integration and expression of positive emotions; (b) high formal complexity combined with low dynamism means formal disintegration and expression of melancholy and depression; and (c) high formal complexity combined with high dynamism means formal disintegration and expression of anxiety and aggressiveness. This is one of the few attempts to investigate how emotional expression is influenced by properties of musical form. However, the indices are complex, and require much analytical work and further validation.

With regard to the dimensional structure of emotional expression, the above studies show similar results converging on two main emotion dimensions: valence (pleasantness–unpleasantness, gaiety–gloom) and activity/arousal (tension–relaxation, excited–calm).

### Continuous recording of emotional expression

As type and intensity of emotional expression usually vary during the course of a piece of music, researchers may want to use a technique for continuous recording of perceived expression. This may also allow a more detailed study of how factors in the musical structure affect perceived expression. Nielsen (1983, 1987) pioneered the development of such a technique for continuous recording of perceived tension in music. While listening to the music, his subjects continuously pressed a pair of tongs in proportion to the perceived tension in the music—the more tension, the harder the press, and vice versa. The pressures were registered on a polygraph showing 'pressure curves' with waves of heightened tension alternating with periods of relaxation. Tension peaks were mainly conditioned by high intensity (fortissimo), but increased tension could also be related to ascending melody, increased note density, dissonance, harmonic complexity, rhythmic complexity, and formal properties such as repetition of various units, condensation of musical material, sequential development, and pauses.

Later studies of perceived tension using other response devices include Madsen and Fredrickson (1993), Fredrickson (1997), and Krumhansl (1996). Krumhansl found that tension peaks followed by a rapid decrease occurred at the end of large-scale sections and that judgments of new musical ideas co-occurred with low tension levels. Continuous recording of perceived emotional expression was also studied by Namba *et al.* (1991), Krumhansl (1997), Madsen (1997), and Schubert (1999) using various computerized techniques (for a more extensive review, see Schubert, this volume).

*Non-verbal responses*

Some methods for studying tension have been mainly non-verbal (e.g. Nielsen 1983), but use of non-verbal responses to indicate emotional expression is rare. Clynes (1977) introduced finger pressure on a so-called *sentograph*—a device for recording the pressure exerted by a finger upon a small disc—to study how subjects expressed different emotions. He found different pressure patterns (sentograms) with regard to duration and dynamics for different emotions (joy, grief, anger, hatred, reverence, love, sex; depicted in Clynes 1977, p. 29 onwards) and then tried to trace corresponding patterns in music (Clynes & Walker 1982). De Vries (1991) had 30 subjects use a sentograph while listening to ten pieces of music and found that sentograms were different for different pieces, and that there were similarities between the sentograms for pieces with a certain emotional expression (anger, grief, joy, love) and Clynes's sentograms for the corresponding emotions. Some evidence in the same direction was found in Gabrielsson (1995) and Gabrielsson and Lindström (1995). (Another example of non-verbal responses—drawings to describe intervals—appears in 10.1.2.)

*Specially composed music*

Thompson and Robitaille (1992) asked composers to compose short monophonic melodies to express joy, sorrow, excitement, dullness, anger, and peace. Their scores were transformed to sounding music using computer software and sampled grand piano sound. Listeners, moderately trained in music, rated the pieces on corresponding emotion scales. In general they perceived the intended expressions. Analysis of the scores showed that joyful melodies were strongly tonal and rhythmically varied. Sad melodies were slow with implied minor or chromatic harmony. Melodies for excitement were fast, and contained intervallic leaps and high pitches. Dull melodies were tonal in a stepwise motion. Angry melodies were rhythmically complex and with implied chromatic harmony or atonality. Melodies for peacefulness were tonal, slow, and often involved stepwise motion leading to melodic leaps.

### 10.1.2 Manipulation of structural factors without musical context

*Intervals*

A distinction must be made between harmonic (simultaneous) intervals (two-tone chords, bichords) and melodic (successive) intervals. Costa *et al.* (2000) used all 12 equal-tempered harmonic intervals (organ sound) contained in an octave, one set in a low register (geometric mean 185 Hz) and another in a high register (geometric mean 1510 Hz) and had listeners rate them on 30 bipolar scales, reflecting 'emotional evaluation' (e.g. happy–sad, pleasant–painful, friendly–hostile), 'activity' (e.g. tense–relaxed, dissonant–consonant, worried–calm), and 'potency' (e.g. strong–weak, vigorous–languid) in accordance with the three dominant dimensions of meaning according to Osgood *et al.* (1957). High register bichords were rated higher in 'activity' (e.g. more unstable, restless, tense) and in 'potency' (stronger) than low register bichords, and low register bichords were evaluated more negatively than high register bichords. Dissonant bichords were judged as more negative, more active, and stronger than consonant bichords; minor bichords as more dull and weaker than major bichords. Females showed greater polarization of scores and judged bichords as more active and tense than males. Difference in musical experience had no effect. Generally, intervals differed more in emotional evaluation and activity than in potency. Earlier, Maher (1980), using 14 different harmonic intervals in just intonation with triangular waveforms in two sets, one high pitched (geometric mean frequency 500 Hz) and one low pitched (250 Hz), obtained some similar results. High-pitched intervals were rated more happy and powerful than low-pitched intervals. Minor and major second, minor and major seventh, and minor ninth were the most displeasing.

Maher and Berlyne (1982) investigated the perception of 12 melodic intervals, sine-wave intervals in tempered intonation (minor second to octave, rising and falling, with the common 500 Hz geometric mean frequency). Larger intervals were judged as more 'powerful' than smaller ones; minor second was considered the most 'melancholic' interval; whereas octave, fourth, fifth, major sixth, and minor seventh were the most 'carefree'.

Smith and Adams (1999) had South African children listen to six ascending intervals performed on a flute and to represent them in drawings. The thematic content of the drawings was assessed by independent raters and also rated by university students using adjective scales. The primary distinction in the findings was between consonance and dissonance, the latter being associated with unpleasant events, the former with home, family, and stability. Major seventh and augmented fourth tended to be associated with danger and violence, perfect fifth with activity, and perfect fourth with being desolate and old. The octave was perceived as positive and strong, and major third as neutral with no particular meaning. The children's responses were influenced by their level of schooling, race, and living environment.

Earlier, Huber (1923) presented short pitch patterns to musical listeners who were asked to freely describe perceived expression. The reports were classified into: (a) mood impressions; (b) impressions of human character, for instance an elderly man; (c) emotionally coloured announcements, such as a call, question, or request; (d) impressions of movement; and (e) various inner images. Referring to Huber, Langer (1957, p. 231) remarked that 'The entire study shows effectively how many factors of possible expressive virtue are involved even in the simplest musical structure'.

*Mode*

Heinlein (1928) studied listeners' perception of major and minor chords in all keys, at different intensities and different pitch levels. Musically trained and untrained subjects described the perceived expression, choosing among adjectives such as bright, happy, joyful (supposed to reflect expression of major mode), melancholy, sad, and soothing (minor mode). None of the 30 subjects got all responses 'correct': there were many sad-type responses to major chords and happy-type responses to minor chords. Loud chords and chords at a high pitch level evoked more happy-type responses than soft chords and chords at a low pitch level, irrespective of mode. Crowder (1984) showed in a reanalysis of Heinlein's data that all but one of the 30 listeners in fact gave more happy-type responses to major chords than to minor chords, that is, in accordance with the conventional association. Crowder (1985) found the conventional major–happy and minor–sad associations in young adults who listened to sine-wave triads in three tonalities and two inversions of each chord. The major–happy and minor–sad associations were also found in many investigations using real music (Hevner 1935*a*; Kleinen 1968; Krumhansl 1997; Nielzén & Cesarec 1982; Peretz *et al.* 1998; Wedin 1972*c*).

*Rhythm and tempo*

Motte-Haber (1968) had ten rhythm patterns, differing in metre, sound event density, and homogeneity (e.g. uniform or dotted pattern), presented at three different metronomic tempos (ratios 1 : 2 : 4) to listeners, who rated them on a large number of bipolar scales (*Polaritätsprofile*). Metronomically rapid rhythms were rated happier (*fröhlicher*) than slow rhythms. Happiness ratings were strongly correlated with ratings of *subjective* tempo, which was related not only to metronomic tempo but also to sound event density and other rhythm characteristics in interaction with metronomic tempo. Similar relations appeared in Gabrielsson (1973, Experiments 1–3) using other rhythm patterns.

*Melodic properties*

Gabriel (1978) investigated the perceived expression of 16 short tone sequences, 'basic terms', which music theorist Deryck Cooke (1959) claimed recur with the same expression in Western music from the late Middle Ages up to the twentieth century. For instance, an ascending major triad (1–3–5) with possible insertions of the intervening notes (2 or 4), was said to express 'an outgoing, active, assertion of joy' (Cooke 1959, p. 115). Its counterpart in minor would be 'expressive of an outgoing feeling of pain—an assertion of sorrow, a complaint, a protest against misfortune' (Cooke 1959, p. 122). Gabriel generated the 16 basic terms using sinusoidals, constant tempo, and uniform rhythm. Students listened to these 'reduced' basic terms and had to judge whether Cooke's characteristics were adequate. The result was mainly negative. However, this experiment has in its turn been criticized regarding the choice of stimuli, lack of context, and use of musically untrained listeners (Cazden 1979; Gabriel 1979; Nettheim 1979; Sloboda 1985, pp. 60–4; for a discussion of Cooke's theory, see Cook & Dibben, this volume).

*Synthesized tone sequences*

Scherer and Oshinsky (1977) investigated the relative importance of several factors by systematic manipulations of synthesized eight-tone sequences (no musical notation was provided, which makes it difficult to judge their musical qualities). The manipulated variables were amplitude variation (small–large), pitch level (high–low), pitch contour (up–down), pitch variation (small–large), rhythm (even–uneven), tonality (major, minor, atonal), tempo (slow–fast), envelope (round, sharp), and filtration cut-off level (intermediate–high). Psychology students rated the stimuli on three bipolar scales: pleasantness–unpleasantness, activity–passivity, and potency–weakness, and also indicated whether each sequence expressed any or more of the following emotions: happiness, sadness, anger, fear, boredom, surprise, and disgust—the last five rarely or never included in earlier studies of emotional expression in music. Multiple regression analysis was used to estimate the predictive strength of each acoustic parameter on each emotion dimension. Most of the results can be found in Table 10.2 (see below). As seen there, any acoustical variable was associated with many emotions, listed in decreasing order of associative strength, in some cases even with seemingly 'opposite' emotions (e.g. low pitch associated with boredom, pleasantness, and sadness).

### 10.1.3 Manipulation of structural factors in musical context

*Manipulation of several factors*

The earliest and still best-known investigations with systematic manipulations of various factors in real music are those by Hevner (1935a, 1935b, 1936, 1937). She arranged a large number of emotion terms in eight clusters in a circular configuration, an 'adjective circle' (Fig. 10.1). The terms within each cluster were supposed to be close in meaning, and adjacent clusters should deviate slightly by cumulative steps until reaching a contrast in the opposite position. Inspection of Fig. 10.1 suggests an implicit dimensionality similar to that described in Section 10.1.1; in other words, valence (sadness–happiness, cluster II–cluster VI) and activity/arousal (exciting/vigorous–serene/dreamy, clusters VII/VIII–clusters IV/III). The circular configuration is reminiscent of the circumplex model by Russell (1980; see also Sloboda & Juslin, this volume) and may be one of the earliest indications of this conception, earlier than that proposed by Schlosberg in 1941 (cf. Remington *et al.* 2000). Listeners were instructed to mark as many of the terms as they found appropriate for each piece. Hevner selected short pieces of tonal music, but besides the original version she also constructed a variant that differed from the original in: (a) mode, a piece in major mode was also played in minor mode; notated example in Hevner (1935a); (b) melodic direction (ascending vs. descending), harmony (simple consonant harmonies vs. complex dissonant harmonies), and rhythm (firm vs. flowing, that is, a firm beat with a chord on every beat vs. a flowing motion in which the chords were broken up); notated examples in Hevner (1936); and (c) tempo (fast vs. slow) and pitch level (one octave or more apart); see Hevner (1937).

Any difference in listeners' choice of descriptive terms between the respective two versions of a piece could then be ascribed to the difference in the manipulated variable. All versions were performed by an experienced pianist, and listeners were hundreds of students, most of them without special musical training. The joint conclusions of several experiments were that variables with the largest effects on listeners' judgments were tempo and mode, followed by pitch level, harmony, and rhythm, whereas melodic direction had little if any effect (Hevner 1937). This order can be seen in Table 10.1, which was Hevner's summary of results from six experiments. It shows the relative

VI

bright
cheerful
gay
happy
joyous
merry

VII

agitated
dramatic
exciting
exhilarated
impetuous
passionate
restless
sensational
soaring
triumphant

V

delicate
fanciful
graceful
humorous
light
playful
quaint
sprightly
whimsical

VIII

emphatic
exalting
majestic
martial
ponderous
robust
vigorous

IV

calm
leisurely
lyrical
quiet
satisfying
serene
soothing
tranquil

I

awe-inspiring
dignified
lofty
sacred
serious
sober
solemn
spiritual

III

dreamy
longing
plaintive
pleading
sentimental
tender
yearning
yielding

II

dark
depressing
doleful
frustrated
gloomy
heavy
melancholy
mournful
pathetic
sad
tragic

**Figure 10.1** Hevner's adjective circle. Adjectives within each cluster appear in alphabetical order. Adjectives used by Hevner (1936, 1937) to represent the respective clusters are underlined (adapted from Farnsworth 1954, p. 98).

weights of each musical factor for each emotion cluster; for instance, minor mode, low pitch, and slow tempo were most important, in that order, for the sad–heavy cluster, whereas major mode, fast tempo, and simple harmony were most important for the happy–bright cluster.

Hevner (1935b, 1937) noted the difficulties of manipulating real pieces of music and still having the manipulated version sound musically acceptable (cf. Behne 1972; Peretz *et al.* 1998, p. 118, footnote). She emphasized the necessity of using pieces with similar emotional expression throughout the whole piece and remarked that the results should only be interpreted in a relative and contextual sense. For instance, although happiness was usually associated with major mode, a piece in minor mode may sound happy due to other factors, such as tempo and rhythm. She warned against drawing too far-going conclusions since results may be dependent on the selected pieces and, above all, since emotional expression usually results from several musical factors in complex interplay. These arguments should be carefully considered by any researcher on emotional expression in music.

Rigg (1939) composed five four-bar phrases supposed to represent two emotion categories: pleasant/happy or sad/serious. They were systematically manipulated regarding tempo, mode, articulation (legato, staccato), pitch level, loudness, rhythm (iambic, trochaic), and certain intervals in an impressively large number of variations. Listeners described perceived expression by choosing first among the above-mentioned alternatives and then among subcategories within each of them (e.g. hopeful longing, sorrowful longing). In a subsequent experiment (Rigg 1940a) the same phrases were transposed up or down an octave, to the dominant (a fifth upwards or a fourth downwards), a second down, and a minor second up. Shifts an octave upward made the phrase happier or less sorrowful, and vice versa. There were less effects for the dominant transposition and practically no effect of the smallest transpositions. Finally, Rigg (1940b) had the same five phrases played by a pianist at six different tempos, from 60 to 160 bpm (beat = quarter note), and found that the higher the tempo, the more pleasant/happy and the less serious/sad judgments were given. However, one of the phrases, supposed to express lamentation, still sounded sad even at the highest tempo, and for another one, supposed to express sorrowful longing, there was about the same number of happy and sad responses at the highest tempo. Both these phrases were in minor mode and had descending minor or major seconds in the upper voice. Rigg (1964) reviewed the results obtained by Gundlach (1935), Hevner (1935a, 1936, 1937), Rigg (1937, 1939, 1940a, 1940b), and Watson (1942).

Juslin (1997, Experiment 2) used synthesized versions of 'Nobody knows the trouble I've seen' manipulating tempo (slow, medium, fast), sound level (low, medium, high),

Table 10.1  Hevner's summary of results from six experiments (adapted from Hevner 1937, p. 626)

| Musical factor | Dignified/ solemn | Sad/ heavy | Dreamy/ sentimental | Serene/ gentle | Graceful/ sparkling | Happy/ bright | Exciting/ elated | Vigorous/ majestic |
|---|---|---|---|---|---|---|---|---|
| Mode | Minor 4 | Minor 20 | Minor 12 | Major 3 | Major 21 | Major 24 | – | – |
| Tempo | Slow 14 | Slow 12 | Slow 16 | Slow 20 | Fast 6 | Fast 20 | Fast 21 | Fast 6 |
| Pitch | Low 10 | Low 19 | High 6 | High 8 | High 16 | High 6 | Low 9 | Low 13 |
| Rhythm | Firm 18 | Firm 3 | Flowing 9 | Flowing 2 | Flowing 8 | Flowing 10 | Firm 2 | Firm 10 |
| Harmony | Simple 3 | Complex 7 | Simple 4 | Simple 10 | Simple 12 | Simple 16 | Complex 14 | Complex 8 |
| Melody | Ascend 4 | – | – | Ascend 3 | Descend 3 | – | Descend 7 | Descend 8 |

The numbers indicate the relative weight of each musical factor (left column) for each emotion cluster.

frequency spectrum (soft, bright, sharp), articulation (legato, staccato), and tone attack (slow, fast). Students rated these versions on six adjective scales: happy, sad, angry, fearful, tender, and expressive. Multiple regression analyses showed that the variance accounted for ($R^2$) by the manipulated factors was typically 0.78–0.88, except for fearful (0.55) and expressive (0.46). Sharp spectrum (higher partials amplified) and high sound level were the most important predictors for angry; fast tempo for happy; slow tempo for sad; slow tempo, soft spectrum (higher partials attenuated), and legato articulation for tender; low sound level and staccato articulation for fearful; and legato articulation for expressive.

Lindström (1997) constructed 72 versions of 'Frère Jacques' by systematic manipulation of tonal progression (choice of notes affecting latent harmony), rhythm (even notes, 1 : 1, uneven 3 : 1 and 1 : 3 ratios, respectively), melodic contour (original and complex), and melodic direction (original and reversed). Listeners' judgments of emotional expression were most affected by changes of harmonic functions, followed by changes of rhythm and melodic contour. Inspection of interactions and most extreme ratings showed intricate interplay between several structural factors (Lindström 2000).

Peretz *et al.* (1998, Experiment 2) manipulated tempo and mode in synthesized versions of 32 excerpts of classical music and found that these factors affected both normal listeners' and a brain-injured listener's perception of happiness and sadness in similar ways. Moreover, exposition shorter than a second was enough for reliable recognition of these expressions. Kamenetsky *et al.* (1997) compared listeners' ratings of emotional expression in synthesized versions of two baroque and two romantic keyboard pieces. The 'original' version with variations in both tempo and dynamics was rated the most expressive. Removing tempo variations but keeping variations in dynamics reduced expressiveness only marginally, whereas removing variation in dynamics but keeping tempo variations significantly reduced perceived expressiveness.

Balkwill and Thompson (1999) asked two professional Hindustani musicians to perform a short *alap* (improvised opening section) from any raga they wanted to choose to evoke each of four emotions: joy, sadness, anger, and peace. Listening to these performances, Canadian students indicated which of the four emotions was most dominant in each performance and rated the degree to which the respective emotion was conveyed. They also rated the performances regarding tempo, melodic and rhythmic complexity, and pitch range. The recognition of intended emotions was successful except for peace, and data show some confusion between joy and anger and between sadness and peace. Judgments by four experts on Hindustani music showed a similar pattern. On the whole, then, Western listeners were sensitive to intended emotions in Hindustani music. Joy was associated with faster tempo and less melodic and rhythmic complexity; sadness with slower tempo and melodic and rhythmic complexity; anger with timbre of stringed instruments; and peace with slow tempo, flute timbre, and less melodic and rhythmic complexity.

*Tempo*

Behne (1972) presented ten pieces of recorded music at three different tempos by means of a so-called Springer machine to music students who rated them using bipolar scales. With decreased tempo of the pieces, listeners rated them as more serious (*ernst*) and complaining (*klagend*). In another experiment, six eight-bar versions of a theme were composed to represent three different basic tempos (slow, midway, rapid) and two levels of harmonic complexity (simple, complex). Each version was then performed at five different tempos by a woodwind trio and rated by 30 subjects. The (complex) results were discussed in relation to conceived tempo, performed tempo, and to melodic and harmonic information density. Hevner's observation that it is difficult to manipulate different factors independently of others in real music was confirmed. The two levels of harmonic complexity were not equivalent across the different tempos: versions with slow original tempo were in fact more harmonically complex than the versions with rapid original tempo at the (assumed) same complexity level.

## Mode

Kastner and Crowder (1990) presented 12 short melodies, each of them in major or minor mode, to 38 children from preschool and elementary school. For each presentation they were asked to choose among four pictures of faces: happy, contented, sad, and angry. All children, even the youngest (3 years), showed a reliable positive-major and negative-minor association, not perfect but significantly different from what would happen on chance basis. In similar studies by Gerardi and Gerken (1995) and Gregory *et al.* (1996), the happy–major and sad–minor association was found in children aged 7–8 years and in young adults, but not in children aged 3–5 years. Thus, in all three studies the conventional happy–major and sad–minor association was present in older children, whereas the results for younger children are inconclusive.

Hill *et al.* (1996) studied which of two alternatives—salvation or condemnation—adults associated with a setting either in Ionian mode or in Phrygian mode of a well-known melody from early seventeenth century, variously known as *Herzlich tut mich verlangen* (promise of salvation, reward) or *Ach Herr, mich armen Sünder* (fear of condemnation, punishment), both in settings by J. S. Bach. Adults as well as children judged the Ionian mode more suitable for the 'salvation/reward' alternative and the Phrygian mode more suitable for the 'condemnation/punishment' alternative. The fact that Ionian mode is identical to major mode may have contributed to its association with the 'salvation/reward' alternative.

## Musical form

Konečni and his co-workers (Gotlieb & Konečni 1985; Karno & Konečni 1992; Konečni 1984; Konečni & Karno 1994) demonstrated that changing the order of movements in Beethoven sonatas and string quartets, randomizing the order of variations in Bach's *Goldberg Variations*, or rearranging the order of different parts in sonata form as in the first movement of Mozart's Sympony in G Minor K. 550 had little or no effect on university students' ratings on various hedonic (e.g. beautiful, pleasing) or emotion-related (e.g. exciting, emotional) scales.

Tillman and Bigand (1996) chunked three pieces by Bach, Mozart, and Schoenberg into (musically adequate) segments of about 6 seconds and then played these either in original or in backward order to university students, who rated them on 27 (mostly) emotion-related scales. There were significant differences among the *pieces* in all scales, but only two significant differences between the two *versions* (original, backward) of each piece. They concluded that for these subjects musical expressiveness was mainly affected by local structures within the chunks, not by global musical structure. This is in good agreement with the main theme in *Music in the moment* by Levinson (1997).

## 10.2 Effects of separate musical factors

Most of the results from the studies reviewed above are summarized in Table 10.2. The first column contains different structural factors in alphabetical order, the second different levels within each factor, and the third column the corresponding emotional expression according to different studies. Authors' names are abbreviated to the initial two letters of the (first) author and publication year to the two last digits (e.g. He36 = Hevner 1936). Studies are grouped into: (A) early studies using choice among descriptive terms; (B) studies based on multivariate analyses; and (C) later experimental studies; thus offering alternative bases for interpretation of the results. As a rule, the emotions are listed in decreasing order of association with the corresponding factor. Following Rigg (1964), results of the early studies (A) are described in terms of Hevner's clusters designated by Roman numbers and the adjective that Hevner used as a label for each cluster (Hevner 1936, p. 265), with the use of shaded areas in the adjective circle.

### 10.2.1. Tempo

Among factors affecting emotional expression in music, tempo is usually considered the most important (cf. Gundlach 1935; Hevner 1937; Juslin 1997; Rigg 1964; Scherer & Oshinsky 1977). Composers as a rule indicate intended tempo, either exactly—for instance, MM (Mälzel metronome) or bpm (beats per minute) = 100—or with designations such as presto, allegro, moderato, andante, and adagio.

The studies under tempo in Table 10.2 indicate that fast tempo may be associated with various expressions of activity/excitement, happiness/joy/pleasantness, potency, surprise, anger, and fear. Slow tempo may be associated with various expressions of

Table 10.2 Summary of results from reviewed studies. Left two columns indicate structural factor and levels within each factor, middle column the associated emotional expression, right column the corresponding clusters in Hevner's adjective circle. Within each factor studies are grouped into (A) early studies using choice among descriptive terms, (B) studies based on multivariate analyses, and (C) later experimental studies. Authors' names are abbreviated to the initial two letters of the (first) author, publication year to the two last digits (e.g., He36 = Hevner, 1936). See text for further explanation.

| Factor | Levels | Emotional expression | Adjective circle (Hevner) |
|---|---|---|---|
| Amplitude envelope | Round | (C) Disgust, sadness, fear, boredom, potency (Sc77), tenderness, fear, sadness (Ju97) | |
| | Sharp | (C) Pleasantness, happiness, surprise, activity (Sc77), anger (Ju97) | |
| Articulation | Staccato | (A) VI: gaiety; VII: agitation (Ri39)<br>(B) Intensity/energy/activity (We72c), gaiety (Ni82)<br>(C) Fear, anger (Ju97) | |

| Factor | Levels | Emotional expression | Adjective circle (Hevner) |
|---|---|---|---|
| | Legato | (A) I: solemn; II: melancholy, lamentation; III: longing (Ri39)<br>(B) Softness (We72c)<br>(C) Tenderness, sadness (Ju97) | VI / V / IV / III / II / I / VIII / VII |
| Harmony | Simple/consonant | (A) VI: happy (He36, Wa42), joy (Ri39; V: graceful; IV: serene; III: dreamy (He36); I: dignified (He36, Wa42), serious (Wa42), solemn (Ri39); VIII: majestic (Wa42)<br>(B) Gaiety, pleasantness (We72c), attraction (Ni82)<br>(C) Relaxation, tenderness (Li97) | VI / V / IV / III / II / I / VIII / VII |
| | Complex/dissonant | (A) VII: exciting (He36, Wa42), agitation (Ri39); VIII: vigorous (He36); II: sad (He36, Wa42)<br>(B) Gloom, unpleasantness (We72c), tension (Ni82, Kr96)<br>(C) Tension (Ni83, Kr96, Li97), fear (Kr97), anger (Li97) | VI / V / IV / III / II / I / VIII / VII |
| Intervals | Harmonic:<br>Consonant | (C) Pleasant, 'non-active' (Co00) | |
| | Dissonant | (C) Displeasing (Ma80), unpleasant, 'active', strong (Co00) | |
| | High-pitched | (C) Happy, powerful (Ma80), 'activity', potency (Co00) | |
| | Low-pitched | (C) Sad, less powerful (Ma80, Co00) | |
| | Melodic:<br>Large | (C) Powerful (Ma82) | |
| | Minor 2nd | (C) Melancholy (Ma82) | |
| | Perfect 4th, perfect 5th, major 6th, minor 7th, octave | (C) Carefree (Ma82) | |
| | Perfect 5th | (C) Activity (Sm99) | |
| | Octave | (C) Positive/strong (Sm99) | |
| Loudness | Loud | (A) VII: excitement (Wa42), triumphant (Gu35); VI: joy (Ri39)<br>(B) Gaiety (Ni82), intensity (We72c), strength/power (Kl68), solemnity (We72c), tension (Ni83, Kr96)<br>(C) Anger (Ju97) | VI / V / IV / III / II / I / VIII / VII |
| | Soft | (A) II: melancholy (Gu35); V: delicate (Gu35); IV: peaceful (Wa42)<br>(B) Softness (Kl68, We72c), tenderness (Kl68)<br>(C) Fear, tenderness, sadness (Ju97) | VI / V / IV / III / II / I / VIII / VII |
| Loudness variation | Large | (C) Fear (Sc77) | |
| | Small | (C) Happiness, pleasantness, activity (Sc77) | |
| | Rapid changes | (A) V: playful, amusing; III: pleading (Wa42)<br>(C) Fear (Kr97) | VI / V / IV / III / II / I / VIII / VII |

| Factor | Levels | Emotional expression | Adjective circle (Hevner) |
|---|---|---|---|
| | Few/no changes | (A) II: sad; IV: peaceful; I: dignified, serious; VI: happy (Wa42) | |
| Melodic (pitch) range | Wide | (A) V: whimsical; VI: glad; VII: uneasy (Gu35) (C) Fear (Kr97), joy (Ba99) | |
| | Narrow | (A) I: dignified; II: melancholy; III: sentimental; IV: tranquil; V: delicate; VII: trimphant (Gu35) (C) Sadness (Ba99) | |
| Melodic direction | Ascending | (A) I: dignified; IV: serene (He36) (C) Tension (Ni83, Kr96), happiness (Ge95) | |
| | Descending | (A) VII: exciting; V: graceful; VIII: vigorous (He36) (C) Sadness (Ge95) | |
| Pitch contour | Up | (C) Fear, surprise, anger, potency (Sc77) | |
| | Down | (C) Sadness, boredom, pleasantness (Sc77) | |
| Melodic motion | Stepwise motion | (C) Dull melodies (Th92) | |
| | Intervallic leaps | (C) Excitement (Th92) | |
| | Stepwise + leaps | (C) Peacefulness (Th92) | |
| Mode | Major | (A) VI: happy (He36), joy (Ri39); V: graceful (He36); IV: serene (He36); I: solemn (Ri39) (B) Happiness (Kl68, We72c), attraction (Ni82) (C) Happiness (Sc77, Cr85, Kr97, Pe98) | |
| | Minor | (A) II: sad (He36); lamentation (Ri39); III: dreamy; I: dignified (He36); VII: agitation (Ri39) (B) Sadness (Kl68, We72c), tension (Ni82) (C) Sadness (Cr85, Kr97, Pe98), disgust, anger (Sc77) | |
| Pitch level | High | (A) V: graceful; IV: serene; VI: happy (He37), joy (Ri40a); III: dreamy (He37), sentimental (Gu35), pleading (Wa42); VII: triumph (Ri39), exciting (Wa42) (B) Gaiety (Kl68, We72c) (C) Surprise, potency, anger, fear, activity (Sc77) | |
| | Low | (A) II: sad (He37, Wa42), melancholy (Gu35), lamentation (Ri40a); VIII: vigorous (He37); I: dignified (He37), serious (Wa42), solemn (Ri40a); VII: exciting (He37), agitation (Ri40a); IV: tranquil (Gu35) (B) Serious (Kl68), sadness, solemnity (We72c) (C) Boredom, pleasantness, sadness (Sc77) | |

| Factor | Levels | Emotional expression | Adjective circle (Hevner) |
|---|---|---|---|
| Pitch variation | Large | (C) Happiness, pleasantness, activity, surprise (Sc77) | |
| | Small | (C) Disgust, anger, fear, boredom (Sc77) | |
| Rhythm | Regular/smooth | (A) VI: happiness (Wa42), glad (Gu35); I: serious, dignified, IV: peaceful (Wa42); VIII: majestic (Wa42); V: flippant (Gu35) | VII VI V / VIII IV / I II III |
| | Irregular/rough | (A) V: amusing (Wa42); VII: uneasy (Gu35) | VII VI V / VIII IV / I II III |
| | Complex | (C) Angry melodies (Th92) | VII VI V / VIII IV / I II III |
| | Varied | (C) Joyful melodies (Th92) | |
| | Firm | (A) I: dignified; VII: vigorous; II: sad; VII: exciting (He36) | |
| | | (C) Sad (We72c) | |
| | Flowing/fluent | (A) VI: happy; III: dreamy; V: graceful; IV: serene (He36) | VII VI V / VIII IV / I II III |
| | | (C) Gaiety (We72c) | |
| Tempo | Fast | (A) VII: exciting (He37, Wa42), uneasy (Gu35) agitation, triumph (Ri40b); VI: happy (He37, Wa42), glad (Gu35), gaiety, joy (Ri40b); V: graceful (He37), mischievous (Wa42), whimsical, flippant (Gu35); VIII: vigorous (He37) (B) Happiness, pleasantness (Kl68, Mo68, We72c, Ga73, Ni82) (C) Activity, surprise, happiness, pleasantness, potency, fear, anger (Sc77), happiness, anger (Ju97), happiness (Th92, Kr97, Pe98), joy (Ba99), excitement (Th92) | VII VI V / VIII IV / I II III |
| | Slow | (A) IV: serene (He37), tranquil (Gu35); III: dreamy (He37), longing (Ri40b), sentimental (Gu35); I: dignified (He37), serious (Wa42), dignified (Gu35), solemn (Ri40b); II: sad (He37, Wa42), lamentation (Ri40b); VIII: excited (Gu35) (B) Sadness (Kl68, Be72, We72c, Ni82), solemnity (We72c) (C) Sadness, boredom, disgust (Sc77), sadness, tenderness (Ju97), sadness (Th92, Kr97, Pe98, Ba99), peace (Ba99) | VII VI V / VIII IV / I II III |
| Timbre | Few harmonics | (C) Pleasantness, boredom, happiness, sadness (Sc77) | |
| | Many harmonics | (C) Potency, anger, disgust, fear, activity, surprise (Sc77) | |
| | Soft | (C) Tenderness, sadness (Ju97) | |
| | Sharp | (C) Anger (Ju97) | |
| Tonality | Tonal | (C) In joyful, dull, peaceful melodies (Th92) | |
| | Atonal | (C) In angry melodies (Th92) | |
| | Chromatic | (C) In sad and angry melodies (Th92) | |

| Factor | Levels | Emotional expression | Adjective circle (Hevner) |
|---|---|---|---|
| Musical form | Low complexity + average dynamism | (C) Relaxation/less tension (Ni83), joy, peace (Ba99) (B) Positive emotions (Im79) | |
| | High complexity (melodic/harmonic/ rhythmic) | (C) Tension (Ni83, Kr96), sadness (Ba99) | |
| | + low dynamism | (B) Melancholy and depression (Im79), | |
| | + high dynamism | (B) Anxiety and aggressiveness (Im79) | |
| | Repetition, condensation, sequential development, pauses etc. | (C) Increased tension (Ni83) | |
| | End of large-scale sections | (C) Tension peaks followed by rapid decrease (Kr96) | |
| | New musical ideas | (C) Low tension (Kr96) | |
| | Disruption of global form | (C) Little effect (Ko84, Go85, Ka92, Ko94, Ti96) | |

calmness/serenity, dignity/solemnity, sadness, tenderness, boredom, and disgust. Which of the different expressions is perceived in each case is highly dependent on the actual context, that is, presence and level of other factors. For instance, although faster tempo tends to increase perceived happiness, other factors may overrule this tendency, such as minor mode and descending seconds (e.g. Rigg 1940*b*; see also Section 10.1.3).

The term tempo may not always have the same meaning, as discussed in Behne (1972), Gabrielsson (1986, 1988, 1999), and Motte-Haber (1968). Usually, tempo refers to perceived pulse rate. However, sometimes the pulse may be felt at, say, half or double pace. Perceived speed may also be affected by note density (e.g. the number of notes per second) as well as density of melodic or harmonic changes. Interplay between tempo (pulse rate) and note density may occur in an infinite number of combinations, for instance, rapid tone sequences (or high note density) but slow pulse (for examples, see Gabrielsson 1986).

### 10.2.2 Mode

Major mode may be associated with happiness/joy and minor mode with sadness, at least from 7–8 years of age. Major mode may also be associated with expressions such as graceful, serene, and solemn, and minor mode with expressions such as dreamy, digni-fied, tension, disgust, and anger.

What expression is perceived depends, again, on the context. For instance, loud chords and high-pitched chords may suggest more happiness than soft chords and low-pitched chords, irrespective of mode. Major mode is not a necessary condition for expression of happiness. An example may be the beginning of the last movement,

'Badinerie', in J. S. Bach's *Second Suite for Orchestra* (Fig 10.2). The theme in B minor with its forward-driving rhythmic pattern is usually played in rapid tempo and can hardly be associated with sadness—the title itself suggests happiness (French: *badinerie*, joke). However, if the same theme were transferred to B major, it may sound even happier (cf. Hevner 1935*b*, p. 202).

### 10.2.3 Loudness

Loud music may be associated with various expressions of intensity/power, tension, anger, and joy, and soft music with softness, tenderness, sadness, solemnity, and fear. Large variations of loudness (amplitude) may suggest fear, small variations happiness or activity. Rapid changes in loudness may be associated with expressions such as playful or pleading, and few or no changes with sadness, peace, and dignity (cf. Juslin, this volume).

### 10.2.4 Pitch

High pitch may be associated with expressions such as happy, graceful, serene, dreamy, and exciting, and, further, with surprise, potency, anger, fear, and activity. Low pitch may suggest sadness, dignity/solemnity, vigour, and excitement, as well as boredom and pleasantness (such a 'contradiction' may depend on the context of other factors). Large pitch variation may be associated with happiness, pleasantness, activity, or surprise; small pitch variation with disgust, anger, fear, or boredom.

### 10.2.5 Intervals

For harmonic intervals, results concerning consonance and dissonance are similar to the corresponding results under harmony (see Section 10.2.7) and concerning high and low pitch level to the corresponding results under pitch (see Section 10.2.4). For melodic intervals, results so far seem rather tentative, for instance, large intervals may be perceived as more powerful than small ones, the minor second as the most sad interval, and the octave as positive and strong.

### 10.2.6 Melody

*Melodic range*

Wide melodic range may be associated with joy, whimsicality, and uneasiness, and a narrow range with expressions such as sad, dignified, sentimental, tranquil, delicate, and triumphant.

**Figure 10.2** Beginning of 'Badinerie', in J. S. Bach's *Second Suite for Orchestra*.

*Melodic direction (pitch contour)*

Ascending melody may be associated with dignity, serenity, tension, and happiness (but not for children, see Gerardi & Gerken 1995), as well as with fear, surprise, anger, and potency. Descending melody may be associated with expressions such as exciting, graceful, vigorous, and sadness (especially when combined with the minor mode; Gerardi & Gerken 1995) and, further, with boredom and pleasantness. According to Gundlach (1935), Hevner (1937), and Rigg (1939, 1964) melodic direction had no or little importance for emotional expression.

*Melodic motion*

There is little research on melodic motion except melodic direction. Stepwise motion may suggest dullness; intervallic leaps, excitement; and stepwise motion leading to melodic leaps, peacefulness. Lindström (1997) found that an interaction between melodic contour and rhythm affected judgments of happiness and sadness.

### 10.2.7 Harmony

Simple, consonant harmony may be associated with expressions such as happy/gay, relaxed, graceful, serene, dreamy, dignified, and majestic; complex and dissonant harmony with excitement, tension, vigour, anger, sadness, and unpleasantness.

### 10.2.8 Tonality

Composers used chromatic harmony in sad and angry melodies. Joyful, dull, and peaceful melodies were tonal, and angry melodies could be atonal (Thompson & Robitaille 1992).

### 10.2.9 Rhythm

Regular/smooth rhythm may be perceived as expressing happiness, dignity, majesty, and peace; irregular/rough rhythm, amusement, uneasiness, and anger; and varied rhythm, joy. Firm rhythm may be associated with expressions of sadness, dignity, and vigour, and flowing/fluent rhythm with expressions such as happy/gay, graceful, dreamy, and serene. Terminology varies among authors, which makes comparisons difficult.

### 10.2.10 Timbre

Tones with many harmonics may suggest potency, anger, disgust, fear, activity, or surprise, and tones with amplified higher harmonics may suggest anger. Tones with few, low harmonics may be associated with pleasantness, boredom, happiness, or sadness; tones with suppressed higher harmonics, tenderness and sadness. Behrens and Green (1993) found sadness best expressed by the singing voice or violin, anger by the timpani, and fear by the violin. With Hindustani music judged by Western listeners, Balkwill and Thompson (1999) found stringed instruments associated with the expression of anger, and the flute with the expression of peace.

### 10.2.11 Articulation

Staccato may be associated with gaiety, energy, activity, fear, and anger, and legato with sadness, tenderness, solemnity, and softness. Articulation is usually more discussed in connection with performance (Juslin, this volume).

### 10.2.12 Amplitude envelope

This refers to the type of attack and decay of tones. Sharp envelope (rapid attack and decay) may be associated with anger, happiness, surprise, and activity; round envelope with tenderness, sadness, fear, disgust, boredom, and potency. The shaping of amplitude envelope is usually more discussed in connection with performance (Juslin, this volume).

### 10.2.13 Musical form

The influence of various aspects of musical form has been little studied. The examples in Table 10.2 concerning the effects of high and low complexity, repetition, condensation of material, and so forth were discussed in Sections 10.1.1 (Imberty 1979; Krumhansl 1996; Nielsen 1983) and 10.1.3 (Balkwill & Thompson 1999). On the other hand, some studies (Konečni 1984; Tillman & Bigand 1996) indicate that various manipulations of musical form may not matter very much (see Section 10.1.3).

### 10.2.14 Interaction between factors

Perceived emotional expression in music is rarely or never exclusively determined by a single factor but is always a function of many factors (see, for example, Hevner 1935*b*, 1937; Rigg 1964). The influence of a certain factor may depend on how it is combined with other factors, that is, on the interaction between factors. A few examples mentioned earlier were mode × loudness and mode × pitch interactions (Section 10.1.2), and tempo × mode interactions (Sections 10.2.1 and 10.2.2). Possibilities for different types of interactions seem almost endless. Apparent contradictions in results, such that two 'opposite' emotions may be associated with the same structural factor may be resolved by examining interactions with other factors. However, interactions are primarily discussed *post hoc*, and there is practically no planned research regarding interaction between factors (Lindström 2000).

## 10.3 Some implications for future research

Despite the considerable amount of results summarized above there are still many gaps, uncertainties, and ambiguities regarding the influence of various structural factors on emotional expression. There is no systematic research on how the timbre of different musical instruments affects emotional expression—certainly something that composers pay much attention to. Research on harmony is very simplistic, usually focusing on consonance/dissonance, while there is practically nothing on chords, harmonic progressions, or implied harmony. There is surprisingly little and fairly tentative research on intervals. The study of melody is limited to the effects of range and direction, while melodic motion, that is, the specific sequences of pitches/intervals during the course of a melody, is almost totally neglected, as is its rhythmic structure. Likewise, the influence of specific rhythm patterns—beyond their degree of simplicity or complexity—is unresearched. Questions concerning how musical form influences emotional expression are touched upon only in a few studies.

However, the most obvious gap concerns potential interactions between different factors. It has been emphasized, again and again (e.g. Hevner 1935b, 1937; Rigg 1964), that no factor works in isolation, its effects are dependent on what other factors and levels are present. Music abounds with interactions. To take but one example not mentioned earlier: the expressive qualities of different intervals can hardly be ascertained in a general manner. How a melodic interval is perceived is obviously dependent on in what tempo, in what direction (up, down), in what rhythm pattern, and at what loudness and pitch level the interval appears, not to mention its position within the musical context in question. Analogous examples may be easily found for other factors as well.

Moreover, most factors are studied only regarding two 'extreme' levels—fast or slow tempo, high or low pitch, loud or soft sound, ascending or descending melody, legato or staccato articulation. Intermediate levels are usually neglected, probably on the implicit assumption that their effects may be inferred from results at the extreme levels. Nor are the effects of transitions from one level to another investigated, such as crescendo or diminuendo, accelerando or ritardando, glissando, transition from minor to major mode, from diatonicism to chromaticism, or from thin to thick texture—not to mention combinations of them, for instance, imagine a glissando towards high pitch combined with diminuendo and ritardando.

The last-mentioned examples hint at another neglected aspect: how expressive qualities vary and change in dynamic ways. Most research has focused on one expression at a time: happiness, sadness, anger, etc., and it is recommended that the investigator choose musical excerpts which are homogeneous with regard to emotional expression (e.g. Hevner 1935b). However, many of music's most expressive qualities relate to structural *changes* across time which make possible expression of, say, shifting emotions, blending emotions, competing or conflicting emotions.

Going beyond emotions, Langer suggested that, because there are certain formal properties that are similar in music and in human feeling, we may perceive expressions such as 'growth and attenuation, flowing and stowing, conflict and resolution, speed, arrest, terrific excitement, calm, or subtle activation and dreamy lapses' (Langer 1953, p. 27), or 'patterns of motion and rest, of tension and release, of agreement and disagreement, preparation, fulfilment, excitation, sudden change, etc.' (Langer 1957, p. 228). These examples represent complex combinations of perceptual, cognitive, and emotional aspects that elude conventional psychological terminology. They remind us of what Stern (1985) called 'vitality affects', which seem intuitively appealing to the study of musical expression (see also Sloboda & Juslin, this volume). Phenomena like these are little investigated in research; the closest examples are studies on tension and release by means of continuous recording (see 10.1.1). Continuous recording of listeners' judgments is a necessary prerequisite to study these phenomena (for a review, see Schubert, this volume).

Research is also hampered by a lack of appropriate definitions and terminology, both regarding structural factors (e.g. on tempo and rhythm; see 10.2.1 and 10.2.9), and regarding categories or dimensions of emotions (see Sloboda & Juslin, this volume).

Should we try to subsume the hundreds of descriptive words for emotional expression under a few dimensions, such as evaluation, activity, and potency (Osgood *et al.* 1957), or valence and arousal in Russell's (1980) circumplex model? (See Remington *et al.* 2000, for a recent review of the circumplex model.) It seems obvious that this reduction goes too far and cannot capture all possible emotional nuances that we may perceive in music. On the other hand, we may have penetrating phenomenological descriptions abounding with suggestive descriptive terms to the limit of overwhelming the reader. In between, there may be something like Hevner's adjective clusters, although criticized and revised (e.g. Farnsworth 1954), which are still useful and referred to. However, emotions such as anger, fear, surprise, boredom, and disgust were missing and were included only in much later studies (e.g. Scherer & Oshinsky 1977).

In order to ensure both adequate control and ecological validity, future research should aim for an efficient interplay between studies using real music and studies using systematic manipulation of structural factors in as music-like contexts as possible. Many gaps, confusions, and contradictions in the present results may be resolved, slowly but safely, by careful research on the interactions between different factors. Techniques for continuous recording, maybe combined with non-verbal responses, should be used in order to better study perceived expression as a dynamic process. Choice of musical examples should be considerably broadened to overcome the present limitation to Western art (and some popular) music. Connections should be sought to studies of emotional expression in other areas, say, speech and body language, as well as to emotion psychology in general, and, furthermore, to music theory, music aesthetics, and music anthropology.

The real experts are, of course, the successful composers, past and present. They know, somehow, how to manipulate different variables in musical structure to attain an intended expression. This knowledge may be in part explicit, in part implicit, in combinations that are different for different composers. Although we may learn some grains of wisdom from the writings of certain composers—for instance, in the volume edited by Fisk (1997)—on the whole, their knowledge is rarely made available to others except for their students and other close persons. Thus, the mystery of composing music may remain—to the satisfaction of those who want to have some mystery in life left untouched.[1]

## References

Balkwill, L. L. & Thompson, W. F. (1999). A cross-cultural investigation of the perception of emotion in music: Psychophysical and cultural cues. *Music Perception, 17,* 43–64.

Behne, K. E. (1972). *Der Einfluss des Tempos auf die Beurteilung von Musik.* Köln, Germany: Arno Volk Verlag.

Behrens, G. A. & Green, S. B. (1993). The ability to identify emotional content of solo improvisations performed vocally and on three different instruments. *Psychology of Music, 21,* 20–33.

----

[1] The writing of this chapter was supported by a grant from The Bank of Sweden Tercentenary Foundation.

Cazden, N. (1979). Can verbal meanings inhere in fragments of melody? *Psychology of Music*, 7, 34–8.

Clynes, M. (1977). *Sentics: The touch of emotions*. New York: Anchor Press/Doubleday.

Clynes, M. & Walker, J. (1982). Neurobiologic functions of rhythm, time, and pulse in music. In *Music, mind, and brain. The neuropsychology of music*, (ed. M. Clynes), pp 171–216. New York: Plenum Press.

Cooke, D. (1959). *The language of music*. London: Oxford University Press.

Costa, M., Bitti, P. E. R., & Bonfiglioli, L. (2000). Psychological connotations of harmonic musical intervals. *Psychology of Music*, 28, 4–22.

Crowder, R. G. (1984). Perception of the major/minor distinction: I. Historical and theoretical foundations. *Psychomusicology*, 4, 3–12.

Crowder, R. G. (1985). Perception of the major/minor distinction: III. Hedonic, musical, and affective discriminations. *Bulletin of the Psychonomic Society*, 23, 314–16.

Davies, S. (1994). *Musical meaning and expression*. Ithaca, NY: Cornell University Press.

Downey, J. E. (1897). A musical experiment. *American Journal of Psychology*, 9, 63–9.

Farnsworth, P. R. (1954). A study of the Hevner adjective list. *Journal of Aesthetics and Art Criticism*, 13, 97–103.

Fisk, J. (ed.) (1997). *Composers on music*. Boston: Northeastern University Press.

Fredrickson, W. E. (1997). Elementary, middle, and high school student perceptions of tension in music. *Journal of Research in Music Education*, 45, 626–35.

Gabriel, C. (1978). An experimental study of Deryck Cooke's theory of music and meaning. *Psychology of Music*, 6, 13–20.

Gabriel, C. (1979). A note on comments by Nettheim and Cazden. *Psychology of Music*, 7, 39–40.

Gabrielsson, A. (1973). Adjective ratings and dimension analysis of auditory rhythm patterns. *Scandinavian Journal of Psychology*, 14, 244–60.

Gabrielsson, A. (1986). Rhythm in music. In *Rhythm in psychological, linguistic and musical processes*, (ed. J. R. Evans & M. Clynes), pp. 131–67. Springfield, IL: Charles C. Thomas.

Gabrielsson, A. (1988). Timing in music performance and its relations to music experience. In *Generative processes in music: The psychology of performance, improvisation, and composition*, (ed. J. A. Sloboda), pp. 27–51. Oxford, UK: Clarendon Press.

Gabrielsson, A. (1995). Expressive intention and performance. In *Music and the mind machine*, (ed. R. Steinberg), pp. 35–47. Heidelberg: Springer.

Gabrielsson, A. (1999). The performance of music. In *The psychology of music*, (2nd edn) (ed. D. Deutsch), pp. 501–602. San Diego, CA: Academic Press.

Gabrielsson, A. & Juslin, P. N. (in press). Emotional expression in music. In *Handbook of affective sciences*, (ed. R. J. Davidson, H. H. Goldsmith, & K. R. Scherer). New York: Oxford University Press.

Gabrielsson, A. & Lindström, E. (1995). Emotional expression in synthesizer and sentograph performance. *Psychomusicology*, 14, 94–116.

Gerardi, G. M. & Gerken, L. (1995). The development of affective responses to modality and melodic contour. *Music Perception*, 12, 279–90.

Gilman, B. I. (1891). Report on an experimental test of musical expressiveness. *American Journal of Psychology*, 4, 558–76.

Gilman, B. I. (1892). Report of an experimental test of musical expressiveness (continued). *American Journal of Psychology*, 5, 42–73.

Gotlieb, H. & Konečni, V. J. (1985). The effects of instrumentation, playing style, and structure in the Goldberg Variations by Johann Sebastian Bach. *Music Perception*, 3, 87–102.

Gregory, A. H., Worrall, L., & Sarge, A. (1996). The development of emotional responses to music in young children. *Motivation and Emotion*, 20, 341–8.

Gundlach, R. H. (1935). Factors determining the characterization of musical phrases. *American Journal of Psychology*, 47, 624–44.

Heinlein, C. P. (1928). The affective character of the major and minor modes in music. *Journal of Comparative Psychology*, 8, 101–42.

Hevner, K. (1935a). The affective character of the major and minor modes in music. *American Journal of Psychology*, 47, 103–18.

Hevner, K. (1935b). Expression in music: A discussion of experimental studies and theories. *Psychological Review*, 47, 186–204.

Hevner, K. (1936). Experimental studies of the elements of expression in music. *American Journal of Psychology*, 48, 246–68.

Hevner, K. (1937). The affective value of pitch and tempo in music. *American Journal of Psychology*, 49, 621–30.

Hill, D. S., Kamenetsky, S. B., & Trehub, S. E. (1996). Relations among text, mode, and medium: Historical and empirical perspectives. *Music Perception*, 14, 3–21.

Huber, K. (1923). *Der Ausdruck musikalischer Elementarmotive*. Leipzig, Germany: Johann Ambrosius Barth.

Imberty, M. (1979). *Entendre la musique*. Paris: Dunod.

Juslin, P. N. (1997). Perceived emotional expression in synthesized performances of a short melody: Capturing the listener's judgement policy. *Musicae Scientiae*, 1, 225–56.

Kamenetsky, S. B., Hill, D. S., & Trehub, S. E. (1997). Effect of tempo and dynamics on the perception of emotion in music. *Psychology of Music*, 25, 149–60.

Karno, M. & Konečni, V. J. (1992). The effects of structural interventions in the first movement of Mozart's Symphony in G Minor K. 550 on aesthetic preference. *Music Perception*, 10, 63–72.

Kastner, M. P. & Crowder, R. G. (1990). Perception of the major/minor distinction: IV. Emotional connotations in young children. *Music Perception*, 8, 189–202.

Kleinen, G. (1968). *Experimentelle Studien zum musikalischen Ausdruck*. Hamburg, Germany: Universität Hamburg.

Konečni, V. J. (1984). Elusive effects of artists' 'messages'. In *Cognitive processes in the perception of art*, (ed. W. R. Crozier & A. J. Chapman), pp. 71–93. Amsterdam: North-Holland.

Konečni, V. J. & Karno, M. (1994). Empirical investigations of the hedonic and emotional effects of musical structure. *Musikpsychologie. Jahrbuch der Deutschen Gesellschaft für Musikpsychologie*, 11, 119–37.

Krumhansl, C. L. (1996). A perceptual analysis of Mozart's Piano Sonata K. 282: Segmentation, tension, and musical ideas. *Music Perception*, 13, 401–32.

Krumhansl, C. L. (1997). An exploratory study of musical emotions and psychophysiology. *Canadian Journal of Experimental Psychology*, 51, 336–52.

Langer, S. K. (1953). *Feeling and form*. London: Routledge.

Langer, S. K. (1957). *Philosophy in a new key*, (3rd edn). Cambridge, MA: Harvard University Press.

Levinson, J. (1997). *Music in the moment*. Ithaca, NY: Cornell University Press.

Lindström, E. (1997). Impact of melodic structure on emotional expression. In *Proceedings of the Third Triennial ESCOM Conference, Uppsala, June 1997*, (ed. A.Gabrielsson), pp. 292–7. Uppsala, Sweden: Uppsala University.

Lindström, E. (2000). *Impact of melodic structure on emotional expression in music.* Manuscript submitted for publication.

Madsen, C. K. (1997). Emotional responses to music. *Psychomusicology,* 16, 59–67.

Madsen, C. K. & Fredrickson, W. E. (1993). The experience of musical tension: A replication of Nielsen's research using the continuous response digital interface. *Journal of Music Therapy,* 30, 46–63.

Maher, T. F. (1980). A rigorous test of the proposition that musical intervals have different psychological effects. *American Journal of Psychology,* 93, 309–27.

Maher, T. F. & Berlyne, D. E. (1982). Verbal and exploratory responses to melodic musical intervals. *Psychology of Music,* 10, 11–27.

Motte-Haber, H. de la (1968). *Ein Beitrag zur Klassifikation musikalischer Rhythmen.* Köln, Germany: Arno Volk Verlag.

Namba, S., Kuwano, S., Hatoh, T., & Kato, M. (1991). Assessment of musical performance by using the method of continuous judgment by selected description. *Music Perception,* 8, 251–76.

Nettheim, N. (1979). Comment on a paper by Gabriel on Cooke's theory. *Psychology of Music,* 7, 32–3.

Nielsen, F. V. (1983). *Oplevelse av musikalsk spænding [Experience of musical tension].* Copenhagen: Akademisk Forlag (includes summary in English).

Nielsen, F. V. (1987). Musical 'tension' and related concepts. In *The semiotic web '86. An international yearbook,* (ed. T. A. Sebeok & J. Umiker-Sebeok), pp. 491–513. Berlin: Mouton de Gruyter.

Nielzén, S. & Cesarec, Z. (1981). On the perception of emotional meaning in music. *Psychology of Music,* 9, 17–31.

Nielzén, S. & Cesarec, Z. (1982). Emotional experience of music as a function of musical structure. *Psychology of Music,* 10, 7–17.

Osgood, C. E., Suci, G. J., & Tannenbaum, P. H. (1957). *The measurement of meaning.* Urbana, IL: University of Illinois Press.

Peretz, I., Gagnon, L., & Bouchard, B. (1998). Music and emotion: perceptual determinants, immediacy, and isolation after brain damage. *Cognition,* 68, 111–41.

Remington, N. A., Fabrigar, L. R., & Visser, P. S. (2000). Reexamining the circumplex model of affect. *Journal of Personality and Social Psychology,* 79, 286–300.

Rigg, M. G. (1937). Musical expression: An investigation of the theories of Erich Sorantin. *Journal of Experimental Psychology,* 21, 442–55.

Rigg, M. G. (1939). *What features of a musical phrase have emotional suggestiveness?* Publications of the Social Science Research Council of the Oklahoma Agricultural and Mechanical College, No. 1.

Rigg, M. G. (1940a). The effect of register and tonality upon musical mood. *Journal of Musicology,* 2, 49–61.

Rigg, M. G. (1940b). Speed as a determiner of musical mood. *Journal of Experimental Psychology,* 27, 566–71.

Rigg, M. G. (1964). The mood effects of music: A comparison of data from four investigators. *Journal of Psychology,* 58, 427–38.

Russell, J. A. (1980). A circumplex model of affect. *Journal of Personality and Social Psychology,* 39, 1161–78.

Scherer, K. R. & Oshinsky, J. S. (1977). Cue utilization in emotion attribution from auditory stimuli. *Motivation and Emotion*, 1, 331–46.

Schlosberg, H. (1941). A scale for the judgement of facial expressions. *Journal of Experimental Psychology*, 29, 497–510.

Schubert, E. (1999). *Measurement and time series analysis of emotion in music.* Unpublished doctoral dissertation, University of South Wales, Sydney, Australia.

Sloboda, J. A. (1985). *The musical mind. The cognitive psychology of music.* Oxford, UK: Clarendon Press.

Smith, L. D. & Williams, R. N. (1999). Children's artistic responses to musical intervals. *American Journal of Psychology*, 112, 383–410.

Stern, D. N. (1985). *The interpersonal world of the infant. A view from psychoanalysis and developmental psychology.* New York: Basic Books.

Thompson, W. F. & Robitaille, B. (1992). Can composers express emotions through music? *Empirical Studies of the Arts*, 10, 79–89.

Tillman, B. & Bigand, E. (1996). Does formal musical structure affect perception of musical expressiveness? *Psychology of Music*, 24, 1–17.

de Vries, B. (1991). Assessment of the affective response to music with Clynes's sentograph. *Psychology of Music*, 19, 46–64.

Watson, K. B. (1942). The nature and measurement of musical meanings. *Psychological Monographs*, 54, 1–43.

Wedin, L. (1969). Dimension analysis of emotional expression in music. *Swedish Journal of Musicology*, 51, 119–40.

Wedin, L. (1972a). *Evaluation of a three-dimensional model of emotional expression in music.* Reports from the Psychological Laboratories, University of Stockholm, No. 349.

Wedin, L. (1972b). Multidimensional scaling of emotional expression in music. *Swedish Journal of Musicology*, 54, 1–17.

Wedin, L. (1972c). Multidimensional study of perceptual-emotional qualities in music. *Scandinavian Journal of Psychology*, 13, 241–57.

# CHAPTER 11

# MUSIC AS A SOURCE OF EMOTION IN FILM

ANNABEL J. COHEN

Emotion characterizes the experience of film, as it does the experience of music. Because music almost always accompanies film, we may well ask what contribution music makes to the emotional aspects of film. The present chapter addresses this question.

It should be said at the outset that in spite of the integral role of music for film, film music has been largely neglected by the disciplines of both musicology and music psychology until the last decade (e.g. Cohen 1994; Marks 1998; Prendergast 1991). The reasons for the neglect are complex, arising from social, technological, economic, historical, and cultural factors. Some of these factors also account for a parallel neglect by psychology of the study of film perception (Hochberg & Brooks 1996a, 1996b). Moreover, unlike other types of popular or art music, much music for film has been composed with the understanding that it will not be consciously attended to. Countering this neglect, the present chapter takes a psychological perspective on the sublime and remarkable emotional phenomena produced by music in the context of film. This chapter has the joint intent of supporting the argument that music is one of the strongest sources of emotion in film and of opening doors to further empirical work that explains why this is so.

The chapter is divided into five sections. The first section briefly establishes a context for discussing emotion in music and film. Section 11.2 focuses on music in film, first establishing a historical perspective and then examining the role of music at the interface of the fictional and non-fictional elements of film. It continues with empirical studies of music as a source of inference and then summarizes the functions that music serves for film. Section 11.3 presents a cognitive framework for understanding musical soundtrack phenomena previously described. Section 11.4 considers the role of the composer as the origin of the source of musical emotion for film, whilst conclusions are drawn in the final section.

## 11.1 Emotion: definitions in music and film contexts

In the present chapter, the term film refers to the narrative dramas characteristic of movie theatres, television, and video with which most people are familiar as a source of entertainment. Music typically accompanies a considerable proportion of the duration of such films. Because of the relative novelty of the empirical study of film music in general, let alone the study of the emotional contribution of music in film, it would be premature to advocate a particular way of considering emotion in the present chapter. What is more important is to show how various 'music-alone' perspectives on emotion translate in the film context. These perspectives include the contribution of music to emotional meaning (Juslin 1997; Levi 1982), the establishment of general mood (Pignatiello *et al.* 1986), and the experience of genuine, deep emotions (Gabrielsson 1998; Gabrielsson & Lindström 1993; Sloboda 1985, 1992; see also Gabrielsson, this volume).

The film context sometimes permits greater terminological clarity than the music-alone situation. For example, consider the terms 'mood' and 'emotion' which are often differentiated with respect to the presence of an object (e.g. Barrett & Russell 1999; Tan 1996). Whereas both moods and emotions may be regarded as dispositions toward appraising emotional meaning structures and a readiness to respond in a certain manner, moods do not have objects; emotions do. For example, experiencing the emotion of relief requires an object of that emotion, such as a safe arrival after a treacherous journey. Objects are not as evident in music-alone contexts, but, as argued by musicologist Nicholas Cook (1998), in a multimedia context music readily finds an object. The emotional associations generated by music attach themselves automatically to the visual focus of attention or the implied topic of the narrative. Because film content provides the object of emotion generated by music, the film helps to control the definition of the object of the emotion experienced during the presence of music.

Considering music and emotion within the context of film also has the advantage of bringing knowledge from psychological studies of film to bear on questions regarding music and emotion. Based on the emotion theorist Frijda (1986), Tan (1996), for example, addresses the question of the genuine nature of emotions in film, a topic that will be addressed later in this chapter. Thus, research on music and emotion in the film context may benefit from research insights derived from studies of film and emotion. Conversely, our understanding of emotion associated with autonomous music may shed light on emotional processes that occur in the film context. All of this information may contribute to the understanding of both the unique accomplishment of composing music for film and the extent to which music provides an important source of emotion in film.

## 11.2 Music and cinema

### 11.2.1 Historical background

*Beginnings*

From the earliest days of film, music played a part. When silent film was first introduced at the turn of the century, the film projector was anything but silent. Music was therefore enlisted to mask the extraneous noise. While serving the masking function, music also was exploited to illustrate and explain the action (Palmer 1980, p. 549). Kracauer (1960, p. 133) emphasizes that the noise problem of the film projection was relatively shortlived, and yet the importance of music remained. An entire music-for-the-silent-film industry developed to support this function of music (Limbacher 1974; Thomas

1997, pp. 37–40). It included the publication of anthologies of music to represent various emotional settings, an increased demand for pianos in the thousands by small movie theatres that sprang up, and architectural plans for movie theatres that included places for pianists and sometimes other musicians.

### Hugo Münsterberg

The first psychologist to direct attention to the new phenomena of film was Hugo Münsterberg at Harvard University (Fig. 11.1). Between 1899 and 1916, he wrote 24 books, one of the last of which was *The photoplay: A psychological study*. In what is regarded as the first book on film theory (Anderson 1997), Münsterberg's views are enlightening. His experience of film was as fresh as a child's although acquired as a highly intelligent adult. His understanding of both introspection and scientific method encourage our confidence in his record of, and insight into, film at that time.

Yes, it is a new art—and this is why it has such fascination for the psychologist who in a world of ready-made arts, each with a history of many centuries, suddenly finds a new form still undeveloped and hardly understood. For the first time the psychologist can observe the starting of an entirely new esthetic development, a new form of true beauty in the turmoil of a technical age, created by its very technique and yet more than any other art destined to overcome outer nature by the free and joyful play of the mind (Münsterberg 1970, pp. 232–3).

**Figure 11.1** Hugo Münsterberg.

He did not live to experience the talking film, but his film experience was not lacking in sound. There were sound effects—he describes a machine, the allefex, 'which can produce over fifty distinctive noises, fit for any photoplay emergency' (Münsterberg 1970, p. 205)—and there was music. In his view, music relieved tension, maintained interest ('keeps the attention awake'), provided comfort, reinforced emotion, and contributed to the aesthetic experience (pp. 204–5).

Münsterberg also used musical metaphor in describing the film experience (e.g. pp. 120 and 128–9). For example, he recounts a narrative cliché of the period, a rapid alternation between three scenes: a jovial boss and his secretary enjoying a private after-hours party in the office, the dismal parents of the secretary awaiting their daughter's return, and the lonely wife awaiting her husband's attention. 'It is as if we saw one through another, as if three tones blended into one chord . . . The photoplay alone gives us our chance for such omnipresence' (p. 105). Yet, to extend his metaphor of the musical chord, it is also music that can represent in rapid succession and perhaps simultaneously the 'emotional polyphony' of these multiple messages.

Possibly because he never experienced the sound film ('talkies'), Münsterberg directed attention to the importance of music within the film and to music as a means of understanding the psychological processes underlying film. He suggested that cinema is more similar to music than to photography and drama, which on the surface are arts that bear a more striking resemblance:

> . . . we come nearer to the understanding of its [film's] true position in the esthetic world, if we think at the same time of . . . the art of the musical tones. They have overcome the outer world and social world entirely, they unfold our inner life, our mental play, with its feelings and emotions, its memories and fancies, in a material which seems exempt from the laws of the world of substance and material, tones which are fluttering and fleeting like our own mental states. (Münsterberg 1970, p. 168–9)

Münsterberg's untimely death (the year of his publication of The photoplay) and the coincident advent of behaviourism, focusing as it did on only objectively observable behaviour, may account for the failure of psychological research in film and music to run in parallel with the technological developments associated with these media. Instead, technology developed and its psychological study lagged far behind in spite of having got off to a good start.

### The sound film

In 1927, approximately 10 years after the death of Münsterberg, The Jazz Singer signaled the advent of the 'talkies' and the demise of the film-music industry. With real voices and sound effects, music would no longer be needed to establish mood and emotional context . . . or would it? To the surprise of many, something was missing without music (Kracauer 1960, p. 138). The screen had lost part of its vitality. As Kalinak (1992, p. 45) says 'when the possibility of synchronized speech and sound effects released sound film from its reliance upon continuous musical accompaniment, it initially rejected music entirely. But the life span of the all-talking picture was brief, the need that music filled quickly reasserting itself'.

Several theorists have commented that music adds a third dimension to the two-dimensional film screen (Palmer 1990; Rosar 1994). Composers also shared this view.

Aaron Copland (1941) stated 'the screen is a pretty cold proposition'. Film composer David Raksin (in Brown 1994, p. 282) referred to Nietzsche's idea 'without music, life would not be worth living'. His statement is extreme (deaf people live worthwhile lives) but paraphrasing the maxim, few hearing people would deny that music contributes to their experience of film.

Since the early days of film, directors have recognized the contribution that film-editing made to the viewer, often referred to as montage. Viewers are typically unaware of the rapid changes in camera angle, the move from close-up to long-shot or from one part of the scene to another and back again. None the less, viewers make sense of the world depicted by these juxtaposed shots. Theories of montage concern the audience's synthesis of juxtaposed information in the film. With the advent of the sound film, Russian director Sergej Eisenstein was among the first to extend the notion of visual montage to sound, and suggested that the listener incorporates the same synthetic process in making sense of the entire audiovisual cinematic presentation.

### 11.2.2 Music and the diegesis and the non-diegesis

Film theory commonly refers to the fictional, imagined, narrative world of the film as the *diegesis*. In contrast, the *non-diegesis* refers to the objective world of the audience, the world of artefact, of film screens, projectors, proficiency of actors, and technical aspects of the film. In terms of physical reality, music as acoustic vibrations belongs to the non-diegesis. Logically—unless such sound were part of a scene portrayed in a film, as in a film about a musical instrument or the life of a great composer—these sounds of music should *detract from* rather than *add to* the sense of reality of the film. This point was well made in Mel Brooks' comedy *Blazing Saddles* (1974). A sheriff rides out on the desert—with seemingly appropriate music in the background—and meets face to face with the Count Basie Band performing the now inappropriate music *Paris in the Spring*. The fictional (diegetic) and the non-fictional (non-diegetic) realities collide and add to the humour of the scene. It is probably not coincidental that Brooks, the director and screen writer of the film, is also a composer of music, including some film scores, and so he would have been particularly sensitive to this film-score convention.

Thus, the audience selectively attends to only the part of the music that makes sense with the narrative. Selective attention is a common perceptual-cognitive operation. The recently discovered phenomenon of 'inattentional blindness' is another example of it in the visual domain of film. Here it has been shown that people rarely noticed or were distracted by impossible visual aspects represented in either a film or in their real-world experience. For example, viewers did not notice that a woman in a film clip began the short scene with a scarf and ended the scene without it (Levin & Simons, 2000). In another study (Levin & Simon, 1998), an experimenter positioned on a college campus solicited directions from unsuspecting subjects. Their conversation was interrupted by two confederates carrying a door. One of the confederates changed position with the experimenter who had initially asked for directions. The conversation about directions then continued. The subject rarely realized that there were two different people to whom he or she had been conversing. Two facts are important here. First, the visual system is blind to much available information, and this inattentional blindness (cf. Mack & Rock 1998) is equally characteristic of vision in the real and in the film world. Thus, the fact that audiences extract the emotional information in music and fail to attend to the acoustical aspects might be described as a case of inattentional deafness, a byproduct of the fact that awareness depends on attention, and attentional capacity is limited. A better parallel can be drawn to the role of prosody in speech perception, which shares with music a greater syntactic similarity than the visual examples given. Here patterns of intensity and frequency from intonation systematically provide emotional meaning to a listener, yet the listener focuses on the meaning and is unconscious of this source of information (e.g. Banse & Scherer 1996; Murray & Arnott 1993).

A good example of the role of music as a source of emotion in the narrative is illustrated in the film *Witness*. Here, a young Amish boy is the sole observer of a violent murder in a train station. He is directed to a noisy police station in order to search through a book of photographs of suspects for a match of his memory to the actual perpetrator of the crime. While left unattended momentarily, he wanders toward a display cabinet that holds a photograph of an honoured senior officer in the force. As he views the photograph, Maurice Jarre's music replaces the background sound effects of the police station. The audience realizes that the boy becomes awestruck with the sudden recognition that the photograph of the police officer depicts the person who he saw commit the crime. The audience takes interest in this scene and is concerned now about the implications for the safety of the boy. This is one of the most critical points in the film; without it there would be no further plot. The criminal within the police force would remain unknown and the boy could continue on his trip without a care. Yet it is this crucial moment, a moment that must be comprehended by the audience, to which the unrealistic music is not merely added but is added at the expense of the more realistic, diegetic sound effects. But the audience, caught up in the drama, is unlikely to have noted this departure from reality.

Film-music scholar Claudia Gorbman (1987) has addressed the unconscious perception of music in her book *Unheard melodies: Narrative film music*. Gorbman's perspective is well captured by Jeff Smith (1996, p. 234): 'By veiling the lacks and deficiencies of other discursive structures, film music, according to Gorbman, lubricates the various cogs and pistons of the cinematic pleasure machine'. If anything, departures from reality via music makes an episode 'more real', more vivid, more emotionally relevant. To date, experimental research has not focused on the subtle uses of music in film (such as its replacement of realistic sound as in the *Witness* example). A number of studies, however, have concerned the role of music in generating inferences, and often those inferences are associated with emotional meaning.

### 11.2.3 Music and inference: empirical studies

Music presumably adds to the diegetic realism while providing non-diegetic, acoustical, information that is completely incompatible with that realism. At the interface of the diegetic and non-diegetic worlds, the use of music in this and in most other film situations is paradoxical (Cohen 1990). To escape the paradox, the analysis of the acoustical information must be regarded as a preattentive step that leads the listener to inferences consistent within the diegetic world of the film. From moment to moment, the audience member extracts information from non-diegetic sources to generate the emotional information he or she needs to make a coherent story in the diegesis. The successful director and film-score composer provide just the right cues to guide the attentional and inferences processes.

One attempt at understanding the phenemenon of diegetic inference comes from the context of psychological situation models described as 'vicarious experiences in narrative comprehension' (Zwaan 1999, p. 15). Zwaan, for example, has focused on how literature enables readers to 'mentally leap into imagined worlds'. The information provided by the text is sufficient to enable a reader to place himself or herself at a spatial, temporal, and psychological vantage point from which events are vicariously experienced. The perspective is termed a deictic centre.

Magliano *et al.* (1996) extended the approach to the study of film. In their study, music was indirectly examined as one of six operationally defined film factors (such as montage) that might contribute to the psychological definition of the situation. In two experiments, they investigated visual, auditory, and discourse conditions that enable viewers to predict future events while viewing a James Bond movie, *Moonraker*. In experiment 1, participants were instructed to generate predictions while watching the movie. In experiment 2, participants provided think-aloud protocols at different locations in the film. In both experiments, the presence of supporting visual and discourse information led to systematic predictions by the participant. Music significantly co-occurred with other cinematic sources of support such as montage and *mise en scène*, which were found to influence inference processes.[1]

The study by Magliano *et al.* (1996) was not specifically designed to show the influence of music in the film context. Studies that have been so designed have been successful in showing this influence. Such studies typically require more conditions than do comparable studies in music-alone situations, because it is necessary to determine the effects of music alone, film alone, music judged in the context of film, and film judged in the context of music. The studies to be reported have often involved several, if not all, of these different comparison conditions.

In a study by Bullerjahn and Güldenring (1994), professional composers of film music (including Peer Raben, composer for all the Fassbinder films) created a total of five different backgrounds (e.g. crime, melodrama) for the same 10-minute film segment. Both quantitative and qualitative analysis showed that the different soundtracks led to different judgments of the appropriateness of emotional categories (e.g. sad, thrilling, sentimental, vivid), choice of genre (horror, comedy, thriller, crime, etc.), reasons for the actions of the protagonist, and expectations about the completion of the film. In some cases, these judgments and inferences could be attributed to specific aspects of the film. For example, the authors suggested that the final closure of the major chord of one of the melodramatic soundtracks accounted for the presumed reconciliation between the film characters though it is preceded by an argument.

In a series of experiments, Thompson *et al.* (1994) specifically examined the effects of musical closure on perceived closure of a film. In their first experiment, a closed soundtrack ended with a traditional 'perfect' cadence (dominant chord to tonic chord ending).

---

[1] When music was entered first into the regression equation, it too was found to be a significant predictor of inference, though accounting for only 6 per cent of the variance (J. P. Magliano, personal communication).

The unclosed soundtrack differed only with respect to the final bar, such that the ending was not on the tonic chord. Subjects viewed a short animation accompanied by one of the soundtracks and were asked to rate the degree of closure represented by the clip. Judgments of closure were significantly higher for the condition in which the closed ending was presented. In a second experiment, a professional composer produced closed and unclosed soundtracks to accompany a short film clip produced by one of the experimenters. Closed soundtracks ended on the tonic chord, in contrast to the unclosed soundtracks. The effect of soundtrack closure was strong for only one of the film clips, suggesting that visual factors may take precedence over musical structure in some cases. In a final study, 12 separate soundtracks were composed for 12 clips from a commercial film, initially chosen for their assumed range in degree of closure. The soundtracks were also composed to represent a range of closure, and the degree of closure needed not to match that of the clip. Participants in the experiment judged the degree of closure of the soundtracks, the clips alone, and the soundtrack and clips together. The influence of independently judged visual and musical closure on judged closure of the film was shown through regression analysis, with a slightly greater contribution arising from visual than musical information. In addition to demonstrating a robust direct effect of musical structure on the feeling of closure of a film narrative, the authors also reported that the role of music was almost completely implicit. When participants were asked for the basis of their judgments, they almost always attributed their judgments to the visual information.

Boltz *et al.* (1991) examined the role of music on inferences in a study that compared music that foreshadowed an outcome versus music that accompanied an outcome. Participants viewed 20 different 3–4-minute clips from feature films and television dramas. Excerpts were selected that ultimately resolved in a happy (positive) or sad (e.g. tragic) way. Music emotionally consistent or inconsistent with these endings (as determined by music-alone ratings) either preceded (foreshadowed) or accompanied the video excerpt. Thus, in some cases the foreshadowing music correctly predicted the mood of the following video event and the accompanying music was congruent with the mood of the video event, and in other cases the foreshadowing music incorrectly predicted the subsequent event and the accompanying music was incongruent with the event. Music accompanying an episode's outcome led to higher recall when the mood of the music and scene were congruent with each other. Conversely, mood-incongruent relations significantly lowered performance to a level comparable to that of the control condition in which no music had occurred. Foreshadowing, however, revealed the opposite pattern. Here, expectancy violations arising from mood-incongruent relations were significantly more memorable than were mood-congruent episodes in which viewer's expectancies were confirmed (Boltz *et al.* pp. 597–8). Boltz *et al.* (1991, p. 602) concluded that their results supported the notion that viewers rely on the emotional expression of music to either generate expectancies about future scenarios or to direct attending toward corresponding aspects of visual activities.

Marshall and Cohen (1988) also observed the ability of music to alter the interpretation of a simple visual presentation. They studied the effects of two different soundtracks on impressions about three geometric forms, a large and small triangle and a circle, in a short animation developed by Heider and Simmel (1944). In their experiment, subjects viewed the 2-minute animation with one of two soundtracks or with no soundtrack (control condition). They then provided 12 ratings for the film overall and for the three figures. Other groups of subjects rated the music on these same scales. Each of the 12 scales represented a bipolar adjective pair (e.g. fast–slow, nice–awful) and specifically tapped one of the three dimensions of emotional meaning—activity, evaluation, and potency—comprising the semantic differential (Osgood *et al.* 1957). The activity and evaluation dimensions are understood to represent the motivation (arousal) and appraisal (valence) dimensions associated with two-dimensional theories of emotion on which many emotion theorists (Barrett & Russell 1999; Lang 1995; Storm & Storm 1987; see also Sloboda & Juslin, this volume) and music psychologists (Gregory 1998; Madsen 1997; Schubert 1998; see also Schubert, this volume) converge.

In Marshall and Cohen's (1988) study, two musical soundtracks were judged to have approximately the same activity level (measured by averaging responses on scales of fast–slow, active–passive, agitated–calm, restless–quiet). The relative activity levels of the three 'characters' in the film, however, differed for the two different musical backgrounds. For example, the large triangle was judged as the most active under one soundtrack while the small triangle was judged as the most active in the other. Marshall and Cohen (1988) argued *post hoc* that shared accent patterns in the music and in the motion of the figures operated to focus attention on the temporally congruent part of the visual scene, and subsequently associations of the music were ascribed to this focus (Fig. 11.2). A similar accent-pattern/association breakdown in the processing of film and music was proposed by Lipscomb and Kendall (1994, p. 91).

Cook (1998), in his book *Analyzing musical multimedia*, has suggested the generality of Marshall and Cohen's (1988) theory to other multimedia examples in which musical meaning alters the interpretation of events that are at the focus of visual attention. In advertisements for cars, for example, the car takes on both the vitality and the high cultural associations of the classical music in the background. Music does more than echo or provide a counterpoint to a concept already present in the film. Music can also direct attention to an object on the screen and establish emotionally laden inferences about that object.

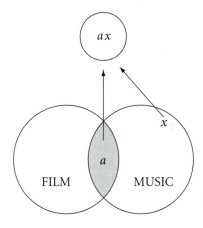

**Figure 11.2** Congruence-associationist model based on that depicted by Marshall and Cohen (1988). The total meaning and structure of the music and film are presented by their respectives circles. The overlap in music and film is depicted by the intersection of the circles (*a*). Attention is directed to this area of visual overlap in the film. Other associations of the music (*x*) are ascribed to this focus of attention (*ax*). Thus, music alters the meaning of a particular aspect of the film.

Regarding the ability of music to focus attention, Bolivar *et al.* (1994), following Boltz *et al.* (1991), noted that attention to a visual object might arise not only from structural congruencies but also from semantic congruencies. Hypothetically, for example, a soundtrack featuring a lullaby might direct attention to a cradle rather than to a fishbowl when both objects are simultaneously depicted in a scene. Subsequently, additional associations from the lullaby would be ascribed to the cradle (and conversely for Schubert's *Trout Quintet*, for those familiar with it). Empirical evidence for the ability of music to focus attention is scant and tends to appear with very simple geometric figures, but has not yet been demonstrated with more complex displays (cf. Lipscomb 1999). Part of the difficulty has been in creation of the materials to study the phenomena; however, rapid advances in the affordability of non-linear editing equipment may make such experiments more practical.

### 11.2.4 Functions of film music

Cohen (1999*a*) described eight functions of music in a film or multimedia context. First, music masks extraneous noises. Second, it provides continuity between shots, for example, when the camera alternates between close-ups of two people who are presumably looking at each other (cf. Magliano *et al.* 1996, p. 205). Third, as Marshall and Cohen (1988) and Bolivar *et al.* (1994) had argued, and as noted by Münsterberg (1970), it directs attention to important features of the screen through structural or associationist congruence. Fourth, when unassociated with a particular focus it induces mood, as often occurs during the opening credits of a film. The ability of music to induce mood has been supported in several experiments (Pignatiello *et al.* 1986) and is used in music therapy (Albersnagel 1988; Bunt & Pavlicevic, this volume). Fifth, it communicates meaning and furthers the narrative, especially in ambiguous situations (Bullerjahn & Güldenring 1994; Cohen 1993; Kalinak 1992; Levinson 1996). Sixth, through association in memory, music becomes integrated with the film (Boltz *et al.* 1991) and enables the symbolization of past and future events through the technique of *leitmotiv*. In leitmotiv, a particular musical theme is continuously paired with a character or event so that eventually the theme conjures up the concept of the character or event in its absence (Palmer 1980, p. 550). The composer Richard Wagner is typically regarded as the first to exploit this principle in opera. In an insightful article by the composer Saint-Saens (1903, p. 259), entitled 'The composer as psychologist', the author remarks that psychological principles must be responsible for the effectiveness of leitmotiv. Mood-dependent memories can also be cued with the emotions established by music (Eich 1995). Seventh, music heightens the sense of reality of or absorption in film, perhaps by augmenting arousal, and increasing attention to the entire film context and inattention to everything else (cf. discussions of reality status by Preston 1999; Qian *et al.* 1999). Finally, music as an art form adds to the aesthetic effect of the film.

## 11.3 A cognitive framework for understanding musical soundtracks

Many of the functions of film music can be explained via notions of congruence or association, because these represent two primary ways in which the brain operates:

through innate grouping principles (Bregman 1990) and by learned connections (Cohen 1993), respectively. Cohen (1999*a*, 1999*b*, 2000) presented a capacity-limited information-processing framework that represented the congruence-associationist concepts in a broad cognitive context (Fig. 11.3).

The framework consists of three parallel channels along the vertical axis, each devoted to one of the significant domains of film: speech, visual information, and music. Each channel is hierarchically organized into four processing levels, with bottom-up levels (A and B) meeting the top-down level (D) at level C, the level of conscious attention and

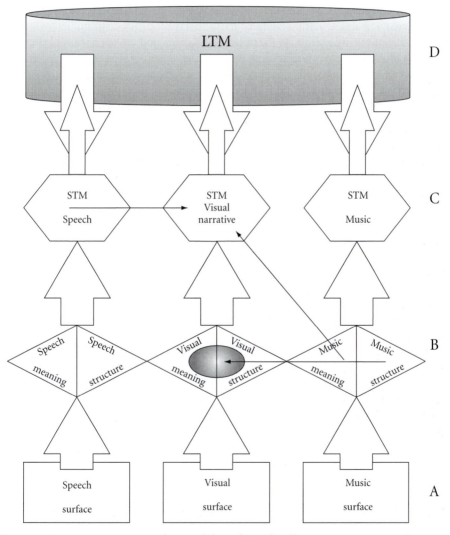

**Figure 11.3** Congruence-associationist framework for understanding film-music communication (see text for explanation). LTM, long-term memory; STM, short-term memory.

short-term memory (STM). Environmental sounds (sound effects) have not been included for the sake of simplicity and because of lack of research to date, but their own grammar and complexity calls ultimately for incorporation as a separate channel. Likewise, the visual channel might admit to further breakdowns, for example, animate/inanimate or background/foreground, but this is secondary to the main concepts presented below.

### 11.3.1 Bottom-up processes: levels A and B

Processing begins at level A with the analysis of physical features of the speech, visual, and musical surfaces into components such as phonemes, lines, and frequencies, respectively. Within each of these domains, at the next level (B), groups of features are subsequently analysed into structural (gestalt-type) and semantic (associationist) information. For music, this means assembly into temporal structures and categorization of cues (e.g. pitch height, tempo, direction) leading to emotional meaning. The outcome of analysis at level B affords the possibility for emergence of cross-modal congruencies, for example, shared accent patterns in audio and visual modalities, to lead preattention to only a portion of the visual information, shown here as the material within the oval in the visual channel.

*Cross-modal structural congruence*

To further explain the concept of cross-modal congruence, cognitive psychologists have typically applied gestalt principles to visual pattern (e.g. Wertheimer 1939) and later to auditory information (e.g. Bregman 1990; Meyer 1956; Narmour 1991). Rarely are the principles applied to the visual and auditory domains at once. But film music provides the necessity for such application. The simultaneous presentation of music and film automatically elicits bottom-up principles that entail perceptual grouping in both auditory and visual domains. When the auditory information and visual information are structurally congruent (e.g. share temporal accent patterns), the visually congruent information becomes the figure, the visual focus of attention (as originally argued by Marshall & Cohen 1988).

As part of a larger study, Iwamiya (1994, pp. 134–5) showed that judgments of degree of audiovisual matching of four short film clips was lower when the original video and music components were desynchronized by 500 ms (the only delay examined). Thus, gestalt theoretical ideas that are typically applied to visual or auditory domains independently can be applied to conjoint visual and auditory dynamic information. It follows that through innate gestalt grouping processes, music can define the visual figure against the audiovisual background; music can sometimes determine what is the visual focus of attention.

More recently, the gestalt account of the phenomenal sense of 'belonging together' has been seen as a forerunner of the current solution to a general problem in cognition, that of consciousness. Lately, cognitive scientists have focused on the concept of 'binding' to explain how 'the unity of conscious perception is brought about by the distributed activities of the central nervous system' (Revonsuo & Newman 1999, p. 123). It is interesting to note the significance cognitive scientists attach to neural synchronization associated with shared temporal patterning across neural ensembles. Film music that shares patterns with visual information on the screen, may therefore contribute to attention and consciousness. Indeed, oscillations (cf. accent patterns) below 10 Hz (the typical limit for the film-score composer's click-track) have been proposed as necessary for information integration and the generation of the stream of consciousness characterizing working memory (cf. Revonsuo & Newman 1999, p. 126).

These notions of congruent patterns in perceptual and cognitive psychology relate to those in the film-music literature on sensitivity to, and effectiveness of, synchronized musical and film structures. Kalinak (1992) suggests that it is this synchronization that contributes to the inaudibility of the music. Synchronization masks the real source of the sound (like ventriloquism):

The vocal track in classical cinema anchors diegetic sound to the image by synchronizing it, masking the actual source of sonic production, the speakers, and fostering the illusion that the diegesis itself produces the sounds. Mickey Mousing [synchronized music and visual accent] duplicates these conventions in terms of nondiegetic sound. Precisely synchronizing diegetic action to its musical accompaniment masks the actual source of sonic production, the offscreen orchestra, and renders the emanation of music natural and consequently inaudible. Musical accompaniment was thus positioned to effect perception, especially the semiconscious, without disrupting narrative credibility. (Kalinak 1992, p. 86)

### 11.3.2 Short-term memeory visual narrative: level C

Returning to the remainder of the framework of Fig. 11.3, information is transferred to STM at level C. Priority of transfer is given to visual information in the gray oval at level B, which has been selected by cross-modal audiovisual congruence. Not all of the visual sensory information that is potentially available reaches the STM. Also, information of musical meaning from B is transferred not only to a music STM but also to the visual STM. Note that visual STM is referred to as the STM visual narrative. This is a unique aspect of the framework: visual STM is construed as the location of consciousness of the film representation. This decision is supported by the evidence for visual primacy and the typical subservience of audio to vision (e.g. ventriloquism, cf. Driver 1997; see also Bolivar et al. 1994; Thompson et al. 1994). The concept is that of constructing a narrative from the information gleaned simultaneously from visual, music, and speech sources. The present depiction illustrates how music transports various packages of information, be they structural or semantic, meeting the (diegetic and non-diegetic) goals of a film director and film-music composer for the minds of the audience. The term narrative is in recognition of the aim of the visual STM process to make sense of the visual information using whatever information is at hand. Thus, the emotional meaning of the music is directed here because it is useful in determining the meaning of the visual scene. However, consciousness of this meaning arises only through correspondence with information from top-down processes based in long-term memory (LTM).

### 11.3.3 Top-down processes: level D

During bottom-up processing, some preattended information from all channels proceeds to the LTM at D and begins a top-down inference process with the goal of constructing the narrative of the film. Thus, both bottom-up and top-down processes simultaneously generate information that meets at level C, the STM. In order to achieve consciousness in the STM of material driven by bottom-up processes, matching of this information by inferences generated from the LTM is necessary. The notion of such a matching process is found in theories of conscious attention (Grossberg's 1995 adaptive resonance theory, ART), comprehension (Kinstch 1998, construction-integration), and consciousness (Baars 1997). These theories assume that preattentive processes are sufficient to initiate the inference processes from LTM.[2]

Because everyday emotional experience associated with events is stored in the LTM, inferences based on past experience would include emotion (e.g. how a protagonist would feel in a certain situation). These inferences generated by the LTM matching process accommodate the visual and emotional information from a film, but not the acoustical properties of the musical accompaniment that are the source of the emotional information. This explains why the acoustical aspects of the music are not generally attended to: in the context of the rest of the narrative, the acoustical aspects of the music do not make sense to LTM (where is that background music coming from?) and no hypotheses would be generated easily to include it (unless, of course, music were part of the diegesis, e.g. the portrayal in the film of attending a concert or taking a music lesson).

An example of this attentional and inference process is provided by consideration of a portion of the film *Apollo 13*, the drama based on the dangerous technical difficulties within the spacecraft, Apollo 13, that prevented the planned landing on the moon and threatened a safe return to earth. Toward the end of the film, Apollo 13 hovers over the moon—so near and yet so far. The film depicts the fantasy of one of the astronauts, Jim Lovell (played by Tom Hanks) imagining his dream of having landed, taking several weightless steps, and slowly brushing his gloved fingers across the moon's surface. The audience has no trouble in inferring the anguish, awe, and exhilaration that he would have felt. Thanks to the composer, James Horner, the musical basis for such emotional information is carried by the musical soundtrack. On the other hand, the story gives no reason to predict that a full symphony orchestra is performing outside the spacecraft; hence, the acoustical aspect of the music is not transported to the STM. It is encoded by sensory memory but it is not predicted by inferences derived from the LTM and hence it is unattended to.

Thus, the main phenomenal experience at the STM visual narrative is one of a narrative with visual, verbal, and emotional components (but not music *qua* sound). Once attended in STM, the information about the narrative can itself be stored in LTM and form the basis of new inferences. In parallel, acoustical aspects of the music can be processed at a conscious level (see levels C and D in the music column, Fig. 11.3), as it is known that simultaneous tasks can co-occur (Neisser & Becklen 1975), and there is evidence that background music is remembered (Smith 1996). A similar process is envisioned for speech as well, but this is not the focus of the present chapter.

--------

[2] In Grossberg's (1996) theory, 'when both bottom and top-down signals are simultaneously active, only the bottom-up signals that receive top-down support can remain active . . . Top-down matching hereby generates a focus of attention that can resonate across processing levels, including those that generate the top-down signals. Such a resonance acts as a trigger that activates learning processes within the system. Resonance is also proposed to be a necessary condition for conscious attention'.

### 11.3.4 Emotion

Emotion cuts through six of the eight functions of film music identified by Cohen (1999*a*): contributing to the narrative's continuity; emotional meaning of events; induction of mood; creation and activation of memory (state dependence, heightening attention to particular events, providing cues in leitmotiv); maintenance of arousal, global attention, and associated sense of reality; and, finally, aesthetic experience. Hence emotion enters at every level of the proposed framework: analysis of structure and meaning, directing emotional meaning to STM, cuing the inference process of LTM, and the matching of LTM and STM representations.

In regard to the nature of experienced emotions generated by music in the context of film, it is useful to consider six criteria of a genuine emotion that Tan (1996) outlined, based for the most part on Frijda's (1986) laws of emotion.[3]

1. *Control precedence.* Music controls emotion response (Thayer & Faith 2000; Thayer & Levenson 1983), hence, like other genuine emotions, emotion created by background music exerts control over the audience member. These effects can result simply from bottom-up analysis of the stimuli, although higher-order learned associations may also play a role.

2. *Law of concern: emotion entails identifiable concern.* When music is combined with other media, the music readily finds an object. Cook (1998) provides clear examples of this with respect to advertising. Marshall and Cohen (1988) explained that music directed attention to an object and ascribed its meaning to that object. Attention is required for concern. Music directs such attention (see horizontal arrow from music to vision at level B in Fig. 11.2).

3. *Law of situational meaning (or stimulus specificity).* Each emotion has a particular 'situational meaning structure', a set of critical characteristics of the stimulus. Characteristics of musical stimuli giving rise to particular emotions have been identified by various researchers (e.g. Juslin 1997; Juslin & Madison 1999; Krumhansl 1997; Rigg 1964), and similarities between these characteristics and visually depicted emotions through gait, posture, and speech intonation have also been noted (for a summary, see Boltz *et al.* 1991; see also Juslin, this volume). Some aspects of the emotional meaning of music transfer directly to film (Iwamiya 1994; Sirius & Clarke 1994; Smith 1999).

4. *Law of apparent reality: the stimulus must represent some reality or other* (see also Tan 1996, p. 67). Music contributes to the sense of reality of the narrative (first demonstrated in the 'talkies' in Steiner's score for *King Kong*; cf. Palmer 1990, p. 28). It accentuates important events. The contribution of only the emotional components of the music to the diegesis has been described in Section 11.2 and explained via Fig. 11.3 (see, in particular, the diagonal arrow between levels B and C).

5. *Law of change: emotion responds to changes in the situation* (see also Tan 1996, p. 56). Music creates an everchanging auditory environment that establishes expectations

---

[3] But see Russell and Barrett's (1999) practical guide to assessment of emotion in which they claim that films do not induce true emotion, what they refer to as emotional episodes.

and implications, some of which are realized and some of which are violated. As such it is a fertile source of emotion (see also Meyer 1956).

6. *Law of closure: an emotion tends toward complete realization of its appraisal and action tendency, and is relatively immune to outside influences such as conscious control.* Music commands interest, especially in a darkened film theatre, as described by Münsterberg (1970). The emotion generated by music is governed by the tension and resolution established by the music of which the audience is unaware (cf. Thompson *et al.* 1994) and over which one seems to have little control, although this is a matter for further empirical work. Rehearing music reproduces emotional responses regardless of prior expectations (e.g. Jourdain 1997).

Thus, having satisfied the six constraints described by Tan (1996), it can be concluded that music contributes genuine emotional experience in a film. The congruence-associationist framework has provided a perspective for understanding how different aspects of music contribute to this outcome, although much still remains to be explained.

## 11.4 Emotion and the film-score composer

It is well to say that music is a source of emotion in film, but the ultimate source is the composer. The average theatre-goer appreciates the emotion established by film music but would be hard pressed to compose this music. Whereas many classical composers have created film scores (e.g. Saint-Saens, Satie, Britten, Honegger, Milhaud, Prokofiev, Shostakovitch, Vaughan Williams, Bernstein, Copland, Schuller, and Corigliano), such composition is often regarded as a special talent and preoccupation, exemplified by George Steiner, Miklós Rósza, Erich Korngold, Bernard Hermann, Dimitri Tiomkin, John Williams, Rachel Portman, and Ennio Morricone among others. Composers known primarily for their film music, have also been recognized for classical music composition, for example, Rósza and Korngold.

According to film-score composer Victor Young, the film-score composer is characterized by exceptional exactitude, diplomacy, and patience, in addition to musical training (cited in Karlin 1994, p. 310). Music composition for film differs from music composition for its own aesthetic sake. Typically film music is music produced for the sake of the story. It is constrained by the intent of the director, narrative, time, and budget. Working within these constraints, the composer may be regarded as exploiting his or her metacognition of the operations described in the framework of Fig. 11.3. The composer must know how shared audiovisual accent patterns can focus visual attention, how musical information avoids conscious attention, how mood is established, how musical associations provoke inferences through reinforcement or counterpoint, and how inferences are cued and generated via LTM to further the diegesis.

The composer is usually called upon at the end of the film production (Palmer 1980; Rózsa 1982, p. 191; some exceptions being Eisenstein and Hitchcock classics) and may be shown the film for the first time with recorded music already in place, known as temp tracks. The temp tracks indicate the director's wishes for type and placement of music, and therefore can restrict the composer's latitude considerably. In Henry

Mancini's opinion, familiarity with the temp tracks may bias the director against new insights offered by the composer (Brown 1994, p. 301). The composer's job is to replace the temp tracks with new material that must meet some or all of a number of constraints: to time the music cue to a fraction of a second to coincide with the rhythm of the action of a particular frame of the film, to match or create the mood or spirit of the film content, to use affordable orchestration and rehearsal time, to be unheard (unless the music is part of the diegesis) but be memorable, and to never drown out the dialogue (cf. Burt 1994, Chapter 6; Rózsa 1982, pp. 69, 108, and 110). In spite of these constraints, some composers, such as classically trained John Barry, claim that composing for film can be the ultimate freedom. Within these constraints, the composer can do whatever he or she wants and is assured of exposure.

Composing for film is one way of transmitting musical culture (e.g. Rózsa 1982, p. 205), because, as shown in Fig. 11.3, although the film music serves narrative function, it is also encoded in an information-processing channel devoted solely to music. Exposure to new compositional styles can be an added aspect of the film experience. For a recent example, *The Red Violin* may provide one's first exposure to the work of the contemporary composer John Corigliano. Films provide a major source for transmission of a culture's musical conventions. Thus, composing for film is a two-way street: the composer learns to code music to match the visual and emotional information of a narrative; at the same time, the film provides the composer with an opportunity to represent this emotional information in musically novel and creative ways, often to a large audience.

For a feature film, the composer may be given only a month of intensive work to score an hour of music. This pace is faster than that of a composer of 'music alone' but the genre is often, though not necessarily, redundant and characterized by cliché. The music does not have to stand independently, yet the possibility of (recent expectation for) a lucrative soundtrack album may create a challenge to compose music that lives on its own yet hardly reaches consciousness during the film.

Knowledge of the techniques and technology of film scoring can be acquired formally through courses, books, apprenticeships, or trial and error. The art of film music, however, perhaps more than other forms of music, requires 'taking the attitude of the other' (Meyer 1956, Chapter 1). Specific messages must be communicated in an aesthetic package, but the aesthetic goals may be secondary, unlike composing music alone. Like other skills, such as chess, bridge, music performance, or knowledge of a discipline, expertise in film-music composition may follow the 10-year rule of concentrated practice (Ericsson 1996). A young McGill University student composer, Aaron Hanson, in scoring an 8-minute film for a friend, spoke of the many hours of experimentation that were entailed until he achieved the effects he wanted. Presumably, like learning any language late in life, extensive effort is required to master the syntax and vocabulary. But the film-score language differs from languages learned from scratch in that the grammar of the film-music language is already known implicitly from exposure to music and film-music conventions. The film-score composer must turn that implicit knowledge into explicit knowledge and, in other words, must become an expert of the rules.

Research by Lipscomb and Kendall (1994) corroborates the notion that the professional film-score composer has the knowledge to create a score that uniquely matches a portion of the film. Moreover, the explicit knowledge of the composer is implicitly shared by the audience. Lipscomb and Kendall (1994) asked participants to select the best fitting of five film scores by Leonard Rosenman for a feature film, *Star Trek IV: The Voyage Home.* One of the scores had been originally composed for the excerpt and the remaining selections were by the same composer but drawn from other excerpts in the film. Confirming the effectiveness of Rosenman's music, the most frequent choice of the subjects was the actual score he had composed for the segment, although not every subject made this choice. Similarly, we recall from research previously reviewed by Bullerjahn and Güldenring (1994), that the professional film-score composer can systematically manipulate the inferences generated by the viewer/listener. Likewise, in the study by Thompson *et al.* (1994), the use of musical closure by the professional composer altered the judged closure in the film.

Some composers may be more suited to film-score composition than others in terms of both personality and motivation (which may play more of a role than talent, as is sometimes the case in regular musical achievement; see Sloboda 1996). The film composer must have a dramatic sense (Rózsa, cited in Brown 1994, p. 278), an appreciation of the visual world of film, and a sensitivity to speech nuances. Unlike many other types of composition, the creation of a film score is a collaborative process. Generally, interpersonal intelligence (Gardner 1993) would be necessary on two fronts: appreciation of the demands of socially shared cognition and the accurate assessment of common ground (Krauss & Fussell 1991), and the willingness to cooperate with the film production team (although the film composer Bernard Hermann was known to be irascible, according to Karlin 1994, p. 270). Korngold describes his positive relations with executive producers and others responsible for the film (cited in Carroll 1997, pp. 298–9) and claims that his artistry was not compromised in film composition. Similarly, Franz Waxman felt 'there was always room for fresh musical ideas in writing for the screen' (in Karlin 1994, p. 307).

## 11.5 Conclusion

Emotion characterizes the primary experience of both music (Sloboda 1985) and film (Münsterberg 1970; Tan 1996). Music typically plays an integral part of film. Kalinak's (1992, p. 87) argument for the importance of music to the emotional experience in classical narrative film finds support in much of the information presented in this chapter:

Scenes that most typically elicited the accompaniment of music were those that contained emotion. The classical narrative model developed certain conventions to assist expressive acting in portraying the presence of emotion . . . close-up, diffuse lighting and focus, symmetrical mise-en-scene, and heightened vocal intonation. The focal point of this process became the music which externalized these codes through the collective resonance of musical associations. *Music is, arguably, the most efficient of these codes,* [italics added] providing an audible definition of the emotion which the visual apparatus offers . . . Music's dual function of both articulator of screen expression and initiator of spectator response binds the spectator to the screen by resonating affect between them.

Kalinak's statement regarding the role of music as a source of emotion is a strong one. She has claimed that music is 'the most efficient code' for emotional expression in film. According to Kalinak (1992, p. 87): 'The lush, stringed passages accompanying a love scene are representations not only of the emotions of the diegetic characters but also of the spectator's own response which music prompts and reflects'. She is arguing that the simultaneity of both the representation and the elicitation of feeling is key. Though her analysis seems correct, more empirical research would be welcomed that compared the relative abilities of music and film to represent and elicit emotion.

That music contributes to the emotional expression and experience of film seems logical, yet surprisingly discussions of emotion in film often ignore music (e.g. Tan 1996). However, Münsterberg (1970) suggested that the psychological processes underlying film were more similar to those of music than to visual art or drama which on the surface might seem more similar. Experimental evidence since then has shown that music influences the interpretation of film narrative and that the music becomes integrated in the memory with the visual information. Music accomplishes other attentional functions through gestalt structural and associationist principles. In addition, the fact that music requires cognitive resources probably plays a role in determining absorption, arousal, and general attention. Music also contributes to the aesthetic experience of the film. More importantly, for present purposes, music in conjunction with film can satisfy Frijda's requirements, as identified by Tan (1996), of a stimulus that can support genuine emotion.

Film-music composition can be regarded as a type of problem solving that exploits knowledge of the musical rules that express and create emotion through specific musical relations. There are many goals that must be satisfied by the film-score composer: providing continuation, directing attention, inducing mood, communicating meaning, cuing memory, creating a sense of reality, and contributing to the aesthetic experience. The ultimate compositional goal is to produce sound patterns that express the emotion consistent with the narrative, the emotion that is jointly recognized and experienced by the audience, binding the spectator to the screen (Kalinak 1992, p. 87). The capacity of music to accomplish the emotional task, arguably far better than the screen itself as Kalinak has suggested, may be based on the ability of music to simultaneously carry many kinds of emotional information in its harmony, rhythm, melody, timbre, and tonality. Real life entails multiple emotions, simultaneously and in succession. Miraculously, yet systematically, these complex relations—this 'emotional polyphony'— can be represented by the musical medium. An example is Korngold's music from the classic film *Sea Hawk* that links romantic love and the spirit of childhood adventure: 'The music for the love scenes still makes an indelible impression with its sweeping heroic lyricism, characterized by arching, repeated rising sevenths that dovetail perfectly with a hypnotic and unforgettable horn call that is redolent of every schoolboy's dream of pirate adventure' (Carroll 1997, p. 254; other examples are provided by Steiner's ability to 'crystallize the essence of a film in a single theme', see Palmer 1990, pp. 29 and 48)

As depicted by the congruence-associationist cognitive framework presented here, and as argued by Cook (1998), music is strong in the representation of emotion in the abstract, and the screen is strong in representing the object to which the emotion is directed. While more research is warranted to further examine the simultaneous contribution of music to emotional meaning, mood, feeling, and absorption, there are sufficient data available now to conclude that music, owing in large part to the explicit knowledge and skills of the composer, provides one of the strongest sources of emotion in film.[4]

# References

Albersnagel, F. (1988). Velten and musical mood induction procedures: A comparison with accessibility of thought associations. *Behavior Research Theory*, **26**, 79–96.

Anderson, J. D. (1997). Introduction to the Symposium on Cognitive Science and the Future of Film Studies. In *Proceedings of Symposium Cognitive Science and the Future of Film Studies*, pp. 2–6. Lawrence, KS: University of Kansas. Retrieved 17 June 2000 from the WWW: http://www.gsu.edu./~wwwcom/ccsmi/vsnipi.htm.

Baars, B. J. (1997). *In the theater of consciousness: The workspace of the mind.* New York: Oxford University Press.

Banse, R. & Scherer, K. R. (1996). Acoustic profiles in vocal emotion expression. *Journal of Personality and Social Psychology*, **70**, 614–36.

Barrett, L. F. & Russell, J. A. (1999). The structure of current affect: Controversies and emerging consensus. *Current Directions in Psychological Science*, **8**, 10–14.

Bolivar, V. J., Cohen, A. J., & Fentress, J. C. (1994). Semantic and formal congruency in music and motion pictures: Effects on the interpretation of visual action. *Psychomusicology*, **13**, 28–59.

Boltz, M., Schulkind, M., & Kantra, S. (1991). Effects of background music on remembering of filmed events. *Memory and Cognition*, **19**, 595–606.

Bregman, A. (1990). *Auditory scene analysis.* Cambridge, MA: MIT Press.

Brown, R. (1994). *Overtones and undertones: Reading film music.* Berkeley, CA: University of California.

Bullerjahn, C. & Güldenring, M. (1994). An empirical investigation of effects of film music using qualitative content analysis. *Psychomusicology*, **13**, 99–118.

Burt, G. (1994). *The art of film music.* Boston: Northeastern University Press.

Carroll, B. G. (1997). *The last prodigy: A biography of Erich Wolfgang Korngold.* Oregon: Amadeus.

Cohen, A. J. (1990). Understanding musical soundtracks. *Empirical Studies of the Arts*, **8**, 111–24.

Cohen, A. J. (1993). Associationism and musical soundtrack phenomena. *Contemporary Music Review*, **9**, 163–78.

Cohen, A. J. (1994). Introduction to the special volume on the psychology of film music. *Psychomusicology*, **13**, 2–8.

Cohen, A. J. (1999*a*). The functions of music in multimedia: A cognitive approach. In *Music, mind, and science*, (ed. S. W. Yi), pp. 53–69. Seoul, Korea: Seoul National University Press.

Cohen, A. J. (1999*b*). Music serves as a vehicle in multimedia contexts. [CD-ROM] *Collected papers of the 137th Meeting of the Acoustical Society of America and the 2nd Convention of the European Acoustics Association* (CD rom, 4 pp). New York: Acoustical Society of America.

[4] The Social Sciences and Humanities Research Council is acknowledged for its support of the author's programme of research in the psychology of film music. Appreciation is expressed to four anonymous reviewers and colleague Thomy Nilsson for their comments on an earlier version of this manuscript. The advice of editors Patrik Juslin and John Sloboda is also gratefully acknowledged.

Cohen, A. J. (2000). Film music: Perspectives from cognitive psychology. In *Music and cinema,* (ed. J. Buhler, C. Flinn, & D. Neumeyer). Middlebury, VT: Wesleyan University Press.

Copland, A. (1941). *Our new music.* New York: McGraw-Hill.

Cook, N. (1998). *Analysing musical multimedia.* Oxford, UK: Clarendon Press.

Driver, J. (1997). Enhancement of selective listening by illusory mislocation of speech sounds due to lip-reading. *Nature, 381,* 66–8.

Eich, E. (1995). Searching for mood dependent memory. *Psychological Science, 6,* 67–75.

Ericsson, K. A. (1996). The acquisition of expert performance: An introduction to some of the issues. In *The road to excellence: The acquisition of expert performance in the arts and sciences, sports and games,* (ed. K. A. Ericsson), pp. 1–50. Mahwah, NJ: Erlbaum.

Frijda, N. H. (1986). *The emotions.* Cambridge, UK: Cambridge University Press.

Gabrielsson, A. (1998). Verbal description of music experience. In *Proceedings of the Fifth International Conference on Music Perception and Cognition,* (ed. S. W. Yi), pp. 271–6. Seoul: Seoul National University.

Gabrielsson, A. & Lindström, S. (1993). On strong experiences of music. *Jarbuch der Deutschen Gesellschaft für Musikpsychologie, 10,* 114–25.

Gardner, H. (1993). *Frames of mind: The theory of multiple intelligences.* New York: Basic Books (originally publisher 1983).

Gorbman, C. (1987). *Unheard melodies: Narrative film music.* Bloomington, IN: Indiana University Press.

Gregory, A. H. (1998). Tracking the emotional response to operatic arias. In *Proceedings of the Fifth International Conference on Music Perception and Cognition,* (ed. S. W. Yi), pp. 265–70. Seoul: Seoul National University.

Grossberg, S. (1995). The attentive brain. *American Scientist, 83,* 438–49.

Grossberg, S. (1996). *The attentive brain: Perception, learning, and consciousness* (abstract). Retrieved 6 June 2000 from the WWW: http://www-math.mit.edu/amc/fall96/grossberg.html.

Heider, F. & Simmel, M. (1944). An experimental study of apparent behavior. *American Journal of Psychology, 57,* 243–59.

Hochberg, J. & Brooks, V. (1996a). Movies in the mind's eye. In *Post-theory: Reconstructing film studies,* (ed. D. Bordwell & N. Carroll), pp. 368–87. Madison, WI: University of Wisconsin Press.

Hochberg, J. & Brooks, V. (1996b). The perception of motion pictures. In *Cognitive ecology,* (ed. M. P. Friedman & E. C. Carterette), pp. 205–92. New York: Academic Press.

Iwamiya, S. (1994). Interaction between auditory and visual processing when listening to music in an audio visual context. *Psychomusicology, 13,* 133–53.

Jourdain, R. (1997). *Music, the brain and ecstacy: How music captures our imagination.* New York: Morrow.

Juslin, P. N. (1997). Emotional communication in music performance: A functionalist perspective and some data. *Music Perception, 14,* 383–418.

Juslin, P. N. & Madison, G. (1999). The role of timing patterns in recognition of emotional expression from musical performance. *Music Perception, 17,* 197–221.

Kalinak, K. (1992). *Settling the score.* Madison, WI: University of Wisconsin Press.

Karlin, F. (1994). *Listening to the movies.* New York: Schirmer.

Kintsch, W. (1998). *Comprehension: A paradigm for cognition.* Cambridge, UK: Cambridge University Press.

Kracauer, S. (1960). *Theory of film: The redemption of physical reality.* Oxford, UK: Oxford University Press.

Krauss, R. M. & Fussell, S. R. (1991). Constructing shared communicative environments. In *Socially shared cognition.,* (ed. L. Resnick, J. M. Levine, & S. D. Teasley), pp. 172–200. Washington, DC: American Psychological Association.

Krumhansl, C. L. (1997). An exploratory study of musical emotions and psychophysiology. *Canadian Journal of Psychology,* 51, 336–52.

Lang, P. J. (1995). The emotion probe. *American Psychologist,* 50, 372–85.

Levi, D.S. (1982). The structural determinants of melodic expressive properties. *Journal of Phenomenological Psychology,* 13, 19–44.

Levin, D. T. & Simons, D. J. (1998). Failure to detect changes to people during a real-world interaction. *Psychonomic Bulletin and Review,* 5, 644–9.

Levin, D. T. & Simons, D. J. (2000). Perceiving stability in a changing world: Combining shots and integrating views in motion pictures and the real world. *Media Psychology,* 2, 357–80.

Levinson, J. (1996). Film music and narrative agency. In *Post-theory: Reconstructing film studies,* (ed. D. Bordwell & N. Carroll), pp. 248–82. Madison, WI: University of Wisconsin Press.

Limbacher, J. L. (1974). *Film music.* Metuchen, NJ: Scarecrow.

Lipscomb, S. (1999). Cross-modal integration: Synchronization of auditory and visual components in simple and complex media. *Collected papers of the 137th Meeting of the Acoustical Society of America and the 2nd Convention of the European Acoustics Association* (CD rom, 4 pp). New York: Acoustical Society of America.

Lipscomb, S. & Kendall, R. (1994). Perceptual judgment of the relationship between musical and visual components in film. *Psychomusicology,* 13, 60–98.

Mack, A. & Rock, I. (1998). *Inattentional blindness.* Cambridge, MA: MIT Press

Madsen, C. K. (1997). Emotional response to music. *Psychomusicology,* 16, 59–67

Magliano, J. P., Dijkstra, K., & Zwaan, R. A. (1996). Generating predictive inferences while viewing a movie. *Discourse processes,* 22, 199–224.

Marks, M. (1997). *Music and the silent film.* New York: Oxford University Press.

Marshall, S. & Cohen, A. J. (1988). Effects of musical soundtracks on attitudes to geometric figures. *Music Perception,* 6, 95–112.

Meyer, L. B. (1956). *Emotion and meaning in music.* Chicago: University of Chicago Press.

Münsterberg, H. (1970). *The photoplay: A psychological study.* New York: Arno (originally published 1916).

Murray, I. R. & Arnott, J. L. (1993). Toward the simulation of emotion in synthetic speech: A review of the literature on human vocal emotion. *Journal of the Acoustical Society of America,* 93, 1097–108.

Narmour, E. (1991). The top-down and bottom-up systems of musical implication: Building on Meyer's theory of emotional syntax. *Music Perception,* 9, 1–26.

Neisser, U. & Becklen, R. (1975). Selective looking: Attending to visually significant events. *Cognitive Psychology,* 7, 480–94.

Osgood, C. E., Suci, G. J., & Tannenbaum, P. H. (1957). *The measurement of meaning.* Urbana, IL: University of Illinois Press.

Palmer, C. (1980). Film music. In *New Grove dictionary of music and musicians,* (Vol 6) (ed. S. Sadie), pp. 549–56. Washington, DC: Macmillan.

Palmer, C. (1990). *The composer in Hollywood.* New York: Marion Boyars.

Pignatiello, M. F., Camp, C. J., & Rasar, L. (1986). Musical mood induction: An alternative to the Velten technique. *Journal of Abnormal Psychology*, 95, 295–7.

Prendergast, R. M. (1991). *Film music: A neglected art*, (2nd edn). New York: Norton.

Preston, J. M. (1999). From mediated environments to the development of consciousness. In *Psychology and the internet: Intrapersonal, interpersonal, and transpersonal implications*, (ed. J. Gackenbach), pp. 255–91. San Diego, CA: Academic Press.

Qian, J., Preston, J., & House, M. (1999). Personality trait absorption and reality status evaluations of narrative mediated messages. Paper presented at the Annual Meeting of the American Psychological Association, Boston, MA, August 1999.

Revonsuo, A. & Newman, J. (1999). Binding and consciousness. *Consciousness and Cognition*, 8, 123–7.

Rigg, M. G. (1964). The mood effects of music: A comparison of data from four investigations. *Journal of Psychology*, 58, 427–38.

Rosar, W. (1994). Film music and Heinz Werner's theory of physionomic perception. *Psychomusicology*, 13, 154–65.

Rózsa, M. (1982). *Double life*. New York: Hippocrene Books.

Russell, J. A. & Barrett, L. F. (1999). Core affect, prototypical emotional episodes, and other things called emotion: Dissecting the elephant. *Journal of Personality and Social Psychology*, 76, 805–19.

Saint-Saens, C. (1903/1951). The composer as psychologist. In *Pleasures of music*, (ed. J. Barzun), pp. 258–64. New York: Viking Press.

Schubert, E. (1998). Time series analysis of emotion in music. In *Proceedings of the Fifth International Conference on Music Perception and Cognition*, (ed. S. W. Yi). pp. 257–63. Seoul, Korea: Seoul National University.

Sirius, G. & Clarke, E. F. (1994). The perception of audiovisual relationships: A preliminary study. *Psychomusicology*, 13, 119–32.

Sloboda, J. A. (1985). *The musical mind: The cognitive psychology of music*. New York: Oxford University Press.

Sloboda, J. A. (1992). Empirical studies of emotional response to music. In *Cognitive bases of musical communication*, (ed. M. R. Jones & S. Holleran), pp. 33–46. Washington, DC: American Psychological Association.

Sloboda, J. A. (1996). The acquisition of musical performance expertise: Deconstructing the 'talent' account of individual differences in musical expressivity. In *The road to excellence: The acquisition of expert performance in the arts and sciences, sports and games*, (ed. K. A. Ericsson), pp. 107–26. Mahwah, NJ: Erlbaum.

Smith, J. (1996). Unheard melodies? A critique of psychoanalytic theories of film music. In *Post-theory: Reconstructing film studies*, (ed. D. Bordwell & N. Carroll), pp. 230–48. Madison, WI: University of Wisconsin Press.

Smith, J. (1999). Movie music as moving music: Emotion, cognition, and the film score. In *Passionate views*, (ed. C. Plantinga & G. M. Smith), pp 146–67. Baltimore, MD: Johns Hopkins University Press.

Storm, C. & Storm, T. (1987). A taxonomic study of the vocabulary of emotions. *Journal of Personality and Social Psychology*, 53, 805–16.

Tan, W. (ed.) (1996). *Emotion and the structure of narrative film: Film as an emotion machine*. Mahwah, NJ: Erlbaum.

Thayer, J. F. & Faith, M. (2000). A dynamical systems model of musically induced emotions: Physiological and self-report evidence. Poster presented at the New York Academy of Sciences Conference on the Biological Foundations of Music, New York, June 2000.

Thayer, J. F. & Levenson, R. (1983). Effects of music on psychophysiological responses to a stressful film. *Psychomusicology,* 3, 44–54.

Thomas, T. (1997). *Music for the movies,* (2nd edn). Los Angeles: Silman-James.

Thompson, W. F., Russo, F. A., & Sinclair, D. (1994). Effects of underscoring on the perception of closure in filmed events. *Psychomusicology,* 13, 9–27.

Wertheimer, M. (1939). Laws of organization in perceptual forms. In *A source book of gestalt psychology,* (ed. W. D. Ellis), pp. 71–88. New York: Harcourt Brace.

Zwaan, R. A. (1999). Situation models: The mental leap into imagined worlds. *Current Directions in Psychological Science,* 8, 15–18.

# PART IV

# THE PERFORMER

# CHAPTER 12

# THE SUBJECTIVE WORLD OF THE PERFORMER

ROLAND S. PERSSON

'A musician cannot move others unless he too is moved', C. P. E. Bach argued in his treatise on the true art of playing keyboard instruments, 'He must of necessity feel all of the affects that he hopes to arouse in his audience' (1985, p. 152). Famed singer Janet Baker, in an interview published in *The Observer*, stated of musicians in general that '. . . [their] business is emotion and sensitivity—to be the sensors of the human race' (quoted in Crofton & Fraser 1985, p. 112).

Clearly emotions, feelings, and affects are paramount issues to musicians in communicating and understanding music. In fact, the musician's role is so intrinsically tied to the subjective world of emotion that attempts to regard a piece of music, or a performance of it, as in any way detached from a positive emotional experience of some kind, is often frowned upon by musicians. In composer Fredrick Delius' words: 'How can music ever be a mere intellectual speculation or a series of curious combinations of sound that can be classified like the articles in a grocer's shop? Music is an outburst of the soul' (quoted in Crofton & Fraser 1985, p. 49).

The reasons that music has emotional significance, however, are complex and often paradoxical. This is particularly true in regarding the interplay between the dynamics of socially determined criteria for what is considered a piece of music, or a performance, of 'good quality' and the different aspects of music cognition (Persson, 2000). Without the potential to evoke some type of emotional response, however, music as a cultural phenomenon would most probably lose its basically universal appeal (Gregory & Varney 1996).

This chapter outlines exploratory research into the *phenomenology* of emotion in musical performance, which includes performance motivation and generation, as well as the learning and conceptualization process of constructing 'musical meaning'. Most of the material providing the framework for this chapter is based on exploratory qualitative and quantitative research in combination, pursued in a real-world research setting; that is, in a tertiary British music institution (Persson 1993, 1995, 1996, 2000; Persson *et al.* 1996; Persson & Robson 1995; Robson 1993). Data were generated interactively between researchers and musicians as co-researchers, to accommodate the potential conflict between representatives of traditional science and art as reported by, for example, Hurford (1988), Kingsbury (1988), and Persson (1993).

The purpose of the presented research was to seek hitherto untried ways in music-behavioural research to explore the understanding of a limited number of expert performers' subjectivity. Hence, the results of the research presented here should not be understood as an effort to generalize findings. They are rather the basis for further research and provide an *initial* understanding of how musicians may construe the subjective aspects of musical behaviour.

## 12.1 Why become a performer?

An obvious first question in seeking to understand the subjective world of the musical performer is to ask what made certain individuals choose a musical career. Nagel (1987), from a largely psychodynamic perspective, has suggested that musicians make such a choice on the basis of gratification of needs, which entails: (a) certain emotion-evoking qualities in the music itself; (b) the potentially positive social feedback of the musical setting: (c) a means to explore devouring and aggressive impulses by the specific motor skills involved in playing an instrument; and (d) a degree of exhibitionism and voyeuristic impulses. However, early relationships, such as the support and encouragement of parents and significant others, also play an important role. One example of this is renowned violinist Ernst Wallfisch (quoted in McDonald 1970, pp. 514–15):

Music played such a big part in my life from the beginning . . . and I recall much . . . my father was a businessman and an amateur violinist . . . music was his big hobby . . . his circle of friends included many like him and chamber music seemed part of living . . . I can remember as a very small boy all of these people in our home talking, laughing, smoking cigars, and making music.

However, relationships in this context may also be understood as finding certain role models, or 'heroes', who possess certain attractive attributes or qualities, which the developing musician wishes to master or in some way emulate. Drummer Steve Gadd, for example, made several famous jazz musicians his role models (quoted in Boyd & George-Warren 1992, p. 125):

When I was a young teenager . . . my father used to take me to clubs to hear a lot of organ groups, where the groove got so intense . . . The music was feeling so good you just couldn't sit still. That feeling made you want to be a part of what was creating it . . . I heard a lot of jazz groups like Dizzy [Gillespie], and Oscar Peterson, Max Roach, Gene Krupa, and I loved them all. Can remember listening to Tony Williams and Elvin Jones, listening to things over and over again . . . They touched me so much. You get something from everyone you hear; you try to take it and use it and pass it on.

Motte-Haber (1984), taking a broader theoretical view of what motivates musicians, proposed that achievement motivation, curiosity, self-actualization, the conquering of failure anxiety, as well as the fear of success should all be considered in understanding the basis of motivation specific to learning and mastering a musical instrument. Hallam (1998) puts forward self-determination as an additional variable.

Persson (1993) and Persson *et al.* (1996), in interviewing piano performers, and combining qualitative analyses of open-ended responses with factor-analytical procedures on given variables, relating to different aspects of motivation as found in the literature, established a tentative typology of motivation specific to performance motivation (Table 12.1). Although a small sample of participants ($n = 15$; of whom ten were male and five were female), the musicians were very eloquent in discussing their interest in music and their choice of a musical career.

Table 12.1 Components of musical performance motivation as elicited amongst pianists ($n = 15$). The main motive categories are listed in order of significance (from Persson 1993)

|   | Type of motivation | Description (and function) |
|---|---|---|
| 1 | Hedonic motive | The search for positive emotional experience |
| 2 | Social motive | The significance of group identity and belonging |
| 3 | Achievement motives: | |
|   | 3a Exhibitionism | A desire to show results of an effort |
|   | 3b Independence | The means to achievement are secondary to success itself |
|   | 3c Dependence | The means to achievement are important, but do not constitute the ultimate target |
|   | 3d Aesthetics | The means also provide the target |
|   | 3e Support | Motives are extrinsically provided, mainly by teachers and parents |

While motives differed considerably amongst the musicians, they all had in common that their musical pursuit offered, for different reasons, satisfaction. Most participants were therefore motivated primarily by a *hedonic* motive; that is, treasuring music as a means to generate positive emotional experiences mostly for one's own satisfaction. A typical response given by the participants was, for example: 'Mood is a big one for me. You have to be in the right mood, because sometimes you can be sort of in a state where you can't exactly get yourself into how the music should be played. Sometimes you sit down and play as if . . . Ahhhh! [The musician sighs profoundly] You can really *feel* everything in the music' (quoted in Persson 1993, p. 150).

Social motives were also significant in choosing a musical career. It is important to belong to a certain group that has certain desirable attributes with which one identifies. While such identification is occasionally prevented by the so-called 'maestro' function (Persson 1996, 2000), the weight of social motive amongst the musicians interviewed may also suggest that performers are not necessarily the self-sufficient 'lone rangers' that the historical and mythical tradition of the musical maestro often would tempt us to believe (cf. Braudy 1997; Osborne 1990). On the contrary, social identification with a certain musical setting, group, or mentor, as some research has shown, is very important, even a key factor in optimizing musical and artistic development (Manturzewska 1990; Ruud 1997).

Achievement motives, interestingly, tended not to be a priority in the studied group. That is not to say, of course, they do not play a significant role in any career or goal setting. Six types of achievement motivation were identified. Some were exhibitionistic and revealed a desire to show off the results of an effort (cf. Nagel 1987). One informant typically exclaimed, when asked whether he liked being alone on a stage to perform: 'Oh lovely! I enjoy that!' Others were categorized as being independently motivated (where the means to achievement are secondary to success itself):

. . . basically, it is the attention to yourself, wanting to achieve something. Music is something I enjoy. I have always had this drive in me to do well in whatever I do, so it is not necessarily just music but any other thing . . . I enjoy cooking . . . and I know I do it well because I enjoy it. (Quoted in Persson 1993, pp. 154–5)

However, some participants were categorized as dependently motivated (where the means to achievement are important, but do not constitute the ultimate target of the musical pursuit): 'I've got this degree. That is motivating for me but I don't wish to be famous by the end of it. I want to do something administrative, which is not so much performance-related really' (quoted in Persson 1993, p. 155).

A few were driven mainly by an aesthetic motive in which the means also provide the target itself. One example of this would be one of the participating performance teachers, who ardently argued that 'Music making is for its own sake, isn't it? You want to feel that you have measured up to what the music demands' (quoted in Persson 1993, p. 266). Well-known violinist Isaac Stern (1979) similarly remarks, in an interview published in *The New York Times Magazine*, that 'somewhere along the line the child must become possessed by music, by the sudden desire to play'.

Finally, some participants felt that the reason they chose a musical career was mainly due to extrinsic motivation. These participants were categorized as displaying a supported achievement motive (where motives are mainly extrinsically supplied by teachers and/or parents). A typical response was the following: 'When you are a child, it is difficult to separate out those [motivational aspects]. I was kind of forced into doing it then, but about the age of twelve I *wanted* to do it' (quoted in Persson 1993, p. 157).

## 12.2 Determinants of performance generation

Although there are many reasons for embracing a musical career, the importance of being able to control and induce pleasant emotional experience by means of playing appears to be the most fundamental consideration amongst the musicians participating in Persson *et al.*'s (1996) study. If emotions and the phenomenology of experiencing music are paramount to many, if not all, musicians, then, which are more specifically the potential determinants of generating and conceptualizing any particular performance?

The question of what makes a musical interpretation 'artistic' has fascinated the cognitive science of music for some time, and the pursuit of understanding just how performers manipulate musical parameters (e.g. tempo, timbre, dynamics, articulation) to obtain an optimal performance has led to the study of algorithms for computer-generated performances (e.g. Friberg 1991), generative principles as based on motor skills and the nature of their programming (Clarke 1988; Parncutt *et al.* 1997), as well as the nature of specific mental representations (Lehmann 1997). As important as these research efforts are, however, the notions of 'feeling' (the term often preferred by musicians) and 'emotional experience' (the term usually preferred by behavioural science), so important to the musicians themselves, are conspicuously absent from this literature.

While questions have been asked how music, and musicians, communicate emotions to listeners and how music-interpretational intentions are perceived by them (e.g. Clynes 1989; Gabrielsson & Juslin 1996; Juslin 1997, 2000; Ohgushi & Senju 1987; Rapoport 1996; Waterman 1996; see also Juslin, this volume), the question of individual conceptualization and its emotional significance is elusive to a traditional psychological research paradigm, and has therefore rarely been asked. Classical in its field, of course, is Meyer's (1956) treatise *Emotion and meaning in music*, but only recently have attempts been made to address the issue of musical meaning by empirical research (e.g. Sloboda 1998; Watt & Ash 1998).

To understand the nature of motor programming, mental representations, and musical meaning more fully, music psychological researchers also need to ask *why* a performer plays in a certain way but not in another, and by what means—other than motor programming strategies and melodic and harmonic memorization procedures—musicians learn a piece of music as well as recreate it in a performance situation. Although there is some controversy about whether or not emotion and cognition should be regarded as separate systems, it is nevertheless well established that cognition and emotion affect each other in different ways in different circumstances (cf. Lazarus *et al.* 1980; Zajonc 1980). Hence, emotions inevitably play a significant role in learning, conceptualizing, and performing music also (cf. Bower 1992). There is therefore a need for music psychology—and perhaps even more so for music education—to begin to understand 'the emotional frame of mind' that generates recall, certain motor patterns, and communicative potential.

### 12.2.1 Performers and imagery

In a series of studies, Persson (1993) endeavoured to explore and chart the emotional aspects of conceptualizing music for a performance. A piece of music (Russian composer Reinhold Glière's *Prelude*, Opus 31, No. 1), unknown to all of the 15 participating pianists from a tertiary British music institution, was chosen because of its manifold interpretational ambiguity, and used as a stimulus in the research design. The musicians were all asked to learn and study the piece for 2 weeks, after which it would be performed, recorded, and discussed in an in-depth interview with the researcher. All interpretational clues provided in the score by the composer, including the title of the piece, were erased. Participants were specifically asked to deal with the music in a way that felt appropriate to them, rather than to consider traditional conventions for any given musical style. In other words, musicians were encouraged to break with perceived conventions should they think it necessary to optimize the conceptualization process.

During the period of study, participants were also asked to supply a descriptive title, which they thought suited the piece and their understanding of it. The title then became the point of departure for the interview on how the performers conceptualized the music at hand. Interview transcripts were verified by the participants themselves and were subsequently subject to analysis (for an exhaustive outline of research strategy and analytical models, see Persson 1993). To prompt musicians to elicit a title was believed to reveal something about the process by which they arrived at an individual understanding of the studied music. Seashore (1938), for example, as possibly the only music psychologist who has addressed the issue, argued in his time that musical imagery is *necessary* in all forms of musical memory:

In vivid musical memory we relive the music. The person who does not have the capacity to do so may recall in abstract terms; such as the musical notation or even the most refined logical concepts of elements in musical performance and musical criticism. But these are only the cold facts. He does not relive the music . . . The non-emotional person can recall the cold facts, but these facts are not the essence of the music, the welling up of musical emotion . . . I have developed a classification of types of musical imagination in terms of which we can readily classify musicians with whom we are acquainted. Basic types in such classification are the sensuous, the intellectual, the sentimental, the impulsive, and the motor. Any given individual may be dominantly one of these types but ordinarily the personality represents integration of two or more. (Seashore 1938, pp. 168–72)

Not all participants in the study succeeded in finding a descriptive title, and not everyone, as Seashore (1938) would have predicted, was keen on labelling a piece of music in such a way. Following instructions, however, all supplied the piano piece with a title (Table 12.2). Even the reluctant musicians' choices were important to the research, since in spite of their reluctance, they nevertheless had to draw from the musical structure to find something appropriately descriptive. Musical structure is related to emotional response (Sloboda 1991; see also Gabrielsson & Lindström, this volume).

Table 12.2 Participating musicians' descriptive titles, types of titles, and duration of performance ($n = 15$). A denotes student performers and B their teachers (from Persson 1993)

| Performer | Chosen title | Type of choice | Duration |
|---|---|---|---|
| A1 | By the water's edge | Mood/semblance | 2' 14" |
| A2 | Lazy Sunday by the river | Semblance | 1' 48" |
| A3 | Rain | Semblance | 1' 47" |
| A4 | Soaring | Mood/semblance | 1' 53" |
| A5 | Thoughts | Semblance | 1' 39" |
| A6 | Falling feelings | Mood/semblance | 2' 13" |
| A7 | Portrait of a lost love | Mood | 2' 40" |
| A8 | The typical romantic | Idiom/mood | 1' 39" |
| A9 | Saturday sprinting | Semblance | 1' 06" |
| A10 | Autumn | Mood/semblance | 3' 20" |
| A11 | Coming home | Mood/semblance | 1' 48" |
| B1 | Souvenir de Chaminade | Idiom | 1' 58" |
| B2 | Song without words | Idiom | 2' 22" |
| B3 | Melancholy (tristesse) | Mood | 2' 00" |
| B4 | I wonder why? Warum? Warum? Pourqoui? Pourqoui? | Structure | 2' 13" |

Mean performance duration was 2' 00".

Titles appear to have been chosen according to mainly four criteria: *semblance* prompted musicians to provide a title in relation to some extramusical association, whereas *mood* made the participants rather focus on their affective response to the music. A musician who appeared to follow a strategy of semblance when learning the music at hand would typically explain his or her choice of title in the following way (quoted in Persson 1993, p. 189):

Sitting by the river, listening to the quiet lap of water. Obviously a warm day! Perhaps going there every day; leisure on the banks, passing dykes, the occasional wildlife here and there . . . well, my descriptive title is rubbish. It is *Lazy Sunday by the river*. The title is rather corny, but—to me—that is what it conjures up . . . It wasn't really telling a story. It was more sort of a scene 'à la Debussy'.

An individual who was categorized as relying mainly on mood would rather respond, for example, in the following representative manner (quoted in Persson 1993, p. 189):

When I read the instruction on the sheet, I thought 'Oh no!', because I remember . . . I could never give pieces and compositions a title. But when I actually started to play [the provided piece], no hassle at all. I was really surprised at the title. I couldn't decide between *Falling leaves* or *Falling feelings*. I wanted 'falling' because I got the impression that the whole . . . The theme is always falling . . . I said falling because I think it is quite a sad piece—melancholy.

Some performers, however, focused on *idiom* when selecting a title as they tried to identify the music stylistically. These participants would argue that the music described nothing but itself. One performer insisted that *structure* was the most significant criterion according to which a title should be chosen. This particular performer argued that there were similarities between melodic phrases and language inflection in several languages, hence her chosen title 'I wonder why? Warum? Warum? Pourquoi? Pourquoi?'.

In further discussions with the participating musicians, the significance of imagery in learning and conceptualizing music was probed. The discussion with each individual was, of course, linked to their choice of title. It would seem that all participants made use of imagery in one way or another in order to construe understanding and meaning, although some would argue that they did not. The analysis of the interviews, however, suggests that learning a piece of music, at least for the occasion staged as part of the research project, most certainly entails a framework of memories that is more extensive than merely relating it to pitch, dynamics, timbre, and the social conventions of interpretation. It also suggests that imagery is used *differently* by musicians.

Participants clearly differentiated between *emotional memory* (associating to anything that might trigger an emotional response, that is also compatible with the qualities inherent in the musical structure) and *memory of an emotion* (recalling a certain emotion, or pattern of emotions, in order to evoke a certain state of mind, which is perceived as appropriate for the piece of music to be studied or performed, and that may, or may not, entail visual imagery; cf. Stanislavsky 1988). The musicians also prioritized one or the other: five participants regarded visual imagery (in terms of emotional memory) as their primary concern in conceptualizing or performing music and memory of emotion was secondary. Eight musicians felt that memory of emotion was primary and visual memory only secondary in importance. Four participants avoided the issue altogether and appeared to feel uncomfortable with discussing music in these terms. However, such a reaction is not to say that these participants did not conceptualize music in a like manner. Their reluctance to discuss and reflect on music in this way is likely, at some level, to be socially determined and to some extent also be influenced by type of personality, as evidenced in participants' sometimes contradictory statements on what they *wished* to do with a particular interpretation and what they felt they *had* to do.

### 12.2.2 Emotion and self-induction to altered states of awareness

One particularly important finding in the exploratory research on the generation and conceptualization of musical performance was how musicians—some more than others—very consciously manipulated recall of certain memories (emotional memories and memories of emotions) in order to 'get into the mood'. Out of 15 participating pianists, eight acknowledged some sort of self-discovered technique to arrive at a particular emotional frame of mind for the sake of learning and/or performing. Three musicians were identified as systematically employing what could appropriately be labelled *mood induction* (that is, to remember the sensation of a certain specific emotion without necessarily conjuring up specific imagery). Five musicians, however, used induction by means of *visualization* in order to evoke a particular emotion. The aim of both strategies was to form the basis of their particular understanding of the music at hand. A musician applying mood induction would typically say:

I find often that to get me into the mood of a piece, say the 'Pathétique Sonata' by Beethoven, and the opening of that, you think something sad. You think *sadly*, not necessarily something that has happened to you, but you think of *the experience of sadness* before you play that chord . . . [it] is a subconscious thing and you are just trying to bring it out' (quoted in Persson 1993, p. 197).

Other performers seemed to combine both mood induction and visualization, depending on circumstance, to attain a certain frame of mind for the performance:

I very rarely resort to just [the technical]. I don't like that! To me, I'd rather have it musical. [That is], you can see a sense in things; see pictures and images, and feel things. If you're not in the mood for that [music, which you have at hand] you are obviously not going to do justice to it. I suppose being a musician you have to get into the mood of it. (Quoted in Persson 1993, p. 198)

Both approaches are reminiscent of what the musicians of the baroque and classical eras, following the influential 'doctrine of affections' (Bukofzer 1947; see also Cook & Dibben, this volume), then prescribed as a necessity for 'true' performing musicians: 'A musician cannot move others unless he too is moved' (Bach 1985). Thus, performers appear to develop strategies by which they succeed to induce themselves into an 'altered state of mind'. Such a state, in this context, and with the different theoretical schools of thought regarding altered states of consciousness in mind, is best defined broadly, such as done by Ludwig (1990, pp. 18–19), as:

. . . any mental state(s), induced by various physiological, psychological, or pharmacological maneuvers or agents, which can be recognized subjectively by the individual himself (or by an objective observer of the individual), as representing a sufficient deviation in subjective experience or psychological functioning from certain norms for that individual during alert, waking consciousness. This sufficient deviation may be represented by a greater preoccupation than usual with internal sensations or mental processes, changes in formal characteristics of thought, and impairment of reality testing to various degrees.

These induction strategies are presumably developed intuitively by musicians, as a result of potentially emotion-evoking structures inherent in the music in combination with striving towards hedonic satisfaction (see also Zuckerman 1994). It is known, for example, that music—at least under certain circumstances—is a particularly efficient medium for inducing an altered state of consciousness (Kenealy 1988; see also Becker, this volume). A number of experiments have shown that induction to an altered state is also subject to a learning process (Kamiya 1990; Shore 1990).

Note that performance teachers never discussed such induction procedures during lessons (Persson 1993), which makes it feasible to propose that mastering such induction procedures is mainly a personal and intuitive matter; it develops over time and—because it is natural and so intrinsically tied to the way we perceive and construe music—is probably often taken for granted in teaching performers.

The pivotal significance of the altered state of mind for a creative effort, however, is fairly well documented in the literature on creativity (cf. Krippner 1999), where phenomena such as inspiration (Kneller 1965), imagination (Stein 1974), peak experiences and being cognition (Maslow 1968), flow (Csikszentmihalyi 1988), and play and fantasy (Russ 1993) are in focus. An extraordinary account of this in the realm of musical performance has been provided by Swedish cellist Frans Helmerson (1990, pp. 250–1), when asked to account for how creativity relates to his artistry (translated from Swedish by the author):

My first point of departure is to evoke the whole [of the piece]. The understanding of the whole is a prerequisite in order to provide the music with a content. It is like assembling the parts in this entire [conceptualization] . . . In other words, it takes a creative process to fit the minute parts of this composition together . . . later in concert I want to—to put it rather solemnly—transcend into a different dimension; one which makes me one with the music. It is a dimension where boundaries between consciousness and intuition are vague and evanescent.

While this 'inspiration-seeking behaviour' certainly could be seen as a social artefact of primarily the romantic era (cf. Persson 2000), the same need for, and use of, the altered state of mind is also found amongst contemporary musicians. Boyd and George-Warren (1992, p. 156), in interviewing 75 popular musicians (such as Eric Clapton, Peter Gabriel, Keith Richards, Ravi Shankar, etc.) regarding their creative process, also note that:

. . . by completely concentrating on the music they're playing or writing, musicians are able to open themselves up to a peak experience. It is as if an intense concentration can push the conscious mind away from 'self-consciousness' and the unconscious is allowed to filter through. The result can be songs that seem to come from nowhere, the ability to suddenly play a riff that had been too difficult before, or an on-stage 'merging' with band mates.'

### 12.2.3 Conceptual flexibility

If a performer conceptualizes a piece of music by constructing a type of affective pattern, related to the musical structure, then how stabile is this conceptual structure? Can a musician generate more than one understanding of a certain piece? These questions were also addressed in Persson's (1993) study. Participants were asked to produce two *different* presentations of the given piece and then discuss both. All participants could produce different versions and understandings of the music at hand, but all but one did not. Most argued that they found one conceptualization which they preferred, and that they did not wish to deviate from.

Above all, the content of their conceptual structure was determined by the chosen tempo (see Table 12.2), which has been shown to be the most potent structural factor in music to determine the type of resulting emotional response (e.g. Holbrook & Anand 1990; Rigg 1940; Wedin 1972; see also Gabrielsson & Lindström, this volume; Juslin, this volume). The participants also argued, however, that they could well imagine another conceptualization of the piece featuring different dynamics, tempi, and articulation, but *only* if it was played by someone else!

This response is likely to indicate that a conceptualization is often inflexible and exists within the cognitive confines of what could be functionally termed a *degree of tolerance.* That is, a musician will often only accept a way of playing a certain piece of music that does not alter the musical parameters to such an extent that they trigger an emotional response different to that which constitutes the way in which they originally construed meaning and understanding in relation to the musical structure. However, there is *some* flexibility in this schema of cognitive-emotional memory structures, the extent of which is likely to be related to personality—and perhaps tolerance for ambiguity in particular (Rogers 1967).

It is possible also that the original conceptualization may change altogether over time in some cases due to accumulated experience and new discoveries that will prompt a musician to re-evaluate 'meaning', thus potentially creating an entirely new schema with a new set of parameters. Pianist Alfred Brendel, for example, argues that:

> . . . as I mold my interpretation and conception I play as instinctively as possible; only later do I attempt to understand what I am doing, why I am doing it. Then I start correcting myself whenever necessary, and from that moment on, I am reassessing my findings as often as I can (quoted in Dubal 1985, p. 91).

In the present research sample, there were apparently limits to a conceptualization, which, when transgressed, prompted the musician to either reject a certain performance or understanding—since it is no longer compatible with the construed 'meaning' of the piece at hand—or construe an entirely new understanding of the music, which takes motivation, effort, and time. However, social context is also likely to play a significant role in determining the degree of tolerance.

It is possible that circumstances and performance tradition *prevented* the participating musicians in deviating from a perceived norm. Although participants knew no details of the piece of music at hand, they still tended to project styles and conventions, typical of the romantic era, onto it—in spite of being encouraged to approach the piece more freely. For example, one performer argued the following in trying to conceptualize the given piece of music in more ways than only one: 'When I think of how my highly respected former piano teacher would have played this, I would know exactly what he would do. I would highly admire that and it would [also] govern what I would do' (quoted in Persson 1993, p. 209). A conservatoire culture is known to often not encourage creative initiatives amongst performers-to-be, but rather insists on conformity and adherence to very elusive rules of tradition and 'authenticity' (Kennedy 1991; Persson 2000; Renshaw 1986).

## 12.3 Musical reality and its further research

Musicians from all eras, and no doubt in all genres of music, are indeed 'sensors of emotion and sensitivity', and subjectivity is, in a variety of ways, most probably the basis of their musical pursuit. It is thus helpful, both for future research and in understanding the phenomenology of musical endeavours, to term the dynamic nature of this emotional basis from which musicians appear to draw motivation, construe artistic understanding, and generate performances, a *musical reality* (Persson 1995), akin to the Kellyan notion of personal constructs (Kelly 1963).

Musicians, at least as evidenced in the research surveyed in this chapter, do indeed construe elaborate meaning based on intrinsic and mainly hedonic criteria, on extrinsic and contextual demands, and on the triggers of emotional responses inherent in musical structures. Musicians further seem to uphold musical reality, pertaining to a particular repertoire, by means of a monitoring function, presumably optimizing different means of achieving a self-serving satisfaction. Haroutounian (1995) has very appropriately labelled such a function *meta perception*: the perceptual and cognitive process of internally manipulating perceptions with expression.

Needless to say, the subjective conceptualization of music needs further study. The results obtained in the discussed research project, as intriguing and suggestive as they are, are still tentative. Above all, the phenomenological excursion in to the subjectivity of musical performers has generated a number of hypotheses that need testing and further exploration in order to arrive at verifiable cognitive models, and no less important, to facilitate application in an educational setting (Juslin & Persson, in press).

While the existence of a subjective musical reality is certain, its nature and function, also in different contexts, need specific research and a theoretical framework. For example, how does musical reality more specifically relate to choice of repertoire, to determining an interpretation, to how a piece of music is rehearsed, and to the actual public performance of it? There are almost certainly differences, as well as common denominators, regarding how emotions (and by implication also the construct of musical reality) will function in these different situations. It is also quite likely, however, that there are *several* strategies available to musicians that govern musical behaviour in these different settings. This was suggested by one participant, who commented: 'Despite the fact when I'm playing to an audience, I play mainly . . . for recognition . . . [I also play at other times] for a pure love of playing' (quoted in Persson 1993, p. 175). Hence, it is one thing to play to an audience (being under public scrutiny and being assessed as artist) and occasionally another to play for enjoyment (with no sense of external scrutiny and evaluation).

Thus, there seems occasionally to exist a conflict between the internal hedonic motive (the largely self-serving positive emotional experience) and the external demand (i.e. socially imposed traditions and expectations). In some circumstances, however, the different strategies employed in different contexts should perhaps simply be understood, in a Kellyan sense, as *several* coexisting musical realities for the same repertoire, but constructed differently for a variety of performance contexts. If so, there would not necessarily exist a conflict, but the existence of several such coexisting realities would perchance be indicative of adaptive 'survival behaviour' rather than artistic persuasion.

In researching how emotions interact with decisions, choices, rehearsal behaviour, and public performance—and, of course, performance under the pressure of a perceived assessment; real or imagined—therefore, it is probably necessary to consider both possibilities: the potential conflict between self-satisfying hedonism and the imposition of context expectations and assessment, as well as the possibility of several concurrent constructed realities. Their common denominator, however, would be a framework of emotional patterns, motives, imageries, memories, and associations.

A pertinent question is how research into the subjective world of the performer might proceed. I envisage three main thrusts of necessary research efforts.

1. Cognitive functions and neurological correlates need to more solidly, and theoretically, outline the nature of the connection between emotion and musical learning.

2. There are developmental aspects to the notion of musical reality, and research questions need to include possible gender differences. How does musical reality develop over time, in what way, and is there possibly a difference between male and female performers in the way they develop and establish preferences for how to learn? Note that, for example, research on music and cognitive styles has so far not demonstrated that such individual differences have much bearing on understanding musical behaviour (cf. Barry 1992; Heitland 1982). But perhaps an extended research effort into musical performance and personality (regardless of theoretical preference) would (cf. Kemp 1996).

3. Also, given that the notion of musical reality is an appropriate heuristic for future research, one particularly interesting question inevitably emerges: how does musical reality—or rather the capacity to generate effectively an emotionally based conceptualization—relate to musical ability and talent? The understanding of musical talent—or giftedness—has not changed much during the hundred years or so that music has been studied as behaviour. The subjective features, which are presumably part of talent and giftedness, have thus far not been studied at all. Hence, to tie musical reality to the notions of expertise and talent would also seem an important future research effort.

## References

Bach, C. P. E. (1985). *Essay on the true art of playing keyboard instruments*, (ed. and trans. W. J. Mitchell). London: Eulenburg Books. (Originally published in 1778.)

Barry, N. (1992). The effects of practice strategies, individual differences in cognitive style, and gender upon technical accuracy and musicality of student instrumental performance. *Psychology of Music*, 20, 112–23.

Bower, G. H. (1992). How might emotions affect learning? In *The handbook of emotion and memory: research and theory*, (ed. S-Å. Christianson), pp. 3–31. Hillsdale, NJ: Erlbaum.

Boyd, J. & George-Warren, H. (1992). *Musicians in tune. Seventy-five contemporary musicians discuss the creative process.* New York: Fireside/Simon & Schuster.

Braudy, L. (1997). *The frenzy of renown. Fame and its history.* New York: Vintage Books/Random House.

Bukofzer, M. F. (1947). *Music in the Baroque Era: music from Monteverdi to Bach.* New York: W. W. Norton & Co.

Clarke, E. F. (1988). Generative principles in music performance. In *Generative principles in music. The psychology of performance, improvisation, and composition*, (ed. J. A. Sloboda), pp. 1–26. Oxford, UK: Clarendon Press.

Clynes, M. (1989). *Sentics: The touch of emotions.* Bridport, UK: Prism Press.

Crofton, I. & Fraser, D. (1985). *A dictionary of musical quotations.* London: Routledge.

Csikszentmihalyi, M. (1988). The flow experience and its significance for human psychology. In *Optimal experience: Psychological studies of flow in consciousness*, (ed. M. Csikszentmihalyi & S. Selega-Csikszentmihalyi), pp. 15–35. Cambridge, UK: Cambridge University Press.

Dubal, D. (1985). *The world of the concert pianist. Conversations with 35 internationally celebrated pianists.* London: Victor Gollancz.

Friberg, A. (1991). Generative rules for music performance: a formal description of a rule system. *Computer Music Journal,* 15, 56–71.

Gabrielsson, A. & Juslin, P. N. (1996). Emotional expression in music performance: between the performer's intention and the listener's experience. *Psychology of Music,* 24, 68–91.

Gregory, A. H. & Varney, N. (1996). Cross-cultural comparisons in the affective response to music. *Psychology of Music,* 24, 47–52.

Hallam, S. (1998). The predictors of achievement and dropout in instrumental tuition. *Psychology of Music,* 26, 116–32.

Haroutounian, J. (1995). Talent identification and development in the arts: An artistic/educational dialogue. *Roeper Review,* 18, 112–17.

Heitland, K. W. (1982). *Cognitive styles and musical aptitudes: An exploratory study.* Unpublished doctoral dissertation, School of Education, Indiana University.

Helmerson, F. (1990). Att tolka musik [How to interpret music]. In *Om kreativitet och flow,* (ed. G. Klein), pp. 250–2. Stockholm: Brombergs.

Holbrook, M. & Anand, P. (1990). Effects of tempo and situational arousal on the listener's perceptual and affective responses to music. *Psychology of Music,* 18, 150–62.

Hurford, P. (1988). *Making music on the organ.* Oxford, UK: Oxford University Press.

Juslin, P. N. (1997). Emotional communication in music performance: A functionalist perspective and some data. *Music Perception,* 14, 383–418.

Juslin, P. N. (2000). Cue utilization in communication of emotion in music performance: Relating performance to perception. *Journal of Experimental Psychology: Human Perception and Performance,* 26, 1797–813.

Juslin, P. N. & Persson, R. S. (in press). Emotional communication. In *The science and psychology of music performance: Creative strategies for teaching and learning,* (ed. R. Parncutt & G. E. MacPherson). New York: Oxford University Press.

Kamiya, J. (1990). Operant control of the EEG alpha rhythm and some of its reported effects on consciousness. In *Altered states of consciousness,* (3rd edn) (ed. C. T. Tart), pp. 600–11. San Fransisco, CA: Harper.

Kelly, G. A. (1963). *A theory of personality: The psychology of personal constructs.* New York: W. W. Norton & Co.

Kemp, A. E. (1996). *The musical temperament. Psychology and personality of musicians.* Oxford, UK: Oxford University Press.

Kenealy, P. (1988). Validation of a music mood induction procedure: Some preliminary findings. *Cognition and Emotion,* 2, 41–8.

Kennedy, N. (1991). *Always playing.* London: Weidenfeld & Nicolson.

Kingsbury, H. (1988). *Music, talent, and performance. A conservatory system.* Philadelphia, PA: Temple University Press.

Kneller, G. F. (1965). *The art and science of creativity.* New York: Holt, Rinehart & Winston.

Krippner, S. (1999). Altered and transitional states. In *Encyclopedia of creativity,* (Vol. 1) (ed. M. A. Runco & S. R. Pritzker), pp. 59–70. San Diego, CA: Academic Press.

Lazarus, R. S., Kanner, A. D., & Folkman, S. (1980). Emotions: A cognitive-phenomenological analysis. In *Emotion: theory, research, and experience. Volume 1. Theories of emotion,* (ed. R. Plutchik & H. Kellerman), pp. 189–217. London: Academic Press.

**Lehmann, A. C.** (1997). Acquired mental representations in music performance: Anecdotal and preliminary empirical evidence. In *Does practice make perfect? Current theory and research on instrumental music practice*, (ed. H. Jørgensen & A. C. Lehmann), pp. 141–63. Oslo, Norway: Norwegian State Academy of Music.

**Ludwig, A. M.** (1990). Altered states of consciousness. In *Altered states of consciousness,* (3rd edn) (ed. C. T. Tart), pp. 18–33. San Fransisco, CA: Harper.

**McDonald, M.** (1970). Transitional tunes and musical development. *Psychoanalytic Study of the Child,* 25, 503–20.

**Manturzewska, M.** (1990). A biographical study on the life span development of professional musicians. *Psychology of Music,* 18, 112–39.

**Maslow, A.** (1968). *Toward a psychology of being,* (2nd edn). New York: Van Nostrand.

**Meyer, L. B.** (1956). *Emotion and meaning in music.* Chicago: University of Chicago Press.

**Motte-Haber, H. de la** (1984). Die Bedeutung der Motivation für den Instrumentalbericht [The significance of motivation in instrumental reports]. *Zeitschrift für Musikpädagogik,* 51, 51–4.

**Nagel, J. J.** (1987). *An examination of commitment to careers in music: Implications for alienation from vocational choice.* Unpublished doctoral dissertation, University of Michigan, Ann Arbor, MI.

**Ohgushi, K. & Senju, M.** (1987). How are the player's ideas conveyed to the audience? *Music Perception,* 4, 311–24.

**Osborne, R.** (1990). *Conversations with Karajan.* Oxford, UK: Oxford University Press.

**Parncutt, R., Sloboda, J. A., & Clarke, E. F.** (1997). Interdependence of right and left hands in sight-read, written, and rehearsed fingerings of piano music in parallel octaves. In *Proceedings of the Third Triennial ESCOM Conference,* (ed. A. Gabrielsson), pp. 702–5. Uppsala, Sweden: Department of Psychology, Uppsala University.

**Persson, R. S.** (1993). *The subjectivity of musical performance: An exploratory music-psychological real world enquiry into the determinants and education of musical reality.* Unpublished doctoral dissertation, School of Human and Health Sciences, Huddersfield University, Huddersfield, UK.

**Persson, R. S.** (1995). Musical reality: Exploring the subjective world of performers. In *Song and signification. Studies in music semiotics,* (ed. R. Monelle & C. T. Gray), pp. 58–63. Edinburgh, UK: Faculty of Music, University of Edinburgh.

**Persson, R. S.** (1996). Studying with a musical maestro: A case study of commonsense teaching in artistic training. *Creativity Research Journal,* 9, 33–46.

**Persson, R. S.** (2000). Survival of the fittest or the most talented? Deconstructing the myth of the musical maestro. *Journal of Secondary Gifted Education,* xii, 25–38.

**Persson, R. S., Pratt. G., & Robson, C.** (1996). Motivational and influential components of musical performance: A qualitative analysis. In *Fostering the growth of high ability: European perspectives,* (ed. A. J. Cropley & D. Dehn), pp. 287–301. Norwood, NJ: Ablex.

**Persson, R. S. & Robson, C.** (1995). The limits of experimentation: On researching music and musical settings. *Psychology of Music,* 23, 39–47.

**Rapoport, E.** (1996). Emotional expression code in opera and lied singing. *Journal of New Music Research,* 25, 109–49.

**Renshaw, P.** (1986). Towards the changing face of the conservatoire curriculum. *British Journal of Music Education,* 3, 79–90.

**Rigg, M. G.** (1940). Speed as a determination of musical mood. *Journal of Experimental Psychology,* 27, 566–71.

Robson, C. (1993). *Real world research. A resource for social scientists and practitioner-researchers.* Oxford, UK: Blackwell.

Rogers, C. R. (1967). *On becoming a person. A therapist's view of psychotherapy.* London: Constable.

Russ, S. W. (1993). *Affect and creativity. The role of affect and play in the creative process.* Hillsdale, NJ: Lawrence Erlbaum.

Ruud, E. (1997). *Musikk og identitet [Music and identity].* Oslo, Norway: Universitetsforlaget.

Seashore, C. E. (1938). *Psychology of music.* New York: Dover Publications.

Shore, R. E. (1990). Hypnosis and the concept of the general reality orientation. In *Altered states of consciousness,* (3rd edn) (ed. C. T. Tart), pp. 281–301. San Fransisco, CA: Harper.

Sloboda, J. A. (1991). Music structure and emotional response. *Psychology of Music,* **19**, 110–20.

Sloboda, J. A. (1998). Does music mean anything? *Musicae Scientiae,* **2**, 21–32.

Stanislavski, C. (1988). *An actor prepares.* London: Methuen Drama. (Originally published in 1937.)

Stein, M. I. (1974). *Stimulating creativity: Individual procedures,* (Vol. 1). New York: Academic Press.

Stern, I. (1979). An interview with Isaac Stern. *The New York Times Magazine,* 23 December.

Waterman, M. (1996). Emotional responses to music. Implicit and explicit effects in listeners and performers. *Psychology of Music,* **24**, 53–67.

Watt, R. J. & Ash, R. L. (1998). A psychological investigation of meaning in music. *Musicae Scientiae,* **2**, 33–54.

Wedin, L. (1972). A multidimensional study of the perceptual-emotional qualities in music. *Scandinavian Journal of Psychology,* **13**, 241–57.

Zajonc, R. B. (1980). Feeling and thinking: preferences need no inferences. *American Psychologist,* **35**, 151–75.

Zuckerman, M. (1994). *Behavioral expressions and biosocial bases of sensation seeking.* Cambridge, UK: Cambridge University.

# CHAPTER 13

# NEGATIVE EMOTIONS IN MUSIC MAKING: THE PROBLEM OF PERFORMANCE ANXIETY

ANDREW STEPTOE

The performance of music induces extraordinarily positive feelings in many players and singers. Participation in a successful and exciting performance often leads to feelings of euphoria, whether it be in a school concert, a piece sung by a village choir, or a public show in a prestigious concert hall. Here is the baritone Thomas Allen (interviewed in the *Independent on Sunday* in 1990) describing his feelings at the end of a performance of *Don Giovanni* in Japan: 'I could have walked over the house tops I was so high'. When the producer came backstage to congratulate him, Allen picked him up and carried him across the stage, 'Oh, I could have run up Mount Fuji!'

The same feelings of joy of creative music making are vividly expressed in a letter written by the 21-year-old Mozart to his father in November 1777. He was playing the organ during a Sunday service in the Court chapel in Mannheim in the presence of the ruler of the state:

I entered during the Kyrie and played the end of it; and after the priest had intoned the Gloria, I played a cadenza. Because this was all so different from what they are accustomed to here, they all turned round . . . The people had enough to amuse them. Now and then was a pizzicato, and each time I just brushed the keys. I was in the best of spirits. Instead of the Benedictus, the organist has to play throughout. I took the subject to the Sanctus and treated it as fugue. Everybody stood there and stared. The pedal is different from ours; that put me off at first, but I soon understood how it worked. (Quoted in Anderson 1988, p. 370)

Unfortunately, musical performance may also induce negative emotions, including distress and anxiety, which in some individuals can approach extreme levels of terror, impair the quality of the performance, and have debilitating effects on professional and amateur careers.

This chapter discusses musical performance anxiety, outlining the psychological and medical literature on this topic, and touches on issues such as the definition and prevalence of musical performance anxiety, its causes and consequences, and methods of alleviating severe problems. Musical performance anxiety is a complex phenomenon. It is no accident that this chapter began with descriptions of positive feelings, because there are close links between negative and positive feelings in the musical performer.

Indeed, sensations of arousal experienced by most individuals prior to a performance may be disturbing to some, but facilitate a good performance in others. As will become apparent later in the chapter, it has proved difficult to demonstrate that physiological arousal is positively correlated with performance anxiety and that musicians with problems in this area are characterized by excessive arousal. Rather it is the interplay between cognitive processes and physiological activation that is central to musical performance anxiety.

Musical performance anxiety is often regarded as synonymous with stage fright, although stage fright is a phenomenon that occurs in non-musical performers such as actors and public speakers as well. I prefer the term musical performance anxiety for several reasons. Firstly, it refers specifically to the feelings experienced by musicians. Secondly, musical performance anxiety occurs in many settings, and not just on the stage. Stage fright has connotations of distress in front of large audiences, but musical performance anxiety may be elicited in quite intimate surroundings, such as a lesson or an audition. It depends on the evaluative nature of the situation, and not on the presence of an audience. Thirdly, the term 'fright' implies a sudden fear or alarm, while musical performance anxiety may be quite predictable and develop gradually over days prior to an important occasion. Finally, the term has implications for the way in which the music is played, and not just the fear that the performer experiences. Stage fright would be bad enough if it were only a feeling of intense fear. But a major concern for many musicians is that it will have an impact on the quality of the performance, and on their ability to carry out the task of playing or singing accurately and effectively. This feature marks musical performance anxiety out from many other types of situational fear.

The empirical literature on musical performance anxiety is sparse, and relatively few investigators have gone beyond describing the phenomenon into disentangling its elements so as to understand how it develops and is maintained (Brodsky 1996). This chapter will therefore draw on research into related phenomena where appropriate, including stage fright in actors and studies of test anxiety. Other potentially negative aspects of the performer's life will also be briefly discussed, since work stress among musicians appears to be related to performance anxiety.

## 13.1 Occurrence and experience of musical performance anxiety

Musical performance anxiety is not an all or nothing experience, but a graduated phenomenon. Different musicians encounter it to a different extent, and the same individual may experience varying degrees of performance anxiety on different occasions. Surveys of the occurrence of musical performance anxiety must therefore be treated cautiously, since they typically rely on somewhat arbitrary classifications. The frequency of performance anxiety is also important, since many more musicians will have suffered occasional bouts of severe anxiety than experience them on a regular basis. The best evidence for the occurrence of musical performance anxiety comes from surveys of musicians who are not specially selected on the basis of problems in this area. Obviously, studies of musicians seeking help for difficulties associated with performance anxiety will be biased, and this may lead therapists to overestimate the magnitude of the problem.

Varying estimates of the occurrence of musical performance anxiety have emerged from different surveys, and it is difficult to know whether these are due to genuine variations or differences in questioning. In probably the largest survey published to date, Fishbein and Middlestadt (1988) studied more than 2200 musicians from 48 orchestras in the USA. Nineteen per cent of women and 14 per cent of men indicated that stage fright was a severe problem. Another large survey involving 56 orchestras throughout the world was carried out on behalf of the Fédération Internationale des Musiciens (FIM) in 1997.[1] Seventy per cent of the 1639 respondents indicated that they sometimes experienced such intense anxiety before a performance that it impaired their playing. For 16 per cent, this happened more than once a week. Fity-nine per cent of symphony orchestra players in a Dutch survey claimed to be acquainted with performance anxiety from their own experience, though only 21 per cent described it as intense or very intense (Van Kemenade *et al.* 1995). A survey of more than 300 students in a faculty from the University of Iowa School of Medicine concluded that 21 per cent experienced marked performance anxiety (Wesner *et al.* 1990). Fifty-eight per cent of the members of the Vienna Symphony Orchestra studied by Schulz (1981) indicated that their 'nervous stress' during concerts was high or very high, while 24 per cent also complained of high levels of tension before performances. These surveys indicate that musical performance anxiety is a serious problem for 15–25 per cent of musicians. Some studies have reported higher levels, probably related to differences in exactly how musical performance anxiety was defined, rather than genuine differences in prevalence (Bartel & Thompson 1995; Marchant-Haycox & Wilson 1992). A pattern of slightly higher levels among women than men is seen in several studies, as it is for other forms of self-reported distress (Mirowsky & Ross 1995).

There have been few systematic comparisons of different types of musician within the same study. However, the author and a colleague (Steptoe & Fidler 1987) compared responses from members of the Royal Philharmonic Orchestra, the London Philharmonic Orchestra, and an amateur orchestra, and orchestral instrumental students at the College of Music, using an adaptation of the state scale from the state-trait anxiety inventory (Spielberger *et al.* 1970). The mean scores were significantly higher among students, and were lowest in the professional musicians in the world class orchestras. Does this mean that performance anxiety declines with experience? Not necessarily, because it is possible that more anxious individuals hoping to become orchestral musicians drop out of the profession at an early stage. Alternatively, it is possible that more anxious musicians fail to be employed by prestigious orchestras, leaving a selected sample of less anxious individuals. Unfortunately, no longitudinal studies have yet been conducted that allow the different explanations of cross-sectional results to be teased out.

There are similar difficulties in understanding associations between musical performance anxiety and age. One might expect performance anxiety to decline with age as musicians become more experienced and familiar with different audiences and challenges. On the other hand, success comes with responsibility, and the acclaimed

---

[1] The FIM survey has not been published in detail. I am grateful to the British Association for Performing Arts Medicine for giving me access to the data.

mature performer may perceive additional burdens in the high public expectations on them. The violinist Nathan Milstein (quoted in the *Guardian* in 1993) recalled how carefree he was when performing in his youth, playing cards or sightseeing during the day before an evening recital. Later in life he was unable to eat lunch and remained pre-occupied for several hours before a performance. Highly successful popular musicians and classical musicians, such as Arthur Rubinstein and Luciano Pavarotti, have admitted to extreme nervousness and distress prior to concerts. Perhaps the most celebrated case is that of the great actor Laurence Olivier, who suddenly succumbed to severe stage fright for several years at a late phase of his career (Olivier 1982).

### 13.1.1 The phenomenon of performance anxiety

Musicians who suffer from performance anxiety describe a wide range of experiences, including fear and terror, trembling, difficulty concentrating, disturbances of breathing, and dry mouth. There is a strong belief among musicians that performance anxiety impairs their playing or singing, and this is corroborated in studies involving objective evaluations. For example, Craske and Craig (1984) had independent judges evaluate the performance quality of piano students divided into anxious and non-anxious groups. Judgments were made from audiotapes recorded when the student played alone, or in the presence of an evaluative audience. Subjective ratings of distress were also collected. Some results are illustrated in Fig. 13.1. It can be seen that the judges' ratings of performance quality were significantly impaired in the audience condition in the anxious group, but improved in the non-anxious group. Subjective distress increased in both groups when an audience was present, but the increase was much larger in the performance anxiety group.

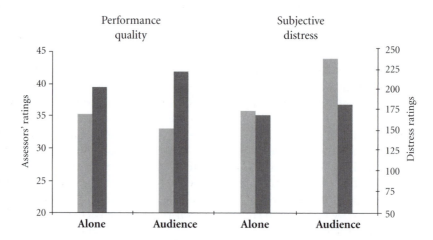

**Figure 13.1** Performance quality and subjective distress in anxious (light bars) and non-anxious (dark bars) pianists playing alone or in front of an evaluative audience. Performance quality (left-hand axis) was judged by assessors blind to the pianists' group, and higher scores indicate superior quality. Distress (right-hand axis) was assessed by combining ratings obtained before and immediately after playing, with higher scores indicating greater distress. (From Craske & Craig 1984.)

Musical performance anxiety is a complex phenomenon. By analogy with other work on stress and emotion (Steptoe 1998), it may be useful to separate four distinct elements. These four components are listed in Table 13.1, along with various examples of the ways in which they are manifested. The primary component is affect or feeling, which forms the central experience of performance anxiety for many musicians. It should also be recognized in this context that the moods and emotions evoked by music are not confined to the audience, but may also affect the performer. However, there are other important aspects as well, including cognitive responses or disturbances in information processing, changes in behaviour, and physiological responses.

Table 13.1 The four components of musical performance anxiety

| | |
|---|---|
| *Affect* | Feelings of anxiety, tension, apprehension, dread or panic |
| *Cognition* | Loss of concentration, heightened distractibility, memory failure, maladaptive cognitions, misreading of the musical score, etc. |
| *Behaviour* | Tremor, trembling, difficulty in maintaining posture and moving naturally, failures of technique |
| *Physiology* | Disturbances in breathing pattern, perspiration, inhibition of salivation (dry mouth), high heart rate, the release of hormones such as adrenaline (epinephrine) and cortisol, gastrointestinal disturbances |

The 1997 FIM survey illustrates the importance of these different elements. Physiological symptoms were frequent before and during performances, with rapid heart beat (67 per cent), sweating hands (56 per cent), and muscle tension (56 per cent) being the most prominent. At the same time, 49 per cent complained that they often lost concentration, and 46 per cent that they experienced trembling and shaking prior to playing. These same four elements are common to many modern conceptualizations of the stress response, which are essentially offshoots of the three system model of fear formulated by Lang and others (Hugdahl 1981).

The various manifestations of musical performance anxiety do not necessarily occur together, and correlations between responses in the different domains are variable (Craske & Craig 1984; Fredrikson & Gunnarsson 1992). One person may show impairment of movement or posture without feeling very upset, while another may experience their principal difficulties in cognitive disturbance. Craske and Craig (1984) showed that concordance between components was greater in more anxious performers, but the correlations between physiological and subjective measures still did not exceed 0.38, suggesting that marked discrepancies remain. Understanding the interrelationships between these domains helps to delineate the core components of performance anxiety.

The framework outlined here and elaborated in the following sections is based on the view that musical performance anxiety is a form of situational stress response. That is, it is similar in some respects to problems such as social phobia or academic examination stress. It should be recognized that this model differs from some approaches that conceptualize performance anxiety as a unique problem related to psychological issues stimulated by performing in front of others. This latter perspective has derived primarily from the psychodynamic tradition. For example, Gabbard (1997) has argued that stage fright can emerge from shame related to genital inadequacy, or impulses that produce feelings of guilt in the unconscious in triumphing over Oedipal and sibling rivals. I have little sympathy with such views, which lack objective verification, and would argue that bringing musical performance anxiety into the mainstream of stress research has major advantages for understanding issues such as the role of cognitive processes or the relations between physiological arousal and performance quality, while highlighting ways in which performance anxiety can be effectively managed.

## 13.2 Physiological arousal during musical performance

Perhaps the simplest model of musical performance anxiety is that it is a consequence of heightened physiological arousal. Certainly, the perception of physiological arousal figures prominently in the experience of many anxious musicians, with symptoms such as palpitations, breathlessness, and perspiration that are indicative of sympathetic nervous system activation. Subjectively, many anxious musicians report symptoms of *hyperventilation*—the pattern of dizziness, tremor, and high heart rate due to overbreathing (and subsequent reductions in arterial carbon dioxide levels) that is characteristic of patients with panic attacks (Widmer *et al.* 1997).

The physiological arousal induced by performing in public has also been established objectively. Two types of study have been carried out: (a) those in which physiological monitoring takes place under conditions specially devised and controlled by the investigator; and (b) naturalistic studies in which musicians are monitored during live performances. Thus, in the study by Craske and Craig (1984) described earlier, heart rate was higher during performances in front of an audience compared with playing alone. Fredrikson and Gunnarsson (1992) studied 19 music students, and reported that adrenaline (epinephrine) increased by an average of 139 per cent and cortisol by 66 per cent with performance in front of an audience compared with playing alone.

The classic investigation of physiological activation during live performance is the work by Haider and Groll-Knapp with the Vienna Symphony Orchestra, first published in German in 1971 and in English in 1981. The heart rate and electroencephalogram (EEG) were monitored during rehearsals and live concerts from 24 musicians. String and woodwind players showed similar responses, with a mean heart rate of 93.9 bpm during concerts, reaching an average maximum of 113 bpm. Since the resting heart rate of these musicians was 66.6 bpm, this means that heart rate increases averaged 27.3 bpm. Interestingly, the heart rate difference between rehearsals and concerts was more than 8 bpm, even though the same pieces were being performed. These substantial increases in heart rate confirmed an earlier study of musicians in concert (Schmale & Schmidtke 1965) and the more recent investigation of members of the BBC Symphony Orchestra (Mulcahy *et al.* 1990). Haider and Groll-Knapp (1981) also used EEG recordings to show high levels of cortical activation during concerts.

In the light of these findings, one possibility is that musical performance anxiety is a consequence of excessive physiological activation. The 'inverted-U' association between tension and performance is a well-established phenomenon in the experimental laboratory, and suggests that information processing and behavioural performance improves with arousal to an intermediate stage, but then deteriorates as physiological arousal rises beyond the optimum (Duffy 1962; Näätänen 1973). However, few studies have documented this pattern in performing musicians. Some evidence for such an association emerged from an interview study I carried out with young professional opera singers (Steptoe 1983). Participants were asked to rank the quality of their performance in five settings: lesson, private practice, audition, dress rehearsal, and public performance. Then, at a different stage of the interview, ratings of emotional tension in these situations were obtained on a nine-point scale ranging from 1 = *extreme tension* to 9 = *extreme relaxation*. I then averaged the emotional tension ratings for each situation, and plotted them against the estimates of performance quality. Figure 13.2 depicts the interrelationship between these measures. It can be seen that the best singing was produced at an intermediate level of tension (in public performances), while the situations associated with greater tension (dress rehearsal and audition) were those in which performance was impaired. The results of this study are consistent with the inverted-U pattern, though they are limited by the use of self-reported measures.

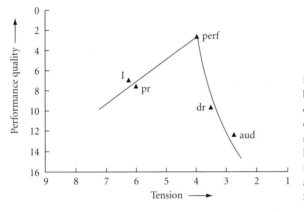

**Figure 13.2** The association between self-rated tension and quality of performance in a sample of opera singers, assessed in five situations: private practice (pr), a lesson (l), public performance (perf), dress rehearsal (dr), and in audition (aud). (For details, see Steptoe 1983.)

When it comes to objective physiological measures, there is much less evidence that musical performance anxiety is associated with excessive arousal. In fact, some studies have shown similar levels of physiological activation irrespective of musical performance anxiety. Thus, Abel and Larkin (1990) show that blood pressure and heart rate increased prior to playing in public, but that responses were not significantly correlated with performance anxiety. Similar levels of heart rate and sweat gland activity response in individuals with high and low levels of anxiety were recorded by Craske and Craig (1984), and adrenaline and cortisol response by Fredrikson and Gunnarsson (1992). The only evidence for excessive arousal to emerge thus far is the observation by Fredrikson and Gunnarsson that anxious musicians showed a mean 39.2 bpm increase in heart rate, compared with 22.6 bpm in the less anxious. It is also possible that musical performance anxiety is manifest physiologically, not in general measures of arousal such as heart rate, but in more specific correlates of breathing disturbance associated with hyperventilation (Widmer *et al.* 1997). An interesting result came from the heart-rate-monitoring studies of the BBC Symphony Orchestra (Mulcahy *et al.* 1990). It was found that the increase in heart rate during concerts was paralleled in measures obtained from managerial and technical staff for the orchestra; even though these individuals were not actually playing music, they responded just as much at a physiological level.

These findings suggest that while physiological arousal may be a necessary condition for musical performance anxiety, it is not a sufficient explanation. Other factors are involved that relate to the cognitive responses to performing, and to perceptions of physiological arousal. However, the results of these objective studies of physiology are also relevant to the issue of the apparently beneficial or facilitatory effects of performance anxiety.

One of the statements that musicians often make about playing in public is that they 'need' stage fright, and that it helps them to perform at the optimum level. This facilitating effect is important, since it may lead musicians not to seek ways of alleviating performance anxiety, because they fear that the quality of their playing or singing may suffer. Some years ago, I interviewed one young professional opera singer whose concern was that she did not get excited enough when performing. She was worried that her lack of 'stress' may have had an adverse effect, giving the impression of little involvement in the music. Her subsequent extremely successful career has given the lie to this fear.

The notion that arousal is facilitative can be understood within a curvilinear model of performance (see Fig. 13.2). However, I would argue that this is not because performance anxiety is beneficial, but because physiological arousal is necessary for a good performance. When musicians say that performance anxiety, or stage fright, is helpful, they may be mislabelling physiological arousal as fear, rather than construing it as an independent entity. Physiological activation may be required for a good performance, but not the negative feelings associated with playing or singing in public. Such empirical work as has been done suggests that facilitating and debilitating aspects of performance anxiety are negatively correlated (Mor *et al.* 1995). The most parsimonious explanation is that the same feelings of physiological arousal are experienced, but while one performer finds these energizing, another perceives them as signs of impending disaster.

## 13.3 Cognitive factors in musical performance anxiety

The musician playing in public tends to be occupied with task-orientated thoughts. That is, the cognitive apparatus is taken up with thoughts related to effective performance. For the orchestral musician, this will include being sensitive to tempo and dynamic directions from the conductor, the volume of sound in relation to the rest of the orchestra, intonation, the particular challenges of the passage, and so on. A member of a rock band will be alert to the way in which the music is being played by colleagues, to improvisations by others, and to maintaining a regular beat. The singer or instrumental soloist often has added cognitive demands related to remembering the music, the actions on the stage, and adjusting performance to the acoustics of the venue.

A characteristic feature of musical performance anxiety is disruption of task-orientated cognitions. Several types of disruption have been identified. One common problem is *catastrophizing*, or exaggerating in imagination the likelihood and effects of negative events during the performance. For example, singers may find that their breath does not hold out in the way they hoped, or the instrumentalist makes a small error of intonation. Musicians with musical performance anxiety tend to believe such occurrences will ruin the entire performance, and will lead to loss of control over the situation. Wolfe (1989) observed that anxious musicians were convinced that a small mistake at the beginning of a performance upset them so much that they tended to make even more simple mistakes later on. Catastrophizing also takes the form of fear of collapse, and the concern that the performer will be sick or faint on stage. We have found in both musicians and student actors that there are strong positive associations between catastrophizing and performance anxiety (Steptoe & Fidler 1987; Steptoe *et al.* 1995).

A second form of distraction comes from preoccupation with evaluation by others. Lehrer and co-workers (1990) carried out a factor analysis of thoughts and worries related to musical performance. Various factors emerged, including worry about anxiety and fear of distraction. In addition, concern about the reactions of other people (ranging from close family to critics) was a prominent feature, and was positively correlated with anxiety. By contrast, we have found that more realistic attitudes, such as the belief that the audience wants the performer to play well and will make allowance for slips, are associated with adaptive levels of moderate arousal, and not with severe performance anxiety (Steptoe & Fidler 1987). Concern about the reactions of others may be coupled with very high internal standards and a perfectionist attitude. An analysis of perfectionism in professional performers was carried out by Mor and colleagues (1995). The perfectionism scale included items such as 'one of my goals is to be perfect in everything I do', and 'the people around me expect me to succeed in everything I do'. It was found that perfectionism scores were positively correlated with debilitating performance anxiety, and that more anxious performers also experienced a lower sense of personal control in their lives.

Cognitive responses of this type tend to divert the musician from concentrating on the task itself, thus increasing the risk of errors in performance. Heightened perception of physical signs also contributes; anxious performers may interpret muscle tension or a rapidly beating heart not as a sign of excitement and involvement, but as signalling loss of control and impending collapse. They may therefore become further distracted by trying to keep themselves physically calm. Thoughts about failure during performance have been shown to predict playing below the standards of which the individual is capable of in other situations (Kivimäki 1995).

## 13.4 Other stresses in the musician's life

Negative emotional experiences among musicians are not restricted to performance anxiety. The musician's life, both during training and their subsequent professional career, is subject to other sources of stress, just as is the case with other types of job. Much of the work on these problems has been carried out in the context of occupational health research.

Parasuraman and Purohit (2000) built on the work of Schulz (1981) to identify five major sources of stress among orchestral musicians. These are issues related to the work environment (air quality, humidity, seating comfort, readability of the musical score, etc.), social tensions (such as conflict within the orchestra, feelings of being undervalued), musical performance anxiety, problems related to artistic integrity (such as unhappiness about how the music is played, being subordinate to the will of a conductor), and concerns about the technical difficulty of the music. They found that social tension, problems of artistic integrity, and poor working conditions all contributed to job dissatisfaction among professional orchestral musicians. To these might be added worries about job security and the financial viability of music making, and boredom arising from playing the same pieces over and over again. In our own work, we found that the principle sources of stress for orchestral musicians were separation from family, irregular working hours, the monotony of rehearsals, travelling, and uncertainty about regular employment (Steptoe 1989).

The 1997 FIM survey asked orchestral musicians to rate more than 40 potential sources of stress. The ten items that were endorsed as being moderately or severely stressful by the largest proportion of players are listed in Table 13.2. It can be seen that the most common sources of stress for professional orchestral musicians were problems with conductors, conflict with fellow musicians, work environment problems, unsatisfactory rehearsal arrangements, and aspects of playing. However, set against these difficulties are the positive feelings of interest and fulfilment deriving from the sheer pleasure of playing in an orchestra, the variety in the job, and the excitement of performing to audiences.

Table 13.2 Stressful aspects of the musician's life.

|  | Proportion of respondents who gave a rating of moderate or severe stress |
| --- | --- |
| Working with a conductor who saps your confidence | 73% |
| Playing an orchestral solo | 73% |
| Illegible music | 65% |
| Disorganized rehearsal time | 65% |
| Problems with your instrument | 63% |
| Making a mistake when performing | 63% |
| Incompetent conductor | 61% |
| Incompatible desk partner | 61% |
| Having medical problems that affect your work | 57% |
| Playing in a cold hall | 55% |

Somewhat similar problems are reported by popular musicians playing jazz and rock (Cooper & Wills 1989). The major concerns reported by a sample of popular musicians were the uncertainty of employment, periods of work overload interspersed with underload coming from being obliged to play routine music in unexciting venues, conflicts with fellow musicians, and the lack of clear structures of career development. The concerns of music students run along the same lines (Dews & Williams 1989).

There are, of course, stressful elements in any work environment, and it is not clear whether the problems of musicians are worse than those experienced by other people. Kivimäki and Jokinen (1994) compared orchestral musicians with industrial and clerical workers, and with people in the health care professions. Average levels of job satisfaction were higher among orchestral musicians than all the other groups, primarily because they enjoyed the variety of the work and the skills they could use in their jobs. However, their sense of autonomy or personal control was relatively low. This same pattern emerged from a comparison of six occupations from a biomedical perspective carried out by Theorell and co-workers (1990). Orchestral musicians felt that they had less autonomy over their work than did all the other occupational groups, including aircraft mechanics, waiters in restaurants, and physicians. Low control at work has been highlighted over recent years as a major source of stress and as a contributor to health risk (Steptoe & Appels 1989).

What is also clear is that these other stresses in the musician's life are not entirely separate from musical performance anxiety. In our own work, we found that musicians with high performance anxiety were more likely to be concerned about other negative aspects of their careers, such as poor financial rewards, social conflict with other professionals, the competitive nature of the job, and uncertainty about employment (Steptoe & Fidler 1987). It is possible that performance anxiety serves to accentuate the individual's perception of other stresses in music making, while these same difficulties may be ignored by musicians who are not troubled with nerves and are able to enjoy their playing.

## 13.5 Coping with musical performance anxiety

Musicians engage in a variety of informal coping efforts in their attempt to manage performance anxiety. Common methods of coping immediately prior to a performance include deep breathing and muscle relaxation, meditation, immersion in the music, reading, and distraction (Steptoe 1989; Wolfe 1990). Relatively small but none the less worrying numbers report using sedatives and alcohol, while a significant proportion of professional musicians use β-blockers to help them cope with the physical manifestations of performance anxiety. Longer-term methods of coping include thorough preparation and practice, and checking on all aspects of the performance venue (lighting, access, acoustics, etc.).

An apparently paradoxical finding in this literature is that coping has been positively correlated with musical performance anxiety. Lehrer *et al.* (1990) showed that more anxious musicians engaged in more coping efforts, while Steptoe and Fidler (1987) found that anxious musicians were more likely to meditate. The use of distraction techniques has been positively correlated with performance anxiety in student actors as well (Steptoe *et al.* 1995), although Wolfe (1990) observed that musicians who use emotion-focused coping techniques felt greater confidence and competence. The explanation for these associations is not clear. One possibility is that anxious musicians are more likely to engage in deliberate efforts at coping than their less anxious colleagues. The methods of coping may be useful, even though anxiety levels still remain somewhat elevated. A second possibility is that some types of coping are effective, while others are maladaptive. That is, musicians may engage in activities that they think are helpful which do not actually alleviate performance anxiety. Such a pattern is difficult to identify, because methods of coping may be helpful on some occasions but not others. When discussing these issues with musicians, it is striking that efforts at coping may become rather rigid.

A good example is the ritual that some instrumentalists and singers carry out on the day of an important performance. They may, for example, remain silent for several hours, feel they have to eat particular foods or wear certain colours, or insist on arriving at the venue at a specific time. These ritual patterns may develop over months or years as the musician comes to believe that he or she performs much better when these routines are fulfilled. The problem arises when these coping routines are disrupted. Perhaps an extra rehearsal is unexpectedly called, or traffic problems lead to a change in travel plans. Under these circumstances, the musician who has learnt to rely on an inflexible coping routine may be more disturbed by these occurrences than other performers, leaving them worse off than before.

## 13.6 Methods of treatment and support

Performance anxiety is not the only serious problem related to health and well-being experienced by musicians. High numbers report pain in their shoulders, backs, arms, and fingers, due partly to overuse and partly to excessive tension. Many wind players experience difficulties in lip control after many years, related to tenderness and inflammation. None the less, performance anxiety is so distressing and intense for some musicians that it seriously impairs their lives and careers. There are a range of popular and self-help guides on managing stage fright, some of which are intended for all types of public presentation (e.g. Ashley 1996; Desberg 1996). The most useful book designed for musicians that I have read is Salmon and Meyer (1998).

Professional support for musical performance anxiety provides two basic approaches: (a) pharmacotherapy; and (b) psychotherapies based on relaxation or cognitive behavioural stress management. Anxiolytic drugs, such as benzodiazepines, have been used to some extent to control performance anxiety, despite side effects and the risk of drug dependence (Lederman 1999). The non-benzodiazepine buspirone has been found to have no beneficial effect on performance anxiety in a small controlled trial by Clark and Agras (1991). Much more popular have been β-adrenergic blockers, originally developed for the treatment of cardiovascular disease. These drugs inhibit the peripheral physiological manifestations of sympathetic nervous system activation, such as rapid heart rate and excessive perspiration. They have been welcomed as peripherally acting drugs that modify the somatic elements of performance anxiety without dulling mental processes.

It is clear that many professional musicians use β-blockers, often without medical supervision. Fishbein and Middlestadt (1988) reported that 27 per cent of musicians in their survey had used β-blockers to help with stage fright, and 70 per cent of these obtained the drugs from informal sources. In the 1997 FIM survey, 20 per cent of respondents had used these drugs over the past year. Musicians who do use β-blockers certainly experience favourable effects, with a reduction in tremor and a greater sense of calm prior to and during performance (Fishbein & Middlestadt 1988).

The scientific evidence for benefits is more equivocal. Liden and Gottfries (1974) compared β-blockers and placebo in a double-blind trial. Musicians' ratings of their own symptoms decreased under both conditions, with no significant differences between them. James and Savage (1984) found no difference in mood ratings prior to performance in β-blockade, benzodiazepine, and placebo groups. However, β-blockers did have superior effects on self-ratings of bow shake and dynamics in string players, and on one of eight ratings of performance quality by professional observers. In another placebo-controlled trial in Switzerland, string players played both with and without an audience (Neftel *et al.* 1982). Tape recordings of their playing were analysed objectively using a sonograph, which allowed subtle aspects of performance—such as the regularity of trills and vibrato of movements—to be assessed. The heart rate increase when playing in front of an audience was effectively blocked in the active drug condition, and the increase in output of adrenaline was also attenuated by β-blockade. There was evidence from the sonographic analysis that fine motor skills were impaired during performance in front of an audience in the placebo condition, but that these aspects were improved by β-blockade. At the same time, there were no significant differences in self-reported anxiety.

The impression from these and other studies is that β-blockers do indeed reduce physiological activation. Aspects of performance that are critically dependent on fine motor control, such as bow movements and vibrato, may therefore benefit. The impact on anxiety, concentration, and other aspects is less clear. The unsupervised use of such potent medications cannot be recommended.

Psychotherapeutic approaches to musical performance anxiety cover the whole range of talk therapies, only a few of which have been evaluated systematically. Psychodynamic therapies such as psychoanalysis have been recommended (Nagel 1993), but there is no evidence involving controlled trials or standardized measurement concerning their efficacy. The best evidence is for cognitive-behavioural programmes based on the model of stress outlined in this chapter.

There are four core elements of interventions that tend to be effective, either alone or in combination. The first is for the musician to acquire self-assessment skills. It is essential that performers themselves become aware of the sensations, thoughts, and reactions to audiences that they experience when they are playing in public. Without this self-awareness, progress in developing coping skills is likely to be limited. Secondly, most successful programmes include some method of helping musicians reduce or control physiological arousal. This might involve relaxation training, although *biofeedback* (providing participants with information about their physiological function) has been used as well (Nagel *et al.* 1989; Niemann *et al.* 1993; Sweeney & Horan 1982). Music-based relaxation has also been shown to be helpful in this context (Brodsky & Sloboda 1997). Thirdly, cognitive methods are used to challenge the negative thoughts that spring into the anxious musician's mind. For example, Kendrick and co-workers (1982) first elicited negative or distracting thoughts from participants, then taught them to substitute task-orientated and positive thoughts through role play, imagined performance sequences, and verbalizing thoughts out loud. The fourth ingredient is practice at using these skills in the performance setting. Controlled exposure to threatening stimuli is one of the key elements of anxiety management (Noyes & Hoehn-Saric 1998), and the same is true for musical performance. Coping skills cannot be imposed prescriptively since the musician needs to experiment with different approaches before deciding what is most useful.

In a number of randomized trials, methods that involve these elements have been shown to be superior to comparison conditions in terms of reducing anxiety and increasing self-reported confidence, and there is some evidence for favourable effects on objective assessments of comportment and playing (Brodsky & Sloboda 1997; Kendrick *et al.* 1982; Nagel *et al.* 1989; Valentine *et al.* 1995). An additional important factor is the application of systematic learning and practice methods, such as those described by Reubart (1985) and Salmon and Meyer (1998).

Despite these benefits, it is clear that the average musician does not seek professional help for performance anxiety. In the 1997 FIM survey, for example, only 11 per cent had consulted a psychologist, psychiatrist, or counsellor over the past year, and many of these consultations were probably not for performance anxiety. This represents only a fraction of musicians who complained of performance anxiety. Fishbein and Middlestadt (1988) found that only 25 per cent of musicians in their large survey who experienced severe stage fright had sought psychological or psychiatric counselling. Reluctance to seek help may stem from three factors. The first is that consulting a psychologist or psychiatrist has connotations of mental illness, and musicians quite reasonably do not see their problems in this way. Secondly, there is ambivalence about arousal stemming from the belief that tension is beneficial for a good performance. This may lead to fears that treatment would have an adverse effect on playing. Thirdly, musicians may not be aware of the availability of effective interventions. More positive attitudes may evolve only gradually. In the meantime, advice and strategies for coping with performance anxiety could usefully be incorporated into the training of musicians in conservatories and colleges of music. Self-help materials based on proven techniques also provide musicians with alternatives to formal support (Salmon & Mayer 1998).

## 13.7 Conclusion

The negative emotions elicited in musicians during performance can be highly aversive, and may lead to the curtailment of promising careers in professionals, and the spoiling of an otherwise enjoyable activity for amateurs. Performance anxiety can be placed within the broader context of stress-related problems, and is not a unique phenomenon limited to actors and musicians. Misconceptions exist about the facilitating role of arousal and the adverse effect of performance anxiety. Promising treatment methods have been devised that are based on cognitive-behavioural stress management. The incorporation of the principles underlying these methods into the training of musicians would almost certainly be very beneficial.

## References

Abel, J. L. & Larkin, K. T. (1990). Anticipation of performance among musicians: Physiological arousal, confidence, and state-anxiety. *Psychology of Music,* **18**, 171–82.

Anderson, E. (ed.) (1988). *The letters of Mozart and his family,* (3rd edn). London: MacMillan.

Ashley, J. (1996). *Overcoming stage-fright in everyday life.* New York: Clarkson Potter.

Bartel, L. R. & Thompson, E. G. (1995). Coping with performance stress: A study of professional orchestra musicians in Canada. *Quarterly Journal of Music Teaching and Learning,* **5**, 70–8.

Brodsky, W. (1996). Music performance anxiety reconceptualized. *Medical Problems of Performing Artists,* **11**, 88–98.

Brodsky, W. & Sloboda, J. A. (1997). Clinical trial of a music generated vibrotactile therapeutic environment for musicians. *Journal of Music Therapy,* **34**, 2–32.

Clark, D. B. & Agras, W. S. (1991). The assessment and treatment of performance anxiety in musicians. *American Journal of Psychiatry,* 148, 598–605.

Cooper, C. L. & Wills, G. I. D, (1989). Popular musicians under pressure. *Psychology of Music,* 17, 22–36.

Craske, M. G. & Craig, K. D. (1984). Musical performance anxiety: The three-systems model and self-efficacy theory. *Behavior Research and Therapy,* 22, 267–80.

Desberg, P. (1996). *No more butterflies.* Oakland, CA: New Harbinger.

Dews, C. L. B. & Williams, M. S. (1989). Student musicians personality styles, stresses, and coping patterns. *Psychology of Music,* 17, 37–47.

Duffy, E. (1962). *Activation and behavior.* New York: Wiley.

Fishbein, M. & Middlestadt, S. (1988). Medical problems among ICSOM musicians: Overview of a national survey. *Medical Problems of Performing Artists,* 3, 1–8.

Fredrikson, M. & Gunnarsson, R. (1992). Psychobiology of stage fright: The effect of public performance on neuroendocrine, cardiovascular and subjective ratings. *Biological Psychology,* 33, 51–62.

Gabbard, J. O. (1997). The vicissitudes of shame in stage fright. In *Work and its inhibitions: Psychoanalytic essays,* (ed. C. W. Socarides & S. Kramer), pp. 209–20. Madison, CT: International Universities Press.

Haider, M. & Groll-Knapp, E. (1981). Psychophysiological investigation into the stress experienced by musicians in a symphony orchestra. In *Stress and music: Medical, psychological, sociological, and legal strain factors in a symphony orchestra musician's profession,* (ed. M. Piperek), pp. 15–34. Vienna: Wilhelm Braumüller (originally published 1971).

Hugdahl, K. (1981). The three-systems-model of fear and emotion: A critical examination. *Behaviour Research and Therapy,* 19, 75–85.

James, I. M. & Savage, I. (1984). Beneficial effects of nadolol on anxiety induced disturbance of performance in musicians. A comparison with diazepam and placebo. *American Heart Journal,* 108, 1150–5.

Kendrick, M. J., Craig, K. D., Lawson, D. W., & Davidson, P. O. (1982). Cognitive and behavioral therapy for musical-performance anxiety. *Journal of Consulting and Clinical Psychology,* 50, 353–62.

Kivimäki, M. (1995). Test anxiety, below-capacity performance, and poor test performance: Intrasubject approach with violin students. *Personality and Individual Differences,* 18, 47–55.

Kivimäki, M. & Jokinen, M. (1994). Job perceptions and well-being among symphony orchestra musicians: A comparison with other occupational groups. *Medical Problems of Performing Artists,* 9, 73–6.

Lederman, R. J. (1999). Medical treatment of performance anxiety: A statement in favour. *Medical Problems of Performing Artists,* 14, 117–121.

Lehrer, P. M., Goldman, N. S., & Strommen, E. F. (1990). A principal components assessment of performance anxiety among musicians. *Medical Problems of Performing Artists,* 5, 12–18.

Liden, S. & Gottfries, C-G. (1974). β-blocking agents in the treatment of catecholamine-induced symptoms in musicians. *Lancet,* 2, 529.

Marchant-Haycox, S. E. & Wilson, G. D. (1992). Personality and stress in performing artists. *Personality and Individual Differences,* 13, 1061–8.

Mirowksy, J. & Ross, C. E. (1995). Sex differences in distress: Real or artifact? *American Sociological Review,* 60, 449–68.

Mor, S., Day, H. I., Flett, G. L., & Hewitt, P. L. (1995). Perfectionism, control and components of performance anxiety in professional artists. *Cognitive Therapy and Research*, **19**, 207–25.

Mulcahy, D., Keegan, J., Fingret, A., Wright, C., Park, A., Sparrow, J. *et al.* (1990). Circadian variation of heart rate is affected by environment: A study of continuous electrocardiographic monitoring in members of a symphony orchestra. *British Heart Journal*, **64**, 388–92.

Näätänen, R. (1973). The inverted-U relationship between activation and performance: A critical review. In *Attention and performance IV*, (ed. S. Kornblum), pp. 155–174. London: Academic Press.

Nagel, J. J. (1993). Stage-fright in musicians: A psychodynamic perspective. *Bulletin of the Menninger Clinic*, **57**, 492–503.

Nagel, J. J., Himle, D. P., & Papsdorf, J. D. (1989). Cognitive-behavioural treatment of musical performance anxiety. *Psychology of Music*, **17**, 12–21.

Neftel, K. A., Adler, R. H., Kappell, L., Rossi, M., Dolder, M., Kaser, H. E. *et al.* (1982). Stage-fright in musicians: A model illustrating the effect of beta blockers. *Psychosomatic Medicine*, **44**, 461–9.

Niemann, B. K., Pratt R. R., & Maughan, M. L. (1993). Biofeedback training, selected coping strategies, and music relaxation interventions to reduce debilitating musical performance anxiety. *International Journal of Arts Medicine*, **2**, 7–15.

Noyes, R. & Hoehn-Saric, R. (1998). *The anxiety disorders.* New York: Cambridge University Press.

Olivier, L. (1982). *Confessions of an actor.* London: Routledge.

Parasuraman, S. & Purohit, Y. S. (2000). Distress and boredom among orchestra musicians: The two faces of stress. *Journal of Occupational Health Psychology*, **5**, 74–83.

Reubart, D. (1985). *Anxiety and musical performance.* New York: Da Capo Press.

Salmon, P. G. & Meyer, R. G. (1998). *Notes from the green room: Coping with stress and anxiety in musical performance.* San Francisco: Jossey Bass.

Schmale, H. & Schmidtke, H. (1965). *Untersuchungen uber die Psychophysiologische Belastung von Musikern in ein Kulturorchestern.* Mainz: Schott.

Schulz, W. (1981). Analysis of a symphony orchestra. In *Stress and music: Medical, psychological, sociological, and legal strain factors in a symphony orchestra musician's profession,* (ed. M. Piperek), pp. 35–56. Vienna: Wilhelm Braumüller (originally published 1971).

Spielberger, C. D., Gorsuch, R. L., & Lushene, R. E. (1970). *Manual for the state-trait anxiety inventory.* Palo Alto, CA: Consulting Psychologists Press.

Steptoe, A. (1983). The relationship between tension and the quality of musical performance. *Journal of the International Society for the Study of Tension in Performance*, **1**, 12–22.

Steptoe, A. (1989). Stress, coping and stage fright in professional musicians. *Psychology of Music*, **17**, 3–11.

Steptoe, A. (1998). Psychophysiological bases of disease. In *Comprehensive clinical psychology. Volume 8: Health psychology*, (ed. D. W. Johnston & M. Johnston), pp. 39–78. New York: Elsevier Science.

Steptoe, A. & Appels, A. (ed.) (1989). *Stress, personal control and health.* Chichester, UK: Wiley.

Steptoe, A. & Fidler, H. (1987). Stage fright in orchestral musicians: A study of cognitive and behavioural strategies in performance anxiety. *British Journal of Psychology*, **78**, 241–9.

Steptoe, A., Malik, F., Pay, C., Pearson, P., Price, C., & Win, Z. (1995). The impact of stage fright on student actors. *British Journal of Psychology*, **86**, 27–39.

Sweeney, G. A. & Horan, J. J. (1982). Separate and combined effects of cue-controlled relaxation and cognitive restructuring in the treatment of musical performance anxiety. *Journal of Counseling Psychology,* 29, 486–97.

Theorell, T., Alberg-Hulten, G., Sigala, F., Perski, A., Söderholm, M., Callner, A., & Eneroth, P. (1990). A psychosocial and biomedical comparison between men in six contrasting service occupations. *Work and Stress,* 4, 51–63.

Valentine, E.R., Fitzgerald, D. F. P., Gorton, T. L., Hudson, J. A., & Symonds, E. R. C. (1995). The effect of lessons in the Alexander technique on music performance in high and low stress situations. *Psychology of Music,* 23, 129–41.

Van Kemenade, J. F. L. M., Van Son, M. J. M., & Van Heesch, N. C. A. (1995). Performance anxiety among professional musicians in symphonic orchestras: A self-report study. *Psychological Reports,* 77, 555–62.

Wesner, R., Noyes, R., & Davis, T. (1990). The occurrence of performance anxiety among musicians. *Journal of Affective Disorders,* 18, 177–85.

Widmer, S., Conway, A., Cohen, S., & Davies, P. (1997). Hyperventilation: A correlate and predictor of debilitating performance anxiety in musicians. *Medical Problems of Performing Artists,* 12, 97–106.

Wolfe, M. L. (1989). Correlates of adaptive and maladaptive musical performance anxiety. *Medical Problems of Performing Artists,* 4, 49–56.

# CHAPTER 14

# COMMUNICATING EMOTION IN MUSIC PERFORMANCE: A REVIEW AND THEORETICAL FRAMEWORK

PATRIK N. JUSLIN

Music is perhaps the most widely practised and appreciated of all art forms. Part of the appeal of music may lie in its ability to induce and represent emotions (cf. Budd 1985; Davies 1994; Meyer 1956; see also Sloboda & Juslin, this volume). Music is often regarded as an effective means of communicating emotions, and this notion pertains not only to the notated or implied structure of the music, but also to the way it is *performed*. Both empirical research (Persson 1995; Persson *et al.* 1996; Woody 2000) and biographical accounts (Blum 1977; Kennedy 1990; Schumacher 1995; Seckerson 1991) have suggested that many performers conceive of performance in terms of emotions, moods, or scenarios. A quote from one of the leading guitarists in the world, Eric Clapton, may serve to illustrate this point: 'Music . . . it's a form of communication and reassurance of feelings . . . what I get out of music is a feeling that I'm not alone' (Clapton 1998, p. 20).

The last decade has seen a steady increase of studies of how performers communicate emotions to listeners. The goal of this chapter is to: (a) review research on communication of emotions in music performance; (b) outline a theoretical framework suitable for organizing the findings; and (c) consider some implications for future research on music performance.

## 14.1 The role of the performer

Music might be viewed as part of a communication system in which composers code musical ideas in notation, performers recode from the notation to musical signal, and listeners recode from the acoustic signal to ideas (Kendall & Carterette 1990). The communicative content in music performance includes the performer's *interpretation* of the musical composition, that is, the performer's individualistic shaping of the piece according to his or her intentions (Palmer 1997). Most music performances involve some intention from the performer's side regarding what the music should 'express' to the listeners. Consequently, interpretation involves assigning some kind of meaning to the music (Persson 1995; see also Persson, this volume).

Although there has been much debate on what constitutes the 'meaning' of music, most accounts seem to involve a reference to the emotional impact of music (Budd 1985). It is not surprising, then, that a great deal of research has explored the expressive properties of various musical compositions (Gabrielsson & Lindström, this volume). However, the *performance* is also important in determining the emotional expression of a piece of music. The same notated structure can be performed in a number of different ways, and the precise way it is performed may affect the listener's impression of the music in profound ways. Both anecdotal evidence and empirical research have suggested that performers attempt to convey particular moods to listeners (cf. Persson 1995; Shaffer 1992; Woody 2000). Such expressive intentions may be more common in certain musical styles (e.g. opera, blues) than in others (e.g. serial music). Similarly, they may be more common among some performers (Fig. 14.1) than among others. Still, they occur frequently enough to be of legitimate interest to artists and scientists alike.

The process of interpretation itself is still largely shrouded in mystery. It is often argued that expertise in music performance involves the synthesis of technical and expressive aspects (Gabrielsson 1999; Sloboda 1996), but music teachers tend to spend more time and effort on the former than the latter (Tait 1992). Many music teachers still regard interpretation as 'the thing that cannot be taught'. Others make efforts to

**Figure 14.1** Expressive performance: blues guitarist B. B. King in concert. King (1996) explained his relationship to the guitar: 'If I was feeling lonely, I'd pick up the guitar; feel like talking, pick up the guitar; if something's bugging me, just grab the guitar and play out the anger; happy, horny, mad or sad, the guitar was right there. It was incredible luxury to have this instrument to stroke whenever the passion overcame me' (p. 41). 'I started experimenting with sounds that expressed my emotions, whether happy or sad, bouncy or bluesy. I was looking for ways to let my guitar sing' (p. 123). (Photographs by Steve Berman.)

enhance performers' expressive skills by using tools such as metaphors, modelling, or mood induction (see Juslin & Persson, in press).

There are various traditions in musical interpretation, and emotions may enter into the process of developing an interpretation in different ways depending on the tradition. In one tradition, the performer's task is mainly to be 'a faithful carrier of the composer's message' (Sloboda 1998, p. 22). In this tradition, interpretation involves a careful study of the score, perhaps accompanied by consultation with the composer or of historical commentaries. The main factors determining the interpretation are performance convention and inferences about the expressive intentions of the composer.

In other traditions of interpretation, the performer has much more freedom. (This is, of course, particularly true in musical improvisation where the performer is also the composer.) In these traditions, the interpretation may be guided by the performer's own emotions while playing the piece (see Woody 2000). Alternatively, the performer may attempt (explicitly or implicitly) to render the performance with an emotional expression that seems suitable for the piece in question, perhaps enhancing a quality of emotion that is already latent in the piece of music. The performer's judgment of what emotion is suitable for the piece may be guided by his or her own listening to the music or by simple intuition.

In sum, the amount of freedom allowed to the performer in his or her interpretation of a piece varies greatly depending on the musical style and culture. This implies that the relative importance of the performance in determining the emotional expression of a piece of music is likely to vary considerably across different contexts. Although the emotional expression of a piece depends *both* on its composed structure and on its realization in performance, one may, in principle at least, separate the two aspects for research purposes. In fact, such a distinction has formed the basis of a series of recent studies of how performers communicate emotions to listeners. In the following, I summarize the main findings from this research and delineate a theoretical framework suitable for organizing the findings.

## 14.2 A brief history of the research

Throughout history, there has been plenty of anecdotal evidence concerning the extraordinary expressive skills of particular performers. Performers, listeners, and critics have all testified to the effectiveness of performance in communicating specific emotions to listeners. This can be illustrated by the following quote from the eighteenth-century violinist Francesco Geminiani:

... with regard to musical performances, experience has shown that the imagination of the hearer is in general so much at the disposal of the [performer] that by help of variation, intervals, and modulation he may stamp what impression on the mind he pleases (quoted in Meyer 1956, p. 201).

Claims of this kind are common in the literature. However, anecdotal evidence can be unreliable. Further, in addition to those authors who have made claims about the expressive powers of music, there are others who have argued that music is unable to express anything whatsoever, like Stravinsky (Fisk 1997, pp. 280–1). The extent to which performers can communicate specific emotions to listeners has thus remained an open question. Given that both performers and listeners regard expressive aspects of performance as important, it may be surprising to learn that research on emotional expression in performance is a fairly recent phenomenon, especially in comparison to research on emotional expression in compositions (Gabrielsson & Juslin, in press).

That this problem did not receive attention earlier is strange. One of the general findings from the early studies of performance was that the performance of a piece of music practically never corresponds to the nominal note values of the notation. In every performance, there are certain 'expressive deviations', or 'systematic variations', from what seems prescribed by the notation. These variations are not random, because performers are able to replicate them with great precision (Shaffer & Todd 1987). This gives rise to a question: what is the *function* of these variations?

One function of expressive variations may be to clarify the structure of the piece to the listener (Clarke 1988; Palmer 1989, 1997; Sundberg 1988). By clarifying the structure, the performer may try to enhance the 'inherent' emotional impact of the musical structure. In this view, then, expressive variations primarily reflect the performer's conceptual interpretation of the structure. However, this explanation has failed to account for all of the variance in musical performances. Repp (1998) analysed 115 performances of a Chopin piece in order to study the individual differences among performers. Based on the results, Repp convincingly argued that individual differences at the phrase level do not arise (mainly) from different interpretations of the musical structure but from different ways of giving 'expressive shape' to one and the same structure. Indeed, a number of researchers have suggested that expressive variations may serve to convey moods to listeners (Gabrielsson 1988; Juslin 1997a; Shaffer 1992).

One of the pioneers in music psychology, Carl E. Seashore, argued that 'deviation from the exact . . . is the medium for the creation of the beautiful—for the conveying of emotion' (quoted in Seashore 1937, p. 155). Seashore did not develop any theory to explain how such systematic deviations convey emotions to listeners. However, he did propose a suitable paradigm for exploring this problem. He was interested in the question of how singers express emotions and asked whether there is 'any possibility of a scientific approach' (Seashore 1947, p. 171). He gave the answer himself by describing a study of vocal expression by Fairbanks (1940), one of his colleagues at the University of Iowa. This study required actors to express different emotions in speech, which was later analysed acoustically. Seashore concluded that 'we can exactly parallel this experiment in the field of music' (Seashore 1947, p. 176).

Strangely, Seashore's plea went unheard, and he did not publish any study of that sort himself. Before the mid-1970s, there was not a single study of emotional expression in music performance. By the late 1980s, only two studies on this topic had been published (Kotlyar & Morozov 1976; Senju & Ohgushi 1987). After this modest beginning, however, there was a virtual explosion of studies in the early 1990s (for a review, see Juslin 1999). Most of these studies used the same paradigm that Seashore suggested 40 years earlier.

## 14.3 The standard paradigm

The paradigm used in most studies of emotional expression in music performance is simple: performers are asked to play a number of brief melodies to express different emotions chosen by the researcher. The resulting performances are first recorded and then evaluated in listening experiments to see whether listeners can recognize the intended expression. Each performance is further analysed to study what acoustic means the performer used to achieve each emotional expression. (The focus in these experiments has primarily been on *represented* emotion rather than *induced* emotion.) The basic assumption is that because the melodies remain the same in different expressions, whatever effects appear in listeners' judgments or in acoustic measures should mainly be the result of the performer's expressive intention. To have performers play the same piece of music with different kinds of emotional expression might seem 'unnatural' from a musical point of view. However, this design is necessary to secure the internal validity of the experiments: If different emotions are expressed by different melodies, it is impossible to know whether the obtained effects on listener judgments or performance measures are due to the melody, the performance, or some complex interaction between the two. This paradigm is not without its problems, but I will temporarily postpone my critique until later sections (for alternatives approaches to studying emotional expression in performance, see Section 14.7.1).

There are about 30 studies of emotional expression in performance. These studies cover a broad range of musical styles, such as opera, classical music, folk music, jazz, and pop/rock. The emotions investigated have usually included happiness, sadness, anger, fear, and tenderness. A variety of musical instruments has also been included, such as the violin, flute, clarinet, electric guitar, piano, trumpet, drums, synthesizer, and singing voice. Studies have mainly focused on two aspects of the communicative process: (a) the accuracy of the communication; and (b) the code used by performers and listeners.

## 14.4 Communication accuracy

The first question of interest to any researcher concerned with emotional communication in music performance is whether such communication is at all possible. It can seem odd to talk about 'accuracy' in the context of music, but most performers are probably concerned about whether their interpretation of the music is perceived in the intended way by listeners. Thus, the extent to which a performer and a listener agree on the expression of the performance can be seen as a measure of the 'accuracy' of the communication. In a pioneering study, Kotlyar and Morozov (1976) asked ten opera singers to sing phrases from various pieces of music in such a way that they would communicate joy, anger, sorrow, and fear to listeners. Musically trained listeners were asked to judge the expression of each performance. The results showed that the listeners were highly successful at recognizing the intended expression.

Since then, many studies have confirmed that professional music performers are able to communicate particular emotions to listeners (Behrens & Green 1993; Gabrielsson & Juslin 1996; Gabrielsson & Lindström 1995; Juslin 1997*a*, 2000; Juslin & Madison 1999; Ohgushi & Hattori 1996*a*; Sundberg *et al.* 1995). However, these studies have also revealed marked individual differences in *encoding* (expression) and *decoding* (recognition) accuracy, consistent with the results from studies of other non-verbal communication channels (Buck 1984; Wallbott & Scherer 1986). Studies of amateurs have indicated that they have a lower accuracy than experts, but that their accuracy can be improved by appropriate feedback (Juslin & Laukka 2000).

Few studies have reported the decoding accuracy in a manner that makes more precise estimates possible. However, Juslin (1997b) used a forced-choice format in order to make the results comparable with the results from studies of vocal expression. Juslin found that decoding accuracy was 75 per cent correct, or about four times higher than what would be expected by chance alone. This suggests that, at least under ideal circumstances, the accuracy of communication of emotion via musical performance may approach the accuracy of facial or vocal expression (cf. Ekman 1973; Scherer 1986). The examination of error distributions shows that certain pairs of emotional expressions are confused more frequently than others. For instance, sadness and tenderness expressions are typically confused with each other, whereas sadness and happiness expressions are rarely confused. On the whole, though, the communicative process is robust.

One objection to this finding could be that the accuracy of the communicative process is boosted because of the response formats used. In most studies, listeners made their judgments by means of forced-choice or adjective ratings, methods which offer only a limited number of response options. To address this problem, Juslin (1997c) investigated the generalizability of decoding accuracy across response formats using a *parallel enrichment procedure* (Rosenthal 1982). That is, quantitative data from forced-choice judgments of musical performances were augmented by qualitative data from free labelling of the same performances. The two methods converged on the conclusions that: (a) communication was reliable regardless of the response format; and (b) what could be communicated reliably was the basic-level emotion categories, but not specific nuances within these categories.

## 14.5 Code usage

The early studies were primarily concerned with investigating whether performers are able to communicate emotions to their listeners at all. However, if we want to study communication as a process, we must also consider its mechanisms, particularly the code used by performers and listeners. Accordingly, researchers have tried to describe the means by which performers express specific emotions (Baroni & Finarelli 1994; Gabrielsson & Juslin 1996; Gabrielsson & Lindström 1995; Juslin 1997a, 1997b, 2000; Juslin & Madison 1999; Rapoport 1996).

### 14.5.1 Expressive cues, emotion categories, and emotion dimensions

One main finding from this line of research is that the performer's expressive intention affects almost every aspect of the performance; that is, emotional expression in performance seems to involve a whole set of *cues*—or bits of information—that are used by performers and listeners. A summary of the code usage established in studies thus far is presented in Fig. 14.2. Included are the five emotions (happiness, sadness, anger, fear, love/tenderness) that have been studied most extensively. These emotions represent a natural point of departure since all are regarded as typical emotions by lay people (see Shaver *et al.* 1987; Shields 1984) and have been postulated as so-called 'basic emotions' by scientists (Plutchik 1994, p. 58). The same emotions have also occurred (some more than others) in the expression marks of musical scores (e.g. *festoso, dolente, furioso, timoroso, teneramente*).

Figure 14.2 combines *categorical* and *dimensional* approaches to emotional expression to illustrate that the code allows performers to communicate both graded signals (e.g. level of activity) and categorical signals (e.g. happiness). Each emotional expression is placed at an approximate point in a two-dimensional emotion space constituted by *valence* and *activity level* (cf. Russell 1980). The placement of each emotional expression in the emotion space is partly based on the results from a study in which participants rated the valence and activity of 400 emotion terms (Whissell 1989). These positions of the emotional expressions are further supported by a cluster analysis of listeners' ratings of various emotional expressions reported in Juslin (1997*b*). Figure 14.2

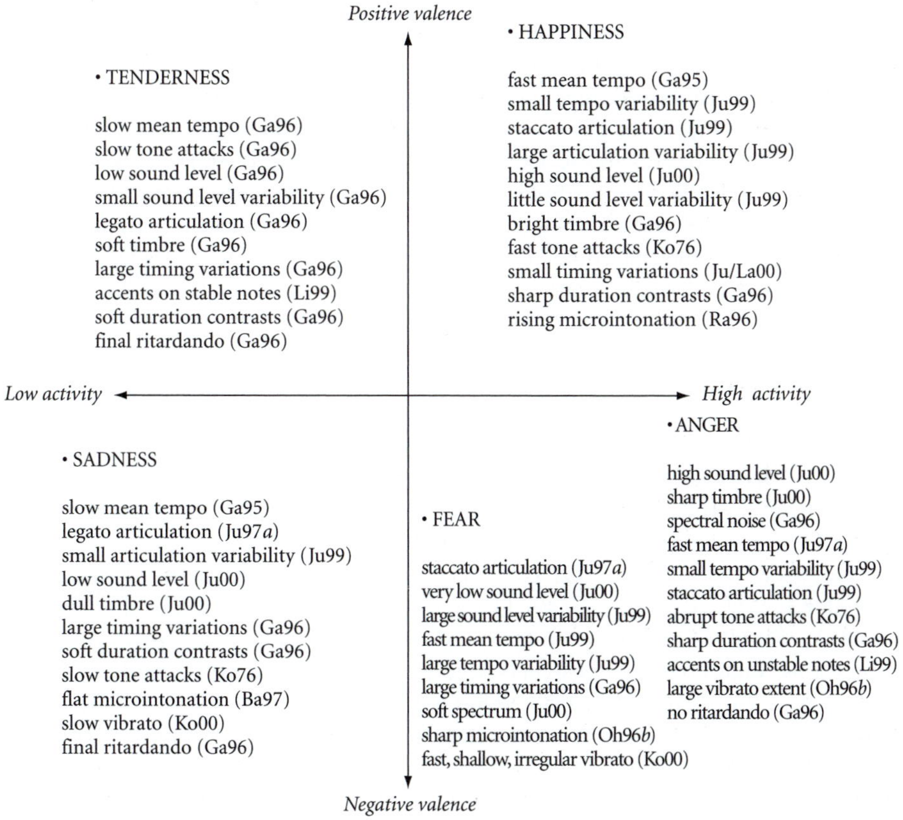

*Positive valence*

• HAPPINESS

• TENDERNESS

slow mean tempo (Ga96)
slow tone attacks (Ga96)
low sound level (Ga96)
small sound level variability (Ga96)
legato articulation (Ga96)
soft timbre (Ga96)
large timing variations (Ga96)
accents on stable notes (Li99)
soft duration contrasts (Ga96)
final ritardando (Ga96)

fast mean tempo (Ga95)
small tempo variability (Ju99)
staccato articulation (Ju99)
large articulation variability (Ju99)
high sound level (Ju00)
little sound level variability (Ju99)
bright timbre (Ga96)
fast tone attacks (Ko76)
small timing variations (Ju/La00)
sharp duration contrasts (Ga96)
rising microintonation (Ra96)

*Low activity* ←——————————————————————————→ *High activity*

• ANGER

• SADNESS

slow mean tempo (Ga95)
legato articulation (Ju97*a*)
small articulation variability (Ju99)
low sound level (Ju00)
dull timbre (Ju00)
large timing variations (Ga96)
soft duration contrasts (Ga96)
slow tone attacks (Ko76)
flat microintonation (Ba97)
slow vibrato (Ko00)
final ritardando (Ga96)

• FEAR

staccato articulation (Ju97*a*)
very low sound level (Ju00)
large sound level variability (Ju99)
fast mean tempo (Ju99)
large tempo variability (Ju99)
large timing variations (Ga96)
soft spectrum (Ju00)
sharp microintonation (Oh96*b*)
fast, shallow, irregular vibrato (Ko00)

high sound level (Ju00)
sharp timbre (Ju00)
spectral noise (Ga96)
fast mean tempo (Ju97*a*)
small tempo variability (Ju99)
staccato articulation (Ju99)
abrupt tone attacks (Ko76)
sharp duration contrasts (Ga96)
accents on unstable notes (Li99)
large vibrato extent (Oh96*b*)
no ritardando (Ga96)

*Negative valence*

**Figure 14.2** Summary of cue utilization in performers' communication of emotion in music. (One representative study is cited for each cue. Authors' names are abbreviated to the initial two letters of the first author (and the second author if needed for clarity), and the publication year to the two last digits, e.g. Ko76 = Kotlyar & Morozov 1976.)

shows that happiness and tenderness expressions are both positive, whereas only happiness is high in activity. Similarly, both anger and sadness expressions are negative, whereas only anger is high in activity.

As seen in Fig. 14.2, the expressive cues include tempo, sound level, timing, intonation, articulation, timbre, vibrato, tone attacks, tone decays, and pauses. Both the mean level of a cue and its variability throughout the performance may be important for the communicative process. For example, sadness expressions are associated with slow tempo, low sound level, legato articulation, small articulation variability, slow tone attacks, and dull timbre, whereas happiness expressions are associated with fast tempo, high sound level, staccato articulation, large articulation variability, fast tone attacks, and bright timbre (for a more detailed review, see Juslin 1999). Although Fig. 14.2 is limited to a few seemingly 'static' emotion categories, it is easy to imagine how the emotional expression can be gradually altered during the course of a performance, along the two emotions dimensions.

Some of the cues described in Fig. 14.2 may be common knowledge to most performers, whereas other aspects, such as those having to do with the *microstructure* (e.g. timing) of the performance, are less obvious. The number of cues available depends on the instrument used. In addition, the cue utilization is not completely consistent across performers, instruments, or pieces of music (Juslin 2000). Notably, even children (4–12 years old) seem to be able to use some of these cues to express emotions in song. For instance, they use a fast tempo and a high sound level in happy expressions, whereas they use a slow tempo and a low sound level in sad expressions (Adachi & Trehub 1998).

The positions of the emotional expressions in the emotion space in Fig. 14.2 suggest that certain cues may have a larger influence on certain emotion dimensions than others. Thus, for instance, tempo, sound level, and articulation seem to be especially important for the activity level, whereas timbre (e.g. the amount of high-frequency energy in the spectrum), perhaps in combination with sound level, seems to be especially important for emotional valence. In the latter case, intermediate levels of sound level and high-frequency energy are associated with positive emotions, whereas more extreme levels (e.g. very high or very low sound level) are associated with negative emotions. This hypothesized two-factor structure can, of course, be tested in future research, using listening tests with synthesized performances.

As suggested by Fig. 14.2, research to date has primarily focused on the expressions of a set of 'basic emotions' (Sloboda & Juslin, this volume). However, it is interesting to speculate whether 'secondary' or 'complex' emotions may be developed from these expressions. Many emotion researchers believe that such emotions constitute 'mixtures' of more basic emotions. For instance, it has been proposed that pride involves the combination of happiness and anger (Plutchik 1994, p. 61). Judging from Fig. 14.2, the expression of pride would then presumably involve some kind of compromise among the cues used to communicate happiness and anger, although perhaps with a slightly lower activity level (cf. Whissell 1989).

Performance analyses have shown that performers may use a number of cues to express specific emotions. However, these analyses do not show that listeners actually *use* the same cues in their judgments. To test the validity of hypotheses derived from performance studies, it is therefore necessary to conduct listening experiments with synthesized and systematically varied performances. Such experiments have mostly confirmed that listeners make the same associations between cues and emotion categories as performers do (Juslin 1997b; Scherer & Oshinsky 1977; see also Bresin & Friberg 2000; Juslin et al., in press).

In addition to the results with regard to relationships between acoustic cues and emotion categories, Juslin (1997b) reported findings on how acoustic cues contribute to the perceived 'expressiveness' of the performance. Juslin manipulated the tempo, sound level, articulation, timbre, and tone attacks of synthesized performances in a factorial design, and asked listeners to rate the expressiveness of the resulting 108 cue combinations. The single cue combination that was most expressive according to listeners had the following characteristics (with cues in order of predictive strength): legato articulation, soft spectrum, slow tempo, high sound level, and slow tone attacks. This raised an interesting question: Is this how performers should play in order to be judged as expressive by listeners? It may be noted that the most expressive cue combination was highly similar to the cue combination that expressed sadness and tenderness best according to the listeners. This seems to suggest that there is a close connection between sadness/ tenderness and expressiveness. This result was confirmed by a cluster analysis of the listeners' judgments, which showed that the ratings of sadness and tenderness correlated more strongly with the ratings of expressiveness than did the ratings of happiness, fear, or anger. It is worth noting in this context that so-called 'separation calls', associated with social loss, are believed to elicit strong sympathetic responses in listeners (Plutchik 1994, p. 331). This could perhaps explain why listeners find performances with a sad expression particularly expressive.

### 14.5.2 The importance of musical time: expressive contours

Most studies thus far have focused on cues that remain 'fixed' during the performance or on 'summary measures' (e.g. mean, standard deviation) of cues that do vary. However, from an intuitive point of view, it would seem that much of music's expressiveness lies in patterns of *changes* in cues during the course of a performance. Frick (1985) used the concept 'prosodic contours' to refer to dynamic patterns of voice cues over time found in vocal expressions. In music, this corresponds to continuously changing patterns of tempo, articulation, and sound level throughout the performance (examples of patterns of articulation for different emotions are presented in Fig. 14.3). In this chapter, I will call these patterns *expressive contours*. Are such expressive contours involved in the communicative process?

Preliminary evidence that expressive contours are really involved in the communicative process was obtained in a study by Juslin (1997b). This study included two kinds of stimulus. The first consisted of a set of musical performances of 'Nobody Knows' on the electric guitar, made with different expressive intentions (e.g. sadness, happiness, tenderness). The second kind of stimuli consisted of synthesized performances of the same melody, in which the same emotional expressions were simulated on the basis of hypotheses from previous performance analyses. The 'human' performances included expressive contours, whereas the synthesized performances included only cues that were 'fixed' throughout the whole performance. Both kinds of performance communicated the intended emotions with high reliability.

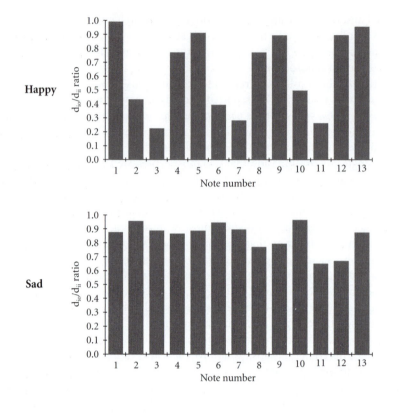

**Figure 14.3** Articulation patterns for happy and sad performances of 'When the Saints' on the electric guitar (unpublished data from Juslin 1997*a*). The duration from the onset of a tone until the onset of the next tone ($d_{ii}$) and the duration from the onset of a tone until its offset ($d_{io}$) were used to calculate the $d_{io}/d_{ii}$ ratio, i.e. the articulation. Articulation close to 1.0 may be referred to as legato, whereas articulation below 0.5 may be referred to as staccato.

To study the relative importance of expressive contours, Juslin played the performances backwards and then asked listeners to decode the intended emotional expression. Playing the sequences backwards changed the expressive contours (i.e. patterns over time) but preserved the summary measures (e.g. tempo) of the performances. The results showed that the human performances suffered from this manipulation (i.e. decoding accuracy was reduced), whereas synthesized performances did not. This suggests that human performances depend, at least to some extent, on the use of expressive contours. However, this study did not provide any clues about what expressive contours were used by listeners.

Further evidence that expressive contours may be of importance comes from a study by Juslin and Madison (1999). They used a combination of analysis and synthesis afforded by the possibility to 'resynthesize' human performances by means of computer technology. This method was used to investigate the relative importance of timing patterns in communication of emotions through musical performance. Juslin and Madison gradually removed different expressive cues (tempo, dynamics, timing, articulation) from piano performances played with various intended expressions (anger, sadness, happiness, fear) to see how such manipulations would affect a listener's ability to decode the emotional expression. The results indicated that: (a) removing the timing pattern yielded a decrease in listeners' decoding accuracy; (b) timing patterns alone were capable of communicating at least some emotions with better than chance accuracy; and (c) timing patterns were less effective in communicating emotions than were tempo and dynamics. The results further indicated that timing patterns (defined as sequences of inter-onset intervals) were particularly important for fear expressions, whereas articulation patterns were particularly important for happiness expressions. This study demonstrated that listeners indeed can use timing patterns to decode the emotional expression of a performance. However, the results did not reveal what it is in the timing patterns that provides the listeners with emotional information.

One way of exploring what it is in the expressive contours that provides the emotional information is to rely on listeners' continuous ratings of expression in performance. In recent years, researchers have increasingly been developing methods for describing the moment-to-moment changes in listeners' emotional responses to music (for a review, see Schubert, this volume). Most of the attempts have involved the use of different pieces of music. However, Sloboda and Lehmann (in press) have applied continuous response methodology specifically to performance. They focused on how music performers use various strategies to enhance the emotional intensity of a performance. Ten expert pianists were required to perform a Chopin prelude as if in a concert. The resulting performances were recorded and the performers were interviewed concerning their interpretations of the piece. Finally, musically trained listeners were asked to rate the concurrent level of perceived 'emotionality' in each interpretation by moving a mouse pointer on a continuous response computer interface.

The results indicated that the different interpretations of the piece gave rise to different profiles of perceived emotional intensity, and that at least some of the differences among the interpretations could be explained in terms of the expressive devices used by the performers. The performers used devices related to timing, dynamics, and asynchronies between melody notes and bass notes (e.g. delaying a note, lengthening a note, changing the dynamic range). Most of the expressive devices occurred at the beginnings of musical phrases. But can such devices be used by listeners to decode different emotions?

One possible answer is provided by research on how notated structure and performed structure *interact* in producing an emotional expression. In a recent study, Lindström (1999) manipulated a brief melody ('Frère Jacques') concerning tonal progression, rhythm, melodic contour, and melodic direction. The resulting versions of the melody were rated by listeners on emotion scales. On the basis of these ratings, Lindström chose 16 versions of the melody that could be regarded as 'good' or 'less good' exemplars of specific emotions (e.g. anger). Then, he asked professional pianists to play the different versions of the melody to express four different emotions (happiness, sadness, anger, tenderness) to listeners. The performers were asked to 'think aloud' throughout the preparation of the performance.

Two findings were of particular interest. First, there was a 'compensation tendency' in the performances, such that the performers used more 'extreme' variations in the performance to achieve the intended expression (e.g. happiness) in those versions of the melody that were 'less good' exemplars of the intended emotion. Second, the results showed that the performers accentuated different features of the melodic structure depending on the intended expression. Thus, for example, if a certain note in the melody structure was seen as particularly 'happy', then the performers emphasized this note (e.g. via accents in timing, dynamics, articulation) in happiness expressions, but de-emphasized it in sadness expressions. However, the general pattern of cues was the same as in previous studies, which suggests that it is mainly the local aspects of the performance that are affected by particular melodies, whereas overall cues (e.g. mean tempo, mean articulation, mean sound level) are used pretty much the same regardless of the particular melody (see Juslin 2000). In sum, it seems that, depending on the intended expression, different parts of the melodic structure are emphasized. This might explain how listeners can arrive at judgments of the expression on the basis of expressive contours.

This section has shown that there are a number of acoustic cues that performers can use to communicate emotions to listeners. But many studies have shown that cue utilization is inconsistent both across and within performers. Similarly, listening experiments have shown that cue utilization is inconsistent both across and within listeners (cf. Juslin 1998). This presents something of a puzzle: how can the communicative process be so reliable if the cue utilization is inconsistent? To explain the characteristics of the communicative process, we need a theoretical framework.

## 14.6 A theoretical framework: the functionalist perspective

One explanation of the scarcity of studies of emotional expression in music performance prior to 1990 might be a lack of relevant theories. This has led to a neglect of expressive aspects of performance in both research and education. One candidate for a useful theory would seem to be Clynes' (1973, 1977) 'sentic' theory, in which he argued for the existence of biologically pre-programmed spatiotemporal forms, or *essentic forms*, for the communication of specific emotions. Unfortunately, independent attempts to replicate these spatiotemporal forms have yielded mixed results (e.g. Gorman & Crain 1974; Nettelbeck *et al.* 1989; Trussoni *et al.* 1988).

The only elaborated theoretical framework aimed specifically at performance aspects has been presented by Juslin (1995, 1997a). Juslin suggested that researchers should adopt a *functionalist perspective* on emotional communication in music performance. This involves the integration of ideas from research on emotion and non-verbal communication with Egon Brunswik's (1956) *probabilistic functionalism*. This framework provides useful questions, hypotheses, and ways of interpreting results. The functionalist perspective is concerned with three aspects of the expressive code: (a) its origin; (b) its description; and (c) its improvement. The following sections focus on the first two of these aspects. For a discussion of applications for music education, see Juslin and Laukka (2000) and Juslin and Persson (in press).

### 14.6.1 Origin of the code

The fact that performers are able to communicate emotions to listeners is something that requires an explanation: What is it that makes this possible? What is the origin of the code used by performers and listeners? According to the functionalist perspective, the key to this problem lies in considering the *functions* that communication of emotions has served—and continues to serve—in social interaction (e.g. Darwin 1872). Although music performance may be a recent addition to the human behavioural repertoire, it must still be constrained by psychological mechanisms that have been shaped by evolution (Juslin 1998). Evolutionary considerations may be particularly relevant for emotional communication, because animals also communicate emotion, for instance, via acoustic signals (e.g. Plutchik 1994, Chapter 10). Accordingly, Juslin (1998) has argued that communication of emotion in music performance reflects two factors: (a) brain programmes; and (b) social learning. Each of these factors will be discussed below.

*Brain programmes*

The first factor hypothesized to govern emotional expression in performance is innate 'brain programmes' for vocal expression of emotion. Studies of both monkeys and humans with brain lesions have investigated the neurological 'substrates' underlying spontaneous vocalizations of emotion (e.g. Jürgens & von Cramon 1982; MacLean 1978; Panksepp 1982; Penfield & Roberts 1959; Ploog 1981, 1986). These studies have yielded evidence of 'brain programmes' that function to initiate and organize 'pre-wired' vocal expressions. Electrical stimulation of particular brain structures in the amygdala and the hypothalamus produces vocalizations that observers cannot distinguish from natural expressions. In humans, at least, these 'pre-wired' vocal expressions can also be executed at will for communicative purposes, thanks to brain structures in the anterior cingulate cortex. Such 'brain programmes' might explain the reported cross-cultural agreement in encoding and decoding of vocal expressions (Frick 1985). There is further evidence that both encoding (Shapiro & Danly 1985) and decoding (Borod *et al.* 1998) of emotion through voice prosody is handled by the right hemisphere of the brain.

What, then, does voice prosody has do to with performance of music? According to the functionalist perspective, music performers are able to communicate emotions to listeners by using the same acoustic code as is used in vocal expression of emotion. The notion that there is a close relationship between music and the human voice has a long history (Helmholtz 1954; Kivy 1989; Rousseau 1986; Scherer 1995; Sundberg 1982). However, it seems unlikely that this link can explain all of music's expressiveness. I have thus suggested that the hypothesis that there is an iconic similarity between vocal expression of emotion and musical expression of emotion applies mainly to those aspects of the music that the performer can control during his or her performance, such as tempo, loudness, or timbre (Juslin, in press). Neuropsychological evidence suggests that certain aspects of music, such as timbre, share the same neural resources as speech, whereas others (e.g. tonality) draw on neural resources that are unique to music (Handel 1991; Patel & Peretz 1997). Further, the same brain hemisphere (the right) seems to be involved in perception of emotion in music and speech (Borod *et al.* 1998; Bryden *et al.* 1982).

In addition, whereas previous formulations of the link have been vague and speculative, the functionalist perspective specifies the actual neurological substrates responsible for these similarities, and leads to research that provides empirical evidence in favour of this hypothesis. Juslin (1999) carried out a systematic review of the code usage in vocal expression and music performance. The results revealed a number of similarities in code usage. For example, vocal expression of sadness is associated with slow speech rate, low voice intensity, low intonation, and little high-frequency energy in the spectrum of the voice (Juslin & Laukka, in press; Scherer 1986). The same acoustic cues are used to communicate sadness in musical performances (cf. Fig. 14.2).

Juslin also argues that encoding and decoding of emotions proceed in terms of a limited number of 'basic' emotion categories (cf. Ekman 1992; Izard 1977; Johnson-Laird & Oatley 1992; Oatley 1992), which provide decoders with the maximum information and discriminability (Ross & Spalding 1994). To be useful as guides to action, expressions are quickly decoded in terms of just a few categories of emotion related to such fundamental life problems as danger (fear), competition (anger), loss (sadness), and cooperation (happiness). It may be noted that even in the first months of life, infants are able to differentiate prototypical vocal expressions in infant-directed speech, and to respond adequately to their categorical messages (Papoušek *et al.* 1990). Indeed, infants may be able to decode vocal expression of emotion even earlier than they are able to decode facial expression (see Oatley & Jenkins 1996, Chapter 6). There is also evidence of categorical perception of emotion in vocal expression in adults (e.g. de Gelder & Vroomen 1996). This supports a conceptualization of the perception of emotion from acoustic stimuli in terms of basic emotion categories.

A related finding is that neurophysiologist and ethologist Ploog (1981, 1992) and his co-workers have managed to identify a limited number of vocalization categories in squirrel monkeys. (Note that the neurological substrates involved in vocalizations are rather similar in monkeys and humans.) The vocalization categories are associated with important events in the monkeys' lives, and include warning signals ('alarm peeps'), threat signals ('groaning'), desire for social contact signals ('isolation peeps'), and companionship signals ('cackling'). It seems plausible that vocal expressions deriving from 'brain programmes' discovered in humans have served—and still continue to serve—similar communicative functions (Panksepp 1982).

It is possible to speculate that vocal expressions associated with the 'basic' emotion categories gradually became meshed with music that accompanied related cultural activities. There is evidence that people can accurately categorize songs of different 'emotional' types (e.g. mourning, love, war, lullaby) that come from diverse cultures (e.g. Eggebrecht 1983). Moreover, there are similarities in the acoustic code used in such songs in different cultures; for example, mourning songs usually have a slow tempo, low sound level, and soft timbre, whereas festive songs have a fast tempo, high sound level, and bright timbre (Eibl-Eibesfeldt 1989). Thus, the acoustic code used by performers today may be linked—in functional ways—to important cultural activities of the past (Gregory 1997; see also Becker, this volume).

### Social learning

The second factor governing emotional expression in performance is social learning or specific memories. This is a life-long process that begins with the socialization of emotions. Certain aspects of music performance (e.g. those not shared with vocal expression) may be completely governed by cultural influences. Others—although based on innate mechanisms—are 'modulated' by experience. This modulation of the code begins with the early interaction between mother and infant (or even earlier, through 'biochemical imprinting' during the prenatal stage). When mothers talk to their infants, for example, if they want to calm their infant, they reduce the speed and intensity of their speech and talk with slowly falling pitch contours. If, on the other hand, mothers want to express disapproval towards some unfavourable activity they use brief, sharp, and staccato-like contours (Papoušek 1996). Thus, as Papoušek argues, the origins of expressive skills in music cannot be easily separated from the earliest stages of emotional communication.

The shaping of the expressive code continues throughout life, along with accumulated experience. Performers learn links between expressive cues and extramusical aspects (e.g. body language, biological motion) through analogies (cf. Sloboda 1996). In the professional career, the code is modulated by advice from music teachers, performance conventions, and the use of metaphors. This second factor of social learning, reflecting cultural influences, could explain: (a) the individual differences among performers; (b) why the cue utilization is inconsistent; and (c) why there are cultural differences in cue utilization. However, Juslin (1999) assumes that the 'core' of the expressive code is provided by the first factor—innate brain programmes for vocal expression. This could explain why expressive skills are often regarded as 'instinctive'.

Predictions based on the functionalist perspective that have received empirical support include: (a) that there are similarities in cue utilization between vocal expression and musical performance (Juslin 1999); (b) that basic emotions are easier to communicate than other emotions (cf. Gabrielsson & Juslin 1996; Gabrielsson & Lindström 1995; Senju & Ohgushi 1987); (c) decoding of emotion from music is quick (Peretz *et al.* 1998); (d) decoding of emotion from music performance is largely independent of musical training (Juslin 1997a); (e) that even children, 3–4 years old, are able to decode such basic emotions as happiness, sadness, anger, and fear in music with better than chance accuracy (see Cunningham & Sterling 1988; Dolgin & Adelson 1990; Kratus 1993; Terwogt & van Grinsven 1988); and (f) that listeners are able to decode basic emotions with accuracy better than chance even from single voice tones (Konishi *et al.* 2000).

One more prediction is that there should be cross-cultural agreement regarding some aspects, at least, of music's expressiveness. A common hypothesis is that there is universal recognition of emotions from vocal expression. For instance, Frick (1985) reviewed a large number of cross-cultural studies of vocal expression of emotion and concluded that 'there is little evidence for . . . cultural differences in the prosodic communication of emotion' (p. 414). If, as I have claimed, there are many similarities in cue utilization between vocal expression and music performance, we would expect to find some degree of cross-cultural agreement in listeners' judgments of emotional expression in musical performances. Thus, Juslin (1997b, p. 248) proposed that 'some aspects of music (e.g. tonality, melody, and harmony) are relatively more culture-specific, whereas other aspects . . . are more culture-independent (because they are based on nonverbal communication of emotion)'. This notion was subsequently turned into a formal model by

Balkwill and Thompson (1999). While few studies have explicitly aimed to address this issue, there is evidence of cross-cultural similarities in performers' utilization of cues from studies in India (Balkwill & Thompson 1999), Russia (Kotlyar & Morozov 1976), Italy (Baroni & Finarelli 1994), Japan (Ohgushi & Hattori 1996*b*), Sweden (Juslin 1997*a*), and Germany (Langeheinecke *et al.* 1999). These studies suggest that cues like tempo, sound level, and timbre are used in a similar manner in different cultures. When it comes to cross-cultural studies that involve other cues (e.g. harmony), there are larger cross-cultural differences (Gabrielsson & Juslin, in press).

The discussion so far has mainly been concerned with the origin of the acoustic code used in the communication of emotion in music performances. However, to truly understand the virtues and limitations of the communicative process, it is also necessary to describe the nature of the code in more detail. The following section describes a conceptual tool that may be useful in describing the essential characteristics of the communicative process.

### 14.6.2 Description of the code: the lens model

Juslin (1995, 1998, 2000) suggested that the communicative process be described in terms of a modified version of Brunswik's (1956) well-known 'lens model' (Fig. 14.4). This model is meant to illustrate how music performers *encode* specific emotions by means of a number of *probabilistic* (i.e. uncertain) albeit partly redundant *cues* in the performance (e.g. tempo, sound level, timbre, articulation). The emotions are *decoded* by listeners who use the same cues to judge the emotional expression. The cues are probabilistic in the sense that they are not wholly reliable indicators of the intended expression. Listeners thus have to *combine* the cues in order to arrive at reliable judgments of the expression. Brunswik's (1956) notion of *vicarious functioning* may be used

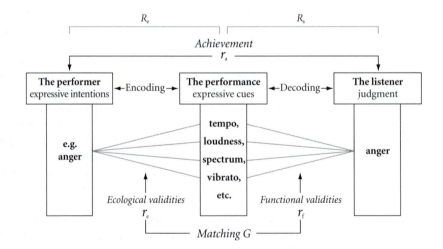

**Figure 14.4** A Brunswikian lens model for communication of emotion in music performance (adapted from Juslin 1995).

to describe how listeners use the partly interchangeable cues in flexible ways, sometimes shifting from one cue that is unavailable to another that is available.

Intercorrelations between cues partly reflect how sounds are produced on instruments. For example, hitting a string harder on the electric guitar generates a tone with increased sound level, but it also generates more high-frequency energy in the spectrum of the tone. However, intercorrelations between cues may also reflect how performers use the cues to accomplish different expressions (e.g. the use of high sound level and fast tempo in both anger and happiness). Empirical studies have confirmed that the cues in performances are probabilistically related to both performers' intentions and listeners' judgments (see Juslin 1997*a*, 1997*b*, 2000), and that there are cue intercorrelations (Juslin 1997*a*; Kratus 1993). Studies using synthesized music performances that are varied in a systematic manner have suggested that the performance cues contribute independently—in an additive fashion—to listeners' emotion judgments, as evidenced by a lack of interactions among the cues (e.g. Juslin 1997*b*). Notably, this is consistent with findings from studies of the vocal expression of emotion, which involve many of the same cues (Ladd *et al.* 1985). However, it stands in contrast to the findings from studies that manipulate aspects of the melodic structure (see Gabrielsson & Lindström, this volume).

The redundancy of the cues reduces the uncertainty of the communicative process. On the other hand, it also limits the information capacity of the communicative channel, because the same information is conveyed by many cues. In Brunswik's own words, the system aims at 'smallness of error at the expense of the highest frequency of precision' (1956, p. 146); such a system leads to 'compromise and falling short of precision, but also the relative infrequency of drastic error' (1956, p. 145). It is easy to see how a system for communication of emotions with this characteristic could have survival value. It is ultimately more important to avoid making serious mistakes (e.g. mistaking anger for joy), than to have the ability to make more subtle discriminations between emotions (e.g. detecting different kinds of joy). The characteristics of the present communicative system can thus be partly explained by evolutionary pressures of the past (Juslin, 2001).

A 'Brunswikian' conceptualization of the communicative process in terms of separate cues that are 'integrated'—as opposed to a 'Gibsonian' conceptualization in terms of more holistic 'higher-order variables' (Gibson 1979)—seems to be supported by studies of the physiology of listening. Handel (1991) points out that speech and music use similar perceptual mechanisms, and that the auditory pathways involve different neural representations for different aspects of the acoustic signal (e.g. timing, frequency) that are kept separate until later stages of analysis. Perception of both speech and music requires the integration of these different representations. (Of course, the question of exactly which acoustic cues are relevant and how they should be defined is an empirical matter.)

In the lens model, the relationship between the performer's expressive intention and a cue in the performance (e.g. articulation) describes the *ecological validity* ($r_e$) of that cue (Fig. 14.4). Ecological validity is a measure of the validity of that cue in predicting the performer's intention. The *functional validity* ($r_f$) of the same cue is indexed by the relationship between the cue and the listener's judgment. Functional validity is a measure of the validity of the cue in predicting the listener's emotion judgment. *Achievement* $(r_a)$ refers to the accuracy of the communication, as measured by the relationship between the performer's intention and the listener's emotion judgment. Finally, *matching* $(G)$ refers to the extent to which ecological and functional validities are 'matched' to each other—that is, whether the performer and listener share a common code (the measurement of each of these quantities is described below).

The Brunswikian lens model has a number of important implications. First, we cannot expect perfect communication accuracy. If cues are only probabilistic, it means that accuracy can only be probabilistic. Second, to understand why the communication is successful or not in a particular situation, researchers need to describe both encoding and decoding in terms of the same concepts. Third, because the cues are intercorrelated to some extent, many different cue utilization strategies can lead to a similar level of accuracy (cf. Dawes & Corrigan 1974). There is a virtue associated with the redundancy of the communicative process: because there is no pressure toward uniformity in cue utilization, performers are able to communicate basic emotions successfully without compromising their unique styles of playing.

One problem in analysing cue utilization is that the strategies used by performers and listeners are largely *implicit* in nature (Juslin & Laukka 2000; Sloboda 1996). Therefore, we need to somehow externalize their expressive strategies. One useful approach to this problem may be to use multiple regression analysis (MRA) to describe the complex relationships between: (a) the performer's expressive intention and the cues (ecological validities); and (b) the listener's judgment and the cues (functional validities). MRA is a data-analytic method flexible enough to handle the complexity of the communicative process (e.g. multiple cues, uncertainty, intercorrelations among cues). MRA also permits us to describe performers and listeners in terms of similar concepts, so that their *cue weights* (i.e. the extent to which they rely on particular cues) can be compared (for details on how this is done, see Juslin 2000).

As demonstrated by Juslin (2000), MRA models of performers and listeners can be mathematically related to each other by means of the *lens model equation* (LME). The LME was originally presented in an influential article by Hursch *et al.* (1964) in the context of studies of human judgment. In such studies, the goal was to relate the judge's cognitive system to a statistical description of the judgment task (Cooksey 1996). However, the LME can also be used to describe communication of emotion in music performance.

The LME (eqn 14.1) embodies the fact that communication accuracy, or achievement $(r_a)$, is a function of two additive components. The first component is usually called the *linear* component because it represents that component of the achievement which can be attributed to the linear regression models of the performer and the listener. The linear component shows that achievement is a function of *performer consistency* $(R_e)$, *listener consistency* $(R_s)$, and *matching* $(G)$. Performer consistency refers to the multiple correlation of the performer model (i.e. performer's intention and cues), whereas listener consistency refers to the multiple correlation of the listener model (i.e. listener's judgment and cues). Both indices reflect the extent to which the regression models fit the cue utilization and are usually interpreted as measures of consistency, or predictability, of the cue utilization. If $R = 1.0$, then the cue utilization is perfectly consistent. Matching ($G$) is a measure of the extent to which the beta weights of performers and listeners are 'matched' to each other; that is, whether they use the same code. This index is obtained by correlating the predicted values of the performer's regression model with the predicted values of the listener's regression model. The resulting correlation is interpreted as the extent to which the performer's beta weights and the listener's beta weights would agree if both regression models were perfect (i.e. $R_e = R_s = 1.0$).

$$r_a = G\, R_e\, R_s + C \sqrt{(1-R^2_e)}\, \sqrt{(1-R^2_s)} \tag{14.1}$$

If the communication under study is unsuccessful, we may ask whether this is because: (a) the performers use a different code than the listeners (indicated by a low $G$ value); (b) the performers apply their code inconsistently (indicated by a low $R_e$ value); or (c) the listeners apply their code inconsistently (indicated by a low $R_s$ value). These three factors set the upper limit of achievement (Hursch *et al.* 1964). By analysing each of them separately, it becomes possible to see how the communicative process could be improved (Juslin & Laukka 2000).

The second component of the LME is usually called the *unmodelled* component of the communicative process. It includes both unsystematic and systematic variance not accounted for by the linear component. This includes effects of inconsistent cue utilization, order effects, distractions, memory intrusions, omission of relevant cues, or *configural cue utilization* (i.e. the use of particular patterns of cue values). $(1-R^2_e)$ and $(1-R^2_s)$ refer to the residual variance of the regression models of performers and listeners, respectively. $C$—or *unmodelled matching*—represents the correlation between the residuals of the performer's model and the residuals of the listener's model. If $C$ is high it indicates: (a) a common reliance on cues in the performance not included in the regression models; (b) chance agreement between random model errors; (c) cue interactions common to both models; or (d) non-linear cue function forms common to both models (Cooksey 1996). However, research indicates that the unmodelled matching of the cue utilization is relatively small in music performance (Juslin & Madison 1999).

Analyses based on the lens model paradigm have generated a number of findings. First, linear regression models provide a good fit to the cue utilization, explaining approximately 70–80 per cent of the variance in expression and judgment (see Juslin 1997b, 2000). Second, achievement seems to depend mainly on the extent to which the cue utilization of the performer is 'matched' to the cue utilization of the listener (at least as regards professional performers; amateur performers may also differ with regard to the consistency of their cue utilization) (Juslin & Laukka 2000). Third, cue utilization is more consistent across different pieces of music than across different performers. That is, performers use pretty much the same code regardless of the melody, but there are considerable individual differences between performers. Fourth, two performers can communicate equally well despite slight differences in their cue utilization (see Juslin 2000). Finally, it has been shown that the lens model paradigm can be used to improve performers' expressive skills through so-called 'cognitive feedback' (Juslin & Laukka 2000).

## 14.7 Implications and directions for future research

Viewing emotional communication in music through a Brunswikian 'lens' has a number of important implications. First, previous studies have tended to focus on either performance or perception. The Brunswikian lens model provides the tool for an ultimately more interesting enterprise: how to *relate* performance to perception. Each of the two aspects can only be fully understood in relation to the other. Second, future studies should consider a whole set of cues to deal with the complete code used and thereby permit both performers and listeners to show their capacity for vicarious functioning. Third, future studies should analyse sufficiently large samples of performers, listeners, and pieces of music to allow for a greater generality and the use of multivariate methods, such as MRA. This recommendation parallels Brunswik's own insistence that we should deal with the phenomenon under study 'on an adequate level of complexity' (1952, p. 1). Lens modelling is an attempt to capture the relationships among *subjective* intentions or judgments and *physical* characteristics of music performances, and can therefore be conceived of as 'emotional psychophysics'.

### 14.7.1 Limitations of previous research

There are a number of limitations of previous research, which provide incentives for further research. First, studies of emotional communication in music performance have mainly been conducted in the laboratory. For obvious reasons, scientists have striven to obtain internally valid results using experimental methods. However, it is now high time to bring the research from the laboratory into the 'field'. We still have limited knowledge about how performers communicate emotions to listeners in real life. How reliable is a performer's communication under realistic conditions? Ways of getting closer to 'ecologically valid' settings might be to analyse existing recordings of performances (Rapoport 1996; Siegwart & Scherer 1995) or to observe performers, from the preparation of a piece to the actual performance in a concert.

Second, the research summarized in this chapter has largely rested on the assumption that the encoding process proceeds more or less independently of the musical structure, but this assumption may be questioned. Performers usually modulate their cue utilization to suit specific compositions, hence there is some inconsistency in cue utilization across different pieces of music (Juslin 2000). Future research should focus on the *interaction* between the composed structure and the performance in determining the expression of a piece of music. The studies of emotional expression in performance in the 1990s measured performance effects separately from structural effects. Now, after 10 years of research, we may be ready to start considering composition and performance together; to study the complete process. One way of doing this could be to expand the lens model further to also include cues associated with the structure of particular pieces, such as rhythm, mode, melodic contour, and tonal progression.

A number of researchers have raised the question whether performances recorded under laboratory conditions produce very different results than performances recorded under natural conditions, such as a concert (Rapoport 1996). Because we lack data on this issue, the jury is still out. However, it seems plausible that similar patterns of effects will be found in realistic settings, but that the effects will be smaller. One reason for this may be that performers often have to coordinate their own playing with that of other performers. This places constraints on their freedom of expression. In addition, the social dynamics within orchestras or bands may influence the expression of the music in ways that merit further research (Davidson 1997).

Only a few studies have explored emotional expression in natural music performances. Siegwart and Scherer (1995) investigated emotional expression in opera singing by analysing existing recordings by famous artists. They reported that: (a) different interpretations elicited significantly different listener ratings of emotional expressiveness; (b) voice samples differed substantially with respect to acoustic cues; and (c) listeners' judgments could be successfully predicted on the basis of the acoustic cues. These are important results, because they suggest that the effects reviewed in this chapter are not confined to the laboratory.

### 14.7.2 Directions for future research: the case of emotion induction

Thus far in the chapter, I have primarily been concerned with how emotion is *represented* in music performance. This simply reflects the fact that most studies to date have investigated representation of emotion—perhaps because *induction* of emotion is more difficult to study. In everyday life, however, the question of why particular performances of music manage to induce strong emotions in listeners is just as important. In this section, I suggest some ideas with respect to how expressive performances might induce emotional reactions in listeners. These ideas are admittedly speculative, but may serve as directions for future research.

First of all, it is possible that the expression of a performance may arouse emotions in listeners through a process of so-called *emotional contagion*, which has been defined as 'the tendency to automatically mimic and synchronize facial expressions, vocalizations, postures, and movements with those of another person and, consequently, to converge emotionally . . .' (Hatfield *et al.* 1994, p. 5). There is a large amount of evidence that people easily 'catch' the emotions of others when watching their facial expressions or hearing their vocal expressions, presumably through some kind of 'motor mimicry'. The fact that certain aspects of emotional expression in music are highly similar to vocal expression of emotion suggests that we get emotionally aroused by the voice-like aspects of musical performances (Juslin, in press).

One objection to this theory could be that most performances do not sound very much like vocal expressions, at least superficially (Budd 1985, Chapter 7; see also Davies, this volume). Why, then, should we react to performances as if they were vocal expressions? One explanation may be that emotional expression is processed by simple, automatic, and independent 'brain modules', which react to certain features in the stimulus (Fodor 1983). Such modules do not 'know' the difference between vocal expression of emotion and other acoustic expression but will react in the same way as long as certain cues (e.g. high speed, loud dynamics, fast attack, many overtones) are present in the stimulus (Juslin, in press). Evidence that we indeed react emotionally to performances of music as we do to vocal expressions comes from studies that use facial electromyography and self-reports to measure emotions (see Hietanen *et al.* 1998; Lundqvist *et al.* 2000; Neumann & Strack 2000; Witvliet & Vrana 1996; Witvliet *et al.* 1998). This modular view of perception of emotion in music is supported by evidence that processing of information about emotion is largely implicit (Niedenthal & Showers 1991), that judgments of emotion in music are quick, and that researchers have obtained brain dissociations between judgments of musical emotion and of musical structure (Peretz *et al.* 1998).

A second way in which a particular performance might arouse emotions in its listeners involves the fact that emotional reactions often occur when musical expectations are violated in some way (Meyer, this volume). It is easy to imagine this happening with regard to music performances. Meyer (1956, p. 206) suggested that expressive variations in a musical performance may serve an aesthetic function by 'delaying an expected resolution', or otherwise 'creating psychological tension'. It should be observed that such effects may be achieved in different ways. For instance, a performer may enhance listeners' emotional responses to the music by emphasizing notes that are of particular 'significance' in the composition, thereby enhancing violations of musical expectations that are already latent in the structure. Support for this idea has been obtained in recent studies (e.g. Sloboda & Lehmann, in press).

However, a performer can also arouse emotions in listeners by performing in a manner that deviates from stylistic expectations with regard to the performance of a certain structure. In this case, the deviation does not serve to enhance significant aspects of the structure, but rather to create psychological tension through deviations from performance conventions. It should be noted that the most 'extreme' performances of classical music are often made by the most well-known performers (cf. Sloboda 1998). In some cases, expressive devices of a performance may have a direct impact on the physiological processes of the listener. Harrer and Harrer (1977), for example, have claimed that it is possible to 'drive' the pulse rate of a listener by dynamic changes in volume (e.g. the crescendo or decrescendo of a rolling drum beat). Moreover, sudden syncopations in a musical performance may be capable of producing premature heart beats. The use of such effects by music performers has been described in the vast literature on rubato. For instance, the famous virtuoso violinist Niccolò Paganini (1782–1840) is known to have used tempo rubato to great effect (Hudson, 1994).

## 14.8 Conclusion

In this chapter, we have seen that performers can communicate specific emotions to listeners by using a number of probabilistic but partly redundant cues in the performance. The relative importance of the performance for the expression of the music is likely to differ depending on the performer, genre, and piece of music—ranging all the way from the faithful rendition of a piece of avant-garde music to the heartbreaking, improvised solo of a blues number.

The vicarious functioning of cues allows performers to simultaneously communicate emotions to listeners in a universally accessible manner and develop a personal expression. This communicative system therefore constitutes the happy marriage of the general and the individual, of the biological and the cultural. The communicative process is fairly robust but has a limited information capacity, ultimately leaving it to the listeners to specify the precise 'meaning' of the music. The phylogenetic roots of the communicative system can explain its powerful impact, and also why many performers regard emotions as 'the essence of musical communication' (Persson 1995, p. 60).

The subtle emotional nuances of music may seem a distant cry from the evolutionary framework of 'basic emotions' that I have described in this chapter. But I would argue that, ultimately, the real force of music's expressiveness—if not its uttermost subtlety—resides in such roots. In writing about the origins of music, Rousseau (1986, p. 65) said:

... how far from understanding the power of their art are those many musicians who think of the potency of sounds only in terms of their air pressure and string vibrations. The more they assimilate it to purely physical impressions, the farther they get from its source and the more they deprive it of its primitive energy. In dropping the oral tone and sticking exclusively to the ... harmonics, music becomes noisier to the ear and less pleasing to the heart. As soon as it stops singing, it stops speaking. And then, with all its accord and all its harmony it will have no more effect upon us.

Thus, the music that touches us the most does not necessarily come from someone who 'plays and sings with the grace of a God', but from someone 'bold enough to act as a messenger of the heart' (Schumacher 1995, p. 314).[1]

# References

Adachi, M. & Trehub, S. E. (1998). Children's expression of emotion in song. *Psychology of Music,* **26**, 133–53.

Balkwill, L-L. & Thompson, W. F. (1999). A cross-cultural investigation of the perception of emotion in music: Psychophysical and cultural cues. *Music Perception,* **17**, 43–64.

Baroni, M. & Finarelli, L. (1994). Emotions in spoken language and vocal music. In *Proceedings of the Third International Conference for Music Perception and Cognition,* (ed. I. Deliège), pp. 343–5. Liége, Belgium: University of Liége.

Baroni, M., Caterina, R., Regazzi, F., & Zanarini, G. (1997). Emotional aspects of singing voice. In *Proceedings of the Third Triennial ESCOM Conference,* (ed. A. Gabrielsson), pp. 484–9. Uppsala, Sweden: Department of Psychology, Uppsala University.

Behrens, G. A. & Green, S. B. (1993). The ability to identify emotional content of solo improvisations performed vocally and on three different instruments. *Psychology of Music,* **21**, 20–33.

Blum, D. (1977). *Casals and the art of interpretation.* Berkeley, CA: University of California Press.

Borod, J. C., Obler, L. K., Erhan, H. M., Grunwald, I. S., Cicero, B. A., Welkowitz, J. *et al.* (1998). Right hemisphere emotional perception: Evidence across multiple channels. *Neuropsychology,* **12**, 446–58.

Bresin, R. & Friberg, A. (2000). Emotional coloring of computer-controlled music performance. *Computer Music Journal,* **24**, 44–62.

Brunswik, E. (1952). *The conceptual framework of psychology.* Chicago: Chicago University Press.

Brunswik, E. (1956). *Perception and the representative design of psychological experiments.* Berkeley, CA: University of California Press.

Bryden, M. P., Ley, R., & Sugerman, J. (1982). A left-ear advantage for identifying the emotional quality of tonal sequences. *Neuropsychologia,* **20**, 83–7.

[1]   I am grateful to Bruno Repp, John Rink, and John Sloboda for helpful comments on a preliminary version of this chapter. The writing of this chapter was supported by the Bank of Sweden Tercentenary Foundation.

Buck, R. (1984). *The communication of emotion.* New York: Guilford Press.

Budd, M. (1985). *Music and the emotions: The philosophical theories.* London: Routledge.

Clapton, E. P. (1998). *Official tour program 1998.* New York: Warner Brothers.

Clarke, E. F. (1988). Generative principles in music performance. In *Generative processes in music. The psychology of performance, improvisation, and composition,* (ed. J. A. Sloboda), pp. 1–26. Oxford, UK: Clarendon Press.

Clynes, M. (1973). Sentics: Biocybernetics of emotion communication. *Annals of the New York Academy of Sciences,* **220**, 55–131.

Clynes, M. (1977). *Sentics: The touch of emotions.* New York: Doubleday.

Cooksey, R. W. (1996). *Judgment analysis.* New York: Academic Press.

Cunningham, J. G. & Sterling, R. S. (1988). Developmental changes in the understanding of affective meaning in music. *Motivation and Emotion,* **12**, 399–413.

Darwin, C. (1872). *The expression of the emotions in man and animals.* London: John Murray.

Davidson, J. W. (1997). The social in musical performance. In *The social psychology of music,* (ed. D. J. Hargreaves & A. C. North), pp. 209–28. Oxford, UK: Oxford University Press.

Davies, S. (1994). *Musical meaning and expression.* Ithaca, NY: Cornell University Press.

Dawes, R. M. & Corrigan, B. (1974). Linear models in decision making. *Psychological Bulletin,* **81**, 95–106.

de Gelder, B. & Vroomen, J. (1996). Categorical perception of emotional speech. *Journal of the Acoustical Society of America,* **100**, 2818.

Dolgin, K. & Adelson, E. (1990). Age changes in the ability to interpret affect in sung and instrumentally-presented melodies. *Psychology of Music,* **18**, 87–98.

Eggebrecht, R. (1983). *Sprachmelodie und musikalische Forschungen im Kulturvergleich.* Doctoral dissertation, University of Munich, Germany.

Eibl-Eibesfeldt, I. (1989). *Human ethology.* New York: Aldine.

Ekman, P. (ed.) (1973). *Darwin and facial expression.* New York: Academic Press.

Ekman, P. (1992). An argument for basic emotions. *Cognition and Emotion,* **6**, 169–200.

Fairbanks, G. (1940). Recent experimental investigation of vocal pitch in voice. *Journal of the Acoustical Society of America,* **11**, 457–66.

Fisk, J. (ed.) (1997). *Composers on music.* Boston, MA: Northeastern University Press.

Fodor, J. A. (1983). *The modularity of the mind.* Cambridge, MA: MIT Press.

Frick, R. W. (1985). Communicating emotion: The role of prosodic features. *Psychological Bulletin,* **97**, 412–29.

Gabrielsson, A. (1988). Timing in music performance and its relations to music experience. In *Generative processes in music: The psychology of performance, improvisation, and composition,* (ed. J. A. Sloboda), pp. 27–51. Oxford, UK: Clarendon Press.

Gabrielsson, A. (1999). The performance of music. In *The psychology of music,* (2nd edn) (ed. D. Deutsch), pp. 501–602. San Diego, CA: Academic Press.

Gabrielsson, A. & Juslin, P. N. (1996). Emotional expression in music performance: Between the performer's intention and the listener's experience. *Psychology of Music,* **24**, 68–91.

Gabrielsson, A. & Juslin, P. N. (in press). Emotional expression in music. In *Handbook of affective sciences,* (ed. R. J. Davidson, H. H. Goldsmith, & K. R. Scherer). New York: Oxford University Press.

Gabrielsson, A. & Lindström, E. (1995). Emotional expression in synthesizer and sentograph performance. *Psychomusicology,* **14**, 94–116.

Gibson, J. J. (1979). *The ecological approach to visual perception.* Boston: Houghton-Mifflin.

Gorman, B. S. & Crain, W. C. (1974). Decoding of 'sentograms'. *Perceptual and Motor Skills,* 39, 784–6.

Gregory, A. H. (1997). The roles of music in society: The ethnomusicological perspective. In *The social psychology of music,* (ed. D. J. Hargreaves & A. C. North), pp. 123–40. Oxford, UK: Oxford University Press.

Handel, S. (1991). *Listening. An introduction to the perception of auditory events.* Cambridge, MA: MIT Press.

Harrer, G. & Harrer, H. (1977). Music, emotion, and autonomic function. In *Music and the brain. Studies in the neurology of music,* (ed. M. Critchley & R. A. Henson), pp. 202–16. London: William Heinemann Medical Books.

Hatfield, E., Cacioppo, J. T., & Rapson, R. L. (1994). *Emotional contagion.* New York: Cambridge University Press.

Helmholtz, H. L. F. von (1954). *On the sensations of tone as a psychological basis for the theory of music.* New York: Dover (originally published 1863).

Hietanen, J. K., Surakka, V., & Linnankoski, I. (1998). Facial electromyographic responses to vocal affect expressions. *Psychophysiology,* 35, 530–6.

Hudson, R. (1994). *Stolen time. The history of tempo rubato.* Oxford, UK: Clarendon Press.

Hursch, C. J., Hammond, K. R., & Hursch, J. L. (1964). Some methodological considerations in multiple-cue probability studies. *Psychological Review,* 71, 42–60.

Izard, C. E. (1977). *The emotions.* New York: Plenum Press.

Johnson-Laird, P. N. & Oatley, K. (1992). Basic emotions, rationality, and folk theory. *Cognition and Emotion,* 6, 201–23.

Jürgens, U. & von Cramon, D. (1982). On the role of the anterior cingulate cortex in phonation: A case report. *Brain and Language,* 15, 234–48.

Juslin, P. N. (1995). Emotional communication in music viewed through a Brunswikian lens. In *Musical expression. Proceedings of the Conference of ESCOM and DGM 1995,* (ed. G. Kleinen), pp. 21–5. Bremen, Germany: University of Bremen.

Juslin, P. N. (1997a). Emotional communication in music performance: A functionalist perspective and some data. *Music Perception,* 14, 383–418.

Juslin, P. N. (1997b). Perceived emotional expression in synthesized performances of a short melody: Capturing the listener's judgment policy. *Musicae Scientiae,* 1, 225–56.

Juslin, P. N. (1997c). Can results from studies of perceived expression in musical performances be generalized across response formats? *Psychomusicology,* 16, 77–101.

Juslin, P. N. (1998). A functionalist perspective on emotional communication in music performance. *Comprehensive Summaries of Uppsala Dissertations from the Faculty of Social Sciences 78.* Uppsala, Sweden: Uppsala University Library.

Juslin, P. N. (1999). *Communication of emotion in vocal expression and music performance: Different channels, same code?* Manuscript submitted for publication.

Juslin, P. N. (2000). Cue utilization in communication of emotion in music performance: Relating performance to perception. *Journal of Experimental Psychology: Human Perception and Performance,* 26, 1797–813.

Juslin, P. N. (2001). A Brunswikian approach to emotional communication in music performance. In *The essential Brunswik: Beginnings, explications, applications,* (ed. K. R. Hammond & T. R. Stewart) pp. 426–30. New York: Oxford University Press.

Juslin, P. N. (in press). Vocal expression and musical expression: Parallels and contrasts. In *Proceedings of the Eleventh Meeting of the International Society for Research on Emotions*, (ed. A. Kappas). Quebec, Canada: ISRE Publications.

Juslin, P. N. Friberg, A., & Bresin, R. (in press). Toward a computational model of expression in music performance: The GERM model. *Musicae Scientiae*.

Juslin, P. N. & Laukka, P. (2000). Improving emotional communication in music performance through cognitive feedback. *Musicae Scientiae*, **4**, 151–83.

Juslin, P. N. & Laukka, P. (in press). Impact of intended emotion intensity on cue utilization and decoding accuracy in vocal expression of emotion. In *Proceedings of the 11th Meeting of the International Society for Research on Emotions*, (ed. A. Kappas). Quebec, Canada: ISRE Publications.

Juslin, P. N. & Madison, G. (1999). The role of timing patterns in recognition of emotional expression from musical performance. *Music Perception*, **17**, 197–221.

Juslin, P. N. & Persson, R. S. (in press). Emotional communication. In *The science and psychology of music performance. Creative strategies for teaching and learning*, (ed. R. Parncutt & G. E. McPherson). New York: Oxford University Press.

Kendall, R. A. & Carterette, E. C. (1990). The communication of musical expression. *Music Perception*, **8**, 129–64.

Kennedy, N. (1990). *Always playing*. London: Weidenfield & Nicolson.

King, B. B. (1996). *Blues all around me*. London: Hodder & Stoughton.

Kivy, P. (1989). *Sound sentiment*. Philadelphia, PA: Temple University Press.

Konishi, T., Imaizumi, S., & Niimi, S. (2000). Vibrato and emotion in singing voice (abstract). In *Proceedings of the Sixth International Conference on Music Perception and Cognition, August 2000*, (ed. C. Woods, G. Luck, R. Brochard, F. Seddon, & J. A. Sloboda), (CD rom). Keele, UK: Keele University.

Kotlyar, G. M. & Morozov, V. P. (1976). Acoustic correlates of the emotional content of vocalized speech. *Soviet Physics. Acoustics*, **22**, 370–6.

Kratus, J. (1993). A developmental study of children's interpretation of emotion in music. *Psychology of Music*, **21**, 3–19.

Ladd, D. R., Silverman, K. E. A., Tolkmitt, F., Bergmann, G., & Scherer, K. R. (1985). Evidence of independent function of intonation contour type, voice quality, and $F_0$ range in signaling speaker affect. *Journal of the Acoustical Society of America*, **78**, 435–44.

Langeheinecke, E. J., Schnitzler, H.-U., Hischer-Buhrmeister, M., & Behne, K.-E. (1999). Emotions in singing voice: Acoustic cues for joy, fear, anger, and sadness. Poster presented at the Joint Meeting of the Acoustical Society of America and the Acoustical Society of Germany, Berlin, March 1999.

Lindström, E. (1999). Expression in music: Interaction between performance and melodic structure. Paper presented at the Meeting of the Society for Music Perception and Cognition, Evanston, USA, 14–17 August 1999.

Lundqvist, L. G., Carlsson, F., & Hilmersson, P. (2000). *Facial electromyography, autonomic activity, and emotional experience to happy and sad music*. Paper presented at the 27th International Congress of Psychology, Stockholm, Sweden, 23–28 July, 2000.

MacLean, P. D. (1978). Effects of lesions of globus pallidus on species-typical display behavior of squirrel monkeys. *Brain Research*, **149**, 175–96.

Meyer, L. B. (1956). *Emotion and meaning in music*. Chicago: Chicago University Press.

Nettelbeck, T., Henderson, C., & Willson, R. (1989). Communicating emotion through sound: An evaluation of Clynes' theory of sentics. *Australian Journal of Psychology*, 41, 17–24.

Neumann, R. & Strack, F. (2000). Mood contagion: The automatic transfer of mood between persons. *Journal of Personality and Social Psychology*, 79, 211–23.

Niedenthal, P. M. & Showers, C. (1991). The perception and processing of affective information and its influences on social judgment. In *Emotion and social judgments*, (ed. J. P. Forgas), pp. 125–43. Oxford, UK: Pergamon Press.

Oatley, K. (1992). *Best laid schemes.* Cambridge, MA: Harvard University Press.

Oatley, K. & Jenkins, J. M. (1996). *Understanding emotions.* Oxford, UK: Blackwell.

Ohgushi, K. & Hattori, M. (1996a). Emotional communication in performance of vocal music. In *Proceedings of the Fourth International Conference on Music Perception and Cognition*, (ed. B. Pennycook & E. Costa-Giomi), pp. 269–74. Montreal, Canada: McGill University.

Ohgushi, K. & Hattori, M. (1996b). Acoustic correlates of the emotional expression in vocal performance. Paper presented at the Third Joint Meeting of the Acoustical Society of America and the Acoustical Society of Japan, Honolulu, Hawaii, 2–6 December 1996.

Palmer, C. (1989). Mapping musical thought to musical performance. *Journal of Experimental Psychology: Human Perception and Performance*, 15, 331–46.

Palmer, C. (1997). Music performance. *Annual Review of Psychology*, 48, 115–38.

Panksepp, J. (1982). Towards a general psychobiological theory of emotions. *Behavioral and Brain Sciences*, 5, 407–67.

Papoušek, M. (1996). Intuitive parenting: A hidden source of musical stimulation in infancy. In *Musical beginnings. Origins and development of musical competence*, (ed. I. Deliége & J. A. Sloboda), pp. 89–112. Oxford, UK: Oxford University Press.

Papoušek, M., Bornstein, M. H., Nuzzo, C., Papoušek, H., & Symmes, D. (1990). Infant responses to prototypical melodic contours in parental speech. *Infant Behavior and Development*, 13, 539–45.

Patel, A. D. & Peretz, I. (1997). Is music autonomous from language? A neuropsychological appraisal. In *Perception and cognition of music*, (ed. I. Deliége & J. A. Sloboda), pp. 191–215. Hove, UK: Psychology Press.

Penfield, W. & Roberts, L. (1959). *Speech and brain mechanisms.* Princeton, NJ: Princeton University Press.

Peretz, I., Gagnon, L., & Bouchard, B. (1998). Music and emotion: Perceptual determinants, immediacy, and isolation after brain damage. *Cognition*, 68, 111–41.

Persson, R. S. (1995). Musical reality: Exploring the subjective world of performers. In *Song and signification. Studies in music semiotics*, (ed. R. Monelle & C. T. Gray), pp. 58–63. Edinburgh, UK: Faculty of Music, University of Edinburgh.

Persson, R. S., Pratt. G., & Robson, C. (1996). Motivational and influential components of musical performance: A qualitative analysis. In *Fostering the growth of high ability: European perspectives*, (ed. A. J. Cropley & D. Dehn), pp. 287–301. Norwood, NJ: Ablex.

Ploog, D. (1981). Neurobiology of primate audio-vocal behavior. *Brain Research Reviews*, 3, 35–61.

Ploog, D. (1986). Biological foundations of the vocal expressions of emotions. In *Emotion. Theory, research, and experience. Volume 3: Biological foundations of emotion*, (ed. R. Plutchik & H. Kellerman), pp. 173–97. New York: Academic Press.

Ploog, D. (1992). The evolution of vocal communication. In *Nonverbal communication*, (ed. H. Papoušek, U. Jürgens, & M. Papoušek), pp. 6–30. Cambridge, UK: Cambridge University Press.

Plutchik, R. (1994). *The psychology and biology of emotion.* New York: Harper-Collins.

Rapoport, E. (1996). Emotional expression code in opera and lied singing. *Journal of New Music Research,* **25,** 109–49.

Repp, B. H. (1998). A microcosm of musical expression. I: Quantitative analysis of pianists' timing in the initial measures of Chopin's Etude in E major. *Journal of the Acoustical Society of America,* **102,** 1085–99.

Rosenthal, R. (1982). Judgment studies. In *Handbook of methods in nonverbal behavior research,* (ed. K. R. Scherer & P. Ekman), pp. 287–361. Cambridge, UK: Cambridge University Press.

Ross, B. H. & Spalding, T. L. (1994). Concepts and categories. In *Thinking and problem solving,* (2nd edn) (ed. R. J. Sternberg), pp. 119–50. New York: Academic Press.

Rousseau, J. J. (1986). Essay on the origin of languages. In *On the origin of language: Two essays,* (ed. J. H. Moran & A. Gode), pp. 5–74. Chicago: University of Chicago Press (originally published 1761).

Russell, J. A. (1980). A circumplex model of affect. *Journal of Personality and Social Psychology,* **39,** 1161–78.

Scherer, K. R. (1986). Vocal affect expression: A review and a model for future research. *Psychological Bulletin,* **99,** 143–65.

Scherer, K. R. (1995). Expression of emotion in voice and music. *Journal of Voice,* **9,** 235–48.

Scherer, K. R. & Oshinsky, J. S. (1977). Cue utilization in emotion attribution from auditory stimuli. *Motivation and Emotion,* **1,** 331–46.

Schumacher, M. (1995). *Crossroads. The life and music of Eric Clapton.* New York: Hyperion.

Seashore, C. E. (1947). *In search of beauty in music. A scientific approach to musical aesthetics.* Westport, CT: Grenwood Press.

Seashore, H. G. (1937). An objective analysis of artistic singing. In *Objective analysis of musical performance: University of Iowa studies in the psychology of music,* (Vol. 4) (ed. C. E. Seashore), pp. 12–157. Iowa City, IA: University of Iowa.

Seckerson, E. (1991). Yuri Bashmet as interviewed by Seckerson. *Gramophone,* June, 26–7.

Senju, M. & Ohgushi, K. (1987). How are the player's ideas conveyed to the audience? *Music Perception,* **4,** 311–24.

Shaffer, L. H. (1992). How to interpret music. In *Cognitive bases of musical communication,* (ed. M. R. Jones & S. Holleran), pp. 263–78. Washington, DC: American Psychological Association.

Shaffer, L. H. & Todd, N. (1987). The interpretative component in musical performance. In *Action and perception in rhythm and music,* (ed. A. Gabrielsson), pp. 139–52. Royal Swedish Academy of Music Publication No. 55. Stockholm: Royal Swedish Academy of Music.

Shapiro, B. E. & Danly, M. (1985). The role of the right hemisphere in the control of speech prosody in propositional and affective contexts. *Brain and Language,* **25,** 19–36.

Shaver, P., Schwartz, J., Kirson, D., & O'Connor, C. (1987). Emotion knowledge: Further explorations of a prototype approach. *Journal of Personality and Social Psychology,* **52,** 1061–86.

Shields, S. A. (1984). Distinguishing between emotion and non-emotion: Judgments about experience. *Motivation and Emotion,* **8,** 355–69.

Siegwart, H. & Scherer, K. R. (1995). Acoustic concomitants of emotional expression in operatic singing: The case of Lucia in Ardi gli incensi. *Journal of Voice,* **9,** 249–60.

Sloboda, J. A. (1996). The acquisition of musical performance expertise: Deconstructing the 'talent' account of individual differences in musical expressivity. In *The road to excellence,* (ed. K. A. Ericsson ), pp. 107–26. Mahwah, NJ: Erlbaum.

Sloboda, J. A. (1998). Musical performance and emotion: Issues and developments. In *Proceedings of the Fifth International Conference on Music Perception and Cognition*, (ed. S. W. Yi), pp. 21–5. Seoul, Korea: Seoul National University.

Sloboda, J. A. & Lehmann, A. C. (in press). Tracking performance correlates of changes of perceived intensity of emotion during different interpretations of a Chopin piano prelude. *Music Perception.*

Sundberg, J. (1982). Speech, song, and emotions. In *Music, mind, and brain. The neuropsychology of music*, (ed. M. Clynes), pp. 137–49. New York: Plenum Press.

Sundberg, J. (1988). Computer synthesis of music performance. In *Generative processes in music. The psychology of performance, improvisation, and composition*, (ed. J. A. Sloboda), pp. 52–69. Oxford, UK: Clarendon Press.

Sundberg, J., Iwarsson, J., & Hagegård, H. (1995). A singer's expression of emotions in sung performance. In *Vocal fold physiology: Voice quality control*, (ed. O. Fujimura & M. Hirano), pp. 217–29. San Diego, CA: Singular Press.

Tait, M. (1992). Teaching strategies and styles. In *Handbook of research on music teaching and learning*, (ed. R. Colwell), pp. 525–34. New York: Schirmer Books.

Terwogt, M. M. & van Grinsven, F. (1988). Musical expression of mood states. *Psychology of Music, 19*, 99–109.

Trussoni, S. J., O'Malley, A., & Barton, A. (1988). Human emotion communication by touch: A modified replication of an experiment by Manfred Clynes. *Perceptual and Motor Skills, 66*, 419–24.

Wallbott, H. G. & Scherer, K. R. (1986). Cues and channels in emotion recognition. *Journal of Personality and Social Psychology, 51*, 690–9.

Whissell, C. M. (1989). The dictionary of affect in language. In *Emotion: Theory, research, and experience: Vol. 4. The measurement of emotions*, (ed. R. Plutchik & H. Kellerman), pp. 113–31. New York: Academic Press.

Witvliet, C. V. & Vrana, S. R. (1996). The emotional impact of instrumental music on affect ratings, facial EMG, autonomic responses, and the startle reflex: Effects of valence and arousal. *Psychophysiology Supplement, 91*.

Witvliet, C. V., Vrana, S. R., & Webb-Talmadge, N. (1998). In the mood: Emotion and facial expressions during and after instrumental music, and during an emotional inhibition task. *Psychophysiology Supplement, 88*.

Woody, R. (2000). Learning expressivity in music performance: An exploratory study. *Research Studies in Music Education, 14*, 14–23.

# Part V

# THE LISTENER

# CHAPTER 15

# MUSIC AND EMOTION: DISTINCTIONS AND UNCERTAINTIES

## LEONARD B. MEYER

I have the gall to divide this chapter into only *two* parts:[1] 'Distinctions' and 'Uncertainty'. The first section considers conceptual/terminological problems having to do with music and emotion, and provides the background and terminology for the matters considered in the second part. The distinctions made in Section 15.1 do not pretend to constitute a coherent argument but are connected by the succession of topics discussed. Section 15.2, the core of the chapter, is concerned with the role of uncertainty in human experience generally, and in musical/aesthetic experience in particular.

## 15.1 Distinctions

I begin by proposing a number of distinctions because, despite its empirical outlook and methodology, the psychological analysis of human emotional experiences—causes and responses—as well as humanistic theory have lacked conceptual specificity and precision. This is evident in the range of behavioural states considered 'emotional'. To take a representative example, Klaus Scherer (1994, p. 31) writes that some terms for emotions 'highlight the physiological, as in the case of "aroused" or "tired." Some are quite cognitive, like "bewildered" or "curious".'

It seems curious, however, to consider 'curious' or 'tired' as being emotions. Such 'states of being'—of awareness (e.g. 'that's an interesting idea') or of feeling (e.g. 'I'm hungry')—are not generally classed as emotions.[2] But are not feelings of sadness, joy, anger, etc., which *are* considered emotions, similarly states of being? So the question is: what are the necessary and sufficient psychological and/or physiological conditions for considering a state of being—a feeling—an emotion?[3]

---

[1] Since my role is supposed to be that of the 'resident humanist', I have taken the liberty of playfully paraphrasing the first sentence of Caesar's *Gallic wars*: 'All Gaul is divided into three parts'.

[2] If tiredness is disturbed or curiosity thwarted, emotion may be evoked; but the 'evoking agent' is the disturbance, the thwarting, and the uncertainty this produces, not the tiredness or the curiosity.

[3] In the course of thinking about these matters, a possible distinction occurred to me: namely, that states of being such as curiosity, hunger, fatigue, cold, etc. depend upon conditions *internal* to an individual, while love and hate, fear and anger, etc. also include conditions *external* to an individual.

Though, to the best of my knowledge, there has been no satisfactory answer to that question, we go on using the concept of emotion and distinguishing different kinds: love and hate, fear and courage, etc. We conceptualize and classify our experiences of the inner as well as the outer world because envisaging and choosing, which lie at the heart of human behaviour, occur primarily in terms of such classes rather than individual instances. So this part of the chapter attempts to distinguish some of the kinds of relationships involved in the interaction between music and emotion.

### 15.1.1 Emotional states versus emotional processes

*States*

*Delineation and association: statistical parameters.*   As a rule, the terms used to characterize emotions denote what I will call emotional 'states'. When listeners or critics describe music as sad, happy, angry, elated, and so on, they are referring to such states. In music, such states are essentially delineated by the action of what I have called the 'statistical' parameters. These aspects of sound vary in *amount* or *degree*—for example, register (lower–higher), dynamic level (louder–softer), speed (faster–slower), continuity (gradual–abrupt), and so forth. Although the configuration of parameters delineating an emotional state fluctuates, state-defining parameters such as register, speed, and dynamic level remain relatively constant over moderate-sized segments of music. And it is this constancy that makes *naming* possible. Indeed, when subjects in psychological experiments identify emotions their answers are, for the most part, based on the disposition of statistical parameters. Put negatively, one cannot imagine sadness being portrayed by a fast forte tune played in a high register, or a playful child being depicted by a solemnity of trombones.

The identification and naming of states is a result of the association of different dispositions of statistical parameters with feelings characteristically evoked in natural or cultural *circumstances*. That is, we deem a passage to portray 'love' or 'anger' or 'jealousy' not because of knowledge of physiological responses or psychological constraints, but because of awareness of, and often empathy with, the feelings and behaviours that occur in particular sociocultural contexts.[4] Thus we recognize the sadness expressed in Macbeth's 'Tomorrow, and tomorrow, and tomorrow' speech because we know the circumstance in which it is delivered—that is, Macbeth's learning of his wife's death. In addition, of course, his feelings are communicated by the repetition of the word 'tomorrow', which in this context signifies sadness and depression, by his performance (slow, soft tone of voice, etc.), and his physical behaviour and facial expression.[5] If this view

......................................................................................................................................

[4] This calls attention to a methodological question: namely, when listeners record their responses to music by, say, pressing buttons or naming emotions, or when psychologists measure the physiological changes (in blood pressure, pulse rate, etc.) of listeners, what do the 'results' represent? Often it seems unclear whether the answers are a result of the subjects' *recognition* of the 'state' delineated by the music or of their own affective *response* to the musical patterning? In this connection, see Sloboda (1992).

[5] Though overt behaviour may be the result of an innate response, behaviour is usually influenced by cultural convention. This is the case because behaviour almost always acts as a sign that is implicative

has merit, then observed behavioural circumstances play an important role in the identification and classification of emotional states.

*Classification.* It is sometimes supposed that our understanding of the world begins with the peculiarities of the individual—person, work of art, landscape, and so on. But, though experiences of phenomena may be peculiar, the peculiar is almost always qualified by, and comprehended in terms of, a conceptual class. This is one of the reasons why understanding and responding to different styles of music depends on learning. For it is largely learning that enables composers, performers, and listeners to internalize the norms governing musical relationships and, consequently, to comprehend the implications of patternings, and experience deviations from stylistic norms.

Just as we classify the phenomenal world into physical and biological realms, styles of music into classic and romantic, folk and jazz, and phrase relationships into antecedent-consequent, so we classify emotions. In most cases, the classifications are fuzzy. They are so because the classes are abstractions from individual, though similar, relationships and experiences. And one of the problems with abstractions is the tendency to treat them as though they possessed a set of objective properties independent of context and culture. But unlike tuberculosis, the biological nature of what we conceptualize as emotional experience has not been ascertained.

Nevertheless we classify emotions. We do so for the same reasons that we classify and categorize the world in general: because to choose effectively, it is necessary to imagine the probability of coming events (whether the behaviour of people or of musical patterns), and such imagining invariably entails classification. One manifestation of the need to classify is our proclivity to give 'to airy nothing/A local habitation and a *name*' (Shakespeare, *A midsummer night's dream*, V. i, emphasis added).[6] Put prosaically— because they threaten our sense of predictive power, nameless phenomena are highly disturbing.

Awareness of, and responding to, the class of some phenomenon need *not*, however, involve conscious conceptualization or naming but rather recognizing and experiencing the relationships presented—that is, knowing how the kind of patterning *works*. The point is important because, as mentioned above, conscious classification and explicit naming tend to undermine uncertainty and weaken emotional response. Something akin to 'the suspension of disbelief' (discussed below) seems at work here. That is, because enjoying music is a matter of experiencing the tension of syntactic and native processes as well as the fluctuations of statistical parameters, listeners generally avoid

---

(both to the individual and to others) of probable subsequent behaviour. Put in evolutionary terms, emotional behaviour was evidently preadapted for communication. There is a need for careful cross-cultural studies of emotional representation. Are the emotional states classified and represented in Western culture differentiated and recognized in non-Western cultures? If so, are they similarly represented?

[6] The fundamental importance of categorization (classification) was the subject of studies that appeared in *Science* (Vol. 291, 12 January 2001) after this essay was written. The result relevant for this essay is summarized in the section, 'This week in science': 'Categories are the fundamental building blocks of nearly all higher level cognitive functions' (p. 207).

consciously classifying and naming kinds of relationships, techniques, or strategies. Just as a reader enjoys a poem not by 'watching the metaphors go by', but by responding to the relationships implicit in the comparisons, so experienced listeners respond to the implicative tension of a gap-fill melody or an antecedent-consequent phrase without conceptualizing its relational class.

*Mapping versus relating.* The conceptualization of feelings as phenomena independent of experiential context has led to a search for the neurological basis of emotion. However, although the areas of the brain that respond to some order of stimuli have been located and mapped, neurologists have yet to explain the nature of *relationships* within or between such areas.

The situation is not unlike that of the astronomers of ancient Greece who were able to map the heavens with considerable precision, but could not *explain* the relationships between the stars, planets, and the like. Neurological studies seem in a comparable position with respect to the mind. The brain has been mapped, and the areas that respond to different kinds of stimuli have been located; and, as with the Greeks, various areas have been given appropriate names. But while the parts of the brain that respond to specific musical stimuli have been identified, the neurological nature of the relationships between such stimuli remains a mystery. For example, the places in the brain that respond to the pitch A (440) and the C# above it, and those stimulated by the pitch E (660) and the G# above it, can be identified; but why both intervals are perceived as belonging to the same relational class (i.e. major third) remains to be explained.

*Processes: native and syntactic*

As observed above, emotional states fluctuate in intensity; and human empathy with the action of the music begets analogous feelings in listeners.[7] But like other fluctuations (e.g. in temperature, energy, or the stock market) changes in intensity or amount do not give rise to processes—that is, to changes involving *functionally differentiated relationships*. And, as argued in Section 15.2 below, crucial facets of the emotional experience of music lie in the realm of processes rather than that of states.

Two kinds of musical processes, 'native' ones and 'syntactic' ones, need to be distinguished.[8] Both are subject to the cognitive constraints of the mind and the physical ones of the body. Syntactic processes, however, also involve learning the norms of a particular

---

[7] Some emotional states require more contextual specification than others. For instance, musical representations of grief and joy, anxiety and calm are readily recognized by competent listeners (see, for example, Gabrielsson & Lindström, this volume; Juslin, this volume); but, because their recognition is more context-dependent, emotions such as jealousy and disgust are more difficult to represent in music alone. Consequently, their representation is, I suspect, relatively uncommon and when it occurs it tends to be accompanied by a text—a vocal part or a programme.

[8] In *Style and music* (Meyer 1989), I emphasized the different roles of syntactic and statistical parameters in creating musical relationships. As will be clear from what follows, though I am keeping the term 'statistical parameters', I now want to use the concept of *process* in connection with syntactic and native relationships. Although implicit in my earlier work, the implication-realization relationship was first made explicit in *Explaining music* (Meyer 1973), Chapters VI–VIII. The relationship has since been thoughtfully analysed, extended, and modelled by Eugene Narmour (1990).

musical style. As a result, native and syntactic processes almost always complement one another in the shaping of musical experience. Those based on the syntax of a style tend to be quite specific, but are historically and culturally circumscribed. Native processes, on the other hand, are less specific. But, as limitations common to humankind, they are essentially universal.[9]

The very existence of sound entails the use of the statistical parameters. Consequently, native and syntactic processes are invariably coordinate with, and qualified by, the action of statistical parameters. Responses to these parameters are also native, rather than learned. But because they are essentially matters of amount, statistical means do not give rise to functional differentiation. Rather what they involve is the *continuation* of prevalent action.

There is, however, an important exception: when amounts—whether of information or redundancy, of speed or intensity of stimulation—become excessive in relation to human cognitive capabilities, the native implication is change rather than continuation. The question is: to what? Because relationships of amount are without specific implications, the probability of the 'what' is uncertain. And when uncertainty is strong, almost any kind of change is welcome. A prolonged crescendo may *end* in silence or a jazzy fox trot, in a soft tremolo or a trumpet fanfare. Whatever the case, the proper term for such termination is indeed 'end', *not* close.

Processes, on the other hand, are functionally differentiated. For instance, the parts of the first phrase of Harold Arlen's 'Somewhere Over the Rainbow' perform different functions. The melody begins with an upward skip of an octave, a 'gap' (native process), whose physical effort implies the relaxation of the following conjunct descent, the 'fill', whose specific pitches are governed by tonal syntax. The fill also involves gradual reduction in physical tension through diminished motor emphasis, lower volume, increased rhythmic regularity, and simplification of texture. This 'abatement' implies ending. And in a tonal piece such as Arlen's, syntax transforms an end into a close. In addition, to 'make assurance double sure'(Shakespeare, *Macbeth*, IV. i), the final pitch of the fill constitutes a return to the first structural tone of the melody.

Like the gap–fill pattern just discussed, many native processes are manifestations of the gestalt principles of pattern perception: for example, once begun processes tend to continue to a point of stability or clear articulation; the mind tends to improve shapes, making them simpler—more regular and complete. Cognitive constraints also result in other native processes: for example, rapid note-succession is associated with high registers and small size; long, slow note-succession is associated with low registers and larger sizes;[10] as mentioned earlier, very high levels either of redundancy or of information imply change; and, as discussed below, forceful motor emphasis tends to weaken the effect of syntactic process.

---

[9] Preoccupied with the evident individuality of different cultures, ethnomusicologists have, it seems to me, neglected the influence of shared, 'native' constraints on the development and organization of the musics of different cultures.

[10] The interrelation among size, speed, and place seems a universal in all realms of being: the physical, biological, social, and perceptual. In this connection, see Schmid *et al.* (2000).

Although syntactic and native processes often complement one another in shaping musical experience, they are essentially independent variables. Thus, while an abatement process generally implies closure, closure could easily be thwarted by syntax—for instance, by an open-ended rhythmic pattern or a non-closural harmony. Or to take a converse case, potential syntactic closure can be undermined by a process whose regularity natively implies continuation. The need to weaken the momentum of a marked continuity process explains why, when a perfect cadence is preceded by regular motion by fourths and fifths, the chord on the second step of the scale is usually inverted (vi–ii6–V–I). Strong syntactic closure is possible because the 'native' continuity process is broken by the first inversion rather than a root-position ii chord.[11]

In other cases, though not congruent, processes may work together to shape experience. Such complementary interaction is evident in the duet of Aida and Radames, 'O terra, addio' at the end of Verdi's *Aida*. Because the initial gap (native) of a major seventh (G♭ to F) strongly implies a fill, the following rise to G♭ functions not only as a poignant, yet delightful, resolution to the tonic (syntactic), but also as an escape tone that descends to D♭, which begins the fill (native).

While syntactic and native processes may complement one another, the relationship of process to amounts is not complementary. Though the statistical aspect of music is a necessary condition for both kinds of processes, its action is inversely related to theirs. That is, the more compelling the action of statistical parameters, the less effective the processes which, as we shall see, shape emotional experience. When, however, syntactic and native processes are primary, statistical parameters tend to be subservient.

### 15.1.2 Implication

The distinctions between emotional states and emotional processes suggest that different kinds of relationships evoke and shape different facets of musical experience. The statistical parameters beget the physical–somatic conditions which, through empathy, characterize emotional states in the primal present. Syntactic and native processes not only beget physical empathy with music, but generate mental arousal that, directing attention to what is still to come, gives rise to implication.

*Implication versus causation*

Both syntactic and native processes generate implications—guesses (feelings) about how present patterns will be continued and perhaps reach closure. But because 'What's to come is still unsure' (Shakespeare, *Twelfth night*, II. iii),[12] implications are never more

---

[11] The desire to enhance closure also accounts for why, instead of continuing directly to the tonic, a descending melodic line (e.g. from the fifth of the scale) often moves from the second to the third step of the scale before closing on the tonic.

[12] I have used quotations from, and references to, Shakespeare's writings throughout this essay not only because I happen to know his works quite well, but because their variety and pertinence so often illustrate (with little qualification) points I want to make.

than *probable*. Consequently, it is important to distinguish implication from causation. As I put the point in *Style and music* (Meyer 1989, p. 96):

The possibility of alternative consequences … may help to account for the difference between implication and causation. For though both involve 'if–then' relationships, causation is a special case in which the antecedent (cause) is a sufficient condition for the consequent (effect). Consequently, alternatives are not possible. The difference in our understanding of the two concepts is reflected in ordinary language. Though it seems entirely proper to assert that 'X *implied* Y, but Y did not occur,' it would seem illogical to assert that 'X *caused* Y, but Y did not occur.'

### Implication: native and syntactic processes

Native as well as syntactic processes can give rise to implications. As observed earlier, the implication created by a gap such as the one that begins 'Somewhere Over the Rainbow' is the result of a native process. At the beginning of Mozart's Piano Sonata in A Major (K. 331), however, a *learned* syntactic process generates the implications that link the antecedent to the consequent phrase. Similarly, an antecedent 'when clause', such as begins Shakespeare's Sonnet 'When to the sessions of sweet silent thought', implies a consequent closure:

But if the while I think on thee dear friend
All losses are restored and sorrows end.

Notice that in both music and language, the 'suspense' created by syntactic or native processes is short range, as compared with 'referential' suspense—for example, about finding the culprit in, say, a detective story. Thus, while the implications of the deceptive cadence at the beginning of Beethoven's Piano Sonata in E Flat, Opus 81a ('Les Adieux') are reactivated during the movement, suspense is experienced locally. And this is also true of language. One cannot, for instance, imagine the implicative tension (suspense) of a 'when' clause at the beginning of a chapter lasting until its close.

Not all implications arise from the presence of orderly processes. As discussed in Section 15.2, some result from the human antipathy to disorder. For instance, whether resulting from unpredictable change or incomprehensible redundancy, uncertainty leads listeners to anticipate the advent of stability and order. Thus insistent repetition (coupled with harmonic instability and a gradual crescendo), such as occurs early in the development section of the first movement of Beethoven's Sixth Symphony (mm. 151ff.), leads listeners to anticipate change. The question is to what extent the expectation of change is a result of culturally acquired goal-directed proclivities; after all, marked beat redundancy does not seem to imply change in contemporary popular music.

### 15.1.3 Emotional expression and emotional experience

The nature of emotional expression versus emotional experiences (and related matters) has been widely discussed in the psychological literature. Accordingly, I have chosen: (a) to offer an early instance (*c.* 1604) of the distinction between expression and experience; and (b) to call attention to a kind of emotional response seldom considered in the psychological literature.

*Expression versus experience*

Seems, madam! Nay, it is; I know not 'seems.'
'Tis not alone my inky cloak, good mother,
Nor the customary suits of solemn black,
Nor the windy suspiration of forc'd breath,
No, nor the fruitful river in the eye,
Nor the dejected havior of the visage,
Together with all forms, moods, shows of grief,
That can denote me truly. These indeed seem,
For they are actions that a man might play;
But I have that within which passeth show,
These but the trappings and the suits of woe.
(Shakespeare, *Hamlet*, I. ii)

*Connotations and recollections*

What is usually meant by an emotional response to music is a response made by accultur-ated listeners to the relationships that shape auditory experience. But, as is well known, an emotional response may be evoked not primarily by the sound patterns presented, but by allusions that those patterns are understood to make to other compositions (e.g. a Bach chorale), to music associated with a cultural activity (e.g. a waltz or a funeral march), or to sounds in nature (e.g. of the wind or of an animal). In these cases, it is not the patterning of the music *per se* that evokes emotion, but the *connotations* that it has for different listeners.

A related kind of response, which I call 'nostalgia' emotion, is not the result of a cul-turally shared reference. Rather, depending on the experience and susceptibility of a particular listener (coupled with the specific circumstance), emotion may be evoked by any sound whatsoever—from the soft sound of waves on the shore, to the singing of birds in the trees, to the rather crude music of 'The Old Grey Mare, she ain't what she used to be many long years ago', to which I marched during basic training 'many long years ago' (in 1943).[13]

## 15.2 Uncertainty: 'puzzles the will'

### 15.2.1 Evolution, choice, and culture

*Evolution and choice*[14]

Although evolution unquestionably influenced human behaviour through the direct action of biological constraints, what most significantly shaped human behaviour and

---

[13] It is important to recognize that emotional responses to the 'remembrance of things past' is depend-ent on the context of the act of remembering. Music that moves us in the concert hall or at a memo-rial service will probably be without affect in an elevator or a supermarket.

[14] I begin the first part of Section 15.2 with a paraphrase of the end of the last chapter of *The spheres of music* (Meyer 2000). I have included it not only because it constitutes the context for my concern with uncertainty, but because I believe it offers an account of how evolution affected human cultures that is significantly different from those proposed by neuropsychologists and sociobiologists.

gave rise to human cultures was not the presence but the absence of adequate innate constraints.[15] It is because evolution resulted in such an animal that human cultures became indispensable. This aspect of evolution is summarized by biologist François Jacob (1982, p. 61):

In lower organisms behavior is strictly determined by the genetic program. In complex metazoa the genetic program becomes less constraining, more 'open' . . . This openness of the genetic program increases with evolution and culminates in mankind.

It seems reasonable to suggest that the growth of cognitive capacity was coordinate with the development of consciousness. And consciousness is aroused when choice is required. Indeed, it seems possible that the growth of consciousness was partly a result of the increased importance of choice. That is, as animal intelligence increased so did the apprehension of differences—of kinds and relationships—in the phenomenal world. This change may well have been accompanied by a diminution of the role of instinct in animal behaviour.[16]

Increased apprehension of kinds and relationships led to the invention and production of usables (from cradles to coffins), to a concomitant increase in the number of conceptual categories, and to a burgeoning of behavioural options. The consequences of these developments were momentous because the proliferation of conceptual categories and behavioural possibilities makes choosing at once inescapable and burdensome. In philosopher Peter Singer's words: 'Our ability to be a participant in a decision-making process, to reflect and to choose, is as much a fact about human nature as the effect of the limbic system on our emotions' (1981, p. 42).

The necessity of choice is a universal that lies at the very heart of the human condition. It constitutes a basis for both ethical and aesthetic judgments. In ethics, as in the law, individuals are culpable only if the behaviour in question can be shown to be a result of choice. In the arts, forgeries are banished to the basement because the relationships reproduced were not created—not *chosen*—by the forger.[17]

*Choice*

A number of interrelated conditions combine to facilitate effective, propitious choosing: the presence of constraints limiting options; the ability to envisage the consequences of alternative choices; concepts of hierarchical structuring; and the power to realize one's choices.[18]

*Constraints.* Without controls limiting the number and ordering the priority of alternative behavioural possibilities, human beings would be caught in distressing indecision—

---

[15] Since writing this passage, I discovered that Clifford Geertz (1973, pp. 45–6) made much the same point in *The interpretation of cultures*.

[16] Put the other way around: as the power of instinct waned, choice became the main basis for human behaviour, and with the necessity of choice came the burden of uncertainty.

[17] See 'Forgery and the anthropology of art' in *Music, the arts, and ideas* (Meyer 1994), Chapter 4.

[18] Because it is not involved in the process of choosing, but in the realization of choices, 'power' is not allotted a separate heading under 'Choice', but is considered below—especially in Section 15.2.2.

an uncertainty that is not only time-consuming, but a source of unwelcome psychological tension. Growing out of and complementing innate constraints, cultures provide the learned, behavioural controls without which human beings could not choose, function, or, indeed, survive.

A single example from the history of music serves to illustrate this point. The abandonment of common-practice tonality by some early twentieth-century composers spawned so many compositional options that limitations were necessary to make choosing feasible. From this point of view, the invention of the twelve-tone method was a response to the need for constraints limiting options. This was the necessary condition for the advent of serialism; the sufficient condition for the constraints actually devised was largely a result of nurture—specifically, of the cultural belief that similarity begets unity.[19] Put succinctly, if too simply: the native need for compositional constraints created the 'problem'; cultural concepts provided a 'solution'.

*Envisaging, culture, and stability.* In order to choose intelligently, the various options available in a particular natural or cultural context must be comprehended and the probable consequences of each envisaged.[20] The need to envisage in order to choose is evident everywhere in human culture—from soothsayers to scientists, from astrological imaginings to the interpretation of dreams, from poll-taking to fortune-telling, from economic forecasting to the postulation of predictable historical processes. Similarly, faith in the existence of an established, unchanging order or, alternatively, in change that occurs in an orderly way is appealing because it seems to assure the possibility of successful envisaging.[21]

Indeed, all our institutions, laws and customs, as well as styles of art, serve to stabilize the conceptual-behavioural environment for the sake of effective envisaging and successful choosing. And the same is true not only of theories (including even those about chaos), but of styles of behaviour, whether in the arts or in culture generally. Conversely, the insane are institutionalized because we are uncertain about how to act in the face of 'irrational'—that is, frighteningly *un*predictable—behaviour.

*Hierarchies: functional versus continuous.* One mode of conceptualization that serves to stabilize our understanding of relationships in the realms of both nurture and nature is that of hierarchic structuring. Because the term 'hierarchy' has been used to refer to

---

[19] In this connection, see the Webern and Krenek quotations in *Music, the arts, and ideas* (Meyer 1994, p. 263). The nature of aesthetic unity has been an enduring concern of artists and aestheticians since Greek times. But the intensity of that concern and the nature of its conceptualization are culture-dependent. Thus, the belief that similarity produces unity appealed to romantic composers, because their repudiation of conventional constraints led to a significant increase in the number of available choices, and the variation and transformation of an existing pattern (motive, harmonic progression, etc.) facilitated compositional choice by limiting options. The role of similarity in creating unity is considered below, in note 36.

[20] Envisaging entails making inferences (based on both native and learned constraints) about the implications of a particular patterning or about the probable course of events in a specific set of circumstances.

[21] Thus, despite manifest differences in belief and method, science and religion have a common goal: namely, to stabilize the perceptual/cognitive world for the sake of explaining, envisaging, and choosing. In other words, both realms are ultimately ways of minimizing unwanted uncertainty.

different kinds of relationships, it seems important to distinguish between two basic types: (a) functionally differentiated hierarchies; and (b) continuous (functionally undifferentiated) ones.[22]

Because their *functional differentiation* specifies relational processes, biological organisms (plants as well as animals), cultural institutions (governmental, educational, industrial), most temporal art works (novels and dramas, sonata forms and rondos), and man-made machines (submarines to space ships) tend to enhance the stability of the behavioural environment. Wealth, power, and celebrity; geological, biological, and technological change; and the fluctuations of climate and populations, all form continuous hierarchies whose elements are related to one another not in terms of function, but of *amount*—for example, of wealth or power; strength, speed, or intensity.[23] In the absence of functional constraints, it seems doubtful whether statistical hierarchies foster stability and enhance the ability to envisage and choose successfully.[24]

## 15.2.2 Uncertainty

A critical corollary of the imperative of choice is the human abhorrence of uncertainty—for instance, the uncertainty surrounding death, which is undoubtedly a crucial reason for the prevalence of religion and for the correlative belief in an after-life. These are the focus of lines from Hamlet's famous 'To be, or not to be' soliloquy:

. . .the dread of something after death,
The undiscover'd country from whose bourn
No traveler returns, puzzles the will
And makes us rather bear those ills we have
Than fly to others that we know not of?
(Shakespeare, *Hamlet*, III.i)

...................................................................................................................

[22] The difference between functionally differentiated and continuous hierarchies is analogous to that between the functioning of syntactic/native processes and the action of statistical parameters. This difference is exemplified by that between the closure created by a functionally differentiated syntactic progression (e.g. from subdominant to dominant to tonic) and that created by 'tonal centring' through the repetition of a pitch, etc. (as, for instance, in the first movement of Béla Bartók's Piano Sonata). After this section was written, one of the readers called my attention to Lawrence Zbikowski's (1997) essay on 'Conceptual models and cross-domain mapping'. That essay also distinguished between two kinds of hierarchy. The first, 'chains of being', is comparable to my 'continuous hierarchies'; but his second type does not seem to consider the role of functional differentiation.

[23] Whether a hierarchy is functional or continuous does not depend on the *kind* of phenomenon, but on the level being scrutinized. For instance, although social history constitutes a continuous hierarchy on the highest level of change, change on lower levels (e.g. of a particular political event) may be governed by functional constraints, and the same can be said of, say, the history of sonata form versus the form of a particular sonata-form movement.

[24] This does not gainsay the fact that statistical change may seem implicative: for instance, the gradual intensification of dynamics, increase in frequency, and shortening of duration may be understood to imply arrival at some kind of goal. But whatever 'arrival' (articulation) occurs necessarily involves either significant repetition of the tonicized pitch (see note 22) or a significant change in other parameters—for instance, a lengthening of the final sound, a change in orchestration, dynamic level, or register.

Here an apparent paradox arises. On the one hand, uncertainty is anathema to humankind.[25] For this reason, as noted above, we devise ways of reducing uncertainty both in the 'out-there' world and in our personal lives. On the other hand, in the arts and in other 'playful' activities such as sports, games, and gambling, we actually relish and cultivate a considerable amount of uncertainty.

### Belief, empathy, and aesthetic experience

The paradox is possible not only because of what Coleridge called 'the willing suspension of disbelief',[26] but more importantly because of a *positive* belief in the competence, integrity, and creativity of the artist and, above all, in the significance of works of art. Such positive belief is indispensable for man-made aesthetic experience (as distinguished from the experience of beauty in the natural world), because it is a necessary condition for the empathy on which perceptual engagement and affective response depend.[27]

The importance of such belief is evident in the ability of criticism to affect the responses of listeners. For instance, the negative reception of avant-garde music was, at least in part, a result of critiques that undermined audience empathy by suggesting that the choices of composers were the result of system-based calculation or of random chance, rather than of 'inspiration' and 'inner feeling'. On the other side, consider this stunning, if preposterous, instance of the power of positive belief to produce a favourable response in an audience. In a book review, 'Fascinating rhythm', David Hajdu writes: 'In 1971, Ravi Shankar, the Indian virtuoso, performed at New York's Madison Square Garden. After hearing a few minutes of Shankar's ensemble, the audience of some 20 000 roared in approval. "Thank you," Shankar replied. "If you appreciate the tuning so much, I hope you will enjoy the playing more."'[28]

The empathy that belief begets is not solely cognitive. Almost always it involves physical behaviour—an inner performative empathy, a kind of imitative identification, with the qualities and patterns of the music.[29] Lack of motor empathy, for example, seems to

---

[25] Uncertainty is evidently also anathema to other animals. Elizabeth Pennisi (2000, p. 577), for example, writes that: 'Although baboons are considered quite aggressive primates by nature, violence tends to be much more prevalent when the troop's structure is unstable . . . if the troop members don't know one another, or if the hierarchy is disturbed, say, by the loss of the top male, the rush to establish rank results in scuffles that subside when everyone knows his or her place.' In short, instability, lack of familiarity, disturbance of social structuring—all create uncertainty which, in turn, begets violence.

[26] *Biographia literaria*, Chapter 14. The 'willing suspension of disbelief' is an important factor in the ability of audiences to re-experience implicative relationships—to 'make believe' that they are experiencing anew.

[27] In addition to being a source of aesthetic enjoyment, music has, since its beginnings, served to foster social cohesion—through the evocation of empathic sharing in religious and secular ceremonies, attending to or participating in theatrical performances, and marching or dancing together.

[28] *New York Review of Books*, Vol. 47, No. 12 (20 July 2000), p. 41.

[29] Many years ago (Meyer 1956*b*), I argued that belief was essential for the success of music therapy. More recently, studies described in the *Harvard Men's Health Watch* (September 1997, p. 6) have demonstrated the importance of belief for longevity and more general well-being. In addition, it seems likely that belief plays a significant role in the placebo effect (see Enserink 1999).

have played a significant role in the negative aesthetic and hence emotional response to avant-garde music, while motorically accessible musics (from Bach to rock) have found ardent audiences. Indeed, I suspect that often contemporary music has failed to find favour with concert audiences, not primarily because it tends to be dissonant, but because it is difficult to empathize with and experience motorically—not just the lack of rhythmic regularity, but such motor-related problems as the prevalence of large descending skips and intervals such as augmented fourths.

The roles of belief and empathy (physical as well as cognitive) help to explain why the uncertainty experienced in relation to works of art, games, and sports differs significantly from that evoked by 'real-life' circumstances.[30] Indeed, in the temporal arts, the arousal and resolution of uncertainty is an essential basis for aesthetic-emotional experience. Because patterns imply alternative possible continuations and realizations, implication invariably involves some degree of uncertainty—uncertainty about *what* will happen, *when* it will happen, and *how* it will happen.[31] Consequently, to paraphrase *Hamlet* again: like sorrows, uncertainties 'come not single spies/But in battalions' (Shakespeare, *Hamlet*, IV. v).

It is important to recognize that uncertainty entails at least an inkling of patterning. Because either too little or too much information precludes the perception of even a modicum of order, neither is compatible with uncertainty. That is, unless there is some degree of order, whether presumed or inferred, there is nothing to be uncertain *about*. And because even a bit of order tends to be implicative, uncertainty is so as well.

*The succession of states*

The role of uncertainty has unfortunately been neglected in the study of the emotional response to music. Neglect has probably occurred because emotional 'states' such as love, anger, and hate are, as mentioned earlier, experienced, classified, and named in terms of the particular real-life circumstances with which they become associated.[32] But uncertainty itself is not 'circumstantial'. And, because it can be coupled with and qualify many states of being or feeling, uncertainty is not thought of as an 'emotion'. However, although not a nameable, circumstantial state, uncertainty is a necessary, though perhaps not sufficient, condition for the emotional experiences and behaviours of human beings.[33]

What I am suggesting, then, is that states of feeling (e.g. love, contentment, hunger, fatigue) become emotional experiences when they are at least tinged by uncertainty. As

---

[30] Another reason for this difference has to do with our relationship to 'roads-not-taken'. In the arts and other pleasure activities, 'roads-not-taken' constitute a source of experiential enrichment. In real life, on the other hand, an abundance of alternatives tends to be disturbing and perplexing.

[31] At times, implications are realized remotely and may, as a result, be recognized largely in retrospect. That is, we did not experience uncertainty when the pattern was presented earlier, but realize subsequently that we *might* have done so.

[32] I suspect that the neglect of uncertainty was, ironically, a result of the psychological and cultural craving for the control that *naming* (separate emotions) provides.

[33] This account represents a modification of that given in Meyer (1956a, p. 16 ff.).

observed earlier, although being 'curious' is not in itself an emotional experience, it may become so if the behavioural inclinations (the needs or goals) associated with it are thwarted. And this appears to be the case with other goal-directed needs—from the need for food to the need to choose. *Qua* feelings, they are states of being. They become emotional experiences or responses when thwarting creates uncertainty about appropriate courses of action.

Seen thus, uncertainty is the result of ignorance—ignorance about how past and present patterns will be continued, eventually reaching stability and closure. In other words, uncertainty is always more or less goal-directed, implying (perhaps unconsciously) resolution to the security of knowing.

Since uncertainty is a function of the amount of information the mind is required to process, if there is so little information that patterning is impossible, the result is a sense of powerlessness and hope-based uncertainty is abandoned. Perhaps this is why during the Vietnam War it was found that, deprived of any stimulation whatsoever, prisoners became mentally deranged. Stimulus overload (too much information), which may be a matter either of amount, or speed, or both, is almost as disturbing as stimulus deprivation. Hence audiences tend to be alienated, when (what for them is) an excessive amount of information in a piece of contemporary music precludes patterning and, consequently, a sense of control.[34]

At the end of *Emotion and meaning in music* (Meyer 1956a) and subsequently in *Explaining music* (Meyer 1973), I grappled with the problem of accounting for the succession of emotional states presented in a piece of music. Much later, in 'A universe of universals' (Meyer 2000), I argued that no necessary, inherent order governs the succession of emotional states or referential subjects presented in a piece of music.[35] We accept such successions because the uncertainty and lack of cognitive control created by intervening instability make the return to mentally manageable patterns satisfying. In short, it is the uncertainty–resolution (or, correlatively, the implication–realization) process, not similarity of melodic, rhythmic, or tonal pattern, that unifies the succession of emotional states presented in a piece of music.[36]

As emphasized in Section 15.1, we conceptualize and understand phenomena not in terms of individual instances, but in terms of *classes*. And classification plays a critical role in our sense of cognitive control and power.

----

[34] If the amount of information is inordinately increased, the result is a kind of cognitive white noise.

[35] A particular succession may, of course, be the result of a programme conceived by the composer, or devised by critics or listeners to account for a succession not linked together compositionally by the tension of syntactic uncertainty. This, together with the diminished sophistication of the audience, may help to account for the increased use of programmes during the nineteenth century.

Also, in order to enhance expressivity, there tended to be an increase in the instability and tension of putatively stable passages. As a result, the difference in degree of uncertainty between presumably stable and unstable passages diminished. When this occurred, the relatively weak level of uncertainty could not unambiguously link successive emotional states.

[36] As observed in note 19, the belief that similarity begets unity became aesthetic doctrine during the nineteenth and early twentieth centuries. But a moment's thought makes it evident that the more

*Power*

When it involves loss of control, uncertainty may also become associated with feelings of angst and terror. This perhaps partly explains why rapid tremolos, which cannot readily be processed by either mind or body, are associated with angst and terror. As in the startle reaction, shockingly unexpected stimuli engender anxiety and fear of the unpredictable and the inexplicable. Writing about the situation in Kosovo, Mark Danner observed that random, indiscriminate violence is more effective than orderly extermination: 'Imposition of terror, *the more "indiscriminate", the better*, breeds fear . . .'[37] Briefly: total uncertainty is unbearably painful.

So too is the frustration created by the impossibility of action. This may help to account for the weeping which seems to come from strong feeling, often evoked by emotion-laden associations and memories, that can find no expression in action. Feelings of hopelessness—an inferno resulting from the inability to choose and hence to act—give rise to strong emotion. For instance, when we recognize that an important goal cannot be realized—that hope must be abandoned—feelings often result in weeping.[38] The action that might-have-been is, as it were, transformed into tears.[39]

This is the source of what I have called the emotion of 'nostalgia'. A personal experience exemplifies this kind of response. At a performance of Verdi's *La Traviata*, when Germont began to sing 'Di Provenza', I began to weep, not only because my father

........................................................................................................................................

*alike* two patterns are, the more they seem separate—the case, for instance, with the motivic repetitions in the Scherzo of Beethoven's Symphony No. 7 (e.g. mm. 37–40 and 49–52). Confusion occurs because unity is equated with *uniformity*.

Unity, however, involves the functional connection of phenomena that differ in some significant respect; uniformity involves connection through similarity of substance and/or pattern. Thus, although the grains of sand on a beach are essentially alike, it would surely seem strange to say that the beach was unified. Similarly, while it is proper to characterize a musical ostinato or a word repetition (such as Macbeth's 'Tomorrow, and tomorrow, and tomorrow') as uniform, it would be wrong to say that they created unity. Whether in music, or in literature, or in biological organisms, unity results not from similarity, but from functional differentiation.

[37] 'Endgame in Kosovo', *New York Review of Books*, Vol. 46, No. 8 (6 May 1999), p. 8.

[38] As Sloboda (1992, p. 37) observed, weeping would seem to be a unambiguous manifestation of emotion. Yet it has been strangely neglected in the psychological literature about music. I can think of two (not mutually exclusive) reasons: (a) because, like uncertainty, weeping is circumstantially variable; and (b) because it is difficult to know whether the tears are a result of acculturation or personal experience.

[39] If weeping comes from within, laughter comes from outside us, from the incongruities of the outside world (in this connection, see note 3). Even when we laugh at ourselves, it is the out-there, 'other' self that we laugh at. Laughter (e.g. at jokes) exemplifies a related facet of uncertainty. Initially, as with any process, we are uncertain as to how stability and closure will be reached. To heighten the tension of uncertainty, the first part of the process is usually elaborated. The tension of patent, though usually playful, delay is resolved by a 'punch-line', and we laugh: first, because of the relief that comes with *knowing* and second because, though apt, the outcome is surprising and amusingly incongruous.

especially loved that aria, but because evoking memories of 'days beyond recall', and beyond empathic reciprocity, made my present powerlessness apparent.[40]

### Risk-taking and culture

Uncertainty can also be associated with what appears to be the opposite of frustration: namely, the thrill and exhilaration of risk-taking. For what sky-diving and the virtuoso performance of a challenging cadenza, or adventurous mountain-climbing and daring modulations to a distant tonality, have in common is the thrilling uncertainty of risk-taking and the illumination of self-discovery.[41] The pleasure of, and empathy with, risk-taking is, however, dependent on the belief of all concerned (composer, performer, and audience) in the existence of expert control.

Risk-taking is in turn related to the heroic. To appreciate, and empathize with, the uncertainty of risk is to move toward and experience something of the heroic. And though it seems *passé* (and a bit theatrical), Samuel Johnson touched on an important facet of human behaviour when he observed that:[42]

Were Socrates and Charles the Twelfth of Sweden both present in any company and Socrates to say 'Follow me and hear a lecture on philosophy'; and Charles, laying his hand on his sword, to say 'Follow me and dethrone the Czar'; a man would be ashamed to follow Socrates . . . The profession of soldiers and sailors has the dignity of danger [of risk-taking]. Mankind reverence those who have got over fear, which is so general a weakness.

But in contemporary culture there has been a significant decline in the valuing of personal honour, the heroic, and the risk-taking associated with them. Hayden White (1973, p. 232) relates the ironic mode of much twentieth-century thought to 'the passage of the age of heros and of the capacity to believe in heroism'.[43] And, according to Admiral Arthur, commander of the American naval forces during the Gulf War, even in the military 'We now have people being taught how to be cautious, not how to be bold' (Schmitt 1995). Construed in terms of the subject of this chapter, tolerance for the tensions of uncertainty has been considerably reduced. One reason for this reduction is

---

[40] Needless to say, not all crying is 'nostalgia-generated'. Infants cry because of unrealized needs—for food, affection, nappy (diaper)-changing, etc. But certainty can, without forcing, also be considered an unrealized need—the need for power, for confidence in our ability to act.

[41] Thus, Garry Wills observed that Robert Kennedy 'courted danger, climbing mountains, shooting rapids. What he was looking for was his true self, so long repressed, so totally held in the service of others' ('Waiting for Bobby,' a review of Ronald Steel's *In love with night: The American romance with Robert Kennedy* published in the *New York Review of Books*, Vol. 47, No. 2, 10 February 2000, p. 20).

[42] Said by Samuel Johnson in 1778 and quoted in Harry G. Summers Jr., 'The men of Company E' (a review of *Band of brothers* by Stephen E. Ambrose published in the Book Review, *New York Times*, 6 December 1992, p. 11). It could be argued that fear is basically a kind of uncertainty.

[43] Also see J. B. Freeman's 'Dueling as politics: Reinterpreting the Burr-Hamilton duel' (*William and Mary Quarterly*, 1996, pp. 289–318), discussed in Gordon S. Wood, 'An affair of honor' published in the *New York Review of Books*, Vol. 47, No. 6, 13 April 2000, pp. 67–8.

that risk-taking, honour, and the heroic are *individual* endeavours that are incompatible with egalitarian, mass culture.

But perhaps the most important reason for the changes taking place in our culture is the altered attitude toward history itself.[44] As the future-oriented perspective prevalent since the Renaissance has weakened, there has been a trend away from risky goal-directed action, in both life and art. This seems evident in the complacent *present*ational character of much minimalist music. Paradoxically, this is also the case with 'bing-bang' popular music whose aggressive force implies no future goal, but rather calls for compliance NOW.[45]

### Further thoughts about uncertainty

*Narratives and plots.* Uncertainty is of vital importance in the aesthetic process of moving from the insecurity of ignorance to the security of knowing. This process, which Aristotle referred to as the 'reversal' of the action in a drama, is at the core of all plots. And this calls attention to the difference between a narrative and a plot.

Most histories (evolution, political, economic, and intellectual), as well as many literary and musical genres (novels and dramas; sonata forms and song cycles), are narratives.[46] But not all narratives are plots. A narrative succession is transformed into a plot when uncertainty is experienced in terms of an imagined goal. One of the problems with many narrative interpretations of music is that they are based on passages that present stable emotional states and referential associations. The result is a succession of largely separate vignettes rather than a plot in which uncertainty reaches resolution in stability.

Here another paradox arises. The human need to envisage leads us to conceptualize the world as being more or less predictable. But continual succession without functionally ordered structure (as in cosmology, evolution, and human history) creates the uncomfortable uncertainty of *un*ordered endlessness. As a result, we tend to transform what are essentially fluctuating continuities (narratives without goals) into plots. To put the paradox succinctly: the uncertainty created by pattern instability begets functional differentiation, which reduces the uncertainty produced by an unarticulated succession of emotional states.

Finally, I suspect that the psychological desire to transform narratives into plots is one reason why we tend to anthropomorphize phenomena. That is, anthropomorphism not only provides conceptual means for envisaging and choosing, but provides goals that change potentially endless successions into implication-realization patterns—that is, into plots with potential for closure.

----

[44] The end of historic optimism is discussed in the 'Postlude' to the second printing of *Music, the arts, and ideas* (Meyer 1994).

[45] Although my aesthetic predilections are obvious, my concern is not with making value judgments, but with trying to understand and explain some of the changes taking place in contemporary culture.

[46] Though implicative, sonnets (as illustrated above) are not narrative—nor are limericks. Both are like propositional 'arguments'. In music, the closest form to 'pure' narrative is the theme and variations which, like high-level histories, are potentially endless successions.

*Motor action, deviation, and implication.* Because it implies virtually automatic continuation, marked motor regularity and strong emotional process tend to be inversely related. And because rapid tempos are usually coordinate with forceful motor action, speed and emotion also tend to be inversely related. For instance, in the opening section of Bach's Brandenburg Concerto No. 2, rhythm, tempo, and (implicit) dynamics evoke strong motor empathy, but only minimal emotional tension.[47]

This suggests why forceful motor action is incompatible with richly implicative processes: namely, because emphatic motor action tends to minimize the imagining of alternative implications—that is, other continuations.[48] For the same reason, however, forceful motor action can be important in the generation of surprise: that is, we are most easily and forcefully surprised when we are *un*aware of the possibility of alternatives.

Mention of surprise reminds us that implications and uncertainties can be recognized, though not experienced, in retrospect. This occurs when the regularity of a pattern and its context make continuation seem highly probable. Then if an abrupt change occurs—as, for instance, in the slow movement of Haydn's 'Surprise' Symphony (No. 94)—we realize that we *should have been* less complacent about the implications of the earlier patterning. Conversely, we may in retrospect recognize that a present pattern is, in fact, the realization of an implication not noticed in a prior process.

In general, not just forceful motor action, but any pattern or behaviour that seems predictable—is stylistically normal and cognitively coherent—reduces uncertainty. By disturbing such predictability, deviation (surprise, delay, etc.) may evoke uncertainty and emotional experience.[49] In short, some degree of regularity (stability) is a necessary condition for an emotional response to music; the sufficient condition is, as I suggested 'many long years ago', the uncertainty created by some degree of deviation.[50]

*Intensity, control, and emotional experience.* As observed earlier, the intensity of uncertainty is variable, depending both on the patterning of events and what is believed to be the importance of their goal(s). In general, as the number and strength of implied alternatives increases so does uncertainty;[51] and the same holds for the richness of their

---

[47] Again, the distinction between an emotional state and an emotional process is critical. Although Bach's opening creates feelings of forceful, confident power, it does not, as I see it, give rise to marked emotional process.

[48] Because they tend to preclude awareness of possible alternative continuations, overly rapid tempi also obscure the relational richness potential in performance.

[49] Briefly, in 'life' we try to conceptualize the world so that it seems regular and predictable. In the arts, on the other hand, we devise regularities as a base for the deviations that, by creating uncertainty, beget emotion and shape aesthetic experience.

[50] In *Emotion and meaning in music* (Meyer 1956a), I argued that deviation, whether one present in the composer's score or one created by the performer, tends to evoke emotion. But I failed to see that deviation does so because it is a source of uncertainty.

[51] Janet M. Levy (1995) distinguishes the multiple meanings (implications) that beget uncertainty from ambiguity which 'gives rise to two or more specifiable meanings' (p. 152).

imagined consequences, both proximate and remote.[52] Thus, when it is said of a novel that 'the plot thickens', what is probably meant is that uncertainty has increased. In music, the degree of uncertainty that is pleasant and enjoyable depends not only on musical relationships, but, as suggested earlier, on the beliefs of the audience about the historical importance and aesthetic value of the music being played. Beliefs are a prerequisite for empathy, and empathy for attentive perception and sensitive response.

The degree of uncertainty appears to be the basis for the distinction made by psychologists between 'pleasant' and 'unpleasant' emotions.[53] This is, I suspect, because intensity influences the sense of control experienced by the listener. Put differently, emotions are felt to be pleasant, even exhilarating, when associated with confidence in the power to envisage and choose; they are experienced as unpleasant when intense uncertainty precludes the sense of control that comes from the ability to envisage with confidence.

Finally, the aesthetic importance of uncertainty lies not only in the shaping of emotional *processes*, as distinguished from the evocation of emotional *states*, but in the articulation of musical structure. When the tensions of instability are resolved to the cognitive security of stable patterning, functional relationships have at once articulated and unified musical structure.

I am, appropriately, uncertain about how to end this essay—and that makes me somewhat sad. Yet, at the same time and for the same reason, I feel glad—glad because connecting puzzled uncertainty with emotion *seems* to confirm my basic argument.[54]

## References

Enserink, M. (1999). Can the placebo be the cure? *Science*, **264**, 238–40.

Geertz, C. (1973). *The interpretation of cultures.* New York: Basic Books.

Jacob, F. (1982). *The possible and the actual.* New York: Pantheon Books.

Levy, J. M. (1995). Beginning-ending ambiguity: Consequences of performance choices. In *The practice of performance*, (ed. J. Rink), pp. 150–69. Cambridge, UK: Cambridge University Press.

Meyer, L. B. (1956*a*). *Emotion and meaning in music.* Chicago: University of Chicago Press.

Meyer, L. B. (1956*b*). Learning, belief, and music therapy. *Music Therapy*, **5**, 27–35.

---

[52] There are significant differences between complexity and relational richness. In this connection, see *The spheres of music* (Meyer 2000), Essay 2.

[53] Anxiety needs to be distinguished from uncertainty. Unlike uncertainty, anxiety occurs when governing constraints are not known and cannot be inferred from the perception of overly complex stimuli. Consequently, anxiety is not implicative but endures, fluctuating in a persistent present. However, because of our beliefs about its special nature, aesthetic experience seldom gives rise to anxiety; it does so only when all sense of order and hence the possibility of cognitive control is lost.

[54] My thanks to the reviewers of this essay—especially to Nicholas Cook—for their helpful comments, criticisms, and suggestions. I am deeply indebted to my wife, Janet Levy, for her leading questions, astute observations, and cogent critiques of the various versions of this study.

**Meyer, L. B.** (1973). *Explaining music. Essays and explorations.* Berkeley, CA: University of California Press.

**Meyer, L. B.** (1989). *Style and music.* Philadelphia, PA: University of Pennsylvania Press.

**Meyer, L. B.** (1994). *Music, the arts, and ideas.* Chicago: University of Chigago Press (originally published 1967).

**Meyer, L. B.** (2000). *The spheres of music.* Chicago: University of Chigago Press.

**Narmour, E.** (1990). *The analysis and cognition of basic melodic structures: The implication-realization model.* Chicago: University of Chicago Press.

**Pennisi, E.** (2000). Personality and rank. *Science, 289,* 577.

**Scherer, K. R.** (1994). Toward a concept of modal emotions. In *The nature of emotion,* (ed. P. Ekman & R. J. Davidson), pp. 25–31. New York: Oxford University Press.

**Schmid, P. E., Tokeshu, M., & Araya, J. M.** (2000). Relation between population density and body size in stream communities. *Science, 289,* 1557–9.

**Schmitt, E.** (1995) The military's getting queasier about death. *New York Times,* The Week in Review, 6 May, p. 5.

**Singer, P.** (1981). *The expanding circle: Ethics and sociobiology.* New York: Farrar, Straus & Girony.

**Sloboda, J. A.** (1992). Empirical studies of emotional response to music. In *Cognitive bases of musical communication,* (ed. M. Riess-Jones & S. Holleran), pp. 33–46. Washington, DC: American Psychological Association.

**White, H.** (1973). *Metahistory: The historical imagination in nineteenth-century Europe.* Baltimore: Johns Hopkins University Press.

**Zbikowski, L. M.** (1997). Conceptual models and cross-domain mapping: New perspectives on theories of music on hierarchy. *Journal of Music Theory,* 41, 193–225.

# CHAPTER 16

# EMOTIONAL EFFECTS OF MUSIC: PRODUCTION RULES

KLAUS R. SCHERER AND MARCEL R. ZENTNER

It is an ancient, and very pervasive, idea that music *expresses* emotion. Apart from the copious literature to this effect contributed by composers, musicologists, and philosophers, there is also solid empirical evidence from psychological research, reviewed in chapters of this book (e.g. Gabrielsson & Lindström, this volume; Juslin, this volume), that listeners often agree rather strongly about what type of emotion is expressed in a particular piece. It is also a pervasive belief that music can, at times, actually *produce* emotion in listeners. The distinction between perception and production is related to the distinction between cognitivism and emotivism proposed by philosophers in their analysis of emotion in music (e.g. Kivy 1989). Whereas 'emotivists' hold that music elicits real emotional responses in listeners, 'cognitivists' argue that music simply expresses or represents emotions. Our view is that it would be premature to prejudge the issue and that both positions may be perfectly appropriate depending on a number of factors outlined below. Our purpose in this chapter is to provide a formalization of the processes whereby music produces emotional effects in the listener that go beyond the cognitive inference of what the music can be said to express. In addition, we review the pertinent evidence to date and suggest ways in which future research might investigate these processes in a systematic fashion. We state at the outset that our discussion and the review of the available evidence are largely based on Western classical music, thereby restricting the generalizability of our claims to other kinds of music and other cultures.

Our attempt at a formalization of emotional effects of music will consist in defining the affective changes that music is supposed to produce in the listener and to identify the determinants of the listening situation (features such as the musical structure of the piece listened to, the interpretation by the performer, relevant state and trait characteristics of the listener, and the respective context). An important issue for discussion will be the relative weighting of the different determinants and the type of their interaction in producing the affective outcome. We follow the senior author's attempt to define the emotional meaning of music in analogy to Bühler's Organon model of language, postulating composition, expression, perception, and production *rules* to model the different facets of emotional meaning (Scherer, 2000*d*). In this context, the term *rule* is used to denote a certain regularity or lawfulness of the effects discussed that can be expressed in concrete predictions or hypotheses. It is not excluded that these rules can be integrated into attempts at computational modelling of the underlying mechanisms (in fact, we consider this a highly desirable option), but we do not feel that the current state of the art provides the necessary precision in specifying the model parameters and the input and output variables that would be required to pursue this aim. Thus, the term *rules* and the pseudo-mathematical formulas to formalize them suggested below are used in a purely descriptive sense in this chapter.

A formalization of the process by which music generates emotion requires, first of all, a definition of what exactly is to serve as the *output variable*, that is, the type of emotional or affective state that is supposed to be produced by music. This is necessary since much of the confusion in the literature is due to a lack of conceptual clarity concerning the hypothetical constructs involved. Scherer (2000*a*) has suggested a design feature delimitation of various affective phenomena, reproduced in an adapted form in Table 16.1. In view of the lack of agreement in the field, we have not attempted to identify the characteristics of *aesthetic emotions*, particularly relevant to music, either as a separate category or as a subcategory of the types proposed. This is a task that remains to be accomplished in future work. We will consistently apply the distinctions suggested in Table 16.1 in this chapter, both in classifying the literature to be reviewed (which at times requires one to speculate what an author meant or what a study measured) and in formalizing mechanisms and discovery procedures. In particular, we will try to distinguish affective preferences, moods, and emotion episodes, all of which might be produced by music. Clearly, any attempt to demonstrate that these different types of states are induced by music requires that the defining characteristics of the respective state are operationalized and measured.

The next step is to operationalize the *input variables*; that is, to specify in greater detail which aspects of listening to a piece of music are involved in the inference and/or induction of emotion (for a more detailed example of such an analytical approach, see Dowling & Harwood 1986). We will distinguish structural, performance, listener, and context features, presuming that these features can, individually or in combination, produce the different affective states described above.

*Structural features*

We subdivide structural features of music—that is, all those qualities of a composer's score that a good performer needs to respect—into segmental and suprasegmental types. *Segmental features* consist of the acoustic characteristics of the building blocks of musical structure: individual sounds or tones as produced by the singing voice or specific musical instruments. In some ways one may presume that such individual sounds correspond to the isolated affect vocalizations that may lie at the source of speech and music. The use of 'Ah' and 'ahimé' in baroque operas illustrates what has been called the domestication of 'brute' affect vocalizations (Kainz 1962; Wundt 1900; for a review of this literature, see Scherer 1994). The closest equivalent in instrumental music is the individual tone, interval, or chord. The acoustic structure of such individual tone segments, corresponding to phones in speech, is described by duration, energy (amplitude), pitch (fundamental frequency), and timbre or harmonic structure (spectral composition) of the complex wave, as well as the energy and pitch envelopes and microchanges in timbre over the duration of the sound. In sound or tone sequences, this acoustic information can be aggregated, yielding measures of central tendencies (mean, median) that, in relatively homogeneous sequences, can be described as the

Table 16.1 Design feature delimitation of different affective states (adapted from Scherer (2000a))

| Design feature / Type of affective state: brief definition (examples) | Intensity | Duration | Synchronization | Event focus | Appraisal elicitation | Rapidity of change | Behavioral impact |
|---|---|---|---|---|---|---|---|
| **Preferences:** evaluative judgments of stimuli in the sense of liking or disliking, or preferring or not over another stimulus (*like, dislike, positive, negative*) | L | M | VL | VH | H | VL | M |
| **Emotions:** relatively brief episodes of synchronized response of all or most organismic subsystems in response to the evaluation of an external or internal event as being of major significance (*angry, sad, joyful, fearful, ashamed, proud, elated, desperate*) | H | L | VH | VH | VH | VH | VH |
| **Mood:** diffuse affect state, most pronounced as change in subjective feeling, of low intensity but relatively long duration, often without apparent cause (*cheerful, gloomy, irritable, listless, depressed, buoyant*) | M | H | L | L | L | H | H |
| **Interpersonal stances:** affective stance taken toward another person in a specific interaction, colouring the interpersonal exchange in that situation (*distant, cold, warm, supportive, contemptuous*) | M | M | L | H | L | VH | H |
| **Attitudes:** relatively enduring, affectively coloured beliefs and predispositions towards objects or persons (*liking, loving, hating, valuing, desiring*) | M | H | VL | VL | L | L | L |
| **Personality traits:** emotionally laden, stable personality dispositions and behavior tendencies, typical for a person (*nervous, anxious, reckless, morose, hostile, envious, jealous*) | L | VH | VL | VL | VL | VL | L |

VL = very low, L = low, M = medium, H = high, VH = very high.

dominant acoustic structure of the sound sequence. This process of aggregation is straightforward for some acoustic variables (e.g. pitch) and rather difficult for others (e.g. timbre). However, even in the more difficult cases approximations can be found (e.g. a rough aggregate measure of dominant timbre might be the mean proportion of the energy above 1 kHz).

Segmental effects on emotion inference or induction are expected to be relatively stable and universal, with the exception of random error, over all types of listeners and performance conditions. Generally, such effects are mediated by evolutionarily evolved iconic signalling characteristics, based on physiological changes in affect vocalization and relatively independent of individual or cultural differences (cf. also Rosar 1994).

*Suprasegmental features* consist of systematic configurational changes in sound sequences over time, such as intonation and amplitude contours in speech. In music, comparable features are melody, tempo, rhythm, harmony, and other aspects of musical structure and form. While iconic coding also plays an important role (e.g. with respect to tempo, rising/falling contours), suprasegmental features seem to carry emotional information primarily through *symbolic coding*, as based on a process of historically evolved, sociocultural conventionalization (see Kappas *et al.* 1991; Scherer 1988; Sloboda 1992).

### Performance features

These refer to the way in which a piece of music is executed by performer(s). Both the stable *identity* (physical appearance, expression, reputation) and *ability* (technical and interpretative skills) of the performer, as well as transient performance-related variables referred to here as *performance state* (interpretation, concentration, motivation, mood, stage presence, audience contact, etc.), may have a major impact on the perception and induction of emotion. The effects of performance features can be based on both iconic and symbolic coding.

### Listener features

Listener features are based on the individual and sociocultural identity of the listener and on the symbolic coding convention prevalent in a particular culture or subculture. They can consist of interpretation rules (e.g. musical systems) that are shared in a group or culture, or of inference dispositions based on personality, prior experiences, and musical talent. These factors can be summarized into *musical expertise*, including cultural expectations about musical meaning, and *stable dispositions* unrelated to music, such as personality or perceptual habits. In addition, transient listener states such as motivational state, concentration, or mood may also affect emotional inference from music (cf. Cantor & Zillmann 1973). In the case of listener features, we suggest a third type of meaning-conferring coding—*associative coding*—in addition to the established semiotic distinction between iconic and symbolic coding. By this we mean the fact that segmental, suprasegmental, and performance cues can be associated with emotional content in an individual's memory due to learned associations and conditioning.

### Contextual features

These refer to certain aspects of the performance and/or listening situation. Thus, the *location* of a performance and/or a listening situation may be a concert hall, church, open-air site, car, or recording studio. The dominant material surrounding the listener/performer may be wood, glass, stone, metal, or cement. In addition to the location, the particular *event* may be a wedding, a funeral, a ball, or the celebration of an outstanding achievement. The music may be transmitted through loud-speakers, headphones, or without any technical support. The music may be heard without interruption or it may be disturbed by the sirens of an ambulance or the coughing of a concert visitor. We submit that all these features can have an influence on the acoustics, the ambiance of the location, or the behaviour of the audience, which in turn may lead to different emotional effects due to objective features of the situation or subjective perceptions of the listeners.

## 16.1 Production rules

### 16.1.1 Predictions

We suggest that an emotion that is actually experienced by a listener while listening to music is determined by a multiplicative function consisting of several factors:

Experienced emotion = Structural features $\times$ Performance features $\times$ Listener features $\times$ Contextual features,

where

Structural features = $W_1$ (Segmental features) $\times$ $W_2$ (Suprasegmental features),

Performance features = $W_3$ (Performer skills) $\times$ $W_4$ (Performer state),

Listener features = $W_5$ (Musical expertise) $\times$ $W_6$ (Stable dispositions) $\times$ $W_7$ (Current motivational / mood state),

and

Contextual features = $W_7$ (Location) $\times$ $W_8$ (Event).

We postulate multiplicative rather than additive functions because it is unlikely that any of the constituent factors in and of themselves, in the absence of other factors, can lead to marked, reliable emotional effects. Furthermore, it seems intuitively reasonable to assume that some listener features (e.g. musical expertise) will strongly interact (in the statistical sense of conveying special strength or significance) with specific structural or performance features. Finally, we submit that the different factors carry different weight. In fact, the order in which the variables are listed above follows the results of a study in which experienced listeners, many of them experts, were asked to rate the extent to which each of the major factors listed above was perceived to influence musical emotion induction (Scherer *et al.*, in press). Clearly, more exploratory studies are needed before more subtle predictions can be made and tested.

After this initial formalization of the output and the input variables involved in emotional responses to music, and the formulation of certain predictions, we now turn to what we call *routes*, that is, particular mechanisms whereby emotion may be generated by music. We distinguish: (a) *central routes* (i.e. implicating the central nervous system (CNS) in emotion generation); and (b) *peripheral routes* (based on direct effects on the peripheral, i.e. the somatic and autonomic, nervous systems (SNS and ANS) with ensuing proprioceptive feedback to central areas). In Sections 16.1.2 and 16.1.3 below, we will briefly describe these different routes and some of the underlying mechanisms. Section 16.1.4 describes the evidence to date.

### 16.1.2 Central route production

*Appraisal*

A parsimonious premise is that musical stimuli provoke emotions in a similar fashion to any other emotion-eliciting event. Thus, the mechanisms described by emotion psychologists may be also applicable to the study of emotion induction via music. There is an emerging consensus that emotion elicitation and differentiation is best understood by assuming a process of event evaluation, or appraisal, that models the way in which an individual assesses the personal significance of an event for its well-being on a number of critieria and dimensions. This process of evaluation is demonstrated in the upper portion of Fig. 16.1: an object or event is evaluated by a specific person, with respect to a number of criteria or dimensions concerning the implications of the event for needs, goals, or values of the individual and his or her ability to cope with the consequences of the event. The result of this appraisal process is an emotion, which is then expressed or externalized in physiological symptoms and, particularly, in motor expressive movements in the face, body, and voice. In this theoretical tradition, the type of ensuing emotion and the patterning of the physiological and expressive responses are seen as dependent on the specific profile of appraisal results on the pertinent criteria (see Scherer 1999; Scherer *et al.*, 2001; for alternative models of emotion differentiation, see Scherer 2000*a*). This appraisal process may occur in a rudimentary, automatic fashion at lower levels of the CNS (mostly the limbic system), especially for evolutionarily 'prepared' stimuli, or in a more elaborated and more effortful process involving the cortical association regions of the CNS as well as the lower centres (see Leventhal & Scherer 1987; Teasdale 1999; van Reekum & Scherer 1998).

The automatic, lower-level appraisal route to emotion elicitation has been well described by Öhman and his colleagues (Öhman 1988) who have suggested that a number of stimuli (e.g. snakes and spiders) can be processed by the lower centres of the brain in an extremely short period of time, outside of awareness, without any apparent

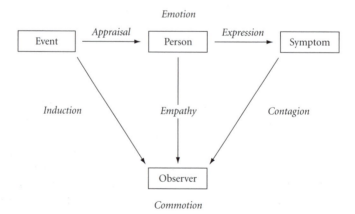

**Figure 16.1** Model of 'normal' emotion induction via appraisal (upper part) and mediated 'commotion' due to empathy or other mechanisms of emotional communication (lower part) (based on Scherer, 1998).

implication of cortical association areas. This research group has demonstrated that facial expressions of fear may have the same effect (Dimberg 1988). While empirical evidence for humans is lacking, one can assume that vocal expressions of emotions comparable to alarm calls in primates (see Jürgens 1988) may be similarly 'prepared' stimuli with respect to immediate, low-level meaning assignment. In consequence, musical stimuli sharing the acoustic characteristics of such fear vocalizations (sudden onset, high pitch, wide range, strong energy in the high frequency range) may be appraised by evolutionarily primitive but extremely powerful detection systems and may provoke, like pictures of spiders or facial expressions of fear, physiological defence responses (see Öhman 1988).

Similar low-level detection mechanisms can be demonstrated for the appraisal criteria of suddenness/novelty and intrinsic pleasantness (e.g. Scherer 1984, 1988). While the results of such rudimentary evaluation processes may not be emotions in the fully-fledged sense, as defined in Table 16.1, they may nevertheless produce positive valence reactions with respect to preferences or other types of affective phenomena short of fully-fledged emotions. There is some evidence that musical sounds can generate strong suddenness/novelty and, in particular, intrinsic pleasantness evaluations.

For example, Zentner and Kagan (1996, 1998) examined the hypothesis of an innate preferential bias favouring consonance over dissonance by exposing 4-month-old infants to consonant and dissonant versions of two melodies. Consonance and dissonance were created by composing the dissonant version in parallel minor seconds, the consonant version in parallel thirds using only two (synthetic) voices (for details regarding the stimuli, see Zentner & Kagan 1998). It was found that infants looked significantly longer at the source of sound and were less motorically active to consonant compared with dissonant versions of each melody. Further, fretting and turning away from the music source occurred more frequently during the dissonant than the consonant versions. Because no relation was found between infants' previous exposure to music (as assessed by questionnaire) and their behaviour in the experiment, the authors suggested that the human infant might possess a biological preparedness that makes consonance more attractive than dissonance. This tentative conclusion is not only consistent with perceptual work on infants' responses to consonant and dissonant intervals (e.g. Schellenberg & Trehub 1996), it is also supported by animal work which demonstrated a preference of consonant over dissonant chords in albino rats (Borchgrevink 1975).

It should be noted that similar automatic evaluation processes can occur for auditory stimuli that are not themselves evolutionarily prepared but that have been conditioned to such stimuli. Thus, LeDoux (1996) has convincingly shown that sounds conditioned to electrical shocks are processed by direct projections from the thalamus to the amygdala in rats (eliciting preparatory neuroendocrine and peripheral responses), before more extensive processing via the auditory cortex and the association areas occur. Similarly, pieces of music that have been consistently associated with evolutionarily prepared (or other powerful, unconditioned stimuli) can be evaluated at very low levels of the brain and evoke emotional responding.

One interesting issue that, so far, has not been much explored in the psychology of emotion, is that, either as a part of intrinsic valence detection or as a separate mechanism, there may be automatic evaluation of aesthetic qualities. Thus, it cannot be excluded that there are some universal criteria of beauty that are evaluated automatically on the basis of visual and auditory stimulation and give rise to an affective response (see Etcoff, 1999). This is certainly the case for the schematic level of appraisal where learned aesthetic preference may play a powerful role.

The capacity of musical stimuli to elicit emotion via processes of higher-level appraisal are virtually unlimited. The appraisal criteria or dimensions suggested by appraisal theorists in particular concern the goal conduciveness/obstructiveness of an event, the individual's potential to cope with the consequences, as well as socionormative and self-ideal norms or standards, (for a summary, see Scherer 1999). Very simply put, appraisal theory predicts that if I have to listen to music that I tend to abhor and that in addition disturbs my concentration on an important task at hand (obstructiveness with respect to desires and goals), I will experience anger or aggravation if I believe it is possible to get the music to stop eventually, and desperation or resignation if I feel powerless.

It can reasonably be argued that music plays only a secondary role in this example, easily exchangeable with any other disturbing stimulus. Future work in this area will need to pay much greater attention to motivational constructs that are specific to music. Why do people listen to music? Why do they go to concerts? Why are some pieces chosen over others? These are the kinds of motivational urges that need to be taken into account when assessing goal conduciveness or obstruction in appraisal processes antecedent to emotions produced by music. More detailed discussions of this point can be found in the chapters by Sloboda and O'Neill, DeNora, and Gabrielsson (this volume).

The evaluation of the compatibility of a stimulus event with external standards (norms, cultural values) and internal standards (personal values) as part of emotion antecedent appraisal is highly relevant for emotion elicitation via music. There seem to be prescriptions specific to culture and/or historical periods as to what is aesthetically pleasing or beautiful and what is to be rejected as a violation of 'good taste' (e.g. Farnsworth 1969; Kenyon 1991; see also Lynxwiler & Gay 2000, for an interesting recent example). Throughout musical history, the social norm or standards criterion has been involved in powerful emotional reactions towards 'modern' music, which was seen as violating established standards of morality and decency. The well-known scandal provoked by the première of Igor Strawinsky's dissonant and polyrhythmic *Sacre du Printemps* or by the première of Edgar Varèse's surreal *Deserts*, both in Paris, are just two particularly drastic examples of strong emotional reactions to the perceived disregard of established standards.

Appraisal processes, then, are one possible route by which emotion may be generated by music. Before turning to other potential mechanisms of emotion production, let us mention certain limitations with this explanatory approach. First of all, the appraisal dimensions pertinent to an evaluation of music may only be in part the same as the dimensions implicated in the generation of everyday emotion. In fact, it has often been claimed by theorists that music does not seem to present stimulus antecedents that are usually implicated in emotion appraisal (e.g. Budd 1985; see also Davies, this volume; Sloboda & Juslin, this volume). Methodologically, examination of this route faces particular challenges, one of which is the microanalysis of specific appraisal processes that continously precede emotional changes in *real time*. Appropriate methods for such sophisticated analyses do not exist and have yet to be invented.

### Memory

Another central route that is well established as a mechanism of emotion induction is imagination or recall from memory. In these cases, a strong emotional reaction that an individual has experienced in the past resurges in memory, spontaneously or triggered by a specific cue, or is evoked due to an experimental instruction to vividly imagine the event. It has been suggested that expressive and physiological reaction patterns to emotion-inducing events are stored in memory together with the experiential content (Lang 1979; Lang *et al.* 1980). In consequence, it is often claimed that recall of past emotional experiences from memory and imagination can evoke similar emotional reactions as in the original experience. The empirical evidence for such memory-induced resurgence of expressive and physiological reactions is still scarce (but see Contrada *et al.* 1991; Dalton 1998; Tarrant *et al.* 1994) except for clinical evidence from the area of post-traumatic stress disorder (Pitman *et al.* 1999; van der Kolk 1997).

Music, like odours, seems to be a very powerful cue in bringing emotional experiences from memory back into awareness. This is not surprising, for two reasons: first, music is quite a pervasive element of social life and accompanies many highly significant events in an individual's life—religious ceremonies, marriage, burial rites, dancing, and other festivities, etc. Thus, there are many associations between musical elements and emotionally charged memories. Second, music, like odours, may be treated at lower levels of the brain that are particularly resistant to modifications by later input, contrary to cortically based episodic memory (e.g. LeDoux 1992).

### Empathy

In the two routes described above, emotion elicitation was based either on the occurrence or the remembering of an event of major significance to the individual. However, emotions are sometimes elicited by just *observing* another person being affected by an event that is very important to him or her but not necessarily to us. Examples are pity with someone afflicted by malfortune or shared joy with someone who has succeeded beyond expectation. The lower part of Fig. 16.1 illustrates three possible origins of such 'commotion' (for further detail, see Scherer 1998). The arrow to the left marks a 'normal' case of emotion *induction* via appraisal: we evaluate the event that has produced the emotion in the person we observe and evaluate it in a similar fashion, with similar results. Even if we are not directly affected by the consequences of the event (e.g. an unreasonable action by a third person), we may evaluate the injustice or unreasonableness in exactly the same fashion as the person that is directly concerned and react equally with anger or irritation (possibly without knowing the reaction of the person concerned). The middle arrow illustrates the mechanism of *empathy*. Here the assumption is that we directly identify with the person concerned and feel 'with' her or him. The process of empathy requires sympathy—were we to dislike the person in question, we might actually feel the opposite emotion (e.g. joy over our enemy's anger). Finally, the right arrow illustrates a mechanism often called *emotional contagion*. Here, the essential feature is the observation of the motor expressions of the person concerned, possibly without any knowledge of the event that caused the reaction. The assumption is that the sheer observation of strong motor expressions can produce similar muscular innervations in ourselves. This process, generally called 'motor mimicry' (Eisenberg & Strayer 1987), has been at the centre of a theory of emotional inference suggested by the German philosopher and psychologist, Lipps (1909). He argued that understanding the emotions of others occurs through *Einfühlung* (empathy), which is based on our mimicking, at least in a rudimentary fashion, the expressive patterns we see in the other (in other words, a contagion, at least of the expressive movement).

Why are these mechanisms of interest to the issues at hand? The link becomes clear when we try to extend the model in Fig. 16.1 to the situation of mass media communication such as film or TV. Assume that you are watching a character in a movie who is experiencing a very sad event, like the loss of a lover. In this case, there is no objective event, only the idea of an event that is the imaginary cause of the actor's acted feelings and the consequent expression manifestations. Assuming that the motor mimicry effect underlying contagion does not require an authentic experience, we presume that the viewer may still reproduce some of the features of the observed expression, albeit in a very weak and rudimentary fashion. In addition, it is not impossible that one will feel empathy, even though we know the emotion of the actor to be prescribed by the script. How else can we explain the tears shed in movie theatres? And, finally, we may even evaluate the imaginary event and be affected by this virtual appraisal. The adaptation of the emotion model to theatre or mass media-generated emotions is shown in Fig. 16.2 (for further detail, see Scherer 1998).

One can argue that listening to expressive music is very close to this example. Rather than an actor playing out a script, we have a musician performing a musical score. We may expect that the expressive movements in the music will lead to some kind of contagion, for example, a certain rhythm producing synchronized movements of the body. This mechanism will be described in greater detail below, because

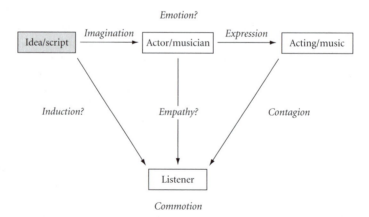

**Figure 16.2** Adaptation of the commotion model in Fig. 16.1 to the case of listening to emotionally expressive musical performances, based on the suggestions concerning emotion communication in the mass media in Scherer (1998). Grey shading indicates the potemtially virtual nature of ideas/scripts.

it may occur on a peripheral rather than a central level. However, there may also be a kind of empathy with the emotion presumed to be felt by the performer that may be construed in our imagination through an underlying 'idea' that is seen as responsible for the emotional state that is expressed (for example, the longing of the composer for his homeland, as in Dvoràk's 'New World Symphony'). Thus, emotion might be induced by the identification with a performer seen as living through an emotional experience produced by an underlying idea. We expect that such a process of musical empathy will be more likely in the case of listening to an admired performer (a listener feature, for example, an attitude) who is performing in a highly emotional manner (performance features such as skill, interpretation, and affective state). Finally, one might wonder whether, even in the absence of such performance cues, the 'underlying idea' might induce an emotional state on the basis of the evaluation of the musical structure of the piece alone. While these hypotheses are highly speculative, they do have the merit of bringing the investigation of the emotional effects of music theoretically closer to other kinds of live or mediated performances (theatre, movies, TV) that are generally considered to have the potential for emotion induction in the viewer, thereby providing opportunities for theoretical and empirical cross-fertilization.

### 16.1.3 Peripheral route production

*Proprioceptive feedback*

This route, while much less established than those described above, provides an interesting alternative, especially for some types of music. It is based on the idea that the emotion system consists of integrated components and that the system as a whole can be activated by manipulating the patterning of one of its components. For example, in a series of studies, Ekman and Levenson have provided some evidence that it may be possible to induce physiological and experiential emotion reactions by asking an individual to produce the facial patterning that is characteristic of certain emotions (without the person being aware of this purpose; see Ekman *et al.* 1983). While these findings are often contested, explaining the effects by a variety of experimental artefacts (e.g. Boiten *et al.* 1994), Ekman, Levenson, and their collaborators have systematically replied to these criticisms by adding further controls in replication experiments (P. Ekman, personal communication). The general idea is also consistent with proprioceptive feedback theories (e.g. facial feedback; see McIntosh 1996) that claim, in their strong form, that subjective feeling can be produced, or in their weak form, enhanced or intensified, by increased or uninhibited motor expression.

Thus, if music could be assumed to systematically influence one of the emotion components, peripheral mechanisms might be invoked to explain a spread to other emotion components, thus in fact producing emotion states that did not exist before. One potential candidate for such influence is rhythm. We all know the contagious effect strong musical rhythm has, at least on susceptible individuals who find it difficult not to move their heads or their legs in unison with the rhythm (e.g. in the case of dance rhythms, marches, or techno beat). Recent evidence suggests that such coupling of internal rhythms to external drivers, as originally described by Byers (1976), might be present at a very early age (Rochat & Striano 1999). If there is, indeed, a fundamental tendency for synchronization of internal biophysiological oscillators to external auditory rhythms, such coupling may provide a promising explanatory venue for the emotion-inducing effects of music. For example, given the close relationship of respiration and cardio-vascular function, a change of respiration through musical rhythm may have an impact on a variety of neurophysiological systems (Boiten *et al.* 1994), in many ways similar to emotion-induced physiological changes.

### Facilitating the expression of pre-existing emotions

So far, we have discussed the production of emotions where there were none before. Another potential effect of listening to emotionally arousing music can be the weakening or the elimination of control or regulation efforts. Due to sociocultural display and feeling rules, or because of strategic considerations, emotional reactions are often highly controlled or regulated, both with respect to motor expression and subjective feeling (Ekman 1984; Goffman 1959, 1971; Hochschild 1983; Scherer 2000*b*). One interesting effect of music, so far reported more often in an anecdotal fashion than empirically established, seems to be a loosening of such control or regulation effects. Movie-goers often report that, while watching a moving film, when the music started they could no longer hold back their tears. This effect may be partly due to similar contagion effects as described in the section above: when a pre-existing tendency toward specific motor expressions and physiological reactions is reinforced by external stimulation, it may be much harder to keep affect under control.

This remark on facilitating mechanisms concludes our overview of some of the mechanisms that may underlie the production of emotion through music. It should be noted, however, that we do not suggest that these mechanisms function in an exclusive manner. Rather, we assume that, generally, all of these mechanisms are operative jointly but having, depending on the circumstances, more or less of an impact on the emotional state produced. Thus, the peripheral route via rhythm entertainment may be particularly powerful for certain types of musical structures (lullabies, waltzes, or marches) and for particular occasions (a ballroom setting or a carnival march). In contrast, the central route, both via appraisal, associative memory, and empathy effects may be dominant in cases where one listens to well-known music in a reflexive mood, as in a concert setting.

### 16.1.4 Evidence

While there is massive evidence that listeners consistently *attribute* specific emotions to certain types of music, it is much more difficult to find convincing evidence that music can indeed *produce* emotion through one of the mechanisms described above. This task is rendered all the more difficult by the problem of deciding on a valid criterion for the *presence* of a certain emotion. As shown below, most studies have used a verbal report criterion, that is, listeners reporting that they are actually experiencing a certain emotion or affective feeling state as a consequence of listening to a particular piece of music. However, the danger of experimental artefacts, demand characteristics, social desirability, and many other problems besetting verbal report make one wonder whether verbal report can really be considered the gold standard as a criterion for genuine emotional experience (see below).

Ideally, the criterion to be used should be linked to the psychological definition of emotion as a hypothetical construct, that is, the operationalization, accessible to empirical measurement, as to the necessary and sufficient conditions to diagnose the presence, including beginning and end, of an emotional episode. So far, there is no consensus on such an operational definition in the literature. However, there is increasing convergence on the notion that emotions need to be seen as multicomponential phenomena (Scherer 2000a), involving at least the components of physiological arousal, motor expressive behaviour, subjective feeling, and possibly also a motivational component in the form of action tendencies and a cognitive component consisting of emotion-constituent appraisal and reappraisal (of external and internal events, including the emotional reaction itself). In addition, there is widespread agreement on the need to conceive of emotions as constantly changing processes, or episodes, rather than steady states. Thus, Scherer (1984, 1993, 2000c, 2001), proposing a *component–process model of emotion*, has suggested that researchers should use the criterion of coupling or synchronization of the different emotion components as evidence that an individual *has* a certain emotion at a particular point in time (see Table 16.1). Using this strict criterion, the claim that music induces emotion would have to be instantiated by studies showing that listening to a piece of music reliably leads (at least for a clearly specified group of listeners and under specified context conditions) to a synchronization of cognitive, physiological, motor-expressive, motivational (in the sense of evoked action tendencies), and experiential (subjective feeling) processes.

Although a few musical mood induction studies have incorporated multiple measures of affect (e.g. Albersnagel 1988; Kenealy 1988; Pignatiello *et al.* 1989; see also below), it may take a while until a study that measures at least three of the different components and determines their synchronization, is designed, executed, and published. In consequence, we will review the available evidence on the basis of individual components, providing an inventory of empirical findings separately for each of the components.

*Cognitive changes*

The philosophical literature across the ages has credited music with multiple effects on the mind, especially the power to provoke specific images or ideas that were, in turn, assumed to produce some of the emotional effects (for recent overviews of the philosophical literature, see Budd 1985; Davies 1994). Similarly, music is often supposed to affect judgment and evaluation. Unfortunately, few of these presumed effects have been empirically validated, demonstrating significant, experimentally induced effects for appropriately operationalized variables. The most frequently examined effects of music on cognitive performance have focused on memory.

For example, Martin and Metha (1997) examined the effects of musical mood induction on recall of childhood memories and found that music had an impact on the total number of memories recalled in the happy condition, but that there was no significant effect of sad music on eliciting sad memory recall. Balch *et al.* (1999) demonstrated mood-dependent memory effects following mood induction through music (i.e. the facilitation of remembering events one has memorized under the effect of a certain emotion when a similar emotion is elicited) (Blaney 1986; Forgas 1991). Their results suggest that it seems to be mostly the valence dimension of the emotional state that triggers the effect.

In one of the few experimental studies on the effect of music on judgmental processes, Bouhuys *et al.* (1995) showed that participants who felt depressed after listening to sad music perceived more rejection/sadness in faces with ambiguous emotional expressions and less invitation/happiness in faces with clear, unambiguous expressions. Some pertinent work may also be found in the studies on the effect of music on consumer attitudes and behaviour (Hargreaves & North 1997; see also Brown & Mankowski 1993, which is discussed below under 'subjective experience').

### Physiological arousal

The idea that music can influence the ANS (also called the peripheral or vegetative nervous system) both in an arousing and a calming fashion is a very old one, going back at least as far as Greek philosophy (Bartlett 1996). Similarly, in many contemporary, popular treatments of this issue, the power of music to affect our autonomic nervous system and even the immune functions of our body are evoked. Thus, Ornstein and Sobel (1989) suggest that music evokes a calmness that may decrease blood pressure and reduce stress, and that it may help control hormones that suppress the immune system.

As to the empirical study of this idea, the French composer Grétry (1741–1813) is credited with the first reported attempt to measure cardiovascular effects of singing by counting the pulse rate by placing a finger on an artery (Diserens 1923, cited in Bartlett 1996). Serious study of the notion that music affects the ANS started as soon as the first instruments for physiological measurement became available and has continued unabatedly for the last 120 years, the period reviewed by Bartlett (1996). In general, researchers were concerned with the arousing or stimulating versus calming or sedating effects of music. Bartlett concludes that in the majority of studies (estimated at 61 per cent), an effect of music on different ANS parameters, corresponding to the prior hypothesis (e.g. increased heart rate and muscle tension for arousing music vs. decreased heart rate, decreased muscle tension, increased skin temperature, increased skin conductance for calming music) was found. There were, however, important differences between physiological variables: while the cardiovascular predictions were confirmed in only 39 per cent of the studies, skin temperature predictions were confirmed in almost all studies.

The large majority of studies reviewed by Bartlett (1996) focused on the issue of arousal versus relaxation as emotional effects of music. Given the period of time in which most of these studies were conducted, this is congruent with the dominant view of emotion during the heydays of behaviourism in psychology. This view defined the emotions as states of the organism characterized by different degrees of psychophysiological arousal or activation (Duffy 1941).

More recently, following the work of Tomkins (1962, 1963, 1984), and particularly his followers Ekman (1984, 1992) and Izard (1971, 1994), the Darwinian notion of a limited number of 'basic' or 'fundamental' emotions serving adaptational purposes (which has been postulated by philosophers since the dawn of time) reasserted itself (see Sloboda & Juslin, this volume, for further discussion). If the induction of emotion via music is seen from this theoretical angle, the issue becomes to demonstrate which of the basic emotions are elicited by a specific piece of music, as judged from the physiological response pattern observed. This question is consistent with the idea prevalent in musical circles ever since the baroque *Affectenlehre* (Mattheson 1739), claiming that music can express specific emotions, a position violently attacked by Hanslick (1854). One could presume that if music can express discrete emotions, it might also be able to generate or induce these same emotions (see 'production rules' above). The evidence required to prove such induction is the production, via music, of the specific patterns of physiological reactions that are postulated for the basic emotions by theorists in that tradition (Levenson 1992) and that have been demonstrated, more or less convincingly, in studies using film stimuli, imagination, or other induction techniques (Ekman *et al.* 1983; but see also Cacioppo *et al.* 1993; Stemmler 1996).

In an exploratory study, Krumhansl (1997) attempted to examine this prediction. She presented 38 Berkeley students with six excerpts from pieces of classical music that are generally expected to induce specific emotional states (and which were consensually rated, by another group of judges, to express the emotions of sadness, fear, happiness, or tension). Eleven physiological parameters, the large majority tapping respiration and cardiovascular functioning, were measured while subjects were listening to the music excerpts (average duration 3 minutes). The results supported the general prediction that music does indeed affect the ANS: during the listening periods, many of the physiological parameters had values significantly different from those during the pretrial (resting) period. Furthermore, Krumhansl was able to show statistically significant differences between the music samples (chosen to express the three emotions, sadness, fear, and happiness) in the extent to which they seemed to influence specific parameters (e.g. sadness excerpts producing large changes in heart rate, blood pressure, skin conductance, and temperature; fear excerpts producing large changes in pulse transit time and amplitude; and happy excerpts producing large changes in respiratory patterns). The author found that these changes were rather well correlated with subjectively reported experiences when analysed on the level of dynamic change over time, but not for the averaged physiological parameters and an overall judgment of emotion for a piece.

However, with respect to the central piece of evidence, the matching of the emotion-specific physiological response patterns, the results were far less encouraging. While, in some cases, the changes for a particular parameter went in a similar direction as the theoretically postulated ones, it would be difficult to argue that complete physiological response patterns, prototypical for 'discrete' or 'basic' emotions, were found. In any case, this would be a tall order, given that even psychologically highly sophisticated induction techniques, designed to produce specific emotions, so far have not yielded the kind of specificity in physiological response patterning that is expected by discrete emotion theorists (see Cacioppo *et al.* 1993; Stemmler 1996).

In a well-designed and higly controlled study using very naturalistic inductions of anger (harassment by experimenter) and fear (dangerous equipment failure), Stemmler and his collaborators (2001) were able to find systematic differences between anger and fear that can be directly linked to the differential action tendencies (i.e. fight and flight; see Frijda 1986; Scherer 1984) for these two emotions. The authors conclude that significant differences can only be expected on the basis of functional demands on behaviour and express some doubt as to the existence of highly specific patterns for many different emotions.

In another music induction study, Nyklicek *et al.* (1997) presented 26 undergraduates with 12 classical music excerpts (of 120–220 seconds' duration), with three excerpts each having been found to reliably express emotional states described as happy, serene, sad, or agitated. Physiological measurement again focused on cardiorespiratory variables. Rather than try to match theoretically defined patterns for discrete emotions, the authors employed multidimensional discriminant analysis to examine whether the reactions to the excerpts with different affective tones could be reliably distinguished on the basis of the physiological patterns. The discriminant analysis classified the reactions to the four types of excerpts with an accuracy of 46.5 per cent, the first discrimination function being largely determined by respiration parameters (reflecting an arousal or activation dimension), and the second dimension being determined by dynamic aspects of the cardiovascular processes (interbeat interval and left ventricular ejection time). While the first dimension was directly linked to subjectively perceived arousal, the second is more difficult to describe with respect to subjective meaning of the emotion space (it did not directly represent the valence dimension of subjective experience). The authors interpret their findings as evidence for both a discrete emotion and a dimensional model, arguing that the lower-order discrete emotions may be discriminated in a space formed by higher-order dimensions. This is reminiscent of the claims made by all dimensional models, starting with Wundt (1974). However, it should be noted that emotion theorists proposing dimensional models generally focus on the subjective feeling rather than the physiological or expressive components of emotion (see Scherer 2000a).

In a recent series of studies, Witvliet and Vrana (1996; Witvliet *et al.* 1998) looked at the effect of music on autonomic measures of skin conductance and heart rate, as well as on the somatic parameters of electromyographic change scores for the zygomatic, corrugator, and orbicularis oris muscles in the face. The music excerpts had been pre-selected with respect to their scores on the valence and arousal dimensions. In line with the earlier literature reviewed by Bartlett (1996), their results showed clear arousal effects on the autonomic measures with increased levels of skin conductance and heart rate, as well as increased tension of the orbicularis oculi muscle, during listening to excerpts judged as high on the activity dimension. In addition, they were among the first to show *valence* effects for music, particularly for the somatic measures. As predicted by discrete emotion and appraisal theorists (Ekman 1992; Scherer 1986, 1992), there was increased corrugator activity (used in frowning) while listening to music with negative valence and increased zygomatic activity (used in smiling) for music with positive valence (especially when combined with high arousal). This is consistent with the results of a more recent study (Lundqvist *et al.* 2000), in which facial electromyography, autonomic activity, and emotional experience were measured while subjects listened to happy and sad music. The happy music elicited larger zygomaticus activity, larger skin conductance, lower finger temperature, more (self-reported) happiness and less sadness compared with the sad music.

Limitations of the studies reviewed above include the lack of sensitivity to the dynamic unfolding of the effects of music over time (often with very rapid changes) and the lack of attention to the determining role of musical structure. Indeed, much of this research only examined physiological reactions integrated over a relatively long time interval. Furthermore, often no expert analyses of the structural features (musical score) were done to examine, or at least derive hypotheses about, what exactly in the music might have been responsible for the reported physiological phenomena.

A pioneering study by Vaitl *et al.* (1993) took both of these aspects into account. In a field study carried out in the festival theatre of Bayreuth in the summers of 1987 and 1988, 27 listeners were psychophysiologically examined while listening to a number of Wagner operas, from *Tannhäuser* to *Parsifal*. However, only data produced by three subjects in response to the leitmotivs during *The Mastersingers of Nuremberg* were analysed in depth. Electrodermal responses, respiratory activity, and ratings of emotional arousal were continuously recorded and analysed during the leitmotivs. It was shown that physiological responses differed markedly with respect to the leitmotivs and their musical features (e.g. melody, rhythm, continuation). An important additional finding was the interindividually variable, but overall weak, correspondence between emotional arousal ratings and physiological responses. Although this case study has obvious limitations, it is a good model to follow for future studies, combining dynamic measurement, on line, of physiological changes and feelings of emotional arousal within a live performance and linking the observed values to particular features of musical structure.

### Motor expressive behaviour and action tendencies

From ancient times, there has been an assumption that movement is a key component, if not the underlying mechanism, of emotional reactions to music. This position is, for example, articulated by Aristotle as follows

Why is sound the only sensation that excites the feelings? Even melody without words has feeling. But this is not the case for color or smell or taste . . . But we feel the motion which follows sound . . . These motions stimulate action, and this action is a sign of feeling (cited in Helmholtz 1954, p. 251).

Among modern philosophers, it is, in particular, Edmund Gurney and Carroll Pratt who gave a central place to movement in their theories of emotional effects of music (Gurney 1880, Pratt 1931).

The fact that much of modern-day music listening occurs under ritualized conditions in the concert hall, under more relaxed conditions in one's living room or car, or via earphones while pursuing all kinds of activities, masks the fact that throughout history much music was composed with very specific action tendencies in mind— getting people to sing and dance, march and fight, or work and play together. Composers of dance music and marches attempt to entice listeners to produce the appropriate rhythmic movements, and many people actually report that they cannot sit still and have trouble suppressing rhythmic body sway and other movements when hearing some bars of a Strauss waltz. On the other hand, lullabies evolved because of their presumed ability to put children to sleep, thus leading to the opposite effect of inhibition of motor arousal (Trehub & Schellenberg 1995).

One would expect, then, to find mechanisms that can produce motor expression and action tendencies via the peripheral production route described above. In one of the few attempts at theoretical foundation, Todd (1992) suggests that expressive sounds may induce a percept of self-motion in the listener via the central vestibular system. The argument is that expression based on elementary mechanics may sound natural because the vestibular system evolved to deal with similar kinds of motions (i.e. gravity and linear and rotational acceleration). As mentioned above, Byers (1976) reviewed potential mechanisms for rhythm induction. Clynes (1977) also argued for pervasive emotion-specific dynamic motor patterns.

Unfortunately, hard empirical, especially experimental, evidence for the production of motor patterns and action tendencies by music is rare (but for some attempts, see Fraisse *et al.* 1953; Harrer & Harrer 1977). Kneutgen (1964) discussed the biological significance of rhythm synchronization in different species and emphasized the role of music in driving biological rhythms. In an interesting pilot study (Kneutgen 1970), an Argentinian lullaby was played to four listeners in sessions lasting from 30 minutes to 2 hours (almost every day for a period of 3 months). It was found that the lullaby had the effect of markedly decreasing heart rate. In addition, the breathing rhythm became synchronized with the rhythm of the music. Interestingly, no such effects were found in a control group exposed to jazz music.

DeVries (1991) used Clynes' (1977) *sentograph* to measure affective motor responses to music and reported that the pressure patterns shown for 11 brief musical excerpts were similar across subjects and seem correlated with the expressive content of the music. However, so far convergent evidence from methodologically sophisticated studies on the validity of the sentograph are missing, and also the theoretical assumptions underlying its use seem rather elusive (but for studies in this area, see Carmean 1980; Gorman & Crain 1974; Nettlebeck *et al.* 1989; Trussoni *et al.* 1988).

Generally, there have been very few controlled studies using measures other than verbal report, on the induction of dynamic motor behaviour or specific action tendencies by music. The same is true for motor expression in the voice and face. In one of the very few studies looking at the facilitation of vocalization by music, Pujol (1994) varied the instrumentation (flute vs. bells) in two types of melodies (pentatonic vs. major) and studied the effects on physiological (respiration and pulse rate) and behavioural responses (eye movement, facial expression, vocalizations, and motor movement) of 15 profoundly handicapped persons. The music (particularly the major flute melody) stimulated the production of vocalizations, an effect which decreased over time.

Given the assumption that the face is 'the primary theatre' of the emotions (Ekman 1992; Tomkins 1984), one would expect to find much evidence for the facilitation of facial expression via music. Again, appropriate studies are rare. However, as reviewed above, Witvliet and Vrana (1996) reported evidence that different kinds of music differentially stimulate the innervation of the zygomatic muscle or corrugator muscles (see also Lundquist *et al.* 2000).

Studies on the effects of music on the tendency to perform certain actions (e.g. prosocial or aggressive acts) tend to be rare. In an experiment by Fried and Berkowitz (1979), different groups heard 7-minute-long musical selections that were either soothing, stimulating, or aversive in nature, while a fourth group was not exposed to any music. Those who heard the soothing music were most apt to show altruistic behaviour immediately afterwards (volunteering for another study). Mood ratings indicated that the soothing and stimulating music created somewhat different positive moods, while the aversive music tended to arouse negative feelings.

*Subjective experience (self-report of feeling)*

Among the methods used to study emotion induction through music, the self-report of feeling has been the most widely used approach. However, most studies having examined emotion *production* via self-report were not carried out within the area of music psychology, where the main emphasis has been on the perception of emotion in music. Assessments of emotion production via self-report is typically found in *mood induction* studies. The aim of such studies is often to examine the effects of different affect states, moods, and emotions on cognitive and evaluative processes, memory, behaviour, and physiology. Such 'instrumental' use of music as a means of emotion or mood manipulation has rapidly increased in recent years, placing music among the most widely used techniques for mood induction in psychology (for a review of mood induction studies, see Westermann *et al.* 1996).

There are two ways to examine the success of a given mood induction. One is indirect, relying on significant effects of the mood conditions on the dependent variables of interest. However, in addition, a self-report of mood or emotion is often used as a so-called manipulation check for the success of the mood induction. Typically, after the mood manipulation, the subject is given a self-report measure of mood. The results are then compared across mood conditions and significant differences among the conditions are interpreted as evidence for the success of the mood induction. Some of the most frequently used self-report instruments to assess emotion or mood production via music include: the multiple affect adjective check list (MAACL(-R-)) (Zuckerman & Lybin 1985); the Nowlis mood adjective checklist (Maslach 1979); the visual analogue scales (VAS) (Bond & Lader 1974); and the brief mood introspection scale (BMIS) (Mayer & Gaschke 1988).

The use of self-report measures as evidence for emotion production has both advantages and disadvantages. It remains the only method that allows access to the subjective emotional experience. Therefore, it should not be replaced by any other measure. However, the data collected in this way are sensitive to the following potential biases and artefacts that need to be carefully considered before conclusions are drawn. Firstly, demand characteristics can be responsible for the mood effects found. Secondly, listeners may confuse the emotions expressed in the music with what they actually feel unless they are specifically requested to distinguish between the two emotion modalities, as has been the case in our recent studies (Zentner *et al.* 2000).

To be taken as indicators of mood effects of music, then, self-report measures have to be validated against other criteria, or they have to be experimentally controlled. Following the latter avenue, Kenealy (1988) has compared self-reported mood effects in two conditions; one in which demand characteristics were intentionally created and one in which the effect of demand characteristics was minimized. She found no effects of demand characteristic on self-reported mood effects, concluding that the 'music procedure is relatively free from demand characteristics' (Kenealy 1988, p. 46). However, one could argue that the so-called 'no demand' condition was in reality also affected by demand characteristics. Subjects were left alone in a room by the experimenter who left on the pretext of having something urgent to attend to. Then, happy or sad music (depending on the condition) was played for 8 minutes. The subject, knowing they were in a psychological experiment and suddenly hearing music, might well have guessed the purpose of the experiment even without explicit demands and even without admitting it after the experiment. Such difficulties in the interpretation of the results notwithstanding, Kenealy's research is important in suggesting possible strategies for controlling demand effects.

The second criticism, confusion of perception and induction, is particularly relevant to studies in which subjects are explicitly instructed to report what they feel in response to the music. Kivy (1989) has argued that listeners make a fundamental attribution error in that they *habitually* take the expressive properties of the music for what they feel. This position is not new. In fact, it has already been summarized by Meyer (1956, p. 8) as follows: 'it may well be that when a listener reports that he felt this or that emotion, he is describing the emotion which he believes the passage is supposed to indicate, not anything which he himself has experienced'.

To our knowledge there is little, if any, empirical evidence to back up this claim. For this reason, we recently conducted a study in which participants were instructed to describe both what they *felt* and what they *perceived* in response to different genres of music. We found that the type of instruction (felt vs. perceived) changed the results quite dramatically (Zentner *et al.* 2000). Overall, the majority of emotions were reported much less frequently when the participants were instructed to focus on the *production* rather than the *perception* of emotion. This does, of course, not suggest that particular emotions are never felt in response to music, as Kivy would have it. (As a matter of fact, for particular emotions the reverse was true—they appeared to be more readily felt than perceived.) However, it indicates that the distinction between perception and production of emotion is empirically valid and that it is essential to take this distinction into account when instructing people to report their emotional responses to music. The studies by Kenealy (1988) and preliminary evidence from our group show that, although verbal reports of moods and emotions have their limitations, there still is much to be done to improve their quality.

In addition to asking listeners directly about their emotional reactions, there is also the possibility of assessing the feeling state without asking subjects directly about their emotional experience. Little use has been made of this possibility in the present area. In a recent review of mood effects on judgments and social cognitions, Forgas (in press) discusses several paradigms that could also be easily applied to the study of music and emotion. In some of these paradigms, subjects are asked to rate something other than affect or mood, for example certain individual dispositions related to attitudes, personality, or self-esteem. In a typical study (Brown & Mankowski 1993), a musical mood induction was used to induce positive, negative, or neutral affect. Afterwards, listeners evaluated *their* specific qualities and characteristics (How smart are you? How kind are you?). It was found that subjects rated themselves more favourably after listening to happy compared with sad music (see also Bouhuys *et al.* (1995), which is discussed above under 'cognitive changes'). Interestingly, this effect was stronger for subjects with low self-esteem, suggesting greater sensitivity to mood manipulation for this particular group.

In sum, because access to the subjective emotional experience of a listener is logically impossible without verbal report, optimization and extension of these methods is indicated. Perhaps, in the future, various brain-imaging techniques can be used as additional indicators of subjective feeling state (cf. Peretz, this volume). At present, verbal report remains the only means to assess this important component of emotional experience. Therefore, it is surprising that there has not been more effort made to systematically develop a vocabulary suited to describe what listeners feel in response to music. This is even more striking if we consider the doubts, expressed by several theorists, that emotional responses to music may not resemble everyday life or basic emotions, such as anger, fear, joy, sadness, shame, and disgust. Thus, Lippmann (1953, p. 569) suggested: 'Musical feelings have their own character: they are not the feelings we know and roughly name in our experience outside of music . . . Thus music may be an emotional experience, and still not represent emotional contexts belonging to other areas of life, for the emotions it formulates are not identical with those accompanying extra-musical experience, nor does the one kind necessarily remind us of the other'.

As is often the case in this domain, there is little empirical evidence to confirm or invalidate this conjecture. Few efforts have so far been made to examine whether the basic emotion categories derived from emotion psychology are theoretically sensible, empirically valid, or musically plausible for describing the emotional experience induced by music. The few systematic attempts at creating a taxonomy of 'musical emotions' (e.g. Hevner 1936; Rigg 1964; Wedin 1972; see also Gabrielsson & Lindström, this volume) were entirely focused on perceived, not aroused, emotions. As has been pointed out by Sloboda (1992, p. 36), 'The relevance of these studies to emotional experience, however, is not proven. It is possible to make character judgements on the basis of conventional characteristics without experiencing any emotion whatsoever'. Moreover, these attempts lacked rigour, as has been pointed out recently by Gabrielsson (1998, p. 2): 'Procedures followed for this purpose are not always explicitly described and are rarely, if ever, based on some theory, rather on the researcher's own experiences and ideas and material used by earlier researchers'. Clearly, then, adopting a systematic approach for deriving a taxonomy of musical emotions while focusing on the aroused, not the perceived, emotions, is an important task for future research in this area.

Such work requires a theoretical background that does not prejudge the issue, as is the case with emotion theories that either, like discrete emotion theories, start from the assumption of a limited number of basic or fundamental emotions or that, like dimensional theories, focus exclusively on the valence and arousal dimensions of emotional feeling (see Scherer 2000a). Unfortunately, neither of these make any provision for emotion processes that may be specific to music. Scherer (1984) has suggested that there may be as many different emotions as there are differentiated outcomes of appraisal processes, rejecting the very limited taxonomy that is imposed by the semantic structure of the 'basic emotion' vocabulary in a specific language. Thus, componential process approaches (Scherer 2001) are perhaps better suited to provide the theoretical underpinnings for research on the specific emotions produced by different types of music. It should be recalled that this does not mean that conscious appraisal implying all criteria is necessarily involved in emotion elicitation via music (see above). It may be necessary to discard the standard, 'fundamental' emotion terms altogether and to focus more strongly on terms for more subtle, music-specific emotions (such as longing, tenderness, awe, activation, solemnity) that seem to describe the effects of music more readily than anger, sadness, or fear (Zentner *et al.* 2000).

## 16.2 Perspectives for future research

The review of the research evidence presented above has suggested that we are far from being able to provide a clear answer to the question of how music can actually *produce* emotional states. Apart from a general lack of sufficient research evidence, particularly with respect to non-verbal measures of affect, it is difficult to avoid the impression that this research domain suffers from lack of theoretical rigour. This is a bad omen for future research, since it is to be feared that additional, isolated research efforts with little or no theoretical underpinnings are more likely to add to the current confusion than to the insight to which the researchers aspire. We believe that much of the problem is due to the lack of differentiation between the different types of affective processes as described in Table 16.1. Clearly, confusion is hard to avoid when researchers apply different criteria for the evidence they require to infer the presence of the successful induction of an affective process via music. Therefore, it would be advisable for researchers to specify more carefully what kind of affective process they attempt to induce through the presentation of musical stimuli.

We suggest the adoption of the distinctions proposed in Table 16.1 for further work in this area. In what follows, we will attempt to specify in greater detail what criteria, both verbal and non-verbal, might be chosen to infer the presence of the respective process. Since it seems unrealistic to assume that music can produce any of the long-term affect dispositions in rows 4–6 of Table 16.1, only the short-term processes in rows 1–3 are discussed. Because there is no established consensus for either the classification proposed or the criteria suggested, the recommendations made below will have to be judged on the basis of their plausibility.

*Preferences*, defined as evaluative judgments of stimuli in the sense of liking or disliking, or preferring or not over another stimulus, are the simplest form of affect manifestations and some theoreticians may deny that they have an affective as well as a cognitive basis. However, because they are treated as emotional phenomena by some theorists (Zajonc 1980; Zajonc & Markus 1984) and because they are directly linked to valence which is seen by many theorists (especially the dimensional theorists) as an essential component of emotion (see Scherer 2000*a*), it seems mandatory to include them here. The verbal criterion for the existence and strength of induced preferences is the verbal claim by a person to like or dislike a certain piece of music with a certain intensity or certainty, or, in a comparative context, to like a piece of music more than (or prefer it over) another piece. One can also ask listeners to sort pieces of music in ascending fashion for greater liking or arrange them on a bipolar scale from extreme disliking to extreme liking.

On the non-verbal level, preferences can be assessed rather precisely by observing choice behaviour, that is, the choice of listening to one type of music rather than another, the length of listening behaviour, and other behavioural measures. Another non-verbal measure of liking is facial expression, measured either through observer coding of visible behaviour (Ekman 1992) or facial electromyography measurement (Cacioppo *et al.* 1993). The presence and strength of musculus zygomaticus innervation (smiling) can be taken as an indicator of degree of liking, and of musculus corrugator innervation (frowning) as a sign of degree of dislike. On the level of physiological measurement,

Lang and his collaborators have suggested that the startle probe (e.g. Lang *et al.* 1990) can be used as a measure of valence (positive or negative feeling state). It should be noted that these behavioural changes are expected to be stimulus-driven, that is, they should only be present in the anticipation, presence, and possibly immediate aftermath of the stimulus, in this case, the music presentation. In contrast, the cognitive judgment, and verbal expression, of liking should be permanently accessible once a stimulus is identified and remembered.

Music seems to elicit preferences almost automatically, as the work on low-level automatic appraisal, reviewed in Section 16.1.2, suggests. Even if there is no comprehensive empirical evidence at present, there is little music that people find completely neutral and for which they are impartial as to whether to listen or not, if given a choice. Judging from informal evidence, most individuals seem to have little trouble in rating the degree of preference or liking (or disliking) on standard scales. However, it seems that there are powerful differences with respect to liking and disliking (e.g. Behne 1997). This seems quite natural since music that nobody likes is unlikely to survive (although detractors of modern music often claim that this is listened to for reasons other than liking). Thus, research on the induction of preference or liking may only be of interest in a differential context.

Contrary to preferences, *moods* are generally not elicited by concrete stimulus events at a particular point in time. Rather, they are defined as diffuse affect states, most pronounced as a change in subjective feeling, of low intensity but relatively long duration, often without apparent cause and thus persisting across encounters with multiple stimulus events. Because the labels for moods and emotions are often similar, care has to be taken to clearly distinguish the two in the instructions by specifying the long-term, non-event-related character of mood states (e.g. scales of good or bad mood, touchy vs. serene mood, etc.). Similarly, behavioural indices have to remain present over a lengthier period of time and not be related to an immediately preceding stimulus. This obviously rules out behavioural choice measures because these are automatically stimulus-driven. However, enduring evidence for morose versus serene facial expression, or prosocial versus aggressive acts, might serve as behavioural indicators.

Music may well be able to produce mood effects. At least this is what the music industry suggests, in particular for positive moods, by selling selections of music destined to produce relaxation or to generally improve one's mood (Bruner 1990; for concrete marketed examples see the mood-inducing compilations by Conifer Classics 1997 and Sony 1995). Similarly, claims for the effectiveness of music therapy are based on the assumption that the effect outlasts the presentation of the music (cf. Bunt & Pavlicevic, this volume). In contrast, music designed to incite customers to buy something or to calm aggression at football games, may rely on co-presence for its effect. There are only a few studies that have addressed the issue by carefully selecting valid *mood* criteria as defined above. Future research in this area, using appropriate measures, seems of prime importance, given the important implications for applied settings.

Can music induce *emotions* in the strict sense of Table 16.1, that is, defined as relatively brief episodes of synchronized responses of all or more organismic subsystems in response to the evaluation of an external or internal event as being of major significance? According to the senior author's theory, this implies that the emotion process is directly produced by an appraisal of the musical event and that the response pattern generated is specific to the event. While it may last beyond the presence of the event, in the case of certain emotions even for relatively long periods (e.g. Frijda *et al.* 1991; Scherer & Wallbott 1994), it is generally expected to be of shorter duration and of higher intensity than moods. Thus, contrary to preferences, valence cues should be accompanied by the presence of arousal indicators in the ANS. While these might also be present for mood, they should be more intense and less stable than in the case of mood. Furthermore, emotion processes should entail motivational changes and preparation of adaptive action in the form of modes of action readiness or action tendencies (Frijda 1986; Scherer 1984).

As mentioned above, Scherer (1984, 1993) suggested that the most salient criterion of the presence of an *emotion* process (in the strict sense defined in Table 16.1) is a high degree of coupling or synchronization of all organismic subsystems, including cognition, during the emotion episode. In order to answer the question of whether music induces emotion in this strict sense, all pertinent indicators in the respective organismic subsystems need to be measured and the degree of their synchronization assessed. So far, none of the studies in this area has attempted to do this, and it is not to be denied that it is a formidable undertaking. Yet, if one agrees to define emotions in this narrow or strict sense, it will be necessary to engage in comprehensive verbal and non-verbal measurement and powerful mathematical modelling of coupling or synchronization.

It is rather probable, of course, that one will not be able to find as intense and highly synchronized response patterns as found in the case of violent rage leading to fighting, for example. Ellsworth (1994) has pointed out that music is quite a special emotion-inducing stimulus in that it is difficult to specify the underlying concerns or goals that tend to be the motor of emotion (cf. Sloboda & Juslin, this volume). One could add, that it is also difficult to see which modes of action readiness or action tendencies that, according to Frijda (1986), define the quality of emotions, can be evoked by music. The exceptions are action tendencies like singing or dancing that are quite regularly provoked by certain types of music. However, it is likely that these action tendencies are provoked by peripheral entrainment, as described above, rather than by centrally controlled motivational changes as is generally the case in the provocation of adaptive action tendencies in 'real' emotions.

We believe that progress in the area will be difficult as long as researchers remain committed to the assumption that real intense emotions must be traditional basic emotions, such as fear or anger, for which one can identify relatively straightforward action tendencies such as fight or flight. Progress is more likely to occur if we are prepared to identify emotion episodes where all of the components shown in Table 16.1 are in fact synchronized *without* there being a concrete action tendency or a traditional, readily accessible verbal label. In order to study these phenomena, we need to free ourselves from the tendency of wanting to assign traditional categorial labels to emotion processes. Take, as an interesting example, the feelings that are rather vaguely described as 'being touched' or 'being moved' for which there is not even a substantive in some languages such as English and French (but there is *Rührung* in German). Examples are the tears shed during sentimental movies in the cinema or the flash of warmth experienced when hearing about a good deed. It would seem that such experiences are what music often produces. One is 'moved' by music (accompanied by symptoms such as moist eyes, chills, thrills, or goose-flesh) without there being a readily accessible label to describe what one is feeling or why. Of course, this does not mean that the lack of suitable verbal labels (or the inability of normal people to discriminate different states) absolves scientists from making the necessary differentiation, falling back to simple arousal models. On the contrary, the task is to develop both suitable non-verbal and verbal indicators that allow one to identify music-induced states that may not correspond to the traditional categories described in emotion textbooks. Finally, and taking this reflection a step further, we have also to be open to the possibility that, in certain instances, responses to music may not fit the states presented in Table 16.1 and may be of a thoroughly non-affective nature.

## 16.3 Conclusion

The suggestions for more principled research efforts in this area, studying several components of emotion, require substantial research investments and competencies in several areas of measurement. It may be unrealistic to expect that such research efforts will emerge in the near future. Yet, even if one is unable to launch such a sophisticated research programme, one still needs to define the theoretical suppositions in greater detail if the work in this area is to achieve a status that permits systematic comparison, replication, and eventually accumulation of findings. Following the specification of the theoretical model to be tested, the appropriate measures would need to be obtained, particularly in the non-verbal domain. This chapter provides an entire spectrum of possibilities for multimodal measurement approaches, encouraging research that does not only rely on standard self-report inventories with their well-known limitations (e.g. Nisbett & Wilson 1977; Scherer & Ceschi 2000). Thus, in future research, the criterion for successful induction should be multimodal, for example verbal report complemented by non-verbal measures such as physiological responses and expressive behaviour. Some of these measures are particularly well suited for this purpose since they provide a continuous, variable signal and are in large parts resistant to conscious regulation.

What are the requirements for measurement for proponents of different theoretical approaches, as outlined above? Researchers adopting dimensional theories would need to specify the expected values for valence and activity for the emotions to be studied and include physiological and expressive indicators in addition to verbal report measurement. Proponents of discrete emotion theories would need to clearly specify the expected emotion-specific response patterns for the emotions studied and include all pertinent variables in their measurement operations. In addition, with respect to the statistical analysis it would seem necessary to use pattern-matching procedures (e.g. profile analyses) rather than simple comparisons for differences (e.g. univariate *F*-tests) between various emotions. Finally, appraisal theorists, in addition to sharpening the predictions for the outcomes to be expected for different appraisal results and the measurement of the respective variables (Johnstone *et al.*, 2001; Pecchinenda 2001), need to indicate how appraisals can be determined in the case of music. Obviously, this requires a much greater research effort than obtaining verbal reports, and one might claim that the suggestions made in this chapter are unrealistic. Yet, similar approaches can already be found in several research domains in the affective sciences and we believe that this tendency will continue.

In brief, we have suggested that by linking research on the emotional expressiveness of music more directly to the progress in the affective sciences generally (see Davidson *et al.*, in press), it may be possible to design empirical studies that are likely to yield results that can be interpreted against a background of theoretical predictions as compared with multiplying studies that have been designed on an *ad hoc* basis and that are difficult to integrate into a coherent body of literature.[1]

# References

Albersnagel, F. A. (1988). Velten and musical mood induction procedures: A comparison with accessibility of thought association. *Behaviour Research and Theory*, **26**, 79–96.

Balch, W., Myers, D. M., & Papotto, C. (1999). Dimensions of mood in mood-dependent memory. *Journal of Experimental Psychology: Learning, Memory, and Cognition*, **25**, 70–83.

Bartlett, D. L. (1996). Physiological responses to music and sound stimuli. In *Handbook of music psychology*, (2nd edn) (ed. D. A. Hodges), pp. 343–85. San Antonio, TX: IMR.

Behne, K-E. (1997) Musikpräferenzen und Musikgeschmack [Music preferences and musical taste]. In *Musikpsychologie: Ein Handbuch*, (ed. H. Bruhn, R. Oerter, & H. Rösing), pp. 339–53. Reinbek bei Hamburg: Rowohlt.

Blaney, P. H. (1986). Affect and memory: A review. *Psychological Bulletin*, **99**, 229–46.

Boiten, F. A., Frijda, N. H., & Wientjes, C. J. E. (1994). Emotions and respiratory patterns: Review and critical analysis. *International Journal of Psychophysiology*, **17**, 103–28.

Bond, A. & Lader, M. (1974). The use of analogue scales in rating subjective feeling. *British Journal of Medical Psychology*, **47**, 211–18.

Borchgrevink, H. M. (1975). Musikalske akkod-prefereanser hos mennesket belyst ved dyreforsok [Musical chord preferences in humans as demonstrated through animal experiments]. *Tidskrift for den Norske Laegefoerning*, **95**, 356–8.

Bouhuys, A. L., Bloem, G. M., & Groothuis, T. G. (1995). Induction of depressed and elated mood by music influences the perception of facial emotional expressions in healthy subjects. *Journal of Affective Disorders*, **33**, 215–26.

Brown, J. D. & Mankowski, T. (1993). Self-esteem, mood, and self-evaluation: Changes in mood and the way you see you. *Journal of Personality and Social Psychology*, **64**, 421–30.

Bruner, G. C. (1990). Music, mood, and marketing. *Journal of Marketing*, **54**, 94–104.

Budd, M. (1985). *Music and the emotions. The philosophical theories*. London: Routledge.

Byers, P. (1976). Biological rhythms as information channels in interpersonal communication behavior. In *Perspectives in ethology*, (Vol. 2) (ed. P. P. G. Bateson & P. H. Klopfer), pp. 135–64. New York: Plenum Press.

---

[1] The preparation of this chapter was facilitated by Grant No. 1114-049680.96 entitled 'Induction of emotional states through music' by the Swiss National Research fund to Marcel Zentner and Klaus Scherer. The theoretical suggestions linked to perception and production rules were first presented by Klaus Scherer in the context of a keynote speech 'Music and emotional meaning: Perception and production rules' at the Sixth Conference of the International Society for Music Perception and Cognition, 5–10 August 2000, at Keele University, UK. The authors acknowledge important suggestions by a group of anonymous reviewers.

Cacioppo, J. T., Klein, D. J., Berntson, G. C., & Hatfield, E. (1993). The psychophysiology of emotion. In *Handbook of emotions*, (ed. M. Lewis & J. M. Haviland), pp. 119–42. New York: Guilford Press.

Cantor, J. R. & Zillmann, D. (1973). The effect of affective state and emotional arousal on music appreciation. *Journal of General Psychology*, **89**, 97–108.

Clynes, M. (1977). *Sentics: The touch of emotions*. New York: Doubleday.

Conifer Classics (1997). *Complete Serenity*. CD No. 51309.

Contrada, R. J., Hilton, W. F., & Glass, D. C. (1991). Effects of emotional imagery on physiological and facial responses in Type A and Type B individuals. *Journal of Psychosomatic Research*, **35**, 391–7.

Dalton, K. M. (1998). Relationships between anterior cerebral asymmetry, cardiovascular reactivity, and anger—expression style during re-lived emotion and coping tasks. *Dissertation Abstracts International: Section B: the Sciences and Engineering*, **59**, 1406.

Davidson, R., Goldsmith, H., & Scherer, K. R. (ed.) (in press). *Handbook of affective sciences*. New York: Oxford University Press.

Davies, S. (1994). *Musical meaning and expression*. Ithaca, NY: Cornell University Press.

DeVries, B. (1991). Assessment of the affective response to music with Clynes' sentograph. *Psychology of Music*, **19**, 46–64.

Dimberg, U. (1988). Facial expressions and emotional reactions: A psychobiological analysis of human social behaviour. In *Social psychophysiology and emotion: Theory and clinical applications*, (ed. L. W. Hugh), pp. 131–50. Chichester, UK: Wiley.

Dowling, W. J. & Harwood, D. L. (1986). *Music cognition*. San Diego: Academic Press.

Duffy, E. (1941). An explanation of 'emotional' phenomena without the use of the concept 'emotion'. *Journal of General Psychology*, **25**, 283–93.

Eisenberg, N. & Strayer, J. (ed.) (1987). *Empathy and its development*. Cambridge, UK: Cambridge University Press.

Ekman, P. (1984). Expression and the nature of emotion. In *Approaches to emotion* (ed. K. R. Scherer & P. Ekman), pp. 319–44. Hillsdale, NJ: Erlbaum.

Ekman, P. (1992). An argument for basic emotions. *Cognition and Emotion*, **6**, 169–200.

Ekman, P., Levenson, R. W., & Friesen, W. V. (1983). Autonomic nervous system activity distinguishes among emotions. *Science*, **221**, 1208–10.

Ellsworth, P. C. (1994). Levels of thought and levels of emotion. In *The nature of emotion: Fundamental questions*, (ed. P. Ekman & R. J. Davidson), pp. 192–6. New York: Oxford University Press.

Etcoff, N. (1999). *Survival of the prettiest. The science of beauty*. New York: Anchor Books.

Farnsworth, P. R. (1969). *The social psychology of music*, (2nd edn). Ames, IA: Iowa State University Press.

Forgas, J. P. (ed.) (1991). *Emotion and social judgments*. Oxford, UK: Pergamon Press.

Forgas, J. P. (in press). Affective infuences on attitudes and judgments. In *Handbook of affective sciences*, (ed. R. J. Davidson, H. Goldsmith, & K. R. Scherer). New York: Oxford University Press.

Fraisse, P., Oleron, G., & Paillard, J. (1953). Les effets dynamogéniques de la musique [Activation effects in music]. *L'Année Psychologique*, **53**, 1–34.

Fried, R. & Berkowitz, L. (1979). Music that charms . . . and can influence helpfulness. *Journal of Applied Social Psychology*, **9**, 199–208.

Frijda, N. H. (1986). *The emotions*. Cambridge, UK: Cambridge University Press.

Frijda, N. H., Mesquita, B., Sonnemans, J., & Van Goozen, S. (1991). The duration of affective phenomena or: Emotions, sentiments and passions. In *International review of studies on emotion*, (Vol. 1) (ed. K. T. Strongman), pp. 187–225. Chichester, UK: Wiley.

Gabrielsson, A. (1998). The study of emotion in music psychology. Paper presented at the Geneva Emotion Week, May 1998, Geneva, Switzerland.

Goffman, E. (1959). *The presentation of self in everyday life.* Garden City, NY: Doubleday Anchor.

Goffman, E. (1971). *Relations in public: Microstudies in the public order.* New York: Basic Books.

Gorman, B. S. & Crain, W. C. (1974). Decoding of 'sentograms'. *Perceptual and Motor Skills*, 39, 784–6.

Gurney, E. (1880). *The power of sound.* London: Smith.

Hanslick, E. (1854). *Vom musikalisch Schönen.* [Of beauty in music.] Leipzig: Weigel.

Hargreaves, D. & North, A. (1997). *The social psychology of music.* Oxford: Oxford University Press.

Harrer, G. & Harrer, H. (1977). Music, emotion, and autonomic function. In *Music and the brain. Studies in the neurology of music,* (ed. M. Critchley & R. A. Henson) pp. 202–16. London: William Heinemann Medical Books.

Helmholtz, H. L. F. (1954). *On the sensations of tone as a physiological basis for the theory of music,* (trans. A. Ellis) (2nd English edn). New York: Dover (originally published 1863).

Hevner, K. (1936). Experimental studies of the elements of expression in music. *American Journal of Psychology*, 48, 248–68.

Hochschild, A. R. (1983). *The managed heart: The commercialization of human feeling.* Berkeley, CA: University of California Press.

Izard, C. E. (1971). *The face of emotion.* New York: Appleton-Century-Crofts.

Izard, C. E. (1990). Facial expression and the regulation of emotions. *Journal of Personality and Social Psychology*, 58, 487–98.

Izard, C. E.(1994). Innate and universal facial expressions: Evidence from developmental and cross-cultural research. *Psychological Bulletin*, 115, 288–99.

Johnstone, T., van Reekum, C. M., & Scherer, K. R. (2001). Vocal correlates of appraisal processes. In *Appraisal processes in emotion: Theory, methods, research,* (ed. K. R. Scherer, A. Schorr, & T. Johnstone) pp. 271–84. New York: Oxford University Press.

Jürgens, U. (1988). Central control of monkey calls. In *Primate vocal communication,* (ed. D. Todt, P. Goedeking, & D. Symmes), pp. 162–70. Berlin, Germany: Springer.

Kainz, F. (1962). *Psychologie der Sprache. I. Band. Grundlagen der allgemeinen Sprachpsychologie.* [Psychology of language. Vol. I. The bases of the general psychology of language.](3rd edn). Stuttgart: Enke.

Kappas, A., Hess, U., & Scherer, K. R. (1991). Voice and emotion. In *Fundamentals of nonverbal behavior,* (ed. R. S. Feldman & B. Rimé), pp. 200–38. Cambridge, UK: Cambridge University Press.

Kenealy, P. (1988). Validation of a music induction procedure: Some preliminary findings. *Cognition and Emotion*, 2, 41–8.

Kenyon, N. (ed.) (1991). *Authenticity and early music.* Oxford, UK: Oxford University Press.

Kivy, P. (1989). *Sound sentiment: An essay on the musical emotions.* Philadelphia, PA: Temple University Press.

Kneutgen, J. (1964). Beobachtungen über die Anpassung von Verhaltensweisen an gleichförmige akustische Reize [Observations concerning the adaptation of behavior patterns to repetitive acoustical stimuli]. *Zeitschrift für Tierpsychologie*, 21, 764–79.

Kneutgen, J. (1970). Eine Musikform und ihre biologische Funktion. Ueber die Wirkungsweise der Wiegenlieder [The biological function of a category of music: On the effect of lullabies]. *Zeitschrift für Experimentelle und Angewandte Psychologie*, 17, 245–65.

Krumhansl, C. L. (1997). An exploratory study of musical emotions and psychophysiology. *Canadian Journal of Experimental Psychology*, 51, 336–52.

Lang, P. J. (1979). A bio-informational theory of emotional imagery. *Psychophysiology*, 16, 495–512.

Lang, P., Bradley, M. M., & Cuthbert, B. N. (1990). Emotion, attention, and the startle reflex. *Psychological Review*, 97, 377–95.

Lang, P. J., Kozal, M. J., Miller, G. A., Levin, D. N., & MacLean, A. (1980). Emotional imagery: Conceptual structure and pattern of somato-visceral response. *Psychophysiology*, 17, 179–92.

LeDoux, J. E. (1992). Emotion as memory: Anatomical systems underlying indelible neural traces. In *Handbook of emotion and memory: Theory and research*, (ed. S. Christianson), pp. 269–88. Hillsdale, NJ: Erlbaum.

LeDoux, J. E. (1996). *The emotional brain*. New York: Simon & Schuster.

Levenson, R. W. (1992). Autonomic nervous system differences among emotions. *Psychological Science*, 3, 23–7.

Leventhal, H. & Scherer, K. R. (1987). The relationship of emotion to cognition: A functional approach to a semantic controversy. *Cognition and Emotion*, 1, 3–28.

Lippman, E. A. (1953). Symbolism in music. *Musical Quarterly*, 39, 554–75.

Lipps, Th. (1909). *Leitfaden der Psychologie* [Primer of psychology]. Leipzig, Germany: Engelmann.

Lundqvist, L. G., Carlsson, F., & Hilmersson, P. (2000). Facial electromyography, autonomic activity, and emotional experience to happy and sad music. Paper presented at the 27th International Congress of Psychology, Stockholm, Sweden, 23–28 July 2000.

Lynxwiler, J. & Gay, D. (2000). Moral boundaries and deviant music: Public attitudes toward heavy metal and rap. *Deviant Behavior*, 21, 63–85.

McIntosh, D. N. (1996). Facial feedback hypotheses: Evidence, implications, and directions. *Motivation and Emotion*, 20, 121–47.

Martin, M. A. & Metha, A. (1997). Recall of early childhood memories through musical mood induction. *Arts in Psychotherapy*, 25, 447–54.

Maslach, C. (1979). Negative emotional biasing of unexplained arousal. *Journal of Personality and Social Psychology*, 37, 933–69.

Mattheson, J. (1739). *Der volkommene Capellmeister* [The perfect musical director]. Hamburg: Herold.

Mayer, J. D. & Gaschke, Y. N. (1988). The experience and meta-experience of mood. *Journal of Personality and Social Psychology*, 55, 102–11.

Meyer, L. B. (1956). *Emotion and meaning in music*. Chicago: University of Chicago Press.

Nettlebeck, T., Henderson, C., & Willson, R. (1989). Communicating emotion through sound: An evaluation of Clynes' theory of sentics. *Australian Journal of Psychology*, 41, 17–24.

Nisbett, R. E. & Wilson, T. D. (1977). Telling more than we can know: Verbal reports on mental processes. *Psychological Review*, 84, 231–59.

Nyklicek, I., Thayer, J. F., & van Doornen, L. J. (1997). Cardiorespiratory differentiation of musically-induced emotions. *Journal of Psychophysiology*, 11, 304–21.

Öhman, A. (1988). Preattentive processes in the generation of emotions. In *Cognitive perspectives on emotion and motivation*, (ed. V. Hamilton, G. H. Bower, & N. H. Frijda), pp. 127–44. Dordrecht, the Netherlands: Kluwer.

Ornstein, R. & Sobel, D. (1989). Coming to our senses. *Advances*, 6, 49–56.

Pecchinenda, A. (2001). The psychophysiology of appraisals. In *Appraisal processes in emotion: Theory, methods, research,* (ed. K. R. Scherer, A. Schorr, & T. Johnstone) pp. 301–15. New York: Oxford University Press.

Pignatiello, M., Camp, C. J., Elder, S. T., & Rasar, L. A. (1989). A psychophysiological comparison of the Velten and musical mood induction techniques. *Journal of Music Therapy*, 26, 140–54.

Pitman, R. K., Orr, S. P., Shalev, A. Y., Metzger, L. J., & Mellman, T. A. (1999). Psychophysiological alterations in post-traumatic stress disorder. *Seminars in Clinical Neuropsychiatry*, 4, 234–41.

Pratt, C. (1931). *The meaning of music.* New York: McGraw-Hill.

Pujol, K. K. (1994). The effect of vibrotactile stimulation, instrumentation, and precomposed melodies on physiological and behavioral responses of profoundly retarded children and adults. *Journal of Music Therapy*, 31, 186–205.

Rigg, M. G. (1964). The mood effects of music: A comparison of data from earlier investigations. *Journal of Psychology*, 58, 427–38.

Rochat, P. & Striano, T. (1999). Emerging self-exploration by 2-month-old infants. *Developmental Science*, 2, 206–18.

Rosar, W. H. (1994). Film music and Heinz Werner's theory of physiognomic perception. *Psychomusicology*, 13, 154–65.

Schellenberg, E. G. & Trehub, S. E. (1996). Natural musical intervals. Evidence from infant listeners. *Psychological Science*, 7, 272–7.

Scherer, K. R. (1984). On the nature and function of emotion: A component process approach. In *Approaches to emotion,* (ed. K. R. Scherer & P. Ekman), pp. 293–317. Hillsdale, NJ: Erlbaum.

Scherer, K. R. (1985). Vocal affect signalling: A comparative approach. In *Advances in the study of behavior,* (Vol. 15) (ed. J. Rosenblatt, C. Beer, M.-C. Busnel, & P. J. B. Slater), pp. 189–244. New York: Academic Press.

Scherer, K. R. (1986). Vocal affect expression: A review and a model for future research. *Psychological Bulletin*, 99, 143–65.

Scherer, K. R. (1988). On the symbolic functions of vocal affect expression. *Journal of Language and Social Psychology*, 7, 79–100.

Scherer, K. R. (1991). Emotion expression in speech and music. In *Music, language, speech, and brain,* (ed. J. Sundberg, L. Nord, & R. Carlson), pp. 146–56. London: Macmillan.

Scherer, K. R. (1992). What does facial expression express? In *International review of studies on emotion,* (Vol. 2) (ed. K. Strongman), pp. 139–65. Chichester, UK: Wiley.

Scherer, K. R. (1993). Neuroscience projections to current debates in emotion psychology. *Cognition and Emotion*, 7, 1–41.

Scherer, K. R. (1994). Affect bursts. In *Emotions: Essays on emotion theory,* (ed. S. van Goozen, N. E. van de Poll, & J. A. Sergeant), pp. 161–96. Hillsdale, NJ: Erlbaum.

Scherer, K. R. (1995). Expression of emotion in voice and music. *Journal of Voice*, 9, 235–48.

Scherer, K. R. (1998). Emotionsprozesse im Medienkontext: Forschungsillustrationen und Zukunftsperspektiven [Emotion processes in the context of the media: Illustrative research and perspectives for the future]. *Medienpsychologie*, 10, 276–93.

Scherer, K. R. (1999). Appraisal theories. In *Handbook of cognition and emotion,* (ed. T. Dalgleish & M. Power), pp. 637–63. Chichester, UK: Wiley.

Scherer, K. R. (2000*a*). Psychological models of emotion. In *The neuropsychology of emotion*, (ed. J. Borod), pp. 137–62. New York: Oxford University Press.

Scherer, K. R. (2000*b*). Emotional expression: A royal road for the study of behavior control. In *Control of human behavior, mental processes, and awareness*, (ed. A. Grob & W. Perrig), pp. 227–44. Hillsdale, NJ: Erlbaum.

Scherer, K. R. (2000*c*). Emotions as episodes of subsystem synchronization driven by nonlinear appraisal processes. In *Emotion, development, and self-organization: Dynamic systems approaches to emotional development*, (ed. M. Lewis & I. Granic), pp. 70–99. Cambridge, UK: Cambridge University Press.

Scherer, K. R. (2000*d*). Music and emotional meaning: Perception and production rules. Paper presented at the Sixth Conference of the International Society for Music Perception and Cognition, 5–10 August 2000, Keele University, UK.

Scherer, K. R. (2001). Appraisal considered as a process of multi-level sequential checking. In *Appraisal processes in emotion: Theory, methods, research*, (ed. K. R. Scherer, A. Schorr, & T. Johnstone) pp. 92–120. New York: Oxford University Press.

Scherer, K. R. & Ceschi, G. (2000). Criteria for emotion recognition from verbal and nonverbal expression: Studying baggage loss in the airport. *Personality and Social Psychology Bulletin*, **26**, 327–39.

Scherer, K. R. & Oshinsky, J. (1977). Cue utilization in emotion attribution from auditory stimuli. *Motivation and Emotion*, **1**, 331–46.

Scherer, K. R., Schorr, A., & Johnstone, T. (ed.) (2001). *Appraisal processes in emotion: Theory, methods, research*. New York: Oxford University Press.

Scherer, K. R. & Wallbott, H. G. (1994). Evidence for universality and cultural variation of differential emotion response patterning. *Journal of Personality and Social Psychology*, **66**, 310–28.

Scherer, K. R., Zentner, M. R., & Schacht, A. K. (in press). Emotional states generated by music: A conceptual and empirical analysis. *Musicae Scientiae*.

Sloboda, J. A. (1992). Empirical studies of emotional response to music. In *Cognitive bases of musical communication*, (ed. M. R. Jones & S. Holleran), pp. 33–46. Washington, DC: American Psychological Association.

Sony (1995). *Rendezvous der Sinne. Die sinnlichste Classic-Collection der Musikgeschichte.* [Rendezvous of the senses. The most sensual CD collection in musical history.] CD No. 60464.

Stemmler, G. (1996). Psychophysiologie der Emotionen [Psychophysiology of emotions]. *Zeitschrift für Psychosomatische Medizin und Psychoanalyse*, **42**, 235–60.

Stemmler, G., Heldmann, M., Pauls, C., & Scherer, T. (2001). Constraints for emotion specificity in fear and anger: The context counts. *Psychophysiology*, **38**, 275–91.

Tarrant, M. A., Manfredo, M. J., & Driver, B. L. (1994). Recollections of outdoor recreation experiences: A psychophysiological perspective. *Journal of Leisure Research*, **26**, 357–71.

Teasdale, J. (1999). Multi-level theories of cognition-emotion relations. In *Handbook of cognition and emotion*, (ed. T. Dalgleish & M. Power), pp. 665–81. Chichester, UK: Wiley.

Todd, N. P. (1992). The dynamics of dynamics: A model of musical expression. *Journal of Acoustical Society of America*, **91**, 3540–50.

Tomkins, S. S. (1962). *Affect, imagery, consciousness. Vol. 1: The positive affects.* New York: Springer.

Tomkins, S. S. (1963). *Affect, imagery, consciousness. Vol. 2: The negative affects.* New York: Springer.

Tomkins, S. S. (1984). Affect theory. In *Approaches to emotion*, (ed. K. R. Scherer & P. Ekman), pp. 163–96. Hillsdale, NJ: Erlbaum.

Trehub, S. E. & Schellenberg, G. E. (1995). Music: Its relevance to infants. In *Annals of child development*, (Vol. 11) (ed. R. Vasta), pp. 1–24. London: Jessica Kingsley.

Trussoni, S. J., O'Malley, A., & Barton, A. (1988). Human emotion communication by touch: A modified replication of an experiment by Manfred Clynes. *Perceptual and Motor Skills*, **66**, 419–24.

Vaitl, D., Vehrs, W., & Sternagel, S. (1993). Prompts—leitmotif—emotion: Play it again, Richard Wagner. In *The structure of emotion: Psychophysiological, cognitive, and clinical aspects*, (ed. N. Birbaumer & A. Öhman), pp. 169–89. Seattle: Hogrefe & Huber.

Van der Kolk, B. A. (1997). The psychobiology of posttraumatic stress disorder. *Journal of Clinical Psychiatry*, **58** (Suppl. 9), 16–24.

Van Reekum, C. M. & Scherer, K. R. (1998). Levels of processing for emotion-antecedent appraisal. In *Cognitive science perspectives on personality and emotion*, (ed. G. Matthews), pp. 259–300. Amsterdam: Elsevier.

Wallin, N. L., Brown, S., & Merker, B. (ed.) (2000). *The origins of music*. Cambridge, MA: MIT Press.

Wedin, L. (1972). A multidimensional study of perceptual–emotional qualities in music. *Scandinavian Journal of Pschology*, **13**, 1–17.

Westermann, R., Spies, K., Stahl, G., & Hesse, F. W. (1996). Relative effectiveness and validity of mood induction procedures: A meta-analysis. *European Journal of Social Psychology*, **26**, 557–80.

Witvliet, C. V. & Vrana, S. R. (1996). The emotional impact of instrumental music on affect ratings, facial EMG, autonomic measures, and the startle reflex: Effects of valence and arousal. *Psychophysiology Supplement*, **91**.

Witvliet, C. V., Vrana, S. R., & Webb-Talmadge, N. (1998). In the mood: Emotion and facial expressions during and after instrumental music, and during an emotional inhibition task. *Psychophysiology Supplement*, **88**.

Wundt, W. (1900). *Völkerpsychologie. Eine Untersuchung der Entwicklungsgesetze von Sprache, Mythos und Sitte* (Band I. Die Sprache). [Psychology of cultures: A study of the developmental laws of language, myth, and customs. Vol. I. Language.] Leipzig: Kröner.

Wundt, W. (1974). *Grundzüge der physiologischen Psychologie* [Fundamentals of physiological psychology], (5th edn). Leipzig: Engelmann (originally published 1874).

Zajonc, R. B. (1980). Feeling and thinking: Preferences need no inferences. *American Psychologist*, **2**, 151–76.

Zajonc, R. B. & Markus, H. (1984). Affect and cognition: The hard interface. In *Emotions, cognition, and behavior*, (ed. C. E. Izard, J. Kagan, & R. B. Zajonc), pp. 73–102. Cambridge, UK: Cambridge University Press.

Zentner, M. R. & Kagan, J. (1996). Perception of music by infants. *Nature*, **383**, 29.

Zentner, M. R. & Kagan, J. (1998). Infants' perception of consonance and dissonance in music. *Infant Behavior and Development*, **21**, 483–92.

Zentner, M. R., Meylan, S., & Scherer, K. R. (2000). Exploring 'musical emotions' across five genres of music. Paper presented at the Sixth International Conference of the Society for Music Perception and Cognition (ICMPC), 5–10 August 2000, Keele, UK.

Zuckerman, M. & Lubin, B. (1985). *Manual for the Multiple Affect Adjective Check List*, (2nd edn). San Diego, CA: Educational and Industrial Testing Service.

# CHAPTER 17

# CONTINUOUS MEASUREMENT OF SELF-REPORT EMOTIONAL RESPONSE TO MUSIC

EMERY SCHUBERT

By definition music requires time to happen. Many styles of music also express or evoke different emotions as time unfolds. Logically, it follows that to understand the relationship between music and emotion, psychologists need to investigate their time-varying relationships. It is therefore surprising to find that the study of *continuous* self-reported emotion in music is less than 20 years old. Continuous response tools measure self-reported emotional responses *during* the listening process and help researchers to better understand the moment-to-moment fluctuations in responses that traditional 'asynchronous' approaches cannot. The approach means that the music does not need to be broken into small portions to enable lucid response, nor does the listener have to compress their response by giving an overall impression at the end of the excerpt. A more realistic listening experience is possible. This 'realism' (Hargreaves 1986, p. 105) contributes to the ecological validity of experimental design at the expense of experimental control.

Given that the methodology is relatively new, there is a need to examine the literature and to provide a framework for future directions. Gregory (1995) and Schmidt (1996) review one kind of continuous response device, and the reviews encompass emotional response as one aspect of a broader scope. The present chapter examines a wider range of continuous measure devices, but restricts the discussion to those studies that investigate self-report emotional response. In this chapter, I will define 'continuous', describe the response formats used for collecting continuous responses, discuss the ways in which researchers have applied continuous response methodology, and then provide an evaluation of the major issues.

## 17.1 Definition of continuous response

The term 'continuous' is arguably used incorrectly in the literature. Continuous means without break, inferring that responses are measured without interruption. Modern techniques of measuring response require some form of sampling because they are associated with digital computers. At best, the frequency of sampling may be high, but is still interrupted. Even a rate of tens of thousands of samples per second is still not, strictly speaking, a continuous measure. Instead, the more correct term is *continual*, or perhaps *multiple equispaced*. It is apparent that the 'erroneous' terminology stems from the kymographic devices used in physiological response studies since the late nineteenth century (Dogiel 1880 cited in Radocy & Boyle 1988, p. 205; Weld 1912), which drew line plots of physiological activities as a function of time. These analogue devices were indeed continuous. And, to be sure, high sampling rates associated with modern digital equipment can give the impression of a continuous measure.

However, the patterns and latency of emotional response makes the need for strict continuity or even high sampling rates of measurement superfluous. For example, a lexical response task alone will take in the order of 1 second (Greene & Royer 1994), and the response latency in the tracking of a musical feature, such as loudness, is 1–1.5 seconds (Geringer 1995). By the same token, the term *continuous* has been used consistently in the literature, and consequently its use will be retained to mean continuous *or* continual.

## 17.2 Response formats

### 17.2.1 Open-ended format

Three of the traditional self-report formats found in the asynchronous emotion–music literature are also found in continuous response research: open-ended (or free-verbal) format, checklist, and rating scale (Gabrielsson & Juslin, in press; Sloboda 1992; see also Gabrielsson & Lindström, this volume). Open-ended approaches (e.g. one part of the study by Watson 1942) are rarely found in the literature because of the obvious problem of the response task *during* listening interfering with the listening process.

### 17.2.2 Checklist

Checklist formats have also been used infrequently (Goins 1998; Hair 1995; Hevner 1936; Mull 1949; Namba *et al.* 1991). An innovative and pioneering example is Hevner's (1936) study, which was the first to use what could be called a self-report continuous response approach. Hevner addressed the problem of collecting an overall response for a piece (that may have actually expressed several different emotions) by asking the listener to make judgments at the end of each section of music as the music unfolded. For example, if a piece of music had several sections, the participant would place the number '1' next to the selected term or terms which best described the emotion in the first section of music, and when the next section of the music began (signalled by the experimenter), a '2' would be placed next to the term characterizing that section. This process continued until all sections were heard. The pieces Hevner reported were divided into three sections and, together, these sections usually made up an entire movement.

In one experiment, Hevner collected responses to *Reflections on the Water* by Debussy. She discovered that responses to the piece were widely distributed across the eight clusters (Fig. 17.1a). The experiment was conducted again using the continuous procedure. In the first section of the piece, the responses were made predominantly in clusters 5 and 7 ('humorous' and 'exhilarated'), whereas in the second section, responses shifted to cluster 4 ('lyrical'). In the final section, clusters 4 and 5 ('lyrical' and 'humorous') were chosen most frequently (Fig. 17.1b). These results demonstrated that different sections of music evoked different, though internally consistent responses.

Despite this and later studies, the categorical approach of the checklist does not easily lend itself to continuous methodology. Categorical responses require the participant to select one or several answers from a range of answers. Unless lengthy training time is administered (e.g. 30 minutes per participant in the Namba *et al.* (1991) study), a large range of choices will require the participant to constantly shift attention between the various response options, in addition to concentrating on the music. In a continuous response task, this may either interfere with the listening experience, or lead to the omission or guessing of some responses so as to minimize interference. This might explain why there are relatively few checklist studies that employ the continuous response approach at high sampling rates. Hevner's approach of gathering responses

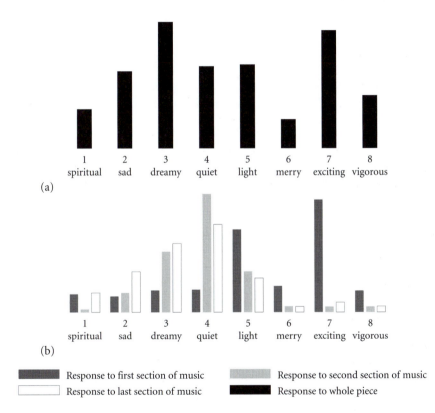

(a)

(b)

Response to first section of music        Response to second section of music
Response to last section of music         Response to whole piece

**Fig 17.1** Hevner's adjective checklist responses to Debussy's *Reflections on the Water* for the whole piece and in sections (adapted from Hevner 1936, pp. 251 and 254). The numbers correspond to the cluster from the Hevner adjective circle with a representative word from each cluster number appearing under each number (the complete adjective circle is presented in Gabrielsson & Lindström, this volume). (a) The relative frequencies of each adjective circle cluster, and (b) the responses to the same piece in a different experiment with separate responses recorded for the three sections of the music.

once only per section of music mitigates the problem, but it does not allow for the investigation of changing shades of meaning within a section of the music.

### 17.2.3 Rating scale

A useful subdivision of continuous response literature employing rating scale measures is according to the number of simultaneous dimensions measured. Most studies use one dimension, and more recently two scales have also been used simultaneously. One-dimensional studies have used a variety of labels representing either one specific aspect or dimension of emotion (such as happiness or tension) to more general labels (such as aesthetic experience or 'when the music causes something to happen to you'). A selection of studies using one-dimensional scales is shown in Table 17.1.

**Table 17.1** Labels used in one-dimensional measures of continuous self-report emotional response, with scale labels and scale poles (or task) indicated

| Self-report label | Poles/task | Examples |
|---|---|---|
| Aesthetic experience | Negative-positive | Capperella-Sheldon (1992) |
| | Negative-positive | Madsen *et al.* (1993*a*) |
| Chills | Raise hand if present | Panksepp (1995) |
| Emotion | Minimum-maximum | Krumhansl (1998) |
| Emotional reaction | Positive-negative | D. Gregory (1998) |
| Emotional response | No emotional response-emotional response | Adams (1994) |
| | Negative-positive | Lychner (1998) |
| Emotionality ('the capacity of the performance at that moment to suggest, communicate, or evoke musically relevant emotion', p. 631) | High-low | Sloboda *et al.* (1997) |
| Fear | Amount of fear | Krumhansl (1997)) |
| Felt emotion | Negative-positive | Lychner (1998) |
| Happiness | Amount of happiness | Krumhansl (1997) |
| Humour | Raise hand if present | Mull (1949) |
| Intensity of emotions | Low-high | A. H. Gregory (1998) |
| Perceived artistic tension | Decrease-increase | Frego (1999) |
| Sadness | Amount of sadness | Krumhansl (1997) |
| Tension | Less-more | Byrnes (1996) |
| | Less-more | Frederickson (1995, 1997, 1999) |
| | Amount of tension | Krumhansl (1997) |
| | Less-more | Madsen & Fredrickson (1993) |
| | Amount of physical pressure on a pair of tension tongs | Nielsen (1983) |
| | Minimum tension-maximum tension | Krumhansl (1996) |
| Thrill | Raise fingers for strength and location of thrill | Goldstein (1980) |
| When the music causes something to happen to you | Frequency of responses | Waterman (1996) |

An important criticism cast against one-dimensional rating scales is that they cannot capture the complexities of emotion satisfactorily (Schmidt 1996). One solution to this problem is to track more than one dimension simultaneously. Since 1996 there has been a trend toward the measurement of two dimensions simultaneously. An early example of what could be referred to as a two-dimensional, continuous response instrument, namely the *sentograph*, was developed by Clynes (Clynes 1977, 1980; Clynes & Nettheim 1982; see also de Vries 1991; Gabrielsson & Lindström 1995). However, because it was used to measure 'inner' emotional experience and 'essentic forms' it is, strictly speaking, not a self-report instrument. Three self-report continuous, two-dimensional 'emotion spaces' (2DES) were developed independently and almost simultaneously by Schubert (1996), Tyler (1996), and Madsen (1997). For each of these instruments, the listener makes responses by moving about a two-dimensional space (computer interface), with each axis (or scale) of the space representing a separate dimension of emotion.

There are various problems associated with rating scale measures. The following sections discuss the kinds of questions asked by continuous response researchers, followed by some of the issues and concerns relevant to continuous response methodology.

## 17.3  When are continuous measures used?

Continuous measures of self-report emotion in music have been used for four broad purposes: validation, comparative investigations, stimulus–response investigations, and system–dynamics investigations.

### 17.3.1  Validation

Continuous response measures have been used to validate traditional asynchronous response formats and vice versa. Goins (1998) compared grand mean categorical continuous response digital interface (CRDI—a dial whose manipulations are recorded on a computer in real time) responses with conventional asynchronous responses using a modified version of the Hevner adjective checklist. He noted a strong similarity between the two methods. This supports the external validity of the approach. However, with just eight categories identified (with asynchronous $n = 30$, and continuous $n = 40$), it becomes difficult to identify subtle differences between the measures and to provide a quantitative index. In a study of intensity in music, Brittin and Duke (1997) found that overall, asynchronous responses tended to be higher in magnitude than the averaged continuous response. Schubert (1999*b*) used an adjective checklist *and* an asynchronous 2DES to investigate the validity of the continuous 2DES rating scales. Participants were required to respond to a piece of music in three ways: continuously, then with an overall judgment, and finally by selecting a word from a checklist. While the checklist responses provided good agreement with averaged responses on the continuous 2DES, the overall 2DES gave a result consistent with Brittin and Duke's findings. Specifically, overall responses were more exaggerated than the average of continuous responses. Continuous responses may gravitate to the centre of the scales being used, or the relationship between averaged and overall responses are in some way scaled.

### 17.3.2 Comparative investigations

An example of the use of the continuous response measure for comparative studies can be found in the Madsen *et al.* (1993*b*) study which used the CRDI to compare non-musicians' and musicians' perceived aesthetic experiences. They concluded that aesthetic experiences do not differ between musicians and non-musicians. Similarly, Lychner (1998) found no significant differences between musicians and non-musicians in their continuous ratings of three classical music extracts and a Sousa march according to felt emotion, aesthetic response, and free response. Another example is the study by Sloboda *et al.* (1997) where 'emotionality' in performances of a Chopin prelude perceived by non-pianists, pianists (a subset of the pianists who had provided the performances), and music jurors were investigated. These researchers found that the pianists responded with significantly lower emotionality scores in the first segment of the piece, and significantly higher scores in the last segment of the piece, compared with the other two groups.

### 17.3.3 Stimulus–response investigations

The use of the continuous response device to investigate the music–emotion system (M→E) is hinted at in several studies. Madsen (1996, p. 106) compared data in studies conducted by himself and John Geringer, producing correlations between musical features (melody, dynamics, timbre, rhythm, and 'everything') that were the focus of listeners' attention with aesthetic response. The highest correlation reported was with melody ($r = 0.67$), and the next highest was dynamics ($r = 0.59$), when listening to an excerpt from Puccini's *La Boheme,* and rhythm ($r = 0.69$) when listening to the first movement of Haydn's Symphony No. 104. A. H. Gregory (1998) observed that higher intensity emotions appeared to occur during vocal passages and periods of higher loudness. In a comparative study (degrees of familiarity with the test piece), Fredrickson (1999, p. 50) described a region of judged high musical tension over bars 32–45 of 'Chaconne' from Holst's *First Suite in E♭*:

There is a *crescendo* to a dynamic peak at measure 41, where a series of running sixteenths begin in the upper woodwinds. The musicians who are unfamiliar with the music (singers and high school pre-test) indicate a higher tension level here that continues through another statement of the melodic material in the trumpets at measure 49, where the melody moves above a heavy (*pesante*) eighth-note section in the low brass. Graphs for musicians who are familiar with the music (wind ensemble and high school post-test) drop off sharply after the *crescendo* and rise only slightly before falling off along with the other groups at the *diminuendo*, which ends the section.

Since Hevner's (1936) early exploration, a small number of studies have used continuous response methodology to focus *specifically* on the issue of the relationship between musical features and emotional response. Nielsen (1983, 1987) and Krumhansl (1996) asserted that there was a relationship between structural features (based on the theories of Lerdahl & Jackendoff (1983) and Narmour (1990)) and tension response. However, graphical examination of the Nielsen (1987) study, and Krumhansl's own observation (1996; p. 415) suggests that loudness matches reasonably well with tension responses; in the case of Nielsen perhaps better than the higher-level structural analysis. Both studies also identified specific locations where the melodic contour was related to the tension response: for Nielsen, in the development section of the first movement of Haydn's Symphony No. 104, and for Krumhansl, in the first movement Mozart's Piano Sonata in E♭ Major, K. 282, Krumhansl found that Lerdahl's pitch-space model (which provides a quantitative coding of pitch and harmonic dissonances) accounted for a significant proportion of the tension response. In another study, Krumhansl (1998) correlated high-level musical features, referred to as 'topics' (Ratner 1980; see also Cook & Dibben, this volume), with judged emotionality. While correlations were not very high, the 'gavotte' and 'alla zoppa' musical topics produced relatively strong emotional responses for the allegro from Mozart's String Quintet No. 3 in C Major K. 515 ($r < 0.2$ and $r < |-0.3|$, respectively), and the 'brilliant style' topic for Beethoven's String Quartet No. 15 in A Minor, Op. 132 ($r < 0.3$).

Sloboda (1991) constructed a list of musical structural features that produced particular physical emotional responses. For example, a harmonic descending cycle of fifths to tonic, a melodic appoggiaturas, and a melodic or harmonic sequence tended to produce a 'tears' response, and a new or unprepared harmony tended to produce a 'shivers' response. Schubert (1996, 1999b) found that the best predictor of arousal was loudness. He also proposed that perfect cadence harmonic progression increased valence response (Schubert 1999a).

Continuous response methodologies have provided an enriching alternative to the study of music as a causal agent of emotional response. While the methodology is inefficient compared with conventional, asynchronous, single-sample-per-stimulus approaches, it has facilitated an understanding of the processes of the M→E system that are difficult to isolate and may require musical context to have an effect. For example, it would be hard to determine empirically the emotional effect of the appoggiatura or the perfect cadence within an ecologically valid framework (musical context) without continuous response methodology.

### 17.3.4  System–dynamics investigations

The single most important purpose of continuous measures is in better understanding the time-dependent, dynamic nature of the M→E system. The analytical method proposed by Schubert and Dunsmuir (1999) provides an example of how lag structure can be better understood. Before continuous response methodologies were accessible, experimental music psychologists could do little more than speculate about the delay in emotional response after a 'causal' musical event. The findings and issues concerned with the dynamic nature of emotional response to music using continuous response methodology are discussed below under Sections 17.4.5 and 17.4.6.

## 17.4  Evaluation of continuous measure devices

The growing interest in continuous measure approaches to emotion in music necessitates the consideration of several issues pertaining to the design, reliability, and validity of continuous measure instruments. Important issues to emerge are the defining and coding of the stimulus and of the emotional response, synchronizing response and stimulus, and determining the optimum and adequate response sampling rates. Pertinent issues in examining the relationship between musical features and emotional response are the response latency (or 'lag structure') and the method used to analyse data. These issues will be discussed with reference to the literature described above and with respect to possible future directions.

### 17.4.1 Stimulus coding

To determine how emotion varies in response to music, the musical stimulus must be analysed and coded. One approach is a *post hoc* analysis where once a significant or important emotional response is identified, the musical features or structures thought to be responsible are then ascertained. Sloboda (1991) and Krumhansl (1996) operated in this fashion. This approach requires a high degree of musicological skill on the part of the researcher. A more objective approach is to code musical feature variables before collecting emotional responses, and to use a statistical method to determine which combinations of musical features can explain the temporally nearby changes in emotion. This technique treats the musical stimulus as a multidimensional set of interacting musical and psychoacoustic features or structures. These features can be coded at a high level, for example in terms of their aesthetic association or 'topics' (used by Krumhansl 1998, based on Ratner 1980), or according to some coding strategy deduced from a theory of harmony or pitch dissonance (Krumhansl 1996, based on Lerdahl's theory of tonal pitch space), or grouping structure (Nielsen 1983, after Lerdahl and Jackendoff's theory of generative grammar in music). Alternatively, low-level musical features could be coded (Schubert 1999a), such as pitch, loudness, duration, timbre, and harmony.

The kinds and levels of variables coded will be a function of the requirements of the researcher, and the feasibility of the coding scheme. Some musical features, such as pitch and loudness, can be coded as perceptually relevant, objective multilevel variables (e.g. Cabrera 1997, 1998; Hall 1987; Moore *et al.* 1997; Rossing 1990; Schubert 1999a). Other musical features, such as harmony and rhythm, require some form of polychotimization to achieve multilevel coding. For example, Schubert (1999a) coded cadential progressions as a continuous, dichotomous variable having the value 'perfect cadence' or 'no perfect cadence'.

### 17.4.2 Response coding

A theoretical consideration that can help to determine response format and coding strategy is the paradigm of emotion. There are two broad systems of classifying emotions: categories and dimensions. Categorical classification of emotion assumes that emotions carrying different meanings, such as happy and sad, are distinct and independent entities. While Goins (1998), Hevner (1936) and Namba and associates (1991) have used the checklist format to obtain data that are essentially continuous, the categorical approach does not lend itself easily to continuous methodology. Categorical approaches require the participant to select one or several answers from a range of answers. A large range of choices will require the participant to constantly shift attention between the various response options, in addition to the experimental task. In a continuous response task, this may either interfere with the listening experience, or lead to omission or guessing of some responses so as to minimize interference. Hevner's approach of gathering responses once only per section of music is an improvement to continual checklist evaluation, but it does not allow for the investigation of changing shades of meaning.

The dimensional classification of emotion holds that all emotions are in some way related within an *n*-dimensional *semantic space* (or, more correctly, *emotion space)*. For example, the dimensional structure suggests that happy and sad are more or less opposite emotions along the *valence* dimension of emotion (Russell 1989). To distinguish distinct emotions having similar valence, such as sad and angry, a second dimension, *arousal,* may be added: Sad expresses low arousal and angry expresses high arousal (see also Sloboda & Juslin, this volume).

Many researchers have assumed that participants can manage concentrating on one dimension only while listening to music (e.g. Madsen & Fredrickson 1993; Nielsen 1983; Sloboda *et al.* 1997). Because emotion is multidimensional, the dimension to choose has been problematic. My review of the literature supports Schmidt's (1996) criticism that most unidimensional continuous response formats refer to a general, abstract construct such as 'aesthetic experience' or 'emotionality', or, even more vague, 'when the music causes something to happen to you' (see Table 17.1). A reasonably specific term was 'musical tension' (Fredrickson 1999; Krumhansl 1996; Nielson 1983), and even this is problematic—what, exactly, is musical tension? Schmidt is critical of vague instructions and non-specific criteria. However, the complexity of the theoretical concepts in some ways demands that the participant uses some implicit and intuitive judgment criterion.

The validity of choosing a non-specific dimension as a means of tapping into emotion is a major issue. For example, when preparing this chapter I compared the response of the first 37 bars of Rodrigo's *Concierto de Aranjuez* obtained from the Schubert (1999a, p. 510) study with that obtained by Waterman (1996, p. 60). The peak responses in the Waterman study ('when . . . something . . . happen[s] to you') occurred at the same locations as the peaks in arousal response gradient in the Schubert study, namely at bars 23, 31, and 33, but no such similarity was found between the valence response gradient and the Waterman data. This prompts me to propose that the more general instruction may actually be tapping into the arousal dimension as a default response, rather than some general, idealized emotional/aesthetic response. I tentatively extend this proposal to include 'tension' because of the large amount of literature which supports a correlation between tension and arousal (e.g. Berlyne 1973; Krumhansl & Schenck 1997).

Another solution attempted by researchers to the problem of measuring emotion on a rating scale is to add more response dimensions. Here, the problem of cognitive load and attentional resources must be considered carefully (Damos 1992; M. Zentner, personal communication). If enough dimensions are responded to simultaneously, researchers will obtain a more complete picture of emotion expressed but, on the other hand, the participant's capacity to execute the more complex task will lead to poorer quality of data. The general consensus in the research community appears to be that two dimensions provide an optimal balance between a parsimonious definition of emotion and limiting the complexity of the task. While there is a lack of agreement on the exact nature of these dimensions, they agree in principle with two of the three dimensions of semantic space proposed by Osgood *et al.* (1957). Through their work on semantic differentials, they asserted that meaning space could be largely described in terms of the dimensions *evaluation, activity,* and *potency.* Labels implying the first two dimensions (evaluation and activity) are commonly found in the music–emotion literature (e.g. Asmus 1985; Collier 1996; Collins 1989; Wedin 1972). The labels used by Madsen, Mulder, Schubert, and Tyler are listed in Table 17.2, grouped so as to reflect the matching dimensional constructs.

Table 17.2 Two-dimensional response labels

| Evaluation | Activity | Examples |
| --- | --- | --- |
| Ugly-beautiful | Relaxing-exciting | Madsen (1997, 1998) |
| Valence | Arousal | Schubert (1996) |
| Unhappy-happy | Not excited-excited | Mulder (1997); Tyler (1996) |

It remains to be seen whether a third dimension will be added by future researchers, what the dimension will be, and how the response format will be interfaced. Based on the literature (Russell 1980; Whissell *et al.* 1986), a possible third dimension is likely to include *potency,* with polar labels of *dominant–submissive.* The participant of two-dimensional continuous studies usually moves the mouse around a two-dimensional surface. Either a three-dimensional mouse could be employed (M. Zentner, personal communication), or the participant's unused hand could be used to provide additional information. A second pass in listening is a problematic solution, because it makes the assumption that the listener is responding on the second pass as he or she would if asked to perform the third dimension task on the first pass. However the 'second-pass' approach (with counterbalancing across listeners) seems to be the most feasible alternative.

The rating scale format is particularly suited to a computer interface. In a study on the reliability and validity of the 2DES, Schubert (1999*b*) found that participants required a resolution of approximately 10 per cent per dimension to distinguish words and pictures of faces expressing different emotions. On a 201-point scale, there was general agreement as to the emotion expressed by a word with a boundary of $20 \times 20$ points. Therefore, a coding that provides a higher resolution than one unit on a ten-unit scale should adequately capture the resolution of human semantic and emotional response. Given that computer displays are restricted by the number of pixels (in the order of hundreds), the issue of resolution and coding of rating scale formats using computer interfacing poses no problem to continuous response research.

### 17.4.3 Synchronization

Early studies had considerable problems with synchronization. Mull's (1949) use of a stop watch as a means of synchronizing response and stimulus was apparently unreliable and the dependent data were discarded. Hevner's (1936) ingenious solution of using numbers for different sections of music was adequate provided that the piece had clearly distinguishable moods or sections. However, it mainly served to distinguish gross characteristics of the M→E system, rather than more subtle ones.

While computer technology has mitigated problems of synchronizing the musical signal with the emotional response, there are other techniques that do not depend on computer technology. For example, Sloboda (1991) used the musical score as a response form. This method ensured precise matching of response and stimulus because the participant was responsible for locating the emotion-evoking episode on the musical map of the stimulus (a musical score). A problem with using the musical score as a response sheet is that it restricts respondents to those who are able to read the particular score in question, although in the Sloboda study respondents unable to read music could refer to recordings. Furthermore, data collection so removed from conventional pen and paper formats could be a precarious task, as the coder searches for some mark, perhaps clear, perhaps esoteric, that signifies an emotional, or some other, event. Sloboda's solution was to have the participant make a mark on the score and then provide a written explanation (J. A. Sloboda, personal communication). The techniques employed by Flowers (1983) and Waterman (1996) also used a physical link between the response and the stimulus, the former by recording the stimulus and response onto an audio tape, the latter by using one of the spare audio tracks, parallel to the stimulus storing tracks, for recording responses.

By far the most common method of synchronization availed to the contemporary researcher is the use of a computer-generated clock which the software uses to track the location of the music and is used as a tag for the participant's response. In the case of Schubert (1996, 1999b), the musical stimuli were taken from an audio CD that was controlled by the software. One routine in the software (Sudderth 1995) was able to read the elapsed time (in seconds) directly from the CD. This value was then tagged with the response in real time. After data collection, the experimenter converted the time into bar (measure) locations so that the concomitant musical structure could be easily identified. This conversion to bars made the analysis independent of the CD recording of the piece under investigation. Another technique of making the music independent of the performance was to employ the method of Sloboda *et al.* (1997), who recorded response after every sixth note. MIDI (Musical Instrument Digital Interface) coding of the performance lent itself to this kind of synchronization strategy.

### 17.4.4 Sampling rate

While a variety of sampling rates have been found in the self-report literature, varying from five emotional response samples per second (Madsen *et al.* 1993a) to one per second (e.g Brittin 1991), the majority of studies have used two samples per second. The choice of two samples per second appears to be based on intuition rather than a firm theoretical foundation. However, the lag structure of the M→E system provides a clue of the optimum sampling rate—optimum meaning the balance between minimum data and maximum information. By applying Nyquist's sampling theorem (e.g. Pohlmann 1995), that the optimum sampling rate is twice the highest frequency which is likely to be encountered, it is possible to posit a suitable sampling rate for measuring continuous emotional response to music. Although no literature was cited which indicated the fastest *emotional* response to a musical feature, the fastest response to a musical feature alone necessarily sets the upper limit (assuming that the listener is not trying to predict an emotional response). Geringer (1995) reported that the response latency in detecting loudness information was in the order of 1.5 seconds (see also Robinson 1988, p. 64). On the basis of this information, responses should be sampled at half this interval—once every 0.75 seconds. Therefore, the popular, slightly higher sampling rate of two per second is a good choice (Gregory 1992).

### 17.4.5 Lag structure

The main benefit to be sought from continuous measures of emotion in music is to determine why responses change as a function of the stimulus. Surprisingly, very few studies have attempted to do this. Unfortunately, the kinds of issues investigated by continuous response studies verge on trivial. Nearly all the studies investigated *describe* the movement of the response time-series, but only a handful have made serious attempts to *explain* these responses in terms of the changing stimulus (e.g. Capperella-Sheldon 1992; Krumhansl 1996, 1998; Nielsen 1983; Schubert 1998, 1999*a*; Sloboda 1991).

Given the primitive state of stimulus-response (M→E) analysis, it comes as no surprise that our understanding of lag structure in emotion in music is minimal. Lag structure refers to the delay in response after an emotion-producing stimulus event. When any stimulus is presented, the response is not instantaneous. Schubert (1998, 1999*a*) proposed that responses are causally related to the stimulus. Consequently, he analysed response according to specific musical features. Using regression analysis (discussed below), he found that a dynamic relationship between emotional arousal and loudness was present. In general, positive changes in stimulus loudness led to positive changes in the arousal dimension of emotion, and these changes occur 2–3 seconds after the change in the stimulus. This is in reasonable agreement with Krumhansl's (1996) identification of a lag of up to 3.25 seconds from the time an event occurs to the time a tension response is made.

Schubert and Dunsmuir (1999) further proposed that the M→E system is nonlinear. For example, sudden changes in loudness produce a faster change in arousal response (1–2 seconds instead of 2–3 seconds). In other words, lag structure is dynamic. Indeed, understanding lag structure is perhaps the single most important application of continuous response methodology. However, the work of Schubert and Dunsmuir is introductory and largely exploratory.

Continuous response methodology provides a fruitful foundation for the investigation of the M→E system dynamics. A hint of the value of this methodology has been provided in Schubert and Dunsmuir's (1999) categories of outliers responsible for altering the hypothetically linear lag structure of the M→E system (or more specifically in the case cited, the 'loudness→arousal system'). They proposed that a faster than typical linear response lag is a *startle* response, while a slower than typical linear lag is an *inertia* response. Three kinds of inertia responses were identified:

1.  *Orientation*, where the participant needs time to adjust to a new piece or section of music.

2.  *Overshoot recovery*, where the participant has overreacted to a change and requires extra time to recover to the linear model-predicted lag.

3.  *After-glow*, where the participant still notices an emotion in the music, even though the music has finished.

An example of an overshoot recovery inertial response is shown in Fig. 17.2 (taken from Schubert 1999*a*). The system-predicted arousal response (based on regression analysis) is shown for seconds 137 to 146 (bars 166–180) of Dvorak's Slavonic Dance Op 42 No. 1. When 142 seconds of the piece had elapsed, the actual change in arousal dropped suddenly at the same time as the change in loudness and spectral centroid (which is related to perceived timbral sharpness) increased. The rate at which the model-predicted arousal gradient changed (Δ) was much slower, and the model was not able to predict the actual response satisfactorily.

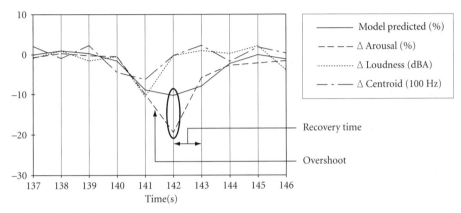

**Fig 17.2** Example of an overshoot recovery inertia response.

Another prudent area for investigating lag structure is in how individual differences affect response time. A common example is the comparison of 'musician and non-musician' responses to music. Capperella-Sheldon (1992) defined such groups and examined where aesthetic peaks and drops in responses occurred while listening to the first movement of Holst's First Suite in E♭ for Military Band. She found five peaks and drops for each group, but could not identify any consistency in response lag between the musicians and non-musicians.

### 17.4.6 Analysis

Perhaps the most grave concern faced by continuous response researchers in music-emotion is the analysis of data. While econometricians and engineers have developed traditions of sophisticated time-series analytical techniques (Box & Jenkins 1976; Hamilton 1994), in the field of self-report emotion research, music psychologists have failed to do much more than provide descriptive, interoccular tests of their continuous response findings. This is somewhat odd because music and emotion are both time series, requiring special analytical techniques. Consequently, an important advantage of continuous response measurement has been neglected, if not resisted. While general empirical psychology publications are subjected to fairly intense statistical rigour and scrutiny, the continuous emotional response to music literature has produced a stream of studies that report simple, weakly substantiated, descriptive claims. This means that the potential benefits of continuous measure methodology are, to some extent, wasted.

Specifically, continuous response enables measurement in response to an entire piece or movement of music. Instead of listening to a few bars of a piece, the music context can be laid out for the listener, and a response can be made in a more realistic listening situation. Measurement of this kind of approach provides the advantage of ecological validity (Lipscomb 1996). In the statistical world, this realistic approach may be best described as a process involving *serial correlation*—that a response or experience at a given point in time is in some way related to something that happened at another point (or points) in time. It is this process of serial correlation that must be addressed to make continuous measures productive tools for research. The analytical approaches used by researchers can be divided into four broad classes that are, in order of (more or less) increasing validity and sophistication: interoccular analysis, correlation of means, analysis of variance, and adjustment for serial correlation.

*Interoccular analysis*

The dimensional rating-scale studies provide potential for a closer analysis of the time-variant relationship between emotional response and musical features (Schmidt 1996). However, there are numerous instances in the literature where a complete analysis will consist of general comments about the appearance of a time-series chart of mean responses. For example, Gregory (1995, pp. 206–7) concludes her review of the CRDI by stating that 'visual comparisons of graphic contours provide immediate discrimination of response similarities across total time spans and at selected samples within time spans. This may be the CRDI's singular contribution to music research instrumentation.'

While visual inspection is an important approach for commencing analysis, it would be unfortunate if this remains the 'singular contribution' of the CRDI or any other continuous response measure. Gottman (1981) points out the foibles of the interoccular test (or 'graphic analysis') that is implied by Gregory's comment. It lacks statistical rigour and is prone to biased interpretation. Further, visual analysis of a chart can be misleading, particularly when deviation scores are omitted—a regular feature of continuous response data reports in the literature under investigation.

*Correlation of means*

A common kind of analysis reported in continuous measure studies is the Pearson product-moment correlation analysis of time-series data averaged across participants. Correlation is used to describe the similarity of two time series, and is the most common statistical approach used for comparative studies (such as comparing non-musicians with musicians). With comparison of categorical data, agreement quotients have been used, where the numerical index is obtained by dividing the number of categories in which there are concomitant agreements across test–retest listenings by the total number of categorical responses (Gregory 1995). None of the studies cited have attempted to provide correlation analyses with serial correlations removed, and only a handful have considered a cross-correlation analysis (Schubert 1999*a*), which provides information about correlations at non-instantaneous lags (i.e. correlations between two time series separated by one sample or more).

Schubert (2000) demonstrated that correlation coefficients were inflated in comparison to correlation analyses made with repeated measures of independent data sets. Indeed, the literature does have a tendency to report boastfully though misleadingly high correlation coefficients, often well above 0.8. For example, Johnson (1996) compared the experimentally obtained correlation coefficient of serially correlated data with the range recommended by Anastasi (1987, p. 106, cited in Johnson 1996) for a reliable measure, without considering this problem. Schmidt (1996) has suggested that, in some cases, a Spearman rank-correlation analysis might be more appropriate because it is more conservative. There are other non-parametric approaches to correlation analyses, and many of the techniques discussed below are applicable (e.g. see Howell 1997). Schubert (2000) proposed that differencing each time series (so as to produce *changes* in response) prior to conventional Pearson product-moment correlation might produce a more valid correlation analysis.

*Accounting for deviation*

A more sophisticated approach than interoccular tests and correlation analyses are techniques that examine variations in responses. The first study of continuous response to emotion in music cited which used mathematical techniques to analyse time-series data was the de Vries (1991) study. While it used the *sentograph* (see Section 17.2.3), and so strictly speaking is not a self-report instrument, it is worth examining the techniques de Vries used. His approach was based on the method of analysis of electrocardiograms developed by Van Bemmel (1982, cited in de Vries 1991). De Vries produced five parameters from a two-dimensional response time series (force and angle of finger pressure). The parameters were: (1) mean angle of pressure direction; (2) roughness (or fluctuation) of pressure angle; (3) roughness of force; (4) pointedness of force; and (5) skewness of force. This produced five time series. Discriminant analysis resulted in three weighting functions that were produced so as to maximize the distinction in responses across musical selections. In other words, de Vries could map musical selections onto a three-dimensional music space using the transformed response parameter weightings. Together, these three functions accounted for 97 per cent of the variance. However, de Vries did not disclose if and how he accounted for serial correlation. Uncontrolled serial correlation may have inflated the explained variance.

The first published *self-report* study among those reported to use some form of inferential statistical analysis (aside from instantaneous correlations) was by Byrnes (1996), who used paired sample *t*-tests to determine the effect of the music as a 'treatment' on the first and last responses. While this is a statistically valid procedure, it seems difficult to justify the collection of so much data between the first and last samples when only the two end-points are used for the analysis.

Another 'early' attempt at using inferential statistical analysis of time-series data was presented by Sloboda *et al.* (1997), who conducted analysis of variance on the grouped responses to performances of Chopin's Prelude No. 4 in E Minor. After eye-balling the time-series plots, the piece was divided into four sections that also coincided roughly with structurally salient points in the music. The repeated measures ANOVA produced significant results, and it was found that adjacent sections were significantly different. Sloboda and associates then used this information to claim that they had captured different levels of 'emotionality'. While it is commendable that inferential statistics were applied, the question of why the analysis was performed remains. It is not clear why it was important to have a piece with varied emotional expression within it (as distinct from across different versions of the same piece). More relevant to the research problem of the study would have been 'what produced these changes?' The notion of musical features as the cause of the response was implied: 'The present study aims to discover how score-based structural indicators, observed performance parameters, and listener characteristics influence the emotional response to music' (Sloboda *et al.* 1997, p. 630). To this end, it would have been of greater relevance if the relationship between response variations and musical structure could be identified using the data obtained.

### Accounting for serial correlation

Krumhansl (1996) used multiple regression to model tension response as a function of musical feature variables based on an analysis by Lerdahl. While no coefficents were reported, the multiple correlation coefficent was estimated as $R_{7\ 177} = 0.79$ ($P < 0.0001$). Krumhansl supported Lerdahl's predictions by leading (or 'shifting backward in time') responses by 0 to 3.25 seconds, and found that the predictions were not as smooth as the actual mean responses. Therefore, Krumhansl smoothed and lagged the predicted response, thus introducing serial correlation and lagging into the model, and hence making it more realistic. A second regression analysis produced an improved fit ($R_{14\ 170} = 0.91$, $P < 0.0001$). However, it is not clear that Krumhansl overtly accounted for the serial correlation in the model: No comment was made about the serial correlation in the residual series (the time series which could *not* be explained by the regression model). This is important, because the presence of serial correlation in the residual violates several assumptions of the linear regression model (Ostrom 1990). Krumhansl's study is ground-breaking because it attempts to explain lag structure. In a later study (Krumhansl 1998), she applied a similar approach by modelling one-dimensional emotional response in terms of dichotomized musical topics. The model fit was $R_{14\ 767} = 0.52$, but again no consideration of modelling serial correlation was mentioned.

Schubert (1998, 1999a; Schubert & Dunsmuir 1999) examined stimulus time-series features including tempo, melodic pitch, and loudness, *and* response time-series dimensions of valence and arousal. His approach was to produce a univariate, linear regression analysis, where each emotional dimension was described in terms of a linear combination of the musical features. The traditional least squares approach was not satisfactory because the assumption of independence was violated. Instead, Schubert used a three-step procedure: (1) differencing all variables; (2) lagging the musical feature variables; and (3) making an autoregressive adjustment (Box & Jenkins 1976; Gottman 1981; Ostrom 1990) to model the remaining serial correlation.

Differencing variables provided a meaningful transformation (it meant 'change in response', denoted by the Greek capital delta symbol, '$\Delta$') and at the same time removed a large amount of serial correlation (see Gottman 1981). In other words, relative values of variables rather than absolute values were modelled. Lagging the variables (by 1, 2, 3, and 4 seconds) enabled the examination of the dynamic lag structure in the M→E system and satisfied the assertion that emotional response is causally affected by musical features. The remaining serial correlation component was modelled using the technique of autoregressive adjustment (Ostrom 1990). Autoregressive adjustment could be described as the addition to the mathematical model that acted as a kind of 'memory', adding a proportion of the linear-system-produced error of the previous point in time. The difference-lag-autoregressive adjusted regression model produced a series of satisfactory models, explaining up to 73 per cent of the variation in response for arousal, and up to 62 per cent of the variation in response for valence in terms of a selection of musical features alone.

The approach taken by Schubert provides researchers with a relatively simple and valid analytical technique for modelling time-series data. However, this approach will not work in all cases. Schubert assumed that the time series investigated were only first-order autoregressive (Gottman 1981; Ostrom 1990). More research is required to determine whether time-series processes in the M→E system may contain higher-order autoregressive processes, or indeed other processes altogether, heading, for example, toward the more sophisticated ARIMA (Autoregressive Integrated Moving Average) models proposed by Box and Jenkins (1976). The possibility of analysing the data in the frequency domain (Gottman 1981) or using other techniques such as neural network models (Todd & Loy 1991) and dynamic system models (Abraham *et al.* 1990) also await investigation in modelling self-report continuous emotional response data (see also Beran & Mazzola 1999).

## 17.5 Concluding remarks and future directions

The literature on self-report continuous response methodology to understand emotion in music has been growing considerably since the pioneering days of Hevner (1936) and, particularly, since Nielsen (1983). The methodology enables researchers to better understand the moment-to-moment fluctuations in emotional response caused by the musical stimulus within an ecologically valid framework (because the listener is usually listening to an uncontrolled, real piece of music rather than an excerpt or contrived auditory stimulus). This methodology has been used to find convergent evidence with traditional asynchronous approaches regarding, for example, the influence of musical features upon emotional response. However, its main advantages are yet to be fully exploited. In particular, continuous response methodology allows researchers to examine the relationship between moment-to-moment fluctuations in music and response as well as the lag structure of response—that is, how quickly people respond after a change in musical structure, or how quickly they respond in comparison to other people listening to the same music.

Important, major issues which remain unresolved are which dimensions of emotional response should be recorded, the dynamic nature of the M→E system, and which analytical techniques to use. Using two dimensions appears to be a reasonable compromise between a meaningful emotional response and cognitive overload. One such combination of emotion dimensions is *valence* (happy–sad) and *arousal* (aroused–sleepy), although the optimal solution is yet to be determined.

A relatively less important issue in continuous response methodology is the genre of musical stimulus to use. Selections have largely been based on the music of romantic

Western art music idioms (I include Holst's band music in these idioms). While it would be interesting to examine different styles, such as contemporary, pre nineteenth century, and popular styles, it is also sensible for the time-being to restrict the number of styles investigated, given that continuous response methodologies are still being established and are already associated with a potentially large number of complex, interacting variables. Restricting stimuli to the romantic music idioms is logical because these are idioms that are defined by the importance of expressing emotion (e.g. Gorbman 1987).

Continuous self-report measures have arisen from a need to provide greater ecological validity in emotion-in-music investigations and through technological developments that have made such an approach to research feasible. However, researchers using this methodology need to remain cognisant as to why they are using the technology. It seems that experimental music psychologists have required a period of exploration and discovery to more fully realize the potential of continuous response measures.

In conclusion, continuous response researchers need to become more aware of the analytical problems created by serial correlation, an inherent part of much time-series data. There are simple, effective solutions available for dealing with the problem, such as differencing, autoregressive adjustment, and other techniques associated with regression-type analysis. It is vital that researchers are willing to apply these methods and other non-parametric techniques to maximize the benefits of continuous research methodology, and in particular to exploit its capacity to provide a basis for understanding the still elusive dynamic nature of emotion in music.

## References

Abraham, F. D., Abraham, R. H., Shaw, C. D., & Garpike, A. (1990). *A visual introduction to dynamical systems theory for psychology*. Santa Cruz, CA: Aerial.

Adams, B. L. (1994). *The effect of visual/aural conditions on the emotional response to music*. Unpublished doctoral dissertation, Florida State University, Tallahassee.

Anastasi, A. (1987). *Psychological testing*, (4th edn). New York: Macmillan.

Asmus, E. P. (1985). The development of a multidimensional instrument for the measurement of affective responses to music. *Psychology of Music, 13*, 19–30.

Beran, J. & Mazzola, G. (1999). Analysing musical structure and performance: A statistical approach. *Statistical Science, 14*, 47–79.

Berlyne, D. E. (1973). Interrelations of verbal and nonverbal measures used in experimental aesthetics. *Scandinavian Journal of Psychology, 14*, 177–84.

Box, G. E. P. & Jenkins, G. M. (1976). *Time series analysis: Forecasting and control*, (rev. edn). San Francisco: Holden-Day.

Brittin, R. V. (1991). The effect of overtly categorizing music on preference for popular music styles. *Journal of Research in Music Education, 39*, 143–51.

Brittin, R. V. & Duke, R. A. (1997). Continuous versus summative evaluations of musical intensity: A comparison of two methods for measuring overall effect. *Journal of Research in Music Education, 45*, 245–58.

Byrnes, S. R. (1996). The effect of audio, video, and paired audio-video stimuli on the experience of stress. *Journal of Music Therapy, 33*, 248–60.

Cabrera, D. (1997). *Db&dba&centr.orc* (Computer software). Sydney, Australia.

Cabrera, D. (1998). *PsySound* (Computer software). Sydney, Australia.

Capparella-Sheldon, D. A. (1992). Self-perception of aesthetic experience among musicians and non-musicians in response to wind band music. *Journal of Band Research,* **28**, 57–71.

Clynes, M. (1977). *Sentics: The touch of emotions.* New York: Anchor Press/Doubleday.

Clynes, M. (1980). The communication of emotion: Theory of sentics. In *Emotion: Theory research and experience,* (Vol. 1) (ed. R. Plutchik & H. Kellerman), pp. 271–300. New York: Academic Press.

Clynes, M. & Nettheim, N. (1982). The living quality of music: Neurobiologic basis of communicating feeling. In *Music, mind, and brain: The neuropsychology of music,* (ed. M. Clynes), pp. 47–82. New York: Plenum Press.

Collier, G. L. (1996). Affective synesthesia: Extracting emotion space from simple perceptual stimuli. *Motivation and Emotion,* **20**, 1–32.

Collins, S. C. (1989). *Subjective and autonomic responses to western classical music.* Unpublished doctoral dissertation, University of Manchester, Manchester, UK.

Damos, D. (1992). *Multiple task performance.* London: Taylor Francis.

De Vries, B. (1991). Assessment of the affective response to music with Clynes's sentograph. *Psychology of Music,* **19**, 46–64.

Flowers, P. J. (1983). The effect of instruction in vocabulary and listening on nonmusicians' descriptions of changes in music. *Journal of Research in Music Education,* **31**, 179–89.

Fredrickson, W. E. (1995). A comparison of perceived musical tension and aesthetic response. *Psychology of Music,* **23**, 81–7.

Fredrickson, W. E. (1997). Elementary, middle, and high school perceptions of tension in music. *Journal of Research in Music Education,* **45**, 626–35.

Fredrickson, W. E. (1999). Effect of musical performance on perception of tension in Gustav Holt's First Suite in E-flat. *Journal of Research in Music Education,* **47**, 44–52.

Frego, R. J. D. (1999). Effects of aural and visual conditions on response to perceived artisitic tension in music and dance. *Journal of Research in Music Education,* **47**, 31–43.

Gabrielsson, A. & Juslin, P. N. (in press). Emotional expression in music. In *Handbook of affective sciences,* (ed. R. J. Davidson, H. H. Goldsmith, & K. R. Scherer). New York: Oxford University Press.

Gabrielsson, A. & Lindström, E. (1995). Emotional expression in synthesizer and and sentograph performance. *Psychomusicology,* **14**, 94–116.

Geringer, J. M. (1995). Continuous loudness judgments of dynamics in recorded music excerpts. *Journal of Research in Music Education,* **43**, 22–35.

Goins, W. E. (1998). The effect of moodstates: Continuous versus summative responses. *Journal of Music Therapy,* **35**, 242–58.

Goldstein, A. (1980). Thrills in response to music and other stimuli. *Physiological Psychology,* **8**, 126–9.

Gorbman, C. (1987). *Unheard melodies: Narrative film music.* Bloomington, IN: Indiana University Press.

Gottman, J. M. (1981). *Time-series analysis: A comprehensive introduction for social scientists.* Cambridge, UK: Cambridge University Press.

Greene, B. A. & Royer, J. M. (1994). A developmental review of response time data that support a cognitive components model of reading. *Educational Psychology Review,* **6**, 141–72.

Gregory, A. H. (1998). Tracking the emotional response to operatic arias. In *Proceedings of the Fifth International Conference of Music Perception and Cognition*, (ed. S. W. Yi), pp. 265–70. Seoul, Korea: Western Music Research Institute, College of Music, Seoul National University.

Gregory, D. (1992). Comparisons of zone delineations, sampling rates, and graphic options of the continuous response digital interface. Paper presented at the Music Educators National Conference, New Orleans, LA.

Gregory, D. (1995). The continuous response digital interface: An analysis of reliability measure. *Psychomusicology*, 14, 197–208.

Gregory, D. (1998). Reactions to ballet with wheelchairs: Reflections of attitudes toward people with disabilities. *Journal of Music Therapy*, 35, 274–83.

Hair, H. I. (1995). Mood categories of lines, colors, words, and music. *Bulletin of the Council for Research In Music Education*, 127, 99–105.

Hall, D. E. (1987). *Basic acoustics*. New York: Wiley.

Hamilton, J. D. (1994). *Time series analysis*. Princeton, NJ: Princeton University Press.

Hargreaves, D. J. (1986). *The developmental psychology of music*. Cambridge, UK: Cambridge University Press.

Hevner, K. (1936). Experimental studies of the elements of expression in music. *American Journal of Psychology*, 48, 246–68.

Howell, D. C. (1997). *Statistical methods for psychology*, (4th edn). Belmont, CA: Duxbury.

Johnson, C. M. (1996). Musicians' and nonmusicians' assessment of perceived rubato in musical performance. *Journal of Research in Music Education*, 44, 84–96.

Krumhansl, C. L. (1996). A perceptual analysis of Mozart's Piano Sonata K.282—Segmentation, tension, and musical ideas. *Music Perception*, 13, 401–32.

Krumhansl, C. L. (1997). An exploratory study of musical emotions and physiology. *Canadian Journal of Experimental Psychology*, 51, 336–52.

Krumhansl, C. L. (1998). Topic in music: An empirical study of memorability, openness, and emotion in Mozart's String Quintet in C Major and Beethoven's String Quartet in A Minor. *Music Perception*, 16, 119–34.

Krumhansl, C. L. & Schenck, D. L. (1997). Can dance reflect the structural and expressive qualities of music? A perceptual experiment on Balanchines's choreography of Mozart's divertiment No. 15. *Musicae Scientiae*, 1, 63–85.

Lerdahl, F. & Jackendoff, R. (1983). *A generative theory of tonal music*. Boston: MIT Press.

Lipscomb, S. D. (1996). The cognitive organization of musical sound. In *Handbook of music psychology*, (ed. D. A. Hodges), pp. 133–75. San Antonio, TX: IMR Press.

Lychner, J. (1998). An empirical study concerning terminology relating to aesthetic response to music. *Journal of Research in Music Education*, 46, 303–20.

Madsen, C. K. (1996). Empirical investigation of the 'aesthetic response' to music: Musicians and non-musicians. In *Proceedings of the Fourth International Conference of Music Perception and Cognition*, (ed. B. Pennycook & E. Costa-Giomi), pp. 103–10. Montreal, Canada: McGill University.

Madsen, C. K. (1997). Emotional response to music as measured by the two-dimensional CRDI. *Journal of Music Therapy*, 34, 187–99.

Madsen, C. K. (1998). Emotion versus tension in Haydn's symphony No. 104 as measured by the two-dimensional continuous response digital interface. *Journal of Research in Music Education*, 46, 546–54.

Madsen, C. K., Brittin, R. V., & Capperella-Sheldon, D. A. (1993). An empirical investigation of the aesthetic response to music. *Journal of Research in Music Education*, **41**, 57–69.

Madsen, C. K., Byrnes, S. R., Capperella-Sheldon, D. A., & Brittin, R. V. (1993). Aesthetic responses to music: Musicians vs. nonmusicians. *Journal of Music Therapy*, **30**, 174–91.

Madsen, C. K. & Fredrickson, W. E. (1993). The experience of musical tension: A replication of Nielsen's research using the continuous response digital interface. *Journal of Music Therapy*, **30**, 46–63.

Moore, B. C. J., Glasberg, B. P., & Baer, T. (1997). A model for the prediction of thresholds, loudness, and partial loudness. *Journal of the Audio Engineering Society*, **45**, 224–40.

Mulder, S. J. (1997). *The identification of the emotional content in choral music: A descriptive study using the two-dimensional continuous response digital interface (2D CRDI)*. Unpublished doctoral dissertation, Florida State University, Tallahassee.

Mull, H. (1949). A study of humor in music. *American Journal of Psychology*, **62**, 560–6.

Namba, S., Kuwano, S., Hatoh, T., & Kato, M. (1991). Assessment of musical performance by using the method of continuous judgement by selected description. *Music Perception*, **8**, 251–76.

Narmour, E. (1990). *The analysis and cognition of basic melodic structures*. Chicago: University of Chicago Press.

Nielsen, F. V. (1983). *Oplevelse af musikalsk spænding [The experience of musical tension]*. Copenhagen: Akademisk Forlag.

Nielsen, F. V. (1987). Musical tension and related concepts. In *The semiotic web '86. An international year-book*, (ed. T. A. Sebeok & J. Umiker-Seboek), pp. 491–513. Berlin: Mouton de Gruyter.

Osgood, C. E., Suci, G. J., & Tannenbaum, P. H. (1957). *The measurement of meaning*. Urbana, IL: University of Illinois Press.

Ostrom, C. W. (1990). *Time series analysis regression techniques*. Newbury Park, CA: Sage Publications.

Panksepp, J. (1995). The emotional sources of 'chills' induced by music. *Music Perception*, **13**, 171–208.

Pohlmann, K. C. (1995). *Principles of digital audio*, (3rd edn). New York: McGraw Hill.

Radocy, R. E. & Boyle, J. D. (1988). *Psychological foundations of musical behavior. Psychological foundations of musical behaviour*, (2nd edn). Springfield, IL: Charles C. Thomas.

Ratner, L. G. (1980). *Classic music: Expression, form and style*. New York: Schirmer.

Robinson, C. R. (1988). *Differentiated modes of choral performance evaluation using traditional procedures and a continuous response digital interface device*. Unpublished doctoral disseration, Florida State University, Tallahassee.

Rossing, T. D. (1990). *The science of music*, (2nd edn). Reading, MA: Addison-Wesley.

Russell, J. A. (1980). A circumplex model of affect. *Journal of Social Psychology*, **39**, 1161–78.

Russell, J. A. (1989). Measures of emotion. In *Emotion: Theory, research, and experience. Vol. 4. The measurement of emotion*, (ed. R. Plutchik & H. Kellerman), pp. 81–111. New York: Academic Press.

Schmidt, C. P. (1996). Research with the continuous response digital interface: A review with implications for future research. *Philosophy of Music Education Review*, **4**, 20–32.

Schubert, E. (1996). Continuous response to music using a two dimensional emotion space. In *Proceedings of the Fourth International Conference of Music Perception and Cognition*, (ed. B. Pennycook & E. Costa-Giomi), pp. 263–8. Montreal, Canada: McGill University.

Schubert, E. (1998). Time series analysis of emotion in music. In *Proceedings of the Fifth International Conference of Music Perception and Cognition*, (ed. S. W. Yi), pp. 257–63. Seoul, Korea: Western Music Research Institute, College of Music, Seoul National University.

Schubert, E. (1999*a*). *Measurement and time series analysis of emotion in music.* Unpublished doctoral dissertation, University of New South Wales, Sydney.

Schubert, E. (1999*b*). Measuring emotion continuously: Validity and reliability of the two dimensional emotion space. *Australian Journal of Psychology*, **51**, 154–65.

Schubert, E. (2000). Unresolved issues in continuous response methodology: The case of time series correlations. In *Proceedings of the Sixth International Conference of Music Perception and Cognition*, (CD rom) (ed. C. Woods, G. Luck, R. Brochard, F. Seddon, & J. A. Sloboda). Keele, UK: Keele University.

Schubert, E. & Dunsmuir, W. (1999). Regression modelling continuous data in music psychology. In *Music, mind, and science*, (ed. S. W. Yi), pp. 298–352. Seoul, Korea: Western Music Research Institute, College of Music, Seoul National University.

Sloboda, J. A. (1991). Music structure and emotional response: Some empirical findings. *Psychology of Music*, **19**, 110–20.

Sloboda, J. A. (1992). Empirical studies of emotional response to music. In *Cognitive bases of musical communication*, (ed. M. R. Jones & S. Holleran), pp. 33–46. Washington, DC: American Psychological Association.

Sloboda, J. A., Lehmann, A. C., & Parncutt, R. (1997). Perceiving intended emotion in concert-standard performances of Chopin's Prelude No. 4 in E-minor. In *Proceedings of the Third Triennial ESCOM Conference*, (ed. A. Gabrielsson), pp. 629–34. Uppsala, Sweden: Department of Psychology, Uppsala University.

Sudderth, J. (1995). *CoreCD (version 1.4)* (Computer software). Core Development Group, Inc.

Todd, P. M. & Loy, G. D. (ed.) (1991). *Music and connectionsim.* Cambridge, MA: MIT Press.

Tyler, P. (1996). *Developing a two-dimensional continuous response space for emotions perceived in music.* Unpublished doctoral dissertation, Florida State University, Tallahassee.

Waterman, M. (1996). Emotional responses to music: Implicit and explicit effects in listeners and performers. *Psychology of Music*, **24**, 53–67.

Watson, K. B. (1942). The nature and measurement of musical meanings. *Psychological Monographs*, **54**, 1–43.

Wedin, L. (1972). Evaluation of a three-dimensional model of emotional expression in music. *Reports from the Psychological Laboratories, University of Stockholm*, **349**, 20.

Weld, H. P. (1912). An experimental study of musical enjoyment. *American Journal of Psychology*, **23**, 245–308.

Whissell, C. M., Fournier, M., Pelland, R., Weir, D., & Makarec, K. (1986). A dictionary of affect in language: IV. Reliability, validity, and applications. *Perceptual and Motor Skills*, **62**, 875–88.

# CHAPTER 18

# EMOTIONS IN EVERYDAY LISTENING TO MUSIC

JOHN A. SLOBODA AND SUSAN A. O'NEILL

There are several key assumptions underpinning our focus on emotion and 'everyday' music listening. Firstly, music is always heard in a social context, in a particular place and time, with or without other individuals being present, and with other activities taking place which have their own complex sources of meaning and emotion. The emotional response to the music is coloured, and possibly sometimes completely determined, by these contextual factors. Emotions should not be thought of as abstract entities such as 'anger' or 'elation', but rather as actual moments of emotional feelings and displays in particular situations within a particular culture. Emotional responses to music are linked to a sequence of events based on conventions and rules that depend not only on shared understanding and representations, but also a common background of knowledge and beliefs. Music is a cultural material (as is language) that provides a kind of semiotic and affective 'power' which individuals use in the social construction of emotional feeling and displays. As such, the impact of music on emotion is not direct but interdependent on the situations in which it is heard. Any meaningful account of music's role in the emotional response of individuals must involve the recognition of these complex, interdependent social factors. We therefore focus in this chapter on several investigations which attempt to preserve, or take account of, as much of the social context of music listening as possible.

Secondly, music is ubiquitous in contemporary life. The prevailing contexts in which we encounter music are, by definition, mundane. They include those contexts in which the most routine activities of life take place: waking up, washing and dressing, eating, cleaning, shopping, travelling. There are, of course, special and 'out of the ordinary' events which music can form a part of, even a crucial and defining part, but we would argue that in order to understand fully these special events and their emotional significance, we must consider them in relation to everyday experience. It is the everyday and normal which frames and helps define the special. This chapter focuses, therefore, on habitual and routine modes of engagement with music.

Thirdly, despite the growing recognition that our experience of emotion is inextricably linked to the social world and the linguistic practices used to make sense of that world, we tend to think of our emotions as personal, 'private' experiences, especially if they do not involve 'public' emotional displays. For example, when we feel angry, we might experience our anger as a private emotion which may or may not be 'acted out' in the things we do or say. However, this is not the case in all cultures. Lutz (1982) describes the way in which the Ifaluk (Samoan and Pintupi Aborigines) use emotion words to describe their relationship to events and other people, and not as expressions of private, internal states. The closest translation of anger in the Ifaluk language is the word 'song' which means 'justifiable anger'. It is not considered a privately owned feeling but rather a moral and public account of some transgression of accepted social practices and values (cf. Burr 1995). As such, emotional feelings and displays are not considered to represent internal states of an individual (whether innate or acquired through learning and experience) that result in physiological reactions to environmental stimuli. Rather, they are meaningful displays that are taken as emotional when they are embodied expressions of judgments, and in many cases, ways of accomplishing certain social acts (Harré & Gillett 1994). Our focus in this chapter is on research which attempts to understand, at least in part, the inextricable connection between individual 'personal' emotional experience and the 'social' forms of meaning associated with music listening.

Our perspective makes it necessary to exclude any significant treatment of three types of phenomenon. The first exclusion relates to the extremely intense, sometimes transcendent, experiences to music which people characterize as defining or life-changing (e.g. Gabrielsson & Lindström 1995; see also Gabrielsson, this volume). These events rarely occur in the lives of individuals, and so are difficult to study empirically. One retrospective study by Sloboda (1989a), which we will discuss in more detail in a later section, provides suggestive evidence that these 'peak' events can occur in childhood, and, when they do, can have a profound influence on a person's attitudes towards, and commitment to, music. Indeed, people who devote their lives to music often include such experiences in the stories of their developing commitment (e.g. Brodsky 1995). This, then, brings us to the second exclusion of our chapter. We shall not be examining the everyday emotional world of the professional musician or the intending professional musician (i.e. the music student). The emotional experiences of these groups are covered in other chapters in this book (Persson, this volume), and we would wish to claim that the everyday contexts in which musicians experience music are so different from those of non-musicians (who form the vast bulk of the population of industrialized nations) that they require separate treatment. Finally, we do not intend to provide a comprehensive review of the literature associated with emotional response to everyday music listening. Much of this literature is covered elsewhere in this book (DeNora, this volume; Becker, this volume; Gabrielsson, this volume). In many cases, previous research in this area include laboratory studies or semiquasi experimental research, which have quite specific social features that make it unlike many other music-listening situations. Rather, our aim is to highlight a number of key features of research in this area which are based on the assumptions outlined above, using examples from several studies, many of which we have been involved in ourselves. In this way, we hope to address important questions that are left unanswered by laboratory research, stimulate further discussion and debate on the topic, as well as indicate some directions for future research.

## 18.1 Capturing everyday experience

One of the problems with studying everyday experience is that it happens outside the laboratory in a wide variety of settings. Although an investigator may make observations (or even attempt to experimentally manipulate) musical engagement in a single setting, it is difficult to observe directly the entire range of settings in which music might be experienced, even in the course of a single day. A second problem is that the everyday is, by definition, unmemorable, and so retrospective studies (such as interviews) may not capture the richness and diversity of musical experience. The more mundane occurrences are simply forgotten or filtered out. Understanding how music interacts with everyday contexts requires a method that not only examines the phenomenon in 'real-world' situations or events, but that does so as the events are unfolding and are experienced by individuals in the course of their daily lives. For these reasons, we (Sloboda *et al.*, 2001) recently conducted a pilot study with eight individuals where we adapted a method developed by Csikszentmihalyi and Lefevre (1989) which enables everyday experiences to be studied in some detail. Our aim in presenting this research is not to make generalizable claims about the frequency of musical occurrences in everyday life. Rather, our aim is to illustrate, through this exploratory research, a method in which we might begin to capture individual subjective experience of emotion concurrent with everyday activities where music is heard, and highlight the heuristic features of the findings in order to inform future theoretical development and research.

The method we employed in our study is known as the experience sampling method (ESM). It involves participants carrying electronic pagers with them at all times during their waking hours. The pagers are connected to a computer that is programmed to call participants at preprogrammed intervals. In our study, participants were paged once in each 2–hour period between 0800 and 2200. The precise timing of a call within each 2–hour block was determined randomly. On each paging, participants were asked to stop what they were doing as soon as practicable and complete one page of a response booklet, which they were also asked to carry with them at all times. The booklet asked questions regarding the most recent experience of music listening since the previous paging. If there had been no music experienced in that period, participants completed the booklet with respect to the activity taking place when the pager sounded.

The eight participants in our study were all adult non-musicians between the ages of 18 and 40 years who were either studying or working at our institution (half of the participants were not involved in psychology). They each carried a pager with them for a 1–week period. Analyses of the data collected provided some quite revealing information about their everyday music use. First, 91 per cent of pagings resulted in a page of the booklet being filled in (we call each event described in the response booklet an 'episode'). This suggested a high level of compliance and involvement in this task over an extended period of time. It also meant that the method provided an almost complete picture of the musical and non-musical experiences of each participant over a normal week (none of the participants reported the week in question being unusual or atypical). The 9 per cent of pagings which did not result in a report sheet being recorded were primarily due to technical problems, participants not having the pager with them at the time (e.g. during swimming or showering), or participants not hearing the pager's signal (e.g. due to travelling or being in a very noisy location).

A second major finding was that 44 per cent of all episodes involved music. In other words, there was a 44 per cent likelihood of music being experienced in any 2–hour period. It has repeatedly been claimed that music pervades everyday life. Our data confirm this and provide a specific estimate of its frequency.

Participants were asked to respond in their own words to the question: 'what was the *main* thing you were doing?' Reported activities were coded *post hoc* according to three main categories: personal, leisure, and work. Personal activities cover those everyday activities that are a necessary consequence of living, and were further divided into states of being (e.g. sleeping, waking up, being ill, suffering from a hangover), maintenance activities (e.g. washing, getting dressed, cooking, eating at home, housework, shopping), and travel (e.g. leaving home, driving, walking, going home). Leisure activities were divided into three subcategories: music listening (there were no examples of performing music), leisure-passive (e.g. watching TV/film, putting on the radio, relaxing, reading for pleasure), and leisure-active (e.g. games, sports, socializing, eating out, chatting with friends). Work activities were categorized according to whether they were primarily solitary activities (e.g. writing, computing, marking/assessing, reading for study) or primarily group-based activities (e.g. planning for a meeting, in a lecture/seminar, making appointments, in a meeting).

It is particularly significant that listening to music as a main activity accounted for only a small percentage of all episodes (2 per cent). This suggests that the concentrated, attentive, focusing on music that is paradigmatic of the classical concert or the laboratory experiment is a rather untypical activity for most listeners. Instead participants were distributing their attention across a complex situation of which music is only a part. In fact, there were three categories of activity which seemed particularly likely to involve music. These were the personal maintenance, personal travel, and active leisure categories.

Emotional reactions to the music were measured by asking participants to rate their state on eleven bipolar scales (e.g. happy–sad, irritable–generous, bored–interested) with respect to how they felt before the music started and how they felt after it had ended. We found that these scales grouped under three main factors. The first factor related to the degree of positivity or negativity, the second factor to the degree of arousal or alertness, and the third factor to the extent to which participants' attention was focused on the present situation or elsewhere (e.g. reminiscing, daydreaming, nostalgic). These factors have characteristics in common with previous research done on emotional response to music (see Sloboda & Juslin, this volume).

We found that, on average, the experience of music resulted in participants becoming more positive, more alert, and more focused in the present. Insofar as such emotional transitions are desired and beneficial, it could be concluded that in general music made these participants 'feel better'. An examination of the number of episodes resulting in change for each of the factors indicated that where there was change, arousal rarely moved in the direction of lower arousal (7 per cent of changes), and little more so in the direction of less positivity (13 per cent). However, present-mindedness showed 35 per cent of change episodes involving moves away from the 'positive pole'. It seems, in other words, as though emotional states arising from a focus on 'things and people not present', such as nostalgia, are a particularly important subcategory within everyday responses to music.

## 18.2  Functional niches within daily life

Our working assumption has been that music has different emotional functions in different contexts (cf. Merriam 1964). In our ESM study we were, therefore, interested to see whether there were any cases in which mood change factors were dissociated from one another (i.e. cases where one mood increased simultaneously with another mood decreasing). Inspection of cases showed that 16 per cent of music episodes were in this category. These cases are particularly important in beginning to identify distinct functional niches for music engagement. The largest group of such episodes ($n = 10$) involved increases in positivity along with decreases in present-mindedness.

One example of this comes from a male participant who reported being at home relaxing with a group of friends and acquaintances. The activity was being done out of choice. There was ambient music playing on a CD, although the participant had not chosen it. The participant commented that 'the music was very tranquil and relaxing', that others present were 'discussing work boringly', and that he was 'very, very tired'. This episode was also associated with a decrease in arousal during the music. It would be reasonable to assume that the participant was using the music as a means of relaxing and disengaging from the surrounding conversation.

A second example from the same category is provided by a female participant who reported being at home, tidying a bedroom as part of the normal basic routine. The participant had chosen to listen to a piece of pop/chart music on a tape. The participant commented that the music was chosen to 'enhance the wonderful experience of cleaning' and was 'very lively'. This episode was associated with an increase in arousal during the music. It seems as if the purpose of this music was to allow the participant to focus attention on the music, and away from the uninteresting domestic chore, and this focused attention was used to increase energy levels.

It was less easy to find examples of episodes where positivity decreased, but one clear episode involved a female participant at home, alone, doing the washing up as part of a basic routine. She had chosen to listen to rock music on the radio and commented that the track was 'a favourite song I had not heard for some time . . . It brought back certain memories'. The music increased this participant's nostalgia, sadness, and loneliness, at the same time as making her more alert. It is clear that this episode reminded the participant of a significant past event which brought on nostalgia. At the same time, it appears that she had chosen the music to engage and arouse during an uninteresting routine task.

In a separate study, using a stratified sample of 76 panel members from the Sussex Mass Observation Archive (Sloboda 1999; see also Sheridan, 2000), respondents were asked to write, in open-ended fashion, about the uses they made of music in their everyday lives. Table 18.1 shows the activities and functions spontaneously mentioned by members of the sample. The most frequently mentioned activities were housework and travel. This mirrored quite closely the distribution found in the ESM study. Functions mentioned were varied but had a predominantly affective character, with many participants (particularly women) explicitly mentioning music as a mood changer or enhancer. The most frequently mentioned function was essentially nostalgic. Participants found it natural to link functions to activities, often mentioning both in the same sentence (e.g. on arrival home from work 'music lifts the stress of work: it has an immediate healing effect').

**Table 18.1** Percentage of mass observation respondents reporting various functions and activities chosen for music

| Activities | |
|---|---|
| To wake up to | 6 |
| While having a bath | 4 |
| Whilst exercising | 4 |
| To sing along to | 6 |
| To work to (desk work) | 14 |
| To work to (housework) | 22 |
| On arrival home from work | 2 |
| Whilst having a meal | 12 |
| Background while socializing | 4 |
| To accompany sexual/romantic events | 4 |
| Whilst reading | 6 |
| In bed/to get to sleep | 14 |
| While driving/running/cycling | 22 |
| While on public transport (Walkman) | 4 |
| | |
| *Functions* | |
| Reminder of valued past event | 50 |
| Spiritual experience | 6 |
| Evokes visual images | 2 |
| Tingles/goose pimples/shivers | 10 |
| Source of pleasure/enjoyment | 6 |
| To put in a good mood | 16 |
| Moves to tears/catharsis/release | 14 |
| Excites | 2 |
| Motivates | 2 |
| Source of comfort/healing | 4 |
| Calms/soothes/relaxes/relieves stress | 8 |
| Mood enhancement | 8 |
| To match current mood | 6 |

In an interview study involving 52 women ranging in age from 18 to 78 years, most of whom were not accomplished musicians, DeNora (1999) also found examples of emotional self-regulation involving a number of musical strategies described by participants as 'revving up' or 'calming down', 'getting in the mood' (e.g. for a particular social event), 'getting out of a mood' (e.g. to improve a 'bad' mood or to 'destress'), or 'venting' strong emotions. For the most part, as in the two previously mentioned studies, these were predominantly described at the 'personal' or intrapersonal level as a means of creating, enhancing, sustaining, and changing subjective, cognitive, bodily, and self-conceptual states. According to DeNora, the women exhibited considerable awareness of the music they 'needed' to hear in different situations and at different times, often working as 'disc jockeys' to themselves:

They drew upon elaborate repertoires of musical programming practice, and a sharp awareness of how to mobilize music to arrive at, enhance, and alter aspects of themselves and their self-concepts. This practical knowledge should be viewed as part of the (often tacit) practices in and through which respondents produced themselves as coherent social and socially disciplined beings (DeNora 1999, p. 35; see also DeNora, this volume).

In addition to the emotional functions at the intrapersonal level, DeNora found examples in which music played a social function in communicating emotions to others. For example, a university student described repeatedly playing at full volume a song from Radiohead entitled 'We Hope You Choke!' not only as way of diffusing her anger against her boyfriend's parents when she lived with them over the summer holidays, but also as a way of communicating her anger to them. In other words, the display of anger or irritation described by the respondent expressed a judgment of the moral quality of some other person's actions. Such a display was also an act of protest directed towards the boyfriend's parents. Music provided one means by which this display was 'acted out' at an interpersonal level. However, as DeNora points out, music is not simply used to express some internal, private feeling or state, nor does it simply 'act upon' individuals, like a stimulus. 'It is a resource for the identification work of 'knowing how one feels"—a building material of 'subjectivity"' (DeNora 1999, p. 41). In this way, music becomes part of the construction of the emotion itself through the way in which individuals orientate to it, interpret it, and use it to elaborate, 'fill in', or 'fill out', to themselves and others, an emotional feeling or display.

## 18.3 Autonomy and individuality

One of the questions in Sloboda, O'Neill, and Ivaldi's ESM study asked participants to rate the music in each episode on an 11-point scale according to the degree of personal choice exercised in hearing the music (from 0 = *none at all*, to 10 = *completely own choice*). There was a significant effect of degree of choice on the degree of emotional change experienced while listening to the music. For each emotion factor this showed a similar effect—the greater the choice the greater the change. We found that high choice situations were most likely to occur when the person was alone, travelling, or working, at home or in a vehicle, or undertaking activities for duty. Low choice situations occurred more often when with others, during active leisure or personal maintenance activities, in shops, gyms, and entertainment venues, and when doing activities because one wants to. Most of these findings are not surprising, although the link between choice and activities undertaken for duty is not intuitively obvious. It may be that choosing music to accompany duties is a way of bringing some autonomy and personalization back to them. DeNora (1999) suggests that the music associated with duties is used as a catalyst to shift individuals out of their reluctance to adopt what they perceive as 'necessary' modes of agency, and into modes of agency 'demanded' by particular circumstances.

The issue of choice and individuality also permeated the responses of the mass observation panel (Sloboda 1999). Many of the musical situations described were solitary, and some participants graphically characterized a difference between the private arena, where emotional work of one sort or another could be accomplished with the help of music, and the public arena, where self-presentation or the conflicting demands of others precluded this kind of activity. One respondent wrote: 'When I'm down I listen to this [a specific track] and go down as far as I can, then I cry, I cry deep from inside. I wallow in self-pity and purge all the gloom from my body. Then I dry my eyes, and wash my face, do my hair, put on fresh makeup, and rejoin the world'. Another reported 'the car is the only place where I can listen to it loud enough without annoying other people'.

Many participants displayed negative, or at best, ambivalent reactions to the music that they experienced in public places, such as shops, restaurants, and bars. These attitudes were sometimes associated with reports of dramatic behavioural consequences with high emotional charge (e.g. abruptly leaving a shop with disliked music, arguing with waiting staff in a restaurant about getting the music turned off). In several responses, the appropriateness of the music was a major theme. Judgments were made both about the situation itself, and about the fit between the music and the person's own identity and preferences. For example, restaurant music could be acceptable so long as it matched the ambience or mood of the venue (e.g. oriental music in an oriental restaurant, 'mellow' music during a romantic encounter), or if its general acoustic characteristics matched the listeners' needs (e.g. not so loud that conversation was difficult, but loud enough to cover potentially embarrassing silences and to prevent people at nearby tables overhearing one's conversation). In other cases, although music in public places might be generally disliked, exceptions were made where the music itself had value for the participant (e.g. 'I have discovered Waterstones Bookshop in Newcastle plays good music: the last time I was there Beethoven's 'Egmont Overture' was playing, and the trouble is that I pay more attention to the music than to finding the book I want'). In this example, because the music was judged to be 'good', the participant was prepared to let his appreciation of the music partially override his main intention of buying a book. The issue of 'fit' between music and its context has been investigated experimentally. For instance, North and Hargreaves (2000) showed that people make consistent discriminatory judgments about the music that is suitable for such activities as aerobic exercise or yoga, and that specific characteristics of the music (e.g. tempo) are implicated in these judgments.

There is evidence that resistance to music in public places increases with age. DeNora (1999) found that most of her respondents over 70 years (and, interestingly, those who were trained musicians) found it antithetical to conceive of music as 'background' to anything. Data from the Sussex Mass Observation Archive also showed that males in the 40–60-year age group reported more negative emotional reactions to music in public places than any other group. It may be hypothesized that the higher average status a group has, the less tolerant it will be of removal of autonomy. However, there are also often more complex subcurrents to do with intergenerational and intergroup stereotypes. The following example reveals much about the attitudes of one middle-aged man to the public self-presentation of some younger men: 'I also dislike the din that some cars make when they pass by, infesting the streets with their thumping noises from within. How they can drive properly with such a din in their cars, God knows. It concerns me too that they wouldn't be able to hear the sound of an ambulance or police car with such a noise going on inside their cars. It seems to me, rather like the fastest drivers, it is usually young men between the age of 17 and 25 who are the main culprits. They usually like to have their driving-seat window open, elbow leaning out of the car and looking macho.' It appears as though young people are more tolerant of, and positive towards, music in public places. Further investigation is needed of these apparent age-related differences.

One phenomenon which deserves greater study and theorizing is the unique position of the busker (street musician) in the affections of even the most hardened opponents of music in public places. Many mass observation respondents spontaneously singled out buskers as evading the opprobrium of other forms of public music. It often was reported as relevant that this music is live rather than prerecorded. Two quotes are provided as representative: 'Both my husband and I have performed on the streets. My husband is still a regular busker. This to me is musical entertainment at its purest form. The joy of busking is its spontaneity. Your audience is free to come and go as it wishes, to pay or not pay, to listen or not listen. There is a beautiful freedom about busking that I love, and I hope we never lose street entertainment.' 'The music in the streets is acceptable. Quite often the musicians are quite good and anyway the noise is dispersed.' Arguably, street musicians do not undermine the sense of agency and autonomy that people like to experience. The musician is potentially amenable to interaction (you can request your favourite song, and audience reactions can be assumed to matter to the busker). There is also a sense of groundedness in a busker. The piped music in shops is produced by unknown people in unknown places, and mediated through hidden production mechanisms (e.g. an under-the-counter sound system), for hidden purposes (e.g. suspected manipulation of buying behaviour). The busker, by contrast, is earning an 'honest' living by aiming to please and entertain through the exercise of visible craft that is the result of personal effort and investment. It may also be significant that modern busking is probably the phenomenon which comes closest to meeting the conditions under which most people in most cultures through history have interacted with music. It is live, public, improvisational, spontaneous, participatory, and social. It creates a small arena of the communal in a pervading culture of individualism and isolation. It may meet an emotional need that is quite fundamental, but which there are few opportunities to indulge in.

## 18.4  Personal and social identity

In recent years, there has been a growing questioning of traditional approaches to the study of identity, which fail to take into account the multiple dimensions of identity as a continual process of negotiation and change. Discursive psychology, which views identity as constructed out of the discourses that are culturally available to us and that we use when communicating with others, has radically altered the way social psychologists conceptualize and study identity. Music provides numerous ways in which musical materials and practices can be used as a means for self-interpretation, self-presentation, and for the expression of emotional states associated with the self. According to DeNora (1999, p. 50), a sense of self is locatable in music, in that 'musical materials provide terms and templates for elaborating self-identity'. For example, one of the respondents in her study described a preferred type of musical material ('juicy chords') as like 'me in life', associating certain musical structures with her sense of self. DeNora (1999, p. 51) suggests that 'music is a "mirror" that allows one to "see one's self". It is, also, however, a "magic mirror" insofar as its specific material properties also come to configure (e.g. "transfigure", "disfigure", etc.) the image reflected in and through its (perceived) structures.'

Nowhere is this more apparent than during adolescence, where identities are being forged, experimented with, and explored. According to Green (1999), music can offer a powerful cultural symbol, which aids in adolescents' construction and presentation of self. Several studies suggest that musical tastes are predictive of a wide range of non-musical activities and attitudes, such as clothing, media preferences, drug use, and degree of sexual activity (Hanaken & Wells 1990; Lewis 1995).

Insofar as the processes involved with the formation and maintenance of adolescent identity are key to an individual's self-image and well-being (e.g. Shotter & Gergen 1989), then we would expect emotions to be deeply implicated in this process. Because most adolescents do not have jobs or family responsibilities they have more 'dis-cretionary' time than many adults do (estimated as up to 50 per cent of waking hours by Csikszentmihalyi and Larson 1984). Much of this time is taken up with media use, mainly TV and music. Eighty-one per cent of young people say that music is an important part of their life, and has influenced how they think about important issues (Leming 1987). This is in direct contrast to TV watching, which most adolescents do not believe has had any major influence on their lives (McCormack 1984). In an experience-sampling study of adolescent daily lives, Larson et al. (1989) found that music listening was associated with greater personal involvement than TV watching (which was asso-ciated with feeling less happy, less alert, more passive, and more bored than at other times). Larson and Kleiber (1993, p. 130) summarize their findings as suggesting that:

. . . the moving lyrics of ballads and the hard-driving beat of rock appear to stimulate a level of personal involvement that is lacking in TV watching. A teenager may be lying face-down on her bed, but her mind is alive and active, thinking about friends, school, or the future'.

In a recent study by North et al. (2000), marked gender differences were found in adolescents' reasons for listening to music. Girls were more likely to report that music could be used as a means of mood regulation, whereas boys reported that music could be a means of creating an external impression with others. It is perhaps not surprising that more girls than boys referred to emotionality in relation to music listening, given that 'masculine' identity tends to be associated with an ability to keep one's emotions out of one's reasoning. However, the boys' reason for listening to music was particularly interesting in that the majority of respondents reported that they usually listened to music on their own. Thus, the external impression the boys sought to accomplish did not necessarily involve direct social contact with others at the time they were actually listening to music. Rather, it appears as though adolescent boys, in particular, were actively involved in the construction of their identity through the use of stereotypes and gendered role models associated with the music they listened to (e.g. the 'macho' and 'sexy' image of male pop/rock musicians playing mainly guitars and drums). In other words, the cultural stereotypes, attitudes, and opinions associated with par-ticular styles of music appears to provide adolescent males with a vision of what it means to be 'trendy' or 'cool', which is 'acted out' or reinforced during their music listening experiences. O'Neill (1997) points out that adolescents' musical values are influenced by culturally defined stereotypes that, once learned, are extremely resistant to change and disconfirmation. In this way, musical associations or 'prevailing discourses' in a culture are both established and maintained through their use as a 'thread' out of which we might fashion or construct aspects of the self and the expression of emotional states associated with the self.

## 18.5  The balance between context and content

Emotional responses to music are a complex outcome of the contribution of a person's reaction to the content (i.e. the musical materials themselves and their associations) and their reactions to the social context in which the music is embedded. For instance, the context may determine the amount of attention available to place on the musical content (e.g. a parent out shopping with an irritable and loudly complaining small child and being embarrassed by the hostile looks of other shoppers may barely notice the 'soothing' Mozart playing quietly in the background). At the same time, the content may be subtly changing the way the person construes the context (e.g. the Mozart excerpt suggests the subliminal message that this is a 'high-class' store for serious, 'well-behaved' adults, and small noisy children have no place here—thus intensifying the feelings in the parent of embarrassment and shame). These effects have been studied experimentally by, for instance, manipulating music–film pairings or music–picture pairings and observing how construed emotional meaning is affected (Cohen, this volume).

However, everyday life does not provide opportunities for controlled manipulation of variables, and so it is difficult to disentangle the unique contribution of content and context. The work that comes the closest to providing an insight into these issues is a study by Sloboda (1989a) in which 70 individuals were asked to recall any incidents from the first 10 years of life that were in any way connected with music. This period was chosen because a major aim of the study was to find connections between early music experience and later attitudes to music. For each incident recalled, participants were asked to say as much as they could about the context (who they were with, what event the music formed part of), and what meaning or significance the event had for them. This allowed each incident to be assigned a value on each of two dimensions—an internal dimension, concerned with the musical content, and an external dimension concerned with the context. On each dimension the significance could be positive, neutral, or negative.

When the 113 incidents elicited were cross-tabulated on these two dimensions, some interesting features emerged. First, there were very few cases where the musical content had a negative significance. One person recalled disliking the sound of a particular set of pipes on a church organ, but there were few other clear cases. This was not, however, the result of a rosy view of childhood where all negative memories had been erased, because there were many cases where the musical context was negative. Many people remembered situations of anxiety, pain, and humiliation, mainly connected with negative appraisal of their musicality by adult authority figures (particularly teachers). The most extreme incident was where a teacher physically beat a child for a performance error. There were, however, positive contexts too. For instance, one respondent recalled rehearsing carols for a school carol concert. What gave the incident its positive significance was the sense of enjoyment among the group, undertaking this festive preparation in place of normal academic classes.

The second important feature was the almost complete absence of incidents where the musical content was appraised positively and the context was appraised negatively.

One might interpret this finding by supposing that where the immediate context is a source of threat or emotional challenge, there is little chance of musical content capturing the emotional system. This study suggests that positive emotions derived from engagement with musical materials is only possible when the context is appraised as, at worst, emotionally neutral. The specific contexts where strong content-related emotions were felt included home, church, and the concert hall, alone or with friends and family. They tended not to include lessons at school, or situations in the direct presence of a teacher. Although hopefully not inevitably so, it seems that formal instructional settings have a tendency to be inimical to emotional engagement with music. This may be because of the emphasis within such settings on achievement, success, and failure, with the concomitant threats to self-esteem and self-worth. It has the paradoxical consequence that people may be driven to express their deepest and most personal relationships with music in private, or in supportive peer reference groups outside, and hidden from, the formal educational process.

## 18.6  Everyday music use as self-therapy

In the preceding paragraphs, we have seen much evidence of music being used deliberately and consciously to achieve psychological outcomes which are reflected in emotional change. Music clearly is used by people to make them feel better or different, or help them accomplish or attune themselves to some concurrent or anticipated activity. These kinds of activity have sometimes been, perhaps rather glibly, cited as examples of 'self-therapy' (Sloboda 1989*b*, 1992). However, therapy, as understood by therapists, is not simply about manipulation of emotions, it is about helping the individual in therapy to develop more appropriate and functional responses to the problems of living (cf. Bayne & Nicolson 1993; Bunt & Pavlicevic, this volume). There is almost nothing in the literature on everyday uses of music that would count as strong evidence that particular self-chosen music improves problem solving or decision making, as compared to no music, or different music. It would be an interesting study to ask people to deny themselves any self-chosen music for a period of time, and compare their adjustment on a number of psychological measures to that found during normal music use. ESM would seem to be particularly well suited to the measurement of the effects of such manipulations.

However, the strong claims made by users of music in a wide range of studies, supported by subjective and anecdotal evidence, make it likely that such effects do exist, although the mechanisms by which they are mediated are poorly theorized. There is, however, one very plausible class of mechanisms by which music could have a therapeutic effect. Much is made in the literature about 'everyday' psychological disorders, such as depression or the effect of cognitive set or narrowing. A depressed person is often locked in a cycle of negative and self-defeating cognitions, unable to call to mind plausible alternatives to the narrow circle of linked aversive scenarios (Blaney 1986; Pollock & Williams 1998). These cognitions are also often accompanied by anomalous states of arousal, such as high anxiety, insomnia, or lethargy. Well-chosen pieces of music may be able to help individuals break out of such cycles by the specific combination of intrinsic and extrinsic cues that they provide (Sloboda & Juslin, this volume).

Extrinsic cues may remind the person of situations, scenarios, people, and emotions that lie outside the closed loop of the pathological state. Intrinsic cues (the ebb and flow of tension, resolution, expectancy, etc.) may provide means for altering arousal states in positive directions. In addition, the unique capacity of music to engender emotional release (as in crying; see Sloboda & Juslin, this volume) may be in itself therapeutic. For reasons that are not well understood, emotional release appears to assist psychological adjustment (through a process sometimes called *catharsis*; e.g. Davis 1988). A fuller working out of some of these ideas in the context of music's role in spirituality is provided by Sloboda (2000).

## 18.7  Conclusion

It is a significant feature of many of the emotional feelings and displays that individuals experience in relation to the everyday musical scenarios that we have outlined that although they may occur in solitude, their point of reference is the relationship between the music user and others. Although viewed as essentially 'private' experiences, involving a great deal of autonomy or agency, emotional feelings and displays are deeply embedded in a social context, which exerts a powerful influence (albeit often implicitly) on our music listening. Reliving past relationships, constructing identity, using music to 'siphon off' emotions that are not for public presentation: all of these depend on, and are used to negotiate and develop, the complex web of cognitions and behaviours that constitute social life. As such, music becomes part of the construction of emotional feelings and displays that are both reflective and communicative 'embodied' judgments used to accomplish particular social acts. In other words, musical emotions are a form of social representation, which is negotiated as an interaction between cultural/ideological values of a society, the values and beliefs operating in a social grouping or subculture in that society, and the individual's own social and personal experience.

Our research highlights the importance of studying emotional feelings and displays as part of a sequence of everyday music listening based on conventions and rules of a particular social context and the unfolding episodes in which they occur. Our recent study (Sloboda *et al.*, 2001) involving electronic pagers and self-reports (experience sampling method) provides one approach which may be used to capture individuals' subjective experiences of emotions during 'real', evolving musical episodes. Another possibility is to approach the analysis of episodes involving music and emotion in a similar way to how we might analyse conversations in discursive psychology. This is not to say that we should analyse the actual vocabulary used by individuals to define emotion words in relation to music. Rather, a 'discourse' in this sense can be thought of as a kind of frame of reference, a conceptual framework in which our emotional feelings and displays can be interpreted. One method of discursive analysis which may prove particularly useful in the study of music and emotions is what has been referred to as the 'positioning triad' (cf. Harré & van Langenhove 1999). It consists of three elements: (a) the story (or content) of an evolving episode; (b) the relative positions of individuals in terms of the cultural/social conventions involved in speaking (and listening) during or about the episode, displaying judgments, and/or expressing acts; and (c) the social act the episode performs. The 'positioning triad' provides a framework for investigating the dynamics of real-life, evolving situations that could be used by researchers seeking to identify and further our understanding of the role of music and the people engaging in emotional displays.

However, a word of caution may be necessary. Most of us are not aware of the fact that our musical activities are completely enmeshed in a social and cultural world. Our engagement with music leads us to 'forget' or become unaware of the grounds on which our feelings and behaviours are based. This 'forgetting' is the product of years of training, socialization, and the institutionalization of music. Not only have our musical practices become routine and invisible, but as musicians and psychologists we are limited in our ability to describe musical materials in a way that is free of the assumptions and biases associated with our own experiences and training. For example, there are many examples of research where specific discourses involving musicological characterizations of emotions (e.g. reference to specific musical works or to structural and symbolic features of these works) are introduced before an attempt is made to characterize the user's emotional responses in relation to them. In doing so, we continue to perpetuate the historical projections and social preoccupations of the various professional elites that have dominated the work of defining what music is and what it is for, not only for themselves but for the wider culture. By turning our attention to the role of emotional 'work' in relation to music, which takes into account individual subjective experience of *both* emotional feelings and displays as they occur in everyday evolving situations, it might be possible to retrieve some of these 'forgotten' or 'hidden' practices. Only by revealing the meanings associated with our evaluative judgments embedded within a particular context or general conceptual framework, can we hope to gain a better understanding of the complexity of emotions and music in everyday life.

# References

Bayne, R. & Nicolson, P. (1993). *Counselling and psychology for health professionals.* London: Chapman & Hall.

Blaney, P. H. (1986). Affect and memory: a review. *Psychological Bulletin,* **99**, 229–46.

Brodsky, W. (1995). *Career stress and performance anxiety in professional orchestra musicians: A study of individual differences and their impact on therapeutic outcomes.* Unpublished doctoral dissertation, University of Keele, England.

Burr, V. (1995). *An introduction to social constructionism.* London: Routledge.

Csikszentmihalyi, M. & Larson, R. (1984). *Being adolescent.* New York: Basic Books.

Csikszentmihalyi, M. & Lefevre, J. (1989). Optimal experience in work and leisure. *Journal of Personality and Social Psychology,* **56**, 815–22.

Davis, P. J. (1988). Physiological and subjective effects of catharsis: a case report. *Cognition and Emotion,* **2**, 19–28.

DeNora, T. (1999). Music as a technology of the self. *Poetics,* **27**, 31–56.

Gabrielsson, A. & Lindström, S. (1995). Can strong experiences of music have therapeutic implications? In *Music and the mind machine: The psychophysiology and psychopathology of the sense of music,* (ed. R. Steinberg), pp. 195–202. Berlin: Springer.

Green, L. (1999). Research in the sociology of music education: some introductory concepts. *Music Education Research,* 1, 159–69.

Hanaken, E. A. & Wells, A. (1990). Adolescent music marginals: Who likes metal, jazz, country, and classical? *Popular Music and Society,* 14, 57–66.

Harré, R. & Gillett, G. (1994). *The discursive mind.* London: Sage Publications.

Harré, R. & van Langenhove, L. (ed.) (1999). *Positioning theory.* Oxford, UK: Blackwell.

Larsen, R. & Kleiber, D. (1993). Daily experience of adolescents. In *Handbook of clinical research and practice with adolescents,* (ed. P. Tolan & B. Cohler), pp.125–45. New York: Wiley.

Larsen, R., Kubey, R., & Colletti, J. (1989). Changing channels: Early adolescent media choices and shifting investments in family and friends. *Journal of Youth and Adolescence,* 18, 583–600.

Leming, J. (1987). Rock music and the socialisation of moral values in early adolescence. *Youth and Society,* 18, 363–83.

Lewis, G. H. (1995) Taste cultures and musical stereotypes: Mirrors of identity? *Popular Music and Society,* 19, 37–72.

Lutz, C. (1982). The domain of emotion words on Ifaluk. *American Ethnologist,* 9, 113–28.

McCormack, J. (1984). *Formative life experiences and the channelling of adolescent goals.* Unpublished doctoral dissertation, University of Chicago, Chicago.

Merriam, A. (1964). *The anthropology of music.* Chicago: Northwestern University Press.

North, A. C. & Hargreaves, D. J. (2000). Musical preferences during and after relaxation and exercise. *American Journal of Psychology,* 113, 43–67.

North, A. C., Hargreaves, D. J., & O'Neill, S. A. (2000). The importance of music to adolescents. *British Journal of Educational Psychology,* 70, 255–72.

O'Neill, S. A. (1997). Gender and music. In *The social psychology of music,* (ed. D. J. Hargreaves & A. C. North), pp. 46–63. Oxford, UK: Oxford University Press.

Pollock, L. R. & Williams, J. M. G. (1998). Problem-solving and suicidal behaviour. *Suicide and Life-threatening Behaviour,* 28, 375–87.

Sheridan, D. (2000). Mass-observation revived: The Thatcher years and after. In *Writing ourselves: Mass-observation and literacy practices,* (ed. D. Sheridan, B. Street, & D. Bloome), pp. 43–78. Cresskill, NJ: Hampton Press.

Shotter, J. & Gergen, K. J. (1989). *Texts of identity.* London: Sage Publications.

Sloboda, J. A. (1989*a*). Music as a language. In *Music and child development* (ed. F. Wilson & F. Roehmann), pp. 28–43. St. Louis, Missouri: MMB Music.

Sloboda, J. A. (1989*b*). Music psychology and the composer. In *Structure and perception of electroacoustic sound and music,* (ed. S. Nielzen & O. Olsson), pp. 3–12. Amsterdam: Elsevier.

Sloboda, J. A. (1992). Empirical studies of emotional response to music. In *Cognitive bases of musical communication,* (ed. M. Riess Jones & S. Holleran), pp. 33–50. Washington, DC: American Psychological Association.

Sloboda, J. A. (1999). Everyday uses of music listening: A preliminary study. In *Music, mind and science* (ed. S. W. Yi), pp. 354–69. Seoul, Korea: Western Music Research Institute.

Sloboda, J. A. (2000). Music and worship: A psychologist's perspective. In *Creative chords: Studies in music, theology, and Christian learning,* (ed. J. Astley, T. Hone, & M. Savage), pp. 110–25. Leominster: Gracewing.

Sloboda, J. A., O'Neill, S. A., & Ivaldi, A. (2001). Functions of music in everyday life: An exploratory study using the experience sampling method. *Musicae Scientiae,* 5, 9–32.

# CHAPTER 19

# EMOTIONS IN STRONG EXPERIENCES WITH MUSIC

ALF GABRIELSSON

In most people's minds there is a strong association between music and emotions. Music can be felt to express emotions as well as to arouse emotions. While musical expression has been given considerable attention in empirical research (cf. Gabrielsson & Lindström, this volume; Juslin, this volume), emotional reactions to music have been less studied. The purpose of this chapter is to describe emotional reactions that occur in particularly strong experiences of music, and further to explore which factors can elicit such reactions.

Strong experiences of music may have many properties in common with other types of strong or exceptional experience, for instance, mystical experience which is described and discussed in many religious contexts. In the following, I first briefly review some earlier research on strong experiences, and then describe a research project on strong experiences of music (Section 19.3) and the associated analysis of emotional reactions (Section 19.4), followed by a discussion (Section 19.5).

## 19.1 Earlier research on strong experiences

In empirical psychology, the best known analysis of strong experiences was furnished by Abraham Maslow, one of the founders of the so-called humanistic psychology. Maslow coined the term *peak experience,* which he originally associated with self-actualization, the highest level in his well-known hierarchy of needs (Maslow 1954, Chapter 5). To explore such experiences, Maslow asked people to describe 'the most wonderful experience of your life; happiest moments, ecstatic moments, moments of rapture, perhaps from being in love, or from listening to music, or suddenly 'being hit' by a book or a painting, or from some great creative moment' (Maslow 1968, p. 71). Surveying the contents of these descriptions, he found several characteristics of generalized peak experience, for example, total attention on the object in question, complete absorption, disorientation in time and space, transcendence of ego, and identification or even fusion of the perceiver and the perceived. Peak experience is good and desirable, there is a complete loss of fear, anxiety, inhibition, defence, and control. Moreover, 'the emotional reaction in the peak experience has a special flavor of wonder, of awe, of reverence, of humility and surrender before the experience as before something great' (Maslow 1968, pp. 87–8), even a fear of being overwhelmed with more than one can bear. The experience may occasionally be described as sacred. Maslow found music, especially the great classics, to be one of the easiest ways of getting peak experience (Maslow 1976, pp. 169–70).

As an extension of Maslow's investigations, Panzarella (1980, p. 71) gathered reports on 'intense joyous experience of listening to music or looking at visual art' from a sample of 103 persons, 51 describing musical experiences and 52 visual art experiences. His analysis (content analysis followed by factor analysis) revealed four major factors of the experience: (a) *renewal ecstasy*, an altered perception of the world ('The world is better, more beautiful than had been thought before'; Panzarella 1980, p. 73); (b) *motor-sensory ecstasy*, physical responses (changes in heart rate, breathing, posture or locomotion, presence of shivers, chills, tinglings, etc.) and quasi-physical responses (e.g. feeling 'high', 'floating'); (c) *withdrawal ecstasy*, loss of contact with both the physical and social environment; and (d) *fusion-emotional ecstasy*, merging with the aesthetic object. Motor-sensory ecstasy and fusion-emotional ecstasy were more pronounced in music reports than in visual art reports.

Earlier, Laski (1961) asked 63 individuals whether they had known an experience of 'transcendent ecstasy' and further analysed texts from selected literary sources and from books on religious experiences. Triggers of such experiences included nature, sexual love, childbirth, religion, art, science, creative work, 'beauty', and others. The contents of the descriptions were classified into four broad categories: (a) feelings of loss of something (e.g. loss of time, place, sense, self); (b) feelings of gain of something (e.g. gain of timelessness, release, satisfaction, joy, salvation, perfection, new knowledge); (c) feelings of ineffability (e.g. the experience is indescribable, eludes verbal communication); and (d) quasi-physical feelings (e.g. light and/or heat words, improvement words, pain words, calm and peace words). Classical music was the most frequently mentioned trigger among the arts.

The concept of *flow* developed by Csikszentmihalyi (e.g. Csikszentmihalyi 1990) has several aspects similar to peak experience and self-actualization. It refers to a state of intense yet effortless involvement in an activity, the experience of which is 'so enjoyable that people will do it . . . for the sheer sake of doing it' (Csikszentmihalyi 1990, p. 4). Some major characteristics of the phenomenon are full concentration on the relevant stimuli, total absorption in the activity; altered perception of time, and loss of self-consciousness. Flow may appear in connection with a manifold of activities, for example, rock climbing, sailing, chess, games, dancing, and making music. With regard to music, the flow concept seems most applicable to performance (see Persson, this volume), for instance, in mastering a difficult piece in a fully concentrated but seemingly effortless involvement, a phenomenon often reported by musicians as the most happy moments in their activities (I agree). Flow experience in listening to music is briefly mentioned as well (Csikszentmihalyi 1990, pp. 68 and 108).

Evidence from the above-mentioned studies indicate many different physical, quasi-physical, perceptual, cognitive, emotional, and transcendental phenomena in strong experiences, whether they are called peak experiences, mystic experiences, ecstasy, flow, or something else. Emotions are important ingredients and may manifest themselves, not only as experience, but also in physical responses (e.g. Plutchik 1994, p. 136).

## 19.2 Physical responses

Physical responses, such as thrills, shivers, and changes in heart rate are often mentioned in descriptions of strong experiences and are commonly associated with strong emotional arousal. From answers to a questionnaire, Goldstein (1980) concluded that thrills—a chill, shudder, tingling, or tickling—are a common response to music, primarily to musical passages with special emotional meaning for a person.

Sloboda (1991) obtained reports from 83 respondents on various physical responses—shivers, tears, lump in the throat, goose pimples, racing heart, and others—that they often experienced to music. In about a third of the cited cases, the response was located to a specific theme, phrase, motif, bar, chord, or moment, all of them belonging to pieces of classical music. Tears or lump in the throat were provoked by melodic appogiaturas, shivers or goose pimples by sudden changes in harmony, and heart race occurred in connection with acceleration and syncopation (see also comments in Sloboda 1999).

Panksepp (1995) investigated chills induced by music. In general, chills were reported more for pieces brought by the participating students themselves than for other pieces, which suggested effects of conditioning. Most examples belonged to popular music. When subjects listened to unfamiliar music, sad pieces produced significantly more chills than happy pieces for females but not for males. Chills tended to peak at the most intense and dramatic crescendos.

## 19.3 The SEM project

Evidence from the studies reviewed above suggests that music may be a common trigger of extraordinary experiences. In the following, I briefly describe a research project aiming to gather further, more detailed knowledge of this topic.

The strong experiences of music (SEM) project was initiated independently of the works described above. The main impulse was my disappointment that music psychology rarely, if ever, comes to grips with the questions that most people consider the most relevant regarding music—simply, how are we affected by music? I was also approached, typically in private, by people who told me about exceptional experiences of music, affecting them deeply in ways that they could not understand.

I started this project at the very end of the 1980s together with psychologist Siv Lindström Wik. We studied Maslow's writings on peak experiences, but found no concrete examples of what people told about their peak experiences, rather 'an impressionistic, ideal, 'composite photograph' or organization of personal interviews . . . and of written reports' (Maslow 1968, p. 71). Panzarella's (1980) pioneering study was very useful as it provided examples of subjects' reports, and procedures for obtaining and analysing them. However, his musical sample was limited to some 50 persons, and in both Maslow's and Panzarella's studies classical music seemed to be the (almost) sole elicitor of peak experiences. This was also stated by Laski (1961). We were also concerned about definitions such as 'intense joyous experience' (Panzarella 1980, p. 71). All this seemed to imply some limitations in relation to the purpose of the SEM project, that is, to obtain descriptions of any type of strong experiences (including negative ones) in connection with any kind of music. In order not to prejudice our potential subjects, we avoided any examples or suggestions of what would define a strong experience of music or of what kind of music could be involved.

The purpose of the project was first of all descriptive, to analyse which phenomena are contained in strong experiences of music—in other words, to find out how people are affected. We also wanted to explore how SEM is related to properties of the actual music as well as to characteristics of the respondent and of the situation in which the experience occurred. Moreover, we were interested in possible consequences of SEM for the individual's future.

The very beginning of the project was briefly reported in Gabrielsson (1989). A classification of SEM phenomena was sketched in Gabrielsson and Lindström (1993), and further elaborated in Gabrielsson and Lindström Wik (2000). Examples of the potential therapeutic effects of SEM were given in Gabrielsson and Lindström (1995); and SEM in relation to musicality is discussed in Gabrielsson (in press). Given the present volume's focus on emotion, the following chapter will be centred on the description of emotional aspects of SEM. Some connections to other aspects and to underlying factors will be briefly discussed within the available space.

### 19.3.1 Data collection

Briefly, subjects were asked to describe 'the strongest, most intense experience of music that you have ever had. Please, describe your experience and reactions in as much detail as you can.' Supplementary questions concerned, for example, if this was the first time the subject had listened to the music in question and if the same strong experience had recurred at later listenings, if any, to the same music; how the respondent felt before and after the experience and what the experience had meant in a longer perspective; how often such strong experiences occurred and if similar strong experiences occurred in other situations than with music; and if the respondent had any idea about what caused the strong experience. The reports were obtained by means of interviews and, mostly, as written reports.

### 19.3.2 Subjects

All participation was on a voluntary basis, and there was no attempt to achieve strict representative sampling of some defined subject population. However, attempts were made to ensure variation with regard to gender, age, occupation, and musical preferences. The present account is based on about 400 reports obtained from some 300 persons (many subjects provided two or more reports). Gender distribution is about equal. Almost 60 per cent of participants are between 20 and 40 years old, about 30 per cent between 40 and 60 years old. About 50 per cent are amateur musicians, about one-third professional musicians, and about one-sixth non-musicians. Although musicians, professional and amateurs, are thus in the great majority, about 80 per cent of the reports refer to experiences as listeners. Musical preferences are spread over many genres.

### 19.3.3 Analysis

Subjects' SEM accounts are subjected to content analysis (see, for example, Patton 1990, Chapter 8), gathering all relevant phenomena mentioned and successively exploring different ways of sorting them into a limited number of fundamental categories. This work was/is conducted independently by the author and his co-worker, also at times by students in connection with writing theses on SEM. After the necessarily tentative analysis of the earliest reports, the agreement between the analysts has usually been very good. However, as human experiences and reactions are hard to fit into truly exhaustive and mutually exclusive categories, there are still some problems regarding proper classification. Some double classifications seem unavoidable, and the classification process may never come to a definite end. A basic problem is, of course, the large interindividual variation in participants' vocabulary and linguistic competence. We stay as close as possible to the descriptive terms used by the subjects themselves, but a certain amount of interpretation from our side is unavoidable. For more complete accounts of methods, see Gabrielsson and Lindström (1993) and Gabrielsson and Lindström Wik (2000).

### 19.3.4 Some general results

The length and detail of the reports vary widely, from only a few lines up to eight pages. A few respondents even wrote poetry to describe their experience. Each report represents a unique case with regard to contents of the experience and influencing factors.

Briefly, the present classification of SEM aspects comprises the following basic categories: general characteristics; physical and behavioural aspects; perceptual aspects; cognitive aspects; emotional aspects; existential and transcendental aspects; and developmental aspects. Each of them contains a number of subcategories as seen in Table 19.1. For discussion and examples of these subcategories, see Gabrielsson and Lindström (1993) and Gabrielsson and Lindström Wik (2000). As noted earlier, we do not pretend that these categories are completely exhaustive, nor quite mutually exclusive. However, repeated application of this classification to lots of SEM reports shows good results. The number of doubtful cases is relatively small and decreases as the classification is successively refined. The classification has also proved useful in pilot studies on strong experiences of dance and of visual art. The present account will be limited to emotional aspects of SEM and related matters.

## 19.4 Emotional aspects of SEM

The emotional aspects of SEM have been classified into four subcategories: (a) intense emotions; (b) positive emotions; (c) negative emotions; and (d) mixtures of emotions/conflicting emotions.

### 19.4.1 Intense emotions

As could be expected, emotional reactions in SEM are typically of unusual intensity, regardless of which specific emotions are experienced. Some illustrative quotations are given here:

I had to close my eyes, it was such an enormous emotional experience.

**Table 19.1** Classification of SEM phenomena

*General characteristics of SEM*
Unique, fantastic, incredible
Hard-to-describe experience, words insufficient

*Physical reactions, behaviours*
Physiological responses
Behaviours
Quasi-physical responses

*Perception*
Auditory
Visual
Tactile
Kinaesthetic
Synaesthetic
Intensified perception
Musical perception-cognition

*Cognition*
Changed attitude
Changed experience of body, time, and space
Changed attitude to music
Thoughts, memories
Imagery
Cognition-emotion
Musical cognition-emotion

*Emotion*
Intense emotions
Positive emotions
Negative emotions
Mixtures of emotions/conflicting emotions

*Existential and transcendental aspects*
Meaning of existence, being
Transcendental states
Religious experiences

*Personal development*
New insights, new possibilities
Confirmation of identity
Feeling of community
Music: new interests, attitudes, motives

. . . overwhelming waves of feelings that were thrown forth as reaction to the music . . . I could absolutely not control the emotional outburst . . . so ABSOLUTELY IMPOSSIBLE to change it.

This song arouses so strong feelings in me that I cannot listen to it more than once a year.

. . . and last an internal peace that words cannot describe.

Although intensity of emotions may seem mainly associated with high arousal, as in the second quotation above, it may as well refer to states of low arousal such as peacefulness (last quotation).

## 19.4.2 Positive emotions

Positive emotions dominate in SEM reports. The by far most frequently mentioned feelings, singly or in various combinations, are happiness, joy, elation, and bliss. In many cases, the feelings are described in even stronger terms, such as a kind of intoxication, rapture, or euphoria boarding on ecstasy. Below are some illustrative excerpts from SEM reports. They are designated E1, E2, etc. to facilitate finding them again when referred to later in text.

A young lady attended an outdoor concert with the artist known as Prince:

[E1] The music began before the curtain rose, and you just stood there as semi-paralysed and screaming . . . Everybody in the audience is exciting each other to a stage next to a climax, and when the artist at last comes on stage he does not have to say more than 'hi' to trigger that climax. It is very much the atmosphere in the audience that gives this concert feeling. If I was standing there all by myself looking at Prince, it would not be the same thing at all . . . One feels so free somehow. At concerts one can dance, jump, scream and sing as much as one wants. You are like a part of it all, not just a spectator. Throughout the whole concert the audience was in total ecstasy. It was only one thing that mattered: the music! You are filled with the wonderful feeling that everything is all right, that you are living only for what is happening 'right now'. You are in a way 'intoxicated with joy' . . . You don't think about what you are doing. You do what you feel like, without even thinking about it.

A young performer was rehearsing a piece by Bach and then:

[E2] . . . suddenly experienced a tremendously strong feeling that was felt both in my body and in my head. It was as if I was charged with some kind of high tension, like a strong intoxication. It made me ecstatic, inconceivably exhilarated, everything concentrated to a single now. The music flowed as by itself. I felt like I was penetrated by Bach's spirit: the music was suddenly so self-evident. There was no doubt any longer how it should be played, as if I had come to the deepest insight and found the genuine, true and correct expression. The intoxication lasted the whole piece, and I staggered out afterwards . . . What a fantastic happy experience!

A woman attended a performance by a band playing Finnish tango in a pub:

[E3] I was filled by a feeling that the music started to take command of my body. I was charged in some way . . . I was filled by an enormous warmth and heat. I swallowed all tones . . . the music became so distinct. I was captured by each of the instruments and what they had to give me . . . Nothing else existed. I was dancing, whirling, giving myself up to the music and the rhythms, overjoyed, laughing. Tears came into my eyes—however strange it may seem—and it was as a kind of liberation . . . Afterwards I was standing there intoxicated with joy. That was a real kick for me.

There are lots of reports of this kind in which happiness and joy abound. In other cases a 'happy end' is attained although actually nothing indicated such a possibility— as in this report by a depressed mother, alone at home with her little child. She felt:

[E4] . . . so tired, so alone . . . grey sky, cold . . . nobody would know if I was to die . . . For some reason, I put on Mozart's *Requiem* (I am not aware of logically thinking in any way about this act) . . . I read the sleeve notes and sink, sink, sink deeper—no time—only the sounds enveloping me in a world aside of this—sinking deeper beyond words, beyond thoughts, only the waterfall of sound cascading around and through me . . . My head is gone, body too, and yet I am here. The grey 4 square table leg is exquisite in its perfection—beyond meaning in the intensity of its greyness, displays a perfection that defies description . . . the whole room, the whole universe is present here in perfect harmony. All colors are vivid beyond description . . .I seem to be experiencing directly and have no words to express this state of bliss, harmony, meaningless beauty. I am totally a part of it all . . . The whole world is dancing before my eyes—I am calm, tears run down my cheeks. I have no idea why . . . I am not happy, I am not sad, am not anything in particular, yet feel the potential for anything to pass through me . . . secure and warm and full of love. I want to kiss the postman, ring the whole world and tell it, it's okay, it's all okay . . . the total qualitative shift in my relating to the world, universe, whatever you can now call it, remains. That pure existence and nothing else could be so beautiful! Satisfaction. Ecstasy.

This is a good example of what Panzarella (1980) named 'renewal ecstasy'. Other commonly mentioned feelings are enjoyment, delight, loveliness, and beauty; for instance, 'I felt an enormous delight' or '. . . it was lovely. It was God and heaven and all angels'. Closely related to this type of responses are also feelings of perfection: 'It can't be better than this!'; 'I remember the feeling of "this is not true, I am dreaming, it is not possible to do like this"'; 'When I came out after the concert, I told my company that I could die happy now'. Performers may feel that they surpass their usual achievements, and manage things that they usually do not master: 'This feeling when everything fits together is wonderful'; 'The music one created was far beyond one's usual capacity'.

While the emotional reactions described so far are associated with high or rather high levels of arousal, another common class of responses reflects feelings at rather low arousal, such as feelings of calm, peace, repose, safety, warmth, and love: 'I experienced a stillness that was not like anything else . . . everything else felt irrelevant . . . the important thing was to be able to exist in the present and the stillness that felt as eternal'; 'I listened to the tape 2–3 times a day . . . it became a safety among all chaos and misunderstandings'; 'I was in a state of warmth and kindness'; 'I felt in love with this music'.

Many feelings seem to represent a mixture of cognitive and emotional aspects. They are contained within the cognition-emotion subcategory in Table 19.1. Feelings of expectancy and tension may occur both before and during the music: 'It is always thrilling to sit down and know that the orchestra is going to perform'; '. . . building up an almost insufferable tension concerning what this would lead up to'. Music may make the listener surprised, amazed, shaken, even shocked (examples of the latter appear under negative emotions): 'I was brought away by the music, amazed and surprised by its beauty'. A common phrase, almost a cliché, is to 'be hit' by the music, feel that it goes straight into oneself, bypassing or crossing all cognitive barriers: 'A pianist played Beethoven's *Appassionata*. It hit the poor, musical child who had neither radio or gramophone at home'; 'The monumental work . . . hit me like a storm'; '. . . the piece goes so directly into me. Quite mercilessly it cuts through all barriers straight into the emotions'.

Still other examples within this subcategory may be feelings of longing ('The music brought me away in dreams, longing'), wonder ('The feeling when you experience this totality is just wonder'), smallness and humility ('It was an enormous experience, I felt small and humble'), gratitude ('I felt so infinitely grateful'), honour ('It was . . . almost an honour having had the possibility to experience this'), solemnity ('I remember the solemn feeling of being present at such an evening'), and sacredness ('I felt myself standing in the midst of a sacred moment in life').

### 19.4.3 Negative emotions

A few extremely negative SEMs were reported. A young man attended an outdoor rock concert:

[E5] After a while, they announced a female's band . . . Malaria was their symptomatic name. They played a hard, heavy, fateful synthetic rock at high volume. We had been sitting quite close but it soon became unbearable. The base was roaring a heavy, deafening monotone sound, that penetrated one's body. The drummer was also beating heavily and tired . . . a saxophone screamed in anguish, completely free from melody . . . accompanied by a singer who completely freely sang the most monotonous and howling song I had ever heard. Their make-up was black and pale, they wore black clothes . . . This naked and gruesome death music that was flowing from the loudspeakers and drowning us made me feel physically ill. I just wanted to get away from the music, and got on my feet to walk away. At the same time whole groups of black-dressed guys and girls came flowing toward the stage and loudspeakers. Everybody looked so pale and listless without life. I tried to remain but felt that it only provoked a destructive feeling of sickness . . . I thought that the Malaria band and the audience, in open anxiety before life and future, allied themselves, horribly and totally, with death and destruction . . . It was a deeply negative experience, strong and gruesome.

One report refers to a special chord in Mahler's Tenth Symphony. A man sat listening to this music shortly after a beloved relative's death:

[E6] But there it was. A chord so heart-rending and ghost-ridden that I had never experienced before. A single tone . . . is added with an endless number of instruments from the orchestra. Not unlike a huge organ where you pull out every organ stop at random. A dissonance that pierced my very marrow. My brother and I reacted the same: we were both filled with such a primitive horror, almost prehistorical, that none of us could utter a single word. We both looked at the big black window and both of us seemed to see the face of Death staring at us from outside.

While the negative emotions in these reports seem to be mainly caused by the music, in other cases the negative experience is associated with various personal and/or situational factors. A female alone at home in a large house a dark evening told:

[E7] I was sitting reading with the radio on. Suddenly Stravinsky's *Rite of Spring* breaks loose without notice. I almost panicked and felt an intense discomfort and had to switch off the radio.

Another negative experience was related to a frightful experience during childhood:

[E8] The Stockholm Philharmonic Orchestra was playing *Finlandia* by Jean Sibelius. The then aged composer was sitting in an armchair a little way from the orchestra. I felt immensely split—not to say that I was in a kind of chaos that would not pass off. The reason was that the work was said to describe the varying nature of Finland, barren landscape, wind and storm—and nothing else. The first time I listened to *Finlandia* was on radio in August 1940 . . . while the war was raging. I was a child living with my grandmother, separated from my parents and did not know when I would meet them again. I was very scared by the piece because I immediately interpreted the trumpet blows as machine guns, bomb explosions and the like. I felt anguish.

Some persons reported strong feelings of sadness associated with a piece of music. Usually the music had originally occurred in connection with negative circumstances, such as unhappy love, illness, attempted suicide, death, or memories of war. Strong frustration was felt by a female in the midst of an SEM when 'the grand mother steps in and turns off the radio telling 'You need not wear out the batteries for such noise'. It felt like she tried to stifle me, I got quite frustrated.' One subject felt anger at a funeral, because quite inappropriate music was played. There was a single report of shame; a child was so affected by the music that 'I started crying by emotion. But I felt ashamed because of this . . . and I did not want to show that I was crying.'

### 19.4.4 Mixtures of emotions and conflicting emotions

While the preceding categories have provided examples dominated by positive or negative feelings, there are many reports with mixed appearances of feelings, feelings that change during the course of listening, feelings that are opposites to one another or in conflict with each other. Musicians' nervousness before a public performance may turn into feelings of joy and inspiration:

[E9] The whole day before I was very restless and tense . . . When I sat down to begin playing I felt, beside tension, increasing feelings of joy. The whole first piece became like a joy-intoxication, particularly as the audience looked very happy and helped to beat time through the whole piece . . . Afterwards I felt both elated and glad and totally relaxed.

Listeners may feel nervous concerning musicians' possibly unsatisfactory capacity, a nervousness that may soon disappear:

[E10] During concerts it often happens that I begin to worry about how it is going to turn out . . . Only a few minutes listening was enough to make me feel quite safe, lean back and let the music speak.

Listeners may be shaken, even shocked by the music, but after a while these feelings may turn into positive ones. A mainly perceptually conditioned shock is the overwhelming loudness and volume perceived when a musician is sitting inside an orchestra for the first time:

[E11] Then came the shock. The sound shock. The sounds that filled all of me, pressed me together into a small louse. Where would I go? I must get away . . . But soon this feeling changed into a courage to grow into the sounds, become a part of the music.

Anxiety or depression may be relieved by music:

[E12] I was in a deep depression, everything was black . . . This day began as all the others. I had great difficulties to bring myself to leave the bed's hiding place and get out into the threats that the new day meant . . . I went to a church where XX as usual was going to play the organ at noon. . . Somewhere in the piece by YY the fantastic happened, my mood was totally changed. Darkness became light and my uneasy mind calmed down . . . I left the church full of appetite on life.

Mixtures of positive and negative feelings may cause confusion:

[E13] One moment I felt like an abandoned child, lost and lonely, the next moment I was like a child in its most carefree moment . . . Suddenly a terrible feeling of confusion came upon me. In what I believe to be but a few seconds, a whole series of conflicting emotions: fright, sorrow, hate, love, anger, and last an internal peace that words cannot describe.

A report that provided penetrating introspective evidence of conflicting emotions was given by a young lady, fascinated by Gustav Mahler's music, when she attended a performance of the reconstruction of Mahler's unfinished Tenth Symphony:

terror' causing a shock in the listener. The notation of this chord (Fig 19.1) reveals a fortissimo chord extending over the whole frequency range of the orchestra with intervals of (mostly) minor thirds between its component tones contributing to very pronounced dissonance (cf. dissonance in relation to critical bandwidth, Dowling & Harwood 1986, pp. 82–5). There is also hardly anything in the immediately preceding music that would make the listener expect such an outburst. The chord thus works as an icon of strong negative emotion and also violates expectations, two ways of representing or arousing emotions (Dowling & Harwood 1986, pp. 205–24). The same chord appears again, further elaborated, in the final movement of the symphony (bars 275–283). To my knowledge, such a complex chord has no earlier equivalent, and it appeared at a time around 1910 when atonal music made its appearance, also in Vienna, with Schoenberg, Webern, and Berg. The listener in E14 also referred to the beginning of the last movement in this symphony, where the beats of 'an enormous wooden club against the largest bassdrum' crushed any attempt by other instruments and caused horror.

Rather than indicating specific moments in the music, many respondents more generally referred to musical factors such as timbre (e.g. an unusual instrument or unusual combination of instruments), loudness/dynamics (e.g. crescendo, diminuendo), tempo (e.g. accelerando), mode (e.g. transition minor to major), rhythm (often in connection with dancing, as in E3), beautiful melodies and harmonies, thick texture, increasing tension followed by relaxation, and still others. It is striking, however, that although many respondents were active musicians, in their reports they did not often use conventional musical terminology but rather terms that can be used by 'anyone': 'brutal chords', 'heavenly beautiful tones', 'majestic sound', 'pure music', 'enormous power and energy', and the like. Metaphors were used now and then: 'every chord goes like waves through yourself', 'in the last bars it is like a light over my closed eyes which more and more goes out in the following diminuendo'. Respondents also often attributed their reaction to the qualities of the performance—the skill, concentration, and involvement displayed by the musician(s), including conductors as well. This was very much due to visual impressions of the musicians, the instruments, and the physical and social environment.

*Personal factors*

Besides common demographic variables such as gender, age, educational level, and profession, our classification of person-related factors influencing SEM includes a variety of factors, for example:

1. *Physical state*, for instance, feeling well, rested, tired, ill.

2. *Cognitive factors*: expectations (positive, negative, not specific, see, for example, E14); feel a need for listening to or performing music; be attentive, receptive, sensitive, open-minded, or not; having heard or performed this music earlier, or not; be familiar or not with musical style, composer, performers, etc.; use or abandon analytical attitude; have pleasant or unpleasant memories of the music (e.g. in E8 trumpet blows were associated with war).

3. *Emotional state*: be in high or low spirits, calm, relaxed, nervous (e.g. E9, E10), stressed, depressed (e.g. E12), in crisis, in love, unhappy love, etc.

Figure 19.1 The chord in bars 203–206 of the first movement of Gustav Mahler's Tenth Symphony arranged by Deryck Cooke (1976). The chord is repeated in bar 208. Copyright ©1966 (Renewed) by Associated Music Publishers, Inc. (BMI). International Copyright Secured. All Rights Reserved. Reprinted by permission.

4. *Personality-related variables* (as suggested by respondents themselves) such as temperament, maturity, and dispositions.

### Situational factors

Factors related to the listening or performing situation included, among others, the following:

1. *Physical factors*: acoustical conditions; listening to live or recorded music; listening or performing at home, in a concert hall, church, restaurant, outdoors, or on a Walkman, etc.; position, close or far away, in relation to performers or among co-performers (e.g. E9); visual conditions (e.g. good sight) and impressions, time of day, season, weather, etc.

2. *Social factors*: listening or performing alone or together with others; size, appearance, and behaviour of audience (see, for example, E1 and E9), of performers, or co-performers (see, for example, E5).

3. *Special occasions/circumstances*: experience during vacations, in another country, in unusual environment, etc.

4. *Performance conditions*: for instance, music well rehearsed or unrehearsed.

### Interactions among factors

A reasonably full treatment of these factors and their effects on SEM goes far beyond the scope of this chapter. It is obvious, however, that emotional reactions in SEM, as in any music situation, depend on interactions between musical, personal, and situational factors (the latter two are sometimes indistinguishable). The relative importance of each factor varies, but none of them can ever be excluded. Even in reports where musical factors appear to be very strong determinants, there are influences of personal and/or situational factors, for instance, in E6 (grief after relative died), E7 (alone at home in a large house on a dark evening), E8 (memories of war during childhood), and E14 (expectancy and fear of disappointment before listening to Mahler symphony).

In many cases, it is obvious that personal and/or situational factors are in fact more important than the music in question, as when, for instance, a piece of music is associated with war (e.g. E8), happy or unhappy love, an exotic environment, beautiful nature, pleasant holidays, certain ceremonies, etc. (for examples, see Gabrielsson & Lindström 1993, 1995). Such cases illustrate what Dowling and Harwood (1986, Chapter 8) call indexical representation, that is, a piece of music is associated with some extramusical object or situation.

In consideration of the ever present interactions between musical, personal, and situational factors it may be appropriate to speak of strong experiences *of and with* music (Gabrielsson & Lindström Wik, 2000) or strong experiences *in connection with* music.

## 19.5 Discussion

In accordance with the title of this chapter and this volume, the focus here has been on emotional aspects of SEM, supplemented by some brief outlooks to other aspects and influencing factors. A look at Table 19.1 shows that this represents but a limited part of the available material on SEM. Cutting out a part of a whole inevitably leads to gaps and imperfections, and the loss of relevant connections and of broader context. For further content and analysis, I refer to our earlier reports as well as to reports in press and in preparation.

### 19.5.1 Comments on emotion

A general difficulty with the concept of emotion is how to make a reasonable demarcation of emotions or emotional feelings versus other feelings. Both psychologists and people in general use terms such as feelings, emotions, and mood in very variable, sometimes idiosyncratic, ways (e.g. Plutchik 1994, Chapter 3; see also Sloboda & Juslin, this volume). This is certainly also true for the corresponding terms in Swedish (for instance, the Swedish word 'känsla' is used in a variety of contexts and meanings). We have therefore simply stayed as close as possible to the terms used by the respondents themselves, provided that they have a reasonable emotional meaning, or at least an emotional connotation. Most of these terms appear in alphabetical order in Table 19.2, divided into positive and negative emotions. No further division is made presently (however, a distinction between different levels of arousal was hinted at in Section 19.4.2). Of course, some reservations must be made regarding the proper translation of Swedish terms into corresponding English ones.

**Table 19.2** Emotions mentioned in SEM reports

*Positive emotions*

Amazement, beauty, bliss, calm, contentment, delight, ecstasy, elation, enjoyment, euphoria, excitement, exhilaration, expectancy, fascination, freedom, gladness, gratitude, happiness, harmony, honour, hope, humility, intoxication, joy, longing, love, loveliness, overjoy, overwhelmed, peace, perfection, pleasure, rapture, relaxation, repose, sacredness, safety, satisfaction, smallness, solemnity, surprise (positive), tension (positive), thrill, warmth, wonder

*Negative emotions*

Afraid, anger, anguish, anxiety, chaos, conflict, confusion, depression, disappointment, discomfort, fear, fright, frustration, gloom, gruesome, hate, horror, mourning, nervousness, pain, panic, sadness, scare, shaken, shame, shock, sorrow, split, surprise (negative), tension (negative), terror, uneasiness, worry

---

In the reports, we find numerous examples of so-called 'basic' emotions. However, opinions differ concerning which and how many basic emotions there are. The survey by Plutchik (1994, p. 58) indicates the best agreement regarding emotions like happiness, sadness, anger, and fear, but proposals by various authors also include (in alphabetical order) amazement, anxiety, elation, enjoyment, expectancy, grief, interest, love, pain, panic, pleasure, satisfaction, shame, shock, surprise, and tension, all of which are represented, to varying extents, in our material. Also proposed, but not represented in the present material, are boredom, contempt, disgust, and guilt—negative emotions which seem less plausible in connection with SEM. However, other negative emotions such as panic, shame, and shock may seem equally implausible, yet they have appeared; so too hasty exclusions should be avoided.

In previous studies on peak experience and flow (Csikszentmihalyi 1990; Laski 1961; Panzarella 1980), rather little was written about emotions. However, Maslow (1968, pp. 87–8) in his survey of 'generalized peak experience' mentioned happiness, ecstasy, rapture, love, wonder, awe, reverence, humility, surrender before the experience as before something great, fear of being overwhelmed, and occasionally a description of the experience as sacred. These feelings are also represented in the present reports (although not all of them in the selected excerpts). None of them, except happiness, love, and fear, appears in lists of basic emotions but rather represent complex mixtures with considerable ingredients of cognitive character. Generally, the borderline between cognition and emotion is blurred, and from the standpoint of investigating strong experiences with music, this distinction may not be very important.

Whether some form of cognitive appraisal precedes emotion or not can be discussed at considerable length. In several SEM reports, respondents described their reaction as a kind of 'direct experience', something that bypasses cognitive barriers and goes 'straight into the emotions'. This suggests that there was no cognitive appraisal, at least not at a conscious level. However, there are also many reports in which the respondent first told about, say, the beautiful timbre of a singing voice, fantastic acoustics, irresistible rhythm, etc., which may be interpreted as rather deliberate cognitive appraisal mediating the emotional reaction. Of special interest are wordings referring to the beauty of the music (which we subsume under enjoyment). In some cases, there is obvious cognitive appraisal behind the beauty response—an insight into, and admiration of, say, the composer's ingenious construction of the music, its formal properties, delicate instrumentation, combination of text and music, etc.—that is, a kind of 'intellectual' enjoyment. In other cases, the response comes as a direct and spontaneous exclamation—'Oh, my God, how beautiful!'—devoid of any analysis or reflection.

The distinction between emotions *expressed* in music and emotions *aroused* by music is not always easy to make in the reports. For instance, 'the music became more and more gruesome' can be interpreted as the respondent's 'neutral' description of perceived expression, or as indicating that the respondent felt anxious, or as a combination of both possibilities.

### 19.5.2 Comments on methodological issues

Verbal reports are associated with several well-known problems (Ericsson & Simon 1993), not least with regard to retrospective reports as here. Many reports refer to experiences which happened many decades ago and are obviously sensitive to memory distortions. Furthermore, subjects differ much in linguistic competence, vocabulary, and willingness to use language to describe their experiences. Many respondents frankly stated that their SEM was impossible to describe by words. Others wrote long and penetrating accounts but still complained about the validity of words to describe what they actually felt—the experience seemed ineffable. However, presently we have no better tools available than language in attempts to approach phenomena like SEM, and I am convinced that language will remain the main instrument for a considerable time still. For some further comments, see Gabrielsson (1989, 1991) and Gabrielsson and Lindström (1993).

### 19.5.3 Continued research

Recently, Lowis (1998) tried to investigate peak experiences under experimental conditions. Subjects listened to prerecorded classical music: five pieces of 'gentle' music (e.g.

'Nimrod' from *Enigma Variations* by Elgar) and nine pieces of 'up-beat' music (e.g. the ending of *The Firebird* by Stravinsky), and used a button device to indicate 'a moment of particularly deep and profound pleasure or joy . . . the sort that produces a tingle in the spine' (Lowis 1998, p. 212). Further definitions of peak experience alluded to phenomena described by Maslow (see Section 19.1). Roughly two-thirds of the subjects pressed the button at least once. The up-beat music generated significantly more responses than the gentle music. Significant correlations were found between frequency of button pressings and ratings for the following feelings evoked by the music: joy, love/tenderness, longing, sadness, reverence/spirituality, action, and memory/thoughtfulness. Waterman (1996) and Sloboda (1999), although not directly referring to peak experiences, used other, partly similar methods for obtaining listeners' continuous and immediate indication of emotionally loaded moments in the music, thereby also increasing the possibilities of relating them to properties of the music in question.

The advantages of experimental procedures are the control of musical stimuli and the immediate, continuous response by the subjects. On the other hand, the situation is by necessity more or less artificial, and a 'button response' does not not tell much about the contents of the experience unless it is supplemented by other information, as is somewhat examplified in these reports. For continued research of strong experiences of music, whatever they are called, a flexible interplay between naturalistic and experimental approaches seems appropriate in order to combine their respective advantages and compensate for their respective drawbacks.

That music is one of the most effective triggers of strong emotional experiences is amply confirmed by several studies referred to in this chapter. 'The power of music' is a cliché that has considerable validity. It remains a fascinating challenge, although frustrating at times, to investigate how, why, and in what contexts we can be so strongly affected by music.[1]

## References

Cooke, D. (1976). *A performing version of Gustav Mahler's draft for the Tenth Symphony.* New York: Associated Music Publishers, Inc.

Csikszentmihalyi, M. (1990). *Flow. The psychology of optimal experience.* New York: Harper & Row.

Dowling, W. J. & Harwood, D. L. (1986). *Music cognition.* New York: Academic Press.

Ericsson, K. A. & Simon, H. A. (1993). *Protocol analysis. Verbal reports as data,* (2nd edn). Cambridge, MA: MIT Press.

Gabrielsson, A. (1989). Intense emotional experiences of music. In *Proceedings of the First International Conference on Music Perception and Cognition,* pp. 371–6. Kyoto, Japan: Japanese Society of Music Perception and Cognition.

Gabrielsson, A. (1991). Experiencing music. *Canadian Journal of Research in Music Education,* **33**, 21–6.

---

[1] My sincere thanks to Siv Lindström Wik for many years of continuous and repeated analysis and discussion of our SEM material. This research is supported by The Bank of Sweden Tercentenary Foundation.

Gabrielsson, A. (in press). Musicality, music performance, and music experience. In *Multidisciplinary perspectives on musicality*, (ed. D. Coffman, K. Gfeller, D. J. Nelson, & C. Rodriguez). Iowa City, IA: University of Iowa Press.

Gabrielsson, A. & Lindström, S. (1993). On strong experiences of music. *Musikpsychologie. Jahrbuch der Deutschen Gesellschaft für Musikpsychologie*, 10, 118–39.

Gabrielsson, A. & Lindström, S. (1995). Can strong experiences of music have therapeutic implications? In *Music and the mind machine. The psychophysiology and psychopathology of the sense of music*, (ed. R. Steinberg), pp. 195–202. New York: Springer.

Gabrielsson A. & Lindström Wik, S. (2000). Strong experiences of and with music. In *Musicology and sister disciplines: Past, present and future*, (ed. D. Greer) pp. 100–8. Oxford, UK: Oxford University Press.

Goldstein, A. (1980). Thrills in response to music and other stimuli. *Physiological Psychology*, 8, 126–9.

Laski, M. (1961). *Ecstasy. A study of some secular and religious experiences*. London: Cresset Press.

Lowis, M. J. (1998). Music and peak experiences: An empirical study. *Mankind Quarterly*, 39, 203–24.

Maslow, A. H. (1954). *Motivation and personality*. New York: Harper.

Maslow, A. H. (1968). *Toward a psychology of being*, (2nd edn). New York: Van Nostrand Reinhold.

Maslow, A. H. (1976). *The farther reaches of human nature*. New York: Penguin Books.

Panksepp, J. (1995). The emotional sources of 'chills' induced by music. *Music Perception*, 13, 171–207.

Panzarella, R. (1980). The phenomenology of aesthetic peak experiences. *Journal of Humanistic Psychology*, 20, 69–85.

Patton, M. Q. (1990). *Qualitative evaluation and research metods*, (2nd edn). London. Sage Publications.

Plutchik, R. (1994). *The psychology and biology of emotion*. New York: Harper-Collins.

Sloboda, J. A. (1991). Music structure and emotional response: Some empirical findings. *Psychology of Music*, 19, 110–20.

Sloboda, J. A. (1999). Musical performance and emotion: Issues and developments. In *Music, mind, and science*, (ed. S. W. Yi), pp. 220–38. Seoul: Seoul National University Press.

Waterman, M. (1996). Emotional responses to music: Implicit and explicit effects in listeners and performers. *Psychology of Music*, 24, 53–67.

# POSTLUDE

# CHAPTER 20

# MUSIC AND EMOTION: COMMENTARY

JOHN A. SLOBODA AND PATRIK N. JUSLIN

The chapters collected here have highlighted a range of dichotomies (or bi-polar dimensions) which 'open windows' to a wider view than that with which most of us will have started our consideration of emotion in music. For many of us who would be naturally drawn to this book, and the enterprise it represents, the assumptions we make about emotion are probably a result of our by now effortless (and hence often unreflexive) accommodations to the specific musical culture which we inhabit. These assumptions often embody one pole of a particular dichotomy. Progress in understanding musical emotions may require the distancing from our own perspective that an articulation of such dichotomies can provide. This postlude highlights five core 'dichotomies' (from a considerably larger potential set), calls for attempts to reach beyond these dichotomies, and concludes with some general evaluative comments about the field as a whole, based on the evidence provided in this book.

## 20.1 Emotion as reception versus emotion as construction

A theme running through many of the chapters concerns the role of the person experiencing the emotion in the causal process. At one extreme is the case where the emotion is 'induced' in someone by the 'force' of the music, in much the same way as the appearance of a snake might induce fear in someone, pretty much independently of whether or not the person concerned had it in mind to feel fear. This case motivates the concern of many contributors to this volume with fundamental emotional processes (see, especially, the chapters by Peretz, Juslin, and Scherer & Zentner). At the other extreme is the case where the person appropriates the music in order to generate an emotional experience, using the music as a resource in a more active process of emotional construction. In such a case, there would be no emotion had the person not decided that there should be. Such a case is driving the arguments of contributors such as DeNora, Cook and Dibben, and Sloboda and O'Neill.

Some of the historical confusions and perplexities engendered by the phenomenon of music's emotionality may have been contributed to by an overemphasis on the 'receptive' rather than 'constructive' pole of the dichotomy within explanatory discourses. The receptive approach has sat comfortably with the apparent role of the listener in both the concert hall and the psychological laboratory. In these settings, the superficial appearance is one of passivity. We sit still and silent, and music is 'presented' to us by powerful others whose purpose is to influence our thoughts and feelings (and, in the case of the laboratory, record them).

Several chapters in this book suggest that the 'active' view of emotional engagement is revolutionizing many of the intellectual approaches to the music. From the 'new musicology' through 'social constructionism' in psychology to the 'interpretive' approach in sociology, a new appreciation is being elaborated. This places the person experiencing music as the crucial agent at the junction of a network of forces and influences—an agent who *makes* emotion happen by his or her 'musicking', to use Small's (1998) deeply appropriate neologism. In one sense, the still silent member of a classical audience is no less active than the performer on the stage. It is simply that the form, vectors, and boundaries of that activity are different.

## 20.2 Emotion as biology versus emotion as culture

A second dichotomy, which is strongly related to the first (in practice if not by necessity), is that between a biological and a cultural approach to musical emotion. On the one side of this dimension, we find the biological perspective on musical emotion, evident in the chapters by Peretz and, to a lesser extent, Juslin, and Scherer and Zentner. This approach recognizes that emotions have a biological basis and reflect the workings of neurological and neurochemical mechanisms developed by natural selection. Emotions have a long evolutionary history, and their neural substrates show 'homologies' with those of non-human primates. The biological perspective takes advantage of the fact that natural selection is the only force in nature that can build functional organization into organisms. Indeed, natural selection is a causal process in which a structure spreads precisely because of its functional consequences, that is, function determines structure (Cosmides & Tooby 2000). The flagship of this perspective on emotion is the 'affect program' approach represented by Paul Ekman, among others. According to this view, each emotion should be defined functionally in terms of how it is adaptive in managing a particular problem scenario that has occurred frequently during evolution.

A biological perspective on music and emotion recognizes that neuropsychological and evolutionary considerations are crucial also for the case of music. Expression, perception, and induction of emotion via acoustic signals did not begin when human beings invented the first musical instrument. Humans have always communicated emotions via the voice, and many animals communicate emotions via acoustic signals as well. Thus, as Juslin notes, it seems plausible that some aspects, at least, of how music intersects with emotion are constrained by psychological mechanisms for acoustic communication that have been 'shaped' by evolution. A biological approach assumes that music recruits essentially the same emotional circuits as other emotion-inducing events, and that we, therefore, can learn a lot about musical emotions by understanding the functional design of emotions in general. Moreover, as Peretz observes, neuropsychological studies may help to resolve some controversies and conceptual problems with regard to the nature of musical emotions.

On the other side of the biology–culture dichotomy, we find a sociocultural approach to musical emotions, represented in this book by the chapters by Becker and DeNora, and also to some degree by Sloboda and O'Neill. Although a greater understanding of emotions in wider non-musical settings is clearly important to the progress of the musical enterprise, we have to remember that music is first and foremost a cultural artefact, and so unlike many of the other things and events to which we may experience emotions. Fearful responses to evolutionarily 'time-honoured' threatening situations (such as snakes) are, in some sense, non-optional. Our genes have designed it so that we have 'quick and dirty' responses to certain situations that impinge directly on our survival (LeDoux 1996). The behaviour of other human beings, and the things they say within practical discourse, can often point directly to these 'basic' event types, and so take on their power and immediacy.

However, cultural artefacts often require a great deal more 'mental scaffolding' to hold them in place. Although this scaffolding quickly becomes second nature within a particular 'habitus' (in the sense outlined by Becker in this book), it can take on different forms, even in superficially similar situations. If even one unnoticed element in the scaffolding is absent in a particular musical event, then the emotion achieved can be quite different, for reasons which may be obscure to the participants. Thus, for instance, the well-known phenomenon among classical performers of the unpredictability of the performance that 'really comes alive', or the perplexity of the adult listener returning to a favourite piece of music and finding that it does not exert the usual emotional power. In both of these cases, it may be a mistake to look for the difference inside the auditory musical object itself, but rather in the way that the participant is construing or appropriating the musical event.

It is important to note that mainstream psychological research on musical emotion has occupied a middle position in regard to this biology–culture dimension. In other words, most psychological studies have taken neither the biological foundation of emotions, nor the wider social context of emotions, into consideration. Thus it seems important that psychologists are willing to broaden their perspectives on musical emotion, keeping themselves informed about the latest developments in neighbouring fields like neuropsychology and sociology. This very book may represent one small step in that direction.

## 20.3 Emotion perception versus emotion induction

One further dichotomy involves the notion (known from ancient Greece) that music may both 'represent' emotions (that are perceived by the listener) and 'induce' emotions (that are felt by the listener). Such a distinction between emotion perception and emotion induction is made in many, if not all, of the chapters in this book. Some (for example, those by Gabrielsson & Lindström and Juslin) focus mainly on perception of emotion. Others (for example, those by Simonton, Meyer, Scherer & Zentner, Sloboda & O'Neill, and Gabrielsson) focus mainly on emotion induction.

It is pointed out by some authors that it is difficult sometimes to separate these different processes in empirical studies. Moreover, the interaction between perception and induction is still little investigated. Research summarized by Scherer and Zentner, however, indicates that it is important to take the distinction into consideration when designing research (this has not always been done in earlier research). Becker reviews some evidence which suggests that the perception–induction distinction may not be unique to the Western world, but also appears in other cultures. There is also some evidence that the distinction has neurophysiological reality, because both expression and perception of emotion seem to be associated with processing in the right hemisphere of the brain, whereas induced emotion seems to be lateralized according to emotional valence—positive emotions processed in the left hemisphere, and negative emotions in the right hemisphere (Blonder 1999). It is possible that brain-imaging techniques, such as PET, fMRI, and ERPs (reviewed by Peretz, this volume), in combination with other measures, might help us to empirically separate felt emotions from perceived emotions in future research. It seems likely that different theories may be required to explain these different processes.

## 20.4 Emotion as private experience versus emotion as public expression

At the heart of some of our dilemmas in understanding how emotion in music 'works' is the common Western view that emotion is primarily a private experience. This view has made it deeply problematical for researchers to confidently identify when an emotion is taking place (cf. previous section). We seem to be required to 'infer' emotion from a variety of unreliable and incomplete cues, such as verbal and physiological data. We are not even sure to what the supposed emotion is a reaction. Within a complex and rapidly changing musical structure, our emotional response may be slightly delayed from the crucial precipitating event, or may be an integrative response to a cumulative series of transitions across time (as discussed in different contexts by Meyer, Scherer & Zentner, and Schubert, among others).

Such problems are unravelled, at least in part, when one considers traditions in which the emotional outcome can be rather more directly read from the emotional behaviour of the participants, or from agreed conventional signals of such outcomes within the musical act. Becker, perhaps, provides the most radical challenge to our common conceptions of emotion by showing how these link to conceptions of the self, which are by no means universal. In some cultures, emotional displays associated with music are the means by which social relations are codified, expressed, and given 'power'. They express an accepted social reality, and the issue of whether a particular individual really feels the emotion expressed becomes secondary. Cook and Dibben remind us that the 'individualistic' approach to emotions in music has had a fairly short history, even within the Western tonal tradition.

Having articulated an important dimension, much work is now needed to locate various types of musical 'habitus' along it. Becker's example of the Pentecostal service is particularly interesting, since the surface discourse suggests a private perspective (the goal of achieving a state of individual ecstasy), yet there would be no 'point' to the occasion if individuals who achieved this state did not display their state through relatively ritualized behaviours which tell other participants 'I've made it'. And, of course, the willingness to indulge in such affect displays creates a kind of self-fulfilling prophecy, through the mechanism that Scherer and Zentner describe as 'peripheral route production'. The mere actions involved in building up to and displaying ecstasy will, along with the 'emotional contagion' of other people providing the same affect display, in themselves help to bring about the desired inner state. Becker also emphasizes the importance of being in a properly receptive frame of mind. Critical responses will 'block' the emotional path to ecstasy. Thus the music will not 'work' for someone unless they have already decided to allow it. Those of us who find it goes against the grain to enter into such activities are only too painfully aware of the complex web of socially engendered beliefs, interpersonal obligations, and dispositions that underpin the Pentecostal 'habitus' (because they are so alien to us). Similar belief systems are, however, there in every 'habitus'. The Pentecostal example highlights the often intricate relationship between private experience and public expression of emotion in relation to musical events.

## 20.5 Emotion as separate from the musical experience versus emotion as constitutive of the musical experience

Many of the chapters in this book express a general perplexity that it has taken so long for emotion to gain even a modest foothold in the arena of academic discourse about music (from whatever disciplinary perspective). Although methodological difficulties have slowed the progress in some disciplines, notably psychology, this cannot be the whole story. The psychology of emotion in general is far more advanced than the psychology of emotion as applied to music. It is more plausible to attribute the delay in progress to two factors.

First, there is the problem of tying down musical emotion to some 'formal object'. The formal object of an emotion, according to Solomon (2000, p. 11), can be described as 'the minimum essential set of 'beliefs' defining an emotion and an emotional experience'. Emotions have intentionality: they are always 'about' something (e.g. an event, person, or state of affairs). This notion is problematic in the case of music. It is difficult to say what musical emotions are 'about'. (Besides the obvious: that they are, in some way, about the music.) As recognized by philosophers, an emotion can also be about some non-existing, merely imagined object (e.g. a 'virtual persona' in the music). An important task for the study of musical emotion (as noted by Davies) is thus to understand how music can come to express and induce emotions despite an apparent lack of 'beliefs' that usually underlie such a response. Many chapters in this book propose possible theoretical solutions to this crucial problem, for instance in terms of 'musical expectancy' (Meyer), 'emotional contagion via independent brain modules' (Juslin), 'melodic originality' (Simonton), 'emotional memories', 'proprioceptive feedback', and 'conditioning' (Scherer & Zentner).

Second, delayed progress in understanding musical emotions partly reflects the cultural assumptions about music that have been shared by those people most well-equipped to move the field decisively forward. At the centre of these assumptions for the last 150 years or more has been the belief that music is epitomized by the canon of masterworks produced by a small circle of 'great' composers. Such works are expressions of things that the composer has grasped (which may include emotions), and the job of the listener is thus to 'learn'. What the listener 'feels' is largely irrelevant to this serious task. This task is traditionally accomplished through a grasp of formal structural descriptions of the work; that is, analysis. This activity can be undertaken at elementary level through the digestion of programme notes and other forms of commentary designed for a wider public, in what has sometimes been called the 'music appreciation movement', or at an advanced level through participation in formal analytical activities.

Since dominant conceptions of music are almost entirely determined by what dominant groups *do* with music, it is inevitable that the belief should have developed that emotion is not core to music. Such a stance has contributed enormously to the disengagement of the general population from entire genres of music. Even among intellectuals in other spheres, the claim that 'I like classical music but don't understand it' is tragically common. Such people engage deeply and thoughtfully with music, are often excellently provocative concert companions, but since they lack a set of vocabularies and techniques which would allow them to coherently address structure independently of emotion they feel 'excluded' from the musical world. In effect, many people feel they are being told 'the thing that strikes you most immediately and powerfully about the music you hear, the thing which keeps you engaged with it and wanting to hear more of it, is really totally irrelevant to a proper appreciation and understanding of it'.

Fortunately, the winds of change are blowing at great speed through the musicological communities. In 20 years, many of the core assumptions of the field have been turned on their head, in favour of emotion (and much else that has traditionally been excluded). Some of the historical and social parameters of this are outlined in this book by Cook and Dibben. However, seeds of change were planted much earlier than 20 years ago, and, in the present context, there can be few more fertile seed-planters than Leonard Meyer. Meyer's (1956) persuasive arguments that structural engagement *requires* emotional engagement have provided music psychologists, philosophers, and musicologists with a firm launch pad to escape the gravitational inertia of traditional historical musicology. (His theory provides one fruitful solution to the problem of the formal object of musical emotions.) Yet, paradoxically, Meyer's theory initially had the opposite effect. Meyer, and later Lerdahl and Jackendoff (1983), implied that understanding musical emotion is best achieved through an understanding of musical structure. As noted by Cook and Dibben, this position could be taken to justify the almost indefinite postponement of consideration of expressive qualities in musicological practice, and a resultant separation between structural analysis and expressive interpretation.

This separation is, in many ways, still with us. The contributions of Persson, Bunt and Pavlicevic, Juslin, and Steptoe show, in their different ways, that a fully articulated discourse (and associated practice) of 'emotional development and management' within the musical profession is a long way off. The core aspects of the training of musicians have remained unchanged for 50 years, largely because those who are most important to the delivery of that training (that is, senior professional performing musicians) received their own training long before any of the ideas summarized in this book were in circulation. These ideas are slow to reach them, and those they teach, because there are few contexts in which the necessary dialogues can take place. However, there are huge changes that economic and cultural factors are forcing on training institutes for performing musicians. These changes provide a unique opportunity for rethinking both what is taught and who gets taught it. In this process, it surely must be inevitable that the world of 'academic and classical' music has to effect a far more thoroughgoing *rapprochement* with popular music, its audiences, and the industries it supports, than anything hitherto achieved.

## 20.6 Sources and components of emotion and different levels of analysis

In the foregoing, we have outlined five dichotomies that characterize this book. In doing so, we do not wish to imply that these dichotomies are valuable as such. Rather we feel that it is important to move beyond these dichotomies, and try to reconcile the different perspectives. Admittedly, this is far easier said than done. None the less, we believe it is important that we attempt to find a common ground upon which different approaches can meet. A case in point is provided by the biology–culture dichotomy discussed earlier. Biology and culture are both crucial aspects of phenotypic development, and it is therefore time to start exploring ways in which neurobiological factors *interact* with environmental inputs to produce phenomena like musical emotions. (How do sociocultural factors, such as learning and language, impact upon the neuronal patterning associated with musical emotions? Do neurological aspects constrain what is learned?) But how can different approaches to music and emotion be integrated? We believe that one key to understanding how the different approaches fit together is to be found in some of the theoretical distinctions introduced in various chapters of this book.

Sloboda and Juslin discuss two primary sources of emotion in music: *intrinsic* and *extrinsic* sources. Intrinsic sources are those that are non-arbitrarily embedded in structural characteristics of the music and that contribute to the creation, maintenance, confirmation, or disruption of schematic expectations (along the lines sketched by Meyer). Extrinsic sources include both *iconic* sources, which come about through some formal resemblance between a musical structure and some event carrying emotional tone, and *associative* sources which are premised on arbitrary and contingent relationships between the music being experienced and a range of non-musical factors, which also carry emotional messages of their own. We believe that failure to specify which source(s) of emotion one is investigating can lead to unwarranted controversies with those who investigate another source; what counts for one particular source may not count for another.

Second, it has been suggested in psychology that emotions can be broken down into various subcomponents, such as eliciting events, appraisal, subjective feeling, physiology, expressive behaviour, action tendencies, and emotion regulation (Mesquita & Fridja 1992). Such a componential approach drives Scherer and Zentner's review concerning emotional reactions to music. Different authors in this book tend to focus on different components. For instance, Gabrielsson focuses on subjective feeling, Peretz on physiological measures, Cohen on appraisal, Juslin on expressive behaviour, and Sloboda and O'Neill on emotion regulation. Again, what counts for one particular component does not necessarily hold for another component. One final distinction (already mentioned here) is that between emotion perception and emotion induction. It is likely that theoretical accounts of musical emotions will differ depending on which of these two processes a researcher is focusing on.

In addition to these different sources of emotion and subcomponents of emotion, it is clear that different authors operate at different levels of analysis, ranging from the biological and the psychological to the social and the cultural. Several commentators have pointed out that, unlike the natural sciences, the social and behavioural sciences lack vertical integration; that is, they are not mutually consistent. However, an increasing awareness of research carried out at different levels of analysis should help to yield such consistency. An important goal for researchers of music could be that the theoretical accounts that they propose at one particular level of analysis should not be inconsistent with the accounts obtained at another level.

Given these distinctions, any research endeavour may focus on a specific combination of features. By being as clear as possible about the particular source(s) of emotion involved, the emotion components studied, the level(s) of analysis applied, and whether perception or induction (or both) is being studied, researchers may be able to integrate their approach with the work carried out by others. While it seems perfectly legitimate to conduct research on one particular level of analysis (or one component of emotion), and to bracket another domain of analysis, researchers should recognize that they are doing so, and acknowledge the legitimacy of other analytical levels.

In some cases, the apparent contradictions of different disciplinary approaches may be reconciled by observing that they focus on different sources of emotion, different components of emotion, or different processes (perception vs. induction). It is further possible that certain approaches may be more relevant for particular combinations of sources, components, and processes than others. A few examples may suffice to illustrate this point: An understanding of *intrinsic* sources of *induced* emotion requires structural analysis of the music and a model of the *appraisal* component involved. For this particular focus, a musicological–psychological level of analysis may be especially suitable. On the other hand, if we want to understand how *iconic* sources of *perceived* emotion are produced via reference to some non-verbal *expressive behaviour* component, a biological–evolutionary level of analysis may be highly fruitful. And, finally, if we want to understand how people talk about musical emotions, and interpret them within the social web of everyday life; how they use music to regulate their own emotions and influence their own self-identities, the *emotion regulation* component, a social constructionist approach may be most suitable. (Of course, this does not preclude that other levels of analysis may have important contributions in each example.)

## 20.7 Is the field of music and emotion in good shape?

On the basis of the chapters collected here, and the work they refer to, there are grounds for considerable optimism. This is not a collection that largely rehashes old work, nor it is a collection of pious platitudes and promissory notes on work not yet undertaken. The vast majority of chapters refer to substantial research programmes yielding new data and new conceptualizations, the great majority of which have been undertaken and published in the last 10 years. A second source of optimism is the high level of theoretical and methodological incisiveness displayed within the research reported.

Emotion work is attracting the attention of some of the best-trained and most rigorous senior exponents of the various disciplines. Younger researchers are, as a result, gaining the confidence to develop focused programmes that branch outwards from PhD projects and find their ways into the most prestigious publication outlets. At least in some parts of the world, and in some disciplines, we have the conditions for what Kuhn (1962) described as 'normal science'. A third source of optimism is to be found in the willingness of researchers from different disciplines to contribute to a book such as this (we do not know of many such resolutely multidisciplinary enterprises).

As psychologists we are particularly pleased that psychology appears to be playing such a central role in the resurgence of emotion studies in music. Psychology may be particularly well suited to such a role at the current time, because of the breadth of its scope (from the neurophysiological to the social), its methodologies (which are rigorous but at the same time also sufficiently 'neutral' to create a meeting place for researchers from different intellectual and ideological traditions), and its well-established record in advancing the understanding of a range of musical phenomena.

On the other hand, optimism should not lead to complacency. Several authors point to deficiencies, some rather major, in what has been achieved, and point out quite significant barriers to further achievement. Deficiencies include a lack of common understandings and definitions of key terms, a piecemeal approach to data gathering, and a narrowness in the domains studied. This narrowness applies to musical traditions (most work is on Western classical music), ages (there is very little work with children and older people), and contexts (a limited range of cross-cultural and subcultural contexts have been addressed). Barriers to further progress include the enormous difficulty of measuring emotions, particularly using multiple measures over extended events, such as pieces of music whose emotional expression may be constantly changing. The recent developments of increasingly non-intrusive methods of measuring brain activity may offer one important way forward.

Another barrier to progress is the relatively independent way in which research in the various disciplines develops. This may be an inevitable consequence of the structuring of the academic world. Researchers can only make substantial contributions if there is relatively secure employment. Employment is only available to those who have important things to contribute to their own discipline, as judged by opinion formers within that discipline. It matters far more to a young musicologist what other musicologists think of his or her research than what a psychologist might think. We have noticed several points within the collection of chapters here where links could have been made to work going on in another discipline but were not. More fundamentally, each discipline has its own trajectory, and issues which seem of great importance to psychologists might seem irrelevant to musicians. Therefore, what constitutes progress in this area may be a matter on which the representatives of the different disciplines will be unable to agree. Several authors end their chapters with a set of suggestions for further research. From outside the specific discipline one can certainly see that the research programmes suggested are possible, rational, and defensible. But are they necessary, or even important? Who would decide? Could the different disciplines ever agree, and would the practising musician or the untrained listener agree with them?

This is an issue that is not specific to music and emotion studies. It is a constant preoccupation of many people involved in the musical sciences. To put the question at its most blunt—does what we do help better music to be made, or for people to obtain more benefits from engagement with music? The answer is not clear. Music scientists sometimes look with envy on medical researchers. Everyone agrees that finding cures for major diseases such as cancer is worthwhile. As a result, governments and industry employ hundreds of thousands of people to research possible solutions.

Interdisciplinary teams are created. Researchers know what the goal is and can assess their success against the goal. What is the goal of music emotion research? There are probably as many answers as there are researchers. However, this book shows that researchers have common and overlapping concerns. Could these concerns ever coalesce into common agreed research agendas, which would direct the shape of the field for the next 10 years? Should they so coalesce? Would any major external body be concerned enough about these questions to provide major long-term funding? We feel that the answers to these questions are not obvious from the contents of the book. However, we hope that the book's existence may stimulate the debates that will lead to clearer answers to these questions, and that a future book on this topic might report progress in a rather more self-conscious and self-confident manner.

## References

Blonder, L. X. (1999). Brain and emotion relations in culturally diverse populations. In *Biocultural approaches to the emotions*, (ed. A. L. Hinton), pp. 275–96. Cambridge, UK: Cambridge University Press.

Cosmides, L. & Tooby, J. (2000). Evolutionary psychology and the emotions. In *Handbook of emotions*, (2nd edn) (ed. M. Lewis & J. M. Haviland-Jones), pp. 91–115. New York: Guilford Press.

Kuhn, T. S. (1962). *The structure of scientific revolutions.* Chicago: University of Chicago Press.

LeDoux, J. (1996). *The emotional brain.* New York: Simon & Schuster.

Lerdahl, F. & Jackendoff, R. (1983). *A generative theory of tonal music.* Cambridge, MA: MIT Press.

Mesquita, B. & Fridja, N. H. (1992). Cultural variations in emotions: A review. *Psychological Bulletin*, **112**, 179–204.

Meyer, L. B. (1956). *Emotion and meaning in music.* Chicago: University of Chicago Press.

Small, C. (1998). *Musicking: The meanings of performing and listening.* Hanover: Wesleyan University Press.

Solomon, R. C. (2000). The philosophy of emotions. In *Handbook of emotions*, (2nd edn) (ed. M. Lewis & J. M. Haviland-Jones), pp. 3–15. New York: Guilford Press.

# AUTHOR INDEX

# SUBJECT INDEX